AN **UNWORTHY**
FUTURE

AN **UNWORTHY** FUTURE

The Grim Reality of Obama's
Green Energy Delusions

JOSEPH TOOMEY

ARCHWAY
PUBLISHING

Archway Publishing books may be ordered through booksellers or by contacting:

Archway Publishing
1663 Liberty Drive
Bloomington, IN 47403
www.archwaypublishing.com
1-(888)-242-5904

Because of the dynamic nature of the Internet, any web addresses or links contained in
this book may have changed since publication and may no longer be valid. The views
expressed in this work are solely those of the author and do not necessarily reflect the
views of the publisher, and the publisher hereby disclaims any responsibility for them.

Certain stock imagery © Thinkstock.
Any people depicted in stock imagery provided by Thinkstock are models,
and such images are being used for illustrative purposes only.

ISBN: 978-1-4808-0892-8 (e)
ISBN: 978-1-4808-0891-1 (sc)
ISBN: 978-1-4808-0893-5 (hc)

Library of Congress Control Number: 2014911736

Printed in the United States of America

Archway Publishing rev. date: 9/22/2014

For Gracelyn, Jeanette and Joseph Jr.
since it is their future and that of their progeny that is at stake.

COMMON ABBREVIATIONS USED IN THIS BOOK

ASES   American Solar Energy Society, a solar energy-promoting lobbying group
AWEA   American Wind Energy Association, a wind energy-promoting lobbying group
BEA   Bureau of Economic Analysis of the U.S. Department of Commerce
BLS   Bureau of Labor Statistics of the U.S. Department of Labor
bpd   barrels per day, a unit of daily oil production
BTU   British thermal unit, the heat required to increase a pound of water 1° Fahrenheit
CAFE   Corporate Average Fuel Economy, an automaker regulation covering fleet requirements on mileage efficiency
CBO   Congressional Budget Office
CCGT   combined-cycle gas turbines, a type of highly efficient natural gas generator
CFL   compact fluorescent lamps, the type mandated for use in the U.S.
CO_2 carbon dioxide, a colorless, odorless, non-toxic chemical compound
CRS   Congressional Research Service
DoD   U.S. Department of Defense
DoE   U.S. Department of Energy
E10   A motor fuel blend containing 10% ethanol and 90% gasoline by volume
E15   A motor fuel blend containing 15% ethanol and 85% gasoline by volume
E85   A motor fuel blend containing 85% ethanol and 15% gasoline by volume
EEG   *Erneuerbare-Energien-Gesetz*, Germany's Renewable Energy Act of 2000
EIA   Energy Information Administration of the U.S. Department of Energy
EISA   Energy Independence and Security Act of 2007
ELCC   effective load carrying capacity, a measure of achievable capacity as % of maximum
EPA   U.S. Environmental Protection Agency
EPAct   Energy Policy Act of 2005
ERCOT   Electric Reliability Council of Texas, grid operator for 85% of Texas' power
ETS   Europe's Emissions Trading System

FDI	Foreign Direct Investment, investment funds from offshore sources
FERC	Federal Energy Regulatory Commission
GDP	Gross Domestic Product, a value measure of domestic economic output
HVDC	high voltage direct current converter, a giant piece of equipment
IEA	Paris-based International Energy Agency
IPCC	United Nations Intergovernmental Panel on Climate Change
kW	kilowatt or 1,000 watts of power
kWh	kilowatt-hour, the amount of energy from one thousand watts flowing for one hour
MBTA	Migratory Bird Treaty Act of 1918 protecting migrating birds
mmgy	million gallons per year
mW	megawatt or one million watts of power
mWh	megawatt-hour, the amount of energy from one million watts flowing for one hour
NAS	National Academy of Sciences, a U.S. scientific advisory group
Nd-Fe-B	a type of magnet made from neodymium (Nd), iron (Fe), and boron (B)
NRC	National Research Council, a blue-ribbon research-advisory group
NRDC	Natural Resources Defense Council, an extremist 'green energy' lobbying group
NYMEX	New York Mercantile Exchange, a commodities trading exchange
OCGT	open-cycle gas turbines, a type of natural gas generator less efficient than CCGT
OECD	Organization of Economic Cooperation and Development
OPEC	12-member Organization of Petroleum Exporting Countries
PTC	Production Tax Credit for producing and selling wind energy
quads	quadrillion BTUs, a standard U.S. measure of energy production or consumption
RIN	renewable identification number, EPA's fraud-plagued biofuel tracking system
RFA	Renewable Fuels Association, a biofuel-promoting lobbying group
RFS2	A Renewable Fuel Standard enacted under EISA in 2007
SPR	Strategic Petroleum Reserve, an emergency reserve to cover supply disruptions
tcf	trillion cubic feet, a standard U.S. measure of natural gas volume
TSO	Transmission Service Operator, an electric transmission grid management entity
UKERC	Energy Research Centre of the United Kingdom, a government agency
UN	United Nations
USGS	U.S. Geological Survey of the U.S. Department of the Interior
WHO	World Health Organization
WTI	West Texas Intermediate, a type of low-sulfur crude oil

CONTENTS

AUTHOR'S NOTE

As with my previous title, I did not start out with the intention of writing a book. The genesis for this work was my apoplectic reaction to a reelection speech given by President Obama at the University of Miami in February 2012. At the time, gas prices were spiking close to $4.00 a gallon. In a panic over the fact that the public might make the obvious connection between the administration's avowed intent to drive up energy prices and the high prices that had subsequently occurred, Obama launched a series of carefully selected visits to deliver the same set of well-rehearsed lines in front of student audiences at colleges and universities intending to plaster over those connections.

Obama's speech was loaded down with so many inaccuracies, inanities, falsehoods, fabrications, and other assorted nonsense that, after reading the text, I immediately set about writing a rebuttal. Within the space of a few hours, the outlines of a book were in place. I continued researching and expanding upon it over the next two years. The Miami speech will be revisited throughout this volume. Written in analytical style from an economic perspective, it is designed to convince an audience of reasonably intelligent people who are not steeped in the arcane aspects of energy policy that Obama's ideas amount to a policy and economic catastrophe. I am convinced that no fair-minded person who reads Obama's Miami speech and then reads this book could possibly support his position on either energy or climate policy.

This work represents my informed viewpoint gathered over a long career as an industry professional and management consultant. My undergraduate and graduate academic background focused on economics and finance, but also included a solid measure of physics, chemistry, and other physical sciences. During the course of my academic career, I concentrated my studies on energy economics, using energy companies or energy economics as the subject for every research project, study or paper that was required. Since then, I have been a close observer of trends and developments in energy markets.

Throughout my industry and consulting career, I have been afforded an opportunity to work with dozens of integrated energy producing, oil-field services, and electric utility clients in a wide array of projects in numerous countries all across the globe. These experiences have deepened my understanding of the complexities of the world's most fascinating industry. The primary focus of my consulting work is on driving out cost in the global supply chain for companies that buy, make, or sell products that need to be sourced, moved, staged, transformed, and delivered. The result of these efforts is to reduce cost and eliminate resource waste in the supply chain. The resource conservation and energy efficiency outcomes might qualify my work as 'green collar' under definitions advanced by the Bureau of Labor Statistics (BLS). Authoring this book probably disqualifies me as a heretic.

While critics will accuse me of being a paid stooge for "Big Oil" or some climate denial conspiracy, I have never received a dime of money from any oil company, energy producer or fossil fuel provider. Nor have I ever worked for, been hired by, or been paid to articulate the viewpoint of any organization, foundation, charitable entity, non-profit organization, or any other advocacy group. The research and opinions expressed herein are mine alone. If my views resemble those of other entities that are routinely demonized or derided in the leftist media or by enviro-left advocacy groups, it is due to the fact that the weight of evidence supports the former over the latter.

In the course of writing this book, I performed hundreds of original macro- and micro-economic analyses, compiling hundreds of separate spreadsheets and simulations. I read and reviewed thousands of reports, academic papers, government documents, and a large variety of original source material. I also read and compiled thousands of newspaper and other media reports. I have downloaded countless numbers of reports from official sources including the U.S. Energy Information Administration, the International Energy Agency, BP, and a variety of government sites from countries including the UK, Germany, Brazil, Denmark, the European Union, and others. Original source material is copiously referenced in the footnotes for readers interested in further research or validation.

Because the subject of energy policy is so wide-ranging, an author necessarily must limit the scope to arrive at a manageably-sized manuscript. The unwieldy length indicates I failed. Indeed, seven exciting chapters dealing with a variety of topics along with some appendices were edited out due to space considerations. Perhaps they will be revisited in a later volume. Nevertheless, many important aspects of energy policy are not covered. If readers are disappointed that there is an absence of discussion on a variety of topics, it should not be inferred that these are considered irrelevant. It was simply a case that other issues can better illustrate the thesis.

I have made strenuous efforts to keep the academic jargon and technical detail to an absolute minimum. In doing so, I strived to adhere to a style of writing such that, were the book to be read by any reader possessed with a reasonable degree of intelligence but little in the way of specialized expertise, it would still be understood. I have also taken pains to edit the prose to eliminate spelling, grammatical, syntax and other errors. If readers spot errors, the fault rests squarely with my editor.

It is said that a picture is worth a thousand words. Nevertheless, many general readers of non-fiction titles may not relish reading a book containing pictorial exhibits like charts and graphs. Those that are included are simple depictions accompanied with copious explanatory notes to enable instant recognition of the key points. Every reader with a solid grammar school education should understand the essential points.

Avid readers of my previous work, *An Unworthy Future: The Obama Legacy of Broken Promises and Failed Policies* will note that a few passages from that book were lifted nearly verbatim for this book. Alert readers will locate some familiar prose in a few chapters of this volume. I beg the indulgence of loyal readers who suffer through monotonous repetition.

Before describing what this book is about, let me caution that it does not seek to argue the truth or falsity of global warming theory. If you were hoping for a work to help bolster your understanding about climate or weather, you'll need to look elsewhere. Instead, this volume will demonstrate that Obama's program to combat climate change with 'green energy' will cost U.S. taxpayers hundreds of billions or even trillions of dollars, but won't have any material impact on the course of future climate events. It will also argue that the cost of climate mitigation will be dozens, hundreds, or even thousands of times greater than the cost of that small portion of climate change it attempts to remediate even under the worst forecasted scenarios. And even if 'green energy' was effective at accomplishing its chief purpose of greatly reducing greenhouse gas emissions, it is not remotely affordable with a U.S. economy permanently locked in stall speed. The moribund Obama economy is incapable of creating jobs necessary to produce the growth and income that could more affordably finance expensive 'green energy.' Our sustained real economic growth rate is lower than at any time in post-War history. The working-age population in the U.S. grew by 2.4 million persons in 2013 but the size of the civilian workforce actually shrank by more than a half a million workers.

Readers of my previous book will harbor no illusions about my political preference. My differences with the Obama agenda are sharp, but they are rooted in philosophy, not party affiliation. The country and indeed the whole world would have greatly benefitted if Obama had followed Jimmy Carter into well-earned single term political exile. Nevertheless, he is already behaving as a lame duck which, if it continues apace, will greatly assist efforts to impede his dangerous energy and climate policy agenda. Public opinion polls show him plumbing new depths of disapproval in the wake of domestic and foreign policy blunders, and for his intransigence in arriving at sensible compromises with his political opponents. I have little doubt that the weight of history will side with me.

A growing share of the American public and even a substantial slice of Obama's core base of progressive supporters are growing weary of the self-absorption, the constant blame-laying, the stomach-turning self-pity, the inability to take ownership of his own shortcomings. Only Obama can deliver an address to the nation like his 2013 State of the Union and invoke the first person — I, me, my — no fewer than 53 times. America is rapidly tiring of the relentless cult-of-personality psychodrama, the narcissism of a man who inhabits a world he believes is insufficiently appreciative of his talents and unworthy of his greatness.

Most sensible Presidents leave the dirty work of partisan bullying to their subordinates.

But not the post-partisan Obama. He relishes it. Only Obama could think of instructing the National Park Service to evict wheelchair-bound World War II veterans from visiting war memorials. Only the post-partisan Obama can deliver an address to the nation putatively designed to soothe national anxieties in the wake of a mass shooting at the Washington Navy Yard and still dedicate 90% of his words to savaging his partisan opposition for what he claimed was their unconscionable disregard for the poor and middle class for doing the unthinkable — opposing the unworkable Obamacare fiscal and economic train wreck. Hilariously, the biggest Obamacare opponent appears to be Obama himself as he unilaterally disregards the law's requirements and delays implementing one after another of the its provisions.

Each new day brings a heightened understanding of the economic damage Obamacare will wreak. Firms are laying off employees fearful that employment costs resulting from the Act will rise inexorably. Workers are finding that employers are unwilling to grant them a full-time work schedule so as to avoid mandatory coverage. That reality is reflected in Labor Department data showing that nearly every Payroll Survey job created since Obama's 2009 inauguration up to August 2013 had been for part-time work. The same data show average hours worked steadily declining. More Americans are now enrolled in one or more means-tested welfare programs than the number who are gainfully employed in full-time jobs throughout an entire year. And those welfare rolls are set to soar as millions more are placed on Medicaid from subsidized Obamacare.

Health care insurance coverage costs are soaring at double-digit growth rates. Like your humble author, millions of privately-insured persons who were promised they could keep their insurance plan if they liked it saw their policies cancelled. The Obama administration has lawlessly suspended implementation of various Obamacare provisions — there were thirty five separate invalidated provisions by the latest count — due to the potential fallout that the policy disaster is likely to have on the 2014 midterm elections. The law becomes more unpopular while the Act's stewardship by the Secretary of Health and Human Services becomes more arbitrary, incompetent, and despotic with each passing day. HHS officials, like their lawless IRS counterparts, spend their days hiding under their desks trying to duck Congressional subpoenas.

Since the 2012 election, Obama has grown progressively weaker and more erratic as the rookie neophyte stumbles from one policy disaster to another. Republicans don't trust him, Democrats don't fear him, dictators around the world laugh at him, and next to no one respects him. He assures the world he is not Bush. So they now think he's Jimmy Carter. Is that better? Like Captain Renault in *Casablanca*, many of Obama's most ardent supporters professed to be "shocked, shocked" when it was revealed that his administration had used the Internal Revenue Service to wage a relentless political war against his opponents. The only thing shocking is why anyone would be shocked.

An article of faith in Washington holds that the cover-up is always worse than the crime. This is just one more instance disproving that belief. Given the close coordination and frequent White House visits by the IRS General Counsel from whence the scandalous program originated, it is clear the lawless conduct has Oval Office fingerprints all over it. Not since the days of Richard Nixon had the IRS been used as a tool against political opponents. Liberal historians and commentators had grown comfortable believing that odious conduct was the exclusive preserve of Republicans. They'll need to rethink their suppositions.

Obama's attempts to utilize the IRS to regulate permissible political speech enjoys the same absence of constitutional authority as does his use of EPA to regulate energy markets. Naturally therefore, he proceeds apace in both efforts undeterred. Administrations come and go. Yet it is Obama's undermining of the integrity of permanent government bureaucratic institutions that represents perhaps the greatest threat to our constitution-based rule of law.

Leftists also affected to be surprised by revelations that the National Security Agency monitored domestic phone traffic. They claimed to be further shocked when the Attorney General admitted he had wiretapped reporters including several who were administration lapdogs. Because Obama enjoyed zero support among ideological and partisan opponents, these revelations merely served to erode support among his own base. When it was revealed that he had been brushing up on his foreign language skills by listening to the private phone calls of world leaders who had slobbered all over their blouses and skirts in elation in 2009 following his election, the feigned outrage seems more like farce.

The administration's foreign policy blundering has resulted in even more wreckage. Obama stood over the lifeless bodies of four American foreign service personnel in September 2012 and, looking the bereaved families in the eyes, lied to them about the nature of the murderous attack on a U.S. diplomatic compound in Benghazi. He knew every critical detail of the Benghazi attack at that pivotal moment. But, in order to rescue a pointless throwaway line he had uttered at the Democratic convention — "al Qaeda is on the path to defeat and Osama bin Laden is dead" — he chose to lie. He pretended the attack was a spontaneous reaction to a ham-fisted video rather than a carefully planned terrorist attack by murderous militants who were armed with mortars, rocket-propelled grenades and heavy machine guns, an attack timed to coincide with the 11th anniversary of the 9-11 terrorist atrocities.

This disgraceful instance alone has disqualified Obama to lead the nation. Even his own party has trouble confronting the reality of Benghazi, preferring to shield their eyes. Only blind partisanship can support his actions in that dreadful affair. He and his partisans were fond of reminding us during the election season that General Motors is alive and bin Laden was dead. In reality, as we now know from the safety of several months, it is GM's headquarters city Detroit that is dead while al Qaeda, with its supremacy in lawless Libya, within the Syrian insurgency, in Muslim Brotherhood-dominated Egypt, in increasingly chaotic Mesopotamia, in the Arabian peninsula, throughout north and central Africa, in east Asia, in the Caucasus, and in a resurgent Taliban in Afghanistan, that is alive and well.

Obama also bungled the Syrian matter in epic fashion. The affair began as did his Libya fiasco, with our self-indulgent narcissist uttering another aimless throwaway line — this time about a "red line" over the use of chemical weaponry in Syria. Whether intended or not, that was interpreted as official Obama administration policy, whatever that means in actual practice. Then chemical weapons were used in Syria and ... nothing happened to the odious Syrian regime that had stockpiled those banned weapons and was thus accountable for their usage. The red line was erased and redrawn. Then they were used again, and again ... nothing happened. But the second time around, catastrophe struck. The President was forced to acquiesce to Vladimir Putin's strategy of propping up the mass-murdering Assad government. This is industrial-strength weakness that will have lasting consequences.

The United States image abroad was destroyed more thoroughly than if Obama had publicly urinated on every national flag in the world. A former British diplomat described September 9, 2013 as "the worst day for U.S. and wider Western diplomacy since records began." Obama's bungling led to him addressing the nation in a televised speech where he laid the blame for the mess he had created on the doorstep of his predecessor as the post-partisan President had reflexively done throughout his tenure. He pretended to have a long-range strategy when it was obvious he was acting moment-to-moment, he urged action he did not himself support, and he outlined a plan he instinctively opposed and actually wanted to see defeated in Congress. Obama had issued a "red line" and wanted Congress to accept responsibility for proving that he had meant what he said.

Whatever the outcome, the U.S. had been made to look ridiculous in the eyes of the world. Maybe this was his intent all along. Like most progressive politicians, Obama is genetically incapable of being embarrassed. So it probably never phased him. But to the world-at-large, the candidate celebrated for his nuanced approach to complex problems, the man who styled himself a multicultural polymath, someone with an innate understanding of the Islamic world, a man who "heard the call of the *azaan* at the break of dawn and the fall of dusk" as he proudly boasted in Cairo, he just looks inept. His carefully-constructed myth about having vanquished Islamic extremism by wishing it away now lies in tatters on the cutting room floor. As the inimitable Mideast observer Fouad Ajami described it, Obama has been swindled like any other tourist at the Arab bazaar, and as it would be with his grandiose 'green energy' dreams, Americans must be made to pay the tab.

Why is this important? What connection do all these considerations have to 'green energy' public policy? There will be plenty enough verbiage devoted within these pages to discussion of that topic. I veer off course to drive home another point. Each self-inflicted wound drains a little more blood from the rotting hulk of Obama's bizarre Presidency. With his growing weakness, he he will be increasingly incapable of imposing his malignant 'green energy' agenda on the nation, his radical attempt to impose a program that would be irreparably damaging to the nation and its economic growth prospects.

One can take great satisfaction from the fact that the ones who have been most disappointed were the legions of pre-programmed media sycophants who, like Bob Herbert of *The New York Times* in 2009, were calling Obama "smart, deft, elegant and subtle."

By 2013, Obama's deftness, elegance, and subtlety extended to him calling his political opponents "hostage takers" and "kidnappers" and "terrorists." It was these realities that reluctantly forced low-wattage luminaries like Barbara Walters to admit, almost seven years after Obama announced his candidacy, that they had finally discovered he was actually not "the next messiah" as they had believed. The ever-vigilant watchdog press that had willingly become lapdogs felt betrayed.

Obama's radical energy program has already been prototyped in Spain, Germany, the UK, and California. The results have thus far been disastrous. These were the very places our policy visionary had offered as shining examples of humanity's bright future, one marked by energy security, millions of good-paying jobs that couldn't be outsourced, copious economic growth, new industries, and a better future for our progeny. Precisely the opposite happened.

His implied promises that you can keep your jobs and affordable energy if you like them are as good as his endless assurances about your health care plan. Obama and his Praetorian Guard of liberal media enablers won't ever admit it. Beneficially for loyal readers, your humble author feels no such forbearance. Soon the evidence will become undeniable. He will then be forced to turn his complete attention back to far more substantive issues like wading into racially incendiary court cases or browbeating NFL teams to change their names.

Some observers like Norman Podhoretz believe that it has been Obama's intent all along to blunder through international crises like Benghazi, Syria, and Ukraine as he has always intended to weaken the nation, to sacrifice America's long-standing global economic and security leadership position, to radically transform the country as he promised he would do back in October 2008, to take a backseat to other nations, to "lead from behind." If that is so, he is doing a remarkably effective job. We're certainly taking it in the behind. His 'green energy' plan fits squarely within that narrative.

It is increasingly apparent that his intent from the beginning was to destroy the private and employer-provided health insurance marketplaces with Obamacare although he will never admit it. It seems at least equally plausible that his 'green energy' program is designed to unleash the same degree of chaos in energy markets as his wreckage in the health insurance markets he created by his brilliant health care policy efforts. By issuing executive orders and unleashing EPA to carry forward his energy destabilization program, he has weakened some of the country's most robust job creators. That assures that great effort will need to be expended over the course of the coming years in political capital, wasted legislative effort, and countless hours of court cases hoping to stem or reverse the damaging trajectory.

Obama's critics often accuse him of devotion to Marxism. If there is truth in that charge, it was not the impenetrable tomes authored by Karl Marx that he follows but the ones from Groucho, Chico, Harpo and Zeppo. Make no mistake, Obama wants to deploy the expertise he brought to remaking health care to energy policy. His 'green energy' program is Obamacare for energy markets. Let's face it, nearly every trademark theme of his administration — "Cash for Clunkers", economic stimulus, green jobs, Obamacare, beer summits, Fast-and-Furious, lead from behind, shovel-ready, hashtag diplomacy, reset buttons, Solyndra, the Chevy *Volt*, cap-and-trade, recovery summer, cellulosic biofuel, pajama boy — you name it, they now only provoke derisive laughter. The Obama agenda has become the preserve of late-night comedians.

Whatever the outcome, it is increasingly clear that Obama does not enjoy a reservoir of public support for draconian measures to boost energy prices, enact new energy taxes, cap energy usage, impose more renewable energy mandates, constrain Americans' freedom to warm their homes during brutal winter weather, or undertake other ruinous measures to combat CO_2 emissions. Instead, he must rely on state mandates, regulatory stealth measures, blatant misrepresentation, discredited UN reports, and compliant media to help him. A deeply cynical press corps continues to amplify worthless claims offered by global warming hysterics that every hurricane, tornado or drought offers further proof that fossil fuel use is damaging the planet, with the only solution being to adopt Obama's draconian 'green energy' program. To their credit, the public ranks climate hysteria at the bottom the list, just below the urgency of rearranging their sock drawers.

Taking his cue from an increasingly shrill Al Gore, Obama likes reminding us how extreme the nation's weather is becoming because of our fossil fuel usage. Consider how difficult it is to take his hysterical claims seriously: Obama's first 60 months in office have seen the fewest number of hurricanes of any President in U.S. history — only three made landfall on his watch and all were weak Category 1 events. Yet between 1885 and 1889 during Grover Cleveland's first 4-year term in office, there were 16 hurricanes to make landfall including the devastating Category 4 storm in 1886 that destroyed Indianola, Texas. The accursed Indianola was clobbered by another hurricane five weeks later leaving the old part of town submerged under Matagorda Bay. Amazingly, the town had suffered a Category 3 storm just eleven years earlier. Today the remnants of the old town are inhabited by sea creatures. Yet no one issued calls to halt coal and oil shipments or to dismantle our fossil fuel way of life in the aftermath.

As these pages went to press, the nation was enjoying the longest sustained period in history back to 1869 without a major Category 3 or larger hurricane striking U.S. territory — over 3,150 days — which was twice as long as the previous major hurricane drought that occurred between 1975 and 1979 and over 30% more days than the twentieth century record established between 1900 and 1906. Despite repeated assurance to the contrary, 2013 had become the calmest Atlantic hurricane season in more than five decades even while carbon dioxide atmospheric concentration reached record levels for the modern era. All of this would be impossible if human-generated CO_2 emissions were the cause of atmospheric instability — "dirty weather" as Gore ridiculously calls it.

By contrast, in 1780, an Atlantic hurricane claimed an estimated 20,000 lives. A Category 4 storm wiped out Galveston, Texas in 1900 killing an estimated 8,000 to 12,000 Texans. A hurricane slammed into Guatemala in 1776 that claimed more than 6,000 lives. A hurricane struck Northeast states in 1938 killing 700 people, leaving tens of thousands homeless, destroying factories, and wiping entire coastal communities completely off the map. The sheer scale of these tragedies is unimaginable. And yet they all occurred before the invention of global warming. Despite the tragic loss of life from the relatively mild-by-comparison Category 1 Hurricane Sandy 2012, you don't need coal-fired power plants and SUVs to cause deadly storm activity. History proves it.

The year 2013 had also set an all time record for the fewest number of tornadoes. And the wildfire count in 2013 was lower than any time in nearly thirty years. Hurricanes, tornadoes, and wildfires supposedly would be soaring out of control with our unchecked carbon fuel usage. Since those dangers are not being observed, the ability to tie unusual weather events to the necessity of driving up energy prices will become increasingly problematic for a thoroughly corrupted Obama White House and their obsequious media mouthpieces. Each time they try, their hysterical claims will be greeted with the derisive laughter they so richly deserve.

Another pivotal event took place in 2013 that is worthy of mention. In early September, Australian voters sent a stinging rebuke to the country's hapless Labour government, throwing them out of office after six dreadful years of pathetic misrule. It was the Labour Party's worst electoral drubbing in more than eighty years. Voters had grown weary of government policy characterized by officially sanctioned climate hysteria. During Labour's time in office, the government managed to enact a deeply unpopular carbon tax despite having solemnly promised not to do so. The unpopular carbon tax had sent electricity bills soaring. Amazingly, on the very same day Australia's Labour Party was wiped out at the polls over a carbon tax, *The Washington Post* ran an editorial proclaiming that the time was right to enact a carbon tax in the U.S. Liberal editorialists are not exactly the brightest bulbs on the Yuletide tree. Even more incomprehensibly, despite the disastrous economic outcome of the carbon tax, the Labour Party had actually been preparing to initiate a carbon cap-and-trade scheme to add to the country's misery in the days just prior to its electoral wipeout. It was these twin economically depressing measures that were uppermost in voters' minds when they went to the polls salivating over the prospect of ridding themselves of the Gillard-Rudd climate-hysterical menace. Would it be too optimistic to hope that politicians in the U.S. with even a shred of self-preservation instinct are paying attention?

Alert readers may note that, in certain cases, some data citations in this volume or graphical depictions herein differ slightly from numbers available on government sites today. This is due to the fact that agencies constantly revise their historical data. For example, on November 6, 2009 when the BLS released the October 2009 employment report, the headline unemployment rate reported was 10.2%. But BLS later incorporated revisions to its Current Population Survey which scrambled all the downstream numbers. If you check today, the October 2009 headline unemployment rate is shown to be only 10.0%. It didn't exactly give great comfort to learn in 2013 that the Census Department had fed false data to the Labor Department in the months prior to the 2012 election, which had the effect of lowering the apparent unemployment rate.

Another more egregious example concerns the magic trick that the Bureau of Economic Analysis (BEA) performed in its July 2013 revisions to the National Income and Product Accounts (NIPA) data. BEA decided that there had actually been more than $1.85 trillion of additional real economic growth than previous estimates indicated, a new understanding which had hitherto escaped the notice of the entire economic community. So BEA inflated its count of economic growth all the way back to 1929 to account of all the activity that they had magically discovered but had never previously been detected.

BEA's revisions fit squarely with the tenor of the times, to wit: if you can't do it the old fashioned way by earning it, then just make it up. Like with NASA global temperature data sets, if the present refuses to grow, then the past must be altered to change the appearance. So in addition to IRS, EPA, DHHS, DoE, BLS, Justice Department, Interior Department, ICE, NLRB, State Department, U.S. Park Police, VA, FERC, and the Census Bureau, you can now add BEA to the list of federal agencies that have, at least in some measure, been debauched purely for partisan gain during the Obama era.

Since much of the analysis and exhibits contained herein were prepared prior to BEA's magical revisions were announced, I have not wasted the countless days of effort that would have been required to revise a number of charts in pursuit of so low a cause. I beg the reader's indulgence for the ever-so-slight, almost completely immaterial differences that might result from this impact. The numbers were accurate when the analytical support was compiled. As reliable media accounts contend, though some growth rate numbers changed slightly, the broad outlines of the dreadful Obama economic non-growth story remain completely intact despite all of BEA's useless efforts.

I wish to acknowledge the assistance I received from various respected authors who were gracious in responding to my requests for help and whose work has greatly influenced my thinking. Professor Paul Joskow of MIT was kind to furnish me some helpful insights and share some of his relevant work. Professor Robert Michaels at Cal State Fullerton helpfully responded to inquiries about issues related to levelized costs of generation, a subject that he has written about extensively. I also appreciate the kind advice and help I received from Robert Bryce, an author who has written extensively of the subject and whose work has been influential to my understanding.

I would also like to acknowledge the invaluable resource that is the Energy Information Administration, the handful of adults among the vast legions of children that work in the federal government on matters concerning energy policy. Readers interested in this subject who have never visited EIA's information treasure trove are encouraged to make copious usage if, for no other reason, to help ground their arguments in a reality that is sorely absent from ideologically-polluted opponents who pretend that America can transition to 'green energy' in a few years' time. I would like to acknowledge some support I received from EIA's renewable energy expert Chris Namovicz and a host of others who were responsive to my inquiries. Their help is greatly appreciated. Unlike so much of the federal bureaucracy or the mass media, the work they do at EIA is usually first rate.

"However beautiful the strategy, you should occasionally look at the results."

Winston Churchill

INTRODUCTION

WHICH PATH TO TAKE?

"One of the keys to understanding the twentieth century is to identify the beneficiaries of the decline in formal religion. The religious impulse — with all the excesses of zealotry and intolerance it can produce — remains powerful, but expresses itself in secular substitutes."[1]

HISTORIAN PAUL JOHNSON, 1980

It is often said that the road to hell is paved with good intentions. As columnist Mark Steyn observes, the truth is, it isn't paved at all. It's rocky, the footing is dangerous, and it's not well lit. Like an endless cavern, it just grows darker and more dangerous as you go deeper.[2] That seems like an excellent metaphor for the unworthy 'green energy' future of Obama. The well-intentioned 'green energy' agenda is our own road to hell.

With almost religious fervor, Obama and his ideological soul mates are fond of telling us that they have "seen the future and it works."[3] They've been telling us that since Lincoln Steffens returned from the Soviet Union in 1919 to proclaim the glorious benefits of Soviet-style centrally-planned collectivism. How well did it go there?

Let's stipulate at the outset: Energy policy is a complex subject. To a lot of folks, it's not terribly interesting. Discussions about it are unlikely to garner substantially larger audiences than important works of literature concerning love affairs among teenage vampires. But as vital as those stories are, we persevere in the hope that the stuff that warms our homes, cooks our meals, runs our workplaces, gets us to and from work, lights and heats schools, powers the ambulance taking a critical patient to the emergency room, jets us off to visit our relatives, and a thousand other things that enable our modern way of life will be seen by most people as reasonably important.

Energy policy is a numbers game. It requires us to delve deeply into numerical analysis. But while much of this volume will be steeped in charts, graphs, economic analysis, numerical examples, and a variety of other cumbersome verbiage, some of the most compelling evidence we could ever hope to collect arises from the stories of real lives that are

1

impacted by the important energy policy choices we now face. Consider some of those stories.

OUR "REAL" ENERGY FUTURE

Edrick Smith is an experienced machinist from Baltimore. He relishes the opportunity he has to learn the operation of various pieces of robotic production equipment at his company, Marlin Steel Wire Works.[4] Edrick spent many months during the recession working temporary assignments, the only work he could find. But with a surge of new orders from industrial accounts that purchase the wire-frame equipment his company makes, new job opportunities opened up and Edrick was hired. The new orders flowing into Edrick's company have come from a variety of industrial accounts that, like Marlin, have seen a ramp up in their own businesses caused by the increasing advantage those firms now enjoy relative to global competitors.

Why are Marlin's customers more competitive today than a few years ago? Because they are benefitting from low cost energy and energy-intensive industrial materials — a competitiveness that has been brought about by the boom in domestic natural gas production. Low cost natural gas is having positive ripple effects throughout the economy that would have been impossible to forecast in detail. Edrick Smith has a job and better future prospects because the oil and gas industry is producing a bounty of new economic activity.

Manufacturing is humming at Fleetwood Homes in Nampa, Idaho. It hasn't always been so. The factory that assembles pre-fabricated houses fell on hard times after the housing bubble burst in 2008. It was forced to close and the company that owned it declared bankruptcy.[5] Dozens of workers were laid off from their jobs, remaining out of work for a long time as the new owners, Cavco Industries, pondered what to do with the plant.[6] Shannon Smith, a mother of two, lost her job and her house. Unable to find work elsewhere, she went deeply into credit card debt.

But within the past few years, the factory has resumed operations, recalling workers including Mrs. Smith. She is happy to be able to pay her bills and put food on the table.[7] Fleetwood has seen a surge of new orders for housing to meet the ever-growing demand from oil field workers in North Dakota, many of whom had previously been sleeping in their cars because of a lack of housing in the Williston area. Oil drilling is remote to Mrs. Smith — she says she has never even seen an oil well. But she is working today because of the economic activity that is flowing from the oil and gas boom taking place in the U.S. on private lands hundreds of miles from her home. She prays that it keeps going strong. It will as long as crusading Luddites in Washington don't make any attempt to kill the goose laying the golden eggs.

A pair of companies are slugging it out in state court in Maine to win the right to construct a natural gas pipeline through the rural Kennebec Valley into Augusta. The pipeline would bring an estimated $240 million in construction-related activity to the community.[8] More importantly, customers in the frigid state would be able to switch from expensive heating oil to lower-cost natural gas which would save them $1,200 per year on heating bills,[9] One of the contenders in the struggle, Summit Natural Gas, outlined a plan to serve 52,000 customers that don't have access to affordable natural gas. That would enable residents to retain more than $62 million each year in disposable income for other necessities.

Trucking companies are poised to expand natural gas service territories far beyond the pipeline's reach, which will substantially expand energy competitiveness, driving down heating costs for rural residents dependent on expensive heating oil.[10] Patrick Woodcock, Director of Governor Le Page's energy office, notes that a typical Maine resident spends more than ten percent of disposable income on energy, a burden that will be substantially reduced when natural gas arrives by pipeline.[11] For a state that ranked 44th for state economic growth rates in 2012,[12] a benefit like that could have a substantial impact.

Thousands of jobs will be created building and maintaining the new Kennebec Valley pipeline. Tina Soucie attended a job fair held by Summit, the company that will be staffing permanent positions for the pipeline. Tina wants to improve her career prospects. She is attracted to Summit because it is bringing lower-cost energy, jobs, and economic growth to her community.[13] She is one of the hundreds of residents who can benefit indirectly from the boom. All of this activity came into fruition because natural gas production in the U.S. from hydraulic fracturing of shale gas has led to a surplus supply that has driven down the residential price to levels unimaginable just a few years ago.

Visitors to Western Pennsylvania marvel at how different the place looks compared to just a few years ago. There are plenty of new cars on the road, new homes are springing up, fences have been repaired, rural properties once in disrepair have been revitalized, the once chronic unemployment rate is dropping, and commerce is returning to previously dormant small towns that dot the landscape. From his office window overlooking Pittsburgh's three rivers, Richard Harshman is reminded of how this region once became the industrial powerhouse of the world. It was due to low-cost, abundant coal supplies and the network of navigable waterways that brought it to market.[14] Today a similar energy-driven economic renaissance is taking place in the region. The benefits are flowing to households throughout the country.[15] Low-cost natural gas being produced in abundance from wells in the nearby Marcellus shale play has brought a bounty of royalties to landowners as well as a powerful economic advantage to local producers.

Mr. Harshman is the CEO of Allegheny Technologies, a company that is building a $1.1 billion metals fabrication plant in nearby Brackenridge.[16] The plant's production will be used in the manufacture of drill pipes for the oil and gas industry and chemicals refining. This renaissance in Beaver County, Pennsylvania mirrors robust economic activity taking place in dozens of other communities across the country. It is taking place not because of very high energy prices that Barack Obama promised during his campaign to bring to America but because of the very low-priced natural gas that he worked overtime after taking office to prevent.

During a very brief visit to Fort McMurray in northern Alberta, Canada, a reporter has time to talk to some workers who have traveled to this remote corner of the world in search of a better life. They're not fur trappers or caribou hunters. They certainly don't come for the climate. At 300 miles north of Edmonton, it is hardly the romantic tropical getaway pictured on a travel poster. With snow on the ground seven months of the year and more mosquitoes than practically any place on earth during the short summer months, no one comes for the weather. One thing this region does offer is steady work with wages far in excess of what workers can earn elsewhere. An annual wage rate in the $150,000 – $200,000 per year range is being paid for a skilled rig operator.[17] Among those who have come are a former IT professional, a lawyer, and a woman from the UK who had trained as a speech therapist. An interviewee tells reporters from *NBC* studios in New York that he can make enough money to save for his children's college education, something he could never have done in any previous occupation.[18]

Fort McMurray is undergoing a gold rush of sorts. A massive amount of capital investment is flooding into the region to mine and process oil trapped in sand near the surface. Solid oily resin called bitumen is the black gold that has brought money and jobs into this otherwise desolate locale.

Mining of bitumen is an energy-intensive process. Copious amounts of natural gas are required to heat water used to reduce viscosity of the solid bitumen trapped inside sandy soils. Unlike just a few years ago, abundant low cost natural gas is now available. And because natural gas prices have plunged, the economics of oil sand production have become favorable, opening the door to western Canada's vast oil production potential.[19] Natural gas prices are low because revolutionary recovery methods have brought forth a flood of gas from North America's vast shale deposits, making the U.S. self-sufficient for the first time in decades.

Visitors to the oil sands pits near Fort McMurray are startled when they see the Caterpillar Model 797 earth moving trucks used to haul the oil-rich material for processing. The truck is a behemoth, larger than most single-family houses. Each truck is capable of hauling 400 tons of earth at a time. That compares to an ordinary dump truck you'd see on the road that can haul a 20-25 ton load. The wheels alone stand 12-feet high meaning that the axle stands higher than the average person's head. But most important for our purpose is the economic impact for U.S. workers.

The Caterpillar 797 is built at CAT's assembly plant in Decatur, Illinois. The engine is built at CAT's engine plant in Lafayette, Indiana. The cab section is manufactured at the Bergstrom Climate Control Systems plant in Joliet, Illinois. These are a few examples of how an oil boom in faraway Canada is producing jobs, income, and economic growth here at home. It's estimated that 90% of the money spent on oil sands production in Canada is funneled back in extended supply chain goods and service in the U.S.[20] Consider a few other examples.

The tires for the CAT 797 are manufactured at a Michelin plant in Lexington, South Carolina. Michelin announced in April 2012 that they would be investing $757 million to expand the earthmover tire plant in Lexington and build a second tire plant for construction equipment in Anderson County.[21] Once Bridgestone and Continental AG complete their tire plants, South Carolina will be the nation's largest tire-producing state. The expansion will add an additional 270 jobs, bringing the plant's employee roster to 1,700 workers.[22] Michelin has become the largest manufacturing employer in South Carolina with more than 8,000 workers in the state.[23] It operates nine manufacturing plants in South Carolina alone.[24] Thirty percent of the tires from the Lexington plant are sent to Canada and used in Alberta oil sands mining.[25] Though Fort McMurray is thousands of miles from Lexington, and most of the Michelin workers in South Carolina will never get close to Fort McMurray, hundreds of them have jobs today because of the oil sands mining.

Michelin has sunk nearly $1 billion in investment projects in South Carolina since 2011. Capital investment is crucial to historically underserved economies like South Carolina. To understand its importance, consider the case of the Philippines, the fastest growing Asian economy in 2012. The country is benefitting from a boom in foreign direct investment with its manufacturing sector posting a 9.7% growth rate in the first quarter of 2013.[26] In 2012, "private sector investment contributed more to [real GDP] growth than household consumption" according to a report in the *Financial Times*. When investment capital pours in, so do jobs.

In a solemn ceremony on September 9, 2003, the Amite Foundry and Machine Company in Louisiana dedicated a casting for the bow section of the USS New York, the fifth of the San Antonio-class amphibious transport ships ordered by the U.S. Navy.[27] The materials used in the casting had been recovered from the World Trade Center wreckage. An emotional Amite spokesman Wayne Peterson remarked that his company was "grateful we've been chosen to do this work." His workers are also very grateful the company was chosen to fabricate the nine immense metal castings that are used in the frame sections of the CAT 797 earthmover. Those sections are machined in Louisiana and shipped to CAT's Decatur plant.

That business won't attract the attention of Washington- or New York-based journalists the way the solemn dedication ceremony for the USS New York bow-section casting did. But it will provide steady work for employees. It is work that wouldn't exist if Canada had chosen to follow the recommendations of environmental zealots that have labored mightily to have the activity stopped based upon a dubious climate justification.

Fortunately for the U.S. and Canadian workers, the Canadian government has ignored the chorus of climate campaigners and is plowing ahead with development of the country's resources.

First time visitors to western North Dakota are struck by the austere quality of the endless desolate landscape. Mile after mile of treeless, gently undulating grasslands are usually covered at least partly with snow from mid-October often until early May. Cows outnumber people about 100-to-one. The wind blows a lot, it's cold most of the time and, in summer, the police don't respond to very many skinny dipping complaints. You won't find the area pictured on the front cover of an up-market travel magazine.

The region witnessed a gradual population decline over the previous seven decades as people fled the prairie desolation for jobs and a better chance for prosperity in far-away locales. Montrail County in the Western part of the state housed fewer residents in 2005 than it did during the Great Depression.[28] The few ranchers who remained — and were wise enough to hang on to their mineral rights — are not sorry they stayed. The United States is one of the only nations on the planet that allows landowners the right to possess the mineral wealth under their feet.[29] North Dakota has plenty of mineral wealth and not many feet.

Barack Obama convinced throngs of well-intentioned dreamers in 2008 that he had a plan for the country's energy independence based upon deploying wind towers, solar panels, and biofuel refineries. His plan doesn't stand a chance of success. The real epicenter of America's drive towards impending energy self-sufficiency can be located near Williston in this desolate landscape in the northwestern corner of North Dakota. Williston sits atop the Bakken shale formation in nearby Williams County. The formation discovered in 1953 was named after local farmer Henry Bakken.[30] Instead of solar panels, they drill vertical holes two miles into the earth's crust, coaxing the drill bit to turn 90 degrees horizontally when it reaches the center of a shale seam. Then they blast water, sand and chemical mixtures under very high pressure to fracture the shale. And viola, oil flows to the surface. Lots of it. More than 900,000 barrels a day by October 2013.[31] That was nine times as much as came out of the ground in 2006. As oil comes out, money, jobs, workers, economic growth, personal income, and prosperity flood in.

Fred Evans is a good example of the kind of people you find in the Bakken region. Unlike many of his neighbors, Fred always believed American technological ingenuity would eventually succeed in bringing the massive reservoirs of oil to the surface despite repeated failures of the past. A former cattle rancher, wheat farmer, and drill rig hand, Evans bought or leased the mineral rights on adjacent properties. His bet paid off making him one of the wealthiest landowners in Mountrail County.[32] As some of his neighbors like to say, Mr. Evans is "bringin' home the Bakken." He's the kind of guy who will drop a $20 tip into the tip jar at Subway after paying for his $10 lunch. As the hourly Subway wage earners will tell you, Mr. Evans is not the only one making money here.

Another resident is Lenin Dibble. While his first name might suggest someone who agitates for the overthrow of the capitalist system, the retired rancher and wheat farmer is fine with the present arrangement. The 75-year old Mr. Dibble lives in a trailer home like many low-income people do. But Lenin Dibble is not really a low-income homeowner, just low-key. That's because he's another resident who's "rockin' the Bakken" as they say. Dibble collects about $80,000 a month in royalty income from the mineral rights on his land, a legacy he plans to bequeath to his children and grandchildren.[33] For his heirs, "if it wasn't for the Bakken, they'd be walkin'" to find better opportunities elsewhere. But instead, their futures are now assured because of America's abundant energy wealth that doesn't rely upon the forbearance of a federal government headed by a politician who wants to see the prosperity extinguished. It all sits on privately-owned lands, so there's little he can do to stop it.

Doing his level best to pretend like there is some major controversy afoot that could cast a pall over the boom, *The New York Times'* self-pitying vegetarian son of the paper's publisher[34] manages to locate a handful of disgruntled malcontents who can always be relied upon to concentrate on the negative aspects of good fortune if it revolves around oil and gas.[35] A.G. Sulzberger of the *Times* is typical of someone who can travel thousands of miles from home, stay for days on end, talk to dozens of people, visit every address in a small town like Stanley and yet, due to ideological obtuseness, never learn the magnificence of the story he was sent to cover. Oil income has brought prosperity to this forgotten corner of the world. Were it not for the oil, the Sulzbergers of New York wouldn't even be able to locate North Dakota on a map. What a headache it must seem to a spoiled trust-fund brat from the Empire State whose pampered future was assured the instant he was conceived. As he masquerades as a reporter, he will never understand the lives of real people who are obligated by circumstances to work for a living.

According to the paper's narrative, North Dakota's 13.4% real economic growth rate in 2012 is supposedly far less desirable than New York's 1.3% rate in the same year.[36] North Dakota ranked number one on the list of state economic growth rates for three straight years while New York ranked 37th.[37] Over the previous four years, New York's economy grew by a combined 5.1 percent. Meanwhile, North Dakota logged a combined 35.0 percent growth rate over the same period.[38] On the date of the media empire heir's visit, North Dakota was posting the country's lowest unemployment rate, below 3.3%, which compared to New York's headline rate above 8%.[39] North Dakota had created jobs during the previous year at a rate nearly six times faster than New York had.[40] It accounted for the fastest personal income growth in the country in five of the previous six years up to 2012, climbing 3.2 times faster than the rest of the country.[41] Between 2006 and 2013, median wages in North Dakota grew 2.3 times faster than in New York.[42] It all happened because of the oil wealth coming out of the Bakken shale. But that's not the story the paper likes to tell.

Instead, the "newspaper of record" affects to be scandalized by the grotesquely uneven wealth distribution — some families are receiving royalty income from oil drillers while others are not. He pretends to be "shocked, shocked" that there is "a great divide over oil riches." This is unseemly to the Ivy League-educated scion from New York. Never mind that they do uneven wealth distribution in New York better than anywhere. The Sulzbergers of New York could hold seminars on the practice.

After spending days talking to local residents, the *Times'* star reporter fails to discover that even the most unskilled workers in the region are benefitting handsomely. The entry-level wage rate at Walmart is $17.50 per hour.[43] Try finding an hourly rate like that for unskilled labor, even in New York. McDonalds in Williston pays $18.00 an hour, covers its employees with a free Cadillac health care plan, and offers a $1,000 signing bonus if the worker agrees to remain on the job for three months.[44] Homeowners with a spare room collect $100 a night in rent. They can keep their rooms booked 365 nights a year if they choose. Those benefits are not being siphoned away by oil giants Halliburton or Schlumberger, the two largest drillers in the region, or by billionaire oil company magnates. They flow into the pockets of local residents all of whom earned a fraction of that amount a few years ago. These are folks who don't have Ivy League diplomas or trust funds. They depend on these jobs and revenue sources for their livelihoods.

Williston and nearby Stanley are examples of America's energy boom towns where employers practically chase you down the street with job offers — "jobs that pay well and can't be outsourced" as Barack Obama promised on a thousand occasions to bring to America.[45] Except Obama was talking about his 'green energy' jobs that never materialized, not oil and gas jobs that are actually available by the boatload.

As Fred Evans or Lenin Dibble will assure you, America's real energy future is here, not in some ridiculously expensive, taxpayer-subsidized solar ranch in California or in the unsightly wind farms that are fouling the pristine vistas of our most majestic landscapes. And certainly not in those biofuel refineries that are burning up 40% of America's corn supply. The benefits from oil are flowing into every corner of the economy. Everyone understands it to be true except the shrill reporters and editors from *The New York Times* — and the ideologues at the Obama White House.

THE 'GREEN ENERGY' STORY

Domingo Tamupsis works on a sugar plantation in Guatemala harvesting sugar cane that is converted to bio-ethanol for shipment to the U.S.[46] There, the imported product is blended into gasoline and sold to motorists. Despite the fact that Domingo's work occurs in the most fertile agricultural region of Guatemala, Domingo and his family go hungry nearly every day. His 23-year old wife Marina is so slender, she could be mistaken for a child half her age. His two year old daughter Yessica has the distended belly typical of children suffering from chronic malnutrition. His third child was stillborn after Marina's difficult eight month pregnancy marked by chronic hunger and sickness.

Conditions are so dire for Domingo and his family because food prices have risen so dramatically over the past year. Given his meager wages, he is unable to keep his family properly fed. But why have food prices jumped so dramatically? Quite simply, the U.S. and the European Union have both established mandatory programs that require massive amounts of biofuels to be used within their respective jurisdictions. Those fuels are either made directly from food crops that are diverted to biofuel production or are made from other crops like palm oil that have displaced food-growing acreage. Domingo's employer grows sugar cane which it converts to fuel and exports. That fuel helps gasoline blenders in the U.S. comply with the Renewable Fuel Standard (RFS2) law enacted in 2007. It also allows 'green energy' activists pretend they're saving the planet. Meanwhile, Domingo and his family go hungry.

The biofuel programs in the U.S. and the EU were enacted under a wildly erroneous belief that they would be beneficial to the planet's climate. While no one in the universe can offer a syllable of proof that the Earth's climate has benefitted from biofuel programs, there is plenty of evidence that they are causing irreversible damage to sensitive ecosystems around the world.[47] Even worse is the toll being taken on the world's poor.[48] Authoritative reports from the World Bank and other agencies consistently show that biofuels programs are causing food prices to soar, resulting in widespread starvation and chronic malnutrition.[49]

The U.S. siphons away nearly 42% of its annual corn crop for ethanol production.[50] That is enough corn to feed 350 million people.[51] The U.S. RFS2 program caused food import costs in Guatemala to increase by $28 million in 2011 according to a report in the *Financial Times*.[52] Coincidentally, that happened to be the exact amount of food aid extended to Guatemala in 2011 by various U.S. food assistance programs.[53] In essence, the RFS2 program incinerated 100% of the food aid U.S. taxpayers extended to Guatemala to enable the country to alleviate the chronic malnutrition.

Biofuels are a form of 'green energy' that are promoted as a solution to global warming. Barack Obama has spoken on hundreds of occasions about how marvelously successful they have been.[54] But Obama's children will never have distended bellies like Yessica Tamupsis. Welcome to the brave new world of climate politics where food supplies that could alleviate hunger in hundreds of millions of the world's poor are incinerated, where concerns about famine are brushed aside to satisfy an angry climate campaigning mob that insanely insists biofuels will help avoid some distant climate cataclysm while ignoring the very real starvation and malnutrition tragedy playing out in poor countries right under their noses, famines their policies helped cause. Domingo Tamupsis and his starving family are the faces of Obama's 'green energy' future.

Retired truck driver Eric Ingram sits in his Gloucestershire flat wearing a heavy coat and gloves on a freezing cold day in late October. With his £144 a week pension and a £300 winter fuel allowance from the UK government, it is simply not enough money to afford the fuel to keep his flat warm — unless he decides to forego food.[55] In Eric's case as with millions of other pensioners, it comes down to a decision whether to heat or eat. The winter fuel allowance will cover only half of the increase he saw in his gas and electricity bill during the previous year.

But people like Eric can be counted among the more fortunate. He was still alive when a reporter came to visit. Rebecca Smith was unlucky in that respect. Well known among her neighbors as someone who lived a "chaotic lifestyle" as press reports antiseptically phrased it, Rebecca was found frozen on the floor of her flat. Her heating had run out.[56] For Rebecca as with millions of poverty-stricken residents, the gas supply is controlled by a token meter. If the money runs out, the heat goes out with it.

Jean and Derrick Randall suffered the same fate. Police who forced their way into the freezing flat of the fiercely independent elderly couple found a tragic scene with Mr. Randall dead on the floor in a hallway and his wife frozen in her bed.[57] Neighbors had been bringing extra clothing and blankets to the elderly couple. But that was no substitute for central heating.

The tragedy of the Randalls resulted in a row in Parliament. A prominent voice in the debate was the Secretary of State for Energy and Climate Change Chris Huhne, who angrily proclaimed that landlords should be forced to upgrade insulation of rented flats if tenants demanded it.[58] But tenants were not dying from a shortage of insulation. They were dying from a shortage of electric and natural gas heat because they couldn't afford the energy prices that Huhne's climate policies were causing to soar.

Huhne is a 21st century model of 'green energy' triumphalism. He boasts that his home is outfitted with its own wind turbine.[59] He brags that he drives a Toyota *Prius*. Fawning media file obscene reports asking in complete seriousness "Is This the Man to Save our Planet?"[60] He likes to brag about the virtues of a 'green energy' future without a shred of understanding about its implications. Huhne thinks that 40% of the country's power that comes from aging coal and nuclear plants can be converted over to unreliable, expensive, intermittent wind power.[61] His plan for thousands of more wind towers ignores the fact that the 3,000 already deployed only produce an average of a single baseload power station using coal, nuclear or natural gas, all of which he opposes.[62] He imagines that imposing life-threatening energy policies will have a material impact on the planet's climactic fate in a country that accounted for only 1.5% of global CO_2 emissions in 2011.[63] Huhne boasted to reporters that his policies were "the most comprehensive and radical policies for reducing carbon emissions in this country" — as if it really mattered — in the same breath as he promised that he wouldn't go "streaking down the high streets of Britain."[64]

But streaking down the high streets of Britain is exactly what he did, receiving a speeding ticket in the process.[65] The trouble was that the selfless savior of the planet coerced his wife to accept blame for the violation so he could avoid the points that would have cost him his license.[66] Huhne and his wife were both convicted of perverting the course of justice and sentenced to prison. It was the wrong offense. Huhne, the man who challenged for the leadership of the Liberal Democrat Party that, had he won, would have put him one election away from becoming the UK Prime Minister, should have been convicted of conspiring to kill pensioners by the thousands. A shocking one fourth of them, like Eric Ingram and the Randalls, suffer from fuel poverty.[67]

Electric utility company E.On estimates that even during mild winters, an additional 8,000 people die for each one degree drop in winter temperatures.[68] But the past few winters have been particularly cold, undercutting the reliability of long-range weather forecasters at the UK's Meteorological Office. With its precision forecasts, the Met Office was once a reliable source of weather forecasting information that helped the Allies win the war over Germany. But in recent years, it has allowed itself to become a thoroughly corrupted appendage of the global warming hysteria industry, forced to admit that the planet had stopped warming nearly 20 years earlier.[69]

The UN Intergovernmental Panel on Climate Change (IPCC) 4th Assessment report — supposedly the world's most authoritative source on the state of global climate science — was released in 2007 and provided cover to UK politicians to enact the economically damaging Climate Change Act of 2008. That measure set the country on its present path of 'green energy' indulgence. The IPCC report's authors included some of the very British climate scientists who had had a hand in steering the Met Office's flawed reporting on impending climate doom.

The 2007 IPCC report has since been discredited, and its lead author Phil Jones has been publicly humiliated, forced to resign his academic post in disgrace.[70] The IPCC-global warming industry hysteria storyline is beginning to crumble.[71] But the 2008 law that will inexorably propel energy prices higher — and claim thousands more lives in the process — will continue unimpeded by the human toll. It is already driving up prices, putting generation plants out of business, and straining the electricity grid, a situation that energy regulator Ofgem calls "horrendous."[72]

The first victims of the program are the pensioners who are freezing to death by the thousands due to a lack of affordable energy. An estimated 7,800 people freeze to death inside their homes each year in the UK.[73] That is more than four times the number of people who die in accidents each year on motorways.[74] The number of hypothermia deaths among the elderly in the UK is estimated to have doubled in the previous five years.[75] An unbelievable 80% of British households are forced to ration energy use due to soaring energy prices that occurred in the wake of the country's ruinous policies.[76] While the IPCC and their evangelizing media sycophants endlessly drone on about dangers of a warmer planet, they keep hidden the basic fact that five times more people die from cold during winter than those who die of heat-related causes during summer.[77]

Incredibly, one fourth of UK households are believed to suffer from energy poverty.[78] Observers point to reliable forecasts that show as many as nine million households, a 50% increase over 2012, will be plunged into fuel poverty by 2016.[79] Household energy prices leaped nearly 20% in just three years since 2009.[80] Rational minds would naturally assume that when such a large percentage of a democratic country's citizenry is adversely affected by deliberate government policy, politicians would hasten to amend it. One would be miserably mistaken for believing so in the case of European nations. Nevertheless, Chancellor of the Exchequer George Osborne announced in late 2012 that the UK government would consider implementing tax breaks to encourage hydraulic fracturing to boost natural gas supply, reduce energy imports, and drive down prices as has occurred in the U.S.[81]

If Eric Ingram thinks his heating costs are expensive now, wait until he gets the bill for the 32,000 wind turbines that the UK government wants to install, 80% of which will be the breathtakingly expensive offshore variety.[82] Once that program is completed, the average ratepayer will be paying an extra £2,400 each year for electricity. That will add an additional £200 to a monthly energy bill that Mr. Ingram already can't afford to pay. But by then, it won't matter how expensive it is because electricity won't even be available at any price. So says Steve Holliday, chief executive of the National Grid, who claims that the days of permanently available power are coming to an end.[83]

Holliday proclaims that "the way that we produce and consume energy today is not sustainable."[84] He says "a large share of our energy will be reliant on the weather."[85] Because the weather is wholly unreliable, Britons will simply have to get used to living without heat and power on the worst days of bitter cold when the wind turbines the nation will rely upon for a majority of its power will stop working. Those instances when the wind stops blowing increasingly coincide with wintertime cold fronts that descend across Northern Europe as they have been doing more frequently in recent years. During those periods, the wind stops blowing for days on end — and pensioners will die in the flats from hypothermia by the tens of thousands each month.

A report in *The Daily Mail* notes that during a particularly nasty cold snap on December 20th in 2010, peak generating capacity across the UK was just over 60,000 megawatts of power. Wind power nameplate capacity was rated at 5,891 megawatts on that day, or nearly 10% of the overall total. Yet, on that crucial day when British consumers needed every watt of power to heat homes and offices, wind was able to supply only 140 megawatts.[86] That amounts to just 2.4% of rated capacity and a laughable 0.2% of overall needs.

BBC meteorologist Paul Hudson cites a peer-reviewed study in the learned *Environmental Research Letters* authored by Mike Lockwood, a University of Reading professor of space environment physics, who claims that the UK is likely to experience even more severe cold weather winters in the future marked by the same anomalous low-wind patterns.[87] This is a situation that would devastate the electrical grid if reliance on wind power for increasing amounts of the country's electrical power were to occur over the next decade or two as wind power supporters like National Grid chief executive Steve Holliday insist it must.

UK Labour Party leader Ed Miliband plans to cap retail energy prices if he is elected in 2015, a plan that might appeal to many struggling UK voters.[88] Miliband's plan would require power producers to buy increasingly expensive 'green energy' from subsidized producers while the prices they can charge retail customers would be fixed. This will result in a slow starvation of capital investment in reliable baseload generation capacity over time as energy company profits plunge. So the fate of Britain's energy companies will be determined not by economic realities but by the whims of cynical politicians catering to public opinion.[89] Shares in energy companies plunged by £2 billion in a single trading day after that announcement.[90]

If enacted, Miliband's plan will end in catastrophe. A similar situation occurred in California when retail prices were fixed at below-market levels while highly volatile wholesale prices were allowed to increase. Wholesale electricity prices that averaged $30 per megawatt-hour during the year 2000 soared to $330 by January 2001.[91] Blackouts occurred across the state as consumers gobbled up cheaper energy while power companies were eventually starved into bankruptcy or sustained on emergency state bailouts.[92] Children were sent to school on cold winter days wrapped in blankets while teachers brought lanterns to see inside darkened buildings.[93] Americans experienced shortages first hand caused by Miliband-style price controls during the era of the 1970s. Basic commodities like toilet paper disappeared from store shelves as a result of President Nixon's ham-fisted attempt to halt an inflationary spiral through price controls.

Central planning expert Miliband's grandiose energy nationalization promise, which may also include seizure of water and rail service as well, is an effort to restore Labour's economic glory days of the mid-1970s when its policies caused the economy to seize up, electrical power shortages and blackouts became commonplace, economic growth collapsed, the exchange rate of sterling plunged, nationwide labor strikes paralyzed the nation, garbage piled up in city parks, unemployment soared, and the country was thrown into chaos. Of course, it was Miliband's program enacted while he was the UK's Secretary of Energy and Climate Change that was partly the cause of soaring energy prices in the first place.[94]

So ratepayers like Eric Ingram may take comfort that his fuel bill might be stabilized at some future level.[95] But by then, energy shortages will assure that electric power and gas heating won't be available at any price. So low prices will offer little comfort. Bundled up in coats and gloves inside his flat to avoid death from hypothermia, Eric Ingram is another face of the Obama-style 'green energy' future being pioneered in Europe, another worthless utopian future that will become increasingly more expensive, regulated, authoritarian, unstable, politicized, and energy-starved.

Press reports indicate that the UK came within hours of running out of natural gas supplies in late March of 2013 as unseasonable cold descended over the entire country.[96] A similar natural gas supply emergency had occurred in 2010 when the worst cold snap in 30 years sent gas prices soaring 70 percent.[97] The nation suffered its coldest March in over 50 years as the number of deaths from freezing in the first two weeks of March soared by 2,000 over the average for the same period during the previous five years.[98] That horrific toll comes on top of an extra 3,057 cold-related deaths the previous month over the five year average for February.[99] To meet its obligation under EU climate policy, the UK has closed eight of its ten coal-fired generation plants and the government, enthralled with global warming hysteria and taking dictation from climate troglodytes in Brussels,[100] has no idea how to replace the shuttered capacity fast enough to avoid blackouts in coming years.[101] But Britons don't need to live this way.

Curiously, the UK is sitting on a massive deposit of Lancashire shale that is estimated to contain as much as 1,800 trillion cubic feet of natural gas.[102] That resource, in conjunction with the country's North Sea deposits, is enough to meet the natural gas requirements of the entire country for hundreds of years — as much as fifteen centuries by some estimates.[103] To get at it, British companies would need to use the proven low-risk recovery method of hydraulic fracturing — or "fracking" as it is often called — a method pioneered in the U.S. With increased domestic supply, it is certainly possible that prices could drop in the domestic market in the same manner as happened in the U.S. where prices plunged to a fifth of their previous high price after fracking volumes flooded onto the market. That would ease concerns of pensioners who struggle to pay their soaring energy costs, allowing thousands of them to continue living more dignified lives rather than freezing to death in their own homes. But it is no sure thing.

Fracking opponents in the UK media like *The Telegraph*'s Geoffrey Lean, the silliest columnist in the country, pretend that fracking is unlikely to produce useful quantities of oil and natural gas because "the rock has to be just right … a rare occurrence."[104] This is imbecility squared. For example, the Marcellus and Barnett shale formations in the U.S. that are largely responsible for America's natural gas renaissance that has driven down prices by 75% from their previous peak are only about 300 feet thick. The Bowland shale in the UK where Caudrilla Resources is exploring is nearly 6,000 feet thick in some places.[105]

Productive shale is supposedly so rare that fracking is happening in North Dakota's Bakken shale, Pennsylvania's Marcellus shale, Texas' widely distributed Barnett, Eagle Ford, and Permian shale basins, Arkansas' Fayetteville shale, Louisiana's Haynesville and Tuscaloosa shales, Wyoming's widely separated Green River and Powder River basins, Oklahoma's Anadarko shale, Kansas' Woodford shale, New Mexico's Avalon-Bone Spring and Raton basins, Colorado's Niobara shale and even in California's Monterrey shale. Fracking has occurred in at least five Canadian provinces.[106] It's already happening in Australia.[107] It has begun in Israel's Levantine basin.[108]

Exploration is underway in Indonesia's largest island of Sumatra.[109] It will be happening in China once infrastructure is in place to get the output to market.[110] It would be happening in Poland if the Polish government hadn't gotten greedy, demanding an 80% revenue split with at-risk producers.[111] It would already be happening in Argentina's massive Neuquén, Golfo San Jorge, Austral and Paraná Basins that are believed to hold the world's second largest deposits of shale oil[112] if global producers weren't fearful that Presidente Cristina Fernández would nationalize their investments as she did with Repsol's Argentine assets.[113] It would be happening in Germany if the climate-hysterical citizenry had any detectable brain wave activity.[114] And it would be happening in large measure in the UK if there weren't so many anti-fracking Luddites like Geoffrey Lean.

According to a report released by the Department of Energy that assessed shale recovery potential in 41 countries outside the U.S., "there has been interest expressed or exploration activities begun in shale formations in a number of other countries, including Algeria, Argentina, Australia, China, India, Mexico, Poland, Romania, Russia, Saudi Arabia, Turkey, Ukraine, and the United Kingdom."[115] Is that rare enough?

The Telegraph's resident global warming hysteric Lean boasts approvingly that fracking opponents bring "music, presentations, poetry … fuelled by freshly prepared vegan and vegetarian foods" to their opposition rallies.[116] But it's clear they don't bother bringing any economic analysis, geological reports, environmental science, or even basic human compassion for elderly pensioners who shiver in the dark. Neither does Mr. Lean. Those are useless commodities to fracking opponents and their media enablers who apparently prefer to see pensioners freeze in their flats rather than be benefitted by domestic production of natural gas that could assure adequate supplies, reduce energy prices, and save lives. Like most of his ideological soul mates, Mr. Lean doesn't believe it better to remain silent and be thought a fool than to speak out and remove all doubt.

But the legislative psychosis that has infused the UK government's global warming hysteria has been called into question.[117] Member of Parliament Peter Lilley rose in the House of Commons in April 2013 to skewer two Tory Party leaders most closely associated with the policy madness.[118] One of those politicians, Tim Yeo, collects hundreds of thousands of pounds each year in lobbying fees from wind farm interests.[119] Lilley's appended words are worth quoting at length:

> *Those whom the gods wish to destroy they first make mad … I do not like seeing hundreds of millions of my fellow human beings wallowing in misery and living lives that are stunted relative to what their material living standards might be if they achieved economic growth. But growth requires energy — it is almost synonymous with the rise in the use of energy … Fossil fuels are the cheapest form of energy. Renewables cost two or more times as much as fossil fuels to produce a given amount of energy.*[120]

As the UK shivered through its fifth freezing winter in a row that saw thousands more freeze to death in their homes from fuel poverty, the UK government plowed ahead trying to solve human-induced global warming by itself. Despite the fact that virtually every industrialized country in the world including 'green energy' leader Germany was busy deploying fossil fuel power plants, that China increased the level of its CO_2 emissions in 2011 alone by 200 million metric tons more than the entire emissions of the UK, the country had set itself on a dangerous alternative path.[121] Not surprisingly, as the thermometer plunged, so did EU residents' trust in government.[122] Politicians have taken a holiday from reality. They are suffering from what author Steve Goreham calls "the tragedy of climatism"[123] where an extraordinary popular delusion — that a single country can materially affect the trajectory of the climate by adopting economically ruinous actions — has caused governments to enact policies that are not only wrong-headed but are actually killing their citizens. Someone should dial up Geoffrey Lean and let him in on the news … if they can get a long-distance connection to the far side of the distant galaxy where he resides.

Britain's largest power plant is located near Drax, a small village in North Yorkshire. With its six boilers, the coal-fired behemoth that sits astride the Selby coal pits is rated at nearly 4,000 megawatts, capable of providing almost 7% of the country's peak load power requirements.[124] Amazingly, the plant will spend £700 million to convert three of its six boilers to burn wood pellets that will be imported from managed forests in Canada and the U.S.[125] Meanwhile, the country is closing coal generation capacity far faster than it can hope to replace it with other sources.[126]

Europe is not running low on coal. It is suffering from a dangerous shortage of sanity.[127] In place of five million metric tons of coal, the UK has decided to source forest timber from the U.S. That will require the utility to construct wood pelletizing plants in Mississippi and Louisiana, load them onto trucks and rail cars destined to Baton Rouge, lift them onto 50,000 ton bulk cargo vessels, and ship them to the UK. From there they will be transferred onto rail cars for shipment to the Drax power plant at a rate of seven trainloads a day. Pellets will then be pulverized and humidified to prevent fires like one that caused millions of pounds of damage to the Tilbury power plant.[128] Other EU utilities are sourcing wood from North Carolina where 100-year old stands of pine, sycamore, cypress, oak, beech, and tupelo gum trees are being clear cut to serve EU renewable obligations.[129] Wood pellet exports hit 2 million tons in 2012 but would double in 2013.[130]

Burning wood permits the plant to qualify for a decarbonization subsidy called a Renewable Obligation Certificate equal to £45 per megawatt-hour.[131] Those certificates come from an office next door to where Certifiably Insane Certificates are issued. The continent's climate campaigners line up outside that office — with poetry and vegan dishes. The renewable energy subsidy alone is 2.3 times more than the weighted average price of electricity on U.S. wholesale market hubs in 2012.[132]

Once complete, the plant's owners will receive £550 million in UK taxpayer subsidies, which compares to the plant's pre-tax profit in 2012 of only £190 million. Hilariously, 'green energy' zealots who are most vocal in their condemnation of energy-company profiteering[133] are also the ones who have cheered most loudly for imposition of these 'green energy' policies that have perverted markets beyond recognition, and cheered moratoriums on fracking that have disrupted the country's pursuit of its natural gas wealth.[134] The plant will cash in on climate hysteria worth four times the earnings it settled for when it had to rely upon the mundane economics of selling electrical power.

Meanwhile, the cost of electricity generation from burning wood may triple according to authoritative estimates.[135] A 2008 study for The House of Lords found that electricity generated from wood costs twice as much as from coal, and even costs more when coal emissions are penalized by £50 per metric ton.[136] Credit Suisse estimates that UK electricity prices will soon be twice those in Germany.[137] Due to its relentless pursuit of 'green energy,' Germany boasts the second most expensive power prices among the core 15 member nations of the European Union.[138] In 2012, German households paid more than three times the level that U.S. residential ratepayers paid.[139] All of the construction costs, subsidies, and higher power generation costs will be borne by British ratepayers to reduce their "carbon footprint."

However, when whole trees are used for fuel in this manner, it will actually increase carbon emissions by 79% over the next 20 years according to analysis from Dr. Timothy Searchinger of Princeton University, who has studied and published his findings in peer-reviewed journals.[140] But even if we accept the UK's lopsided carbon avoidance calculation — and we'd be ill-advised to do so — what will be the price tag per metric ton of CO_2 avoided? Under even the most optimistic economic assumptions, UK taxpayers will be shelling out £225, or U.S. $372, per metric ton.[141]

That £225 cost compares with a price of carbon emission certificates on Europe's Emission Trading System which averaged less than £4 per metric ton during the first few months of 2013.[142] But the UK can't offset emissions from coal use in this manner because Parliament passed a law that set a floor price on carbon at far higher levels, which British electricity rate- and taxpayers will need to absorb.[143] Wood, the energy source pioneered by Paleolithic cave dwellers 300,000 years ago[144] — the EU's twenty first century "fuel of the future" — is an example of climate lunacy in hyper-drive.

Like many Spaniards, Juan Antonio Cabrero exuded optimism when Spain's government announced its plan to adopt a 'green energy' transformation. Unfortunately, the sales professional of a hybrid bus manufacturer embraced that plan more wholeheartedly than was good for him. Señor Cabrero was enthusiastic when leftist former Spanish Prime Minister Jose Luis Rodriguez Zapatero proclaimed his vision for transforming Spain into a twenty first century economic miracle through massive deployment of renewable energy like solar and wind. All these 'green energy' investments would be supported by generous subsidies from the public treasury.

Cabrero poured all of his life's savings and took out an €80,000 bank loan to invest in a large solar energy producing plant near his property.[145] He pledged his family home as loan collateral. The solar investment was predicated upon assurances from the government that the promised subsidy flow would run unimpaired for at least twenty years, enough to pay off the loan and help fund the 60-year old Señor Cabrero's retirement. That solar power produced by the plant was many times more expensive than traditional forms of energy that Spain relied upon was no impediment to the leftist ideologue Zapatero — or to Señor Cabrero.

Zapatero was elected in 2004 proclaiming an end to nuclear power that supplied 23% of the country's electricity, vowing to replace it with subsidized solar and wind.[146] As a candidate, Obama regularly extolled Spain's virtues, claiming America needed to act aggressively to establish its leadership.[147] Obama wanted to transform America in the same way Spain was transforming itself, substituting low cost baseload power for new, revolutionary, intermittent, onerously costly 'green energy.' Sure, that would drive up energy costs on every segment of the economy. But visionaries like Zapatero and Obama promised a flood of new, high-paying jobs that couldn't be outsourced.[148] Spanish citizens salivated.

Perhaps the most specious claim from 'green energy' promoters was that the program would create a tidal wave of 'green jobs.' That conceit was thoroughly dismantled by a very influential study published in 2009 by economist Gabriel Calzada Alvarez of Spain's King Juan Carlos University. Professor Alvarez's study showed that the country's 'green energy' program had actually destroyed more than twice as many jobs as it created.[149] Extremists like the Natural Resources Defense Council have discredited themselves trying to counter the damaging impact of this study.[150] But despite these low-road efforts, the debt load from the ruinous subsidy program continued to pile up.[151] That aspect of their program was undeniable.

By 2008, Spain was installing half of the entire world's solar energy capacity.[152] Domestic and global investors poured in to soak up the lucrative financial returns promised by the Zapatero government. This led to an unsustainable bubble, piling up a mountain of debt that the country could ill-afford. Companies that had been planning to monetize their holdings by offloading worthless equity shares on European bourses were forced to abandon those plans.[153] Suddenly, the economic equation that relied upon an uninterrupted spigot of public funds had been upended and the government was forced to curtail subsidies.[154]

Spanish voters delivered a stinging rebuke to Zapatero in May 2011, throwing his Socialist party out of power, a vote which ended his political career.[155] But that was a small price to pay for the destroyed futures those policies had engendered in a nation that could not afford his senseless vision. Spaniards like Juan Antonio Cabrero will be paying the debt burden for the rest of their lives.

As of early 2013, Spain was groaning under a public debt load from 'green energy' subsidies estimated at $38 billion.[156] That number pales in comparison to the private debts that were amassed by unfortunate Spaniards like Señor Cabrero, who faces the prospect of losing his family home and life's savings to pay off his dubious wager. Spain's debt burden will stand north of 100% of GDP by the end of 2014, a level considered to be a death knell by credit agencies.[157] Amazingly, having spent an economically crippling fortune on solar subsidies since 2000, Spain still derived less than 3% of its electricity from solar power in 2012.[158] Spain spends more on 'green energy' subsidies each year than it does on higher education. By the end of the century, with the hundreds of billions of euros that will go down the drain hoping to stem climate change, global warming will only be postponed by 61 hours from all these exertions.[159] Does this sound like money well spent?

And what about the harvest of 'green jobs' the visionaries had promised? By the first quarter of 2013, unemployment in Spain had reached 27.2%.[160] That was more than twice the level in any other European Union member nation.[161] Britain's leftist rag *The Guardian*, one of the world's noisiest promoters of these publicly-funded 'green energy' programs, notes that conditions in Spain are so dire, middle class families regularly rummage through dumpsters for food.[162] This is the same future that Señor Obama hopes to import to America.

Obama unleashed a vicious, sarcasm-drenched barrage on his electoral opponent at an election rally in Elkhart, Indiana in August 2008. He promised his heavily unionized audience that his novel energy plan would create at least 5 million union jobs:

> ... *we'll invest $150 billion over the next decade and leverage billions more in private capital to harness American energy and create five million new American jobs — jobs that pay well and can't be outsourced, good union jobs that lift up our families and communities.*[163]

Obama was talking about 'green energy,' mostly wind power. With federal and state taxpayer assistance in the form of tax credits, grants, mandates, and other market interventions, wind farms would spring up across the country bringing a flood of new jobs. Or so went the promise.

Consider the example of a 150 megawatt wind farm project in Webb County, Texas.[164] Situated near the town of Bruni, the Cedro Hill Wind Farm promoters promised there would be lots of permanent and temporary jobs that would benefit struggling local communities.[165] Like Señor Cabrero in Spain, Webb County resident Alfredo Garcia took the 'green energy' job creation promise to heart. Assuming there would be a flood of hungry new workers in the area from the $108 million federal taxpayer assistance, Mr. Garcia borrowed and spent a bundle expanding his 80 seat Aimee's Mexican restaurant to accommodate 120 patrons.[166]

But as with all 'green jobs' promises, they tend to be long on 'green' and short on actual jobs. The $300 million project produced only three permanent jobs in the Bruni area. Nobody showed up at the newly expanded restaurant. Mr. Garcia declared bankruptcy and he was forced to close, putting eighteen employees out of work.[167] Another local business, the C&C grocery store, was forced to lay off a worker when one of the wind farm subcontractors ran up a $2,000 bill for gas and failed to pay.[168]

The very few permanent wind energy jobs that are created in Texas come with a very stiff price tag. The State Comptroller's office issued a report in 2010 estimating that each wind job costs the state $1.6 million in tax breaks.[169] And that number did not include the federal wind energy tax credit of $23 per mWh, which would add another $8.6 million per year in subsidies to the price tag.[170] Nor did it include the $108 million federal economic "stimulus" funds squandered.

Texas can spend $1.6 million to create a wind power job but could only pay its public school teachers about $47,311 a year during 2010.[171] So the state can boast that it is number 1 in the country in wind power.[172] But it is ranked number 44 in outlays per student enrolled in primary and secondary education.[173] And it's dead last among states in high school graduation rates.[174]

Wind promoters counter that we can't overlook temporary jobs created during the construction phase. Typical of that bounty is truck driver Richard Castillo who worked for a total of six weeks on the Cedro Hill project.[175] He wonders if he is counted in the Obama total of five million 'green energy' jobs that were promised.

Helle Thorning-Schmidt, Denmark's first female Prime Minister, presented her newly installed cabinet ministers in early October 2011 to Queen Margrethe II at Amalienborg Castle, the royal residence in Copenhagen.[176] At the traditional credentialing ceremony, cabinet members were animated by a desire to flout their "green" virtue. A roar of approval rose from the environmentally conscious crowd when several self-approving ministers arrived by bicycle.[177] However, photos of the ministers in the moments prior to arriving for the elaborately staged display show the ministers were actually driven to a nearby point in a gas-guzzling minivan where they were discharged for the short bicycle ride to the palace.[178] It was just elaborate theatre for gullible audiences.

But first prize that day for conspicuous display of environmental absurdity went to the now-disgraced Christian Friis Bach, the Social Liberal Party Minister for Development Cooperation. Friis Bach chose to arrive in a tiny three-wheeled electric vehicle to the acclaim of his admirers who believe, as he does, that electric cars offer humanity hope for salvation from their sinful, fossil-fuel powered, carbon-belching, industrial lifestyles.[179] Like his bike-riding colleagues, there was more to the Friis Bach electric car story than meets the eye. Friis Bach's electric contraption had an eight kilometer range but the round trip distance from home to palace is 60 kilometers. So he loaded the electric toy car into a horse trailer, dragged it by automobile to the vicinity of the palace, and then unloaded it for the last mile to a warm reception. He ended up burning more gas and liberating more CO_2 dragging trailer and kiddie car into town than if he had just driven his car.

Get used to it. These are the inanities we must endure in a culture that places a far higher price on environmental pieties than on energy policy substance. At least nobody froze in their flat. A few liters of gasoline burned or avoided would hardly matter one way or the other for the fate of humanity. But in an atmosphere choked by hyper-politicized climate hysteria, this is the theatre of the absurd we must endure when a leftist-aligned media culture serves as our information gate-keeper.

Tory leader David Cameron, easily the worst Conservative Party leader in modern history, enjoyed establishing his 'green' credentials by biking to work each day. He applauded reporters from *The Daily Mirror* for rapidly recovering his bike after it had been stolen while he shopped at the Portobello Road Tesco in Notting Hill.[180] Cameron shares the same adolescent narcissistic sensibilities as his U.S. counterpart. He pines for the day when some deranged media hagiographer writes a puff piece asking if he, rather than Chris Huhne, is the man who will save the planet. Like Huhne, the planet will not even notice his passing — and neither will history. But Cameron's carefully crafted environmental credentials took a hit when press photos revealed that his car followed closely behind him carrying his papers which, he claimed, were too voluminous to carry on his bike.[181] As in Denmark, it was just cartoonish environmental theatre.[182]

Drew Ryun is the son of the famous distance runner Jim Ryun who established a number of world track records.[183] Jim Ryun later became a Republican member of Congress from Kansas. Drew Ryun is also a Republican. Drew attempted to establish a non-profit group called Media Trackers under Section 501(c)(3) of the tax code by filing the necessary paperwork with the IRS. After 15 months had elapsed, he had still received no response. Ryun's application suggested his Media Trackers non-profit group might be dedicated to educating the public about the institutional corruption and bias at work within the prestige media. Ryun believes the media is innately hostile to conservative viewpoints, especially opinions that question the uniformly-enforced explanation that humans are solely responsible for causing catastrophic climate change. Ryun didn't know then that the Obama administration was using the IRS to wage a relentless assault against constitutionally-protected rights of people who oppose administration policy. Opponents are routinely harassed, hounded, audited, derided, consigned to bureaucratic limbo, and have their confidential IRS filings leaked to leftist groups affiliated with Obama's party.[184] They even have their telephones tapped and computers burglarized. Obama routinely jokes about subjecting his opponents to IRS audits.[185]

Sensing he would never hear back from IRS on his first try, Ryun filed another identical application under an eco-fuzzy name Greenhouse Solutions. That application was approved by the IRS in three weeks.[186] The IRS is the agency Obama is counting on to administer his Obamacare program in a fair, impartial manner. Outfits with names like Greenhouse Solutions saw their path smoothed if they appeared to be organized for the purpose of spreading the gospel of 'green energy' salvation among the moral defects who continue to believe in the primacy of fossil fuels. Groups that support the 'green energy' agenda of the President escaped the jackboot treatment meted out to ideological opponents. This was stuff that longtime observers of Washington's worst had not seen since Nixon administration days.

There shouldn't have been any surprise. As Richard Milhous Obama promised his supporters, "we're gonna punish our enemies and we're gonna reward our friends who stand with us on issues that are important to us."[187] 'Green energy' is obviously on that issue list. Punishment included unleashing the IRS or EPA on opponents. Ryun's experience was a classic example of how political dissent against the liberal catechism would be dealt with under the new ethical standard of green energy's biggest promoter.[188] It is Obama's brave new era of liberal thugocracy.[189] It's a place where constitutional protections of free speech and statutory safeguards against enforcement discrimination on the basis of political affiliation are effortlessly swept aside when offenders deviate from the approved path.

OBAMA'S 'GREEN ENERGY' FUTURE WON'T WORK

Many of the problems posed by 'green energy' will be examined within these pages. One such problem is that it doesn't provide very much energy. That's okay if you live in a place like Yemen or Burundi and don't use much. But if you live in the United States where the typical household has thirty five to forty electrical appliances and more than one car in the garage, where per capita consumption in 2012 was about 307 million BTUs, it's terrible.[190]

Another unpalatable feature is that 'green energy' costs far more than conventional energy. That drains discretionary income from those household budgets required to consume a lot of it. And that's not good in an economy where median personal household income in 2011 was lower than anytime back to 1996.[191] It's an economy where, for men working in full time occupations, inflation-adjusted personal income was lower than any time since 1978,[192] where 11 million receive disability payments, where a record 72.6 million are enrolled in Medicaid, where more than 108 million people were enrolled in one or more means-tested public assistance programs at the end of 2011,[193] and where almost 50 million people receive food stamps.[194] More spent for energy means less is available for everything else. The real 'green' in Obama's program is all the money required to sustain it.

Most 'green energy' applications are highly intermittent. They often don't provide energy at peak periods when it's most needed. That's not good if you want to power a world whose energy needs grow each year. To balance intermittency, you need to build a lot of load storage systems that would make already expensive 'green energy' even more expensive.

Still another aspect is that Obama's beloved 'green energy' doesn't create very many jobs but is very effective at destroying lots of other jobs that previously existed. That's not so good in an economy suffering from the lowest labor force participation rates observed in over thirty five years,[195] where almost twelve million are listed as unemployed,[196] where less than one out of every ten new adult entrants to the working-age population finds their way into the civilian labor force,[197] where the number of persons receiving government-supplied food aid outnumber the number of full-time workers on private sector payrolls,[198] where there were fewer workers are on private sector payrolls than seven years earlier,[199] where the number of people enrolled in means-tested public assistance programs outnumbered the number of workers employed full-time throughout the year.[200] It is an economy that, in fifty two months since inauguration day 2009, had added 10.8 new food stamp program enrollees for every job created.[201] And almost every single new job was for low paying part-time work.[202] It is an economy where even the Obama-cheerleading *Associated Press* is forced to admit that "Four out of five U.S. adults struggle with joblessness, near-poverty or reliance on welfare for at least parts of their lives, a sign of deteriorating economic security and an elusive American dream."[203] Nice to hear it. But some honesty earlier might have helped a bit more.

Moreover, for most 'green energy' manifestations, technical problems have not been overcome. Many of the long-promised practical applications are still far from commercial-scale realization. That doesn't sound too promising when you recognize that, as a nation, we've been pouring super-tanker loads of public money into perfecting these sources for five decades.

Despite claims to the contrary, 'green energy' is not even effective at accomplishing its primary task of reducing CO_2 emissions. Even when we accept at face value the most optimistic carbon-reduction scenarios advertised by 'green energy' proponents, CO_2 reductions that do occur come at extraordinary expense, far in excess of putative external emissions costs that are abated.

Lastly and perhaps most important, 'green energy' isn't even very green. It pollutes the planet. We will examine how millions of poor workers around the world, but especially in China, suffer premature cancer deaths due to toxic runoff of rare earth metals that are mined and smelted to create devices like solar panels, wind turbines, plug-in hybrid electric car batteries and other gadgets. Wind towers take a dreadful toll on sensitive species of migrating avian life. Direct effects of fertilizer runoff from biofuel cultivation are poisoning sensitive marine ecosystems. Direct and indirect land-use changes are propelling massive tropical deforestation that endangers mammalian species and threatens the planet's very ability to sustain oxygen-breathing life. These pages will examine other examples of how environmentally destructive 'green energy' has been.

'Green energy' promoters often use the lexicon of religion to establish and embed the authority of their program. Listen to the way Dr. Ralf Fuecks, head of the Heinrich Böll Foundation in Berlin, describes his country's ruinous quest to reduce its relatively insignificant share of global CO_2 emissions — Germany produced only 2.3% of emissions in 2011:[204]

> *Green is not about departing from the modern lifestyle. We are progressing into a moral economy. Morality is not a contradiction to economic success. It is the other way around.*[205]

He says this with the certitude of a bible-thumping Calvinist preacher. Renewable energy is a religious crusade with its proponents on the side of the angels. The rest of us are moral lepers. Never mind that his moral crusade has caused nearly a million Germans to lose their power because they can no longer pay their soaring electricity bills,[206] that renewable energy surcharges will have grown by 86% in just two years,[207] that Germany's real GDP rate is one of the lowest in the industrialized world,[208] that business are shifting investment capital and jobs to lower cost regions,[209] that thousands of Germans are fleeing the labor market wasteland,[210] that old-growth forests are being clear cut by Germans for firewood to heat homes,[211] that the inverted power market landscape favors continuity from aging CO_2-belching coal plants over low-emission gas turbine plants that would emit half as much CO_2 and would be twice as energy efficient,[212] that Germany actually increased its CO_2 emissions in 2012 over the previous year even as its 'green energy' grew,[213] etc. Contrary evidence is unimportant to moral crusading green-left evangelists like Herr Dr. Fuecks.

Obama's 'green energy' future will accomplish the same outcomes in America. It is already driving up the cost of living to unaffordable levels for ordinary citizens, destroying jobs and prosperity, impairing economic and personal income growth, reducing energy availability, expanding public employee payrolls, bloating federal and state budget deficits, increasing tax burdens, expanding the thicket of regulatory excess, increasing welfare rolls, sending businesses, taxpayers, and jobs fleeing to more favorable climates, adding enormous integration challenges to grid operators, and so forth.

Obama's vision of utopia includes driving up the cost of cheap conventional energy so that high-cost 'green energy' can become more competitive. It relies upon adopting economically crippling environmental regulations that will outlaw America's most abundant domestic energy sources. It requires enactment of taxes and penalties on fossil fuels to make them less affordable. It includes imposing caps on the emission of carbon dioxide to limit our ability to exploit abundant domestic supplies of coal, oil and natural gas. It is characterized by massive public expenditures for ruinously expensive 'green energy' schemes that will drive up budget deficits and debt in a country that borrowed thirty five cents of every federal dollar it spent during the first Obama term in office.[214] It depends upon a set of job-killing subsidies, handouts, and tax breaks in an economy with ninety two million working-age Americans who are unemployed, under-employed or out of the workforce. It survives on a set of onerous federal and state mandates that obligate us to purchase it whether we want it or not. It includes shoveling taxpayer-financed benefits to campaign-contributing cronies through government sponsorship of lucrative deals that enrich the well-heeled millionaire, billionaire, corporate jet-owning 1% at the expense of the 99% of taxpayers. It is built around erecting a massive regulatory monolith that will govern every public and private transaction involving any form of energy, a regulatory structure that will serve to curtail energy use and act as a permanent impairment to economic growth. It relies upon perpetuating a colossal fraud, preying upon the decency of conscientious Americans by promoting exaggerated hysteria over impending planetary doom. And it relies upon demonizing anyone who utilizes fact or logic to highlight its falsehoods, incongruities, and absurdities. To paraphrase Thomas Jefferson, it is falsehood that requires staunch government support. Truth can stand on its own.

As Obama explained in 2008, what he seeks is a "complete transformation" of the American economy.[215] "Breaking our oil addiction ... will take nothing less than a complete transformation of our economy," he says.[216] A partial transformation won't do. We must replace the proven economy, the one we know actually works, with a roll of the dice, with one we already know and which these pages will demonstrate, clearly does not.

Again in Obama's own words, it is a "transformation that will require more than just a few government programs."[217] That's right. It will require countless government programs. In essence, Obama's 'green energy' vision is a suicide pact built with oceans of taxpayer money funneled through an endless maze of new government programs, rules, mandates, unelected bureaucrats, and agencies. And all of it resides atop a mountain of exaggerations, falsehoods, ideological extremism, media distortions, and pseudo-intellectual conceits that appeal to a narrow segment of elites but will be poisonous to America's economic competitiveness, survival, and twenty first century leadership.

But the good news is that this doesn't need to be our future. Americans have a say in the decision. It is our misfortune to live in an age where all that is required to offend is to disagree with someone's viewpoint. Thus, many will claim to be offended. But irrespective of how deeply one cares about the environment, it is no justification for pursuing a program that will harm us far more than will help by simply labeling it 'green.' Nor does it provide cover to a media culture that, in the name of 'green' virtue, willfully distorts the truth, withholds information unhelpful to its cause, and deliberately steers its agenda-driven reporting toward realization of a future wholly unworthy of a great nation and people.

This book will analyze the 'green energy' program advocated by Obama, examining in detail the horrific and yet undeniable truths. Readers will discover that:

- ✓ 'Green energy' deployments are economically infeasible in most of their proposed applications despite massive infusions of taxpayer funding over decades.
- ✓ The world is far from exhausting its supply of fossil fuels despite resolute assurances from 'green energy' cheerleaders that the well is running dry.
- ✓ 'Green energy' is not affordable in a country posting its lowest sustained economic growth in post-War history.
- ✓ 'Green energy' cannot possibly scale sufficiently to make major contributions to America's overall requirements, much less serve as a complete replacement for fossil fuels.
- ✓ 'Green energy' destroys far more jobs than it could possibly ever create.
- ✓ The 'green energy' vision is championed by a cynical, deeply flawed politician who knows exactly nothing about energy or economics, but who has never allowed that to interfere in his relentless campaign to bring his vision into fruition.
- ✓ In states that have pioneered 'green energy' mandates, a competitive disadvantage has resulted. Energy costs are higher, unemployment has increased, and economic growth has declined measurably vs. those states that ignored the mandates.
- ✓ The more resources we squander and mandates we impose, the greater will be the permanent impairment we will suffer in relation to global trading partners that have ignored 'green energy' promises and are winning the race for twenty first century economic supremacy.
- ✓ The claim that 'green energy' will enable American energy independence is meritless because its adoption relies upon materials and components that originate from a very small number of the world's most illiberal regimes.
- ✓ 'Green energy' performs poorly at its primary mission of reducing greenhouse gas emissions. In certain instances, its usage actually causes a substantial increase in emissions compared to even the most CO_2-intensive fossil fuels.

✓ In instances where its usage reduces CO_2 emission, the abatement cost is anywhere from ten to a thousand times more than the cost of climate change that could ever result from using fossil fuels. Even worse, the U.S. will enjoy less than 5% of any climate benefits from its 'green energy' outlays since Americans represent only a small fraction of the planet's population.

✓ Even if America were to eliminate its CO_2 emissions in the next few decades — a completely impossible supposition — it would not materially impact global climate change because the rest of the world's emissions will overwhelm any CO_2 emission reductions we could make.

✓ Most disturbingly of all, 'green energy' really isn't 'green' at all. It results in some of the most hideous pollution on the planet, exacting an unimaginable human death toll upon some of the poorest people on Earth, a situation often described as "environmentalism's dirty little secret."

✓ Lastly, it will be shown how easily it will be for Americans to turn their backs upon this 'green energy' fantasy and adopt a set of social justice policies that will have real, measureable, sustainable, lasting, beneficial impacts upon humanity.

SECTION 1

THE CLOUDED VISION
OF A VISIONARY

CHAPTER 1

A 'GREEN ENERGY' SUICIDE PACT

"The curious task of economics is to demonstrate to men how little they know about what they imagine they can design."[1]

F.A. HAYEK

In the early part of the twenty-first century, America finds itself struggling with two radically different views of itself and its proper role in an increasingly dangerous world. One school of thought has been heavily influenced by authors like Noam Chomsky and the late Howard Zinn. Both men believe that America is a negative force on the planet. To these observers, the U.S. is a reckless superpower that has wielded its disproportionate power exploiting the resources of the poor, despoiling the planet's fragile environment through ecologically degrading activities like using fossil fuels, instituting a corporate-driven societal model that devalues individuals, and fomenting imperial wars of conquest inspired by greed against peaceful indigenous populations.

This angry, deeply pessimistic viewpoint holds that America's only hope resides in a complete transformation of the country's economic and social model away from using the fossil energy that powers our modern way of life. Not only must we do this, but it must be done quickly. Indeed, most of the adherents to this view are influenced by the extremist rhetoric of Al Gore who proclaimed in 2008 — without a shred of embarrassment — that America can and must eliminate its use of fossil fuel for electricity generation within ten years.[2] Of course, Gore also absurdly proclaimed that there was a 75% chance the Arctic ice cap would melt in five years.[3] But he also goes around the country pleading with hotel masseuses to help him release his "second chakra."[4]

According to Gore and his ilk — call them the Cassandras — America can supposedly eliminate fossil fuel use through a crash program of wind turbine and solar panel deployment. While we're at it, we'll need a lot of biofuels that would presumably be able to replace gasoline, diesel and jet fuel. We would also need to make deep lifestyle changes, doing away with modern conveniences, reducing our resource consumption, using much less energy, living in more cramped conditions, sacrificing personal freedoms, and getting by with far less or everything except politicized rhetoric. By following this plan, proponents contend that America would eliminate CO_2 emissions that they claim are causing hurricanes, droughts, floods, and other damaging effects of climate change that supposedly never occurred prior to humanity's exploitation of carbon-based energy.

This pessimistic view is closely aligned to an apocalyptic theory of population growth espoused by an eighteenth century British philosopher named Thomas Malthus in a 6-volume compilation of essays. Malthus believed that since resources grow arithmetically while population grows exponentially, eventually people outgrow food supply.[5] In Malthus' view, the planet would eventually host a population too large to be able to be sustained. Those "Malthusian" viewpoints have been thoroughly discredited by the incontestable verdict of human history. And yet, despite a wealth of contrary evidence, these slightly updated views still find fertile ground.

A front-page story in *The New York Times* encapsulated the cramped thinking of Malthusians, darkly warning readers in 1948 that "Population Outgrows Food, Scientists Warn the World."[6] Remember when the world's population outgrew its food supply in the late 1940s and early 1950s? Neither does anyone else. In more recent years, the most prominent advocate of this discredited school of thought has been a Stanford University quack "scientist" named Paul Ehrlich whose co-author colleague John Holdren serves as President Obama's White House science advisor.[7] It figures. Most strains of present-day anti-fossil fuel environmentalism are deeply influenced by Malthusian charlatanism. Modern eco-pessimists couple this philosophy with a decided preference for empowering governments with coercive powers to enact society-altering measures.

The competing, optimistic vision was embodied by the nation's founding fathers who established a representative republic as a refuge from tyranny. It would become a nation where people would be free to pursue their own enlightened self-interest without undue interference from repressive, despotic government, where basic liberties would be inviolable, and essential God-given rights would be enshrined in a document that limited the powers of the federal government. Abraham Lincoln proclaimed that America was humanity's last, best hope on Earth. The optimistic viewpoint holds that, whatever its faults, America's engagement with the world has led to an era of unprecedented prosperity, social progress, improved health, economic opportunity, longevity, peace, and basic well-being for billions of people.

Coupled with this viewpoint is a philosophy that relies upon the indisputable verdict of history that the gloomy future of Malthus has never and will never come to pass. Adherents of this philosophy — call them the Cornucopians — posit that human ingenuity, powered by the forces of a free market allowing individuals to maximize their talents, will assure that innovation, adaptation, and the forces of supply and demand will enable society to meet whatever challenges nature places in its way.[8] As author Indur Goklany carefully documents, this prosperity has fostered progress that is unprecedented in human history, allowing its beneficiaries to live longer, healthier, better educated, more affluent lives on an increasingly cleaner planet.[9] More than any other factor, it was humanity's exploitation of fossil energy that enabled it to prosper, overcome immense physical obstacles, conquer poverty and disease, and improve our human condition.

It is to our everlasting misfortune that a book supposedly dedicated to setting the record straight about practical energy policy must find itself mired in discussions about the planet's climate. During the two centuries of our country's existence, Americans have become accustomed to politicians with callous disregard for accuracy who offer soaring visions of the future delivered in lofty prose which, in the end, predictably turned out to be just empty rhetoric. But never have Americans encountered a politician whose empty pieties included a promise to fix the weather.

Barack Obama's speech in St. Paul, Minnesota in June 2008 amounted to a quantum leap into the realm of the ridiculous. And yet his followers cheered wildly when he piously proclaimed that future generations would look back upon his nomination as "the moment when the rise of the oceans began to slow and the planet began to heal."[10] His mere presence on the scene along with the program he espoused would repair the damaged climate and heal the broken planet. The planetary healing underway in Libya, Egypt, Ukraine, Syria, Iraq, Central Africa and dozens of other places offers clues to the potential for success of his climate fixing agenda.

It is difficult to find another example that throws into such stark relief the cultural divide contrasting the two competing visions of America. On the one hand, a little more than half of the electorate voted for a man who reinforced their adolescent belief that America possessed the power to repair the weather — it could slow the rise of the oceans — by enacting some nebulous version of his 'green energy' program.

The other half of the electorate is composed of more sober-minded souls. Like adults tasked with the responsibility of supervising misbehaved children who spend their days breaking the toys someone else paid for, they can't afford the luxury of pretending. Most sensible people recognize the immense importance of a strong and capable America, of the historic role it must shoulder in a world where, on average, another country is added to the list of nuclear-armed nations every six years. If America is going to continue serving as Lincoln's last, best hope on Earth, it must remain resolute in its founding principles, possessed of the might to safeguard its own liberties and vital interests, and willing to honor its commitments to its allies. This can only be enabled by economic growth and prosperity that provides the wherewithal required to carry out this unique role.

Few Americans possess a deep appreciation of how close the country came to committing voluntary economic suicide in 2010. America was within a hair of imposing a cap-and-trade mechanism upon the economy that would have resulted in permanent impairment, the kind that would have endangered the country's very ability to perform its planet-stabilizing role. A draconian version of such legislation called Waxman-Markey was ramrodded through the House of Representatives during the 111th Congress. Obama applauded the bill as a good first start toward even more damaging measures to follow.[11] It was only due to opposition by a handful of wavering Senate Democrats that prevented Congress from passing some version of that crippling legislation. Cap-and-trade would have driven energy prices far higher on every segment of the economy. Had Obama and his allies succeeded, it would have rendered the country increasingly incapable of competing against rising nations that will pose substantial challenges to our best efforts at helping to maintain a peaceful, orderly world free from despotic tyranny.

Obama and his allies contend that his cap-and-trade economic wrecking-ball was an essential element in a broad deployment program that would bring about much higher energy prices. He claims his program will eliminate the threat of global warming for which he pretends we are solely to blame and over which we have complete control to reverse with clever policy-making. Neither assertion is remotely accurate. And yet many otherwise intelligent and even highly educated people believe in both of these impossible notions.

Part of our problem is that basic media dishonesty or outright ignorance about climate change has led to substantial public confusion. Media accounts typically conflate the nebulous term "climate change" that encompasses many distinct considerations with a narrow interpretation positing a lengthy chain of contentions all of which, they claim, must be believed in total. The climate is always changing, the planet has seen some gradual atmospheric warming over the past three centuries, human activities have increased the concentration of CO_2 in the atmosphere, 80% of human-generated CO_2 emissions since pre-Industrial times occurred after 1958, human emissions of CO_2 do trap some extra amount of heat, and that extra heat will impact the climate in unpredictable ways. All of those statements are factual.

But media depiction of climate change usually requires us to accept that the planet had previously been delicately perched in an optimum climate condition prior to human intervention, that CO_2 emission from burning fossil fuel is solely responsible for upsetting this delicate planetary balance by causing rapid and dangerous global warming, that the warming is unprecedented in human or even planetary history, that natural forces do not contribute to any of the measured changes, that all of the impacts are uniformly bad, that the warming will inevitably lead to human and animal extinction, that the only solution is to adopt an onerously expensive, radically transformative 'green energy' program no matter the cost, that 'green energy' is capable of fixing the problem at a moderate cost or even a net savings to society, that every respectable scientist on the planet agrees unquestioningly with every aspect of these unsupported, faith-based contentions, and that anyone who disagrees with any aspect of the foregoing is an ignorant, knuckle-dragging Neanderthal, a bigoted, Holocaust denying troglodyte. And yet every one of these statements is false.

The first description is incontestable. Climates are always changing. The climate has been changing since the beginning of the planet's atmospheric history. We know the planet's atmosphere has been warming gradually since the late 1600s and may continue to do so for centuries or perhaps thousands of years. That's what happened during the last inter-glacial period about 120,000 years ago — the brief period of relatively mild conditions wedged in between two ice ages — when the Earth's atmospheric temperature rose by as much as 14° Fahrenheit higher than at present.[13]

The second of these two contentions is highly debatable. An overwhelming body of scientific evidence suggests that today's climate is relatively mild by the planet's historical standards, that the atmosphere began warming gradually centuries before humans began emitting carbon dioxide in substantial quantities, and that today's rate of climate change is far from unprecedented in human history even if it is true that human activity is causing some portion of recent atmospheric warming. Reliable, long-standing scientific research shows that global temperatures have undergone far greater and more abrupt changes over much shorter periods of time through purely natural causes within the span of human existence. Those abrupt climate changes sharply contrast with the relatively mild, gradual changes we have experienced over recent decades or centuries.[14] Today's temperatures are not even close to the maximum achieved during the last inter-glacial period.[15]

CAN WE REALLY CHANGE THE CLIMATE CHANGE?

Irrespective of what people choose to believe about "climate change" or global warming, several things are beyond reasonable debate. First, despite claims to the contrary, any alteration in America's carbon dioxide emissions in the short, medium, or long term will have little or no material impact upon whatever amount of human-induced climate change is in store for humanity. That is because the rest of the world's emissions will simply overwhelm any efforts made by the U.S. to reduce its amount of CO_2 discharge. The evidence for this is incontestable.

China already emits 59% more CO_2 than the U.S.[16] That country accounted for 29% of global emissions in 2011.[17] China's emissions of CO_2 in the year 2030 could equal the entire planet's output today by some estimates.[18] The country will account for 83% of the entire planet's emissions increase between 2011 and 2014.[19] China's current development plan shows two coal-fired power plants being deployed every week.[20] Coal is the most CO_2-intensive energy source. A report from the World Resources Institute tracks the progress of 1,200 CO_2 belching coal plants that are planned for the near future which will possess a capacity to generate a combined 1.4 terawatts of power.[21] Three quarters of these plants will be built in China and India.[22] These new plants alone will be capable of generating nearly three times as much electricity as the entire U.S. consumes in a typical year.[23] In 2012, China consumed more coal than all other nations on the planet.[24] That amounted to 4.3 times more than the U.S. consumed.[25] China increased its coal consumption in 2012 by 6.3% while the U.S. decreased its coal usage by 11.7%.[26] Its oil imports are forecasted to grow from 4 million barrels per day (bpd) to 12 million a day by 2025.[27] The two countries are headed in precisely the opposite direction in terms of economic growth, energy consumption, energy security, and CO_2 emissions.

Media reports leading up to the Copenhagen climate gabfest in 2009 misrepresented China's pledge about curbing carbon emissions. They conflated China's promise to reduce carbon "intensity" — CO_2 per unit of GDP — claiming wrongly that the country would cut absolute carbon emissions.[28] There's a huge difference. China will not begin reducing carbon dioxide emissions until 2035 and possibly not even until 2050.[29] The country is forecast to triple its generation of electricity by the year 2030. Most of that increase will come from coal-fired plants, the dirtiest and most CO_2-intensive form available. It will also account for half of the world's growth in liquid fuel demand by 2030.[30] The U.S. Energy Information Administration (EIA) — think of them as the energy policy adults among government officials in the age of Obama — forecasts that global primary energy consumption will grow 56% by 2040.[31] China and India will account for half of that growth.

The planet increased its emissions of CO_2 by a compound rate of 3% per year between 2005 and 2011.[32] The global CO_2 emission growth that took place between 2004 and 2011 produced an amount greater than the entire CO_2 emission footprint from energy generation from every source in the U.S. during 2011. As this was happening, America had reduced its own CO_2 emissions by an annual rate of 2.3% during the previous four years using market self-correcting mechanisms without imposing economically ruinous cap-and-trade or carbon tax programs advocated by Obama. America's total contribution to the UN Intergovernmental Panel on Climate Change (IPCC) modeled twenty first century midrange 2.96 degree Celsius global temperature increase amounts to less than 0.2 degrees.[33] America could cease to exist tomorrow and it would have almost no appreciable impact on global CO_2 emissions or global warming over the next 50, 100 or even 1,000 years.

The UN IPCC climate mitigation models are driven by four factors that determine future atmospheric CO_2 concentration: (A) population, (B) real Gross Domestic Product (GDP) per capita, (C) energy intensity, the amount of energy required to produce one dollar of GDP, and (D) carbon intensity, the amount of carbon dioxide emitted per unit of energy.[34] A careful examination of each of these variables shows that a developed economy like the U.S. will become increasingly less important to global emission scenarios over time relative to developing economies. Nothing any U.S. politician says or does can or will reverse these trends. Examine each of these factors in detail:

(A) Population — Global population is growing fastest in developing countries while birth rates in developed countries have slowed even below replacement rates in most of them.[35] Non-OECD countries, those in the least developed part of the world, will account for 90% of population growth between 2012 and 2030.[36] Japan was once the world's second largest economy and was spoken about triumphantly in the 1980s as destined to surpass America.[37] But now it is locked in a demographic death spiral, with the population on course to drop by a million persons each year.[38] Retailers in Japan sell more adult diapers than baby diapers.[39] South Korea has the lowest fertility rate of any developed nation.[40] America's birth rate at 1.93 births per woman of child-bearing age is below the 2.1 replacement rate.[41] The country established an all-time low birth rate in 2012 of 63.2 births per 1,000 women aged 15 to 44, with fewer total births than in any year since 1998 when the overall population was far smaller.[42] There are more Germans aged 65 and older than there are children in that rapidly aging country.[43] None of the core 15 nations in the affluent European Union have fertility rates even close to the replacement rate.[44] The average fertility rate for the European continent is 1.58, a recipe for demographic extinction.[45]

(B) Real GDP per Capita — Developing economies are growing at much faster rates than developed economies. The dollar-weighted compound annual real GDP growth rate among the 156 developing countries in the International Monetary Fund's World Economic Outlook country database over the 10-year period from 2003 to 2012 is 4.2 times higher than the average annual GDP growth rate for the 29 developed countries on the list, and almost 4 times higher than the 10-year compound annual growth rate for the U.S.[46] Non-OECD countries will account for 70% of GDP growth and 90% of energy consumption growth by 2030.[47] Developed economies are hitting stall speed while developing economy jackrabbits are leaving them in the dust.

(C) Energy Intensity — The energy intensity of developing countries is substantially higher than that of developed countries. Developing economies account for increasingly larger amounts of low-value, energy-intensive production of basic commodities like cement, steel, iron ore, glass, paper, chemicals and so forth than developed nations that have outsourced these needs to offshore suppliers. Developed nations grew GDP per unit of energy by an average annual growth rate of 3.8% over the 10 years up to 2012.[48] By contrast, developing nations improved their energy intensity by only 3.3% per year over the same period.[49] These trends are forecast to continue. America's per capita energy use declined by 12.3% between 2000 and 2012.[50] The average American consumed less primary energy in 2011 than in 1970 even as per capital real GDP grew by 214% over that time.[51] Developed nations have also made far more impressive energy efficiency strides than developing nations have, a factor which exacerbates energy intensity differences.

(D) Carbon Intensity — Each of the major developing nations is investing heavily in very carbon-intensive energy generation capacity while the developed world appears intent on doing precisely the opposite. University of Colorado researcher Roger Pielke Jr. observes that the rate by which global energy decarbonization is taking place has declined markedly over recent years.[52] The rate of improvement in CO_2 emission reduction from energy usage has steadily declined over the past twenty years. Emerging nations are undergoing industrialization and urbanization. Their development path includes relatively inefficient energy- and carbon-intensive capital investment.[53] The world needs and wants a lot more energy. They'll be getting it with CO_2 emitting fossil fuels.

Two other factors are worth mentioning. The forecasted future growth rate for electricity usage is higher than the growth rate for overall energy consumption. DoE forecasts that U.S. electricity usage between 2010 and 2040 will grow 2.5 times faster than the growth rate for overall energy consumption.[54] This continues a trend that has been in place since Edison threw the switch on his first generating station in New York. The rest of the world is forecast to exhibit a similar, albeit less pronounced trend. Since coal is used almost exclusively for power generation, the proportion that coal contributes to overall primary energy will continue to increase for decades to come.[55] In addition, between 2010 and 2040, the less developed world is forecasted to grow its consumption of primary energy at a rate more than seven times the growth rate that the U.S. will experience during those years.[56] Electricity generating capacity in the developing world will grow more than three times faster than in the U.S.[57] Coal will be the fuel of choice.

Moreover, unless every nation on earth cooperates in a carbon dioxide abatement scheme, the costs imposed upon those economies that do participate will be comparatively inordinate. We are already seeing that effect occurring in Germany, the UK and Denmark, nations that are pretending they can solve global warming all by themselves. Yale economist William Nordhaus, the man who invented climate change economics, notes that if only half of nations on earth participate in a global CO_2 abatement regime, a cost penalty of up to 250% would be imposed upon them vs. those outside the program.[58] For a climate treaty to work, every nation on earth must participate. But as Walter Russell Mead notes, there is zero chance that could ever happen.[59]

Between 2011 and 2030, developed nations will increase primary energy by only 6% in total, an absolute decline in per capita terms, while developing nations will increase consumption by 61%.[60] Thus, developed countries will only account for 37.6% of CO_2 emissions by 2020, a number that declines to 34.2% of the total by 2030.[61] So the penalty on developed nations that will account for only a third of global emissions, the only nations likely to participate in an emissions abatement program, will be far more onerous than Nordhaus' 250% figure suggests. There is little doubt that China and India have read the economic literature and are counting on the U.S., Western Europe, Japan, Canada, Australia, and other industrialized nations to adopt increasingly futile, ruinously expensive abatement schemes while they watch the unfolding gladiatorial suicide spectacle from the stands.

Second, America has no practical ability to eliminate its use of fossil energy anytime in the foreseeable future. During 2011, the United States consumed more than 97.3 quadrillion BTUs of primary energy, 82% of which was derived from fossil fuel sources like coal, oil and natural gas.[62] Fossil energy powers America's modern way of life, providing motor fuels for transportation, heating oil and natural gas for homes, coal and natural gas for electricity, fuel oil and gas that powers our industrial economy, and so on. EIA, in its reference case, forecasts that even by 2040, America with all its frantic, hyper-politicized hysteria over global warming, will still derive more than 80% of its primary energy from fossil fuel sources.[63] That's barely different than today.

The same is true everywhere. Global energy use is growing because it is the most essential ingredient for economic growth. Fossil fuels form the backbone that enables that growth. In the first decade of this century, global usage of renewable energy grew by 2%, but fossil fuel usage increased 2.7%.[64] Despite all the hype and blather, renewables can't even keep pace. The world more than doubled its consumption of primary energy in the years between 1973 and 2011, but over that time the share contributed by coal and lignite, the most CO_2-intensive sources, actually increased from 24.6% of the total in

1973 to 28.8% in 2011.[65] The pace at which coal is capturing market share is increasing. During the 10 years up to 2012, the world's consumption of primary energy increased at a 2.7% compound annual rate while coal usage increased at a 4.6% yearly rate.[66] Energy consultancy Wood Mackenzie estimates that coal will surpass oil as the largest source of primary energy by 2020.[67]

In the words of distinguished Professor Emeritus of the University of Manitoba Vaclav Smil, "the world has been running into fossil fuels, not away from them."[68] A prolific author of energy policy, Smil notes that energy transitions take generations to complete. While the U.S. is blessed with hydrocarbon resources in dozens of locations, it still required twenty five years for the country to increase oil consumption as a share of its primary energy from 5% to just 25%.[69] More than a hundred countries export oil, and yet it required the world forty years to increase primary energy share from oil from 5% to 25%.[70] These facts are not offered as fossil fuel triumphalism, but as the cornerstone for energy realism. Just laugh when you hear someone tell you we can easily move away from carbon-based energy.

Third, despite claims by 'green energy' proponents that other countries will follow America's moral example if we undertake a crash program of eliminating fossil fuels, this isn't ever going to happen. Believers in this line of reasoning are as naive as those who advocated unilateral disarmament during the 1970s and 1980s in the preposterous belief that the imperial warlords of the Soviet Union would have destroyed their nuclear stockpiles if only America would have disarmed first. Apparently impossible for leftists to assimilate, it was America's possession of an overwhelming, survivable nuclear retaliatory capability that prevented a nuclear exchange between the U.S. and the Soviet Union during the most intense instances of Cold War standoff like the Berlin crisis, the Cuban missile crisis, and the 1973 Yom Kippur War.

Nothing America does will alter the trajectory of global economic development using fossil fuels. Some observers even contend that the two issues of energy usage and nuclear weapons are intertwined. Energy policy gadfly Amory Lovins wrote an astoundingly bizarre article in *Foreign Affairs* in 1976 claiming that America could seize the moral high ground by eliminating nuclear weapons, halting nuclear energy plant construction, and embarking on a morally superior 'green energy' program.[71] He promised other nations would follow our nuclear weapon-and-energy disarmament lead.[72] That policy might work on Planet Fuzzy Bunny where most progressive policies originate, but it's useless down here on Earth.

Not surprisingly, Obama subscribes to the completely discredited unilateral disarmament delusion that he couples with fossil energy disarmament. In his own words, if America simply eliminated its nuclear weapons capability, that "will then give us a greater moral authority to say to Iran, don't develop a nuclear weapon; to say to North Korea, don't proliferate nuclear weapons."[73] How well has the "moral authority" of the Nobel Peace Prize laureate worked thus far with these nuclear-arming rogue nations? How will 'green energy' authority work with developing nations like China, India, Brazil, Indonesia, and others whose citizens need access to cheap, reliable energy? *Kumbaya* is not a foreign policy. It doesn't work well as energy policy either.

Lastly, recent scientific evidence suggests the threat to the global climate posed by CO_2 emissions has probably been greatly exaggerated by hysterics.[74] The science appears to be far from settled. Despite the vaunted climate models used by the IPCC, winner of the 2008 Nobel Peace Prize for its supposedly unquestioned authority as the final word on the scientific basis for climate alarmism, the planet has failed to obey the climate models and hasn't warmed for almost twenty years.[75] Every single one of the climate models the UN IPCC relies upon to frighten the developed world into eliminating fossil fuel usage and make massive wealth transfers to developing nations appears to be wrong.[76] Year after year in steady progression since the 1980s, climate alarmists have been forced to revise downward their doom-laden forecasts of future warming.[77]

Atmospheric CO_2 has increased 12% since 1990 yet instead of the 0.2 to 0.9 degree warming they forecasted, we have seen less than a 0.1 degree change.[78] A draft fifth IPCC assessment report leaked to reporters in January 2013 demonstrated that the previous four IPCC reports had greatly overstated the influence of human activities on warming over the past several hundred years.[79] The IPCC struggled with a face-saving way to admit it and predictably fashioned some unsupported speculations about why the atmosphere hadn't warmed in its latest report. The panel suggested that the missing heat is hiding in the deep ocean, the scientific equivalent of "the dog ate my global warming."[80] Nevertheless, the IPCC increased its confidence level in its discredited climate models to 95% from 90%. They cut their level of uncertainty in half even while admitting they haven't a clue why global warming stopped.[81] Government officials from the U.S. and the EU actually huddled in panic prior to a September 2013 climate conference in Stockholm — a panic over the potential absence of public panic — to craft a cover story on why they believe the hiatus is not really a hiatus.[82] It is they who appear to be the real climate deniers.[83]

When Obama and his fellow cap-and-trade enthusiast John McCain were both running for President in 2008, America's electric utilities used coal for almost 50% of their electricity output,[84] citygate natural gas prices averaged $9.59 per thousand cubic feet,[85] the spot price of a barrel of crude oil at Cushing, Oklahoma traded as high as $147 per barrel,[86] America was only producing about 70% of its primary energy consumption,[87] the country was importing nearly 60% of its oil requirements,[88] and it was suffering its worst trade deficit impact from oil imports in its history.[89] Most politicians believed that global warming caused by fossil fuel burning was the most pressing problem humanity had ever faced, which required heavy government intervention.

But in the interim, production of crude oil and natural gas on private lands has soared, CO_2 emissions have declined substantially, natural gas prices have been more than cut in half, utilities are transitioning away from coal to clean-burning natural gas at a furious pace, the unfavorable trade balance from oil imports has been cut by two-thirds, authoritative reports forecast complete energy self-sufficiency by 2020, and grandiose legislative cap-and-trade measures, which have descended into a hilarious cesspool of centrally-planned economic failure in the European Union, have been blessedly relegated to the slag heap of history. Additionally, carbon tax proposals are rightly seen by most sentient observers as naked efforts to pick the pockets of America's taxpayers to maintain a ruinously high level of government spending rather than as a mechanism to slow climate change. Thankfully the momentary psychosis that animated our energy discussion in 2008 has responded well to the curative provided by a stiff dose of market-based reality. The "inconvenient truth" is that every vestige of this occurred without government intervention.

Unfortunately, we are saddled with a leader who hasn't seemed to notice. At what was billed by his dwindling cadre of compliant media worshipers as a major speech on climate change, Obama outlined a plan in June 2013 to reduce emissions from energy production by 2020 to a level 17% lower than 2005 levels.[90] Given that the EIA's 2020 reference case in its *Annual Energy Outlook 2013*[91] shows U.S. emissions in 2020 will already be lower than 2005 levels without his help,[92] the Obama plan amounts to only about a 13.8% decrease from the level EIA believes is already baked into the cake. But even a 14% reduction in CO_2, which Obama expects to achieve by shutting down most of the country's remaining coal-fired electricity generation capacity, will still cost the economy tens of thousands of jobs and hundreds of billions of dollars.[93] At the rate China grew emissions between 2009 and 2011, it will take only nine months to replace the entire emissions cut that Obama wants to achieve over seven years, at a staggering cost to jobs, livelihoods, and economic output.[94]

Obama claims "We don't have time for a meeting of the Flat Earth Society."[95] He thinks anyone opposed to his fossil fuel elimination plan is a moron. And what will be the impact on global CO_2 emissions when we achieve his 17% emission reduction goal? Will we be saved forever from the ravages of global warming? Will we be able to cut half of the world's emissions total, or a quarter of it or even 10% of it? No, the reduction will amount to less than 2.3% of the total.[96] And what will we achieve in terms of climate benefit when this is accomplished? The 17% reduction in CO_2 emissions in the U.S. will reduce the planet's temperature by 0.034 degrees Celsius 100 years from today, an amount too small to distinguish from natural variability.[97] Proposed mitigation solutions to the problem impose costs on society far out of proportion to the claimed harm that climate change will ever incur.[98] The people who are members in good standing of the Flat Earth Society are the ones who, like Obama, believe that ruinously expensive climate mitigation measures will offer any tangible benefit over any timeframe.

A FAMILIAR PATH

America has found itself wrestling with national energy policy in crisis terms for the past four decades. The idea of energy as a crisis to be solved by concerted federal policy was given birth during the 1970s. Crude oil production in the U.S. peaked at around ten million barrels of oil per day in late 1970.[99] By that year, America's consumption of oil and petroleum liquids was 30% higher than the quantity of domestic production, requiring the country to import the balance from foreign producers.[100] In 1973, Arab members of OPEC imposed an embargo on oil shipments to the U.S. in retaliation for U.S. support to Israel during the October War. The embargo sent world prices spiking upwards from about $3 per barrel to the $12-13 per barrel level in the space of a few months.[101] Even U.S. ally the Shah of Iran supported the large price increase.[102]

In the mid-1970s, supposedly authoritative mass media outlets like *Time* magazine proclaimed that the country was facing an energy crisis.[103] In August 1971, President Nixon imposed what he termed "emergency" wage and price controls which extended to petroleum products and a wide variety of other commodities as a method to control domestic inflation.[104] The predictable result from this policy blunder was shortages of a wide variety of basic commodity products, everyday items like gasoline and toilet paper whose assured supply ordinary Americans had long taken for granted.[105] Popular legend contends that 1970s gasoline lines were caused by the Arab oil embargo. But in reality it was a result of price control measures imposed by the federal government. Did the oil embargo cause the toilet paper shortage that occurred at the same time? It became Americans' first taste of waiting lines for day-to-day consumer products mirroring the kind experienced in the workers' paradises of the Soviet Union and Warsaw Bloc countries.[106] In addition to those tender government-crafted outcomes, dramatically higher fuel and electricity prices spread across the entire energy complex, driving up utility rates along with the energy input price component of every product or service, further boosting the cost of living for American consumers. This helped ignite a "cost-push" inflationary spiral that would last for a decade.

The American economy would have been well equipped to handle external shocks like a temporary Arab oil embargo. Absent price controls, higher market-based prices resulting from the embargo would have provided a powerful economic incentive to producers to discover, produce, and supply more oil. It would have also served as an incentive to consumers to curtail consumption. So the logical responses in a dynamic economy like ours would have eventually driven down the price of oil without the need for any government intervention. But such was not the case because the federal government intervened to dampen both supply- and demand-based incentives.

The arcane minutiae of the interminable succession of oil price control missteps during the 1970s is more detail than readers who value their sanity should be expected to withstand.[107] Suffice to say, the net effect of the burdensome, counter-productive set of regulations would lead to a decade of blundering as America's first peacetime excursion into government-orchestrated national energy policy played itself out as tragicomedy across the landscape. Each announced price control policy initiated by central planners resulted in an unanticipated negative consequence that needed to be solved by a succeeding measure that produced more unfavorable results that were solved by yet additional measures that then boomeranged, and so on ad infinitum.[108]

To compound matters by an incalculable degree, in November 1976, Americans suffering from the debilitating effects of post-Watergate trauma went to the polls and, to their later regret, elected an insufferable, moralizing, deeply pessimistic, Bible-thumping scold named Jimmy Carter as their 39th President. Carter was a man who knew something about peanut farming but absolutely nothing about macroeconomics and even less about energy policy. As President, he maintained one form or another of price controls on oil and gas for almost the entirety of his tenure in office.

A second oil crisis occurred in 1979 following the overthrow of the interim regime in Iran, a situation that resulted in a second and even deeper wave of gasoline lines. The price of imported crude oil more than doubled over the course of a few months.[109] Oil price controls remained in effect until full deregulation was ordered on January 28, 1981 by Carter's timely, desperately needed successor, President Ronald Reagan. The moment that logical economic forces were allowed to prevail, gasoline lines were forever consigned to the history books and oil prices promptly fell.[110] And clueless media set about constructing a fairy tale that the Arab oil embargo, rather than big government blundering, had caused the gas lines. During the price control era, a two-tier market developed. The price of imported crude oil not subject to price controls soared above $40 a barrel. Within a few years after price decontrol, the benchmark NYMEX price of crude oil sank below $10 per barrel.[111]

Carter believed passionately that government needed to insert itself in energy markets in a big way. The same federal government geniuses that had conceived the price control program on oil and gas markets years earlier — the program that brought Soviet-style gasoline lines[112] — would now exert their similarly unparalleled expertise across every facet of the energy policy spectrum.[113]

Included in Carter's policies would be tax credits for renewable fuels, burdensome energy regulations, government funding for a broad array of breakthrough energy schemes, expansion in the scope of environmental rule-making, and increasing reliance on conservation measures to reduce demand. But even more ubiquitous would be Carter's trademark accent on empty, sanctimonious moralizing. He famously described his energy crusade as "the moral equivalent of war,"[114] a statement as incomprehensible today as it was in 1977. America had fuel shortages that accompany wartime experience. The only things missing were color-coded ration coupons.

A key plank in Carter's plan was that the federal government would now act as venture capitalist promoting dubious energy schemes through his Synthetic Fuels Corporation.[115] Synfuels was enacted in 1980 and funded with $20 billion in seed capital.[116] Its purpose was to help achieve energy independence with biofuel subsidies, coal gasification, solar energy, and thermal energy projects. Does this sound familiar? The justification for the program was that uncertainties about economic potential prohibited private capital funding for such high-risk endeavors. So it was necessary for the government to step in to do what the private sector was unwilling to do or, in reality, had better sense not to try with other people's money. The federal government then — as now — feels no such sense of forbearance. After a series of spectacular failures, the Synfuels Corporation was terminated in 1985.[117] Not surprisingly, the period of Carter malaise saw the American economy slide into a deep recession beginning in the second quarter of 1980 that the country would not fully emerge from until the third quarter of 1982.[118] Does this sound familiar?

In November 2008, Jimmy Carter's soul mate Barack Obama was elected after promising to unleash a flood of taxpayer money on a similar program of dubious energy ventures. A deluge of funds would be showered on 'green energy' schemes like solar power, wind turbines, plug-in hybrid electric cars, advanced batteries, cellulosic and algae-based biofuels, and a variety of other ideas. While the justification for the 1970s policy disaster was a desire to achieve energy independence, the primary motivating factor behind Obama's energy policy disaster was his ideologically rigid certitude that fossil fuel usage was causing a planetary emergency. Indeed, he contended that these debilitating impacts were already being felt with rising ocean levels, droughts, floods, famines, mightier storms, shorter ski seasons and an array of other effects.[119]

Obama decried America's lack of global leadership on adopting stringent, economically onerous mitigation policies. It was, in his view, a failure of leadership that the Bush administration did not agree to Kyoto Protocol limitations on emissions, something he vowed to adopt once elected. Never mind that Kyoto was negotiated during the Clinton administration and withheld by Clinton from ratification because the Senate had voted 95-0 against the treaty without major changes.

Of course, Obama proclaimed that his plan could also help America achieve energy independence. But that theme played a subordinate role to "the planet's greatest threat,"[120] catastrophic global warming. Needless to say, exactly how America would ever achieve the promised goal of energy independence while simultaneously curtailing usage of its immense reservoir of fossil fuels was an incongruity he has never bothered to explain.

At the outset of Obama's campaign, energy independence was cited only as a bonus, one that took a back seat to the supposed ecological imperative posed by global warming. Later, as American voters began to distrust the doom and gloom narrative, particularly in the wake of the Climategate revelations that severely undercut its credibility and made a laughingstock of the IPCC,[121] energy independence jumped into the front seat of Obama's energy rhetoric. Climate change was less frequently invoked.

In his State of the Union speech to a joint session of Congress on January 24, 2011, Obama heralded the glorious potential of his 'green energy' future, vowing to set the nation on a path toward achieving a goal — what he termed a new "Sputnik moment" — of deriving 80% of the country's electricity from "clean energy sources" like solar power and wind turbines.

We've begun to reinvent our energy policy. We're not just handing out money ... With more research and incentives, we can break our dependence on oil with biofuels, and become the first country to have a million electric vehicles on the road by 2015. Tonight, I challenge you to join me in setting a new goal: By 2035, 80 percent of America's electricity will come from clean energy sources.[122]

It was literally true. Obama wasn't "just handing out money." He was dumping it out in truckload quantities. He was shoveling it out the door so fast in so many directions, nobody could even keep track of it all. The hope in Washington, as in European capitals, was that if government established enough crippling mandates and soaked consumers with enough costly subsidies — the "incentives" he advocated — low-carbon technologies would become self-sufficient in a short period of time.[123] It has never worked and likely never will. The list of Treasury and Energy Department 'green energy' grant, loan guarantee, and seed capital failures is endless.

Sadly for America and its vital interests, Barack Obama is not now and never has been a student of history. He wouldn't know the painful history of America's energy policy failures regarding 'green energy' schemes that preceded his arrival. But if he did know, he wouldn't even care. That's because the man is possessed with an arrogant self-certitude of his own limitless capability to overcome the most intractable obstacles. Ordinary pedestrian influences like the forces of supply and demand or price mechanisms that efficiently allocate resources can, in his view, be effortlessly swept aside by brilliantly conceived policy measures. Countless studies along with mountains of evidence have shown that massive, Soviet-style, centrally-planned, interventionist, government-directed renewable 'green energy' schemes are doomed to fail.[124] Thus, to our detriment, out of a combination of historical ignorance, willful blindness, ideological obtuseness, Cateresque incompetence, and strong sympathetic backing from a hagiographic, philosophically aligned, complicit mass media, he was destined to repeat the mistakes of the past.

CHAPTER 2

THE ENERGY OF ADOLESCENCE

"I'm proud of the fact that under my administration, oil production is higher than it has been in a decade or more."[1]

PRESIDENT OBAMA
FEBRUARY 20, 2013

*"**Fossil Fuel Production on Federal Lands at 9-Year Low:** Fossil fuel (coal, oil, and natural gas) production on Federal and Indian lands is the lowest in the 9 years U.S. Energy Information Administration reports data and is 6 percent less than in fiscal year 2010."*[2]

INSTITUTE FOR ENERGY RESEARCH
MARCH 15, 2012

*"**Oil and Gas Production Decline on Federal Lands ... Again**: Department of Interior ... oil and natural gas production on federal lands dropped again in FY 2012."*[3]

INSTITUTE FOR ENERGY RESEARCH
FEBRUARY 28, 2013

*"**Fossil Fuel Production on Federal Lands at a Ten Year Low:** Fossil fuel production of federal lands is at a 10-year low, and oil production on federal land fell in fiscal years 2011 and 2012.*[4]

INSTITUTE FOR ENERGY RESEARCH
JUNE 10, 2013

What do you do if you're a politician who has built an energy policy around making conventional fossil fuel energy exorbitantly expensive to create a market for costly renewable energy? It's easy. You rush out the door and crisscross the country making dozens of speeches pretending it was never your intention to drive up the price of energy. "Deny everything," they said on *X-Files*. Obama was obviously paying close attention.

In the midst of the oil price spike in early 2012, Obama traveled to the University of Miami in Coral Gables, Florida to deliver a speech on energy policy. Speaking to a wildly enthusiastic audience of adolescent students who understood as much about a balanced energy policy as he did — which is to say nothing — Obama tore into his partisan opponents. He derided them using the same venom he had employed for the past seven years in Washington for supporting more oil drilling as if increasing the supply of oil were precisely the opposite of a sensible approach to reducing oil prices.

"The American people aren't stupid," he thundered. Apparently the guy who doesn't believe in the forces of supply and demand as determinants of price gets to define stupidity. To prove to the American people just who is stupid, Obama claimed that if "we start using less, that lowers the demand, prices come down." But just a few moments later, he also stated that no matter "how much oil we produce at home … that's not going to set the price of gas worldwide."[5] Got that now? If we increase supply, there will be no impact on price. But if we reduce demand, then prices will promptly come down:

> *You can bet that since it's an election year, they're already dusting off their 3-point plan for $2 gas. And I'll save you the suspense. Step one is to drill and step two is to drill. And then step three is to keep drilling. We heard the same line in 2007 when I was running for President. We hear the same thing every year. We've heard the same thing for 30 years. Well, the American people aren't stupid.*[6]

Obama was betting that his audience wasn't aware that the nationwide average price for gasoline was $1.89 per gallon on the day he was inaugurated. Now that gasoline was in the $4.00 range, it was heresy to speak of a plan aimed at boosting supply. The man who could undo federal law with a stroke of his mighty pen could also negate the left half of the law of supply and demand.

Let's have a quick look at whether Obama's claims that "there are no quick fixes" and "we can't drill our way out of this" have any merit. In the month Obama delivered his Miami eulogy to low gas prices, the country managed to produce 180.6 million barrels of crude oil.[7] Meanwhile, motorists were demanding 8.6 million barrels a day of gasoline.[8] The average nationwide price that week was $3.78 per gallon.[9]

One year later, domestic production had soared over 20% to 217.2 million barrels.[10] Gasoline demand had dropped to 8.2 million bpd, a 4.7% decline.[11] But the small drop in demand was swamped by the 20.3% jump in crude oil supply. In other words, the rate of demand decline was less than one fourth of the increase in supply. So largely as a result of increased supply, the average nationwide gasoline price had dropped by a sizeable 9.3%.[12] America had achieved a "quick fix." It had drilled its way to lower gas prices.

For decades, oil industry analysts were accustomed to seeing a price differential between spot prices for West Texas Intermediate (WTI) crude oil in Cushing, Oklahoma and spot prices for Brent North Sea crude oil. WTI consistently priced at a premium. Between 1987 and March of 2006, the WTI premium averaged about $1.54 per barrel, reaching as high as $7.63 a barrel in November 2004.[13] America's light sweet crude oil was always preferred in international markets to heavier, dirtier, higher sulfur-content product from the North Sea.

But everything changed in Cushing in early 2006 as North Dakota crude oil from the Bakken fields unexpectedly began to pour into the terminal. Suddenly, the price premium enjoyed by WTI turned into a substantial price discount that, for the most part, has remained in place ever since. In January 2011, the WTI discount reached double-digit levels. Between the months of January 2011 and the end of May 2013, the WTI discount averaged an astounding $16.60 per barrel.[14] America's fuel consumers were the beneficiaries. In the absence of this glut, they would have been forced to pay higher prices. Despite the blather tossed out to his impressionable student audience, America had "drilled its way" to lower prices.

Shortly after oil was discovered in Titusville, Pennsylvania in 1859, oil traded for $10 per barrel. Following massive production expansion, prices dropped within one year to ten cents a barrel.[15] In October 1930, the East Texas field was discovered, the largest oil find in U.S. history. Around the time of discovery, East Texas oil was selling for about one dollar a barrel. But within a single year as East Texas production increased dramatically, prices plummeted to as low as thirteen cents a barrel.[16] In both examples, America drilled its way to lower prices.

The favorable price impact from American oil production could become even more pronounced in coming years. As U.S. gasoline demand continues to slacken while domestic oil production soars, as more Canadian oil from Alberta finds its way into U.S. markets, and as the country maintains its prohibition against crude oil exports, the domestic glut could become exacerbated.[17] Railcar shipments of crude oil, a hitherto uncommon service-line for Class I railroads, increased by 356% in 2012 over the year earlier.[18] New pipelines are transporting stranded inland oil from Texas and Oklahoma storage depots to Gulf refineries and ports. But since many of those refineries are optimized to handle heavier crude imports from Saudi Arabia, Venezuela, and Mexico, the likely impact will be to transfer the glut to Gulf storage terminals.[19] Domestic crude oil supply may actually exceed the country's capacity to refine it by 2014 or 2015.[20] So it's possible that U.S. oil prices could become even further decoupled from global prices.

THE 90% GAP

So the guy who claimed "there are no quick fixes to this problem" announced three weeks later that he wanted to tap the Strategic Petroleum Reserve (SPR) as a quick fix.[21]

The guy who angrily denounced a policy position supporting increased oil supply as "a strategy to get politicians through an election year" wanted to tap the SPR to help nervous Democrats get through the 2012 election year. The man who pretended he had the power to command ocean levels to rise and fall was incapable of merely commanding gasoline prices to fall. His solution to high energy prices is to impose more regulatory impediments on oil and gas production. And he does this while criticizing policies that favor oil and gas drilling that actually produces jobs, and lower cost energy.

At the outset of his remarks, Obama praised the work of engineering students at the University of Miami. As he admitted, "I understood about 10 percent of what they told me." That was precisely the problem and it was not limited to recitations delivered by engineering students. It was the issue that had plagued his entire approach to the country's energy situation. On energy, Obama only "understood about 10 percent of what they told" him. He proclaimed:

> When gas prices go up, it hurts everybody — everybody who owns a car, everybody who owns a business. It means you've got to stretch a paycheck even further … high gas prices are like a tax straight out of your paycheck.[22]

The guy complaining about high prices acting like a tax straight out of your paycheck supports enactment of a carbon tax straight out of your paycheck.[23] The man who made these remarks got himself elected President on the wisdom of an energy policy that was built around his own ironclad assurance that energy prices "would necessarily skyrocket."[24] Even worse is the fact that he doesn't understand the direct correlation between low energy prices and economic growth, how lower prices can improve the economic climate.[25]

How could he be complaining about skyrocketing energy prices? They were the very foundation of his policy from Day 1. His carefully enumerated plan all along had been to supplant relatively cheap, abundant, easily obtainable fossil fuels in favor of ruinously expensive wind and solar energy coupled with regulatory measures designed to cap the amount of carbon-emitting fuel that could be used in the U.S. economy. But when elements of that catastrophic idea had, by legislative and bureaucratic measures,[26] come into fruition and the intended higher energy prices had resulted, Obama traveled all the way down to Coral Gables to whine.[27]

Obama's answer to the wildly erroneous claim that more oil drilling could never lead to lower prices was to urge more widespread adoption of far costlier "wind and solar and nuclear and biofuels, and more." So the answer to high fossil fuel energy prices was to expand usage of wind power that was three to four times more expensive than fossil fuels[28] and solar power that was even more expensive,[29] and biofuels which cost 35-to-40% more than gasoline during 2013.[30] Pay no attention to the obvious incongruity that practically zero amount of wind and solar power is used as transportation fuel.[31] Also, petroleum accounts for less than 1% of electricity generation.[32] Thus, the direct substitution impact on gasoline usage from these new energy sources would be close to zero.

Listeners who were not college sophomores instantly recognized that, where energy economics and policy was concerned, Obama "understood about 10 percent of what they told" him. And that problem had now become America's most pressing energy problem. It wasn't unwarranted oil price speculation in the NYMEX trading pits, it was not Iran's threats to close the Strait of Hormuz, nor SPR drawdown policy, nor price gouging, nor profit margins by oil companies, nor restrictive OPEC policies, nor Wall Street, nor millionaires, billionaires, and corporate jet owners that were to blame. The problem was the self-admitted 90% knowledge gap of the guy who was indecipherably orchestrating the nation's dissonant energy policy.

In his remarks, Obama praised the fact that "the wind turbine at the Miami-Dade Museum can meet about 10 percent of the energy needs in a South Florida home." A small wind turbine of that size, about 10 kilowatts, carries an installed cost of $40,000-50,000.[33] Florida homeowners spent an average of $136.61 a month in 2010 for electricity.[34] So, for that amount of capital, the typical Florida home could save $13.66 per month.[35] It would take more than 274 years to payback the initial outlay.

But that payback would only occur if the equipment survived into infinity, never needing to be repaired, maintained, or replaced. But turbines do require regular maintenance and repair along with complete replacement every ten or fifteen years. This surreal absurdity is what our energy theorist was promoting. The Princeton, Massachusetts municipal budget was overwhelmed by maintenance and component replacement costs for a turbine it deployed after being goaded into that policy by wind zealots.[36] A similar situation occurred in nearby Portsmouth, Rhode Island where a $3 million wind turbine at a local high school had to be idled due to a faulty gearbox whose replacement cost could not be afforded with the town's resources.[37] So on these projects, there will never be a payback. That becomes a perfect metaphor for the value we can attach to the Obama 'green energy' program.

YOU DIDN'T BUILD THAT — PRIVATE COMPANIES DID

Obama proudly took credit for the increasing proportion of American petroleum demand satisfied by domestic sources of oil and gas in recent years:

Under my administration, America is producing more oil today than at any time in the last eight years. That's why we have a record number of oil rigs operating right now … And we've opened millions of acres for oil and gas exploration … In 2010, our dependence on foreign oil was under 50 percent for the first time in over a decade.[38]

Obama was the rooster claiming credit for the dawn. Despite his claim that America's increased domestic oil production had occurred "under my administration,'" the truth was that it had occurred despite his efforts, solely from oil and gas ventures that had long predated his arrival in office as Figure 2-1 clearly shows.[39] The Obama administration's actual record boasted a double-digit percentage drop in crude oil production on federal lands where the federal government actually has direct control. In the first year of the Obama administration, the number of new oil wells on federal lands declined by 35% from the level posted just one year earlier.[40] On-shore oil and gas drilling leases on federal lands during Obama's term had dropped to levels not seen since 1984.[41] In November 2013, Obama laughingly boasted in his weekly radio address that the impressive decline in oil imports was due to his support for wind and solar power which has no offsetting impact on oil supply and also to his support for an increase in automobile mileage standards, a policy that had yet to go into effect.[42]

FIGURE 2-1. **Domestic Percentage of U.S. Petroleum Consumption**

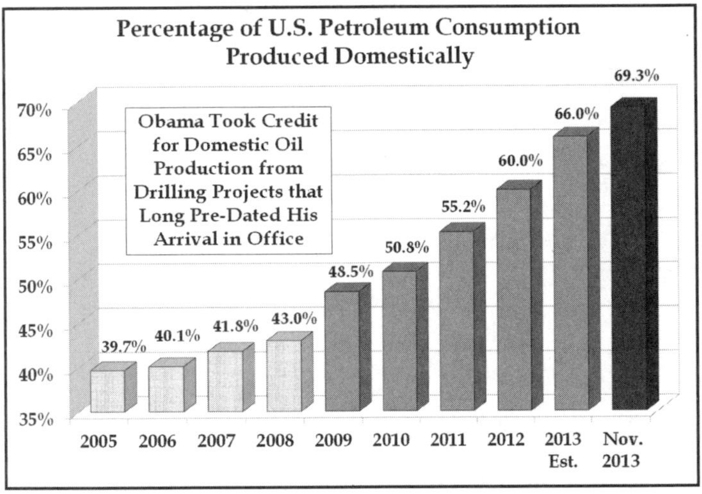

Source: Energy Information Administration

A political furor over plunging fossil fuel production on federal lands erupted in early 2012. Fossil fuel production on federal lands had sunk to a 9-year low.[43] Federal production had declined in every year of the Obama administration.[44] All of the increased domestic oil and gas production Obama had been crowing about had occurred on privately-owned lands in places like North Dakota and Texas.[45] In that very same month, the Congressional Research Service (CRS) published a report showing that 96% of the increase in domestic production since 2007 had occurred on private lands.[46] One year later, DoE reported that fossil fuel production had declined again in fiscal year 2012, setting a 10-year record low for production on federal lands.[47]

Crude oil production on federal leases in the Gulf of Mexico hit a peak in 2009 at 565.8 million barrels.[48] Within two years, production had declined by more than 18% to 463.6 million barrels.[49] Eighty percent of production on federal lands occurs in offshore fields, and 95% of that takes place in the Gulf of Mexico.[50] So Gulf production is a proxy for all federal oil production.

FIGURE 2-2. **Fossil Fuel Production on Federal and Private Lands**

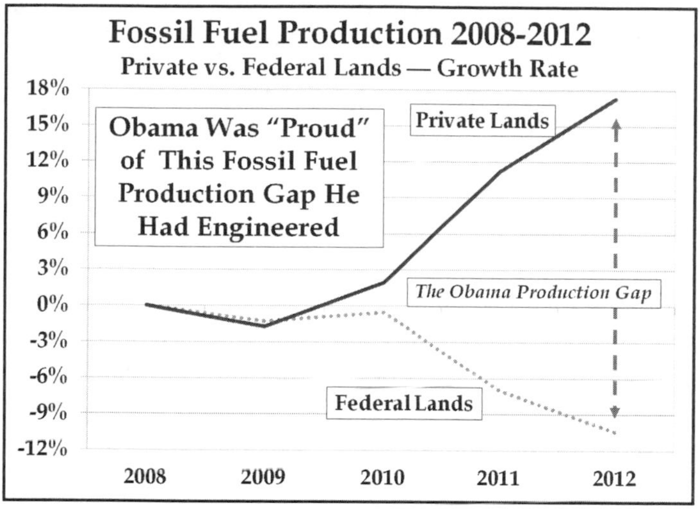

Fossil Fuel Production 2008-2012
Private vs. Federal Lands — Growth Rate

Obama Was "Proud" of This Fossil Fuel Production Gap He Had Engineered

Private Lands

The Obama Production Gap

Federal Lands

Source: U.S. Energy Information Administration

The subject was revisited during the second Presidential debate when, after another empty boast, Obama was reminded by his opponent that drilling on federal lands which he controlled had declined during his term while increasing on private lands over which he had no control. Naturally, Obama dishonestly denied it. There was no Candy Crowley to rush to his aid and cover up his deceit. Figure 2-2 shows the truth.[51] The data comes from the DoE.

Obama even boasted in late February 2013 that he was "proud of the fact that under my Administration oil production is higher than it has been in a decade or more."[52] But on the very same day he issued that disingenuous statement, the CRS released another report setting the record straight, implicitly calling the President a liar.[53] CRS made clear that all of the increased production had occurred on private lands. By using the word "all," CRS understated the share attributed to private lands, since private production increased while federal production declined:

> All of the increased production from FY2007 to FY2012 took place on non-federal lands, causing the federal share of total U.S. crude oil production to fall by about seven percentage points. Overall, U.S. natural gas production rose by four trillion cubic feet (tcf) or 20% since 2007, while production on federal lands (onshore and offshore) fell by about 33% and production on non-federal lands grew by 40%.[54]

Was Obama was proud of this? CRS data made clear that federal production declined in every year since FY2010.[55] Examination of the report from the Interior Department showed that production on federal lands declined in each of the four categories of hydrocarbons between FY 2011 and FY 2012 even though Obama claimed that he was "proud of the fact" that oil and gas drilling had increased under his watch.[56] The only reason America was increasing fossil fuel production was that private operators were bringing new production to market faster than Obama could shut down federal activity.

Had oil and gas production on federal lands merely kept pace with FY2010 output, GDP would have been $16.3 billion higher than it actually was, more than 0.1% on an annualized basis. Since 2012 GDP had posted a woeful 1.67% and fourth quarter 2012 had come in essentially flat,[57] it could have helped the economically-challenged President. But job creation, oil and gas production, economic growth, and real personal incomes are clearly not priorities to Obama.

Obama never tires of reminding us that there was no point in increasing domestic production of oil and gas, that there were no short term fixes to America's energy situation because the projects required to bring increased fossil fuel supply into fruition might require ten years to complete. It is one of the reasons often cited by climate zealots against approving the Keystone XL pipeline.[58] Ten years will never arrive so it can't possibly make a difference.

The Obama administration had gone out of its way to delay, disrupt, and restrict domestic production of oil and gas.[59] In addition to the moratorium on Outer Continental Shelf drilling in the wake of the Deepwater Horizon disaster, Obama slowed deep-water drilling permits by more than half and shallow water permits by more than two thirds.[60] Between 2006 to 2011, the time required to obtain a permit for drilling on federal lands had grown 41% to 307 days.[61]

The administration also proudly announced a ban on drilling in the Eastern Gulf of Mexico as well as off the Atlantic and Pacific coasts.[62] The ban would essentially cordon off these potentially rich areas to oil recovery for at least seven years.[63] The announcement was a classic double-cross, a reversal of administration policy that had been announced eight months earlier where the President proclaimed that, while he was cancelling four lease sales in Alaska, he would be opening up the Eastern Gulf and offshore Atlantic and Pacific coasts to drilling.[64]

In October 2011, the Obama administration lifted the moratorium on deepwater drilling it had imposed following the Deepwater Horizon disaster.[65] But at the same time, it also established a set of onerous new regulations that acted as a de facto extension of the moratorium.[66] Indeed, five months after the administration announced its lifting of the moratorium, the Interior Department had still not managed to approve a single new exploratory deepwater drilling plan.[67] The agency charged with evaluating and approving offshore drilling plans, the Bureau of Ocean Energy Management Regulation and Enforcement, was still sitting on 103 deepwater drilling plans that were awaiting review.[68]

The slowdown in Gulf of Mexico drilling would result in a decrease of 220,000 barrels of oil per day.[69] The reduced production would not only restrict energy supplies resulting in higher prices at the pump. But, given the federal government's 18.75% royalty rate, it would amount to a reduction in royalty revenues to the Treasury of more than $1.6 billion in 2012.[70] It's not like a country that ran a federal budget deficit of $1.3 trillion that year actually needed to find ways to decrease revenues.

As a result of the moratorium and the de facto drilling halt from approval rope-a-dope, drilling companies moved deepwater drilling rigs out of Gulf waters to other global markets where prospects were far more promising. By early 2011, eight of the thirty deepwater rigs contracted to work in the Gulf had been moved to other regions.[71] That number had reached eleven by early 2012.[72] And the moratorium resulted in the loss of tens of billions dollars of potential capital investment, destroying thousands of American jobs in the process.[73]

Despite of all of Obama's triumphant claims about expanding domestic oil and gas production, his administration's actions in the wake of the Deepwater Horizon spill had been to cancel four lease sales in Alaska, ban both shallow and deepwater drilling in the Gulf, lift the Gulf drilling ban but impose a de facto moratorium by spiking the approval process, and open the Eastern Gulf, Atlantic, and Pacific coastal areas to drilling only to close them off again months later.

ALL OF THE ABOVE, BUT NOTHING BELOW

The Obama administration's strange, ideologically-motivated war on oil and gas producers didn't stop with these moves. From the moment he took office, Obama had set about shutting down domestic fossil fuel generation to try and jump-start his quixotic 'green energy' quest. Obama:

✓ Imposed new taxes on oil and chemicals production under provisions of the Comprehensive Environmental Response, Compensation and Liability Act (CERCLA).[74]

✓ Proposed repeal of favorable LIFO inventory accounting rules on oil and gas projects, increasing amounts subject to taxes, reducing project returns and discouraging production.[75]

✓ Tendered a 2010 budget proposal that sought to eliminate a wide variety of incentives on oil and gas production while imposing new fees to discourage drilling.[76]

✓ Proposed a 13% excise tax increase on Gulf of Mexico oil and gas drilling hoping to stifle production.[77]

✓ Removed more than two million acres of federal lands from oil and gas recovery.[78]

✓ Proposed a 2012 budget that imposed a schedule of much higher inspection fees and royalty payments on offshore drilling.[79] The proposals included $60 billion in new taxes and fees on production.[80]

✓ Proposed to repeal intangible drilling cost expensing, requiring longer asset write-downs that would degrade the economic potential of oil and gas projects.[81]

✓ Proposed eliminating expense treatment of tertiary injectants used to enhance oil recovery in aging wells that would reduce return on investment and discourage marginal production.[82]

✓ Proposed elimination of passive loss write-down on working wells that would boost tax liabilities, curtailing marginal production.[83]

✓ Proposed repealing percentage depletion allowance on drilling projects that would degrade economic returns.[84]

✓ Supported "use or lose" fees on nonproducing leases, a proposal designed to stifle future production on temporarily idle wells.[85]

✓ Sought to extend the amortization period for independent geological and geophysical producers to seven years, increasing income tax liability, rules designed to degrade drilling project net present value and rate of return[86]

✓ Announced new rules restricting drilling on federal lands in five Western states.[87] Companies had already paid over $100 million for leases to which they had been denied access.[88]

✓ Proposed other taxes and penalties on oil and gas producers contending they had distorted the industry by over-investing and over-producing, that carbon emissions concerns were more important than fossil fuel production, and that 'green energy' schemes suffer when the fossil fuel industry benefits.[89]

✓ Cancelled 77 oil leases in the state of Utah that had already been awarded during the previous administration.[90]

✓ Proposed a 50% increase on onshore oil and gas royalties on federal land drilling designed to curtail production.[91]

✓ Blocked oil exploration activities in Alaska's Beaufort and Chukchi Seas[92] leaving the state with the highest oil production potential holding the fewest drilling rigs[93]

✓ Proposed fiscal year 2013 budget rules that sought to remove tax incentives, harming small oil and natural gas producers, a move designed to reduce production and destroy jobs[94]

✓ Proposed increasing the corporate tax rate on oil and gas producers by 3 percent in a country that has one of the highest corporate tax rates in the world.[95]

✓ Supported his Interior Secretary's efforts to delay an Outer Continental Shelf drilling plan[96] that had been previously approved.[97]

✓ Announced a plan to reduce lease terms on federal lands from ten to five years, degrading the economic return on oil drilling projects to discourage domestic production.[98]

✓ Unleashed nuisance attacks against producers working the Bakken shale in North Dakota, alleging companies were responsible for twenty eight bird deaths, while waiving prosecutions against wind farm operators that kill millions of birds each year.[99]

✓ Ordered the Bureau of Land Management to withdraw sixty one previously awarded Montana drilling leases, using a ridiculous "climate change" rationale.[100]

✓ Supported EPA's baseless attacks against oil and gas companies in Texas, Pennsylvania, and Wyoming. EPA was forced to withdraw after the meritless allegations were exposed.[101]

✓ Supported EPA's restrictions on chemicals used in natural gas drilling.[102]

✓ Supported Interior Department's effort to curtail acreage that lessors could utilize on natural gas wells on public lands while boosting royalty rates and filing fees.[103]

✓ Sat on his hands as North Alaska's Chukchi region's oil drilling development plans got bogged down in federal and state permitting disputes.[104]

✓ Proposed eliminating foreign tax credits for oil and gas producers, provisions available to all taxpayers, in an effort to impair economic returns and reduce production.[105]

Collectively, his policies had kept 87% of offshore drilling acreage off-limits to oil and gas recovery through his first three years in office.[106] But, despite these strenuous efforts, when oil prices predictably began to rise in early 2012, Obama crisscrossed the nation in a panic pretending that his policies had had nothing to do with increasing gasoline prices. Suddenly it was important for Obama to pretend to be the "oil drilling President."[107]

In April 2009, Obama traveled out to a manufacturing plant in Newton, Iowa that makes towers for wind turbines to deliver his Earth Day speech. In that speech, the President invoked "climate change" or "climate crisis" six times.[108] In 2009, gasoline prices weren't important. Climate change took center stage. But his 2012 Earth Day speech didn't mention the word "climate" a single time in any context.[109] Nor did it appear in his University of Miami speech.

A look at the White House Energy and Environment web page in the Summer of 2012 showed a picture of the President proudly walking past a long stack of 36-inch diameter oil pipes. You don't stuff expensive wind and solar energy into those.[110] The headline blared that oil imports declined one million barrels a day between 2010 and 2011.

On Earth Day 2009, Obama told listeners that the choice between the environment and the economy was false — "the choice we face is not between saving our environment and saving our economy," he claimed.[111] The correct choice to Obama was that "we can remain the world's leading importer of oil, or we can become the world's leading exporter of clean energy."[112] Nowhere in 2009 was there any mention that the U.S. possessed the ability to become the world's leading producer and net exporter of oil and refined petroleum products. That choice did not enter into Obama's 2009 calculus, nor did it in 2010, nor in 2011. It only became important in 2012 when gas prices spiked, when voters became angry, and as reelection neared. By 2012, the newly-converted oil enthusiast was bragging that oil imports had declined "1 million barrels per day" in a single year.

But even while Obama was doing all this, at the same time he was promoting windmills, solar energy, biofuels, and electric cars under the rubric of an "all of the above" energy program. His assurances notwithstanding, it is abundantly clear to any fair minded observer that his "all of the above" program excluded all of the stuff below ground. Sermons about reducing imports, pictures of oil guy Obama walking past oil pipes, claims about "all of the above" was all a smokescreen.

Just to highlight the total incomprehensibility of the administration's energy policy, Obama had deliberately curtailed permitting to U.S.-based producers for production in the Gulf of Mexico while offering to assist Mexico's state-owned Petróleos Mexicanos

(Pemex) in deep-water drilling in Gulf waters.[113] He chose that path even though Pemex has far less experience and capability than the U.S. has to undertake these complex activities.[114]

Obama had also traveled to Brasilia in March 2011 to offer U.S. assistance to Brazilians intent on exploiting newly discovered offshore deposits of oil and natural gas.[115] Two years earlier, he had offered more than $2 billion of Export-Import Bank loan commitments to Brazil to enable offshore discovery in the giant Tupi oil field located off the coast of Rio de Janeiro.[116] Brazil is home to seven of the world's ten largest deepwater oil fields discovered in the past decade.[117] While there, he assured business leaders that the U.S. would become an eager trading partner for its production volumes. This would further degrade America's balance of trade. If we did that, it would worsen the imported oil problem, the security risk that he was complaining about in Coral Gables.

Would that Obama exerted even a fraction of the same effort toward U.S. oil and gas producers, something that would actually improve U.S. economic growth prospects, job creation, balance of trade, balance of payments, and energy security. But America's burden is that Obama is either oblivious or is indifferent to the direct connection between abundant, low-cost energy and improved economic performance. We all pay a price for that.

CHAPTER 3

GIVE HIGH ENERGY
PRICES A CHANCE

"The current high oil prices have the potential to strangle the economic recovery in many countries."[1]

FATIH BIROL
CHIEF ECONOMIST, INTERNATIONAL ENERGY AGENCY
DECEMBER 14, 2011

"My plan isn't just about making ... energy expensive, it's about making [expensive] energy affordable [by comparison]. Once we make ... energy expensive, the second step in my plan is to invest $150 billion [of borrowed money] over the next decade [creating a lot of expensive energy]"[2]

BARACK OBAMA
PORTSMOUTH, NEW HAMPSHIRE
OCTOBER 8, 2007

It was early 2011, shortly after his political party, the party that supported higher energy prices and more expensive health care, had suffered a hard-earned and well-deserved shellacking in the mid-term elections. President Obama faced the politically inconvenient prospect of rising gasoline prices. A handful of House Democrats wrote a letter to Obama calling upon him to stage a late night raid on the Strategic Petroleum Reserve (SPR) to help lower prices.[3] Shortly thereafter, a group of six Democratic Senators joined their House colleagues in the same call.[4] In response to the political pressure, Obama raided the SPR for 30.6 million barrels of Louisiana Light Sweet Crude oil.[5] The sale contracts awarded to 15 companies brought in $3.3 billion, $107.80 per barrel.[6]

To gain momentary political advantage, Obama had spoken favorably in the past about SPR drawdowns. In early August 2008, candidate Obama told an audience in Lansing, Michigan that he was in favor of making a 70 million barrel release:

We should sell 70 million barrels of oil from our Strategic Petroleum Reserve for less expensive crude, which in the past has lowered gas prices within two weeks.[7]

So the guy who told University of Miami students that more supply wouldn't reduce oil prices was claiming more supply would reduce oil prices. This came just weeks after crude oil had hit an all time intra-day high of $147.24 a barrel on the NYMEX.[8] But Obama's Lansing position represented a reversal of a position he had taken only one month earlier where he went on record opposing that approach.[9] He had told reporters in St. Louis on July 7th that releases from the SPR should only come in a real emergency:

I do not believe that we should use the strategic oil reserves at this point. I have said — and, in fact, supported a congressional resolution that said — that we should suspend putting more oil into the strategic oil reserve, but the strategic oil reserve, I think, has to be reserved for a genuine emergency.[10]

That position echoed one Obama had taken back on August 31, 2005 in the wake of Hurricane Katrina when President Bush authorized the release of 11 million barrels to cover spot supply disruptions after Gulf refineries had been damaged and shut down. Obama made it clear that:

The reserve should only be used in the event of an emergency, and that we shouldn't be tapping the reserve to provide a small, short-term decrease in gas prices.[11]

Clearly this was a man of bedrock principles. Plunging poll numbers as indicated by a fifteen point advantage for McCain among unaffiliated voters in early August 2008 offered an example of precisely the type of extreme national emergency Obama had in mind.[12] Alert observers of Obama's career had become accustomed to these highly principled, abrupt policy reversals from the rock-solid energy policy expert over the years. For instance, Obama had pandered to listeners at a press conference in Jacksonville in June 2008, assuring Floridians he would remain resolutely opposed to offshore drilling off their coasts:

When I'm president, I intend to keep in place the moratorium here in Florida and around the country that prevents oil companies from drilling off Florida's coasts. That's how we can protect our coastline and still make the investments that will reduce our dependence on foreign oil and bring down gas prices for good.[13]

A month later and safely away from Florida's pristine shorelines, Obama was showing flexibility on the question of offshore drilling to listeners in Dayton:

I understand the politics. In a country desperate for action, ideas like a gas tax holiday or expanded oil drilling in the waters off our coasts are popular. And I'll say this — if there were real evidence that these steps would actually provide real, immediate relief at the pump and advance the long-term goal of energy independence, of course I'd be open to them. But so far there isn't.[14]

No one could prove to him that greater supply could help reduce prices and secure energy independence. He doesn't "do" economics. Supply and demand don't figure in his playbook. He was impervious to truths that clashed with ideological certitudes.

FIGURE 3-1. **U.S. Energy Production % of Demand 2005 to 2016**

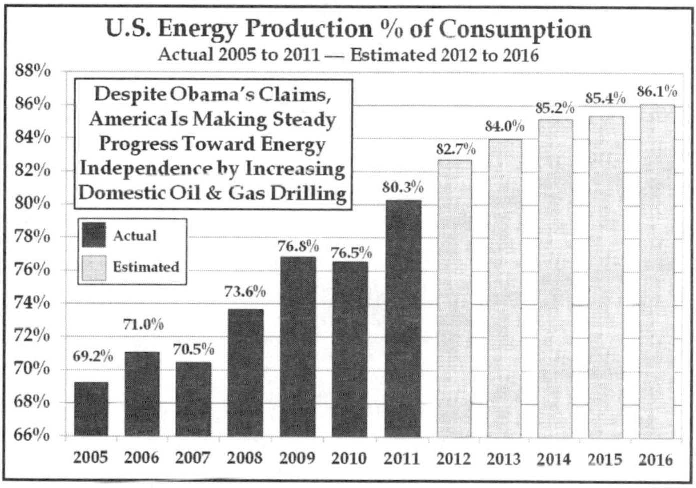

Source: Actual data from Annual Energy Review 2011 and estimated data from Annual Energy Outlook 2013, U.S. Energy Information Administration

All Obama needed to do was check with DoE to understand the impact increased domestic oil and natural gas production had upon America's strides toward achieving real energy self-sufficiency. Figure 3-1 shows the U.S. produced only 69.2% of the energy it consumed in 2005.[15] By 2012, America was producing 82.7% of its energy needs.[16] The improvement was a result of a slight 3% reduction in demand and a significant 12.5% increase in domestic production.[17] DoE estimates this trend will continue well into the future. By 2016, America will be producing more than 86% of its energy requirements without any decrease in demand.[18] This is the evidence that will "advance the long-term goal of energy independence," the evidence Obama said didn't exist.

Nevertheless, only one month after telling his Dayton audience that no one could prove to him otherwise, that there was no evidence to the contrary, Obama was adapting his message to a public unhappy with $147 per barrel oil prices. They were not inclined to vote for a man who did not understand the impact that expanded supply might have on commodity prices. So Obama performed another one of his trademark energy policy pirouettes, telling *The Palm Beach Post*:

> *My interest is in making sure we've got the kind of comprehensive energy policy that can bring down gas prices. If, in order to get that passed, we have to compromise in terms of a careful, well thought-out drilling strategy that was carefully circumscribed to avoid significant environmental damage — I don't want to be so rigid that we can't get something done.*[19]

Translated from Weasel into English, that means he was willing to consider drilling in Florida's coastal waters. It is worth noting that the political pressure brought upon Obama by his Congressional colleagues to make releases from the SPR in early 2011 was in response to the price of benchmark West Texas Intermediate (WTI) crude oil that was between $90-$100 per barrel range. But, eleven trading days after the July 2011 release, WTI had actually jumped by 4.7%.[20]

History shows that SPR releases have little or no sustained impact on the price of oil. In 1991, within 10 days of the January 16th release of 17.3 million barrels, crude prices had dropped by 34.5%. But that action was due to the market euphoria from the launch of Operation Desert Storm that got underway the next day rather than from a token release of oil from the SPR. It was, in no small part, also due to the fact that Saudi Arabia had made massive supply additions to global crude oil shipments at the request of the U.S. whose troops were fighting to protect the Saudi royal family and its exclusive oil franchise.[21]

After 11 million barrels of oil were released from the SPR on September 2, 2005, crude oil prices declined 6.7% within 10 trading days. That limited release was designed to cover spot shortages caused by supply disruptions in the wake of Hurricane Katrina. But that release coincided with the end of the driving season in the U.S. which typically sees energy prices fall. The price drop also resulted from a reduction in supply uncertainty in the wake of improved hurricane damage assessments. By the start of the next year's summer vacation season, crude oil prices were trading well above the peak levels suffered during the Katrina price spike.[22]

Even the usually reliable voices of political support at *The Washington Post* editorial page saw through the transparent scam regarding the June 2011 SPR release announcement, correctly identifying its political dimensions rather than supply disruption concerns.[23] To Obama, reelection-minded price management during the summer driving season was a critical national security objective that required triggering the President's emergency drawdown authority.[24] Obama certainly didn't want to suffer the same fate as his sixty three House colleagues the previous November.

Obama never replaced the oil he had siphoned from the SPR in 2011, even after prices dropped well below the levels obtained by DoE in its sales contracts. By early March 2012, prices for the Louisiana crude that had been removed from the SPR were trading in the $125-130 per barrel range, meaning that it would take about $3.9 billion to replace the oil that Obama sold for $3.3 billion one year earlier purely as a political expedient.[25]

The reason why that March 2012 date was important was because, under pressure from nervous Democrats who had been receiving angry phone calls from constituents about high gasoline prices, Obama began preparing plans to make additional sales of crude oil from the SPR.[26] The situation in March 2012 represented another emergency as the President's poll numbers began to move in the opposite direction of oil prices.[27]

The SPR authorizing legislation, the Energy Policy and Conservation Act of 1975,[28] permitted drawdowns from the SPR upon a Presidential finding that there has been a "severe energy supply interruption."[29] Following the Exxon Valdez oil spill, a later amendment, the Energy Policy and Conservation Act of 1990,[30] permitted releases when there are supply disruptions within the U.S.[31]

The President's drawdown authority under the enabling legislation specifically excludes price as a drawdown trigger.[32] It doesn't mention anything about polling numbers either. But never mind those inconveniences. Legal impediments did not trouble the man who had sworn in January 2009 to faithfully execute the laws of the land. After all, he was the Constitutional law professor who revered the Constitution as he never tired of reminding us.[33]

The SPR had only been tapped three times in its existence. The first President Bush tapped it in the wake of the supply disruption during the Mideast War of 1990-91. The second President Bush tapped it following the domestic supply disruptions caused by Hurricane Katrina that shut down damaged pipelines and refineries for weeks on end. The third instance occurred when Obama tapped it in 2011 … to salvage his political standing among angry voters and wavering Democrats. To Obama, that easily constituted an emergency triggering a drawdown authorization.[34]

Having done it once, he'd consider doing it again. He was receiving air cover from former administration flaks who argued the perfectly preposterous idea that there was too much oil in the SPR anyway.[35] In early 2012, crude oil prices spiked due to a variety of reasons, not the least of which was the risk premium attached to threats from Iran to close the Strait of Hormuz. Congressional Democrats naturally began pressuring the Constitutional law professor to undertake a second lawless SPR drawdown.[36]

Those calls received greater urgency when Nancy Pelosi joined in to urge the law scholar to show his reverence for the Constitution by once again disregarding the EPCA law and acting in the political interests of vulnerable House Democrats.[37] After all, you have to tap the SPR to see what's in it. Pelosi badly wanted to grab the Speaker's gavel once again, which would become difficult if pump prices continued to rise. The hurdle would become even higher if voters were treated to video reminders of Obama proclaiming that his 'green energy' paradise necessitated higher prices.

OBAMA'S PLAN FOR HIGHER PRICES

It was difficult to understand why Obama and Democrats were complaining about high energy prices. This was the political party that nearly succeeded in imposing ruinous carbon cap-and-trade, champions the mutual suicide pact called the Kyoto Protocol, supported the moratorium on offshore drilling, advocates carbon taxes, advocates drilling prohibitions in the Arctic National Wildlife Refuge, applauds efforts to impede domestic drilling, favors measures that degrade economic returns on drilling, backed the Presidential candidate who supported higher energy prices, regularly demonizes oil companies, ignores the risk premiums attached to foreign policy missteps of an administration that blunders its way from one disaster to another in the Middle East, lionizes myth-makers who peddle hydraulic fracturing hysteria, urges cancellation of the Keystone XL pipeline, empowers energy-curtailing environmental regulatory excess, etc. Why was that party crying about higher energy prices? Democrats were blaming oil market speculators, calling for Congressional investigations into oil trading, proposing to outlaw energy exports, and advocating windfall profits taxes. Higher energy was their plan. Their program had worked as intended.

It wasn't exactly like they were going to have a lot of luck hiding their true intent. Obama's Secretary of Energy Steven Chu ended the debate once and for all, if there had ever been one. Chu told a House Committee in late February 2012 that the Obama administration was not interested in lowering gasoline prices.[38] He was reiterating his honest but injudicious 2008 comment that "somehow we have to figure out how to boost the price of gasoline to the levels in Europe."[39] Europe is where people were paying $7 and $9 per gallon on the day Chu testified.[40]

Obama claimed in numerous instances that "there is no magic bullet" when it comes to lowering the retail price of fuel.[41] It's true. There is no magic bullet. But there are sensible energy policies, and insensible ones. Obama has a decided fondness for the insensible with a judicious helping of incomprehensible. There are policies that can help to lower the cost of fuel, and those that drive up prices. Obama and Chu favor higher prices,[42] they are both on record testifying as much,[43] and they had taken a lengthy series of steps designed to make their preferences reality.

Obama proclaimed before inauguration day that he wanted to "end the age of oil in our time," demanding there be "real results by the end of my first term in office."[44] Such a program would "take nothing less than a complete transformation of our economy. This transformation will be costly."[45] A key part of that transformation was a rapid increase in prices that would assist the transition to less cost-competitive options. The cost increases Obama had in mind were to be borne by fuel consumers, the ones paying higher prices in 2012.

Even if the U.S. took Secretary Chu's advice adopting crippling gasoline taxes to boost prices, it would likely have only a marginal impact on reducing mileage. Crippling European motor fuel taxes have had little impact on driving in Europe.[46] Numerous studies have confirmed that, despite ever increasing taxes on transport fuels in Europe, passenger transport continues to grow inexorably. A 2007 report from the European Environment Agency noted that:

Between 1990 and 2003, passenger transport volumes in the EEA member countries grew by 20% while GDP increased by 30%. Air transport grew the most during this period (96%), followed by private car transport.[47]

The only thing Europeans received for the crippling taxes imposed on transport fuels was a substantial reduction in disposable income. The promised environmental benefits Obama and Chu heralded never materialized.

More recent studies show that, while overall transport demand in Europe slightly declined during the 2009-2010 recession, passenger automobile demand actually rose. In addition, over the past decade, demand for motorized passenger transport outpaced the rate of economic growth in the twelve core countries of the European Union despite some of the highest motor fuel taxes in the world. The EEA report found:

The car accounts for 77% of all motorised intra-EU passenger transport (road, rail, air and sea) and is the only mode for which overall demand has not fallen in recent years. Between 1999 and 2009, passenger car demand in the EEA has increased by 14%. This trend has been strongest in the EU-12, where demand swelled by 55%, compared to a rise of 8% in the EU-15. This may be because vehicle sales tend to develop in line with economic growth.[48]

Chu was certainly not alone in his quixotic viewpoint. Other leftists have made similar statements urging higher energy prices. Jay Hakes, the head of the U.S. Energy Information Administration during the Clinton administration, proclaimed "There's no way we can create a better future without the price of [fossil-fuel-based] energy going up."[49] Got that? Your future will only improve if you pay much higher prices at the pump, if your utility bills skyrocket, if the cost to heat and cool your home soars, if the cost to cook your meals, wash your clothes and take a shower increases to crippling levels, if your disposable income sinks and you have far less to spend on other needs like food, education, or health care because you have to spend so much more on energy, if America's gross domestic product declines precipitously because personal consumption expenditures that account for 70% of GDP are siphoned away on energy purchases, a large portion of which is imported from other countries.[50] George Orwell had these people in mind when he said "there are some ideas so absurd that only an intellectual could believe them."

Secretary Chu is even more forthright in his sarcasm-drenched condescension. He tells the American public that it acts like a pack of wayward children who need to be constantly disciplined by their parents, by which he obviously means our superiors in the federal government. To progressives like Obama and Chu, Americans who have driven down their energy usage per dollar of real GDP by 250% since 1949 are simply too intellectually primitive to understand what is in their best interest. "The American public … just like your teenage kids, aren't acting in a way that they should act," he said at a conference in Washington.[51]

It turns out that it is Chu, or his own agency, that is the real wayward teen. DoE regularly fails energy efficiency audits conducted by the Office of Inspector General.[52] Employees leave lights on, fail to turn off computer monitors, keep thermostat settings too high, and are guilty of many other wasteful energy management practices.[53] The Department won't even meet its energy intensity reduction obligations set forth in the Energy Independence and Security Act of 2007 .[54]

Chu had mentioned in a 2008 interview that his ultimate objective for the country was energy efficiency, a laudable goal on the surface. Like Obama, he enjoys dismantling straw man arguments. He said it was a misconception that "if you went to an energy-efficient economy, you will kill the economy. That is just demonstrably not true," he proclaimed.[55] But who said otherwise?

Chu's comment highlights the danger of sending a physicist to do an economist's job. The relative benefit or damage done to the economy depends upon the amount of investment required compared to the energy improvement benefit derived. As an economist would say, it depends upon your return on investment. If you invest modest amounts of capital and receive large returns in energy reduction, you improve the economy. The cost-benefit numbers look good. But if you spend mountains of capital and receive comparatively little benefit in return, it's bad. For example, if you spend $535 million on a solar scam like Solyndra as Chu did, lose all your money and get zero benefit in return, it's terrible for the economy. Unfortunately, physicists don't traffic in concepts like capital efficiency. And politicians like Obama are ideologically indisposed to consider them.

When Mississippi Congressman Alan Nunnelee asked the Energy Secretary in late February 2012 if it was the Obama administration's "overall goal to get our price" of gasoline lower, Chu cut off the Congressman in mid-sentence, curtly replying "No, the overall goal is to decrease our dependency on oil, to build and strengthen our economy."[56] It was a response that demonstrated better than any that, as an economist, Chu makes a great physicist. The issue of soaring gasoline prices is mainly a concern to people who drive. It didn't bolster his case when Chu freely admitted during Congressional questioning that he doesn't own a car.[57]

A few days after his remarkably candid testimony to the House Committee, a no doubt deeply chastised Secretary Chu appeared in front of the Senate Energy and Natural Resources Committee bearing the visible scars and bruises of his political shellacking he had taken for being forthright about Obama energy policy. He promptly disavowed his earlier honest but politically inconvenient remarks.[58] When pressed by Utah Senator Mike Lee about his 2008 comment favoring higher gasoline prices, he disingenuously replied:

I no longer share that view. Of course we don't want the price of gasoline to go up. We want it to go down. Since I walked in the door as Secretary of Energy, I have been doing everything in my powers to do what we can to reduce … those prices.[59]

It was true; he doesn't share that view any longer. He still believes it. But he keeps it to himself. The rest of his statement was a patent lie uttered by an administration official exhausting his last vestige of credibility on orders issued by a reelection-minded White House overcome by panic. No doubt Chu favors $2 gasoline — as long as it's sold by the pint.[60] The comments underscored the panic that led the White House to hurriedly schedule four falsehood-strewn energy policy speeches within the space of a few weeks.[61]

THE OVAL OFFICE SPEECH

Obama's Coral Gables speech was substantially similar to an earlier televised energy policy speech delivered by the President from the Oval Office to a national audience. He opened his remarks warning Americans that an economy built around a steadily increasing demand for fossil fuels in the face of shrinking supply was doomed. He claimed that "we simply must balance our demand for energy with our rapidly shrinking resources." Some of his proposals would be unpopular he warned and would lead to shared sacrifice. Otherwise, we would face "national catastrophe."

In the Oval Office speech, the President claimed that oil supply was dwindling, a fact that was evident with the increasing imbalance between supply and demand. As with Obama's Miami remarks, energy conservation and efficiency were constantly repeated themes:

We simply must balance our demand for energy with our rapidly shrinking resources. By acting now, we can control our future instead of letting the future control us. The oil and natural gas we rely on for 75 percent of our energy are running out. Unless profound changes are made to lower oil consumption, we now believe that … the world will be demanding more oil that it can produce.

Americans had once depended upon wood, the President explained. That era gave way to coal, which was more versatile, particularly as wood was no longer available in many areas. Coal made the Industrial Revolution possible. The next transition occurred when Americans began tapping oil and gas, which enabled automobile and airplane travel. But this era was now drawing to a close as supplies dwindled.

The President assured Americans that the reduced availability of oil and natural gas would necessitate "strict conservation." Americans would also need to switch to his favorite alternative energy, solar power:

Because we are now running out of gas and oil, we must prepare quickly for a ... change, to strict conservation and to the use of ... permanent renewable energy sources like solar power.

As he had done many times in the past, the President again assured Americans that the country would not be able to drill its way out of its dwindling oil supply problem. We could not continue on our current path because "we could use up all the proven reserves of oil in the entire world by the end of the next decade."

The handwriting was clear. The world had only another 15 to 20 years before the planet would run out of fuel. Americans had to make major changes now. The country needed to hear the harsh truth:

World oil production can probably keep going up for another six or eight years. But ... it can't go up much more. Demand will overtake production. We have no choice about that.

To highlight the urgency for adopting conservation measures, the President scolded listeners saying Americans were wasteful:

Ours is the most wasteful nation on earth. We waste more energy than we import. With about the same standard of living, we use twice as much energy per person as do other countries like Germany, Japan, and Sweden.

The President pleaded with the country to end its oil addiction, saying that if we did not mend our ways, we were in danger of "losing American jobs and becoming increasingly vulnerable to supply interruptions." In a sputtering economy, preserving and enhancing job growth was high on the agenda. Nevertheless, there was hope if the nation was willing to change:

If we fail to act soon, we will face an economic, social and political crisis that will threaten our free institutions. But we still have another choice. We can begin to prepare right now. We can decide to act while there is time.

The plan that the President laid out would solve our energy supply problems in an economically and environmentally sensible way. The principles he enumerated included (1) placing the government at the forefront of national energy policy, (2) adopting energy conservation measures, (3) protecting the environment by reducing waste, (4) reducing oil consumption, (5) limiting oil company profiteering, and (6) setting up a public investment plan for unconventional sources like solar, wind and geothermal power.

The President promised that America could overcome its energy problems even if the road ahead was difficult:

I can't tell you that these measures will be easy, nor will they be popular. But I think most of you realize that a policy which does not ask for changes or sacrifices would not be an effective policy.

As he had so often in the past, he repeatedly protested that the country had squandered the respect of the entire world that it had won through two centuries of moral leadership, a theme that was often reiterated by other Democrats and partisan supporters in the press. But the President proclaimed that America could earn back that respect if it was willing to show leadership:

Now we have a chance again to give the world a positive example. And we have been proud of our vision of the future. We have always wanted to give our children and grandchildren a world richer in possibilities than we've had. They are the ones we must provide for now. They are the ones who will suffer most if we don't act.

He summed his remarks, pleading with Americans to join him in his vision for a secure energy future:

Other generations of Americans have faced and mastered great challenges. I have faith that meeting this challenge will make our own lives even richer. We will again prove that our great nation can lead the world into an age of peace, independence and freedom.

The speech resembled many others that the President had delivered as a candidate and while in office. The President's Coral Gables speech was essentially a reiteration of the Oval Office speech and resembled it in dozens of instances. It was delivered in the same monotonous moralizing tone that Americans had come to associate with this President's preferred style. All of the familiar themes enumerated in each of the two speeches were clear. America needed an effective national energy program directed by the federal government, led by a true visionary.

The only difference between the two speeches worthy of note was that the Oval Office speech had been delivered by the insufferable, moralizing scold Jimmy Carter on April 18, 1977 while the Coral Gables speech had been delivered by America's newest insufferable, hectoring scold, Jimmy Carter Jr., also known as Barack Obama.[62] Why does anyone think the failed energy policy delivered by a failed President a generation ago will suddenly work when they are tried again by another failed President?

SECTION 2

A DETACHMENT FROM REALITY

CHAPTER 4

ARE WE ALMOST OUT OF OIL AND GAS?

"The global energy landscape is changing at a stunning pace. North America is close to energy independence, which once seemed unattainable. Better yet, the U.S., long dependent on supplies from potentially hostile nations, will attain self-sufficiency in 20 years ... The surge in domestic oil and gas production — spurred on by such new techniques as hydraulic fracturing ... did not come about as the result of government energy polices, but largely in spite of them."[1]

EDITORIAL, USA TODAY, AUGUST 2013

"It is commonly asked, when will the world's supply of oil be exhausted? The best one word answer: Never."[2]

MORRIS A. ADELMAN
MIT PROFESSOR OF ECONOMICS

After bragging about what a wonderful job he was doing to reduce imports, Obama reverted to disingenuousness in front of a Miami student audience. He praised his daughters' environmental and natural resource awareness,[3] their supposed unparalleled understanding about the importance of energy conservation.[4] He poured scorn on the country, implying that America was guilty of natural resource injustice:

The United States consumes more than a fifth of the world's oil — more than twenty percent of the world's oil — just us. We only have two percent of the world's oil reserves. We consume twenty; we've got two.[5]

His adoring members shouted "Preach it, Mr. President." But ignore the natural resource injustice angle. Concentrate instead on his claim that the United States possessed only "two percent of the world's oil reserves." Obama was probably referencing Energy

Information Administration (EIA) data showing the U.S. in possession of 20.7 billion barrels of proven crude oil reserves in 2009, which was 1.5% of 1,341.6 billion barrels of crude reserves worldwide.[6] The U.S. consumed 18.8 million barrels of petroleum per day, which was 22.4% of the worldwide total consumption of 84.7 million barrels per day (bpd).[7] Media reports filed by shallow reporters echo these same figures as if that is the beginning and end of the story.[8] So his statistics were close enough for government work.

FIGURE 4-1. **Proved Reserves and U.S. Oil Production**

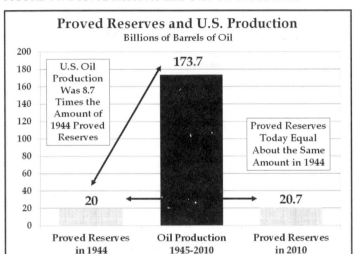

Sources: U.S. Field Production of Crude Oil (Thousand Barrels), *Energy Information Administration*, 'North American Energy Inventory: December 2011,' *Institute for Energy Research*

Nevertheless, while EIA lists proven reserves at 20.6 billion barrels, a better estimate of technically recoverable oil supply within the U.S. given current capabilities is closer to 1.4 trillion barrels.[9] That's no small difference. That estimate is derived from a pair of studies from the RAND Corporation and the U.S. Geological Survey.[10] The 1.4 trillion barrel figure is nearly 70 times more than Obama claimed and amounted to a number greater than DoE's estimate of the entire world inventory of proven reserves. The figure Obama was citing to his Miami audience excludes the massive amounts located in off-shore fields, in Alaska, in the Rocky Mountain West, and in other fields where the federal government prohibits recovery. It also excludes enormous quantities that can be recovered using improved techniques like hydraulic fracturing and horizontal drilling.

Just in case you're wondering how much faith we should have in the EIA figures on proven reserves, consider this: In 1980, the Department of Energy (DoE) estimated proven reserves at only 29.7 million barrels. Nevertheless, between the years 1980 and 2010, the U.S. managed to squeeze more than 77 million barrels out of reserves and still end up with 20.7 million barrels remaining.[11] The U.S. managed to produce 77 million barrels of crude oil while proven reserves declined by only 9 billion.

Consider another example. In 1944, proved reserves in the U.S. were estimated by the Interior Department to be 20 billion barrels, about the same as today.[12] Yet between 1944 and 2010, the U.S. produced 173.7 billion barrels.[13] Figure 4-1 shows how the country managed to produce 8.7 times as much oil as we had on hand in our 1944 stash and still have 20.7 billion barrels remaining. How much credence should be given to someone who claims that America has the same amount of oil today as the government claimed it had in 1944 when the country had managed to produce nine times the claimed inventory on hand?

HAVEN'T YOU NOTICED? WE'RE ALREADY OUT OF OIL

How was this possible? To answer this, one needs to recognize that crude oil reserve estimating is a slippery slope. There has been a steady progression of revisions to America's crude oil reserves ever since Drake drilled his first oil well in Titusville, Pennsylvania in 1859. There has also been a steady drumbeat of claims that oil reserves would soon be completely depleted.

The moment the first barrel of oil was brought to the surface, the world began running out of oil. So should we start worrying? Examining the trail of oil supply forecasts over the last 140 years highlights the skepticism we should accord anyone who tells you reserves will soon be exhausted.

Predicting the imminent exhaustion of oil reserves has a long, storied history. Pennsylvania's chief geologist Alex Taylor III wrote an article in *Fortune* in 1874 forecasting that kerosene use would exhaust America's oil reserves by 1878.[14] Taylor's colleague John Strong Newberry, Chief Geologist of neighboring Ohio, made a similar prediction in 1875 that oil supply would soon be gone.[15]

In response to concerns about imminent resource exhaustion, the U.S. Geological Survey was formed in 1879 "to study the geological structure and economic resources of the public domain."[16] The country needed to know for certain the date when our natural resources would be gone. Three years later in 1882, the Institute of Mining Engineers estimated that only 95 million barrels of oil remained in the U.S. reservoirs.[17] The U.S. produced that amount of oil every nine days during 2011.[18] The U.S. Bureau of Mines issued a forecast in 1914 claiming that the entire world's oil supply would be depleted in ten years.[19] In 1919, the once learned journal *Scientific American* estimated there were only 20 years of oil remaining.[20]

In 1920, the U.S. Geological Survey estimated that there were 6.7 billion barrels of reserves, plus or minus 25%.[21] Yale University professor Harold Hibbert, citing data in the USGS report from the year earlier, warned in 1921 that, within 10 to 20 years, the U.S. would run out of domestic oil supplies and would become dependent upon foreign sources.[22] Like Jimmy Carter and Barack Obama, Hibbert fretted that the public was unaware of the implication that the exhaustion of domestic reserves posed.[23]

The Federal Oil Conservation Board provided an estimate of 4.5 billion barrels remaining in 1926, a seven-year supply.[24] The Board increased its estimate to ten billion barrels in 1932. In 1939, the U.S. Interior Department assessed the state of global oil supply and concluded that there was only thirteen years of inventory remaining.[25] The Department updated its gloomy forecast in 1951, proclaiming that now the world had just thirteen years of supply remaining.[26] In 1946, the *Los Angeles Times* warned its readers about a State Department forecast that America's domestic supply would be exhausted within twenty years after which the U.S. would be reliant upon Middle East suppliers.[27]

By 1950, the American Petroleum Institute estimated there were only 100 billion barrels of oil remaining in the entire world.[28] In a 1970 issue of *Scientific American*, a National Academy of Sciences geochemist named Harrison Brown forecasted that the world would have completely exhausted its physical supplies of lead, gold, tin, silver and zinc by 1990, and that copper and crude oil would be gone by the year 2000.[29] This helped propel the notorious Club of Rome to publish its best selling quackery entitled *The Limits to Growth* that famously predicted that the world was rapidly exhausting its supply of a vast range of critical materials such as tin, copper, zinc, natural gas, oil and gold. The book, which sold 10 million copies worldwide, claimed that the planet's oil supply would be fully depleted by 1992.[30] The authors have since reissued at least two updated versions making the same discredited forecasts without any hint of embarrassment.

Stanford University professor and Malthusian crackpot Paul Ehrlich testified before a committee headed by Senator John Tunney of California in 1974, proclaiming that global petroleum reserves were "going to be gone by the end of the century."[31] In 1977, Ehrlich and his Malthusian charlatan wife Anne Ehrlich along with a young geologist assistant named John Holdren, who would be named President Obama's science czar in December 2008,[32] proclaimed that recoverable oil reserves would be fully depleted within 25 years.[33] The world would be forced to derive its energy supply from sources other than petroleum. The world didn't run out of oil in 2002 as Ehrlich, Holdren, and Ehrlich — or was it Dr. Howard, Dr. Fine, Dr. Howard? — had predicted.

Oil was first produced at the Kern River field just north of Bakersfield, California in 1899.[34] In the 50 years between its discovery and 1949, a total of 303.9 million barrels had been produced in the reservoir that spreads out over twenty square miles of the San Joaquin Valley and Sierra foothills.[35] Geologists estimated in 1949 that there were only 47 million barrels of oil remaining in the reservoir.[36] But over the next twenty eight years, another 469 million barrels, or 10 times the prior reserve estimate, was produced.[37] At that point in 1977, the State Oil & Gas Supervisor reported estimated reserves in the field to be 640 million barrels.[38] Despite this, between 1978 and 2012, the Kern River field produced another 1.4 billion barrels of oil, more than twice the 1977 reserve estimate. And after all that production, the State Oil & Gas Supervisor estimated in 2009 that the Kern River field still contained a reserve of 569 million barrels.[39]

Besides disco balls and polyester leisure suits, one of our most enduring images from the dismal 1970s was moralizer-in-chief Jimmy Carter scolding Americans in April 1977 for their energy prolificacy, telling them that they would use up all of the proven reserves in the entire world by the middle of the next decade.[40] In 1980, while the positively awful Carter was still President but preparing his well-earned political exile, he welcomed the findings of a panel of "experts" who forecasted in their doom-laden *Global 2000 Report* that "during the 1990s world oil production will approach geological estimates of maximum production capacity, even with rapidly increasing petroleum prices."[41] The report went on to forecast that "engineering and geological considerations suggest that world petroleum production will peak before the end of the century."[42] The authors of Carter's *Global 2000 Report* made the same mistake nearly all forecasters make, failing to consider on-going energy efficiency improvements, and thus wildly over-estimating future consumption. The report forecast that global production of crude oil would top out at 101.4 million bpd in 1995.[43] In actuality, crude oil production only hit 70.3 million bpd that year.[44] By 2012, global petroleum production had climbed 26.7% above 1995 levels.[45] But at 89.1 million bpd, it was still way shy of the Carter's forecast for seventeen years earlier.

The same year as Carter was fretting over his report forecasting the imminent collapse of society due to exhaustion of oil supply, DoE announced that there were 642 billion barrels of proved reserves in the world, about seven and a half years of supply at today's global consumption rate.[46] But by 2009, EIA was reporting 1.3 trillion barrels of global reserves, more than twice as much as they believed existed in 1980.[47] Nevertheless, in the intervening period between 1980 and 2011, the world had seen 841.9 billion barrels of oil production.[48] Somehow the world had managed to produce 31% more oil than the entire available supply in 1980 and still have another 1.3 trillion barrels under the ground.

Forecasts of imminent oil depletion are collectively known as the "peak oil" theory, a belief that the world's production curve had already or would very soon reach a peak in production from whence we would see irreversible decline. The modern installment of the "peak oil" hypothesis was the brainchild of Shell petroleum geologist Marion King Hubbert, who delivered a remarkable paper to a meeting of petroleum geologists at the American Petroleum Institute conference in San Antonio in June 1956.[49] Hubbert's address forecasted that the U.S. would reach its maximum production of oil in 1970.[50] Exactly in line with his prediction, the U.S. logged its highest oil production volume in November 1970 at 10.04 million bpd.[51]

Hubbert was a geologist, not an ideological polemicist. Nevertheless, the astounding accuracy of his prediction made him an unlikely rock star in the American declinist camp, a community of pessimists that really came into its own during Carter's dreadful 1970s. In a farewell address as he left his post, Jimmy Carter's Energy Secretary proclaimed in 1979 that the world had already reached a peak in oil production.[52] Promoting a philosophy of America's eventual decline that was influenced by pseudo-academic strains of hatred for Western civilization and an absurd belief in the inevitable triumph of Soviet socialism, this ridiculous ideology reached its apogee with the election of the dreary, moralizing pessimist Carter who subscribed to some of these viewpoints.

Petroleum geologist and longtime "peak oil" theorist Colin Campbell has been forecasting the imminent exhaustion of oil supply since the 1980s.[53] In 1989, Campbell predicted that world production had already peaked at 65.5 million bpd.[54] But since 1989, global oil production had climbed 33.5%.[55] In 1998, Campbell wrote in *Scientific American* "that within the next decade, the supply of conventional oil will be unable to keep up with demand. " This is profoundly absurd since supply always comes into equilibrium with demand. It's the price that changes. Campbell's assessments are often more rooted in politics than geology though he seldom acknowledges it.[56] He conveniently cited declining output in Indonesia and Mexico as proof of his theories. But, as any reasonable analysis would conclude, the reasons for production drop-off and reserves adjustments in those countries has far more to do with political dysfunction than geology.[57]

Campbell addressed a conference of Malthusian pessimists in March 2000 proclaiming that conventional oil production would peak during that year.[58] In 2002, Campbell assured us that "peak oil" would bring about "war, starvation, economic recession, possibly even the extinction of homo sapiens."[59] Is that all? We were afraid it would be serious. Despite the evidence of ever-growing world oil supply, Campbell reiterated his gloomy forecast in 2003.[60] A year later, he proclaimed that the peak would occur within the next 12 months.[61] In 2006, Campbell helpfully volunteered to lead the world in a series of negotiations and workshops designed to avert wars, terrorism, and global economic catastrophe certain to arise from impending oil depletion.[62] In 2007, Campbell issued yet another forecast proclaiming that the global peak in oil production would come in 2011.[63] But in 2012, world production climbed 700 million barrels higher than the year before.[64]

Like other perennial pessimists, Campbell has gained a reputation for continually shifting the goal posts. Despite seeing all his prior forecasts invalidated, he clings to his doom-and-gloom thesis. Obama has been strongly influenced by these schools of thought as his appointment of John Holdren clearly demonstrates.

Geophysicist Kenneth Deffeyes forecasted that global oil production would peak sometime during the first decade of this century.[65] His 2001 book entitled *Hubbert's Peak: The Impending World Oil Shortage* largely escaped notice until later in the decade as eco-pessimists latched on to the idea as a potent pathway for justifying their claims that society needed to adopt an immediate shift to renewable energy.[66] As his doom-laden views caught the media's attention, Deffeyes revised and updated his book in 2008 reiterating his earlier forecast, which had not yet come to pass. Deffeyes boasts that he has "no professional expertise in economics."[67] That was precisely why he was wrong.

Flamboyant Texas oil tycoon T. Boone Pickens appeared on *CNBC*'s *Kudlow and Cramer* cable TV show in August 2004 and proclaimed that "never again will we pump more than 82 million barrels" per day.[68] A year later, he gave an address to the 11th Clean Cities Conference where he claimed that "I don't believe you can get it any more than 84 million barrels. I don't care what [King] Abdullah, [Vladimir] Putin or anybody else says about oil reserves or production."[69] He didn't care what the production data said either. Two years later, Pickens told the Forbes CEO Conference in Dallas that oil production had peaked at 85 million bpd.[70] By November 2012, daily oil production reached 89.3 million barrels despite Pickens' earlier assurances it could never surpass 82 million.

An investment banker named Matthew Simmons, whose business catered to oil producers, was known throughout his life as a consistent "peak oil" pessimist. Claiming that global oil production would peak in 2007, Simmons forecast in 2004 that Saudi Arabia would need to curtail its production to "3 to 4 million bpd so that their oil might last another 30 to 50 years."[71] Using midpoints, Simmons estimated the country had only about 51.1 billion barrels of oil left in its reservoirs.[72] But between 2004 and 2012, Saudi Arabia managed to produce 35.3 billion barrels of oil.[73] So, under the Simmons calculus, that would entail a remaining reservoir in 2013 of only 15.8 billion barrels. But EIA estimated Saudi proved reserves at 267.9 billion barrels in 2012,[74] which is in close agreement with the International Energy Agency reserve figure of 264.5 billion.[75] Simmons' estimate was wrong by a factor of 17 at least. That factor will grow over time as both production and reserve estimates increase. Simmons told a reporter he hoped he was wrong but he was "waiting and hoping for someone to prove him wrong."[76] History has proven him wrong, hilariously so.

Simmons reiterated his faulty analysis in a 2005 book *Twilight in the Desert: The Coming Saudi Oil Shock and the World Economy*, saying that Saudi production was at its peak production capacity or already in decline, particularly at the Ghawar field, the world's largest reservoir.[77] Simmons claimed that 2005 daily production level of nine million barrels could not possibly be exceeded.[78] Since then, the world's swing producer Saudi Arabia has seen production of over 11.5 million bpd.[79] That included at least a million and a half bpd of excess capacity on standby.[80] Simmons spent years in a futile attempt to resurrect the reputation of The Club of Rome.[81]

Simmons told an interviewer in 2003 that he had examined "more than 100 very technical production reports" about Saudi oil production indicating the country had already reached its production peak and was in permanent, irrevocable decline.[82] Saudi Arabia produced about 8.81 million bpd in 2002, which would have been the most recent "technical" data Simmons could have examined.[83] Despite Simmons assurances, in 2012, Saudi Arabia's production had risen to well over 11.5 million bpd, a 31% increase.[84] Oil industry analysts see 2013 production growing in new fields like the giant offshore Manifa basin faster than decline rates in existing fields can remove supply.[85]

In the same interview, when asked for his solution to dwindling natural gas supply, Simmons offered that "I don't think there is one. The solution is to pray. Under the best of circumstances, if all prayers are answered there will be no crisis for maybe two years. After that it's a certainty."[86] The certainty he referred to was gradual economic collapse from exhaustion of oil and gas supplies. So it was incontestable that the end of the world would arrive in 2005, or 2006 at the latest. In 2005, America managed to produce less than 18.1 trillion cubic feet of gas to satisfy domestic demand that was 22% higher.[87] Yet by 2012, America's domestic production of natural gas had soared more than 33% above its 2005 level.[88] As domestic production had outstripped consumption, all the talk in 2012 was about the potential for natural gas exports. It happened without anyone's prayers. Simmons' "certainty" about economic collapse was averted.

Just like Paul Ehrlich, whose highly publicized wager with economist Julian Simon should have served to discredit Ehrlich, Simmons also made a high-profile wager about resource prices.[89] Simmons bet Julian Simon's widow Rita, a professor of public relations at American University in Washington, and *The New York Times* reporter John Tierney each $2,500 that the price of oil during the year 2010 would average at least $200 per barrel in 2005 dollars. The spot price of crude oil at Cushing, Oklahoma never even reached $91.50 during the year 2010 and averaged only $79.48 a barrel.[90] That was about $71 in 2005 dollars. Sadly, Simmons passed away in August of 2010, so he never lived long enough to make good on his wager. More importantly, he was spared the humiliation of having to eat crow over another of his doom-laden forecasts which was off by a country mile.[91] Nevertheless, the executors of the Simmons estate reviewed the data and agreed to pay off on the wager to Mrs. Simon and Mr. Tierney.[92]

Popular eco-catastrophist Bill McKibben has enjoyed a successful career preaching impending planetary collapse resulting from climate cataclysm timed to coincide with the exhaustion of the world's oil supply. McKibben has gained a large degree of notoriety in recent years leading legions of adolescent college students agitating their university endowments to divest from oil and fossil fuel company holdings.[93] He assured his loyal eco-worry warts in 2008 that "we're running out of oil and running out of atmosphere."[94]

McKibben, a long-time "peak oil" theorist, pointed to a 2008 report from the International Energy Agency (IEA) that proclaimed 2006 as the year when the world had reached its maximum production of crude oil.[95] To leftist purveyors of eco-doom, these views find fertile ground. *The New York Times*, America's bible of leftist eco-pessimism, assured us in 2010 that "Peak oil is not just here — it's behind us already."[96] The Paris-based IEA had forecast that world oil production had topped out at 70 million bpd in 2006 and would slowly decline from there. Someone forgot to tell the world's oil producers. They produced a steadily increasing supply of oil since 2006, averaging 87.2 million bpd in 2011.[97]

Perhaps to avoid humiliation, McKibben pulled a complete 180° in 2012 and began preaching that the problem was that there was too much oil.[98] McKibben really should not feel embarrassed by his sudden reversal. Eco-doom is a crowded field. If you're forecasting planetary destruction, you need to stand in line. There are countless others who made precisely the same ideological pirouette at precisely the same moment in time.

George Monbiot, Europe's highest profile eco-catastrophist at London's leftist rag *The Guardian*, has been preaching the society-wrecking implications of "peak oil" for years.[99] But, in a sudden reversal, Monbiot admitted in 2012 that he had been completely wrong. "We were wrong on peak oil. The facts have changed, now we must change too," he proclaimed.[100] The facts hadn't changed; only the slow-learning Monbiot's awareness of them. Suddenly, the problem with respect to the world's oil supply according to Monbiot is that "There's enough to fry us all."[101] At the same time, *CNN* proclaimed "Peak Oil Doomsayers Proved Wrong."[102] *Business Insider* wrote an epitaph saying "Peak Oil Is Dead."[103]

McKibben says we need to "do the math" about fossil fuels. He probably says that because he fears that we might otherwise "do the history." If we did, he and his ideological soulmate Naomi Klein, with whom he is joined at the hip in their anti-fossil fuel jihad, would both be laughed out of the room and rightfully consigned to the dustbin where they belong alongside all of the other discredited utopian visionaries and eco-pessimistic Malthusian step-children.

The late University of Maryland economist Julian Simon, winner the high-profile wager against Malthusian charlatan Paul Ehrlich, once observed that you can make a lot of headlines proclaiming doom-and-gloom but you can make a lot of money betting against them.[104] But doom and gloom never seems to go out of style. A *CNBC* headline in September 2013 screamed that the world had only 17 years before it was tapped out of resources.[105] It purpose was to call attention to the annual Clinton Global Initiative conference, whose 2013 theme was dedicated to mobilizing the planet for impending collapse timed to arrive by 2030.[106] I'll wager it doesn't happen. Does "the Big He" wish to bet?

FIGURE 4-2. **World Proved Oil Reserves (Billions of Barrels)**

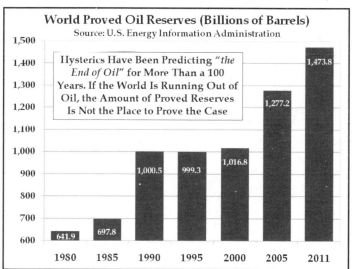

Source: U.S. Energy Information Administration

Between 1970 and 2000, global proved reserves doubled.[107] This happened despite the fact that the world's population had soared by 64% and the planet's inhabitants had boosted oil consumption by 69%.[108] By 1996, the amount of global proved reserves had jumped to over a trillion barrels.[109] From 2000 to 2009, reserves grew by another 32% even as consumption in populous, rapidly developing countries soared.[110] Figure 4-2 shows global proved reserves steadily growing to more than 1.47 trillion barrels by 2011.[111]

Each year, the amount of proved oil reserves increases. If the world were really in imminent danger of running out of oil, the opposite would be happening. We'd see declines in reserves. Such realities lend credence to remarks delivered by Abdallah S. Jum'ah, President & CEO of Saudi Aramco at the Third OPEC International Seminar in September 2006:

> ... *we are looking at more than four and a half trillion barrels of potentially recoverable oil. That translates into more than 140 years of supply at today's current rate of consumption. To put it another way, the world has only consumed about 18% of its conventional and non-conventional producible potential even leaving aside oil shale potential. That fact alone should discredit the argument that "peak oil" is imminent, and put our minds at ease concerning future petroleum supplies.*[112]

So there was not just 13 years of supply as a long list of hysterics had been proclaiming since 1859, but perhaps 140 years without even including the immensity of shale oil. America alone had enough recoverable shale oil to equal the entire world's existing proven reserves. If the world was running out of oil as Carter had claimed and Obama implied, reserves data was certainly no place to go looking for proof.

Some old truths about natural resource supply that were revealed long ago must continually be relearned.[113] First, consistent undershooting of production peaks reveals an inherent bias. Second, continuing upside resource "surprises" are oxymoronic since it's not a surprise if you keep making the same mistake. Third, reserves are not a measure of fixed quantity but a constantly changing dynamic measure of capability at specific prices. Fourth, conservatism in resource estimating is often misinterpreted as a cause for pessimism. Fifth, the ability to forecast future production requires the ability to forecast future technology capabilities, an impossibility. Sixth, investment in pipelines and drilling rigs to recover large deposits reduces recovery cost in adjacent marginal fields, which increases ultimate recovery potential. Seventh, in the long run, resource raw materials prices usually decline in "real" terms. Eighth, converting potential resources to proven reserves is an on-going process that depends upon technology that grows in unpredictable ways. Lastly, resource depletion curves are often fitted around marketplace realities unrelated to geology, things like price controls, export constraints, end-use regulations, political instability, zoning, environmental prohibitions, and so on. "Peak oil" theorists and reserves confabulists ignore these realities.

"WE CAN'T DRILL OUR WAY OUT OF THIS"

Consider another example offered by the energy obfuscator-in-chief to convince his Miami student audience. Obama proclaimed "that anybody who tells you that we can drill our way out of this problem doesn't know what they're talking about." For years, he had grown fond of recounting the experience of Brazil to his prove his point. He told an audience in Chicago in 2006 that America should follow the example of Brazil and triple-down on biofuels. That would, he promised, be our ticket to freedom from foreign imports:

Brazil, a nation that once relied on foreign countries to import 80% of its crude oil, will now be entirely self-sufficient in a few years thanks to its investment in biofuels.[114]

Obama claimed that Brazil had been importing 80% of its oil in 1980 but, due to its determination to become energy self-sufficient, the country had embarked upon a crash development effort to convert sugarcane into ethanol. Brazil had completely done away with oil imports. What an inspirational story. What a magnificent achievement. What a terrific example for the U.S. to follow. What a load of BS.

Ethanol production got underway in earnest in the late 1970s when Brazilian domestic oil production had declined to as low as 18% of demand.[115] To address the economically damaging drain on the country's current account arising from its worsening trade deficit, the government embarked upon a crash program aimed at eliminating the need for imports.[116] Between 2000 and 2010, Brazil increased its production of ethanol by more than 161%.[117] Ninety percent of new cars on the road are flex-fuel capable.[118] Brazil produces 30% of the world's supply of fuel ethanol, second only to the U.S., which accounts for 58%.[119] The country has enough land area to produce up to 20% of the fuel needs of all the cars in the world today without deforesting the Amazon basin according to UNICA, the Brazilian ethanol industry association.[120] That all sounds so convincing.

But it doesn't mean the Amazon forests aren't being destroyed. As *Time* correspondent Michael Grunwald describes, ethanol mandates in the U.S. entice Midwest farmers to switch from soybeans to corn for conversion to ethanol, which entices Brazilian farmers to fill the soybean market void by expanding into cattle grazing lands. This indirect land-use displacement forces ranchers to destroy Amazonian forests, converting forest into grasslands to feed and support herds.[121] You can draw a straight line. Congress and EPA mandate more ethanol, the Amazon rainforest gets burned down — at the rate of sixty two square miles every year.[122] UNICA may be technically correct that sugar cane plantations are not being established in the Amazon rainforest. But their sugar cane plantations are displacing newly-established soybean plantations that displace cattle ranchers who destroy the Amazon.

Despite what Obama says, the real truth resides elsewhere. Brazil's energy independence with respect to motor fuels has precious little to do with its production of ethanol. What Obama always neglects to tell audiences was that Brazil had increased its domestic oil production by 876% over the previous two decades.[123] That factor, not biofuels, had enabled the country to become self-sufficient in its motor fuel segment.

Brazilian government figures show that in 2010, ethanol only accounted for 18.8% of total transportation fuel by volume.[124] Since a gallon of ethanol is only about 65.6% as energetic as gasoline when burned,[125] Brazil derives only 13% of its motor fuel needs on an actual mileage-equivalent basis from ethanol. Brazil is set to become a major oil producer due to recent offshore oil discoveries.[126] Those were the offshore oil discoveries that Obama has effectively prohibited in the U.S. but hailed in Brazil.[127] The stark truth is that Brazil "drilled its way out" of its oil imports problem. And, just like Brazil, America could easily drill its way out of its oil imports situation if prohibitions on oil drilling on federal lands and offshore deposits had not been emplaced by Obama.[128] It was Obama who didn't know what he was talking about — or did and was lying.

But he is hardly alone. Cellulosic ethanol hucksters egged on by shallow media luminaries have been peddling this falsehood for years. In 2006, *Dateline NBC* traveled down to Brazil to hype the same distortions that Obama has been peddling for years. Standing in a sugar cane field, *NBC*'s Stone Phillips proclaimed:

> *What you're looking at is a field of dreams: Homegrown security that has helped this country to completely free itself from foreign oil. Last month, Brazil announced it no longer has to import oil from the Middle East or anywhere else. And much of the credit goes to ethanol.*[129]

NBC Dateline's implication was clearly misleading and false. *NBC* called ethanol "a simple solution for pain at the pump." It was simply false. Of course, the overwhelming majority of the credit for eliminating oil imports goes to domestic offshore oil drilling, not ethanol. Phillips could have easily checked the numbers. It takes seconds to retrieve the data from the Brazilian Ministry of Mines and Energy to uncover the truth. That was too much to ask of the vaunted *NBC* brand.

In 2006, the year of the *Dateline NBC* report, Brazil derived only 13.1% of its volume of highway motor fuels from alcohol.[130] That equates to less than 9% of the total highway energy requirements on a mileage-equivalent basis.[131] Phillips also falsely implied that "most drivers choose ethanol" when they fill up their cars. Sure Stone. If that's so, why doesn't it show up in the volume statistics? How about his "pain at his pump" claim? Pull up a Brazil street view on Google and look at pump prices in any Brazilian city. Ethanol is 20-30% more expensive than E20 gasoline blends on a mileage-adjusted basis.[132] Or pull up the consumer price data on the UNICA website for an additional validation point.

The plain truth is that Brazil's energy future is closely tied to oil and gas. Why is Petrobras, Brazil's state-owned petroleum company, building two oil refineries rather than more ethanol distilleries?[133] And why is it in talks to build another two?[134] *Reuters* observed in June 2013 that:

> *Despite running at record levels, Petrobras' 12 existing refineries have been unable to keep up with demand for gasoline, diesel, cooking gas and jet fuel. Gasoline consumption alone rose more than 12 percent.*[135]

Nothing about ethanol. By the end of 2012, ethanol production had dropped 26% from 2008 levels and more than 40% of refineries had closed.[136] Obama and his media apologists have been peddling snake oil using Brazil as their straw man. Brazil forecasts much higher gasoline and diesel fuel demand in the future. Most Brazilians seem to understand that ethanol made from sugar cane belongs into their caipirinhas while gasoline made from the crude oil goes into their fuel tanks. When will someone let Obama and Stone Phillips in on the secret?

DO THE MATH ... AND FORGET THE RHETORIC

A great example of how unreliable proved reserves estimates really are can be seen with the recoverable crude oil in Bakken shale located in the Three Forks-Sanish region of North Dakota's giant Williston Basin. In 1995, the U.S. Geological Survey (USGS) estimated that there were only 150 million barrels of "technically recoverable" oil in all of the Bakken shale formation.[137] In April 2008, the agency revised its estimates of recoverable Bakken shale oil upward to 4.3 billion barrels.[138] That represented a number 2,867% larger than earlier. Then in 2013, the USGS doubled its 2008 estimate, increasing the amount of technically recoverable reserves in the Bakken and Three-Forks formations to 7.4 billion barrels.[139]

Since USGS's 2008 survey, more than 4,000 wells had been drilled in the Williston Basin.[140] Those findings showed that the Three Forks formation contained even more reserves than the Bakken.[141] The region's largest driller, Continental Resources, puts the amount of oil that can be recovered with current technology at anywhere from 8 billion[142] to 24 billion barrels.[143] Continental's CEO Harold Hamm confidently places the estimate of recoverable reserves at the higher end of that range.[144] Who are you going to believe? Do we trust Obama, a guy who couldn't find North Dakota on a map if he had help? The only time he ever went there, he claimed the U.S. had fifty seven states.[145] Or do you trust Harold Hamm, who is up there every week drilling and moving oil to market?

With advances in technology, the amount of recoverable oil just from Bakken shale could exceed 500 billion barrels.[146] According to a report by the Rand Corporation, the Green River Formation (GRF) spread across Colorado, Wyoming and Utah may actually contain a mind-bending amount of recoverable shale oil estimated at between 500 billion and 1.1 trillion barrels.[147] But the USGS disagrees with the Rand survey saying its own estimate is not 1.1 trillion but 4.3 trillion barrels.[148] And the federal government estimates that the Monterey shale formation spread across 1,750 square miles of California's Central Valley holds up to four times more oil than its estimate of recoverable potential in North Dakota's Bakken formation.[149] America suffers from a shortage of media integrity and executive leadership, not crude oil.

Another significant reserves estimate growth story concerns Russia's Bazhenov formation. Geological estimates now place the recoverable crude oil potential of this area recently considered to be fully played out at 80 times as much as North Dakota's Bakken formation.[150] Russia's state-owned oil giant Rosneft has entered into joint a venture with Exxon, with its deep expertise in horizontal drilling and hydraulic fracturing, to assist in development of the tight oil locked away in this massive shale formation.[151] Oil industry analysts estimate that Russia could be producing a million barrels a day from the 2.3

million square kilometer shale formation that is as large as Texas and the Gulf of Mexico combined.[152]

Another mistake that pessimists make when they forecast "the end of oil" is failing to take into account the impact that technology advances have upon our ability to recover deposits that, like the Bazhenov formation, had long since been played out. Occasionally a major discovery is announced such as the Prudhoe Bay field in Alaska in 1970. But those instances are relatively rare.

Most of the growth in U.S. crude oil reserves is derived from new estimates for the recovery potential of existing fields, called *ultimate recovery appreciation*. Those revisions to prior estimates come about primarily through a reassessment of the recovery ability of new advances in technology. The quantity of recoverable hydrocarbon resources is not a function of geology, but of the economics of applying available technology.[153] As *Oil & Gas Journal* observed in a special report section in 1996:

> … *the most important reserves trend in the 1990's has been the additions of large volumes through activities other than new-field exploration.*[154]

Before leftist polemicists discovered they could make a living off of it, the majority of history's doom-laden forecasts were issued by geologists, not economists. This is no knock on geologists. We need them. We could use more. They can all wear plastic pocket protectors if they want. But resource estimation is not strictly a matter of geology, but of economics.

Hydraulic fracturing in shale gas deposits provides an example. Despite the fact that USGS had mapped virtually all of America's shale basins over 100 years earlier, recoverable reserves of shale oil and gas didn't even exist in any meaningful measure before 2003. Today shale production promises to make the country energy self-sufficient by 2020.[155] The world's three largest oil field services companies are boosting capital budgets, focusing their efforts on enhanced recovery methods in an effort to improve yields from existing shale deposits, which currently only recover a fraction of the oil and gas contained therein.[156] "Most of the oil we will discover is from oil we've already found," says energy industry analyst Lawrence Goldstein.[157] As EIA noted years ago:

> *Most significantly, from 1977 through 1995 approximately 89 percent of the additions to U.S. proved reserves of crude oil and 74 percent of the additions to U.S. proved reserves of dry natural gas were due to ultimate recovery appreciation (URA) rather than to the discovery of new oil or gas fields.*[158]

Another problem in crude oil reserves estimating is that, due to Securities and Exchange Commission regulations, U.S. producers have been required to report only "proven" reserves, at least up to 2009,[159] while outside the U.S., other countries report not just proven reserves but also potential and possible reserves.[160] So Obama was making apples-and-oranges comparisons when he bellowed about the U.S. having only 2% of proved reserves.

In 1980, Iraq was reported to have thirty billion barrels of crude oil.[161] But between then and 2012, despite tumult and turmoil that has wracked the country and its oil industry, Iraq produced 21.5 billion barrels.[162] And how much remains in its reserve today? BP claims Iraq holds 150 billion barrels, five times more than in 1980.[163] This is probably a woeful understatement.

Consider the mechanism by which the twelve member countries of the Organization of Petroleum Exporting Countries (OPEC) estimate their reserves.[164] Each OPEC member country is allocated its production quota based upon an estimate of country reserves. If a member country holds 10% of total OPEC reserves, it is permitted to produce that percentage of OPEC's output volume each year. For nearly every member country, oil production revenues comprise the majority of sovereign foreign exchange revenues earned each year since these countries produce little else but oil and natural gas. Because sovereign foreign exchange revenues are so dependent on oil sales, each country has a strong incentive to boost their own estimates of reserves to maximize income.

This sparked a reserve estimating scramble. In 1985 when OPEC adopted its reserves-based production quota system, Kuwait increased its reserves estimate by 50% overnight. Iran, Iraq and the United Arab Emirates followed suit shortly thereafter.[165] Saudi Arabia boosted its reserves estimate three years later. In 2009, the twelve nations of OPEC accounted for over 70% of world reserves, a figure that was no doubt wildly inflated relative to other global producing countries due to the quirky nature of its quota allocation system.

OPEC member country Venezuela more than doubled its reserves estimate in 2011 to 211.2 billion barrels within the space of a single year, a number that grew to 297.6 one year later.[166] OPEC's statistical bulletin, based upon numbers furnished by the Paris-based International Energy Agency, estimated that Venezuela's crude oil reserves were 296.5 billion barrels, substantially surpassing Saudi Arabia's 264.5 billion barrel reserve, making it the largest holder of crude oil resources in the world.[167] But even these substantially increased estimates are far lower than the USGS estimate of 513 billion barrels of technically recoverable reserves in Venezuela's Orinoco Oil Belt.[168] Whether Venezuela's astounding estimated reserve increase was due to better geology, better economics, better recovery technology, or a desire by its left-wing dictator Hugo Chavez to grab a larger slice of OPEC's revenue pie to fund his Bolivarian revolutions is not precisely known. Needless to say, Mother Theresa didn't design the global system for estimating crude oil reserves. USGS was alluding to this recognition when it observed:

> In the United States, proved reserves are rather rigidly defined. Worldwide, however, a set of uniform reporting requirements does not exist. Criteria for the estimation of remaining reserves differ widely from country to country, as do the technical, economic, and political incentives that drive the reserve-growth process.[169]

A good example of the unreliability of estimates for proven reserves concerns Israel. EIA figures for 2011 indicate that Israel had an oil reserve of less than two million barrels.[170] The same data for 2012 shows 12 million barrels, a six-fold increase in just one year.[171] Nevertheless, neither of these estimates is even remotely close to the true potential. Offshore drilling in Israeli waters over the Levantine Basin indicates up to five billion barrels of recoverable oil and 16 trillion cubic feet of natural gas.[172] If those finds pan out, it would amount to crude oil reserves 2,500 times larger than those estimated by EIA in 2011.

News reports suggest that the promise in the Levantine Basin is so enormous, it has propelled global gas giants like Russia's Gazprom, France's Total, and U.S.-based Exxon Mobil to go scrambling to establish beachheads in the region long believed to be completely devoid of hydrocarbon resources.[173] The U.S. Geological Survey in 2010 pegged the Levantine Basin potential at 122 trillion cubic feet of natural gas[174] and 1.7 billion barrels of oil. These estimates had obviously not found their way into DoE reserve figures.[175] The recovery potential is so large that there is a growing unease about the possibility of military conflict involving Israel, Turkey, Greece, and other actors in the region.[176]

Former Israeli Prime Minister Golda Meir, daughter of a Milwaukee grocer, once observed that Moses had "dragged us forty years through the desert to bring us to the one place in the Middle East where there was no oil."[177] She spoke too soon. Israel is projected to earn $60 billion in foreign exchange earnings over the next twenty years from natural gas exports alone.[178] Only about 40% of the production will be exported.[179] Sovereign revenue from the Tamar fields is expected to boost Israel's real GDP by at least one percentage point in 2014, and yet Tamar is believed to hold far lower reserves than the adjacent Leviathan field.[180]

Cyprus is also prepared to share in the bounty of hydrocarbon reserves in the Levantine Basin. EIA data shows zero natural gas proved reserves for tiny Cyprus.[181] The Cyprus government invited France's Total to help it develop its massive natural gas resources that lie just off the southern shores of the island. Despite EIA's claim that Cyprus has zero reserves of natural gas, some analysts estimate there could be as much as sixty trillion cubic feet of gas residing in the thirteen blocks that comprise 51,000 square miles of the country's exclusive economic zone.[182] There is so much potential that royalties could reach €600 billion before the basin is exhausted using today's recovery methods.[183] Cyprus was teetering on the edge of extinction in early 2013 over a mere €17 billion bailout package to refinance its insolvent banks.[184] It seems like a small down payment of a very large future potential. While Cyprus seeks an EU bailout, it could very well be Cyprus that bails out the EU in a few years.[185]

Yet another example concerns estimates of global natural gas proved reserves from the International Energy Agency, supposedly the world's premier energy information source. As with the DoE's estimate of Venezuelan crude oil reserves, IEA doubled its estimate of the world's natural gas reserves in a single year's time.[186] Suddenly, within the space of twelve months, IEA said there was not 15,000 trillion cubic feet of natural gas in the world but 30,000.[187] If there was a pollution problem with the global energy business, it most significantly concerned crude oil and gas reserves estimating.

One of the world's largest beneficiaries of the natural gas bonanza is the U.S., which may suddenly have 1,000 trillion cubic feet more of natural gas reserves than believed just a few years ago.[188] The Potential Gas Committee (PCG), a group of over a hundred fossil fuel industry geologists, geoscientists, and petroleum engineers provided an estimate of 2,170 trillion cubic feet of recoverable natural gas in 2011.[189] That is about an 86-year supply at current consumption rates. In 2013, PCG increased its technically recoverable natural gas resources estimate to 2,384 trillion cubic feet.[190] Compare that reserves number to DoE's year 2000 estimate for natural gas reserves of just 177 trillion cubic feet, or even its 2010 estimate which had been boosted to 305 trillion cubic feet.[191] PCG makes clear that:

> ... *our present assessment, strengthened by robust domestic production levels, demonstrates an exceptionally strong and optimistic gas supply picture for the nation.*[192]

EIA issued an estimate of technically recoverable natural gas reserves from six shale plays in its *Annual Energy Outlook 2006* that totaled 83 trillion cubic feet.[193] When EIA released its *Annual Energy Outlook 2012*, the agency was showing 482 trillion cubic feet of technically recoverable reserves residing in fifteen shale gas basins, a six-fold increase in six years.[194] America is benefitting from a massive increase in natural gas supplies that can now be economically recovered from shale deposits. Shale basins had been known to exist for eons of time, but were never seriously considered part of our natural resource base until application of improved technological processes.

With the issuance of the *World Energy Outlook 2011* report from the Paris-based International Energy Agency, in the space of a single year the world's supposedly most authoritative source of energy data had completely reevaluated their prior World Energy Outlook 2010 position on natural gas recovery potential. By 2011, IEA proclaimed what it called a Golden Age of Gas where "unconventional natural gas resources are now estimated to be as large as conventional resources."[195] The agency noted that conventional resources were equivalent to 120 years of supply at current consumption rates. So, within the space of a single year, the planet was suddenly sitting on twice as much recoverable natural gas as the world's most trusted authority for energy information had believed just one year earlier. Of course, IEA was the most authoritative source of energy data in 2010 when they were looking at much lower reserve numbers. The same was true in 2006 when they were peddling "peak oil" theory.

Even more astounding was a revision to the UK's shale gas reserves provided by the British Geological Survey (BGS) in early 2013. Prior estimates indicated that Britain had gas reserves of 5.3 trillion cubic feet.[196] But a leaked version of the BGS report indicated that the earlier estimate had been revised upward to between 1,300 to 1,700 trillion cubic feet.[197] If the UK recovers just 10% of the lower estimate — 130 trillion cubic feet — that would amount to far more gas production than the 85 trillion cubic feet of gas that had been recovered from all of Britain's North Sea fields during the forty one year period from 1970 to 2011.[198] Shale gas discoveries may end up boosting global natural gas reserves by 900% according to an analysis by researchers at Texas A&M University.[199]

How many of us think of Australia as an oil-producing powerhouse? The country only accounted for about a half a percent of global oil production in 2012. [200] EIA data shows the country held less than a billion and a half barrels of oil reserves in 2012.[201] But recent shale oil discoveries in the Arckaringa Basin indicate the reserve potential may rival Saudi Arabia's crude oil reserves.[202] Independent analysis indicates the potential is larger than Canada's giant oil sands deposits.[203] If these estimates pan out, Australia could earn as much as AUS$20 trillion in sovereign revenues, transforming the country into one of the world's largest oil exporting countries.[204] Reassessments of Australia's natural gas reserves indicate the country may hold ten times the amount that had been previously reported.[205]

In 2013, DoE updated an earlier assessment of shale resources throughout the world. Within the space of just two years, the amount of technically recoverable oil resources from shale deposits had been boosted eleven-fold.[206]

Recent estimates of America's total hydrocarbon potential are nothing short of mind-boggling. A report from the Manhattan Institute observes that North America's hydrocarbon resource base comprising coal, oil and natural gas is four times larger than the entirety of the Middle East.[207] The U.S. is now the fastest growing producer of oil and natural gas in the world.[208] The Green River Formation in the states of Wyoming, Colorado and Utah, may contain up to three trillion barrels of oil.[209] Estimates suggest that 50% of this oil could be potentially recoverable.[210] If so, that deposit alone would exceed EIA's estimate of proven reserves in the entire world.

So the impressionable student audience at the University of Miami was listening to their President tell them that America only had 2% of the world's proven reserves of oil while he was knowingly sitting on authoritative reports from his own executive branch agencies telling him that America had more oil in the Green River Formation alone than the reserve figure for the entire world. Between 2008 and 2010, the U.S. produced a volume of just less than 42 trillion cubic feet of dry natural gas.[211] But during this time, proved reserves increased by sixty trillion cubic feet.[212] America is piling up reserves of natural gas at a rate 50% faster than it is exhausting its supply. How much credence should listeners accord to a cynical, dishonest, ideologically obtuse politician who cries about the implications of proven hydrocarbon reserves, the same discredited tantrum thrown by Jimmy Carter in his 1977 Oval Office speech, when the country's proven reserve estimate of natural gas had increased by almost 800% over the course of just the previous seven years?[213]

Usually found peddling pessimistic tracts forecasting America's inevitable demise,[214] *Financial Times* writer Edward Luce observes that America could soon be producing fifteen million barrels of oil per day compared to Saudi Arabia's eleven million per day output.[215] Obama's absurd Carteresque claim was that America's only hope to become energy independent, free from the scourge of imported oil, resided in energy conservation and biofuels rather than natural resource exploration. But analysts are forecasting the oil shale boom taking place in various states will allow the country to become a net exporter of oil and natural gas by the end of the decade.[216]

While EIA forecasts that America won't become energy self-sufficient until 2035,[217] this is likely too conservative. EIA administrator Adam Sieminski alludes to that:

> *One thing I can say with absolute certainty ... is that our long-term forecasts are going to be wrong. It looks like the direction we're going ... on oil is there's going to be more of it.*[218]

Energy self-sufficiency will happen much sooner than EIA forecasts unless Obama or some other Luddite tries to stick a fork in it. This is not just idle rhetoric. Obama's cabinet picks signal his clear intention to make good on his inaugural threat to drive in the fork using an executive authority he believes he possesses if Congress fails to enact destructive measures for him.[219]

Citibank published a research note in February 2012 observing that the vast increase in Bakken and Eagle Ford shale oil is primarily responsible for a decades-long reversal in the price premium that West Texas Intermediate typically enjoyed over Brent crude.[220] The Citibank authors noted that the glut in production, together with softening demand, had reduced U.S. oil imports from 13 million bpd down to eight million bpd. The number of producing wells in the U.S. increased 500% in the three years previous to 2012.[221] For the first time in more than 60 years, the U.S. became a net exporter of refined petroleum products in 2011.[222] America's refineries were producing fuels to meet global demand while domestic demand declined.[223] Since 2011, the net export position of the U.S. had strengthened well beyond EIA forecasts.[224] Citibank forecasted the U.S. would become energy self-sufficient by 2020.[225] These and other findings compelled Citibank's researchers to proclaim the death of the "peak oil" hypothesis.

One year later, Citibank issued a follow-up report announcing that progress toward energy independence during 2012 had exceeded earlier expectations. Researchers noted that :

> *The robust growth in North American production over the last two years helped to keep a lid on oil prices globally ... A half-decade from now, combined U.S. and Canadian oil output could be in surplus of projected needs. And over the next five years, demand for natural gas in the U.S. should catch up with supply, opening up unexpected opportunities in transportation and igniting a reindustrialization of the country.*[226]

Citigroup made clear that beneficial impacts from enhanced oil and gas recovery would spark renewed economic growth, reduce fuel prices, ignite a resurgence in industrial production, produce high-wage industrial job growth and, at long last, result in a resumption of personal income growth in a country that had seen a steady decline for more than a decade.

PEAK OIL … OR PEAK POLITICS?

The U.S. reduced imports of crude oil in October 2012 to the lowest level since the year 2000.[227] The reduction in imports to 8.091 million bpd in October had been accomplished by an increase in domestic production to the highest level since December 1993.[228] By the end of 2013, America was producing more crude oil than anytime back to 1988.[229] That enabled the country to reduce net petroleum imports to levels last seen in 1990.[230]

Leading the way in America's energy resurgence was the continuing crude oil production boom in North Dakota which reported 945,906 barrels of output per day during October 2013.[231] That amounted to an amazing 93% increase over just two years earlier.[232] North Dakota crude oil production growth is an amazing story. Figure 4-3 shows North Dakota averaged about 102,500 bpd over the 27-year period from February 1980 up to July 2006.[233] But shortly thereafter, production exploded with crude oil output growing at a compound annual rate of 34%. By July of 2013, North Dakota was producing 874,234 bpd, an 8-fold increase over the level in 2006.[234] Each year, another 1,500 wells are added that increase state-wide production by about 200,000 bpd.[235]

FIGURE 4-3. **North Dakota Crude Oil Production Explodes**

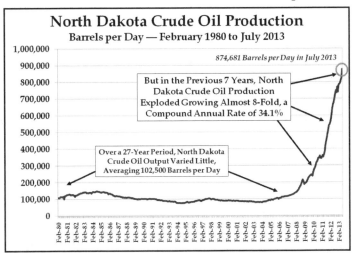

Source: North Dakota Department of Mineral Resources

Texas has gone from producing less than 20% of the nation's crude supply to more than one third.[236] The state has doubled its output in just three years, producing more crude oil than OPEC nations like Venezuela, Kuwait and Nigeria.[237] Shale oil potential is considered by observers to be so large that it prompted Prince Alwaleed bin Talal, nephew of Saudi King Abdullah, to issue a warning to his country to diversify its economy to protect from the destabilizing impact of massive U.S. oil production volume.[238] Saudi Arabia derives 92% of its budget from oil revenues.[239]

For the first time since 1995, the fourth quarter of 2013 saw domestic crude oil production come in at a higher level than imports.[240] Coupled to these encouraging signs are revised forecasts from DoE that pegs America's 2014 imports to decline below six million bpd, the lowest level in twenty five years.[241] Domestic production will soon greatly exceed imports for many years to come.[242] The International Energy Agency forecasts that by 2018, the U.S. will exceed its previous high of domestic crude oil production that occurred in 1970, the "peak oil" forecast issued by the aforementioned Marion King Hubbert.[243] We are not running out of oil. Instead, we're running out of evidence to support "peak oil" hysteria.[244]

America is enjoying an unprecedented renaissance in oil and gas production. The growth in domestic oil production of 311.7 million barrels[245] that occurred in 2012 was greater than in any year since Drake drilled his first Titusville, Pennsylvania well in 1859.[246] DoE's prediction that 2013 would shatter that record[247] easily came to pass.[248] For the first time since 1987, America's production of natural gas had just about drawn even with its consumption.[249] Natural gas production will easily outpace consumption in 2014.

MIT economics professor Morris Adelman addressed the oil supply issue in a 2004 article in the scholarly journal *Regulation*, writing "It is commonly asked, when will the world's supply of oil be exhausted? The best one-word answer: Never."[250] Addressing the Society of Exploration Geophysicists in 2013, Barry Smitherman, chairman, of the Texas Railroad Commission which handles oil and gas permitting in the state, claims that advances in geophysical recovery capabilities has led to what he calls a "relatively boundless supply" of oil and gas worldwide.[251]

EIA published a research note about changes to proved reserves estimates in August 2013, the wording of which requires no elaboration:

In 2011, oil and gas exploration and production companies operating in the United States added almost 3.8 billion barrels of crude oil and lease condensate proved reserves, an increase of 15 percent, and the greatest volume increase since the U.S. Energy Information Administration (EIA) began publishing proved reserves estimates in 1977.[252]

Yet amidst all of this promise, we've been saddled with a President who leads a political party that sniffs its way through life crying about the tyranny of oil, America's supposed addiction to imported oil, and its dwindling energy reserves, its supposed need to substitute other forms of energy that are more costly, and are far less reliable. He wastes his time peddling hysterical scare stories about impending climate doom, expending all of his efforts attempting to cap fossil fuel usage, and trying to impose carbon taxes on fossil fuel that would drive up its cost without even creating an incentive to produce more. He heads a government that was able to get oil production resumed in Iraq but is incapable of getting it started on federally-owned lands in Alaska, Colorado, California, and numerous other states. He travels to Brazil and Mexico to offer help with offshore drilling while shutting it down in the U.S. He pursues a program that stifles domestic oil and gas resource development while, at the same time, complaining about America's dependence on foreign oil. And while he does that, he pretends, like Jimmy Carter before him, that the country is within a few short years of complete hydrocarbon supply exhaustion.

Oy vey.

CHAPTER 5

A BASKETBALL PLAYER WHO
DOESN'T DO REBOUNDS

"Whenever ... a given quantity of output costs less to produce than ... before, we may be sure ... that there has been innovation somewhere. It need not necessarily have occurred in the industry under observation, which may be only applying, or benefitting from, an innovation that has occurred in another."[1]

JOSEPH SCHUMPETER

During his speech at the University of Miami, Obama repeatedly invoked energy efficiency and conservation as central planks in his multi-faceted energy program. He assured his listeners that conservation would help solve America's energy problems, praising students by saying "you guys are so much more aware than I was of conserving our natural resources and thinking about the planet." He claimed that "We've got to develop new technology that helps us use less energy, and use energy smarter."[2]

Obama was referring to two related but distinct concepts, conservation and energy efficiency. Conservation refers to reducing consumption by avoiding its use — turning off lights when you leave a room, turning down the heat, avoiding car trips, etc. By contrast, energy efficiency refers to adopting improved technology that accomplishes the same task with less energy, things like replacing incandescent light bulbs with energy efficient fluorescent bulbs or replacing your energy-gobbling refrigerator with a newer, more efficient model. Conservation relies upon changing behavior. Efficiency requires an investment which we hope to recoup later through energy savings. Most of the discussion in this chapter concerns energy efficiency rather than conservation.

Obama assured his audience there would be more fuel efficient cars that students would buy in the future. These cars would reduce demand for oil."It means this country will reduce our oil consumption by more than two million barrels a day. That's not only good for your pocketbook, that's good for the environment," he promised. So naturally, if you get better gas mileage, you use less gasoline, and save money. And if you switch to more efficient appliances, you use less energy, and lower your total cost of energy. The country's energy requirements will be lowered substantially. It was reasonable, sound, logical … and, unfortunately, inaccurate.

When Obama remarked that "I understood about 10 percent of what they told me," he was not only referring to the lecture he had received from engineering students. He was also referring to the knowledge gap of his coursework in basic economics.

In 1865, a British economist named William Stanley Jevons was intrigued by the vast increase in coal consumption brought about by large efficiency enhancements in steam engine technology.[3] Efficiency improvements should have reduced coal consumption — but precisely the opposite had occurred. James Watt's steam engine offered pronounced improvements in engine efficiency vs. William Newcomen's outmoded design, making coal-burning steam engines more affordable. More efficient engines meant that more work could be accomplished for a given amount of coal. It had become more affordable at the margin to use coal-burning steam engines rather than horses, mules, and men to do any specific task. The economic appeal of coal usage had increased. The practical result was that, instead of a decrease in coal consumption, coal usage greatly increased because coal became cheaper when denominated in terms of the output of work it could achieve.

Jevons postulated a theorem regarding energy efficiency and resource consumption, to wit: "It is wholly a confusion of ideas to suppose that the economical use of fuels is equivalent to a diminished consumption. The very converse is the truth."[4] Less elegantly, any increase in the efficiency with which a resource is utilized will result in an increase rather than a decrease in the use of that resource.[5] For instance, if you could suddenly double the gas mileage of your car overnight, the practical result might not be a proportional reduction in your gas consumption but rather an offsetting increase in the miles you would be able to drive for the same amount of money.

Air conditioning tends to have a self-reinforcing effect: If you work in an air conditioned office, it is almost unendurable to come home to an un-air conditioned dwelling. If you replace a less efficient window unit with a more efficient one, you might not necessarily save money on fuel costs because you might be more inclined to get a second unit or run air conditioning throughout longer periods of time. This is what economists refer to as a "rebound effect." Obama apparently slept or choomed through the lecture on the Jevons Paradox and missed his follow up reading assignment. It's hard to imagine an avid basketball player like Obama who doesn't understand rebounds.

Mexico recently implemented an energy efficiency effort dubbed cash-for-coolers in honor of Obama's laughable Cash-for-Clunkers program. The program was designed to replace aging, inefficient refrigerators and air conditioning units in an effort to drive down energy consumption, improve economic efficiency, and reduce emissions of CO_2. The World Bank undertook an engineering study attempting to forecast the impact that the program would have.[6] They estimated that new refrigerators would reduce refrigerator energy consumption by 30%.[7]

But a follow up by economists at the University of California and the UN Development Fund published by the National Bureau of Economic Research discovered that Mexico only achieved energy savings of 7% from the program.[8] That was because consumers decided to choose larger capacity units with greater storage space that incorporated modern features like automatic ice making equipment and frost-free devices. The World Bank had sent engineers, not economists, to perform the original forecast.

Another example is electric lighting. Artificial light from electricity arrived with Edison's invention of the incandescent light bulb. Cities in the U.S. and other advanced countries rushed to deploy its revolutionary labor-saving features — it displaced manual lamplighting and candles. Consumers demanded it in their homes to brighten the dim condition of oil lamps, remove the odor, eliminate the soot, and reduce the risk of fire. As efficiency of artificial lighting increased with improvements in incandescent filament technology, to more energy-efficient gas-plasma fluorescent lighting, to solid-state high-intensity discharge technology such as light-emitting diodes, the ubiquity of lighting has grown inexorably. Improvements in lighting efficiency always lead not to an absolute reduction in energy consumption but to an increase in the amount of lighting we use. The demand for more and more lighting is insatiable.

Two economics researchers have identified a direct relationship between national wealth and the amount of lighting consumed by a country. Examining data over three centuries on six continents, Jeffrey Tsao at Sandia National Laboratory and his French colleague Paul Waide conclude that 0.72% of the planet's GDP and 6.5% of its consumption of primary energy is used for lighting.[9] In other words, demand is related more to wealth and income and weakly correlated with the efficiency of various types of lighting devices employed. As income grows, so does the use of lighting.

Among the most astonishing photographs anyone is likely to view are night time satellite images of the Korean peninsula showing vibrant, heavily illuminated South Korea sitting side-by-side with the dreary Stalinist graveyard of North Korea. With the exception of its capital Pyongyang, the entire country is shrouded in complete darkness.[10] If you have never seen these photos, drop what you're doing and dial up "North Korea at Night" on the internet.

CIA's World Fact Book of GDP in 2011 shows that South Korea has an economy thirty nine times larger than its warlike northern neighbor, a figure that understates the practical difference. The overwhelming share of North Korea's national income is consumed by its inept, inefficient, blood-thirsty, totalitarian government.[11] It's not a case that North Koreans don't need or want electric lighting. They'd use tons of it if they were afforded the opportunity. They simply suffer the misfortune of having been born in the world's worst hellhole and are denied the basic necessity of life that almost everyone else on the planet takes for granted.

In a modern society like the U.S., as lighting efficiency has improved by three orders of magnitude over the first Edison light bulb, we have responded by deploying lighting devices in more places and consume countless more lumens. As income grows, we use more lighting because it represents a quality-of-life improvement.

LEFTIES DON'T DO REBOUNDS

Rebound effects have been well documented in the scientific literature at the macro-level but can often be problematic on the micro-level. To sensible minds, they are beyond reasonable debate when viewed across a broad spectrum.[12] They have been studied exhaustively in a wide variety of modern-day applications. A good example are the wide-ranging studies of motor vehicle efficiency improvements. This work provides very strong support for rebound theory.[13]

Enthusiasm for energy efficiency as a route to energy self-sufficiency and climate change mitigation are accepted as articles of faith among the environmental left.[14] Most notable among the rebound effect deniers is the Natural Resources Defense Council, an organization dedicated to reversing the arc of human progress.

Sensible people who remember the *Alar* hoax break out in laughter when the discredited acronym NRDC is invoked. Award-winning *CBS 60 Minutes* allowed itself to be scammed after accepting at face value bogus NRDC assertions.[15] Most people recognize this is all one needs to know to dismiss further consideration. Unfortunately, given the immense budget NRDC wields and their dreadful influence on policy, lots of energy must be wasted countering the absurdities.

NRDC has been peddling the theme of energy-efficiency-as-salvation for eons. In April 2003, they published a report claiming that the state of California could reduce overall electricity demand by 5.9 terawatt-hours over ten years by adopting a program of energy efficiency measures.[16] This would reduce electricity costs by $12 billion, they claimed.[17]

Despite enacting some of the country's most rigid environmental and energy efficiency standards, ten years later California was consuming 23.2 more terawatt-hours of electricity than in the 2002 base year.[18] Per capita electricity usage was higher in every single year after 2002.[19] If there was a factor holding down consumption, it was because electricity rates had risen nearly nine times faster over that period of time than had usage.[20] As opposed to a $12 billion in savings, Californians were shelling out $68.8 billion more for electricity by 2012.[21] That amounted to an *Alar*-scale $80 billion miss.

In 2010, NRDC issued a congratulatory report claiming that California's efficiency program had saved energy users billions of dollars and thousands of gigawatt-hours of energy.[22] NRDC based its 2010 findings on a long-established trend that is attributed to physicist and former California Energy Commission member Arthur Rosenfeld that has been in place for decades. Rosenfeld is credited with helping enact a program of efficiency standards that its boosters credit with holding per capita usage constant over decades while the rest of the U.S. saw consumption increase 50% or more.[23] The relationship is referred to as the Rosenfeld Effect, depicted as a graph of rising per capita electricity consumption for the U.S. compared to a flat usage line for Californians over decades. Rosenfeld and his supporters attribute this "achievement" to legislative mandates. Rosenfeld's authorship of the trend catapulted the bespectacled physicist into rock star status.

But did Rosenfeld's mandates deserve all the credit? That was the question Stanford graduate researcher Anant Sudarshan and his faculty advisor James Sweeney addressed in one of the most widely-cited research projects ever undertaken on the subject. In June 2008, the researchers acknowledged that "since the early 1970s, electricity consumption in California has stayed nearly constant, while rising steadily for the United States as a whole."[24] This would seem to provide powerful evidence that the enacted mandates had their desired impact. Nevertheless, after examining a wide range of factors, the team demonstrated that only "about 23% of the overall difference between California and the United States could be due to policy measures, the remainder being explained by structural factors."[25] Sudarshan continued his research into the subject and submitted a 184-page doctoral dissertation in March 2011 indicating that only about 20% of the difference can be adequately explained by the efficiency program.[26]

Sudarshan found that per capita consumption remained constant in California because the state had undergone transformative structural changes. A large influx of Hispanic immigrants had much less disposable income than existing residents, which held down per capita consumption. Increasing urbanization also meant greater reliance upon mass transit, higher density living conditions, comparatively larger family sizes of immigrant populations within single dwellings, and correspondingly lower energy footprints per family member. Sky-high residential real estate prices shifted the property market toward smaller homes.[27] Other factors like changes in commercial sector floor space and an exodus of energy-intensive industry served to reduce per capita energy use. Much of that industry moved offshore. But the portion that remained relocated to other states. So only one fifth of the credit for the per capita energy decline use was due to mandates.

A study prepared by Arik Levinson of Georgetown University for the National Bureau of Economic Research takes Sudarshan's a step further. Levinson concluded that three factors: (1) a population shift to a warmer Southwest climate, (2) the relatively small income elasticity of energy use in California, and (3) California's demographic profile as described in the research above, can account for "around 90 percent of California's apparent residential electricity savings, thus providing no lessons for other states or countries considering adopting or tightening their energy efficiency standards."[28] Levinson observed that long run trends in residential electricity unrelated to efficiency measures can explain nearly all the improvement in per capita energy consumption.[29] So other states can gain little by emulating California's regulatory mandates.[30] The largest share of energy usage in California is for transport. But efficiency does not explain the per capita usage improvement over time. Instead, a reduction in miles driven is the primary cause.[31]

It is undeniable that Rosenfeld's efforts have had a pronounced impact upon California energy consumption. He was an early proponent of demand-side management (DSM) which led to so-called Time of Use (TOU) pricing, which imposes a higher price on electricity consumed during peak demand periods than at other times of the day.[32] While

TOU schemes don't reduce aggregate electricity demand — you still run the washing machine the same as before — they do help redistribute electricity demand to periods that enable utilities to better smooth out daily loads. TOU pricing can have an impact upon total cost of service since utilities invest to meet peak demand. Reducing peak demand helps reduce the number and capacity of generating stations required.

Some of Rosenfeld's ideas like requiring white roofing on buildings are effective in reducing local heating effects and have been utilized elsewhere. Floridians were doing it long before anyone heard of Rosenfeld. Many appliance efficiency standards have been adopted by manufacturers for models sold in every state. Still, most of the credit for the Rosenfeld Curve resides elsewhere.

The Sudarshan findings have been borne out in other research. A UC Berkeley student named Howard Chong studied the impact of California's strict building codes upon energy efficiency improvements. Chong noted that "California since the 1970s has implemented increasingly strict building and appliance codes and [has] claimed via engineering calculations, energy-electricity decreases of 14-18% of total load."[33] But Chong noted that there are "reasons to be cautious about these claims of energy efficiency."[34] He concluded that those who give the lion's share of credit to legislated energy efficiency programs:

> ... should temper declarations that they are a success and especially temper the interpretation of the Rosenfeld Curve for California as "evidence" that California energy efficiency policies are the cause of California's impressive energy efficiency performance.[35]

Today there are no auto manufacturing plants in the state compared to eight that were there twenty five years earlier. Max Schulz of the Manhattan Institute summarizes the situation:

> Californians still enjoy the fruits of those manufacturing industries — driving cars built in the Midwest and the South, importing chemicals and resins and paints and plastics produced elsewhere, and flying on jumbo jets manufactured in places like Everett, Washington. California can pretend to have controlled energy consumption, but it has just displaced it.[36]

In a hilarious 2006 post, NRDC applauded California, saying the state "illuminates the world." NRDC credited the state's energy efficiency standards for enabling it to weather the highly embarrassing series of rolling blackouts during 2000 and 2001.[37] Of course, the blackouts couldn't possibly have been due to the fact that the state had only approved 10% of the 45,000 megawatts of capacity additions that had been proposed in the 1980s, or that it had shuttered 1,900 megawatts of nuclear generating capacity at Rancho Seco and San Onofre.[38]

NRDC posits the counter-factual claim that there are no rebound effects from energy improvements, ridiculously proclaiming that:

Throughout almost four decades of societal progress in getting more work out of less energy, those who deny the promise of energy efficiency have persisted in a bizarre claim: any energy savings from efficiency are offset by activities that demand additional energy consumption.[39]

Uh, memo to NRDC: this effect was first published in 1865, not four decades ago. Promoters of the rebound effect do not "deny the promise of energy efficiency." They like it as much as the next guy. Instead, they recognize its promise at promoting economic efficiency and arrive at the perfectly logical, empirically defensible conclusion that as any resource becomes cheaper, you'll get more consumption of it. NRDC labels this contention "bizarre." Who are the denialists here? This is Econ 101, a course that Choom-smoking Obama and his mates at NRDC skipped.

NRDC demonstrates its absence of understanding about the economic history of the U.S. and all industrialized societies, pretending that improved energy efficiency offers a refutation of rebound effects:

The most obvious rebuttal to "rebound effect" claims is the performance of the U.S. economy since the early 1970's: between 1973 and 2009, U.S. economic production more than tripled even as total U.S. energy use increased by less than a third. If "rebound effect" advocates were right, that record would have been flatly impossible, since savings in energy use would be offset by activities that demand energy, keeping energy use trends in lockstep with economic growth (just as they were for the first three decades after World War II).[40]

This is a completely ridiculous claim. It might satisfy environmentalist extremists in Washington nervous about being laughed at by serious people. But it won't suffice to win the debate about energy policy. It is undeniable that America has made steady improvements in energy efficiency over the past four decades. Cars go further on a gallon of gas, light bulbs consume less electricity producing a given amount of brightness, we require less energy to heat or cool a given volume of space, appliances are more efficient than before, insulation protects against loss more effectively, window units shed less energy, etc. We all benefit from energy efficiency improvements. But America is not the only nation on Earth.

It is NRDC that hasn't been paying attention. Indeed, the International Energy Agency (IEA) claimed in a 2008 report that:

… improved energy efficiency has been the main reason why final energy use has been decoupled from economic growth. Without the energy efficiency improvements that occurred between 1973 and 2005 energy use would have been 58% higher in 2005 than it actually was.[41]

The reasons why America uses less energy today to produce a dollar of real GDP than four decades ago are complex and in no way offer a refutation of the Jevons Paradox. In

2001, Arthur Rosenfeld, the same man mentioned above, published a relationship between energy efficiency and economic growth, a relationship that NRDC was certainly aware of, but blithely ignored:

> *From 1845 to the present, the amount of energy required to produce the same amount of gross national product has steadily decreased at the rate of about 1 percent per year. It took 56 BTUs (59,000 joules) of energy consumption to produce one (1992) dollar of GDP in 1845. By 1998, the same dollar required only 12.5 BTUs (13,200 joules).[42]*

FIGURE 5-1. **Energy Intensity of U.S. Economy 1949-2012**

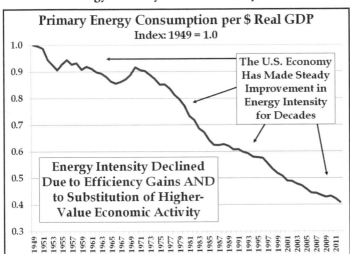

Sources: Annual Energy Review 2011, Annual Energy Outlook 2013, *Energy Information Administration*; Real GDP Annual Data, *Bureau of Economic Analysis*

America has wrung more economic activity out of a single unit of energy each year since the Civil War, and probably even before. The single most important reason why the American economy is less energy-intensive than it was in 1970, as shown in Figure 5-1, is due to the enormous structural shift that has taken place. Rosenfeld shows that the pace of improved economic activity per unit of energy consumed has actually increased in recent decades.[43] The curve keeps getting steeper.

This shouldn't be surprising. Most forecasts of future consumption have significantly overestimated the amount of energy that would be required to support levels of future economic activity.[44] This is largely due to the inability of forecasters to anticipate changing dynamics of economic activity and how those changes impact energy intensity. Jevons himself should figure on this list. In his 1865 book *The Coal Question*, he estimated that Britain would need 2.2 billion metric tons of coal annually by the year 1961.[45] The country actually used less than 10% of that amount in the early 1960s.[46] A Ford Foundation report in 1974 concerning future consumption assumed primary energy growth of 3.4%

per year from 1974 onwards.[47] Extrapolated to the year 2013, that assumed growth amounts to three times the level the U.S. actually consumed.[48] Between February 1973 and February 2013, the U.S. economy actually reduced its consumption of oil by 2.3%.[49] As improbable as it seems, we used less oil in early 2013 than we did 39 years earlier even though the population grew by nearly 50% over that time.

FIGURE 5-2. **DoE Forecast of 2020 and 2025 U.S. Energy Consumption in the AEO**

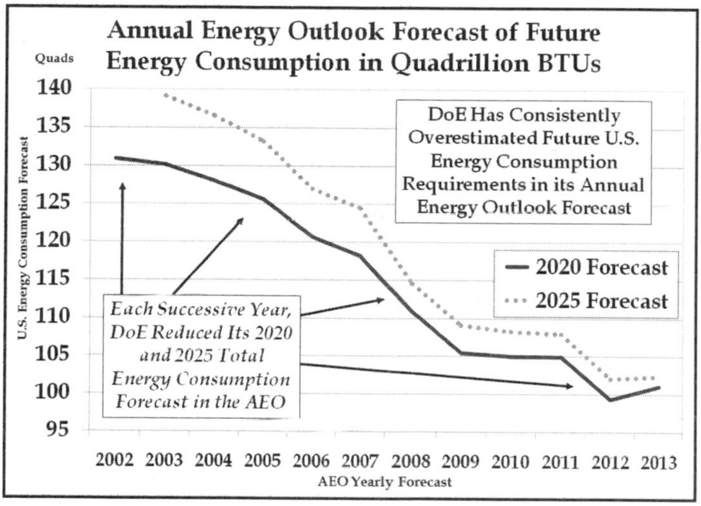

Source: Annual Energy Outlook, Reference Case Forecasts, 2002 to 2013

DoE itself would be a classic case of overestimating future demand. Forecasts embodied in the "business as usual" reference cases for each of the last ten years of Annual Energy Outlook reports show consistent overestimates of future demand. Each successive year's forecast for a future period is lower than the previous year's estimate. Figure 5-2 shows how DoE reference case forecasts for future years 2020 and 2025 have gradually descended back toward Earth with each passing year's estimate. For instance, in 2003, DoE's forecast for 2025 consumption at 139.1 quadrillion BTUs (quads) was 36% higher than its 2013 estimate of only 102.3 quads.[50] Despite the exponential growth in the number of cars, electric appliances, and electronic devices used today compared to an earlier era, per capita energy consumption in 2010 was lower than in 1970.[51] It has only been recently that DoE has fully grasped this essential aspect of economics.

The fact is, today we do more valuable things and we do them with much less energy than we needed in the past. In addition, when we achieve energy efficiency improvements, the savings are employed elsewhere in the economy, increasing economic growth and GDP performance. It's hilarious that NRDC celebrates Rosenfeld's energy efficiency curve while pretending not to notice his energy intensity relationship.

For better or worse, American has greatly reduced the size and importance of energy-intensive industry. The U.S. used to be the world's largest producer of primary aluminum and a net exporter of aluminum products. Aluminum production is highly energy-intensive. Aluminum production involves bauxite mining, reduction of ore into alumina, conversion of alumina into primary aluminum, and fabrication of primary aluminum ingots into finished products. Each of these steps consumes gobs of energy. Because aluminum is one of the most chemically reactive metals — its ion has one of the highest electrical potentials on the metallic ion chart — you need a lot of energy to pry it loose from other elements in the compounds where it is found in nature.

By 2011, America accounted for only 4.5% of global primary aluminum smelting.[52] China produced more than nine times as much primary aluminum as the U.S.[53] The same story is evident in dozens of other energy-intensive basic commodity industries like steel, coking, glass, primary non-ferrous metals, petroleum, inorganic and petrochemicals, pulp and paper, cement, etc.

The U.S. economy has "migrated up the value chain." Our workers spend their efforts on higher value activities, and are compensated thusly. While many Americans decry the loss of basic manufacturing jobs that have been shifted offshore, most of these jobs involve very low value-added activity for which economic competitiveness can only be maintained when the daily wage rate is exceedingly low. It is the reason why we can go to Target or Walmart and buy an $18 toaster or a $12 pair of children's shoes. That's about what we paid for those items in 1980.

The U.S. economy derives about 70% of its GDP from personal consumption, and the high-value services sector is nearly twice the size of the goods producing sector.[54] In 1970, the goods producing sector was the same size as the services sector.[55] These factors, together with the inexorable growth of government as a percentage of the economy, have displaced the value component of GDP formerly occupied by the energy-intensive manufacturing sector.

But even with the remaining segments of manufacturing, the value added per hour of productive effort and per unit of energy input is far higher today than it was decades ago. The auto industry provides a good illustration. In 1970, auto plants employed many more workers than today. The labor input per finished automobile produced was far higher. Countless numbers of workers performed low value-added tasks like welding, stamping, manual paint application, material handling and conveyance, manual sub-assembly and assembly tasks, and so forth. A high proportion of the total production value occurred right at the finished assembly plant. By contrast, today's assembly plant employs very high-value robotic capital equipment performing most of these tasks. Instead of a mountain of piece parts being utilized at the auto assembly plant to fabricate a major sub-assembly such as a dashboard, all of those labor-intensive tasks have been outsourced to components suppliers with production facilities in low labor cost markets like Mexico and China. In place of thousands of dashboard piece parts assembled by hand on the factory floor, a single dashboard sub-assembly incorporating hundreds of piece-parts is supplied to the auto plant where it is dropped into and affixed to the unit by computerized robotic appliances.

In addition, the actual value of the car is greater today because the value of the components is greater. A typical new car in 1970 might have an AM radio that cost the car company $20 per unit to acquire. Today, even with low- and mid-range models, you're likely to find AM-FM-Satellite-CD-DVD player units with an independent set of controls wired into the steering wheel that cost hundreds of dollars. Instead of crank windows and manually locking doors, you find power windows and door locks. Instead of keyed ignition switches and door entry locks, there are computerized remote starting and locking devices wired into anti-theft devices. Rather than simple drum brakes on rear wheels, you find computer-actuated anti-lock disk brakes on front and rear wheels. Solid state digital ignition systems requiring maintenance every 100,000 miles have replaced manually-timed distributor caps and rotors that failed frequently and needed constant maintenance. Body moldings made from highly-engineered plastic resins have replaced heavier weight steel to reduce weight and improve gas mileage. On-board computers with dozens of logic devices have replaced a handful of simple analog monitoring gauges. Catalytic converters remove more than 99% of harmful tailpipe emissions compared to earlier generation cars that spewed smog-creating soot. The list of safety- and value-enhancing qualitative improvements goes on forever.

The net result is that a new car now costs ten or twelve times more than it did in 1970 but its assembly does not require anything close to ten to twelve times more energy. The energy embedded in a few truckloads of steel plate worth $100,000 is about the same as the annual energy consumption of a medium-sized medical office building that generates $25 million in value each year. Today, the U.S. economy does a lot more of the latter than the former compared to decades earlier. The economic value of output derived per unit of energy input is far higher today than in 1970. NRDC's claim is preposterous. The real tragedy is that so much effort needs to be squandered dismantling their deliberate academic malpractice.

FIGURE 5-3. **Per Capita Energy Consumption 2000-2012**

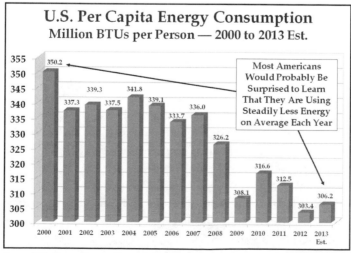

Source: U.S. Census Bureau, *Energy Information Administration* Annual Energy Review 2012, Annual Energy Outlook 2013

The obvious impact is that per capita energy usage in the U.S. has seen a fairly steady decline in recent years. Each American requires less energy today than we did previously due to efficiency, conservation, and structural shifts in the economy as Figure 5-3 shows. Despite the steady drumbeat of politicized conditioning positing that Americans' wasteful consumption of energy grows inexorably each year, the truth is exactly the opposite.

BREAKTHROUGH DISMANTLES THE FABLE

Hoping to settle the matter, NRDC published an article in *Energy Policy* in May 2011 laying out their case.[56] NRDC restricted their analysis to end-use consumption in rich developed countries where rebound effect impacts are often less pronounced.[57] It is certainly true that you won't be inclined to do more vacuuming if you buy a more efficient vacuum cleaner. It's also true that your commute to work won't become longer just because you now buy a car with better gas mileage. So NRDC says, case closed. Not so fast. The U.S. is not a hermetically sealed economy. They ignored the impact of global trade, on energy-intensive sectors of the economy, and the developing world where the largest increase in energy consumption is occurring, and where the rebound impacts are most in evidence.

In less developed countries, there is a very high propensity to consume more energy when efficiency improvements are achieved. The example of Mexico was cited earlier. In other countries where energy penetration is low, improved energy efficiency acts as a powerful inducement to increased consumption.[58] The UN IPCC,[59] the Stern Review,[60] and McKinsey & Company[61] have all advanced similar drivel that ignores rebound effects. Each entity postulated that the most effective strategy to reduce CO_2 emissions is efficiency improvement, which they contend will reduce consumption. They uniformly assume a direct linear relationship between energy efficiency savings and reduced demand.

We might all be able to agree that lower CO_2 emissions, improved energy efficiency, and reduced energy consumption are beneficial outcomes. We don't all agree that an improvement in energy efficiency necessarily results in a proportional reduction in total energy consumption and CO_2 emissions. It never has and never will.

NRDC returned to its ridiculous contention that it could refute the rebound effect by demonstrating that energy consumption does not grow "in fixed proportion to the economy — to GDP."[62] That notion has been safely debunked in the foregoing discussion. NRDC pats itself on the back, claiming "our analysis found that energy efficiency policies are not only the fastest way to reduce energy use but continue to be most the [sic] effective solution to combat climate change."[63]

Don't bet on it. NRDC's frenzied activity appeared to be in response to a February 2011 study published by the liberal Breakthrough Institute. They analyzed ninety six published journal articles and other relevant peer-reviewed literature to assess the current state of academic understanding on the question of the rebound effect, concluding:

Below-cost energy efficiency is critical for economic growth and should thus be aggressively pursued by governments and firms. However, it should no longer be considered a direct and easy way to reduce energy consumption or greenhouse gas emissions.[64]

This was exactly right in every respect. Breakthrough observed that rebound effects were first postulated in 1865 and have never really been controversial among economists. The authors destroyed the conceits of NRDC and each of the above studies, which all contend that humanity's climate mitigation salvation can be effected by efficiency improvement:

Rebound effects are real and significant, and combine to drive a total, economy-wide rebound in energy demand with the potential to erode much (and in some cases all) of the reductions in energy consumption expected to arise from below-cost efficiency improvements.[65]

Breakthrough's study is especially disconcerting to central planning enthusiasts for two reasons. First, Breakthrough is usually considered to be a reliably liberal think tank. So when they heretically challenge liberal catechism, it provokes incontinence among green-left progressives. Secondly, Breakthrough shows there is no painless approach to carbon emission reduction despite assurances from central planning enthusiasts to the contrary:

... there is no substitute for the difficult work of decarbonizing the global energy supply. Below-cost efficiency measures, while contributing indirectly to this effort, do not them-selves offer a shortcut toward that objective, nor do they appear to offer a quick and easy means to reduce carbon emissions in the interim.[66]

Breakthrough discovers six indisputable economic impacts that reinforce the rebound effect. First, as the effective price of energy falls, consumers use more to produce more output, capturing a *direct output-income effect*.[67] Second, cheaper energy results in a rearrangement of relative prices for the materials, labor, and other inputs required, *a substitution effect*.[68] Third, when consumers save money from efficiency improvements, it can be spent on energy-intensive activities elsewhere, yielding *an income-multiplier effect*.[69] Fourth, efficiency improvements always require some energy expenditure to accomplish, subtracting from the tally of anticipated energy savings, *an embodied energy effect*.[70] Fifth, efficiency enhances overall economic productivity, which increases economic growth spurring secondary energy demand, *a macroeconomic growth effect*.[71] Lastly, efficiency improvements promote structural changes from demand rearrangement as relative input price changes take place, *a market price effect*.[72]

Professor Robert Michaels identifies two additional rebound effects. Efficiency technology improvements in one industry usually see migratory application impact in adjacent industries, an economy-wide *migratory technology innovation effect*.[73] In addition, when more advanced economies undergo widespread adoption of efficiency-enhancing equipment upgrades, it is common for outdated technology to be exported to capital-starved, less developed countries. This sparks an incremental increase in energy consumption, a *global technology transfer effect*.[74]

An obvious example of this last effect occurs when U.S. railroads upgrade locomotive fleets to more efficient models. Older fuel-guzzling locomotives are often exported to developing nations where capital constraints prohibit acquisition of more costly new equipment. As a consequence, new rail service can be inaugurated in previously underserved areas. This causes a net increase in global energy consumption.

NRDC laughingly complains that economic researchers have thus far been unsuccessful identifying precise impacts from each of these undeniable efficiency improvement economic effects:

> *Rebound enthusiasts rarely define what they actually are predicting. This is an important failing because the science of economics demands that theories be tested in such a way that the evidence either disproves or supports the hypothesis.*[75]

This is not even true as Breakthrough estimates relative contributions from each major effect.[76] But as Hillary Clinton would say, it's hard to understand what difference it makes since all of these effects act in concert. They all occur and they all contribute to measureable rebound effects. NRDC is demanding a debate about how many angels can dance on the head of a pin.

WHO ARE THE DENIALISTS?

NRDC and promoters of the discredited idea of energy efficiency as a pathway to global energy and CO_2 emission reduction have been influenced by energy economics Luddite Amory Lovins, a policy gadfly who has become the go-to guy for lazy, clueless, disinterested journalists trying to push a narrow point of view. Lovins, a spokesman for eco-left advocacy group Friends of the Earth, was an early supporter of 'green energy' that he claimed, if strenuously adopted, would enable America to avoid a society-destroying fate.

Lovins wrote an error-riddled article in the quarterly journal *Foreign Affairs* in 1976 making a series of outlandish predictions.[77] A college dropout,[78] he billed himself as a consultant physicist. He would have done well to finish his coursework, especially in elementary physics. He asserted in his article that "the capital cost per delivered kilowatt of electrical energy emerges as roughly 100 times that of the traditional direct-fuel technologies on which our society has been built."[79] Ignore the incomprehensible prose and faulty arithmetic. A kilowatt is not a measure of electrical energy, but of electrical power. There's a difference. A real physicist could have explained it to him. Energy is a quantity of work. Power is merely a flow rate.

Lovins added his name to the list of those like William Stanley Jevons, the Ford Foundation, and DoE, that have all made wildly over-hyped estimates of future energy demand. In his article. Lovins predicted that America's current energy use was rising so rapidly that catastrophe was inevitable. He provided a graphical depiction of steadily growing energy demand that would reach 165 quadrillion BTUs (called quads) by the year 2000 and 235 if extended to 2011.[80] Actual energy consumption was only about 98.8 quads in 2000.[81] By 2011, consumption declined to 97.3 quads.[82]

Lovins estimated that, to meet our rapidly growing needs, there would be 450 to 800 nuclear reactors in place by the year 2000, of which 80 would be breeder reactors. This giant fleet of nuclear reactors would be used to help power 15 million electric automobiles that would be on the road by then.[83] At the end of 2012, there were only 65 nuclear stations with a total of 104 reactors, or about 17% of his mid-range estimate.[84] Not a single breeder reactor had been built for commercial generation. Blessedly there were fewer than 100,000 electric cars on the road at the end of 2012 despite $7,500 federal tax credits offered as inducement. Lovins missed his forecast by a mile.

Because consumption would grow so fast according to Lovins, capital availability to replace aging assets would become a major obstacle for conventional energy, particularly electricity. The capital cost of new power plant construction would soar to unaffordable levels. He offered an estimate of the replacement capital cost for the amount of nuclear generating capacity equal to the energy content of one barrel of oil per day, about 626 megawatt-hours.[85] He claimed that would be about $200,000 to $300,000.[86] EIA data in the 2012 Annual Energy Outlook 2012 report for the capital cost of advanced nuclear generating capacity entering service in 2017, stated in 1976 dollars, is around $16,987 for that amount of electricity.[87] Lovins missed his mid-range estimate by a factor of nearly fifteen. He went on to claim that capital costs of centralized electrification would become so exorbitant that "no major country outside the Persian Gulf can afford these centralized high technologies on a truly large scale, large enough to run a country."[88] That was a claim worthy of immediate induction into the Absurdity Hall of Fame.

Lovins forecast that the cost of electricity in 1976 dollars would triple by 1985. He claimed utility base-load generation would suffer because "the current-dollar cost of a kilo-watt-hour will treble by 1985, and that two-thirds of that increase will be capital charges for new plants."[89] Rather than the cost tripling as Lovins predicted, it increased by only 21% in constant dollars.[90] He missed by a factor of fourteen.

He projected that renewable energy sources such as wind, solar, and cellulosic biomass would account for about 40-45% of primary energy needs by the year 2000 and 100% by 2025.[91] The country derived only 3.3% of its primary energy consumption needs from non-hydroelectric renewable sources in the year 2000.[92] DoE's reference case in the Annual Energy Outlook 2013 forecasts that non-hydro renewables will account for only 7.5% of primary energy by 2025.[93] That's probably an overestimate since most of that assumed growth would be for biofuels that won't likely be produced. Lovins was off by a factor of thirteen.

With side-splitting hilarity, Lovins proclaimed that the conventional approach to energy policy — he calls it the "hard path" —the one America has been on for over a century, the one providing most of our energy needs, will result in "a world of subsidies, $100-billion bailouts, oligopolies, regulations, nationalization, eminent domain, corporate statism."[94] He also claimed our current conventional approach would require "centralized management." His preferred future — he calls it the "soft path" — of decentralized village commune-style power stations, efficiency enhancements, wind, solar, and biomass generation, tie-dyed fabrics, chanting beads, incense, *Kumbaya*, poetry readings, vegan dishes, organic farming, and Roman sandals would not. Okay, I made up the last part about Roman sandals.

In actually, the soft 'green energy' program advocated by Lovins is the one requiring huge subsidies per unit of energy produced. That approach has been fed over the years by hundreds of billions of dollars in cash grants, low-interest loans, feed-in tariffs, mandates, tax credits, and other costly subsidies. It relies upon a massive regime of regulations, mandates, central planning, and other heavy-handed, market-distorting mechanisms. It is sustained by the statism embodied in an endless maze of federal and state bureaucracy. It will require extensive expansion of eminent domain, along with a revamping of traditional utility regulatory policy, to enable far-flung 'green energy' producing locations to be connected with distant consuming markets. It also requires these exorbitant costs be spread among ratepayers all across the country. In short, everything Lovins claimed would occur by maintaining the "hard path" has come to pass to enable even small portions of the "soft path." Meanwhile, none of it is a feature of the energy markets and infrastructure of the "hard path," the conventional approach he claimed would result in catastrophic societal collapse.

Lovins was very influential during the latter half of the 1970s. He performed a pirouette, fashioning an entire career out of promoting the idea that efficiency improvements would result in plummeting demand for electricity as consumers began making wholesale shifts to efficient lighting, weather stripping, fuel efficient cars, and so on. Energy demand wasn't going to grow, it would collapse according to the newly re-invented energy guru. In essence, Lovins forecast that a completely new energy production sector would materialize out of the surplus energy derived from efficiency improvements. Decades ago, Lovins proclaimed that this would cause equity shares in utilities, power providers, oil companies, and other energy companies to plummet.

A 1977 article in *Business Week* captures the energy conservation plan that Lovins advocated, showing how deeply rooted it had become in the "consensus" viewpoint of the day:

> *The idea is rapidly gaining support that conservation may be a cheaper and better — if unfamiliar — way to solve the nation's energy problem than developing new supplies. And there is a deep-rooted feeling in Washington that if energy conservation is to be effective on the scale that federal planners now believe is essential, it will require demand management on an unprecedented scale.*[95]

Central planning at the federal level with authoritarian "demand management on a massive scale" again became the prescription *du jour* among elite thinkers in the media. Lovins is famous for telling *Business Week* in a 1984 interview that the U.S. would never need to construct another power plant because efficiency improvements would be cheaper and be able to supply ever-increasing requirements for a growing economy and population. Even blind squirrels find acorns. Yet one strives in vain to locate a single Lovins quote throughout his entire life that turned out to be accurate.

Try not to fall off your chair laughing at this 1984 pronouncement:

> *The long-run supply curve for electricity is as flat as the Kansas horizon. We will never get, we suspect, to a high enough price to justify building centralized thermal power plants again. That era is over. The efficiency improvements are there to be bought. It is up to the utilities to choose participation rather than obsolescence.*[96]

It never occurred to Lovins that if we began making massive efficiency-related savings, as we certainly did, the effective cost of energy would go down, and so we'd use more of it, so we'd need more of it. History has not been kind to Lovins or his energy prognostications, a fact that media luminaries who continue to seek him out for his supposedly sage advice seem able to ignore effortlessly without a shred of embarrassment.

Between 1984 and 2010, total electricity generation in the electric power sector increased from 2.42 terawatt-hours to 3.97 terawatt-hours.[97] The era of the centralized thermal power plant was not finished. Any sensible person could have forecasted this in 1984, or at any other time. Electricity demand increased at a far faster pace than primary energy growth, a factor that Lovins ignores. Out of that substantial increase, nearly two thirds came from thermal plants burning coal and natural gas, the ones Lovins told us we would never need.[98]

There were large efficiency improvements during that period along with immense structural transformations. But electricity growth occurred anyway. How did all of that energy efficiency enhancement work out for CO_2 abatement? This empirical history has been ignored by the UN IPCC, the world's supposed final word on energy policy for the twenty first century and beyond.

Lovins, in the same interview, confidently forecast that electricity prices would plummet to the point that it would become uneconomic to operate most power generation plants. He told his interviewers, all of whom should have been doubled over in derisive laughter:

> *Full use of the best devices now on the market — most of which did not exist last year — would roughly quadruple the long-run efficiency of using electricity in this country at a cost under 2 cents a kilowatt hour, in today's dollars. That is less than the operating cost of coal or nuclear plants. In other words, something like 80% or 90% of the electricity*

now sold is uncompetitive with electricity-saving technologies. Even if you've just finished
building a new reactor, it would be cheaper to write it off than to operate it.[99]

Remember when all the nuclear and coal-fired power plants were suddenly shut down in the 1980s because they were uneconomic to operate? Neither does anyone else. In 1984, when Lovins offered his 2 cents per kilowatt-hour (kWh) forecast about electricity prices, the country was paying 6.25 cents per kWh in constant 1984 dollars.[100] Five years later, electricity cost 5.55 cents in 1984 dollars. And five years after that, it was 5.15 cents. Between 1994 and 2010, nominal all-sector electricity prices ranged between 6.74 cents and 9.99 cents per kWh. In 2010, a kilowatt-hour was priced at 9.83 cents. We're still waiting for that 2 penny electricity Lovins promised.

Similar forecasts about the death of baseload generation are being made today as a proliferation of exorbitantly expensive, taxpayer-subsidized solar panels and even a few bird-blending wind turbines find their way onto the roofs of upper-income dwellings.[101] Absent regulatory warping of market dynamics, forecasts for the death of baseload generation through existing grids are as wildly exaggerated now as they were in 1976 when Lovins issued his laughably inept proclamation. As a utility executive observed, "I don't characterize distributed generation in and of itself as a threat. I characterize the regulatory scheme that supports it as a threat."[102] Even as utilities make inroads in distributed generation markets, baseload power is not going away.

These visionaries forget that their schemes rely upon a limitless flow of taxpayer-funded subsidies and an unlimited political appetite to finance ever-expanding public outlays in an era of widening municipal and state deficits, defaults, and bankruptcies. They also assume that the hyper-politicized environment in the U.S. can long endure the glaring social injustice inherent in this arrangement. To effect this future, upper-middle income homeowners who can afford to install taxpayer-subsidized distributed power-generation systems on their McMansion rooftops utilize a program called "net metering" to sell vastly over-priced energy back into the grid. That causes the high fixed costs to be borne largely by lower- and middle-income ratepayers who cannot afford to do this. Distributed generation causes a wealth transfer from poor to rich. Why are social justice champions like Obama such enthusiastic supporters of this completely indefensible situation?

Incidentally, Lovins' discredited views are shared verbatim by Jon Wellinghoff, Obama's former chief at the Federal Energy Regulatory Commission. He proclaimed in a report carried in *The New York Times* that new centralized baseload nuclear or coal plants would never need to be built since there was such bountiful wind, solar, and biomass resources.[103] He also claimed America could wring an astounding 50% efficiency savings out of the system using existing technology.[104] This is almost word-for-word from Amory Lovins' 1976 *Foreign Affairs* quackery. Nobody on Team Obama does rebounds — or even history.

Lovins advised Google on its Clean Energy 2030 plan, the most important part of which assumed the country could reduce energy consumption 33% by 2030 through efficiency improvements.[105] So the country won't need 103 quads of energy in 2030 as the Annual Energy Outlook 2013 forecasts but something closer to 67 quads according to the adolescent brain trust. Too bad Google didn't bother using Google to research the history and economics of energy efficiency. One can easily understand the appeal that gadflies like Lovins and his ilk have for UN IPCC authors, Sir Nicholas Stern, NRDC, or even the adolescents running Google. But why on earth would a well-regarded global management consultancy like McKinsey promote such charlatanism?

The Energy Research Centre (UKERC) in the UK performed a study in 2007 similar to the one by the Breakthrough Institute. The intent of the UKERC study was to help guide policymakers who were required to devise a policy response to the mutual suicide pact known as EU 2020, the agreement obligating signatories to derive 20% of their energy from renewable sources by 2020. Policymakers would need to know if their grandiose plans to save the planet by renewable energy use would actually do anything other than drive up the cost of energy and throw more British subjects into fuel poverty.

More than 19% of British households were considered to suffer fuel poverty in 2010,[106] a number that had tripled in just six years.[107] Energy costs doubled in the six years from 2006.[108] The British government estimates that 2,700 Britons freeze to death in their homes each year because they can't afford heating.[109] But the real number is closer to eight thousand.[110] More people are found frozen in their homes each year than die on UK motorways.[111] The number of indoor freezing deaths among elderly pensioners doubled in the five years up to 2012, chiefly due to rising fuel bills.[112] Naturally therefore, to UK central planners, CO_2 abatement must take precedence over energy affordability.

The UKERC team followed the same approach as the Breakthrough Institute, reviewing over 500 studies. Not surprisingly, UKERC reached the same conclusions as Breakthrough:

> *Rebound effects have been neglected by both experts and policymakers — for example, they do not feature in the recent Stern and IPCC reports or in the Government's Energy White Paper. This is a mistake. If we do not make sufficient allowance for rebound effects, we will overestimate the contribution that energy efficiency can make to reducing carbon emissions. This is especially important given that the Climate Change Bill proposes legally binding commitments to meet carbon emissions reduction targets. We need to get the sums right.[113]*

Clearly policymakers in the UK don't have "the sums right." Nor do they have their priorities right. And neither does the UN IPCC, nor Sir Nicholas, nor NRDC nor the Obama administration. And neither does the European Commission that gave birth to the *Frankenpolicy* known as EU 2020. As UKERC authors note:

> *Potential 'energy savings' from improved energy efficiency are commonly estimated using basic physical principles and engineering models. However, the energy savings that are*

realised in practice generally fall short of these engineering estimates. One explanation is that improvements in energy efficiency encourage greater use of the services which energy helps to provide. Behavioural responses such as these have come to be known as the energy efficiency "rebound effect." A key conclusion of this report is that rebound effects are of sufficient importance to merit explicit treatment. Failure to take account of rebound effects could contribute to shortfalls in the achievement of energy and climate policy goals.[114]

Proponents of the rebound effect do not shun economically feasible energy efficiency as NRDC falsely implies. The exact opposite is true. Where feasible — below-cost energy efficiency is how they describe it — efficiency improvements yield economic gains. A 2010 National Academy of Sciences (NAS) study cluelessly puzzles over this aspect, decrying implementation barriers to more efficiency measures. Among these barriers NAS cites are high initial capital costs, alternative investment options for capital, payback time uncertainty, and lack of perfect clarity about potential rates of return on efficiency investments.[115] But this is precisely how it is supposed to work. The optimum strategy of capital owners is not to reduce energy usage but to achieve optimum return on invested capital. It is difficult for the NAS to grasp this essential facet of economics.

Increased economic welfare is a desirable outcome in and of itself. Few dispute that. But cheaper energy input leads to an increase in output for the same cost. NRDC and the behavioral science deniers have a hard time understanding this aspect of basic human response. If people who are skeptical that global circulation models have properly defined and quantified all the planet's physical climate response mechanisms exactly correctly can be labeled "deniers — the climate models celebrated by the IPCC and the organized climate mafia —then it is entirely appropriate for clear-headed economic analysts to label as "deniers" the Luddites at NRDC, and IPCC, and Google who deny the undeniable aspects of behavioral science upon which rebound effects are derived.

The counter-factual catechism about rebound effect denial is so firmly embedded into "denialist" liberal theology, it has become folklore.[116] The certitudes that mandating improved fuel efficiency will result in proportional reductions in fuel use, CO_2 emissions, and oil imports are never questioned by leftist visionaries.[117]

ENERGY EFFICIENCY AS A WAY OF LIFE

The U.S. government has been meddling in energy markets and mandating efficiency for decades.[118] The most noteworthy example is the corporate average fuel economy (CAFE) standards on auto manufacturer fleets. Since 1970, the federal government has boosted the CAFE mileage by more than 50%. The average mileage per gallon of all vehicles on the road improved from 11.9 miles per gallon in 1973 to 17.4 mpg in 2008.[119] Nevertheless, despite the obvious intent to drive down fuel consumption, Americans have more than doubled their average miles driven.[120] Precisely the opposite outcome occurred from the one intended by Congress and CAFE boosters.

Government has also mandated more efficient appliances and central heating and air conditioning equipment. That wasn't necessarily wrong. But do we use proportionately less energy today? The actual result is that we live in much larger houses further from work.[121] Homes in the U.S. that were built after the year 1999 are 30% larger on average than homes built earlier, but consume about the same amount of energy.[122] Advances in low emission window panes and heat-trapping argon window inserts have not driven down energy usage. They have led to much larger window units. If you're not convinced, just hop in your hybrid car and take a drive sixty miles outside of town and take note of the McMansion developments crowding the ex-urban landscape.[123]

Over time, the practical result of more efficient heating and cooling and better insulation is not energy savings that are permanently pocketed, but larger houses. The only place that can happen affordably for most home buyers is far from town where land values are lower. Hence, we have longer commutes in higher horsepower, more fuel efficient cars, and we spend about the same amount of money as before.[124] As energy efficiency improvements drive down the real cost of using energy, we invent a proliferation of new appliances that gobble up even more energy. Yet the only ones who don't seem to have noticed are Barack Obama, NRDC, the IPCC, Obama's student audiences, and shallow media cheerleaders. They continue to peddle the energy efficiency evangelism as the only feasible route to CO_2 emission reduction.[125]

Efficient markets working in concert with unimpeded price signals will make mincemeat out of a super-tanker load of central planners when it comes to integrating economically feasible efficiency in our homes, cars, appliances, and offices. It's been happening since caveman days and it will continue even without government mandates.

Businesses and consumers have enjoyed constant improvement in energy efficiency without relying upon the heavy hand of government to effect changes. Residential heating systems in 2000 delivered more than twice the heat content per unit of energy as those of 1950.[126] By the year 2000, we were able to generate 500 times more light in lumen-hours per kWh of electricity than in 1900.[127] We achieved 555 times more passenger miles per gallon in 2000 than we did in 1900.[128] Certain models of Energy Star refrigerators can be 70% more efficient than comparable models sold just twenty years earlier.[129] During the previous five decades, the fuel efficiency of commercial jetliners improved 70%.[130]

The man who brought us unprecedented wreckage in health care markets with Obamacare thinks government can do better. He showed us how in February 2013. On the day before Super Bowl XLVII at the New Orleans Superdome, DoE bragged on its website that it had brought government expertise to New Orleans in time for the start of the game, helping the Superdome install an energy efficient lighting system and undertaking other energy-saving efforts around the city.[131] But then that same lighting system failed during the game, and football fans were treated to a hideous thirty four minute delay.[132]

A twenty three watt compact fluorescent flood light (CFL) will deliver about the same luminosity as a 100 watt incandescent bulb using 77% less energy.[133] The CFL might last two and a half times longer.[134] If the flood light stays on for ten hours a day, the incandescent would cost \$43.22 per year compared to \$9.94 per year for CFL[135]. In this example, a desire to save money would induce most homeowners to substitute CFLs for their incandescent bulbs.

Fleet optimization toolsets are increasingly being deployed on commercial vehicles, resulting in large fuel, labor, variable maintenance, and capital cost savings. Fleet leasing company PHH Arval improved its fuel economy by 10% when it installed a mobile resource management capability that computes optimal routing solutions for fleet drivers working delivery schedules.[136]

Walmart reduced its fleet operating costs 20% by installing GPS position tracking equipment and cell phones in their trucks. Those enhancements permit fleet managers to arrange driving assignments and schedules that minimize non-productive mileage.[137] An optimal routing software system enables a dispatcher to provide a driver with a complete turn-by-turn instruction set which optimizes truck and driver time while substantially lowering fuel usage. Smart phone apps that provide optimal navigation software are readily available today. Airlines employ highly sophisticated fuel management software that computes an optimal fuel load that permits safe operation and allows for unplanned in-flight traffic- or weather-related loitering without requiring the plane to lift and carry more fuel weight than is necessary. These capabilities improve efficiency.

As a management consultant, the author advised a snack food manufacturer that operates a product distribution network plagued with numerous inefficiencies. The company made thousands of needless truckload shipments, engaged in redundant product re-handling, fulfilled replenishment orders from less than optimal origin points, and often shipped product over long-haul routes when shorter movements could have sufficed. A transformation blueprint permitted the company to continue shipping the same volume of product to its customers each year under the same service specification while eliminating \$20 million in needless transport. Once put into action, the company avoided more than 11.7 million truck miles, which equated to almost two million gallons of diesel fuel each year. Despite ridiculous assurances from NRDC that such a thing was impossible, the snack food giant was able to maintain the same revenue level, boost its bottom line, and eliminate millions of gallons of fuel consumption each year. Businesses and consumers do these things every day, figuring out how to do more with less.

The author visited a Texas lumber mill years ago that had deployed a software system enabling the plant to optimize usage of timber. The three-dimensional geometry of each log is scanned seconds before it is cut. Its external dimensions are analyzed and recorded. An algorithm matches the known and anticipated customer orders for various board sizes and lengths with the geometry of the log, instantly computing an optimal cutting solution that maximizes usage of the available timber to best meet customer demand. The result is a 30% improvement in yield and a commensurate reduction in cellulosic waste. That means 30% fewer inbound truck shipments and far less plant electrical power is required to satisfy a given order volume. Much less energy is required to manage the waste stream since there is less of it. Demand can be more effectively fulfilled through improved operations, so less inventory of various board sizes and dimensions is required to manage day-to-day order flow. Much less plant and warehouse footprint is required for a given base of business. All of these features deliver tangible energy savings.

Like the snack food company, the forest products company is not in the business of saving the planet. Neither company had been swayed by trendy advice to busy themselves counting their carbon footprints — or is it feetprint?[138] Both companies only wanted to remain competitive and put more money on the bottom line. They were able to do so by enhancing efficiency. To paraphrase a clever academic, the hidden hand did not require a regulatory glove to develop a green thumb.[139]

An author who attempted to write a heavily annotated book of this nature twenty five years ago would have needed to make countless energy-intensive trips to dozens of university libraries, would have required hundreds of government and other publications to be sent by energy-intensive mail deliveries to his home or office, would have needed to make dozens of expensive investigatory field trips, and so forth. Today, a manuscript of this nature and length can be completed almost entirely in the comfort of one's home or office.

IS EFFICIENCY A ROUTE TO ENERGY INDEPENDENCE?

None of the foregoing should be mistaken as advocacy for wasting energy or even under-appreciation for the value of saving it. On the contrary, any *economically feasible* measure to increase efficiency amounts to good economic practice, good public policy, and good environmental stewardship. Note the key ingredient here: economic feasibility. It does suggest that any effort to base public policy upon an expectation that efficiency mandates or CAFE standards will automatically lead to a substantial decrease in the public's demand for energy is doomed.[140]

Consider the disastrous experience in Europe, which made large public expenditures hoping to achieve efficiency gains. A damning report from the European Court of Auditors released in January 2013 made clear that the "investments" were squandered:[141]

> *None of the projects we looked at had a needs assessment or even an analysis of the energy savings potential in relation to investments. The member states were essentially using this money to refurbish public buildings while energy efficiency was, at best, a secondary concern.*[142]

Energy conservation may rank well among the set of available personal virtues. But it performs poorly as a results-oriented national policy designed to reduce energy consumption. Just ask the Europeans who squandered €5 billion pretending they were saving the planet.[143] Instead, they just wasted taxpayer money. The auditors made clear that the funds went to projects where "the cost in relation to the potential energy savings was high."[144] That's putting it politely. In many cases, payback time was as high as 150 years, longer than the useful lives of the refurbished buildings.[145] Projects like these produce negative rates of return when the cost of capital is included in the calculation. This doesn't qualify as "economically feasible" energy efficiency. But it is model public policy in the age of Obama.

That doesn't mean we shouldn't avoid resource waste wherever possible. It does mean that we shouldn't expect to suddenly achieve energy independence based upon our efficiency efforts. The inescapable paradox is that all of our sustained efforts to use less energy will result in our using more. Get used to it.

Obama told his audience at the University of Miami:

We need to keep developing the technology that allows us to use less oil in our cars and trucks, less energy for our buildings and our plants and our factories — that's the strategy we're pursuing. And that's the only real solution to this challenge.[146]

Developing energy efficiency technology is useful. We're doing it now and we'll keep doing it. We don't need his help. He already helped our health care markets. And he helped Super Bowl XLVII . And he helped the solar industry with Solyndra. Sadly, Obama thinks more domestic energy supply couldn't possibly improve the situation. Only reduced consumption works in his playbook. He sounds like Jimmy Carter in a cardigan sweater holding fireside chats trying to sell weather-stripping out of the Oval Office.

Whether Obama admits it or not, energy demand can only be reduced by increasing its price. Again, as the Paris-based IEA noted in its 2008 report:

… the changes caused by the oil price shocks in the 1970s … did considerably more to control growth in energy demand and reduce CO_2 emissions than the energy efficiency and climate policies implemented in the 1990s.[147]

Indeed, after the oil price shock of 1973, it took 17 years for the U.S. to return to its previous oil consumption level.[148] In their 2005 book *The Bottomless Well: The Twilight of Fuel, the Virtue of Waste, and Why We Will Never Run Out of Energy*, authors Peter Huber and Mark Mills observed that "To curb energy consumption, you have to lower efficiency, not raise it. But nobody, it seems, is in favor of that."[149] Nobody except Obama.

An elegantly named bi-partisan measure called the Shaheen-Portman Energy Savings and Industrial Competitiveness Act of 2013 was making its way through Capitol Hill as these pages were written.[150] The bill is designed to boost energy efficiency. Terrific. How does it propose to do that? It will devolve much discretionary rule-making to DoE.[151] Given DoE's disgraceful track record with its 'green energy' venture capital business and its own conservation efforts, we can hardly wait.

Obama is completely mistaken that energy efficiency is "the only real solution to this challenge." No doubt he envisions coercive, heavy-handed federal mandates like the ones in Obamacare that he used to fix our health care system. If we get any energy usage reduction from efficiency improvements at all, it will be slight. Enhancing energy efficiency lowers its effective price, which boosts consumption. If you really wanted to curtail energy use, you'd need to increase its price, not decrease it. But increasing the price of stuff like energy or health care is something Obama already knows how to do quite well.[152] Just consult your current health insurance premiums and deductibles. Boosting energy costs will only depress economic growth. That's something Obama is really good at also.[153]

CHAPTER 6

ALL THOSE DREADFUL SUBSIDIES

"Although wind farms still depend on tax credits, they are likely to be economical without this support within a few years."[1]

CHRISTOPHER FLAVIN
WORLDWATCH INSTITUTE, 1985

"Production tax credits (for wind farms) play a key role in securing the profitability of Renewable Energy projects."[2]

MICHAEL WEBER
WORLDWATCH INSTITUTE, 2012

As with nearly every aspect of energy policy, the subject of public "subsidies" is poorly understood, deliberately distorted, and vastly different from the crude caricature painted by Obama. He hates subsidies when they are used to promote the use of low-cost, economically beneficial, high-value energy sources like oil and natural gas. But he adores them if they are steered to campaign-contributing cronies and doled out in copious quantities to promote expensive, economically infeasible, technically unworkable, and environmentally damaging sources like wind, solar, and biofuels. Obama mirrors his leftist allies the world over positing a preposterous belief that, were it not for oil and gas subsidies, 'green energy' would dominate the new energy investment landscape.[3]

The President has devoted his career decrying the supposedly indefensible conduct of oil and gas companies being granted subsidies that were enacted to promote oil and gas exploration and drilling. To a President trying to wean the nation off of its fixation with fossil fuels, it was unimaginable that taxpayers were actually according favorable tax treatment to producers to increase proved reserves and domestic supply:

Over the long term, an all-of-the-above energy strategy requires us having the right priorities. We've got to have the right incentives in place. I'll give you an example. Right now,

$4 billion of your tax dollars subsidize the oil industry every year — $4 billion. They don't need a subsidy. They're making near-record profits. These are the same oil companies that have been making record profits off the money you spend at the pump for several years now. How do they deserve another $4 billion from taxpayers and subsidies? It's outrageous. It's inexcusable. [4]

The President was throwing down a marker to politicians, daring them to justify their previous votes in favor of establishing favorable tax treatment subsidies to oil and gas explorers and producers. Those votes, he claimed, were "outrageous." They were "inexcusable."

Of course, Obama didn't bother to point out to his Miami audience that he had voted in favor of those same subsidies when he was a Senator back 2005.[5] It probably slipped his mind. Were those votes outrageous and inexcusable? In 2005, Obama had voted in favor of the Energy Policy Act of 2005, breaking ranks with his Democratic colleagues in the Senate.[6] That measure, among a range of other measures, included $2 billion in subsidies to oil and gas companies. Nor did he complain about the Section 1603 Program enacted in his American Recovery and Reinvestment Act of 2009 that had approved $16 billion in 'green energy' giveaways, a fourth of which — or $4 billion — had gone to foreign firms.[7] That $4 billion subsidy was also okay. The other kind, the one that actually creates jobs and income, clearly was not.

Observers of the mercurial career of this most dour, petulant, thin-skinned man had come to recognize Obama's penchant for breath-taking sanctimonious hypocrisy. His Miami rhetoric was in perfect accord with the same hypocrisy he exhibited during the summer of 2011 as he geared up his reelection strategy. That was when he began road-testing his program of demonizing corporate jet owners for a razor-thin federal tax benefit accorded private aviation manufacturers. At every speech or press conference he held, he sanctimoniously asked his audiences, "Are you willing to compromise your kids' safety so some corporate-jet owner can get a tax break?"[8] As in Miami, Obama had not bothered to point out that it was his own economic "stimulus" program he had signed into law, the measure he had claimed was essential to the survival of the republic, that had enacted those aviation tax breaks in the first place, the ones he later denounced.[9]

THE TRUTH ABOUT OIL AND GAS SUBSIDIES

Overlook the obvious incongruity that Obama had supported the very energy subsidies he was wailing about in Miami. How much truth was there in his criticism? Complaining about subsidies being extended to oil and gas producers is likely one of those issues that tests well in focus groups. Obama has developed a well-earned reputation of latching on to issues that offer little in the way of substance but sound persuasive on the stump.

Just five weeks after his Miami speech, Obama delivered a Rose Garden speech entirely devoted to the topic of oil and gas "subsidies." In his remarks, Obama singled out oil and gas producers for heavy-handed treatment:

Right now, the biggest oil companies are raking in record profits — profits that go up every time folks pull up into a gas station. But on top of these record profits, oil companies are also getting billions a year — billions a year in taxpayer subsidies — a subsidy that they've enjoyed year after year for the last century. Think about that. It's like hitting the American people twice. You're already paying a premium at the pump right now. And on top of that, Congress, up until this point, has thought it was a good idea to send billions of dollars more in tax dollars to the oil industry.[10]

Congress did this. Senator Obama of Congress had had no role in it. There were three categories of "subsidy" in Obama's crosshairs that accounted for the overwhelming majority of the $37 billion he was hoping to recoup over the next ten years: (1) Section 199 deductions to domestic manufacturers, (2) deductions for percentage depletion for oil and gas wells, and (3) deductions for intangible drilling costs.[11]

The first on the list of "subsidies" to oil and gas producers involves a provision in the Internal Revenue Code enacted in 2004 called Section 199. The intent of this provision was to offer a tax preference for companies that produce goods in the United States. It was designed to spur domestic job creation. But Obama's Fiscal Year 2013 Budget Plan proposed to raise $11.6 billion over ten years by eliminating the provision.[12] This Obama proposal is exceptionally strange.

Obama enjoyed significant mileage over the years promising to punish companies that ship jobs overseas. He built his 2012 reelection strategy around demonizing Mitt Romney for what Obama falsely contended was Romney's cardinal sin of outsourcing jobs to foreigners. So Obama should be a wildly enthusiastic supporter of any tax measure designed to keep American jobs here at home. He had demonized his 2008 opponent John McCain in the same way, telling a rally in Des Moines just days before the 2008 November election that:

The truth is, we won't be able to bring back every job that we've lost, but that doesn't mean we should follow John McCain's plan to keep giving tax breaks to corporations that send American jobs overseas and promoting unfair trade agreements. I will end those breaks as President, and I will give American businesses a $3,000 tax credit for every job they create right here in the United States of America.[13]

But now in Miami and again in his Rose Garden remarks, here was Obama complaining about tax subsidies that had been enacted solely to spur domestic manufacturing and production. Producers of identical products in offshore locations do not qualify for Section 199 "subsidies." The Obama proposal to remove the domestic manufacturer tax benefit was targeted solely at domestic oil and gas producers. All other domestic producers would continue to enjoy the preferential Section 199 treatment. Obama was all for job creation, except in the oil patch. He's for jobs before he was against them.

The second of these "subsidies" involves percentage oil depletion allowance. Obama hoped to collect $11.5 billion over ten years by eliminating these provisions.[14] The percentage depletion allowance was first enacted in 1926 to recognize that when a driller produces a unit of product, it is merely transferring one unit of inventory from underground to above ground storage.[15] Each unit of product brought to the surface, in effect, represents a degradation of the future potential production value of the underground deposit. But more interestingly, while Obama's hot rhetoric was aimed at integrated oil majors like ExxonMobil, BP, Chevron and Conoco Phillips, percentage depletion allowances for major integrated oil companies were eliminated from the tax code in 1975.[16] Those oil giants that Obama was singling out in the Rose Garden don't even qualify for these tax breaks. The only companies that can benefit are the small drillers who account for ever greater shares of domestic oil and gas production. Obama's rhetoric was a complete fraud. And he knew it.

To a small producer, percentage oil depletion allowance represents a major item on their tax return. More importantly, it represents a substantial portion of the overall net present value and economic return on a marginal drilling operation. How can Obama claim to be a supporter of small businesses, to claim to favor more domestic oil drilling, to claim to favor retention of domestic job-producing activities, to claim to support U.S. job creation, to be on the side of the small guy, while at the same time proposing to eliminate the provision that keeps many of these businesses, marginal projects and workers in operation? Obama has made these same proposals in every budget plan he has submitted to Congress since he was elected President.

Furthermore, oil depletion is similar to the tax provision that permits a manufacturer to deduct depreciation of capital assets. An auto manufacturer, even one owned by American taxpayers, builds and equips an assembly plant to produce cars that it attempts to sell for a profit. The company raises capital to acquire and clear land, build a plant, purchase and install production equipment, hire and train workers, and all the rest. It assembles cars which, with the exception of the Chevy *Volt*, it hopes to sell for a profit. The company then pays income taxes on the profit from those sales. But the profit is only the amount left over after it has paid out all of its deductible expenses. Included in those deductible expenses is a portion of the capital that it initially spent to build, improve, and equip the production plant.

Every company regularly deducts as depreciation an amount that reflects a gradual degradation of invested capital, a fact which recognizes that buildings and equipment don't last into perpetuity. They need to be replaced on a regular basis. But no one considers the deductibility of periodic depreciation of capital assets in a manufacturing business to be a taxpayer subsidy. Instead, it is a completely legitimate cost of doing business. Amazingly, Obama even proposed to allow all other businesses to deduct 100% of their capital outlays in the year they were made rather than being required to charge off the cost over a period of years.[17] Obama has actually been on both sides of this issue at the same time.[18] But he chose to demonize oil producers for doing what every business does and what he previously advocated.

The third item on Obama's hit list concerns something called expense deductions for intangible drilling costs. Obama's 2013 budget plan proposed collecting $13.9 billion over ten years from eliminating those write-downs.[19] These tax code provisions have been in place since the U.S. enacted its first income tax law in 1913. The provisions permit oil producers to deduct incidental expenses that are not directly related to the producing well itself such as site surveys, grading, drainage, environmental impact assessments, and so forth. Any company that expends capital funds for these same kinds of outlays putting up a manufacturing plant or office building is entitled to capitalize and deduct them. These are completely legitimate business expenditures that are accorded similar treatment regardless of the type of business.[20]

Small oil and gas producers are eligible to expense 100% of these costs in a single year, whereas integrated oil majors are only entitled to recoup them over a five year period. As with percentage depletion, faster write-downs improve the net present value and rate of return, and are designed to spur production by enhancing financial viability of projects at the margin.

Again as before, these provisions do not even benefit companies like ExxonMobil, the oil giant that Obama singled out in the Rose Garden — "Exxon pocketed nearly $4.7 million every hour," he told his incontinent listeners. Interestingly, the top three oil producers ExxonMobil, Chevron and Conoco-Phillips, had paid a combined $289 billion in federal and state taxes between 2007 and 2012.[21] Energy companies actually paid the highest effective corporate tax rates of any class of industrial companies.[22] If companies needed to be demonized for being tax scofflaws, there were certainly far better targets — Google and Apple for example — than oil producers. But those companies are headed by executives who contribute copiously to Obama's campaign. Those companies have hundreds of billions sitting idly in offshore accounts solely to avoid repatriation tax burdens. But we never hear Obama complain about their tax avoidance efforts.

Energy consultancy Wood McKenzie performed an economic analysis on the probable impact of Obama's proposal to eliminate intangible drilling cost expense treatment over the ten year period from 2013 to 2023. Obama wants drillers to treat these expense items as capital costs subject to periodic depreciation, requiring the industry to delay cost recovery. By 2023, Obama's plan would result in lost oil production of 3.8 million bpd, a reduction of at least 260,000 jobs, and foregone investment of $407 billion in income-producing capital outlays.[23] That volume of lost output would equate to more than 60% of the country's crude oil production during the month Obama was sobbing to his Rose Garden audience.[24] The foreign trade impact alone would shave nearly one percent off of the moribund real GDP growth rate. Impeding economic recovery, destroying jobs for middle-income workers, reducing personal and corporate incomes, eliminating America's energy self-sufficiency, and endangering the country's national security is the real agenda behind the Obama rhetoric on oil and gas subsidies.

Most interesting is that the 100% intangible drilling deduction for small producers was extended by the terms of the elegantly-named Tax Relief, Unemployment Insurance Reauthorization and Job Creation Act of 2010.[25] You'll never guess who signed that one into law. Yep, it was President Barack Obama, the guy who was now complaining about those very provisions he was solely responsible for putting into place. There was only one person in the known universe who could have made his wishes a reality. And now he was weeping about it.

After spending his entire adult life demonizing provisions contained in the year-end 2010 tax deal, Obama staged one of his trademark policy flip flops, announcing his sudden enthusiasm:

> *What all of us care about is growing the American economy and creating jobs for the American people. Taken as a whole, that's what this package of tax relief is going to do. It's a good deal for the American people.*[26]

Apparently in the 2012 election year, growing the economy was not important. Back in 2010, Obama used the signing ceremony as an occasion to lambaste howling leftist colleagues within his own party who hitherto had been fully aligned with his opposition. That is, they were aligned with him until he flipped on them. He unleashed a barrage of criticism at Congressional Democrats:

> *Somehow, that was a sign of weakness and compromise. If that's the standard by which we are measuring success or core principles, then, let's face it, we will never get anything done. People will have the satisfaction of having a purist position and no victories for the American people. And we will be able to feel good about ourselves and sanctimonious about how pure our intentions are and how tough we are.*[27]

So in December 2010, it represented "a good deal for the American people," a victory. It created jobs, he proclaimed. Nevertheless, despite those cringe-inducing flip-flops, Obama was shirted up and back on the Democrat roster in early 2012, reverting to his familiar script of castigating oil and gas companies, once again proposing to eliminate tax measures that hold down the cost of oil and natural gas. It was apparently no longer a "good deal for the American people." He no longer cared about those jobs. He had rediscovered his pure intentions.

Fortunately for those same American people, the consumers of oil and natural gas, that "special interest" worthy of endless demonization, that infinitesimal sliver of the population that needs to drive, cook, heat and cool a home, take mass transit, work in a heated environment, buy consumer goods trucked to market, fly in airplanes, use power equipment, keep lights on, send kids to school, or do any of a thousand other things requiring oil and natural gas, the Democratic-controlled Senate defeated Obama's plan on the very day he was whining about "subsidies" in the Rose Garden.[28] Maybe it was payback for his treatment of them in December 2010.

HOW MUCH IS ENERGY SUBSIDIZED?

How much do we really spend on energy subsidies? To learn the answer, the Senate Energy and Natural Resources Committee requested the Congressional Budget Office (CBO) to prepare a report based upon fiscal year 2011 budget numbers. Their report indicated that:

> *The federal government has used both tax preferences and spending programs to provide financial support for the development and production of fuels and energy technologies in recent decades. In 2011, federal support totaled an estimated $24 billion, which was provided in the following ways:*
> - *Tax preferences — such as special deductions, special tax rates, tax credits, and grants in lieu of tax credits — which totaled $20.5 billion, or about 85 percent of the total.*
> - *The Department of Energy's spending programs, which received funding totaling $3.5 billion, or about 15 percent of the total.*[29]

The interesting thing to note about the CBO report was that, of the $24 billion in subsidies, $16 billion went to renewable technologies while only $2.5 billion went to fossil fuel programs.[30] Among the recipients of tax breaks for renewables was $6 billion that went to promote Obama's favorite fuel, ethanol.[31] To hear Obama talk, you'd think fossil energy companies were mugging widows and crippled orphans in back alleys and stealing their purses while noble, forlorn solar, biofuel, and wind companies were eating out of dumpsters. The other interesting thing to note was that the largest increase in energy subsidies in history was enacted in the "economic stimulus" measure that Obama pretends saved the U.S. from extinction, the one he signed into law.[32]

A year earlier, DoE had performed a similar study at the request of Congress.[33] The study determined that subsidies totaled $37.2 billion, of which only $2.8 billion were targeted to oil and natural gas producers.[34] The largest recipients were renewable energy programs, which raked in $14.7 billion. Subsidies for renewables, smart grids, conservation measures and aid to low income families — the programs Obama supports — amounted to 82% of all federal energy subsidies.

When viewed in relation to the actual amount of energy produced, the comparisons become even more interesting. Based upon energy production figures in the Annual Energy Outlook 2012 reference case for 2010,[35] the latest data available when Obama was complaining, the subsidy per million BTUs of actual energy produced looks like this:

FIGURE 6-1. **Federal Subsidies by Energy Source**

Energy Source	FY'2010 Subsidies (Millions)	Quadrillion BTUs Produced	Subsidies (per Million BTUs)	Ratio vs. Oil & Gas
Coal	$1,358	22.06	$0.0616	0.8
Oil and Gas	$2,820	36.47	$0.0773	1.0
Nuclear	$2,499	8.44	$0.2961	3.8
Biofuels	$7,761	4.05	$1.9163	**24.8**
Other Renewables	$6,913	3.85	$1.7956	**23.2**

Source: Direct Financial Interventions and Subsidies in Energy in Fiscal 2010, *Energy Information Administration*, July 2011

The salient point would be the two numbers in the lower right-hand corner of the table. Renewable energy subsidies were anywhere from 23 to 25 times higher per unit of energy than for oil and gas. Astoundingly, the subsidy level alone for a million BTUs of wind energy in 2012 was greater than twice the *market price* to purchase an equivalent amount of natural gas.[36] Those staggering oil and gas subsidies, the ones that Obama was apoplectic about, the ones that caused him to nearly collapse under the sheer weight of their moral indefensibility, the ones he had lost sleep over, they cost less than eight cents per million BTUs. A million BTUs is the amount of energy the average household in the U.S. consumed in four days during 2009.[37] Those were the subsidies that induced Obama to proclaim to another student audience in Nashua, New Hampshire in early March 2012:

> *Right now, $4 billion of your tax dollars — $4 billion — subsidizes the oil industry every year. Four billion dollars.*[38]

The poor man nearly fainted. He had to say it three times in Nashua just in case they were hard of hearing. Those oil and gas subsidies that prompted Obama to crisscross the nation giving dozens of speeches, that consumed months of the administration's time and attention, that crowded out other substantive policy positions that might have boosted employment, incomes and output, they cost American taxpayers less than eight cents per million BTUs.

If we could only recoup that $4 billion each year, the country would be able to balance its budget. Well okay, maybe not. The deficit Obama projected for fiscal 2012 would be $1.3 trillion.[39] All this frenzy was over $4 billion, about 0.1% of federal outlays.[40]

By contrast, subsidies to biofuels, the fuel Obama claims will save the planet, snagged about $1.92 per million BTUs. Other renewables like wind and solar energy snared subsidies to the tune of $1.80 per million BTUs. This was an administration that loudly claims its "energy priorities were not about picking one energy source over another."[41] Despite this provably counter-factual boast as the evidence clearly demonstrates, Obama vocally advocates making all renewable energy tax credits and subsidies permanent, including the 2.3¢ per kilowatt-hour wind energy production tax credit.[42]

America, a country that spends $6 billion a year on potato chips, must suffer a President who burns oceans of jet fuel crying about $3 or $4 billion in "subsidies" — and most of it is not even subsidies but expense deductions similar to those accorded every other business — to an industry that accounts for nearly 50% of all of the domestic energy produced. In fiscal year 2012, it took the federal government nine hours and 14 minutes to spend $4 billion. Obama spent more time than this on his trip down to Miami. John Edwards spends more time each day combing his hair.

The lion's share of those deductions Obama cries about are taken by marginal producers, the very ones that produced all of that extra domestic oil and natural gas that Obama bragged about to his Miami audience, the petroleum that caused America to import less than 50% of its needs, the energy that fueled Air Force One that brought him to Miami to cry like an infant with a soiled diaper about those very "subsidies" he had signed into law:

> We're focused on production. That's not the issue. And we'll keep on producing more homegrown energy. In 2010, our dependence on foreign oil was under 50 percent for the first time in over a decade.[43]

American had indeed reduced oil imports. And it happened in spite of, not because of, Obama energy policy. "We're focused on production," he said. It was true. They were focused on production — making it as difficult as possible to occur. That's what he really meant to say. Because that's precisely what his laments on the stump and his overall energy policy from Day 1 and his enforcement approach and his 2010 budget plans forward through to 2014 had entailed.

THE PROFITS OF DOOM

Had the nation been able to harness a fraction of the energy Obama expended crying over oil and gas subsidies, America would be completely energy independent today. Nevertheless, the worst aspect of his complaint was not that the case had been so dishonestly overstated. The real scandal over subsidies concerned those extended to crony-connected projects his administration funded.

A classic story that puts squarely into context where the real energy subsidy scandal resides concerns a massive deployment of wind power in Oregon at a project called Shepherds Flat. With 338 General Electric turbines each rated at 2.5 megawatts for a total nameplate capacity of 845 megawatts, the Shepherds Flat wind energy complex was, at completion, the largest wind energy project in the world.[44] Lead sponsor of the project is a New York-based outfit called Caithness Energy. Shepherds Flat will sell all of its output to Southern California Edison under a 20-year guaranteed purchase contract.[45] This will help the utility meet the state's stringent requirement to derive one third of its power from renewable sources. Because the turbines are scattered across more than 30 square miles of Oregon real estate, it was also necessary to construct 85 miles of additional roadway and 90 miles of high-voltage transmission grid to enable power gathering among its far-flung towers.[46] The price tag for the completed project will be north of $1.9 billion.[47]

Interestingly, Caithness drew intense scrutiny during the planning stages by offering to pay residents in the nearby town of Ione a "noise easement" of $5,000 to forestall complaints about the racket that swirling turbine blades create.[48] It was hush money for noise. The wind farm will result in 35 permanent jobs, which comes to $35.4 million per job.[49] At that rate, it would only cost taxpayers $177.1 trillion to create the five million 'green energy' jobs Obama promised.

But the real scandal concerns the amount of public subsidy the project will receive. Sponsors subdivided their project into three phases and made separate applications for Oregon's controversial Business Energy Tax Credits, receiving $30 million in state benefits under rules that explicitly govern which proposals qualify as separate, distinct projects.[50] The Shepherd Flat project should have been eligible for only one $10 million payout because it is only one project.[51] But the Oregon Department of Energy (ODoE) had no trouble ignoring legislative intent or its own rules in approving the corporate welfare arrangement.[52]

This scam has been tried before. One sponsor broke a single wind farm project into nine phases and applied for subsidy handouts on each phase.[53] Amazingly, four of those phases were approved for taxpayer handouts by ODoE. But that relatively insignificant exercise in taxpayer-funded corruption can be overlooked. This was minor league stuff.

The major leagues of corruption concerns the fact that more than $1.2 billion of the $1.9 billion construction cost was funded under five separate subsidy arrangements.[54] The example was so extreme that it prompted administration flaks Lawrence Summers and Carol Browner to draft a memo to Obama complaining about the indefensible arrangement. They noted that lead sponsors "would provide little skin in the game," putting up less than 11% of the construction cost.[55] The White House duo claimed the project would have proceeded anyway without subsidies, meaning the generosity amounted to a taxpayer gift to GE and the project's crony-connected partners.[56]

Given the low investment requirement for Shepherds Flat sponsors, the project will generate an astounding 30% annual rate of return.[57] At that outlandish growth rate, a $1,000 initial one-time investment would be worth more than $190,000 after 20 years.[58] If a worker set aside $5,000 in savings each year in an account offering a compound annual 30% growth rate, after a 30-year period, his $150,000 in contributions would have grown to more than $73.7 million.[59]

Even better was the fact that other partners in the scam beside Caithness Energy included the billionaire founders of Google.[60] Who was more deserving of taxpayer-funded welfare than the world's 20th and 21st wealthiest billionaires on the *Forbes* 2013 list of the richest people on earth?[61] Of course, the tab for all the over-priced energy that Shepherds Flat will sell to Southern California Edison will be picked up mostly by lower- and middle-income ratepayers in California, while the exorbitant profits will be pocketed by billionaires and corporate jet owners. Not only do taxpayers and ratepayers get to subsidize expensive energy. But they are also afforded the opportunity to line the pockets of campaign-contributing billionaire Obama cronies.

Green-bleating media triumphantly proclaims that Shepherd Flat will eliminate 1.2 million tons of CO_2 from the atmosphere.[62] We await proof of that stupendous claim. But even if every syllable is true, that would amount to a taxpayer subsidy abatement cost of $130 per metric ton of CO_2.[63] If you accept the Obama administration's wildly sandbagged estimate of the "social cost of carbon" — and you'd be crazy if you did — that abatement cost compares to an inflated social cost of about $55 per metric ton. Since the U.S. only accounts for 4.4% of the planet's population, we can only expect to receive 4.4% of that inflated $55 benefit, or about $2.42 for every $130 outlay. Does this sound like a good use of $1.2 billion of taxpayer resources? And yet these are the type of projects Obama insists the country needs to subsidize at far greater degrees.

The economic model is simple and straightforward. Government entities like DoE provide federal subsidies such as construction loan guarantees and other economic incentives to cover a portion of the cost to build and operate renewable energy installations. The far higher costs of generating electricity from these projects are off-loaded onto electric utilities that are obligated to buy the power at rates far in excess of prevailing market levels. The utilities, in turn, charge electricity ratepayers much higher electricity rates through a "feed-in tariff" that compensates the utility for its much higher energy generation costs. This permits the operators of these projects to earn above-market returns on equity. In other words, the higher costs from renewable energy are socialized among federal taxpayers and ratepayers while the much higher financial returns of these zero-risk renewable energy projects are privatized among wealthy, politically-connected, campaign-contributing sponsors.[64]

Another good example is Warren Buffett-owned Berkshire Hathaway's MidAmerican Energy Holdings' purchase of Topaz solar farm in California.[65] Lest anyone think the Oracle of Omaha has suddenly gotten 'green energy' religion, we have Wall Street solar analyst Michael Horwitz to set them straight:

Let's be clear, this is not Warren Buffett taking a bet on solar technology. This is Warren Buffett investing in a power plant that is guaranteed to yield large cash flows for at least 20 to 25 years. The power plant just happens to be solar powered.[66]

For all Buffett really cared, it could have been a toxic waste dump. Middle- and lower-income electricity ratepayers in California will cough up the overwhelming majority of the surcharges that support the expensive solar power. The burden will impact low-income ratepayers the worst.[67] Meanwhile, all of the excess returns will help fatten the wallet of the world's second wealthiest person. But Buffett is hardly alone in this indefensible shakedown racket.

Yet another solar project adjacent to the Topaz plant called the California Valley Solar

Ranch is being built near Santa Margarita. That project will sell power to Pacific Gas & Electric (PG&E) under a 25-year power purchase agreement.[68] The price PG&E will pay will be in the 15-to-18 cents per kWh range.[69] Meanwhile, wholesale power that traded at California's two major hubs was priced well below 4 cents per kWh during 2012.[70] Virtually the entire construction cost of this zero-risk endeavor will be subsidized by middle-class taxpayers.[71] Lead partner in the project is NRG Energy, whose CEO David Crane unashamedly boasted to well-heeled Wall Street analysts:

> *We intend to do as much of this business as we can get our hands on. I have never seen anything that I have had to do in my 20 years in the power industry that involved less risk than these projects.*[72]

No kidding. Neither have we — and we'll be the suckers paying for it. The entire cost of the project is paid for by taxpayer largesse, utilities in the state of California are obligated to purchase the power at four times the wholesale price of power available under other arrangements, middle-class tax- and ratepayers will pay the excess cost for another 25 years, and all the above-market financial benefits will flow into the deep pockets of the Obama-crony billionaire investors. To paraphrase Lord Acton, power corrupts and 'green power' corrupts expensively.

Among the owners of this boondoggle are the billionaire founders of Google, who are also busy shaking down ... er, investing in other 'green energy' projects in other states.[73] Some might say these 'green energy' visionaries are putting their money where their mouths are. But since every one of these projects relies upon public subsidies for its existence, a more accurate description would be that they're putting their hands where your wallet is. Liberals like Obama consider these kinds of arrangements to be model public policy.

To understand the pernicious nature of the rip-off taking place, examine an S-1 registration document for an initial public offering (IPO) of common stock filed with the Securities and Exchange Commission by a solar panel company. Solarcity is a California company headed by Elon Musk, the billionaire Chairman of Tesla Motors, another 'green energy' company feeding at the public trough. Tesla recorded tens of millions of dollars in profit in 2013 from zero emission vehicle credits it sold to other auto manufacturers.[74] Those credits are purely an invention of the California state government's effort to warp markets to favor certain industries, and certain 'green energy' billionaire entrepreneurs, over others.

Solarcity offers residential power customers a deal whereby they agree to have solar panels installed on their rooftops and, in turn, surrender tax credits and other subsidies to Solarcity. The company survives solely on an uninterrupted flow of money chiseled out of taxpayers and electricity ratepayers. But don't take my word for it. Just examine Solarcity's IPO filing for various risk factors that the company identified:

(1) *Existing electric utility industry regulations, and changes to regulations, may present*

technical, regulatory and economic barriers to the purchase and use of solar energy systems that may significantly reduce demand for our solar energy systems.[75] If federal and state governments decide to discontinue looting lower- and middle-income ratepayers to enrich solar power billionaire entrepreneurs, the gravy train could turn into an economic train wreck for Solarcity.

(2) *We rely on net metering and related policies to offer competitive pricing to our customers in some of our key markets.*[76] Net metering is a program in place in numerous states where power generated by solar rooftop systems is sold back to the grid at full retail prices. So what's the problem with that? First, power companies ordinarily sell power to customers that they can acquire for a much lower cost. Wholesale power contracts traded on California's two major hubs in 2012 were priced at 3.6 cents per kWh.[77] But with net-metering, power companies are forced to "buy back" power from well-to-do homeowners who can afford residential solar installations at a price of 15.7 cents per kWh, the residential electricity price paid by Californians during 2012.[78] That rate is 4.3 times more expensive than the utility's cost to acquire wholesale power. Second, homeowners can often generate enough solar power to "zero out" their bills in certain months. What's the problem with that? By doing so, they become system "freeloaders" because they do not pay any of the fixed costs of capital embedded in the system that they rely upon to deliver power during months when availability of solar power is low and they need to rely upon the grid.[79] Those avoided fixed system costs don't go away. They get offloaded onto the backs of all the other users. So "net metering" becomes a method that drives power prices higher for system users who can least afford to pay. Net metering has, in effect, become a regressive tax mechanism where income is transferred from lower-income ratepayers to higher income residents courtesy of 'green energy' policies enacted in various "blue" states. Left-leaning politicians would ordinarily faint at proposals to tax poor people to enrich wealthy residents. But those inhibitions are easily overlooked when 'green energy' is served.

(3) *Our business currently depends on the availability of rebates, tax credits and other financial incentives. The expiration, elimination or reduction of these rebates, credits and incentives would adversely impact our business.*[80] So it's not a business at all, not in any real sense. It is merely a welfare scam designed to extract value from market imperfections that have resulted from legislative tampering. It can only exist because public policy has warped the competitive landscape allowing slick operators to enrich themselves at our expense.

(4) *Our ability to provide solar energy systems to customers on an economically viable basis depends on our ability to finance these systems with fund investors who require particular tax and other benefits.*[81] If there were not a flood of tax credits and public subsidies being funneled from low- and middle-income taxpayers and ratepayers through government channels into the pockets of billionaire solar welfare recipients, there would be no Solarcity.

(5) *A material drop in the retail price of utility-generated electricity or electricity from other sources would harm our business, financial condition and results of operations.*[82] This is perhaps the most damning indictment of all. The economic viability of this indefensible arrangement that benefits these billionaire solar entrepreneurs enrolled in public assistance

programs depends upon ever-increasing residential power prices being extracted from the pockets of lower- and middle-income ratepayers. If residential ratepayers were to benefit economically through lower power prices, that would hurt crony billionaires on welfare who are raking in billions from this arrangement.

(6) *We have incurred losses and may be unable to achieve or sustain profitability in the future.*[83] So have we. Join the crowd. It would be a real shame to see you go down the toilet.

It is indisputable and you don't need to rely upon some obscure author who penned a polemical tract for proof. You can get it straight from Solarcity billionaire entrepreneurs in their public document filings. There is a direct transfer of funds from lower- and middle-income taxpayers and ratepayers into the burgeoning coffers of 'green energy' millionaires, billionaires, and corporate jet owners.[84] This is what passes for "climate justice" in the upside-down world of Obama 'green energy' economics.

SUBSIDIZING POND SCUM

Obama also found time to promote some breakthrough energy technologies that he claimed could have enormous beneficial impact. He claimed that algae was one of those revolutionary solutions to America's future energy needs. Without a hint of embarrassment, Obama proclaimed:

> *We're making new investments in the development of gasoline and diesel and jet fuel that's actually made from a plant-like substance — algae. You've got a bunch of algae out here, right? If we can figure out how to make energy out of that, we'll be doing all right.*[85]

Obama was promoting an idea to grow pond scum and convert it into jet fuel.[86] He wasn't even joking. Apparently Obama was hoping that his Miami audience wasn't aware of the sole-source contract his administration awarded to a crony company called Solazyme to supply algae-based jet fuel to the U.S. Navy that will cost American taxpayers $16 per gallon for fuel that usually costs around $4 per gallon.[87] Fuel at $16 a gallon was Obama's answer to high fuel prices. Obama was also hoping audience members were unaware that, under pressure from the his White House, the Navy had rejected two RAND Corporation studies concluding that "the use of alternative fuels offers no direct military benefit over the use of conventional petroleum-derived fuels."[88]

Following his algae gaffe, lapdog leftist commentators were quick to cover the President's exposed flanks[89] for reminding voters about his $16 per gallon crony socialism boondoggle for algae-based biofuel. His Navy Secretary Ray Mabus idiotically claimed it "makes us better fighters."[90] The President was right about one thing. We can produce scads of energy from a variety of sources not currently used today, even pond scum. We could convert our soiled underwear into synthetic fuel if we wanted to. The question is not about how much energy we can derive. As the $16 per gallon jet fuel crony contract demonstrates, the key question is: How much energy at what cost?

It's that stubborn economic feasibility question again. Cost is never a consideration that Obama and his allies in the media ever want to discuss. Remember, these were the guys that forked over $1.2 billion in subsidies for an Oregon wind farm that created 35 permanent jobs at $35.4 million each to abate CO_2 emissions at a cost of $130 per metric ton in exchange for over-valued climate benefits of $2.42 per ton. Nevertheless, given that the entire point Obama's visit to South Florida was specifically to address concerns about high energy prices, cost should be relevant.

Even Obama's DoE claims that massive-scale algal biofuel plants could only produce algae-based fuel at a hideously expensive $8 per gallon level.[91] And that figure is almost certainly wishful thinking at current enzyme technology capabilities given the $16 per gallon contract awarded to the Obama crony. DoE currently funds 30 algal biofuel projects to the tune of $85 million, to which the Obama White House proposes to add tens of millions more.[92]

Obama says "We'll be doing all right" if we can figure out how to make fuel out of algae. But we've already figured it out. It's costing taxpayers $16 per gallon. Whether it costs $8 per gallon or $16 per gallon, it would likely not allay the concerns of an anxious public complaining about gasoline priced at $4 per gallon. Still, it serves as an adequate reminder of how preposterous the energy policy of Obama has become, that their proposed solution to the high cost of $4 per gallon gasoline is algae fuel that costs $8 to $16 per gallon. Not surprisingly, Obama's supporters in Miami deliriously applauded this excursion into public policy senility.

Of course, Obama could not avoid engaging in outright lies. When you're talking to college students enrolled in humanities courses who don't routinely keep abreast of DoE or DoD contracts, you can easily slip a few blatant falsehoods. Consider this claim:

> *Believe it or not, we could replace up to 17 percent of the oil we import for transportation with this fuel that we can grow right here in the United States. And that means greater energy security. That means lower costs.*[93]

"Believe it or not," he said. They would do well not to believe it because it was a lie. It was "the big lie" as George Orwell called it, mixing a truism with an obvious falsehood to make the whole statement appear true. As G.K. Chesterton said, "the whole truth is generally the ally of virtue; a half-truth is always the ally of some vice." Or some deliberate deception. Sure, "we could replace up to 17 percent of the oil we import for transportation with this fuel." Why not 100 percent? And it could all happen here in the U.S. It is possible if we were willing to pay a high enough price. But that was the key consideration. It won't mean lower costs. It will mean far higher costs. Just ask Ray Mabus. He buys $16 algae-based biofuel for a U.S. Navy accustomed to paying $4 a gallon.

Cost was not the only problem inherent in algae-based fuels. Another major problem is location. Commercial scale algae growth requires substantial amounts of sunlight, nutrients, water, warm temperatures, and carbon dioxide.[94] Southwestern deserts in the

U.S. provide plenty of sunlight, warm temperatures, and nutrients but not a lot of water. Since heavy CO_2 fertilization is required, co-location with coal-fired power plants is the only practical approach. But there aren't many coal-fired plants in the desert. There are plenty in the Midwest and in Northern prairie states. But there isn't too much in the way of warm temperatures. So, while it all sounds fine in a speech to university students, the idea collapses when you look at the details. Expect DoE's $85 million in algae projects to pay off as well as Solyndra did.

Obama used his Saturday radio address following his February 2012 trip to the University of Miami to reiterate the points he had made to impressionable students in attendance. All of this disingenuous, self-contradictory, indecipherable mania and more is what Obama described as a comprehensive, cohesive policy to "get our priorities straight, and make a sustained, serious effort to tackle this problem."[95] Remember, the "problem" Obama was talking about was high energy prices, for which his solution was higher-priced subsidized energy like $16 algae fuel, and solar power that costs four times the wholesale price of conventional power.

A few days later, the President mocked a *Fox News* reporter for asking a wholly impertinent question about high gasoline prices.[96] *Fox*'s Ed Henry had the temerity to remind the energy-strategist-in-chief that, amidst the panic about higher fuel prices, "you have said before that [higher prices] will wean the American people off fossil fuels onto renewable fuels."[97] The reason Ed Henry mentioned that Obama had supported much higher fuel prices is because he had done exactly that. Higher fuel prices was his highest priority goal. It formed the centerpiece of his program.

The President abruptly shot back in classic self-pitying fashion, saying "Do you think the president of the United States going into re-election wants gas prices to go up higher? Is there anybody here who thinks that makes a lot of sense?"[98] Needless to say, the President thought it made great sense back in 2008, and 2009, and 2010, and even in 2011. He had always wanted gas prices to go up. He just didn't want anyone to notice during an election year. And he didn't want to have impertinent reporters reminding him or the American public about his position, which remains in effect today.

SECTION 3

WE KNOW HOW THE STORY ENDS

CHAPTER 7

THE 'GREEN ENERGY' PIONEERS

"We should not expect that the current production level of European industry will remain the same in the next 10, 20 or 50 years. We will have to downsize industrial facilities in Europe in the long term."[1]

WOLFGANG EDER
CEO, VOESTALPINE

"The U.S. has become much more attractive to companies than Europe. Germany is in the process of getting sandwiched between eastern Europe with its low labor costs and the U.S. with low energy costs."[2]

MARTIN WANSLEBEN
ASSOCIATION OF GERMAN CHAMBERS
OF COMMERCE AND INDUSTRY

"We are suffering from the high energy prices, our companies are affected by it, because there are German companies that are deciding in favor of other locations and do not want to set up their business in Germany. The challenge is to promote and expand renewable energies without jeopardizing competitiveness."[3]

PHILIPP ROESLER
GERMAN ECONOMIC MINISTER

"Good luck with that."

JERRY SEINFELD
PHILOSOPHER

Americans do not need to engage in a lengthy debate about the promise of 'green energy.' We don't need to ponder the likely impact that Obama's 'green energy' future would have upon the country. The evidence about the potential to either improve or degrade America's economic position has already been established. The debate is over.

The 'green energy' future has been pioneered in Europe. We can look at the slow-motion collapse of the European Union, its descent into double-dip economic recession,[4] record unemployment levels,[5] expanding deficit and sovereign debt,[6] intractable political dysfunction, and successive waves of insolvency of various Western European countries for clues to how this idea will play out. Europe's self-imposed economic stagnation is the result of burdensome regulations, soaring wages, ruinously expensive welfare policies, expanding debt and deficits, and though often overlooked, its deeply damaging descent into a 'green energy' regulatory super-state.

Germany is the best benchmark because it is so far along toward realization of this unattractive future. It long-ago embarked upon an aggressive program of 'green energy' deployment enabled by high subsidy payments, a program whose pace has steadily increased over the years. The result is that Germany now boasts the second highest electricity rates in the core EU-15.[7] Not coincidentally, between 1998 and 2007 Germany posted the lowest average annual real GDP of any of the 12 core EU countries with the exception of Italy.[8] In the five and a half year period from January 2008, Germany logged an annual real GDP growth rate of just 0.47%.[9]

Each member nation of the Eurozone faces an obligation under the EU 2020 law requiring it to derive 20% of its energy from renewable sources by the year 2020. To achieve compliance, Germany began erecting a Byzantine array of rules, subsidies, mandates, regulations, feed-in tariffs, carbon trading schemes, and corporate exemptions that have transformed the energy sector into an economic hall of mirrors.[10] The result is that, beside the highest energy bills in the EU, its power grid regularly suffers reliability problems.[11] Businesses and citizens suffer occasional power outages and voltage fluctuations due to the highly unstable nature of intermittent renewable energy.[12] The country must often import electricity to overcome production deficiencies. At other times, power overflows it can't control produced during surge periods must be offloaded upon reluctant neighbors.

According to Germany's Federal Ministry of Economics and Technology, the cost associated with energy consumption increased 20% in one year between 2010 and 2011, more than doubling since the year 2000.[13] Amazingly, despite this staggering increase, the costly 'green energy' program seems to enjoy widespread popularity, at least among media cheerleaders.[14] It is regularly extolled as a model for America to follow in hundreds of error-riddled media paeans offered by faithful believers.[15] The country is both allergic to nuclear power and apparently unconcerned about the price tag of its 'green energy' ambitions.[16] Yet despite the media assurances about the supposed popularity of high cost energy, the Merkel government announced a cap on subsidies to contain runaway costs in order to assure political survival.[17] Since the German public has ruled out nuclear power,[18] fracking,[19] carbon capture and underground burial,[20] and with the Bundesrat, Germany's upper legislative body, having blocked tax incentives to promote energy efficiency,[21] renewable energy appears to be the only option for the country to achieve its carbon reduction goals.

In the wake of the Fukushima nuclear catastrophe in 2011, former nuclear supporting Chancellor Angela Merkel made an abrupt U-turn. She suddenly announced that

Germany would close all of the country's seventeen nuclear plants by the year 2022, which generated one quarter of the country's electricity.[22] Seven of the oldest nuclear plants were shut immediately for "safety" concerns as the world watched the Fukushima disaster unfold.[23] An eighth plant was added to the list shortly thereafter.[24] The loss of 8.8 gigawatts of generating capacity transformed Germany from a net electricity producer to a net consumer, from net exporter to net importer. Japan made a similarly precipitous move also shuttering nuclear power plants. But rather than relying upon renewable energy to make up the difference, the Japanese shifted their focus to fossil fuels.[25] The Japanese government, looking at the breathtaking $622 billion price tag to build a 'green energy' grid, decided to jettison its 25% carbon reduction goal rather than agree to commit economic suicide.[26]

In its 2011 Annual Report, European Network of Transmission System Operators for Electricity noted that the only reason why the European grid has not faced a major catastrophe is because recent winters have very mild by comparison with other years.[27] But if an extended period of severe cold sets in as it did in 2010, many areas could experience crippling power curtailments.[28] That would be especially problematic in France as many households use electric heating. The country had hitherto been a major importer of surplus German electrical power. That becomes more problematic with the loss of eight nuclear base-load generating plants. A cold snap in February 2012 that coincided with shutdown of two gas-fired power plants caused by a Gazprom supply cutoff very nearly caused a collapse of the grid.[29] German grid operator TransnetBW issued an advisory in December 2012 warning of anticipated power shortages during the coming winter.[30]

Oddly, though Germany proclaimed loudly to the world that it would be exiting the nuclear power business, the immediate power shortfalls were covered mostly by Czech and French nuclear power stations.[31] One of the Czech stations in Temelin is only 62 miles from the German frontier. It experienced more than 130 failure incidents in recent years including a radioactive fluid leakage.[32] If Merkel's intent was to safeguard the public from Fukushima-type nuclear incidents, she had not entirely succeeded. Given higher energy imports, neither had she improved Germany's energy security, trade balance, or economic growth.

A FLOOD OF NEW GREEN JOBS — IN OTHER COUNTRIES

The German energy dilemma helps highlight the deep political and economic dissonance afflicting the European populace. Public support for mothballing Germany's nuclear plants remains high.[33] To make up the difference, the government wants to replace that capacity with wind and solar rather than affordable base load fossil power. Support for that appears high also. They have also ruled out fracking of Germany's abundant natural gas resources.[34] But wind and solar, which rely upon massive subsidy levels for their existence, are far more expensive than nuclear and conventional sources. To effect the transition to renewables, feed-in tariffs that unload the additional costs onto the backs of consumers are deeply unpopular, economically calamitous, and impose dreadful outcomes on low-income families.[35]

One tenth of German households struggle to pay the increased costs resulting from the country's energy revolution.[36] Environment Minister Peter Altmaier claims he "knew from the start that the energy switch can't be realized for free. However, I want to prevent costs that can be prevented."[37] Altmaier replaced the previous Environment Minister Norbert Röttgen who was fired by Merkel in May 2012 after the electoral defeat in Germany's most populous state, North Rhine-Westphalia. The voting outcome was heavily influenced by voter disgust with the government's energy fiasco.[38] Röttgen's dismissal was less related to the electoral defeat and more about his poor performance implementing what Germans call the *Energiewende* (or energy change) without the politically damaging cost increases. But that was Mission Impossible.[39] Altmaier is not so delusional as to pretend there is even a remote chance this attempt to rewrite the laws of economics and physics will actually succeed as Angela Merkel, a physicist by training, wants it to.[40]

Germany's power grid suffers from unreliability issues that had hitherto never plagued it prior to the Chancellor's decision to shut down nuclear power plants. Blackouts and large voltage fluctuations are far more common today than just a few years earlier before high penetration levels of wind and solar power. Unreliability is destroying German heavy industry.[41] Munich endured a city-wide power outage in November 2012, the first one that the city had suffered in 20 years.[42]

Arcelor Mittal's energy-gobbling blast furnace steel mill in the Finkenwerder district of Hamburg was forced to shut down during a cold day when a power surge risked a blackout in the city.[43] The mill was compensated for the forced closure, with the bill being sent to German power consumers.[44] A power interruption at the Hydro Aluminum mill in Hamburg lasted for only milliseconds. But it was enough to cause serious damage to the plant's equipment.[45]

Germany's largest steelmaker ThyssenKrupp was forced to sell off its Krefeld stainless steel mill employing more than 400 workers. The purchaser, Finnish competitor Outukumpu, promptly announced its intent to close the mill.[46] The reason: high electricity prices and unreliability of supply. Similarly, Düsseldorf-based conglomerate GEA shut down a zinc plant in Datteln for the same reasons.[47] Hamburg-based Aurubis, Europe's largest copper producer, shifted production offshore to avoid the high costs and vagaries of Germany's increasingly unstable power markets.[48] Norsk Hydro suffered substantial losses at its Neuss aluminum mill near Düsseldorf due to power fluctuations that cause equipment seize-ups.[49] German car maker BMW selected Moses Lake, Washington as the site to build its energy-intensive carbon fiber plant — the output will be used in the BMW i3 urban electric vehicle — because industrial power from the Bonneville Power Administration is available to industrial customers for three U.S. cents per kilowatt hour.[50] The company never considered putting the operation in Germany, where industrial power prices are six times higher. Opened in 2011, the company started a second production line in 2013.[51]

German chemical maker BASF has poured $5.7 billion of investment into the U.S. since 2009 to take advantage of low natural gas and electricity prices.[52] Workers in Wyandotte, Michigan and Monaca, Pennsylvania will soon be enjoying the job security that the company's plant expansions will provide, courtesy of competitive energy and raw material prices unavailable in Germany.[53] The U.S. subsidiary of Munich-based Wacker Chemie, AG announced plans to expand its polymer plant in Calvert City, Kentucky.[54] The company is planning a $2 billion polysilicon plant in Charleston, Tennessee, and a research and development facility in Dalton, Georgia.[55] Wacker has twice increased its original production targets for the Charleston plant.[56]

Munich-based industrial conglomerate Siemens chose Charlotte, North Carolina as a site to expand its worldwide 60 Hz gas turbine manufacturing.[57] After the Charlotte plant completion, Siemens announced it would eliminate 1,400 jobs at three assembly plants in Erlangen, Offenbach and Leipzig.[58]

The CEO of German chemical giant BASF pretends that the world is looking at the colossal failure of Germany's 'green energy' experiment with *Schadenfreude*, the perverse pleasure one gets from the misfortune of others.[59] But he has repeatedly warned that if the company is required to absorb ruinous grid fees, BASF will be forced to locate its operations abroad.[60] So it's a lot less about our *Schadenfreude* and much more about his survival instinct. BASF's competitor Dow Chemical announced plant closures in the Netherlands, Belgium, the UK, and Spain while opening new plants in the U.S., with its CEO singling out Europe as a place to avoid due to its soaring costs of operation.[61]

Airbus announced plans to build a mid-range A320 jetliner assembly plant in Alabama, which is due to begin production in 2015.[62] The company broke ground on the new $600 million plant in April 2013.[63] The move will help the Boeing competitor avoid the high-cost of European production.[64] Numerous other German companies like BMZ GmbH, Prufrex Innovative Power Products, Thomas Magnete GmbH, Kayser Automotive, and The Kübler Group have all announced plans to shift production and research facilities away from high-cost Germany to the U.S.[65]

Austrian steelmaker Voestalpine is building a $715 million iron ore processing plant in Texas that will create 150 jobs when it opens.[66] The company is unequivocal about its plans to abandon domestic European manufacturing. Its CEO unabashedly admits the company never seriously considered reinvesting in Europe.

This flood of foreign direct investment (FDI) has brought with it a wealth of high-paying industrial jobs that could have remained in Germany. Company officials predict that even more FDI will flow out of Germany due to its increasing competitive disadvantage and unreliable power supply. Subsidy payouts have doubled in three years since 2010.[67] Irrespective of the course of political outcomes, annual subsidy costs of at least €20 billion for renewables are baked into the cake until at least 2030.[68] Projections show these payments could actually soar to over €40 billion a year by 2020.[69] There is nothing the country can do to stem the self-inflicted drainage of jobs. Germany is fast becoming an industrial wasteland courtesy of 'green energy.'

Companies are facing enormous cost increases installing stopgap approaches like batteries and backup power generators. But these measures don't offer a permanent solution and many producers are looking to shift production overseas.[70] Germany is slowly strangling its domestic energy-intensive industries like glass, aluminum, chemicals, ferrous and non-ferrous metal fabrication, fertilizers, building equipment, and pulp and paper out of existence.

European Energy Commissioner Günther Oettinger has warned repeatedly that Germany needs a "speed limit" on how fast energy costs can rise.[71] Oettinger sees Germany's 'green energy' program as a mad dash toward de-industrialization.[72] That outcome may be the ultimate goal of program proponents. Amazingly, as her 'green energy' program drives away employment, Chancellor Angela Merkel's advice to unemployed workers was: "Move"[73] Employers are busy heeding the Chancellor's advice.

ROLLING LOADED DICE ON OFFSHORE WIND POWER

Germany's first foray into promotion of renewable energy occurred in 1991 with implementation of the Electricity Feed-In Act. This law established the first feed-in tariff which promoted hydroelectric and wind energy.[74] The Renewable Energy Sources Act (known by its German acronym *Erneuerbare-Energien-Gesetz* or EEG) came along in 2000, overhauling and expanding the renewable subsidy arrangement that gave renewable energy a preferential position on the grid. EEG needed to be amended in 2004 to repair economic dislocations not initially foreseen by Germany's social engineers.[75] That prompted a second amendment in 2008 to correct new deficiencies.[76] Predictably, another amendment passed in 2012 to repair some of the new damage.[77] Following that amendment, central planners busied themselves developing new changes to repair yet more damage to the energy marketplace in a never-ending cycle.

The long-range EEG plan calls for massive deployment of offshore wind energy generation in the northern Baltic and North Seas eventually accounting for a sixth of Germany's total electricity requirements. But northern Germany is sparsely populated and can't possibly absorb all the power that will be produced. The only way the program can succeed would be for the majority of that power production to be consumed in the more densely populated central and southern regions. To accommodate the regional imbalance, Germany will spend €37 billion for a network of long-distance power lines.[78] Other estimates place the figure north of €52 billion, a plan that includes massive upgrades to existing power lines.[79]

Former Economics Minister Rainer Bruederle estimates that Germany will need 3,600 km of new high-voltage grid lines to integrate offshore wind power.[80] Citing figures from the German energy agency DENA, the country will also need 200,000 kilometers of upgrades to existing distribution grids.[81] This will not only require a lot of money but a major overhaul of the country's legal framework to assure grid operators are adequately compensated for this staggering cost increase.[82] Transmission service operator (TSO)

TenneT is being relied upon to provide grid build-out for 25 gigawatts of offshore wind power by 2025.[83] But the cash-strapped, Netherlands government-owned TSO has neither the stomach nor the resources to take on the task. TenneT required a €600 million cash infusion from the Dutch government in 2011.[84] The Dutch don't understand why they should pay to make Germany's 'green energy' program succeed.

At present, the four major grid operators have no incentive to undertake costly system overhauls. Financial incentives built into the EEG law go exclusively to power producers, not distributors. So grid upgrade work is far behind schedule.[85] Hoping to adopt a Solomonic solution, the Merkel government adopted a modified grid build-out and overhaul plan that involves constructing only 2,800 kilometers of new grid extensions.[86]

Recognizing the central planning incongruities of the EEG, Merkel cabinet minister Ilse Aigner recommended nationalizing the entire grid.[87] These ideas have gained some currency. Everything will then be fixed once the necessary nationalizing is complete — just like it was in the Soviet era. People like Aigner argue that the current unbundled structure put in place a few years ago — grid operators are independent of power generators — represented a historic mistake that the European Commission must now fix.[88] But it was the European Commission that forced utility companies to divest their grid operations in the first place.[89]

The trouble with the grid expansion master plan is that the southern consuming regions are opposed to this expensive, inefficient idea. Instead, they plan to deploy regional and local solutions to their power requirements, at lower cost. The uncertainty in the compensation arrangement has prompted German utility operator RWE to announce plans to postpone construction of its €5 billion Nordsee I wind park.[90] Why spend billions on generation capacity if you can't assure a consumption market?

But these concerns are not forestalling most of the construction plans for littering the Baltic and North Seas with massive arrays of wind farms. Reaching out into the turbulent, storm-tossed waters as far as 150 kilometers from shore, Germany expects to derive up to 25,000 megawatts of electric capacity from offshore wind power by the year 2030.[91] This is the equivalent of 25 nuclear power stations. Once complete, the offshore power complex will consist of 5,000 turbines each sitting on top of a tower as high as a 20-storey building, spreading across an area six times larger than the boroughs of New York City.[92]

A portion of one of these wind parks, a 30-tower complex called Borkum Riffgat,[93] sits in waters claimed by both Germany and the Netherlands. That prompted a diplomatic row that had not been resolved prior to construction of the site.[94] Once in operation, Riffgat promises to be able to provide power to 116,000 households from its 30 wind turbines which are rated at a combined 108 megawatts.[95] Grid connections to the Borkum wind park were delayed because the seabed is littered with unexploded World War II munitions.[96] Operators are forced to burn massive amounts of pollution-spewing diesel fuel running turbines to prevent corrosion to mechanical components.

Germans, like the Kennedys of Hyannis Port, prefer not to foul their million-Euro seaside views with wind towers.[97] It's the excess cost of offshore wind energy they seem able to ignore. To avoid the vicious opposition campaigns, the type that the Kennedy clan is waging against Cape Wind, these massive German off-shore wind farms are being located far out into the seas. This is adding enormous technical and environmental challenges — and massively to the cost burden. Onshore wind power is already an expensive proposition, far more than conventional combined-cycle natural gas according to understated DoE figures.[98] Offshore wind power is at least 2.5 times more expensive than onshore generation.[99] Just as cost and complexity increase when outer-continental shelf oil recovery operations migrate from shallow to deepwater locations, offshore wind generation cost begins to soar when towers are located far beyond sight of land.

These offshore wind parks will likely pose a risk to shipping. Ships operating in foggy conditions may collide with wind towers sitting hundreds of kilometers out to sea. To avoid accidents, ships will be forced to divert far away, taking long circuitous routes to minimize risk. As *The Daily Telegraph* observes, ship owners:

> *... claim that diverting large cargo ships and tankers around wind farms will lead to an increase in carbon dioxide emissions from heavy shipping, which would cancel out much of the carbon dioxide savings wind farms are intended to deliver.*[100]

Despite steadily lower operations and maintenance costs, offshore wind gets overwhelmed by its unaffordably high capital costs.[101] Global energy consultancy BTM Consult estimates German offshore wind projects cost as much as $5.1 billion per 1,000 megawatts of nameplate capacity, which is double the amount estimated for earlier generation of offshore installations.[102] If offshore wind delivers 40% of nameplate capacity, the $5.1 billion number goes to $12.8 billion per megawatt of actual deliverable power. That compares to $3.8 billion for advanced "always-on" nuclear plants.[103] In an era of low-cost capital, this is far less of a problem than when interest rates begin to rise, as they undoubtedly will.

One reason why offshore wind generation is so costly is that German offshore wind parks require installation of a massive piece of expensive equipment called a High Voltage Direct Current (HVDC) converter station. The HVDC prevents loss of the power that needs to be transported over long distances just to make it onto shore. HVDC converters sit on platforms near the wind towers. They collect alternating current generated by the wind turbines and convert it to direct current for transmission over undersea cables. An example is the ABB-built Borwin Alpha HVDC converter that serves the Bard 1 turbine complex. The yellow box-like converter sits atop a platform in about 50 meters of water, rising 80 meters above the wave crests. Displacing 431,000 cubic feet of volume, it occupies 15 to 20 times more space than a typical single-family house.[104]

It is not known if the colossus will even work. Despite the project being years behind schedule, the HVDC can't be tested in the field because there is no power being generated by the turbines.[105] But even when the turbines begin rotating, there is nowhere to send the power because the major components of the grid to distribute it are not in place. Nevertheless, project contractors will qualify for payments for power that won't even be generated and can't be used.[106] German households will pay project sponsors for all the non-existent power.[107]

WHAT IF THE WIND STOPS BLOWING?

Even if the technical aspects of wind power can be overcome, there still remains the problem of intermittency. Occasionally, the wind stops blowing — and not just in one location where load drop could be handled by an adjacent wind fleet some distance away. There are numerous instances where the wind stops blowing across the entire country for extended periods.

The intermittent, unreliable nature of wind energy is portrayed in Figure 7-1. The data is derived for the month of January 2012 from German grid operator TenneT which provides electrical grid service to Northwest Germany and the Netherlands.[108] Extensive analysis on this topic is provided in the Appendix. The curve shows onshore wind-generated power flow fed into the German grid at 15-minute intervals throughout the month. A look at the curve shows a highly variable pattern of wind power ranging between a high power flow of 9,769 mW at 4:30 PM on January 3rd to a low value of 54 mW at 12:30 PM on January 15th.[109]

Throughout the month, power flow averaged 3,891.5 mW, about 40% of rated capacity. But on January 15th, a low pressure system descended over Northwestern Germany that shut down wind power almost completely in every region. Throughout a nine and a half hour period beginning at 10:15 AM, power flow dropped to double digit levels and remained below 100 mW until 7:30 PM. It was fortunate that January 15th was a Sunday, so demand was low. During a sustained 54 ½ hour period between 11:15 AM on the 27th and 5:30 PM on the 29th, power output dropped below 1,400 mW throughout the entire period, averaging only about 747 mW.

FIGURE 7-1. **TenneT Wind Power Fluctuations — January 2012**

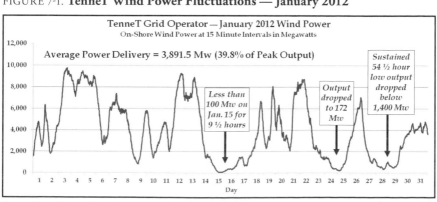

Source: TenneT Actual Wind Energy Feed-In for January 2012

Skeptical readers might conclude the results shown in the chart are atypical. In actuality, January was the second windiest month of the year in terms of wind power output as Figure A-8 in the Appendix shows. Despite that fact, January still exhibited a high level of power intermittency. Throughout the entire year, TenneT was able to feed an average of only 2,341.2 mW into the grid. This amounts to about 17% of TenneT's rated power capacity.[110]

To underscore the nightmares that highly variable loads present for German grid operations, it's important to understand the magnitude of wind power intermittency. Nothing represents that severity better than the fact that more than 40% of the 15-minute power flow intervals recorded by grid operator TenneT during the year were feeding power at levels less than one-tenth of total rated capacity.[111]

A look at the annual wind power flow depicted in Figure A-2 in the Appendix shows a same highly variable pattern. Throughout most of the year, the total wind power output is well below 3,000 mW. During the 167 day period from the morning of April 2nd until the morning of September 16th, some 86% of 15-minute interval readings from the grid operator were feeding less than 3,000 mW. More than 40% of those readings were below 1,000 mW, just 7% of rated capacity. Despite claims that the rated capacity would be able to power 14.8 million homes, the actual capability was only a small fraction of this amount throughout most of the year.[112] And when power dropped to almost nothing as it did on at least twenty three occasions, the system was able to power essentially zero homes. Power flow actually dropped to below 1% of rated capacity during 450 of the 15-minute segments in the year representing more than four and a half total days of operation. Intermittency causes grid controllers to intervene more than twice as often to prevent grid collapse as they did just a few years ago.[113]

Another problem concerns the abruptness with which severe power drops and surges occur due to highly variable wind conditions. Figure A-5 in the Appendix shows sixteen instances where sudden power drops of 85% or greater magnitude occurred within twenty four hour periods during 2012. Section 12 of the EEG law obligates grid providers to notify renewable energy providers at least a day in advance of how they plan to manage the provider's output twenty four hours hence. But power levels can be wiped out within time intervals less than the notification window the law requires. The EEG law requires grid operators to become fortune tellers.[114] One can foresee liability litigation arising in future from grid operators' negligence for failing to forecast weather events to a high degree of certainty.

STORAGE "SOLUTIONS" TO BALANCE INTERMITTENCY

It is generally recognized that the 'green energy' vision won't work without massive deployment of electrical storage capacity — the "holy grail" of intermittent power integration.[115] The long-term vision to overcome renewable energy intermittency involves constructing a massive network of energy storage systems that could provide steady dispatchable power to accommodate smooth demand patterns in conjunction with highly variable supply. Germany's "environmentally-friendly" solution will be to shear apart thousands of breath-taking mountain vistas to construct dams and pumped-storage plants to accommodate a technically unworkable 'green energy' plan.[116] Backers insist upon being granted exemptions from lawsuits and environmental regulations.[117]

One idea is to transport surplus intermittent power to pumped-storage plants in neighboring Norway.[118] Some of these hydroelectric facilities work both uphill and downhill, so they can accommodate pumped-storage. But there are numerous problems associated with this idea.

First, there would need to be a massive network of high-capacity underground cables to transport surplus power hundreds of kilometers to storage stations. This would entail heavy extra costs. But this option seems remote as Norwegian power industry sources observe that there is little incentive for them to participate.[119] The EU wants member countries of its cross-border grid management system to cough up contributions more than 16 times higher than current payment levels.[120] Norway has little incentive to build links after seeing its annual contributions rise from 70 million kroner to 1.15 billion.[121]

Secondly, other Baltic and North Sea neighboring countries have also deployed copious amounts of wind power. Experiencing the same intermittency problems, they are looking to dump their extra surge power onto Norway's storage dams. Both Germany and the UK want to build 1,400 megawatt undersea cables to Norway.[122] There is not enough storage capacity in Norway to accept all of the surplus power. So German utility companies are looking at even more distant regions like Balkan countries where existing hydroelectric and pumped-storage exploitation is low.[123] In addition, there is enormous energy lost in this inefficient storage solution.

By contrast, under pressure from environmentalists, the U.S. has been following a long-term program of dismantling hydroelectric dams to restore natural habitats.[124] While they don't liberate CO_2, hydroelectric dams wreak profoundly negative environmental impacts on the landscape and the animals that inhabit the surroundings.[125] Since NOAA adopted the Open Rivers Initiative in 2005, it has removed more than 90 dams and stream blockages.[126] But environmentally advanced Europe is busy scouring its natural landscapes, blocking pathways for migrating fish, flooding terrestrial habitats, chopping up its open spaces, submerging vibrant forest lands, and wiring the ocean floor to install high-voltage transmission cables to make its 'green energy' program more expensive and slightly more workable. This is an example of how twenty-first century environmentalists destroy the environment in the name of saving the planet.

The sheer scale of additional hydroelectric pumped-storage, and the amount of investment required, brings perspective to the issue. Holger Gassner at RWE Innogy observes that annual electricity consumption in Germany amounts to about 450 terawatt-hours.[127] That breaks down to about 12.3 terawatt-hours for a ten-day period. But current pumped storage capacity in Germany only amounts to 7,000 megawatts, enough to generate 0.04 terawatt-hours of energy when emptied. To meet ten days of power needed during periods of sustained wind inactivity, pumped storage capacity would need to expand 313 times larger than at present.[128] So the back-breaking cost increase that German energy consumers are suffering under at present is only the tip of a very large iceberg. There will be plenty more in store when renewables account for a majority of power requirements if the country wants to provide a load-balancing mechanism to overcome intermittency.

And all these grandiose visions assume that the German public will simply accept a program that would require massive changes to natural landscapes, disruption to water protection zones, and degradation of natural habitats of endangered species to install holding ponds and pumped storage stations. Widespread public opposition to expansion plans at the storage plant at Schluchsee Lake in the Black Forest makes clear, there is little chance this vision could ever come into fruition.[129]

Another even wilder idea in the works to overcome intermittency involves drawing excess electricity into a hydrogen-hybrid station to produce hydrogen gas for storage and eventual re-conversion to electricity. At an opening ceremony for a proof-of-concept technology demonstration plant at Prenzlau in November 2011, Brandenburg Prime Minister Matthias Platzeck was effusive in his praise for the project telling physics-challenged members of the press corps:

> *The hydrogen-hybrid power station is providing a real boost! This project is an innovative, practicable and efficient contribution to be more climate-friendly.*[130]

Physicist Angela Merkel attended the plant's groundbreaking ceremony in 2009.[131] Green media hailed it a "first," extolling its revolutionary, innovative, and path-breaking design. Why hadn't anyone thought of this before? Just utilize excess electricity in electrolytic separation and use the stored hydrogen to power turbines when you need the power. It seemed so simple. PM Platzeck had assured media attendees that the project was "efficient."

Let's see how efficient the concept really is. Platzeck never mentioned and no one in the media was well enough schooled in the laws of thermodynamics to ask about all the energy loss that occurs with each conversion in the storage and release cycle. As any physics student knows, every time energy is converted from one form to another, energy in the form of waste heat is lost. Look at the concept in each successive stage. When the alternating current from the wind turbine is converted to direct current for electrolysis, about 10% of the energy is lost. Another 25% of the energy is lost in waste heat during electrolysis as electrical energy splits apart a molecule of H_2O to produce hydrogen. Finally, when the hydrogen output from electrolysis is burned in gas generators to re-convert back into electricity, a 70% energy loss is suffered.[132] Collectively, the energy loss amounts to about 80% of the originally produced electricity. So this process becomes many times more expensive than the original surplus wind power when it is ultimately harvested.

Based upon the relative cost data of German energy production, onshore wind electricity was 1.5 times more expensive and offshore wind was 2.5 times more expensive to generate as coal-fired electricity.[133] Then the surplus wind electricity undergoes inefficient hydrogen storage and reconversion, which causes at least 80% of the surplus energy to be sacrificed. That means the stored electricity now costs about 7.5 times more to deliver as conventional power sources. In addition, the staggering capital, maintenance and operations costs of these hydrogen storage and conversion plants will add greatly to this relative cost disadvantage. This is a 'green energy' proponent's idea of "efficient" energy. This is the real reason why no one had tried this before. It's idiotic.

A vestige of Soviet era days is that Germany's grid interconnections with its Eastern neighbors are better developed than those between Germany's north and south. Most of Germany's wind turbines are located in the country's northern and eastern regions.[134] Excess wind power from those wind farms pours into the grids of Poland and the Czech Republic during winter peak generation months. But with 8,885 megawatts of wind power having been deployed between 2007 and 2012, the power surges that occur on windy days are threatening the stability and safety of Polish and Czech grids.[135] Both countries have installed phase-shifter transformer switches to shut off German wind power during such periods, which will make the German grid more unstable as it won't be able to offload wind power surges onto its former Warsaw bloc neighbors.[136]

To forestall this outcome, German grid operators agreed to install an expensive "virtual transformer," the cost of which German ratepayers will be forced to absorb.[137] The region-wide instability has rendered Germany "the electric island in the European energy network."[138] Germany's 'green energy' has caused it to overstay its welcome on Polish, Czech, Hungarian, and Slovak grids. Its ability to export ever greater amounts of excess wind power is rapidly reaching its limit.[139]

Excess wind power is not the only problem. On a sunny day, Germany will see its output of solar power ramp from zero at 6AM, to 16,000 megawatts or even higher by midday, and then back down to zero by 6PM. Between January and October 2012, Germany exported 10.3 terawatt-hours (tWh) to France and 4.8 tWh to the Czech Republic at very low prices.[140] The portion that cannot be absorbed on neighboring grids gets grounded.[141] France has substantial hydro capacity that can more easily absorb and balance excess power. The Czech grid cannot, forcing the Czechs to build a switch to shut off Germany's excess. So Germany subsidizes production of vast quantities of solar power at between €0.30 to €0.60 per kilowatt-hour, exports some of it to neighboring countries at a fraction of the cost, and electrocutes the dirt wasting the rest that can't be offloaded.[142]

Another curious aspect about excess flow of power pouring into neighboring country grids is the impact it has upon market pricing. The flood of wind power depresses wholesale power prices in Poland and the Czech Republic which undercuts the economic incentive to construct new baseload power capacity in those countries.[143] And some of that excess power actually finds its way through "loop flows" back into Germany via interconnections in Austria.[144] Efforts to maintain grid stability cost more than €500 million for power plant shutdowns and restarts across eight northern and central EU member states in 2008, costs that were borne by ratepayers.[145]

Germany's embrace of 'green energy' has caused industry, capital, and jobs to flee, led to massive increases in the cost of power for consumers, increased the level of uncertainty in the utility and grid operator industries, unbalanced the economic landscape of traditionally low-risk baseload power generation investments, boosted emissions of CO_2, stressed the grids of neighboring countries, caused a massive drain on public finances as subsidies are paid to produce power that can't be used, and fomented a rent-seeking and lobbying free-for-all in Berlin. This is the arrangement that Europe's 'green energy' enthusiasts refer to as a "sustainable" energy future.[146]

CHAPTER 8

PROMOTING ECONOMIC DECLINE

"It's a complex fate, being an American, & one of the responsibilities it entails is fighting against a superstitious valuation of Europe."[1]

HENRY JAMES

"Things are a mess. If you want to solve the climate problem, you have to begin at the international level. It's going to be very hard to convince Europe to go it alone and impose costs on itself that the rest of the world isn't accepting."[2]

BRIAN RICKETTS
SECRETARY GENERAL OF THE EUROPEAN COAL ASSOCIATION

The EU is on a collision course with fiscal and economic ruination. Its 'green energy' program deserves a large measure of the credit. In what can only be described as a "Fox Butterfield moment," *The New York Times* observed that "Europe is lurching through an energy crisis that in many respects parallels its seemingly unending economic crisis."[3] To the paper's Stanley Reed, it was a tragic, inexplicable coincidence. The *Times'* clueless correspondent Fox Butterfield years ago was similarly puzzled over the bewildering paradox of "more inmates despite drop in crime," unable to make the causal connection between higher incarceration rates and the corresponding drop in crime as more bad guys were taken off the streets.[4] Reed seems equally incapable of recognizing that Europe's wholehearted embrace of ruinously expensive 'green energy' is one of the chief culprits in the region's economic demise. Just as Butterfield was ideologically obligated to doubt that incarceration was a potential solution to high crime rates, Reed is predisposed to genuflect at Europe's renewable energy mandate, laughingly describing Germany's costly program a "success."

Amazingly, *Reuters* seconds Reed's silly sentiments, also calling Merkel's plan a "success." This is the plan that is bleeding the country's ratepayers dry, causing as many as 800,000 Germans to lose their power completely, ballooning subsidy payments that may reach into the trillions of Euros, degrading the viability of the electric utility sector, and causing a virtual shut-down of energy-intensive industry that employs a million workers.[5] Credit Suisse estimates that the subsidies enacted to incentivize implementation of the EU's costly "success" carry a present value price tag of $725 billion. The Swiss banking house describes the arrangement as already "unaffordable," draining away as much as 6% of gross domestic product from Europe's largest power markets.[6] Most people hold a different view of "success" than the ideologues at *The New York Times* and *Reuters*.

Bloomberg claims that utilities are expected to absorb a quarter of the cost while consumers will be on the hook for the rest.[7] The notion that utility investors will simply absorb these punitive cost increases without causing capital flight that will need to be backfilled through public subsidies is wishful thinking. Europe's system ratepayers will eventually foot 100% of the bill.

In the eyes of the Swiss bank advisory team, the negative impact this liability imposes "should be considered a problem alongside the Eurozone crisis."[8] Like Stanley Reed, Credit Suisse also has trouble making the connection. The renewable build-out, even at relatively low penetration rates in place in 2012, has resulted in a reduction of wholesale power prices by between four to nine Euros per megawatt-hour, which has decreased utility earnings by €10.2 billion per year.[9]

On one side of the ledger, large increases in expensive renewable energy have stressed the cost structure of utilities' power production. On the revenue side, a surplus of renewable power has driven down power prices and revenue streams to conventional power producers leading to a surge in price volatility.[10] The proliferation of solar panels on residential rooftops producing power at peak times when power prices are highest has also greatly reduced the amount of high-margin power demand, cutting into once-profitable revenue streams for utility suppliers.[11] Formerly stable companies that relied upon predictable revenue, cost and earnings patterns offering investors a low-risk, stable return proposition have seen their risk profiles upended.[12] Hardest hit are pension funds whose recipients rely upon payouts from securities offering stable, predictable returns.

Credit rating agency Moody's observed that Germany's focus on renewables has had "a profound negative impact" upon prices and power producers. The basic creditworthiness of German utilities has been degraded as a result:

> *Large increases in renewables have had a profound negative impact on power prices and the competitiveness of thermal generation companies in Europe. What were once considered stable companies have seen their business models severely disrupted and we expect steadily rising levels of renewable energy output to further affect European utilities' credit-worthiness.*[13]

A peculiar result of the law is that it has driven conventional power generation into unprofitability because grid operators are obligated to give preference to subsidized 'green energy' sources over reliable fossil fueled power.[14] To prevent overload, conventional power plants frequently need to be shut down, cutting further into utilities' revenue base.

By the end of 2012, the German Wind Energy Association boasted that over 30,000 mW of rated wind power had been installed from 22,614 wind turbines.[15] But over the course of the year, the country would derive an average of only about 5,100 mW from all of that rated capacity. Intermittency highlights the absolute necessity for fossil-fuel backup capacity in the grid. But as opposed to a steady flow of power generation revenues, those plants will also experience highly variable patterns of stop-start operation, and highly uncertain revenue patterns to match. As the level of revenue uncertainty for fossil fuel standby increases, so too will the cost of raising capital funds in the future. Moody's warns this is not a temporary condition:

Given that further increases in renewables are expected, these negative pressures will continue to erode the credit quality of thermal-based utilities in the near to medium term.[16]

With fossil fuel generators operating at a loss, some may be forced to close. Utility giant RWE announced in August 2013 they would shut down as much as 7% of Northern European generating plant capacity because the plants are no longer profitable to operate.[17] The company's statement makes clear that "Due to the continuing boom in solar energy, many power stations throughout the sector and across Europe are no longer profitable to operate."[18] A total of 3,100 mW of generating capacity will be shuttered.[19] RWE's operating profit in the first half of 2013 plunged by two-thirds over the year earlier.[20] The profit decline was limited by the fact that RWE had sold most of its output in forward markets years earlier at higher prices than in 2013.[21] Had it not done so, profits would have plunged even further. RWE and competitor E.On which is making similar moves, have warned that the instability will eventually endanger Germany's long-term energy generating security.[22] E.On took 6,500 mW of capacity offline in 2013 in response to the market deterioration, which was in addition to 11,000 mW of idled capacity previously announced.[23]

These two power providers have experienced steady erosion in their financial conditions, which has taken an enormous toll on their market valuations. Each company's valuation declined by more than two-thirds over the five years from 2007. RWE's market capitalization declined at a compound annual rate of 20.5% over the 5-year period to early December 2012[24] while E.On market capitalization declined by 22.7% per year over the same period.[25] A combined €26.8 billion in market value of the two utility operators was wiped out in 2011 alone.[26] E.On cut its dividend in 2013, sold off assets, and cut capital spending.[27] The utility also placed its 2014 and 2015 earnings outlook under review.[28] The top 20 European utility companies shed more than a half a trillion euros in capitalization value from 2008 through September 2013.[29] To stay afloat, utility operators will be required to seek government subsidies.[30] Moody's foresees a three-way subsidies battle-royale between renewable generators, utility companies, and network operators.[31]

Businesses unable to cope with higher energy prices and grid unreliability have shifted production and jobs offshore.[32] The domestic investment climate suffers from the uncertainties of an ever-evolving political landscape.[33] German citizens pick up the tab for subsidies paid to 'green energy' producers.[34] The European Commission estimated that these subsidy outlays had already totaled €130.2 billion by 2003.[35] Eight years later, those outlays had soared to a staggering €636.7 billion, which were predominantly borne by German electricity ratepayers.[36] Figures from the German Federal Ministry for the Environment, Nature Conservation and Nuclear Safety show feed-in tariff payments since 1991 growing at a compound rate of more than 25% per year over a 20-year period. Solar energy subsidies alone had surpassed €100 billion by 2011.[37]

As the proportion of renewable energy grows, the amount of fossil energy will continue to decline. But substantial conventional power capacity will always be required to deal with the intermittent, unreliable nature of renewable sources. This may necessitate capacity mechanisms where governments would guarantee revenue levels to fossil fuel providers through yet another subsidy arrangement, the cost of which would be passed on to consumers.[38] These subsidies will become quite expensive because the intermittent nature of renewable energy necessitates an amount of under-utilized standby fossil capacity that could be a very high proportion of total German power requirements to avoid service outages. Experience in California and Texas that have deployed a large wind capacity footprint show that backup generation needs to be 100% of peak capacity to cover the periods throughout the year when renewable energy disappears.

Massive publicly-funded infrastructure investments are being channeled into high-risk, low-return, hugely uncertain energy projects. And worst of all, Germany must endure a media culture that continuously counsels the wisdom of bearing any burden and suffering any economic hardship to maintain the disastrous course.[39] America must also suffer its own 'green energy' zealots who, with their willful blindness and their highly fictionalized one-sided portrayals, pretend that Germany's energy fiasco is a model worth emulating in the U.S.[40] Take it from 'green energy' cheerleaders at *The Economist*:

Renewable energy has grabbed a growing share of the market, pushed wholesale prices down and succeeded in its goal of driving down the price of new technologies. But the subsidy cost also has been large, the environmental gains non-existent so far, and the damage done to today's utilities much greater than expected.[41]

SUBSIDIZING ECONOMIC INEFFICIENCY

At the same time as her nuclear plant closure announcement, Merkel established a goal that by the year 2050, the country will derive 80% of its electricity from renewable sources like wind, solar and biomass.[42] As of the end of 2012, Germany was already deriving about 25% from these costly sources.[43] Fossil fueled electricity generating plants were mothballed, prices for power at the consumer level soared, shortages occurred, and the net result was a political catastrophe that could have even endangered the Chancellor's political survival.[44] Indeed, it would have if not for the fact that her opposition is an even more vocal proponent of the 'green energy' arrangement.

Under the German program, individual consumers, businesses and co-ops are incentivized to deploy investment capital installing distributed solar and wind power capacity through a subsidy arrangement. While wind capacity additions have become ubiquitous, particularly in coastal regions, solar installations represent the source of deepest renewable energy penetration. By the end of 2010, the EU accounted for 74% of the entire world's solar power capacity with Germany accounting for more than half of that.[45]

All of this investment has occurred despite the fact that the entirety of Germany's land mass resides above of 47 degrees north latitude. Of course, a steep angle of incidence like this means that it does not represent ideal solar power generation conditions. Cloud cover is also problematic. German cities receive between 1,250 and 1,850 hours of sunlight per year and average only about 1,600 hours.[46] That paltry amount compares to a city like Phoenix that gets about 4,000 hours of sunlight each year.[47] Jürgen Grossmann, former CEO of German utility giant RWE, calls subsidizing solar energy in Germany about as sensible as subsidizing pineapple farming in Alaska.[48]

Nevertheless, when conditions are favorable, Germany can pump out record-breaking amounts of solar power. On May 26, 2012 when the sun was just a few weeks from its northern latitude summer solstice maximum, temperatures were mild and cloud cover across the country was minimal, Germany established a world record 22 gigawatts of solar power production during midday, an amount of power output equivalent to over 20 nuclear power stations at full capacity.[49] That equated to almost 50% of the country's entire power requirements. The surge lasted for about an hour. The event occurred on a weekend when most offices and factories were closed and air conditioners were turned off.

Even more salient was the hugely variable power generation profile of the two primary intermittent sources, wind and solar power, on that day. Grid operators were forced to manage wildly erratic power output that ranged from less than 5,000 megawatts just before dawn to about 27,000 megawatts at around 1:00 PM.[50] Because May 26th was a Saturday, midday power needs were far lower than on a weekday when a surge of this magnitude could have more easily been integrated into the grid.

A similar thing happened on June 16, 2013 when solar power flooding onto the grid amounted to 60% of total country-wide demand, forcing wholesale electricity prices into negative territory.[51] The renewables output surge reached nearly 28 megawatts.[52] While this sounds impressive, Germany only derives about 4% of its total electricity requirements from solar power throughout the entire year.[53] By contrast, the country derives about 7.7% of its annual electrical power requirements from onshore and offshore wind.[54]

Not surprisingly, Natural Resources Defense Council attorney Robert F. Kennedy, Jr. perpetrated an *Alar*-style hoax in the pages of *The New York Times* falsely claiming that rooftop solar panels in Germany "provide close to 50 percent of the nation's power."[55] The paper had to print a deeply embarrassing retraction several days later after being inundated with rebuttals.[56] It might be thought surprising that the *Times* would allow itself to be scammed by a notorious anti-science zealot like Kennedy who has earned a reputation for peddling crackpot theories that have all been thoroughly debunked.[57] But it's not.

It's hardly surprising that Germany can harvest so much solar power despite its unfavorable climatic and geographic positioning. The high solar penetration level is due to exorbitant subsidies for solar deployment. The EEG law established a feed-in tariff that guaranteed producers of solar power €0.57 per kilowatt-hour (kWh) for the solar energy.[58] At exchange rates in effect in April 2013, that electricity subsidy rate equated to more than 6.3 times the average of residential electricity rates paid by American home-owners in 2011.[59] *Der Spiegel* ridiculously describes the arrangement where ratepayers fork over staggering amounts of money as a mechanism to bring about "fair market competitiveness":

> *The goal of the law was to encourage investment and help bring the cost of energy from technologies like solar panels and wind farms into fair market competitiveness with coal, nuclear or gas.*[60]

Der Spiegel thinks that this subsidy arrangement where German ratepayers pay an amount more than eight times the cost of wholesale power constitutes fairness. Would you think it was fair if your co-worker earned eight times your pay rate for doing exactly the same amount of equivalently-valued work? Even taking into account the relatively high cost of solar photovoltaic (PV) power — the U.S. DoE pegs solar photovoltaic generation at 3.2 times more expensive than conventional combined cycle natural gas generation[61] — this generous subsidy represents a powerful economic inducement to install solar capacity. For the same amount of subsidy expenditure, wind power supplies five times and hydroelectric generates six times the amount of power as does solar.[62] Solar energy soaks up 56% of all renewable energy subsidies but produces only 21% of subsidized electricity.[63] But German media describe this highly unbalanced arrangement as a "fair market." Presumably it would have also been "fair" if Usain Bolt had been required to carry a refrigerator on his back to even out competition at the Olympic 100-meter sprint.

Since all of these imponderable arrangements were put into place to reduce CO_2 emissions, it's useful to consider the relative economic efficiency with which competing carbon-reduction schemes achieve that goal. To eliminate the same quantity of CO_2 emission, Germany could spend €1 on building insulation or, €4 on installing a natural gas power generation capacity. But to achieve that same CO_2 reduction with solar energy, €100 is required.[64] Naturally, as with any central planning approach, all the money is going into solar generating capacity since it offers the lowest possible return on investment for taxpayers.

Another economic incongruity to consider is the sheer cost of photovoltaic solar panel production. It takes anywhere from four years to as many as nine years of solar power generation before the energy required to produce a PV panel is even recouped in solar power output.[65] Solar photovoltaic electricity in Germany is still five times more expensive than a new nuclear plant being built in Finland even though that plant was originally projected to cost $4 billion but will eventually cost $11 billion and will be delayed by seven years.[66]

In October 2012, Germany's four largest power grid operators announced surcharge increases of 47% for 2013, from 3.6 to 5.3 Euro cents per kilowatt-hour.[67] It will rise another 17-22% in 2014.[68] The surcharge is calculated as the difference between guaranteed prices allotted to producers of the higher cost renewable energy and the cost of conventional sources.[69] The German government promised consumers that "the amount paid by every electricity consumer to subsidize renewable energies is to remain unchanged at around 3.5 Euro cents per kilowatt-hour."[70] That promise has a familiar ring: "if you like your affordable power, you can keep it. " Electricity is fast becoming a luxury good in Germany.[71]

A surcharge of 6.5 Euro cents scheduled for 2014 would boost electricity rates to the average residential ratepayer in the U.S. by over 74% and add more that $987 per year to the average American consumer's electricity bill.[72] Chancellor Merkel assured the country in a Bundestag speech in 2011 that the country's transition to renewable energy would not lead to any increase in cost — "the EEG assessment should not increase above its current level" she said. There might even be "room for decreases" claimed German Economics Minister Philipp Rösler.[73] The only decreases that occurred were in personal income and consumer discretionary spending. Due to the unaffordable explosion in solar deployment since 2000, solar power installations will have to be capped at 1,000 megawatts per year through the year 2020.[74]

All of the previous predictions about the amount of solar and wind power that would be deployed have turned out to be disastrously wrong by astonishing degrees. A 1998 study by German think tank Prognos forecasted solar photovoltaic deployment would produce 0.44 terawatt-hours of energy by the year 2020.[75] Germany was deriving ten times as much as that by 2008, a full 12 years earlier than forecast. As late as 2005, the soothsayers at Prognos were back at it again, preparing a forecast for the Federal Economics Ministry of the amount of 'green energy' that would be produced in 2030. That predicted level was achieved just two years later in 2007.[76] The odious Greens Party leader Jürgen Trittin[77] infamously predicted in 2004 that the EEG law would cost German households "only about one Euro per month — as much as a scoop of ice cream."[78] That forecast was off by a factor of nearly twenty. The German Institute for Aerospace baseline estimate of the amount of solar power that would be deployed by 2010 was only one sixth of the 7,400 megawatts actually installed.[79] The Association of Renewable Energy (BEE) assured German ratepayers in 2009 that subsidies would amount to only €5.6 billion by 2013.[80] At €20.4 billion, subsidies had already reached nearly four times that amount in 2012.[81]

FIGURE 8-1. **Residential Electricity Prices in Germany 2008 to 2013**

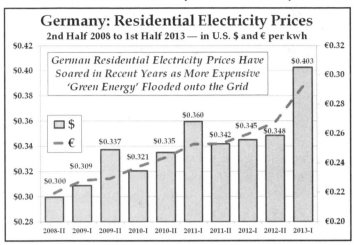

Sources: Eurostat, European Commission, Electricity prices for domestic consumers, second half 2008 to first half 2013, bi-annual data; *Yahoo Finance* U.S. Dollar—Euro exchange rate

As a result of the massive cost of subsidies for renewable energy, German households pay the second highest electricity rates in the EU at 29.2 Euro cents per kWh for the first half of 2013, more than $0.40 in U.S. dollar terms.[82] This is 3.4 times the $0.1184 rate that U.S. households paid on average in 2012.[83] Figure 8.1 shows how residential electricity prices have continued to soar relentlessly upward over recent years.

It's not difficult to understand why electricity prices continue to climb to unaffordable levels in Germany. As more and more costly renewable energy floods onto the grid, the subsidy costs that need to be borne by residential ratepayers are layered into the rate structure that consumers must pay. According to an industry analyst, German onshore wind is about 50% higher in cost than coal power while solar photovoltaic energy more than 3.2 times more expensive.[84] So the rate continues to climb. Those relative ratios closely track DoE figures in the Annual Energy Outlook 2012.[85]

But there is a problem with the values given above since German wind only achieves about half of the capacity yield that U.S. wind turbines generate on average. DoE cost numbers assume a 34% capacity realization from wind while Germany only achieved 17.3% in 2012.[86] In other words, German on-shore wind costs about 96% more than U.S. wind does.[87]

German consumers complain that the EEG arrangement has led to a two-tiered system of rates and charges. Residential ratepayers and many small companies pay far higher electricity rates than large manufacturing companies.[88] An estimated 1,550 large companies received lucrative exemptions from paying renewable energy surcharges in 2013.[89] Industrial corporate consumers paying spot prices at the European Energy Exchange (EEX) in Leipzig enjoyed rates as low as six Euro cents per kilowatt-hour compared to residential rates that are five times higher.[90] Meanwhile, surcharges on companies not exempt exceeded €4 billion in 2013.[91]

With a flood of solar energy continuing unabated, wholesale rates continued to set record low levels, with forward contracts for electricity delivered in 2014 plunging €0.0362 in August 2013.[92] Consumers are not the only ones complaining. Competitors that do not qualify for the low-cost power have complained to the European Commission's competition authorities.[93] If the Commission rules against the subsidy arrangement, it may result in elimination of the two-tiered pricing, even requiring companies to repay billions of Euros.[94] This would speed up the exodus of Germany's industry. A German antitrust court in Düsseldorf ruled in March 2013 in favor of five utility companies that complained the arrangement violated the German constitution.[95]

Meanwhile, residential electricity rates increased 12.5% in 2013, the largest increase in over a decade.[96] Since 2000, the year when the EEG plan was enacted, residential electricity rates in Germany increased at an annual rate of 5.5% per year.[97] By contrast, residential electricity prices in the U.S. rose only 1.4% per year between January 2008 and mid-2012.[98] Observers forecast that residential rates will reach 40 Euro cents per kWh by 2020.[99] That would be almost five times the amount the average U.S. household pays.

Writing in the pages of *Forbes*, Cato Institute economists Jerry Taylor and Peter Van Doren characterize the situation in place today as an example of a phenomenon called "price suppression" where a surplus of renewable power produced during inopportune periods is offloaded onto wholesale markets at very low prices.[100] Many 'green energy' enthusiasts proclaim that this is beneficial to power consumers because they enjoy lower prices. But this claim is unfounded. In reality, the savings enjoyed by wholesale power buyers is far less than the cost of subsidies required to produce it. The subsidies are paid mostly by modest-income consumers while the savings are enjoyed exclusively by deep-pocketed corporate consumers. The lower wholesale prices have been accompanied by a severe spike in price volatility, a measure of chaos in the system.[101]

Existing base-load power producers suffer as renewable power surges force shut-downs at lower-cost non-renewable generation stations.[102] Worst of all, this wealth transfer from poor to rich consumers does not result in enhanced economic performance. Taylor and Van Doren point out that the "wealth transfer from existing non-renewable energy producers to consumers is the source of the reduced prices rather than an overall improvement in economic efficiency."[103] It is tragic that Germany's 'green energy' program inspired by collectivist impulses results in efficient wealth distribution — from poor people to the wealthy.

The predictable result is that fuel poverty has exploded.[104] Over 800,000 households in Germany can no longer afford to pay their electricity bills.[105] To help contain the political fallout, Chancellor Merkel reined in the subsidies paid to residential producers of renewable energy.[106] The German Parliament cut solar subsidy payments by 29%.[107] This measure was adopted to stem the highly unpopular runaway cost increases of renewable energy.[108]

EXPANDING ARRAY OF ECONOMIC DISLOCATIONS

Germany's program of subsidizing uneconomic 'green energy' has resulted in a number of destabilizing economic distortions. One distortion has led to a series of perverse incentives in renewable energy compensation schedules. As expected, renewable energy generators operate in a manner designed to maximize subsidies rather than in a way that optimizes power output.[109]

A distortion in the pricing mechanism causes wind farm operators to deploy generating capacity to take advantage of temporarily lucrative subsidy rates long before transmission infrastructure is in place to connect the power they produce to the grid.[110] And arcane rules force grid operators to build grid links long before wind farms that would be served by those installations have even been built.[111] So subsidy payments will flow to operators of offshore wind projects long before the power generated can flow onto the grid. Likewise, Germans pay for grid connections long before wind farm power begins to flow.

Another distortion concerns the imbalance between the amount of power consumed vs. the method by which consumption costs are apportioned among users. The country's largest power-intensive industries consume 18% of Germany's electricity but bear only 0.3% of the subsidy costs associated with the EEG arrangement.[112]

Yet another distortion requires renewable power producers to be paid for power even when the output they produce can't be accepted onto the grid. Section 12 of the EEG law requires mandatory compensation to power providers whenever any of their output is lost. Power curtailments subject to Section 12 reimbursement payments more than tripled between 2010 and 2011.[113] The Ministry of Environment's EEG progress report indicated that those same payments had increased 700% between 2004 and 2009.[114] As 'green energy' scale expands linearly, curtailment reimbursement increases exponentially. German energy consultancy EIKE explains that Section 12 establishes a perverse incentive to destabilize the grid as these payments increase to 100% of expected compensation if the payment amounts exceed 1% of the provider's annual revenue.[115]

Still another distortion is the fact that the pricing structure for wholesale power can often become inverted due to competitive pressure. Prior to introduction of large amounts of wind and solar power, wholesale prices for daylight power that coincided with peak demand would be many times higher than night time prices. These pricing differentials reflect a rational demand-based pricing mechanism as seen elsewhere. But high solar power output during daylight hours drives down daytime wholesale prices to the point that the market often sees zero or even "negative prices" as payments must be made to hydroelectric pumped-storage plants in Austria to accept surplus power produced in Germany.[116] Negative prices had never occurred prior to the EEG law.[117]

A similar situation occurs for wind power. Historically, wholesale prices for night time generation were already at very low levels reflecting the substantial decrease in demand. But during some months, winds are stronger at night. Power levels fed from wind power installations at night are higher during those periods than during daylight hours. As more offshore wind installations are deployed, market analysts expect wholesale pricing structures for night time power to collapse due to supply-demand mismatch as night time supply surges occur when demand drops substantially.[118]

Conventional power producers traditionally relied upon higher daytime prices to augment revenues and return on capital. But with a bountiful output of solar power on some days and not on others, opportunistically higher daylight prices are no longer available on a predictable basis. As revenue patterns have become variable and unstable, utility risk levels are much higher, causing the investment prospect for capacity replacement to become distorted and deeply degraded. These realities come as no surprise to economic historians who marvel at the power of technocratic social science geniuses to delude themselves into believing they can out-think rational market mechanisms.

RENEWABLE ENERGY BOOSTS CO$_2$ EMISSIONS

The EU adopted the world's first carbon "cap-and-trade" scheme in 2005 called the Emission Trading System (ETS).[119] By limiting the amount of CO$_2$ emissions from power production, the system was designed to drive up the cost of fossil fuel usage and provide an economic incentive for alternative energy. Instead, it provided an economic incentive to reduce levels of economic activity in Europe as a flood of producers moved investment and operations offshore.[120]

Rather than doing what it was designed to do, exactly the opposite outcome resulted. Carbon emission permit prices have sunk to all-time lows after a few short years of trading.[121] Leftists are in a panic noting that carbon prices are "inching ever closer to zero."[122] After carbon prices on the ETS plunged to an all-time low price below €4.80 per metric ton in late January 2013,[123] the carbon market opened on January 24th and prices promptly dropped 40% to an intra-day low of €2.81 per metric ton within the first 30 seconds of trading.[124] Germany cancelled a carbon credits auction in early 2013 because there were no bids received at the minimum price established under the rules.[125] Stated more forthrightly, the auction cancelled itself.

Editors at *The Economist* attribute the ETS failure to an over-supply of permits, saying the carbon-trading scheme "had not been working well, largely because too many permits to emit carbon had been issued."[126] It reality, it was due to a lack of demand resulting from reduced economic growth caused by Germany's 'green energy' policies. On April 16th, the European Parliament rejected a proposal to boost emission permit prices by limiting the number of new permits.[127] *Der Spiegel* called it "the end of a European climate policy."[128] News of the vote outcome sent permit prices plunging to €2.55 per metric ton at one point.[129] In a second contentious vote, the Parliament approved the measure ten weeks later.[130]

Carbon prices plummeted almost 90% during the five years up to early 2013.[131] When emission prices were high, leftists cheered, a sign they said of market mechanisms were working properly. When prices dropped to just above zero, it was an indication the

EU needed to meddle more deeply to "fix" the problem. It should now be abundantly clear that cap-and-trade was never intended to be a "market solution" as its promoters ridiculously claimed but blunt force trauma to kick-start a wholly unsustainable 'green energy' future. Indeed, the EU's central focus has always been on climate politics rather than rational energy policy. Delusional observers blame declining economic activity for the erosion of climate policy effectiveness, when exactly the opposite is true.[132] The EU's climate policies have been effective at promoting economic decline.

The EU's beloved carbon-pricing mechanism has always been described by supporters in reverential, moralistic tones. The European Parliament's renunciation of it was hilariously described by *The Wall Street Journal* as "the true-believer equivalent of the pope renouncing celibacy."[133] The slow learners of the left should be re-discovering that centrally planned economies are a recipe for failure. One need only consider the case of socialist paradise Venezuela, awash in $100 per barrel oil — the world's largest proven reserves according to the International Energy Agency[134] — and yet with over $100 billion per year in oil revenues, the country still can't locate enough food to feed its populace,[135] keep the lights on,[136] or even supply basic necessities like toilet paper.[137]

The fictitious mechanism to control energy markets was greeted with enthusiasm when first implemented. But the scandal-plagued ETS is now widely viewed as a complete failure.[138] Absurdly, it has actually resulted in coal-fired electricity generation, the worst CO_2 emitting source, looking even more attractive.[139] Emitting carbon from even inefficient coal-fired plants is cheaper than undertaking energy efficiency measures. Incongruously, given that CO_2 causes or contributes to climate change, emissions trading is actually accelerating rather than inhibiting it.[140]

It should be hardly surprising that the ETS is not working properly, let alone helping advance the cause of economic efficiency. Since 1990, Germany has been subsidizing the installation of solar power at a furious pace. And how much do Germans pay to eliminate a single metric ton of CO_2 given their nine-figure investment in solar photovoltaic capacity? According to the economists at RWI, a German economic consultancy, the abatement cost is €716 per ton.[141] This number is an understatement. The International Energy Agency estimates the cost at €1,000 per ton.[142] This is a central planner's concept of cost-effective climate protection.

In what can only be fairly described as a hilarious perversity, the phase-out of nuclear power and the highly intermittent pattern of rapidly growing renewable energy in Germany have together resulted in a pronounced shift *toward* coal power. Coal-fired electricity in Germany had grown from 53% to 68% of total power generation needs in the year up to May 2012.[143] The same thing happened in the first half of 2013.[144] An identical pattern has occurred in the UK, where coal generation plants were all operating at full capacity during 2012, the year when coal usage was supposed to be strangled out of existence by ETS emission permit prices.

Coal is the worst of the CO_2 emitting sources. So naturally the 'green energy' program designed to eliminate CO_2 emission from coal-fired power generation has produced exactly the opposite outcome.[145] Germany commissioned a modern, 2,200 mW coal-fired behemoth at Grevenbroich-Neurath near Cologne in 2011.[146] Since Germany's phase-out of nuclear power in 2011, the EU will emit 43 million metric tons more of carbon dioxide due to increased coal usage for power than in the previous year.[147] The new coal plant near Cologne, though more efficient than its predecessors, will emit more CO_2 in one year than all of Germany's 17 nuclear plants would emit over the next 20 years.[148]

The $3.4 billion Grevenbroich-Neurath lignite coal plant's operator RWE boasts that its revolutionary design permits rapid start and stop to accommodate highly intermittent wind and solar power that receive priority on the grid.[149] This is advertised as a positive feature — that a coal-burning plant which operates more efficiently in steady operation can be stopped and re-started in just minutes to smoothly integrate with variable wind and solar. Just like an automobile which gets about 50% better gas mileage in steady operation on a highway vs. the frequent stop-start profile of city driving, the Grevenbroich-Neurath plant will emit far more CO_2 per unit energy produced due to rapid cycling than if wind and solar were unplugged and the coal plant allowed to operate continuously. This perversity has been seen elsewhere, notably in Colorado and Texas, where engineering studies show that cycling coal plants to accommodate intermittent wind results in a higher emissions footprint than if coal plants were permitted to operate without cycling.[150]

RWE generated only 66% of its power from coal and lignite in the first nine months of 2011. But one year later, the utility was getting 72% of its power from the dirtiest source available during the same nine-month period.[151] This is the polluting fuel that Germany's EEG plan was designed to eliminate. Because natural gas prices are high in Europe, renewable energy is actually displacing natural gas, not the far more emission-intensive coal and lignite.[152] Logic and reason get inverted when renewable energy takes center stage. But this is not new. Germans have known, or at least should have known, for years that all of its investment in renewable energy had never "prohibited the emission of even a single gram of CO_2," according to Der Spiegel.[153]

In conjunction with the hilarious outcomes of Germany's 'green energy' experiment are a few deeply tragic realities. The rising cost of energy is prompting Germans to chop down trees and steal firewood to heat their homes.[154] Increasing numbers of tenants are turning to wood-burning stoves — some 400,000 were purchased in 2011 alone — to pay for heating costs that increased 22% during the winter of 2012-13.[155] A similar situation is taking place in Greece, as the forests slowly disappear to provide wood for heating.[156] So not only is cleaner-burning, more efficient, base-load power being displaced by dirty, soot-belching, CO_2 emitting, local heating appliances like wood stoves. But in addition, the carbon sequestering potential of woodland is being degraded by the 'green energy' program designed to reduce CO_2 emissions.

It is not only economically-distressed householders who are felling trees for energy. Lumber from felled trees is finding its way into wood pellet heaters and biomass-consuming power plants.[157] Timber cutting emits thousands of tons of CO_2 into the atmosphere and does incalculable additional damage, depriving the planet of essential carbon sequestering capability. More than half of the timber harvested from Germany's forests is consumed in this manner.[158] The ancient beech forests of Germany, which were added to the UNESCO list of World Natural Heritage Sites in 2011, are being clear cut to provide "environmentally friendly" biomass to the country's energy portfolio.[159]

Germany could easily reduce its CO_2 footprint substantially by switching coal plants to natural gas, which emits far less CO_2 per unit of energy produced than coal. But gas is much more expensive in Germany than in the U.S. because gas prices are keyed to oil prices under long-term contracts with Russian supplier Gazprom, the continent's largest supplier.[160] Against better advice from the Reagan administration, countries in Western Europe agreed to permit building of natural gas pipelines from the Soviet Union to Western European countries in the 1980s.[161] Countries like Germany and Poland are now largely dependent upon Russian gas supplies imported at prices that are far higher than prices paid elsewhere in the world.[162]

Pipelines are like a marriage.[163] It takes substantial effort to get out. But the lesson apparently hasn't sunk in as the UK is seriously considering extension of Gazprom's Nord Stream pipeline from Germany to the UK.[164] Due to Germany's "marriage" with Gazprom and the high costs it entails, gas-fired generation plants cannot compete with their coal-energy equivalents.[165]

Europe's leading companies and trade groups recognize the competitive disadvantage that wildly overpriced natural gas imposes on Europe's energy-intensive industries, as these costs are spread all throughout the industrial and consumer value chains.[166] German trade group BDI forecasts that the cost of U.S. natural gas-fired electricity generation would remain at around €16 per mWh through the year 2020.[167] That compares to its forecast for the cost of German electricity that would rise from €47 to €61 per mWh over that same time.[168] This is a bone-crushing economic disadvantage for German industries to suffer for an industrial input so essential to modern society. And with complete phase-out of German nuclear power by 2022, the gap will only worsen, further degrading Germany's industrial competitiveness.

A utility that would lose €11 per mWh burning natural gas can profit by €14 per mWh from burning coal.[169] The "clean spark spread," which determines whether gas generation can occur profitably, traded in deep negative territory in forward markets all throughout 2012.[170] In October 2009, when Brent North Sea crude oil prices were trading in the $67 to $77 per barrel range[171] and carbon emission permit prices were far higher, gas generation could yield a profit of about €21 per megawatt-hour.[172] But no longer.

Accordingly, utilities have put gas-fired plants into cold reserve. By the middle of November 2012, German utility giant E.On's 415 mW Irsching-3 gas fired unit had only operated nine days during the year.[173] The company also announced that its 622 mW gas-fired Staudinger-4 unit would be placed into cold reserve.[174] Ridiculously, state-of-the-art, low-emission gas plants are being mothballed in favor of obsolete, inefficient, decades-old, carbon-belching coal plants.[175] This is Euro-style, low-carbon, planet-saving, environmentally exhibitionist climate policy in action.

If you're following here closely, you find the European Union, which never tires of lecturing humanity about how it leads the world in undertaking the necessary actions to save the planet from CO_2 poisoning, now deploying coal-burning power plants at a furious pace.[176] Not only do coal plants emit much more CO_2 than natural-gas fired generation, but by cycling on-and-off to integrate with the vagaries on 'green energy' intermittency, all of these coal plants are required to operate inefficiently. So they emit far more CO_2 than they otherwise would. Meanwhile, the U.S., which failed to sign onto the Kyoto Protocol, regularly a recipient of copious criticism and even condemnation from its moral tutors in Europe for its climate backwardness, is busy unplugging coal-fired utility plants, replacing them with natural gas-fired stations which liberate far less CO_2.[177]

Natural gas power generation has allowed the U.S. to reduce CO_2 emissions by 500 million tons annually compared to a reduction of only half that amount by the Kyoto signatory EU.[178] Accordingly, Kyoto non-signatory U.S. is on pace to reduce its CO_2 emissions derived from energy production to levels lower than 20 years earlier.[179] Hilariously, it has been recognized by proponents for years that Germany's 'green energy' program would not yield any reductions in CO_2 emissions by itself, even if that stunning reality is never acknowledged in public.[180] In truth, the only realistic hope the EU has to reduce CO_2 emissions stems from its strenuous efforts at destroying economic activity, to which the 'green energy' program has been a significant contributing factor.[181]

The EU was the driving force behind the Kyoto treaty limiting emissions of CO_2 by signatory nations. Ever wonder why Kyoto signatories are obligated to reduce emissions below 1990 emission levels? Why not 1995 levels, or 2000 levels for that matter? Why was 1990 such a magical year? To answer that question is to gain an appreciation of the scam that underlies the EU's intense support for the Kyoto Protocol and its various hoped-for successor agreements — Johannesburg, Poznan, Copenhagen, Durban, etc. Without a doubt, the EU has been at the forefront of global climate advocacy, hoping to force adoption of the emissions reduction targets to levels below those in place in 1990.[182] And, as if part of a predefined script, the global leftist media have praised that position as one of selfless diplomacy, real 21st century political leadership, a model to be emulated by moral lepers like the U.S.

In the year 1990, Europe was in the throes of geopolitical chaos as the regimes of Eastern Europe had just begun collapsing, an event touched off by the dramatic dismantling of the Berlin Wall in November 1989. At that time, all of Eastern Europe was still operating under the Soviet production model characterized by massive-scale state-run electrical generation and industrial combines powered by hugely inefficient coal-burning plants. Eastern Europe emitted enormous quantities of CO_2 from these inefficient, world-scale plants that consumed copious quantities of coal while generating only modest amounts of electrical power per ton of coal consumed compared to their far more efficient Western counterparts.

After the collapse of the Soviet Bloc and economic integration with Western

European countries, many of these highly inefficient, uneconomic, state-run plants were shut down in favor of vastly more efficient generation plant and industrial power technology in the West. The EU, during the Kyoto Protocol negotiations, was adamant that the target emission reduction baseline year should be 1990. They were equally adamant that all of Europe be counted as a single entity for compliance purposes. Under the terms of Kyoto, Europe received the credit of CO_2 emission reductions that had already taken place by the shuttering of obsolete Soviet-style power and industrial plants whose closures had had absolutely nothing to do with climate change policy. To its EU designers, Kyoto was strictly about obtaining an economic advantage over global competitors.

Being largely deprived by nature of bountiful supplies of hydrocarbon resources with which countries like the U.S. are blessed, Europe would forever find itself at a disadvantage if it had to rely upon far more expensive renewable energy.[183] The 1990 peg was intended to become a noose around the necks of every country on Earth except the EU since they were expected to have met and far exceeded their reduction targets before the treaty was even signed. Kyoto was a clearly and deliberately enacted piece of global economic competitive advantage engineering masquerading as environmental altruism. It has been used over the years as a bludgeon to tout European moral superiority over the U.S. and other industrialized countries.[184] Yet, and here is the delicious part, the EU still has failed to observe the mandate it was certain it would achieve by rigging the rules of the game. Meanwhile, the U.S. has made enormously greater strides on an equivalent post-1995 basis by substitution, transitioning to energy sources with lower carbon-intensity.

A handful of observers contend that Germany's 'green energy' experiment will result in a decrease in CO_2 emissions that will eventually forestall the onset of catastrophic global warming. One such observer is Bjørn Lomborg of the Copenhagen Consensus Center. Lomborg is a wholehearted believer in the theory that the atmospheric temperature increases observed over the past 50 years were entirely driven by human emissions of CO_2. And yet Lomborg readily admits that all of the mountains of cash that Germans are pouring into their 'green energy' experiment will only forestall global warming by thirty seven hours.[185] Time to break out the *Schnaps* and celebrate.

SPREAD THE MISERY

To protect local industries from the negative consequences of these policies, the EU is making efforts to share the burden it has imposed with the rest of the world. Various EU and OECD countries have advocated erecting a set of carbon tariffs called "border carbon adjustments" that would impose a series of duties on imported goods. The purpose would be to equalize the higher costs and economic non-competitiveness suffered by domestic producers operating under onerous CO_2 emission reduction regimes with global suppliers free from this curse.[186] In essence, it is an attempt to export the high-cost of the EU's 'green ' policies onto other global trading partners who have taken a more sober approach to growth and economic development.

But the EU was not alone in this approach. The Waxman-Markey cap-and-trade bill of 2009 proposed a similar protectionist trade harmonization arrangement, erecting a tariff on trade goods imported into the domestic commerce of the U.S. originating from countries that did not impose similarly ruinous CO_2 emission reduction commitment costs on their own domestic economies.[187]

The EU's first and most ambitious attempt at exporting its 'green energy' regulatory framework to the rest of the world involved imposing taxes upon airlines flying between the EU and anywhere else on the planet. Recognizing the political unpopularity of the measure, President Obama signed into law a bill giving the Secretary of Transportation authority to shield U.S. airlines and passengers from the law's impact.[188] In February 2012, an EU official announced that "The EU will not suspend the legislation."[189] Press reports indicated that, because of its urgency, the EU "will not back down on the plan."[190] According to EU climate spokesman Isaac Valero-Ladron:

We're not modifying our law and we're not backing down. We're confident that compa-nies will comply. The penalties for non-compliance are much higher (than complying).[191]

Nevertheless, due to the increasingly ferocious international response, in early November, the EU did precisely that, backing down in the face of withering opposition, particularly from China.[192] After announcing that its airlines would ignore the law,[193] China began blocking orders for Airbus long-range commercial aircraft as a retaliatory measure.[194] The U.S. also announced it was prepared to take unspecified "appropriate action" if the measure was enforced.[195] It appeared that the cost on non-compliance was going to be quite high indeed — for the EU.[196] What began as a typically harmless EU effort at environmental preening on the world stage, had instead metastasized into a full-fledged trade war.[197]

The *BBC*'s shallow, climate campaigning activist Richard Black, who occasionally pretends he's a journalist, was quoted to be mystified how it could possibly come to this:

The dispute is hard to understand on one level because the sums of money involved are so trifling.[198]

It's not just the sums that are trifling, but also any measureable impact upon the climate. If the amounts are so trifling, why should the EU risk a global diplomatic and trade war over them? It is clear that the exercise is far less about raising money and far more about incrementally imposing the EU's hysterical climate agenda upon the rest of the skeptical world — and in the usually insufferable manner to which non-EU countries have become accustomed to enduring from their moral exemplars in Western Europe.

Black's slow-wittedness is shared by other Europeans. Connie Hedegaard, the EU commissioner for climate action, observed that "Many Europeans don't get why, politi-cally, this should be controversial."[199] A former head of the International Airline Transport

Association fearlessly agrees, telling reporters "I don't get why opposition is so fierce given that this is relatively straightforward and the cost is typically low and passed on to passengers."[200]

Germans seem to inhabit a parallel universe. Blathering to an unquestioning *Time* magazine reporter, the EU's ambassador to China Markus Ederer notes that his carbon tax on airlines would drive up the price of a Beijing to Brussels ticket by only 17.5 Yuan, about $3.00. Without a shred of embarrassment, he obligingly offers "I leave it to you to make a judgment on whether this is too much for saving the earth."[201] That's it. Just spend an extra three bucks on an airline ticket and the planet is saved. If that's all it takes, the problem must not be very severe. Whatever they serve in Berlin cafes, we only wish it was legal everywhere.

Who knew there were so many low-wattage intellects operating in positions of prominence? None of these leading lights can understand why the world might balk at an EU program designed to siphon billions of dollars from the rest of the world into EU coffers in the name of climate virtue, pursuing a climate mitigation scam that every sentient soul on the planet admits will have zero impact on the climate. Sorry, that's wrong. By 2100, all of Germany's climate mitigation exertions — and countless billions of Euros wasted on it — will reduce the IPCC's twenty first century mid-range modeled global temperature increase of 2.96 degrees Celsius by a grand total of 0.002 degrees.[202] Why would anyone complain?

Since when did highway robbery come with its own set of climate benefits? Despite libraries of biographical research material having been assembled about Abraham Lincoln, most Americans learned for the first time in 2012 that their 16th President had spent his adult years hunting vampires.[203] Maybe it's also time to reassess the career of notorious train robber Jesse James, who might now be fondly remembered as the planet's first climate campaigner.

But the EU was not going to limit its 'green energy' trade war with China to airline levies. It will also include anti-dumping duties with a potential for real long-term economic damage to the EU. China now supplies some 80% of solar photovoltaic panels to the EU.[204] Like their U.S. counterparts, the EU announced plans to slap punitive tariffs on Chinese solar panels. The plan would impose tariffs of 37.3% to 67.9% in an effort to protect the few remaining German solar panel makers.[205] This had the potential to drive up the cost of solar photovoltaic energy being deployed in Germany at a furious pace, the extra costs of which would have been borne by German ratepayers.

AN ECONOMIC MISDIAGNOSIS

Given the reckless disregard for economic growth and competitiveness that allowed the EU to establish their 'green energy' program in the first place, it is hardly surprising that they would completely misdiagnose their current dilemma. With their attempts to export their high cost climate hysteria through border carbon adjustments and airline surcharges unlikely to meet with success, the next step is to pretend that Europe's current economic straits are merely coincident with or somehow unrelated to high energy prices.

Spain plunged headlong into 'green energy' believing a high level of subsidizing would result in a permanent competitive advantage over other nations leading to a deluge of high-paying jobs. But when the money ran out, the country was left with a crushing debt load that threatens its fiscal survival.[206] By 2013, unemployment in Spain rivaled levels not seen since the days of the Spanish Civil War in the late 1930s.[207] Each day brings new record levels of deficit and unemployment to the headlines.[208] Yet it is nearly impossible to locate an EU official who makes the obvious connection between 'green energy' policies and the current economic wreckage.

Policy geniuses rely upon assurances from the Paris-based International Energy Agency that, were it not for massive global oil and gas subsidies, 'green energy' would be capturing the lion's share of investment capital for new energy capacity.[209] This belief is evidence of dementia. Global governments subsidize energy, but only to make it affordable and promote economic growth. 'Green energy' only stunts growth. Germany has poured over €600 billion of subsidies into 'green energy' and, like the tee shirt might say, all it got was a lousy economy.[210]

The EU is saddled with legions of officialdom who think, as does European Commissioner for Energy Günther Oettinger, that the absence of "astronomical" prices for carbon emissions is something to lament, that a lack of Europe-wide coordination is undermining a 'green energy' future in a Eurozone which is collapsing due to an over-reliance on that same style of coordination from monetary authorities, that "the next logical step" for Europe is to boost renewable energy mandates to 40% from the current targeted 20% level that has already proved to be fiscally ruinous and economically catastrophic, that the EU's policy priority of focusing upon energy "affordability" can be achieved by boosting the level of renewables.[211] As we observed previously, Oettinger warned about the dangers of "de-industrialization," which makes him one of the more moderate voices on the continent.[212] EU officials think failure to achieve its target of generating 20% of its energy from renewable sources by 2020 — if it only reaches 19% or 18% for instance — will have "major consequences."[213] I'll wager it won't.

Europe's embrace of an Obama style 'green energy' future has brought a bountiful harvest of needless hardship to consumers, businesses, and EU member nations. The harvest includes steadily rising energy costs, power reliability problems, frequent blackouts, electricity service curtailments, destabilizing market distortions, deeper government involvement in power markets, inefficient cross-subsidizing, massive network investments for poorly utilized electrical distribution infrastructure to transport power from remote source locations, highly unpredictable power production, fluctuating voltage patterns, utility company credit downgrades, higher imports of base-load power from neighboring countries, impaired economic growth, low power plant utilization, degraded wholesale power pricing structures, widespread energy poverty, reduced economic competitiveness, increased diplomatic friction, protectionist trade measures to preserve economic competitiveness, punitive trade retaliation, destabilizing market distortions, a widening disparity between rich and poor, etc. Worst of all, it is promoting a steady exodus of jobs and industry to more favorable climates.[214] To the aforementioned Stanley Reed at *The New York Times*, this harvest represents "success."[215] And it is exactly the kind of "success" America can expect to achieve if it follows the path Obama laid out — think of it as Obamacare for energy markets — a trail of epic failure that has been blazed in Europe.

While the EU has been busy waging a pointless carbon jihad against climate catastrophe by enacting ruinous subsidy schemes, driving up energy costs, driving away energy-intensive industry, and seeing their economic growth plummet as a result, the rest of the world has been securing their real energy futures. Private entrepreneurs in the U.S. invented an innovative method to extract copious amounts of oil and gas out of once-useless shale, the Chinese have been locking up oil resources in every remote corner of the planet, the Russians have been forcibly annexing the subsea Arctic's oil and gas resource base believed to hold about 22% of the world's remaining hydrocarbon reserves, the Qataris have been moving aggressively into midstream and downstream markets to improve their oil and gas market potential, the Israelis have been exploiting the vast gas and oil recovery potential in the Eastern Mediterranean, and the Japanese have been working on a method to extract natural gas out of hydrates of methane which could extend global gas supplies nearly into infinity.[216] There is enough frozen methane on the Atlantic sea floor off the coast of the Eastern U.S. to meet 100% of America's natural gas requirements for 75 years.[217] There are also vast methane hydrate deposits in U.S. waters in the Pacific, Gulf of Mexico, and adjacent to Alaska's North Slope sea floors.[218] It's fortunate Europe has beautiful castles, picturesque Gothic cathedrals, unparalleled cuisine, and quaint Medieval hilltop villages for tourists to enjoy. Because if the EU remains on its present path, that's all it will have left in a few decades.

Germany, as some observers contend, is Europe's "indispensible nation."[219] If that is so, then the U.S. is without question the whole planet's only indispensible nation. As costs soar through the solar-paneled roof to sustain Germany's unsustainable approach to "sustainable" energy, dependent client states on the European periphery will quickly discover that her ability to serve as their fiscal backstop will become irreparably eroded.

By the same token, if America is to impose calamitous costs upon its already degraded fiscal and economic condition by emulating Germany's 'green energy' folly, its ability to serve as the world's anchor for stability against primitive barbarity will also rapidly disintegrate. The world would scarcely need to worry about a gradual atmospheric temperature increase due to CO_2 emissions from using fossil fuels. It will be civilization itself and our democratic way of life that will go up in flames. The heat from that will be far more unbearable.

CHAPTER 9

BLAZING THE 'GREEN ENERGY' TRAIL IN AMERICA

"It is to be regretted that the rich and powerful too often bend the acts of government to their selfish purposes … when the laws undertake to add to these natural and just advantages artificial distinctions, to grant titles, gratuities, and exclusive privileges, to make the rich richer and the potent more powerful, the humble members of society — the farmers, mechanics, and laborers who have neither the time nor the means of securing like favors to themselves — have a right to complain of the injustice of their Government."[1]

ANDREW JACKSON
JULY 10, 1832

While the European Union is way out in front of the U.S. in its voluntary 'green energy' suicide program, at least one part of the U.S. is furiously playing catch up. Our own 'green energy' index case is California. As with many societal transformation ideas, some good, most bad, and a few absolutely horrible, California is America's laboratory for government-led social experimentation. Obama's 'green energy' future, already having been prototyped in Western Europe, is also unfolding at a hurried pace in California.

California passed its own 'green energy' implementation measure that included a cap-and-trade provision, hilariously entitled *The Global Warming Solutions Act of 2006* but referred to more commonly as AB32.[2] This laughable piece of moral exhibitionist theatre with its grandiose-sounding name — Californians think they have the "solution" to global warming — was enacted as a model for the rest of the country to emulate. Twenty nine states and the District of Columbia have enacted some form of renewable energy mandates. But none thus far has been as aggressive as California. Nor have any followed California's mandatory cap-and-trade example.[3]

Not surprisingly, the sensible part of the country declined California's offer to join the deep-green fun,[4] despite Obama's repeated threats to impose renewables mandates and a cap-and-trade scheme onto the wallets of American consumers. Obama had been a proponent of transitioning away from an oil-based economy long before he became a candidate. Obama's vision for America has been enacted in California. We won't need to wait around for decades to learn the results.

From his earliest recorded pronouncements, Obama made it clear that America needed to make a radical shift away from fossil fuels to a robust 'green energy' program. Like other political cynics, Obama opportunistically piled on in the wake of Hurricane Katrina in September 2005, contending that it should serve as America's wake-up call. He claimed that Katrina was a reminder that "the days of running a 21st century economy on a 20th century fossil fuel are numbered — and we need to realize that before it's too late."[5] A few months later, he revisited this theme at the Governor's Ethanol Coalition, recounting all the "reasons why it's a good idea for this country to move away from an oil-based economy."[6]

Obama also claimed America needed to enact renewable energy mandates as has been done in Europe for his 'green energy' plan to succeed. At a speech in Dayton in July 2008, Obama had vowed to impose a Renewable Portfolio Standard on the U.S. that was even more stringent than the EU's paltry 20% target:

> *To create a market for alternative sources of energy like solar and wind, I'll require that 25% of our electricity comes from renewable sources by 2025, and that we produce two billion gallons of advanced cellulosic biofuels by 2013.*[7]

Marvel at the boundless confidence of the man who can summon political, economic, and technical realities into existence on command. Obama would *require* that 25% of our electricity be derived from renewable sources. And he would *require* that the country produce two billion gallons of cellulosic ethanol by 2013. His command was all that was needed to make these things a reality. The Energy Independence and Security Act of 2007 *requires* America to consume one billion gallons of cellulosic ethanol by 2013 and three billion by 2015.[8] Yet despite the *requirement*, only 20,069 gallons of cellulosic ethanol had been produced in commercial-scale plants since enactment through the first five months of 2013, even though the federal government had squandered a king's ransom trying to make it a reality.[9] Obama was promising to double-down on the unachievable by the sheer force of his mighty pen. Obama is also a vocal proponent of California's cap-and-trade program. He expended considerable effort advocating for it on the campaign trail.

AB32 directs the California Air Resources Board to adopt a series of regulations to drive down CO_2 emissions in California by the year 2020 to the same levels experienced in 1990.[10] The law established seven emission reduction requirements,[11] three of which will be exorbitantly costly.[12] Those three are (1) a cap-and-trade mechanism on CO_2 emissions, (2) a Renewable Portfolio Standard obligating the state to derive a threshold amount of energy from renewable sources, and (3) a low-carbon fuel standard that requires the state to reduce the carbon intensity of transportation fuels 10% by the year 2020.[13]

The California Air Resources Board (CARB) commissioned an economic study whose updated findings were published in March 2010. CARB's study authors found that AB32 would only cost the state 0.2% of Gross State Product (GSP) in 2020, just $4 billion in 2007 dollars.[14] The low-ball figure was based upon an analysis that magnanimously attributed a lengthy list of imaginary benefits that would accrue to California residents living under the bill's dictates.

Despite those overly optimistic findings, the California Manufacturers & Technology Association (CMTA) commissioned its own economic impact study of the effects of AB32. Needless to say, the real impact is likely to be far worse — for the state, for the taxpayers, for workers, and for businesses. CMTA found that in its "optimistic case," AB32 will cost California consumers nearly $136 billion by 2020.[15] By that year, annual costs will soar to $35.3 billion, an amount equal to 40% of the state's general fund revenues.[16] A 26% emissions reduction will actually materialize solely as a result of depressed economic activity resulting from the damaging impact of AB32.[17]

Want to drive down CO_2 emissions? It's simple. Just drive out people and businesses while stifling the ones that remain. It's how Germany is doing it. Instead of a 0.2% reduction in Gross State Product as CARB believes, the actual reduction will be closer to 5.6%[18] costing the state not $4 billion in lost economic activity as CARB contends, but $153.2 billion.[19]

An example of how this will occur in practice is provided by Pacific Coast Producers in Woodland, just west of Sacramento. Pacific uses copious amounts of natural gas to remove water from pureed tomato sauce to make tomato paste. The company's CEO Dan Vincent observes that the only realistic way he has to reduce the company's carbon footprint to comply is to reduce plant output — to lower the amount of economic activity.[20] Reduced output will lead to job cuts in the already depressed job market of the Central Valley.[21] Vincent is looking to shift production to Texas as one option. They grow tomatoes there and don't do cap-and-trade.

The law will destroy an estimated 262,000 jobs by 2020,[22] costing the average household $2,500 per year.[23] While the U.S. added a half million manufacturing jobs in the 2011 to 2012 period, California was not a beneficiary, having shed on third of its manufacturing base over the previous decade.[24] State revenues from the economic wreckage left in AB32's wake will decline by an estimated $7.4 billion per year.[25] *Sacramento Bee* columnist Daniel Weintraub makes clear the scale of the challenge presented by the law's aggressive objectives:

> *What will it take to achieve the benchmark? Consider that California could take every one of its 14 million passenger cars off the road and still be less than halfway toward its goal. Shutting down 100 state-of-the-art natural gas-fired power plants still wouldn't get us there. Closing the entire cement industry, although it is a major source of greenhouse gases, wouldn't finish the job.*[26]

Another study that measured the impact of AB32 was commissioned by the Western States Petroleum Association, which retained Boston Consulting Group. BCG found that "policies like the Low Carbon Fuel Standard are not feasible and can't be sustained."[27] Supplies of low carbon fuels like cellulosic ethanol or Brazilian sugarcane ethanol will not be available in sufficient quantity to meet the thresholds. The effect would be to increase fuel cost by as much as $2.50 per gallon and result in fuel shortages as early as 2015.[28] Fuel prices could top $6.00 per gallon by 2020.

Five to seven of California's fourteen oil refineries could be forced to close. Four have already closed in the past two decades.[29] A large chunk of the state's refinery capacity would vanish. Energy intensive businesses, the few that remain, will be driven away to other states or countries. Tens of thousands of jobs will be lost. Billions in tax revenues will be sacrificed. The economic climate will likely worsen substantially from its already depressed levels. Most difficult to justify, the negative impact upon low and moderate income residents will be greatest.[30]

The fact is inescapable. AB32 will drive up the cost of energy far higher than it is today while destroying what is left of the state's manufacturing base — and the middle income jobs that go with it. As in Europe, California companies pay much higher rates for energy than their neighbors, nearly 50% more than companies in the rest of the country.[31] The governor actually brags about the supposed benefits of cap-and-trade, but is always careful to avoid mentioning its cost.[32]

California practices a form of energy bigotry. It produced only 70% of the electricity it consumed in 2011 and 2012.[33] It is unwilling to approve construction of new generation capacity, but is content to source power from neighboring states that get stuck with the emissions and resulting pollution. In essence, California exports its emissions to neighboring states. To salve its collective consciences, California moved to prohibit imports of coal power.[34] This has added to the sense of arrogance its actions engender. A senior Bush administration Energy Department official observed that California was "clearly trying to trim down the growth of coal, not just in California, but elsewhere. California is using their regulations to direct the economic development of the West. And it is arrogant and it is appalling."[35] California is content to let other states assemble the cars, refine the petroleum, produce the cement, fabricate the plastics and chemicals, manufacture the consumer products, build the aircraft, and produce the other energy-intensive products its citizens enjoy.

Between 1979 and 1999, the California Energy Commission approved only 10% of the 45,000 mW of generation capacity that was proposed.[36] During that time, the state ordered the 900 mW Rancho Seco nuclear plant and the 1,000 mW Unit One nuclear reactor at San Onofre to be closed.[37] The results of those actions were predictable. By 2001, the state suffered its infamous rolling blackouts, which the California Energy Commission blamed on electric utilities.[38] An initiative will likely appear on the 2014 ballot which would require remaining nuclear plants to close prematurely.[39] If the ballot measure succeeds, 18.3% of the state's generating capacity would disappear without any replacement capacity.[40] Southern California Edison announced in June 2013 that it would permanently close the San Onofre nuclear plant rather than fight an uphill battle.[41] A 2011 study by the California Council on Science and Technology makes abundantly clear "there are no technical barriers to large-scale deployment of nuclear power in the state."[42] But Californians don't do science or technology when it comes to energy policy. So the barriers are impassible.[43]

AB32 establishes a mechanism that allows utilities to receive emission permits for free. But these operators will then be obligated to invest the proceeds they receive on renewable energy projects, which will automatically drive electricity rates higher.[44] The state expects to collect as much as $14 billion per year in cap-and-tax revenues by 2015.[45] But that expectation assumes the law will have no deleterious effects on economic activity and associated income-based remittances to the state treasury, which is a completely fanciful belief.

The state's first carbon auction under the cap-and-trade program was a huge disappointment in terms of revenues to the state coffers, bringing in only about 14% of the amount anticipated for the fiscal year that ended in June 2013.[46] The price established for carbon emissions in the auction was very near the floor price below which bidders were not permitted to bid.[47] The rules had been rigged to favor the government.[48] The Brown administration promptly snatched all the revenues to fund welfare programs.[49] The transportation sector, the largest emitter of CO_2 in California, won't be covered under the program until 2015.[50] But even without inclusion of this volume, the auction was a megaflop.

Europe's Emission Trading System is so plagued with fraud, they might as well throw in a deed to the Brooklyn Bridge when you buy carbon offsets for all the real climate mitigation likely to occur.[51] Europol estimates that as much as 90% of the carbon credits originated in some countries are fraudulent.[52] Billions of euros are being squandered each year in these utterly worthless pursuits.

Some American companies are involved in carbon trading scams. Dupont was caught gaming a carbon offset system, collecting $4 million a year to destroy a potent greenhouse gas called HFC-23 that it could have easily destroyed with very low-cost equipment upgrades.[53] California's cap-and-trade folly permits emitters to purchase carbon offsets in lieu of actually making CO_2 emission reductions. As much as 85% of emission allowances traded on California's exchange originate from carbon offsets, the fraud-plagued mechanism run by organized crime.[54] So it's entirely possible that the overwhelming majority of "climate benefits" supposedly achieved through the state's silly cap-and-trade experiment could actually be non-existent. California businesses and citizens will pay through the nose for carbon offsets that quite possibly would entail transfers of cash to fraudulent operators and organized crime groups without any real climate benefit.[55]

AB32 also established a Renewable Portfolio Standard (RPS) that mirrors Europe's program. The law initially obligated electric utilities to incorporate 20% of the energy generation from renewable sources like wind and solar. But unlike in the EU where each country is obligated to generate 20% of its energy from renewable sources by 2020, California set a far more ambitious target. Governor Brown signed a bill in April 2011 obligating the state to acquire 33% of its electricity from renewables by 2020. He has been advocating for a 40% threshold.[56] The Southern California Public Power Authority warned that power rates would likely be hiked 30% because of the mandate.[57] More than two-thirds of Americans live in states that have enacted some form of renewable portfolio standard.[58] But none are as aggressive as California's.

To reach its 33% mandate level, a massive renewable energy infrastructure will need to be deployed. The California Public Utility Commission (CPUC) estimates it will require $115 billion to accomplish.[59] That amounts to $3,087 per person.[60] So, as will be the case in Germany, California will need to ravage forests, wildlife refuges, and pristine public spaces to install a network of high-capacity transmission wires.[61] This is the way 'green energy' is helping to save the environment.

INCOME REDISTRIBUTION — FROM POOR TO RICH

Cost increases from renewable energy projects began to kick in at a time when the state was staring fiscal ruin in the face. By late 2012, California ratepayers were already absorbing an estimated $1.3 billion per year in solar energy subsidies paid mostly to well-heeled homeowners who had placed solar panels on their properties, exactly as has happened in Germany.[62] California was looking at a budget shortfall of $23 billion for fiscal year 2012 and at least another $16 billion budget shortfall in fiscal year 2013.[63] The governor laughingly labeled this outcome "unexpected."[64] That wasn't anywhere as bad as the $60 billion shortfall the state experienced two years earlier.[65]

To demonstrate that the California Assembly is serious about getting their fiscal house in order, they also voted in July of 2012 to install a high-speed rail line between Los Angeles and San Francisco that will cost a projected $68 billion just to build.[66] The final figure for "the train to nowhere" will likely be far higher than this lowball estimate[67] — it carried an estimated price tag of "only" $33 billion in 2008.[68] Stanford University watchdog group California Common Cause published a report in June 2012 estimating the final cost at $200 billion.[69]

California's residential electricity rates at $0.1475 per kWh in 2010 were the 10th highest in the nation.[70] At the end of 2012, the state had jumped up to eighth place on the list at $0.1565 per kWh.[71] By September 2013, the state had leaped into the fifth place on a year-to-date basis at $0.1635 per kWh.[72] It won't be long before the state jumps into third place. The California Division of Ratepayer Advocates (DRA) discovered in February 2011 that California's four major public utilities had accepted virtually every renewable energy contract offered to them, and 59% of those contracts were priced at levels higher than comparable market rates.[73] The cost was almost 60% greater than for combined cycle natural gas power.[74] "Of the 184 renewable-energy contracts presented to the CPUC for approval since 2002, only two had been rejected," found DRA.[75] This has forced the state to pay utilities an extra $6 billion, which "is over seven times CPUC-specified amounts."[76] The issue is so sensitive that utilities refuse to disclose the prices they pay on renewables projects because they are so expensive.[77] As more of these get layered into the supply portfolio, it won't be long before the 17.1 cent rate California residents paid in September 2013 will seem like a bargain.[78]

Pacific Gas & Electric is at the top of DRA's list. PG&E has contracted over a 25-year period to buy every kilowatt-hour of the solar energy offload produced by Warren Buffet's new Topaz Solar and Google founders' California Valley Solar Ranch scams.[79] The Renewables Portfolio Standard has created a situation that is "signaling to the market that California will accept overpriced renewable energy, and that it is willing to lock customers into higher prices for decades to come" as DRA phrases it.[80]

The current situation with AB32's impact on the car market offers another example of Sacramento's love affair with 'green' excess. To meet its 80% emission reduction goal below 1990 levels by the year 2040, virtually every car sold in the state will need to be an electric or plug-in hybrid car.[81] Never mind the strain that will place on the electric grid that already can barely handle peak demand requirements in a state that deploys net new generation resources at about 60% the rate at which demand needs to grow. Governor Brown stepped out in front of this freight train issuing an executive order requiring 1.5 million zero-emission vehicles to be on the roads by 2025.[82]

But the public must be induced to cooperate. Thus far, there is little appeal among the proletariat for electric cars. To make up for the shortfall in the overall fleet sales, auto makers can purchase zero-emission vehicle credits, a sort of Medieval indulgence with a left coast flavor that permits purchasers to continue their sinful ways without fear of incurring the wrath of the 'green' commissars. Electric car maker Tesla earned nearly $120 million in the first half of 2013 from credit sales.[83] It was the only reason they were profitable.[84] A federal tax rebate of $7,500 and a state rebate of $2,500 offers some taxpayers an inducement to buy an electric car. These are not cash refunds per se but reductions in federal and state tax liabilities. Almost half of California's wage earners pay no federal income tax. So only very well-heeled households can participate.

Surveys reveal that the most popular rebate filing in the state is for the Tesla Model S sports sedan which carries an "all-in" sticker price north of $105,000.[85] This is not Henry Ford's Model T car for the masses. Nearly every Tesla buyer has another conventional gas-power auto parked at home in the garage.[86] A study in 2011 found that the average electric car buyer has a median income of $150,000 and more than half of these owners own two other cars.[87] Electric car owners fancy themselves moral exemplars teaching society how to curtail wasteful consumption.

The increasing popularity of the 6-figure electric cars strained the state's rebate program budget, requiring additional appropriations from Sacramento.[88] The state wanted to snare cap-and-trade revenue but the Governor had cleaned out the cupboard.[89] So, as with solar panels on rooftops, or solar ranches and wind farms owned by wealthy investors, California's electric car fetish has become one more example of how lower- and middle-income households — the 99-percenters — are forced to transfer wealth to the undeserving, ultra-rich one percenters.

In early 2011, Los Angeles Mayor Antonio Villaraigosa boasted that his city had already met a 20% renewable energy level. But Department of Water and Power officials disclosed the painful truth that the percentage of renewable energy would decline over time to 13% without substantial cash infusions.[90] And even if the city is to maintain its current 20% level, much less the 33% required under law, retail electricity rates will need to increase between 28% and 47% from 2012 to 2017.[91] These realities will serve to drive even more jobs and taxpayers out of the state to more favorable locales while doing absolutely nothing toward remediating global warming.

As the degree of penetration from renewable power increases, the amount of grid instability also increases due to intermittency of renewable sources. This means that the margin of coverage from standby backup fossil fuel generation needs to increase also. The California Independent System Operator (ISO) which manages the statewide electrical grid estimates that reserve capacity will need to double when the state hits the 33% renewables target.[92] The number they assign is 3,100 megawatts of additional, poorly utilized standby power by 2017.[93]

One of the problems created by this situation is that operator revenue for reliable power declines as a greater amount of standby plant capacity is idled. There needs to be an economic incentive to build additional generating capacity or it won't get built. These revenue declines need to be offset by additional subsidies to be borne by ratepayers, driving up the cost of power.[94] And grid instability increases from the management challenges posed by extreme intermittency. This may result in brownouts as early as 2014.[95] The ISO counsels that there is no reason to worry. They offered that advice a decade ago as the state experienced a wave of embarrassing blackouts.[96]

An example of 'green energy' success is Blue-Lake Energy which operates a generating station using biomass feedstock. The plant sells its power to a San Diego utility at twice the market competitive rate. Even better, when the previously-idled plant restarted in 2010, it spewed forth so much black smoke and soot that the town of Blue Lake had to be evacuated. Some residents did not return home for several days. The reward for that stellar performance was a $5.4 million grant from the federal government for being a "clean burning" plant.[97]

Blue-Lake Energy has been a recipient of numerous clean air violations during the short time since its resurrection. Some environmental advocates wonder aloud why government policy subsidizes activity more damaging to the environment than coal-fired generation.[98] Don't we all. Unlike California, the Commonwealth of Massachusetts issued new regulations that eliminated renewable energy subsidies to biomass-burning plants unless they meet an unattainably high-level efficiency threshold.[99] Those rules were issued after a study commissioned by the state determined that biomass plants usually liberate more CO_2 on a full life-cycle basis than plants that burn fossil fuels.[100] California is so desperate, it doesn't care about inconvenient details.

Another biomass plant in the Central Valley has been cited for environmental violations more than two dozen times for spewing sulfur, carbon monoxide, and nitrogen oxide pollution as well as for prohibited burning of plastics and rubber. Its website boasts that the company produces "green renewable electricity,"[101] the kind that requires city-wide evacuation to avoid airborne toxicity. Naturally, on the strength of its pattern of repeated environmental violations, the plant qualified for over $6 million in taxpayer subsidies steered to producers of 'clean energy.'

California is willfully adopting a strategy that results in far more damaging nitrogen oxide emissions from renewable energy plants than fossil fueled plants would ever release, all to avoid carbon dioxide emissions. Nitrogen oxides react with water vapor and sunlight in the atmosphere to form nitrous and nitric acids. These corrosive compounds acidify rivers and lakes, causing severe damage to trees, particularly to the most fragile species at higher elevations. N_2O or nitrous oxide is 310 times more potent a greenhouse gas than CO_2.[102] Carbon dioxide, on the other hand, is plant food and promotes the acceleration of green growth through photosynthesis, plants that remove CO_2 from the atmosphere.

About 80% of the biomass-burning plants in the U.S. like Blue-Lake Energy have received fines from federal or state enforcement agencies for air or water pollution violations.[103] There are four power generation stations in the vicinity of the Blue-Lake plant. Three of these are biomass-burning plants and have all been cited repeatedly for environmental violations. The fourth plant has an absolutely spotless environmental record. Needless to say, it burns natural gas, a fossil fuel. Accordingly, it doesn't qualify for inclusion under AB32 renewable portfolio rules. The plant with the clean environmental record, the one that liberates plant food, that spews no damaging nitrogen oxides, is not considered 'clean energy.'

ALLERGIC TO JOB-CREATING ENERGY

In addition to a wildly optimistic belief in the promise of 'green energy,' California shares another trait with its Euro-sclerotic statist counterparts that it aspires to emulate, a deathly aversion to fossil fuels. During the 1920s, California produced as much as one fourth of the entire world's oil supply.[104] But following the 1969 oil spill off the coast of Santa Barbara, California made it increasingly difficult for producers to receive drilling permits. A quirky feature of AB32 actually makes imported crude oil more attractive to refiners in the state because fossil fuel burning is required for steam injection to recover domestic crude oil.[105] California crude has a higher carbon intensity relative to competing imported oil which is not penalized. Nevertheless, California still produces copious quantities of crude oil, including in Beverly Hills of all places. The drilling equipment resides in buildings carefully hidden from view adjacent to Olympic and Pico Boulevards.[106] Upscale Californians don't want to be reminded that their Bentleys, Ferraris, and Lamborghinis actually burn fossil fuel that must come from somewhere.

Despite EIA estimates that there are 15.4 billion barrels of recoverable crude oil in the state's Monterrey Shale formation,[107] oil production plummeted by 45% over the previous 25 years.[108] The Monterrey Shale formation, which runs a sizeable percentage of the length of the massive state, may actually hold 500 billion barrels of oil.[109] Were only half of the 15.4 billion barrels of recoverable oil to be tapped over the next 30 years, the state's economy would receive a boost of $48.9 billion per year using average 2012 crude oil prices.[110] That amount would bring in $18 billion per year in royalty revenue to the state each year,[111] more than enough to close California's FY 2012 budget gap.

That figure doesn't take into account the job creation impact from the increased economic activity that would inevitably result. Economists Peter Passell of the Milken Institute and Robert Hahn at American Enterprise Institute estimate that California derives between $30 and $80 billion in broad social and economic benefits from each billion barrels of oil recovered.[112] Job gains could exceed 43,000 by the year 2020.[113] So California can continue along its AB32 path and see an estimated 262,000 jobs destroyed. Or it can chuck aside its climate hysteria and embrace its real energy future, creating an estimated 43,000 jobs in the process.

But the likelihood is bleak that the state would ever reap such a bountiful harvest to which it is entitled. That is due to the thicket of state land use and environmental regulations that severely impede oil recovery.[114] Incredibly, in early 2013, there were at least ten bills in various stages of consideration in the California Assembly designed to block fracking in the Monterey shale.[115] One such bill was defeated on a 35-24 vote in June 2013.[116] That vote was interesting for the fact that there were 12 Democrat abstentions who might have voted to permit fracking had they been unafraid to cross their Party leadership.[117] Even more interesting was the regional breakdown with nearly all the Nay votes hailing from wealthy coastal districts while nearly all of the affirmative votes came from poorer districts in the interior populated by working-class people who desperately need jobs.[118]

While it is potentially hopeful that the federal Bureau of Land Management holds subsurface mineral rights for most of the Monterrey shale deposits, leadership would need to originate in Sacramento to proceed.[119] That possibility seems remote. The majority of California voters, perhaps the most automobile-centric people in the world, ape their European counterpart's schizophrenia and seem not to mind, or even applaud, the current politicized energy paralysis.

A curious aspect about this is that while the state has been drowning in deficit and debt, it seems a remote likelihood that the Sacramento political culture would ever consider a change of mindset on fossil fuel recovery that could bring prosperity, balanced budgets, and debt reduction. The State Budget Crisis Task Force reported in September 2012 that California is groaning under the weight of $372.5 billion in debt obligations, which comes to $10,079 per man, woman and child.[120] The state's 2012-2013 budget included $8.8 billion in debt service payments alone, almost 10% of budgetary outlays.[121] Governor Brown's 2013 budget merely kicks the can down the road.[122]

California's population grew by only 15% between 1996 and 2012. But over that time, state spending doubled.[123] So naturally, given this flood of increased public spending, California's school system must be pumping out the highest performing graduates, and the state should be able to boast the nation's finest roads, right? Actually California's

8th graders performed the worst of any state school system in the country in standard-ized math and reading tests in 2011 with the exception of Mississippi and the District of Columbia.[124] Its school system used to rank first in the nation in the 1960s.[125] That was when California was the nation's second largest producer of oil. The federal government rates only half of California's roads as acceptable while private surveys rate the road system near the bottom.[126] But all of those high scores were logged before progressivism took control of the state and improved things. Today, nearly one quarter of the state's residents live in poverty and its welfare caseload is four times higher than the next highest blue-state economic basket-case, New York.[127]

Interestingly, although California sits atop a shale formation that contains almost two-thirds of all the recoverable shale oil in the country, the state is mired in political paralysis.[128] By contrast, North Dakota has foregone the eco-extremist handwringing and has surged to become the second biggest producer of oil in the country, leapfrogging Alaska and California.[129] And how has North Dakota fared? It posted a 3.3% unemploy-ment rate in March 2013 compared to California's 9.4%.[130] It ran an economic growth rate of 13.4% in 2012, which was almost four times higher than for California,[131] and eight times the national average.[132] North Dakota posted the highest real economic growth rate of any state for three straight years.[133] It also ran a $1.6 billion fiscal surplus in 2012 compared to California's double-digit deficit.[134] Its population is at the highest level since the Great Depression as workers stream in to fill vacancies while California's working populace shrinks.[135]

The U.S. Chamber of Commerce ranks North Dakota number one on its list of the most enterprising states with a composite score in five performance categories nearly twice the next highest state, Texas.[136] Professor Mark Perry of the University of Michigan calls North Dakota "America's Miracle State."[137] The four highest states on the Chamber's list are all major oil producing states. North Dakota's economic performance could provide a powerful lesson for Sacramento to emulate if it weren't for the hyper-politicized, progres-sive hothouse psychosis that has warped the state's political culture.

IS THIS AMERICA'S FUTURE?

California earns its fair share of derision from other parts of the country. All of it is deserved and most of it is generously understated. An example of the laughable measures for which the state has garnered its hard-earned reputation is Executive Order S-3-05 signed by Governor Arnold Schwarzenegger in 2005 that proclaims confidently that the state will "by 2050, reduce Greenhouse Gas emissions to 80 percent below 1990 levels."[138] Since an executive order lacks the force of law, a bill known as Assembly Bill 284 (AB284) was introduced by a freshman legislator that would embed the order into law.[139] How the state could ever hope to reduce CO_2 emissions to 80% below 1990 levels while simul-taneously shuttering nuclear generating capacity and prohibiting coal-fired power to be imported from other states is anyone's guess. But that's why people laugh at California.

Consider just a few of the implications of the policy objective taken from a comprehensive two-year study published in 2011 by the California Commission on Science and Technology. That study attempted to identify measures the state must undertake to achieve the 80% reduction goal over the remaining 39 years.[140] The authors used 2005 as a baseline, noting that the population of 37 million state residents would likely increase to 55 million by 2050.[141] Emissions of CO_2 would need to be cut to 85 million metric tons of CO_2-equivalent from the 2005 level of 470 million.

Forget about 80% for a moment. Just to get to a 60% reduction, every existing building in the state must either undergo a complete renovation to achieve better energy efficiency or must simply be demolished and replaced with new designs.[142] At least three-fifths of light duty vehicles must operate either on electricity or hydrogen rather than CO_2-producing fuels.[143] And the entire portfolio of the state's electricity generation must be completely replaced with zero carbon-emitting sources — and then doubled — to meet projected demand.[144] Achievement of the 80% goal will require exploitation of technologies that are neither on the market nor even in demonstration phase today.

Buildings can be constructed today that deliver 40-50% energy efficiency improvements for no additional outlays. But to achieve a 70-80% improvement, the retrofit cost would be in the range of $30,000-100,000 per unit.[145] The total price tag for the state just to meet an interim year 2025 building retrofit target of a 25% to 30% energy intensity reduction is estimated to run between $1.5 to $2.0 billion per year. No one knows how much it would cost to hit the 70-80% target.

Electricity generation is asked to do the heavy lifting when it comes to decarbonizing the energy portfolio. To meet the target, one new nuclear plant would need to be built each year beginning in 2020. A typical light-water reactor is rated at 1,000 megawatts of baseload power. But California has deployed an annual average of only 635 megawatts of utility-scale power generation capacity since 1980.[146] In addition, the state has shut down two of its nuclear plants, Rancho Seco and San Onofre.[147] Without nuclear power, the state has no realistic hope of meeting its 2050 target.

As all this is sinking in, there are 17 gas-fired plants and 1 remaining nuclear facility that use coastal and estuary water resources for cooling.[148] They may all be forced to close by 2020 to comply with the state's stringent interpretation of Section 316 of the Clean Water Act.[149] Each of these plants utilizes "once through cooling" (OTC) where ocean water is pumped into and through the cooling system and then discharged back into the ocean.[150] California's powerful State Water Resources Control Board (SWRCB) ruled in 2010 that because marine life is either sucked into or pinned against intake screens, these plants must eliminate this form of cooling.[151] SWRCB provided a low-ball cost increase estimate of 1 cent per kilowatt-hour to remediate the problem, an estimate which excludes the effect of lost revenue.[152] Still, that amount will boost electric bills by 7%. Most of the plants will not undergo retrofit because the estimated cost of $11 billion is far too high.[153]

Collectively, these eighteen plants account for 20,873 megawatts of power generating capacity.[154] That equates to 38.3% of total generating capacity under normal operating conditions according to the California Independent System Operator.[155] Two nuclear plants, Diablo Canyon and San Onofre, together generated 13% of the state's entire power requirements in 2011.[156] San Onofre is already closed.

Amazingly, the state is willing to bear these costs and potential severe grid impacts without carefully assessing if these wildlife protection measures were even warranted. Virginia-based utility AES operates three of the affected plants. A study they conducted at their Huntington Beach generating station discovered that only four pounds of fish and other aquatic life were being destroyed each day.[157] As the *Los Angeles Times* observed in a widely circulated report, this is equal to the daily dietary intake of a single pelican.[158] Obviously California doesn't do cost-benefit analysis.

The Electric Power Research Institute (EPRI) performed another assessment and provided the results to SWRCB prior to the Board's decision. EPRI found that for most of these affected plants, "few options exist besides either converting facilities to closed-cycle cooling at a cost of billions of dollars or retiring facility/generating units."[159] Even more interesting is that the closed-cycle cooling method advocated by SWRCB "causes its own adverse social and environmental impacts such as increased plant air emissions and the resulting decreases in local air quality."[160] Even more amazing is the fact that EPA's own interpretation of Section 316 does not encompass a statutory obligation to protect zoo-plankton, the most plentiful adversely impacted species. As EPRI observes, 95% of marine losses "were to commonly occurring forage species (e.g., gobies) not subject to commercial or recreational fishing."[161] California will impose billions of dollars in regulatory costs to comply with requirements of a rule that doesn't exist to protect a few dozen pounds of fish nobody wants, an outlay equating to about $400,000 per pound of fish each year.

Partly as a result of all of this 'green energy' excess, California is choking in red tape, high taxes, an expanding welfare caseload, the nation's largest Medicaid expenditures — a fourth of Californians are enrolled in the program — ruinous budget deficits that threaten the state's credit rating, the second highest unemployment rate in the nation, and an ever-shrinking taxpayer middle class. Indeed, 47% of Californians are members of a semi-permanent underclass, paying no income tax.[162] The state now has the highest sales tax rate, the highest marginal income tax rate at 13.3%, and the highest gasoline taxes.[163] While California has only one-eighth on the nation's population, it accounts for one third of its welfare caseload.[164] Eight out of every eleven new residents in the state enroll in Medicaid.[165] Over the previous 20-years, 70% of California's 10 million population increase enrolled in the program.[166] A middle class family making just over $48,000 a year pays a marginal income tax rate of 9.3%, which is a higher tax rate than millionaires and billionaires and corporate jet owners pay in 47 other states. California also enjoys the distinction of having the worst credit rating of any state in the country.[167]

California Democrats succeeded in getting an initiative placed on the ballot for November 2012 that raised marginal income tax rates and the highly regressive state sales tax even higher.[168] California's sales tax rate on election day was already the highest in the country.[169] Perhaps not surprisingly, the measure was approved by a comfortable

8-point margin by voters.[170] The state also approved by a lopsided 60-40 margin a ballot initiative that would impose higher corporate taxes on out-of-state corporations to fund more 'green energy' projects.[171]

And in the midst of all this, the legislature that brought its citizenry AB32 is busy grappling with much bigger issues like putting farmers out of business to preserve irrigation canal habitats for a three-inch fish called the delta smelt that is not even listed as endangered,[172] outlawing the sale of *foie gras* in restaurants,[173] pushing for a national lesbian, gay, bisexual, transgender and queer bill of rights,[174] and assuring that children can be raised in households by multiple sets of legally recognized parents.[175] California's assembly can find time on its crowded calendar to grapple with bills honoring the 100-year anniversary of the Sikh American community, gender pay equity, bullying prevention day, Assyrian Martyrs Day, Kwanzaa, and Philippine Independence Day.[176] But it can't find enough time to consider restoring fiscal sanity, ramping up energy production, or removing onerous 'green energy' mandates that are crippling the state's economic competitiveness.

Over the past two decades, California has lost more than four million taxpaying workers as it groaned under a double-digit unemployment rates that remained in place for forty five straight months from February 2009.[177] Between the years 1992 to 2008, 4.4 million taxpaying Californians exited the state while only 3.5 million arrived to take their place.[178] The 869,000 taxpayers who left were more prosperous and paid more in taxes, with an average adjusted gross income of $44,700 compared to only $38,600 for those who took their place.[179] The net loss in tax revenues over that time period is estimated to total $44 billion.[180]

As many as 2,000 upper-income Californians leave the state each week, fleeing high taxes and costly regulations.[181] From Obama's inauguration to late 2013, the state's unemployment rate averaged 270 basis points higher than the national rate.[182] It is an economy that has witnessed nearly 5% of its jobs disappear over the past decade to more favorable climates.[183] This is the real climate change California should worry about. The pace of business exodus is accelerating, with a quintupling in the business departure rate just since 2009.[184]

California is ranked last among 50 states in a May 2012 survey of overall business climate by *Chief Executive* Magazine.[185] At 50th on a survey of 50 states, the state may not be able to sink lower on the list. But the gap between 49th and 50th can certainly widen. Already there has been a steady succession of key city bankruptcies, a trend that will surely gain momentum as more California cities experiencing declining tax rolls and higher cost exposure from the state's excessive zeal to rewrite the rules of physics and economics join the casualty list alongside Vallejo,[186] Mammoth Lakes,[187] Stockton,[188] San Bernardino[189] and Compton[190] into bankruptcy court. Some cities may simply cease to exist.[191] An estimated thirty more municipalities were on the bankruptcy watch-list in early 2013.[192] How many more bankruptcies are in the offing?[193] The state's auditor says the state had a negative net worth of $127.2 billion at the end of its 2012 fiscal year.[194] If unfunded retiree obligations were to be included on the state's balance sheet, the number would be several hundred billion dollars worse.[195]

Analysis of 2009 California tax returns provides a stark depiction of the problem the state faces as it grapples with its unfriendly climate. Between 2007 and 2009, the number of returns reporting income of $500,000 or more dropped from 146,221 to 98,610, a decline of 33% in the space of just two years.[196] Amazingly, while returns of a half million dollars or more in 2009 accounted for only about one half of one percent of all tax returns, those high-income taxpayers accounted for 16.8% of California's reported adjusted gross income, 18.8% of taxable income, and 33% of tax receipts.[197] High-income taxpayers are crucial to California's solvency. Driving them out of state or out of existence is not good public policy. Economists may be in some doubt about whether the steep drop is mostly attributed to an exodus of high-income taxpayers from the state, or simply a reduction in personal incomes. Without doubt, both trends are at work. What is undeniable is the impact that the loss of taxing power is having upon the state's economic and fiscal climate.

Democratic lawmakers in Sacramento may be lulled into thinking that their next move would be to go hat-in-hand to Washington for a bailout. Good luck with that. There are legions of leftists advocating for a federal bailout of Detroit which, six decades earlier, had the highest per capital income of any city in the nation.[198] An Ingham County, Michigan Circuit judge named Rosemary Aquilina vacated the Chapter 9 bankruptcy petition filed by Michigan's governor claiming that it violated the constitution.[199] But her real complaint was that it "was not honoring the president" who had bailed out the auto industry.[200] Former Obama administration auto bailout czar Steven Rattner argued in *The New York Times* that U.S. taxpayers should relish the opportunity to bail out Detroit. After all, as Rattner says:

> ... *apart from voting in elections, the 700,000 remaining residents of the Motor City are no more responsible for Detroit's problems than were the victims of Hurricane Sandy for theirs, and eventually Congress decided to help them.*[201]

But that was exactly the reason why voters were to blame for the toxic conditions — and why they must now be forced to foot the bill. Sandy was an unfortunate accident of nature. Six decades of progressive policies that leftist voters supported had bankrupted the Detroit and now they want everyone else to pick up the tab.[202] When California collapses, *The New York Times* will devote generous allotments of column space urging federal tax-payers to bail out the state.

Just ask taxpayers in Nebraska, Texas, South Carolina or any other state how much they'd like to fork over extra tax money to bail out profligate Californians. Just ask the Finns threatening to exit the Euro over the debt crisis how much they'd like to fork over their hard-earned savings to bail out Greece, Cyprus, Portugal, Italy, Spain, and Ireland.[203] In a moment of side-splitting hilarity that makes sensible observers wonder about the safety of the water supply in DC, *The Washington Post* reflected in a December 2012 editorial that "California's experiment might not work well enough to persuade others to follow along."[204] Ya think? Who would want to follow along? Actually, the experiment will succeed beyond anyone's wildest dream. It will serve as a model of public policy to avoid at all costs.

California, with its high taxes, Democrat-driven demands for even higher tax rates, expanding welfare rolls, ruinous budget deficits and debt, soaring energy costs, shrinking worker and taxpayer base, high unemployment, unaffordable cost of living, bloated unionized public employee payrolls, lavish public sector benefit packages, institutional hostility to job creators, bankruptcies, mandates and ever-expanding miasma of suffocating regulatory excess is a microcosm of Obama's term in office. It is not coincidental that the state with the most aggressive 'green energy' policies exhibits all of these unpalatable characteristics. If you want to see what Obama's 'green energy' future looks like and what it will do to the United States, look closely at California.

SECTION 4

THE 'GREEN ENERGY' FLIM FLAM

CHAPTER 10

ENERGY BONDAGE WITH 'GREEN ENERGY'

"Increasing the United States' reliance on a "clean" energy, as touted by President Obama, is a risky policy that leaves Americans dependent on China for supplies of critical energy resources. Key components of every green energy technology ... are made from of a small class of minerals known as the rare earth elements. China is increasingly choosing to sell finished green products to the world, rather than exporting its rare earths in raw form. The push to adopt rare earth-powered energy technologies involves swapping one form of dependence for a much more restrictive one. The old saying, out of the frying pan into the fire comes to mind."[1]

H. STERLING BURNETT
SENIOR FELLOW, NATIONAL CENTER FOR POLICY ANALYSIS

"President Obama's plan creates a much stronger dependence on China's virtual monopoly on rare earth production."[2]

INSTITUTE FOR ENERGY RESEARCH

In a typically doom-laden, pessimistic speech, Obama articulated his new 'clean energy' vision in Portsmouth, New Hampshire in October 2007. He justified his claim that America needed to migrate away from fossil fuels toward "clean energy," assuring listeners that the country would be able to "make real progress toward energy independence" by following his advice.[3] Obama's approach mirrors countless other visionaries on the left-most fringe of reality.[4] If America would simply forsake fossil fuels that the country produces in abundance from the largest natural hydrocarbon reserves on earth, in favor of wind turbines and solar panels of which it has just a small portion of global production capacity, it would finally free itself from foreign sources of supply. Pause for side-splitting laughter. This simplistic, improbable, absurdly fact-free vision was offered before an adoring crowd of sympathizers whose grip on reality was even more tenuous than Obama's.

For a country that derives most of its energy from fossil fuels as the U.S. does —
87% of primary energy consumption over the previous decade[5] — energy independence
is typically defined as the ability to deliver virtually all of its requirements from domestic
supply sources. But if the country were to transition to a 'green energy' model, the definition of true energy independence would need to change to accommodate the fact that
fuel would no longer become critical to energy production.[6] Instead, energy independence
would rely upon assured access to the critical finished products and components required
for renewable energy and other energy-efficient technology.

No country could deprive America of wind or sunshine. But if the U.S. were to harvest
these sources, it would need a wealth of materials and critical components to make that
happen. To achieve energy independence through Obama 'green energy' plan, instead of
access to domestic supplies of oil, natural gas, and coal, America would need to be able
to produce all of the wind turbines, solar panels, hybrid cars and engines, energy efficient
lighting, advanced batteries, smart meters, biofuel enzymes and catalysts, along with all
the other assorted flotsam and jetsam required.

So if America were to follow this path, achieving true "energy independence" would
necessitate not just transition of the country's energy generation sources. It would also
require a wholesale transition of its economy to permit complete self-sufficiency in the
production of 'green energy' technologies. Otherwise, America would be just as hostage
to foreign suppliers as it would be if, like Japan or South Korea, it needed to import all of
its coal, oil and natural gas.

The U.S. Code defines the term *energy security* to mean "having assured access to
reliable supplies of energy and the ability to protect and deliver sufficient energy to meet
mission essential requirements."[7] So self-sufficiency for "reliable sources of supply" would
entail not just finished product manufacturing of these gadgets. The country would need
to be able to supply all critical sub-assemblies and strategic raw materials required in their
production as well. How realistic is this vision? How likely is it that America could become
self-sufficient in production of wind turbines, hybrid engines, advanced batteries, solar
panels, biofuel refinery catalysts, and energy efficient lighting along with the necessary
sub-components and raw material supplies in the near future?

RARE EARTH METALS SUPPLY

About 76% of all the elements that exist in nature are metals. There is a group of
metallic elements that are referred to by chemists as inner transition lanthanides or, more
commonly, rare earth elements. There are 17 of these rare earth metals, 15 of which are
the lanthanides with atomic numbers between 57 and 71 on the periodic chart. They are
joined by two others having atomic numbers 21 and 39. Although many of them are not
excessively rare, there are very few places on earth where these elements can be mined
economically. For example, the most plentiful rare earth metal is cerium which occurs in
greater abundance in the earth's crust than copper.[8] The rarest of the rare earth metals

are thulium and lutetium and yet they are 200 times more plentiful than gold according to geologist Thomas Monecke at the Colorado School of Mines.[9]

Few if any of our valued readership will ever even remember hearing the names of these elements. Yet they are crucial to the operation of many 'green energy' technologies. Among the unique properties of these metals is that they possess extraordinarily strong magnetic properties, they conduct electricity very well without heat-producing resistance, they exhibit interesting catalytic properties, they are efficient electrodes in batteries, and some of them are notable for their phosphorescent capabilities. These attributes make them crucial to Obama's 'green energy' plan. More than two-thirds of rare earth demand by dollar value is for magnets and phosphors.[10]

Rare earth metals are key ingredients in things like wind turbines, electric car batteries, hybrid engines, energy efficient lighting, super-conducting circuitry, and so forth. Each Toyota *Prius* engine contains at least one kilo of neodymium and the battery requires more than ten kilos of lanthanum, both of which are rare earth metals.[11] The permanent magnet used within a three megawatt wind turbine weighs two tons.[12] It is produced from a sintered neodymium-iron-boron (Nd-Fe-B) alloy, 27% of the weight of which — more than 1,100 pounds — is the rare earth metal neodymium. Energy-efficient compact fluorescent light bulbs rely upon phosphorescent elements like terbium, europium, and yttrium, all of which are rare earths.[13] Nickel-metal hydride batteries used in plug-in electric cars require rare earth metals like lanthanum and cerium.[14]

The United States used to be the world's largest supplier of rare earth metals. Up to the 1980s, the U.S. supplied the world with the majority of all rare earth elements and oxides.[15] But that situation changed dramatically in the 1990s as the U.S. exited the market due to environmental concerns and China quickly filled the vacuum. And the supply situation is not expected to change anytime in the foreseeable future as China is the only country able to produce enough volume of both heavy and light-weight rare earth materials to meet global demand.[16] While the U.S. Geological Survey estimates that China controls less than half of the world's 110 million metric tons of reserves, it takes more than a decade to construct and outfit a world-scale mining operation.[17]

But it is not as simple as rare earth raw material mining. The U.S. capability to manufacture finished goods using rare earth metals disappeared over time as ever greater shares of the complex supply chain migrated to China including raw ore mining, smelting, reduction and refining, element separation, alloying, strip casting, extrusion, magnetic powder production, and finished product manufacturing of both sintered and rapidly-solidifying permanent magnets.[18] As a Department of Energy report makes clear, "maintaining the availability of materials for clean energy is not simply a mining issue. Manufacturing processes across the full supply chain must also be considered."[19]

An interesting example of our present difficulty concerns a company called Magnequench. The company was founded as a division of General Motors that, along with competitors from Japanese electronics firm Hitachi, had jointly invented the Nd-Fe-B magnet.[20] GM sold the company in 1995 to a company called Sextant, a front controlled by two Chinese companies, China National Non-Ferrous Metals Import & Export Corporation and the Beijing San Huan New Materials High-Tech Inc.[21] Both of these two companies have close ties to the Chinese government and their corporate heads are each sons in-law of former Communist Party strongman Deng Xiaoping.[22]

The deal was approved by the U.S. Committee on Foreign Investments (CFIUS) on condition that its operations remain in the country for at least ten years. Sextant's CEO Archibald Cox, Jr., son of the Watergate special prosecutor, assured Magnequench workers that manufacturing operations would remain in the U.S. for decades.[23] But within three years after deal closure, Cox closed Magnequench's Anderson, Indiana plant, fired the workers, and shipped the entire assembly line to China.[24] Within a few days after expiration of the ten-year lock-up, Magnequench's Valparaiso, Indiana operation was shuttered, its employees were fired, and all of the equipment and proprietary know how was shipped to China.[25] It was a sign of things to come.

It's not entirely clear why this deal was even approved. The Commerce Department had not done its homework and Archibald Cox had failed to disclose material information. Only months before the Sextant-Magnequench deal closed, San Huan New Materials had been cited by the U.S. International Trade Commission for patent infringement and industrial espionage.[26] Even more curious was the fact that Magnequench supplied 85% of the neodymium magnets that power a range of critical components in precision guided munitions, laser range-finders, and other defense weaponry.[27] It also supplied 80% of the world's neodymium magnets that power computer and high-capacity data storage systems.[28]

Rare earth element mining is considered a strategic industry in China. Export of nearly all of the country's most critical minerals has been restricted or completely curtailed.[29] This has driven up prices for these critical commodities to exorbitant levels over the past few years.[30] In September 2010, China halted exports of rare earth materials to Japan, the world's second largest consumer, citing a maritime dispute.[31] Soaring prices made rare earth elements mining an even more lucrative proposition, greatly exacerbating heavy metal contamination in China's waterways.

In 2004, China imposed a rare earths export quota.[32] By 2010, the announced quota available for export was pared to 31,130 metric tons.[33] But in 2011, the country further restricted supply, permitting only 60% of this volume to be shipped abroad.[34] Through ten months of 2012, China had exported only 9,967 metric tons of product.[35] This compares with 70,000 metric tons exported in 2003.[36] Independent non-ferrous metals industry analyst Jack Lifton, who correctly forecast the trade dispute that would emerge between the U.S. and China over rare earth export quotas, believes China intends to completely prohibit neodymium exports in the future.[37] A Chinese government report entitled *Rare Earths Industry Development Plan 2009-2015* indicated that the Ministry of Industry and Information proposed a complete ban on exports of rare earth metals including yttrium, terbium, lutetium, dysprosium, neodymium, and thulium.[38] This would preclude the ability of the U.S. from producing wind turbines, advanced batteries, energy efficient lighting, and a host of other 'green energy' technologies that rely upon these materials. Every wind turbine or major sub-assembly using a permanent magnet would need to be sourced from China if Lifton is correct.

Another rare earth metals expert, the Australian geologist Dudley Kingsnorth, made a similar prediction. In 2007, Kingsnorth prepared a chart forecasting that China's internal consumption of rare earth metals would match 100% of its available production by the year 2012, leaving nothing available for export.[39] He revised his chart after the 2009 economic slowdown when global demand for raw materials in manufacturing declined significantly, pushing that critical date out to 2014.[40] But when Kingsnorth updated his forecast to accommodate the previously unforeseen rapid growth in permanent magnets for wind turbines, the new intersection date when Chinese internal consumption would exactly match its production demand returned to 2012.[41] Kingsnorth also foresees rapid growth in supply availability for at least some of these materials outside China as mines in the U.S., Canada, Australia, Africa and South America eventually come on line.[42] But the U.S. will still only account for a small fraction of the worldwide total.

So Obama's "energy independence" program requires reliance upon a set of technology solutions whose supply is completely controlled by one of the world's most illiberal regimes and most unreliable trading partners on the planet. Chinese companies also follow a state policy of assisting the country's intelligence agencies by undertaking massive intellectual property theft.[43] Western-based 'green energy' companies doing business in China routinely see their trade secrets stolen. U.S.-born Tom McGregor, China's modern day version of Tokyo Rose, denies that China engages in such conduct.[44] But no serious person takes those denials seriously.

China is the world's most aggressive practitioner of industrial espionage.[45] China's industrial espionage is run by a special unit of the Chinese Red Army.[46] Housed in a headquarters building in Shanghai, its primary targets are U.S. infrastructure assets like electricity grids, pipelines, water works, and communication systems.[47] The danger is so serious and has been for so long that the Obama administration finally got around to issuing a public threat to undertake actions against China if its program persists, which it undoubtedly will.[48] Threats against the similarly massive Soviet espionage program undertaken against U.S. scientific, industrial, and military targets over decades of time never produced any tangible change in behavior. Soviet spies continued to siphon classified U.S. military and industrial intelligence without interruption.

The material supply situation is so dire, and more importantly, the potential to render Obama's 'clean energy' policy such a complete laughing-stock is so pronounced, that the Department of Energy commissioned a study in 2010 to address the problem and devise a long term strategy to reverse the supply problem.[49] The report examines materials required to produce four basic categories of products essential to Obama's vaunted program: (1) permanent magnets for wind turbines, (2) advanced batteries used in electric and hybrid cars, (3) thin-film semiconductors like cadmium telluride used in photovoltaic solar panels, and (4) phosphors for compact fluorescent and other energy-efficient lighting.

The bottom line is that the U.S. has zero hope of achieving the goal of energy independence in the short, medium, and even long term if it is based on 'green energy.' The U.S. will be at the mercy of China for its supply of 'green energy' components for a very long time to come. No matter the outcome any trade dispute, Obama cannot wish away the governing supply constraint of his energy independence vision. This renders the whole idea useless.

It is difficult to grasp why this problem snuck up upon 'green energy' promoters. Chinese leader Deng Xiaoping embarked his country on a path of economic supremacy in 1992, deciding to utilize China's economic advantage in rare earth metals in the same manner that oil-rich Middle Eastern countries utilize abundant hydrocarbon resources to their advantage.[50] That was seventeen years before Obama became President.

Deng's successor Jiang Zemin took the program a step further, creating a worldwide stranglehold on the global supply while also expanding China's downstream research and development efforts to achieve economic superiority over the rest of the world.[51] China would not just produce rare earth raw materials. It would migrate up the value chain, becoming the manufacturing hub for the world's supply of finished products that incorporate these materials.

These twin capabilities would be exploited as a weapon to facilitate manufacturing, technology transfer, and price control to China.[52] China today controls as much as 97% of the world's supply of these critical materials.[53] Rare earth resources are located throughout many areas of China including Shandong, Fujian, Sichuan, Hunan, Baotou, Guangxi, Jiangxi, Guangdong, and other regions and provinces.[54] The government has periodically halted operations at the country's largest production locations in a conscious effort to boost prices and further constrain global supply.[55] In late 2012, the world's largest rare earth producer halted operations for three straight months in an effort to boost prices.[56] It is also clear that China intends to consume the vast majority of the rare earth metal production that does occur, further constricting exports.[57] There may be a hundred Chinese companies producing Nd-Fe-B magnets compared to zero in the U.S.[58]

Another complication to Obama's program concerns China's imposition of export controls and tariffs. This has led to a two-tiered price structure where the prices of certain rare earth elements like neodymium can be fifteen times higher on the world market than within China.[59] That creates a strong inducement — it acts more like an obligation — for multinational companies to relocate manufacturing operations to China to avoid the high prices for essential strategic components.[60]

The extreme price differentials led to the growth of a rare earth smuggling industry. The Chinese government claims that 20,000 metric tons of rare earth oxides were smuggled out of China in 2008.[61] The Chinese Society of Rare Earths is on record stating to a *Reuters* reporter in 2010 that the country intends to shut off exports of rare earth materials completely in a few years.[62] The government pretended it was misquoted, which seems unlikely.[63] China is also stockpiling rare earth ore for strategic purposes to help assure a supply for years to come.[64] So Obama's 'green energy' future depends almost entirely upon perpetuation of global smuggling. How reassuring.

The strategic rare earth element supply problem is considered by the Department of Energy to be so acute that, in January 2013, DoE announced plans to spend $120 million establishing a Critical Materials Institute at the Ames Research Laboratory in Iowa to develop potential solutions.[65] Nevertheless, whatever DoE eventually decides to do, they'll know about it in Beijing before word reaches Washington. That's because half of the foreign graduate students who come to study at the Ames laboratory are from China. Anytime a Chinese student leaves, another Chinese national arrives as a replacement.[66] The Chinese are playing for keeps to win the game of global economic supremacy while Obama kowtows to climate hysterics.

The only domestic supply potential in the U.S. at present is a mine in Mountain Pass, California owned by Molycorp. As recently as the 1980s, the Mountain Pass mine was the largest producer of rare earth metals in the world.[67] That facility, once fully restarted, may be able to contribute about 10 to 15 percent of today's global supply of rare earth metals.[68] That amounts to a drop in the bucket if Obama's vision for massive increases in 'green energy' manufacturing is to be launched in the states. Hilariously, the EPA shut down the Mountain Pass mine in 1998 citing environmental concerns.[69] That was the mine that supplied America's only hope to achieve Obama's 'clean energy' future.

But even if output from Mountain Pass reaches the highest levels that Molycorp's most optimistic estimates promise,[70] the mine will not be able to supply significant quantities of heavy rare earth metals like dysprosium.[71] That element is critically important for hybrid electric motors and batteries.[72] China is the world's only supplier of dysprosium. Since late 2007, it has reduced its exports to zero.[73] None of the mines in development elsewhere in the world will be able to supply substantial amounts of heavy rare earth elements such as dysprosium, terbium or yttrium.[74] And Molycorp would still lack the critically important downstream assets to refine and manufacture 'green energy' components even if it could produce these elements in quantity.

U.S. Department of Energy metallurgist Karl A. Gschneidner Jr. has been studying rare earth metals since the 1960s. Gschneidner makes clear, "There is nearly zero rare-earth mining, processing, and research going on now in the U.S."[75] This reality won't change anytime soon.[76] Too bad Obama is not paying attention to this easily obtainable counsel offered from within his own administration ranks. And if he is, it certainly doesn't figure in any of his public pronouncements.

Amazingly, some years ago, China came close to getting its hands on the Mountain Pass mine. Unocal acquired Molycorp in 1977.[77] Chevron and Unocal agreed to merge in 2005 in a transaction valued at $16.8 billion.[78] But two months after that deal was announced, the state-owned China National Overseas Oil Company (CNOOC) made an unsolicited $18.5 billion all-cash offer for Unocal.[79] Though it went completely unnoticed at the time[80] — The New York Times offered the seemingly plausible explanation that the Chinese state-controlled oil company merely wanted access to Unocal's crude oil reserves[81] — it is now clear the real reason for the unsolicited offer was China's intent to lock up 100% of the world's supply of rare earth metals.

Observers at the time cited their concerns about Chinese access to Unocal's oil reserves.[82] A House hearing elicited frantic testimony from foreign policy stalwarts R. James Woolsey and Frank Gaffney, both of whom condemned the proposed deal over concerns about oil supply.[83] A resolution opposing the deal passed the House by a margin of 398 to 15.[84] All of the discussions centered around oil or Chinese military expansionism. There wasn't a syllable of concern about control of rare earth materials in any of the hearings or press reports at the time.

The state-owned China Non-Ferrous Metal Mining Co. also attempted to gain control of an Australian company called Lynas Corp. which had announced plans to construct a world-scale rare earth metals mine.[85] Australia is believed to possess about 4% of global proved reserves of rare earth metals.[86] The Chinese government backed out of the deal only after the Australian government's Foreign Investment Review Board refused to permit more than a 49% stake in Lynas.[87] China is not shopping for investments. It wants to lock up complete control of rare earth supply and pricing.

Instead of rapidly developing U.S. capability to produce rare earth materials and the complex supply chain components required to become self sufficient in these strategic industries, the Obama administration decided it would be better to join the EU and Japan in filing a formal complaint with the World Trade Organization (WTO).[88] No doubt the Chinese are sweating bullets over this. The complaint alleges that China uses unfair trade practices to limit exports, manipulate prices, pressure companies to relocate operations to China, and create unfair material price differentials that favor domestic manufacturers over foreign producers.[89] China, for its part, filed a complaint against EU countries alleging they offer preferential treatment to domestic solar photovoltaic producers over Chinese suppliers.[90] All of these allegations are incontestably true. And all of them are completely beside the point. The U.S. is not going to win this game by crying over Chinese practices, or complaining to transnational trade bodies.[91]

When Joseph Stalin was reminded that the Vatican had condemned his brutal subjugation of Eastern Europe, he rightly asked how many divisions of troops the Pope could put into the field to oppose him. The Chinese leaders were students of Stalinist power politics. How many divisions does the WTO have? The U.S. will only win this contest by securing its own domestic supplies of rare earth materials and downstream manufacturing process capability or, in the absence, by broadly diversifying its supply base.[92] That day is a long way off; even longer if it is left up to the Obama administration and its preferred instrument of blunt-force industrial policy trauma, the EPA.

Meanwhile, the race is on to find rare earth metals substitutes for permanent magnets. General Electric is evaluating superconducting alternatives to Nd-Fe-B magnets in its larger wind turbines.[93] Toyota is planning to eliminate Neodymium-based motors from its hybrid car lineup.[94] But irrespective of substitutions at the margin, rare earth metals will continue to dominate 'green energy' technology applications. And China will continue to control the majority of rare earth supply. It will thus effectively control 'green energy' technology supply markets for a long time to come. And all the empty Obama rhetoric or platitudes issued by ignorant media boosters and equally clueless enviro-left promoters of 'green energy' won't be able to change this.

'Green energy' proponents never tire of reminding the world that supplies of hydrocarbons are finite while the resources of their preferred energy sources, sunlight and wind, are inexhaustible. Wind and solar may be infinite. But the supply of materials required to harness these inexhaustible sources are definitely finite. None of those materials are controlled by the U.S. at present. And, if production levels are ramped up to massive scale required to satisfy the deployment demands envisioned by 'green energy' promoters, economically recoverable rare earth metal supplies will likely be exhausted far sooner than hydrocarbons ever will be.[95] This is the inescapable truth that destroys the 'green energy' independence argument.

SOLAR PHOTOVOLTAIC SUPPLY

In addition to rare earth materials required to produce various elements of Obama's future vision, true 'green energy' independence will also require complete control of the manufacturing and supply chain for solar energy applications. Leading that parade would be production of photovoltaic panels and the semiconducting photovoltaic materials that produce electricity.

Thin film photovoltaic production technology has made great strides in recent years in lowering cost per unit of electrical energy produced far below levels measured just a few years earlier. Three major developments have combined to accomplish this outcome. First, there have been technology advances that have produced a steady downward slope in the cost of manufacturing a solar panel. This was achieved by concentrating efforts on thin film technology based upon semiconducting materials like cadmium telluride over more costly panels using crystalline polysilicon technology.[96] Cadmium telluride deposition rates are three orders of magnitude faster than for polysilicon panels, which greatly lowers the effective capital cost embedded in the production of each panel produced.[97] And thin film cadmium telluride surfaces require far less material than their polysilicon predecessors, with thicknesses in the active layer of only two to three microns.[98] Cadmium telluride panels have crossed the magic barrier of $1.00 per watt with Arizona-based First Solar claiming production costs of 70 to 80 cents a watt, a number that solar analysts just few years ago thought would not be achievable for decades.[99]

Second, there has been a notable improvement in both yield efficiency as well as reliability of photovoltaic technology. Cadmium telluride panels can convert as much as 17% of the light energy from the sun into electrical energy.[100] Hitherto, a 15% efficiency threshold had been considered the holy grail, the minimum amount necessary to permit entry to the big leagues of power production for solar photovoltaic power generation. Improved reliability has lengthened the effective life of a photovoltaic panel. These factors together have combined to reshape the economic dynamics of photovoltaic solar power generation.

Third, the Chinese government has allocated billions to subsidize photovoltaic solar panel production. This has permitted Chinese companies to greatly lower production costs and drive down prices.[101] That led to an explosion in the number of Chinese photovoltaic panel producers, a massive build up of unsold inventory and a steeply dropping price curve.[102] Polysilicon-based solar panel prices plunged by 80% over the five year period up to 2012.[103] Fremont, California-based Solyndra cited cutthroat competition from Chinese panel producers as the reason why it was forced to declare bankruptcy in 2011.[104] So did another failed solar panel maker, Abound Solar. Solyndra filed suit against several Chinese panel producers alleging they had engaged in illegally collusive business practices.[105]

In March 2012, the Commerce Department imposed a series of countervailing duties on imported solar Chinese panels ranging between 2.9 and 4.73 percent.[106] The action originated with a German solar manufacturer's complaint that Chinese companies were subsidized by the government.[107] Of all the companies in the world to launch such a trade complaint, it fell to one from a country whose government has poured more than €100 billion in subsidies into solar energy since 1991, most of which went to its domestic solar photovoltaic panel manufacturers.[108] In a related ruling two months later, Commerce issued a preliminary ruling slapping duties of 31% on several of China's largest solar panel manufacturers.[109] Commerce finalized its May ruling in October 2012, greatly boosting duties to between 18.32 percent and 249.96 percent.[110] This will drive up the cost of solar energy in the U.S.

But China is hardly alone in subsidizing solar panel manufacturing. Obama is a proponent of the same approach. His solution to kick start America's solar panel manufacturing industry was to appropriate oceans of taxpayer dollars through the Obama "stimulus" plan. His 'green energy' programs will have consumed $150 billion of public spending between 2009 and 2014.[111]

There is no doubt that ruinous competition in the solar photovoltaic panel market has had a profound effect. General Electric announced plans in 2011 to construct the largest U.S.-based PV panel manufacturing plant to be located in Colorado.[112] But just a few months later, GE shelved its $300 million panel manufacturing plan citing intense competition from low-priced Chinese imports as the reason for at least an 18-month delay.[113] GE had planned to use a cadmium telluride thin film process technology at its new plant.[114] GE is not alone. First Solar had also been driven to the edge of extinction by ruinous competition from Chinese panel manufacturers. It was forced to close plants in the U.S. and Germany, further straining the domestic panel supply picture.[115]

The landscape is littered with the carcasses of solar PV companies driven out of business by low-cost Chinese competition.[116] Given the deluge of solar company market exits, fire sales, plant closures and bankruptcies in recent years — Evergreen Solar, Solyndra,

Soliant, Q-Cells, Solar Trust of America, Stirling Energy Systems, Solar Millennium, BP Solar, SpectraWatt, Abound Solar, Energy Conversion Devices, and Solon to name some examples — China's market dominance is likely to grow in the future.[117]

Amazingly, in the 1990s, China unleashed a deliberate strategy of flooding the market with rare earth materials, driving down prices and completely eliminating global competition in this space.[118] Then a few years after eliminating global competition in the rare earth metals industries, China boosted prices and restricted or completely eliminated exports. An identical picture could be emerging in the solar photovoltaic panel market-place. The first stage of eliminating global competition is nearly complete. Does wagering our future on photovoltaic panels that will soon be supplied almost entirely by Chinese manufacturers sound like energy independence?

Tellurium is most commonly recovered as a by-product of copper mining.[119] The world's largest copper mines reside outside the U.S., notably in Chile, Canada and China. Principal tellurium import sources are China, Canada, and Belgium.[120] Other materials critical to competing solar photovoltaic panel technologies include gallium and indium. As the DoE report referenced earlier makes clear, in 2009 the U.S. produced zero gallium and zero indium while information about the amount of tellurium produced in the U.S. was withheld by DoE.[121] One supposes that it's some sort of big secret that the U.S. produced zero tellurium also.

Solar energy is crucial to Obama's energy independence promise. America will presumably achieve that by deploying solar panels on every available square inch of rooftop, desert floor, and prairie. The plan is to blanket the landscape with photovoltaic panels produced from a supply of strategic materials that are currently sourced almost 100% from outside the country and are as abundant on Earth as platinum, a precious metal that sold for $1,550 per troy ounce in 2012. Good luck.

ENERGY-EFFICIENT LIGHTING

Obama boasted to his Portsmouth, New Hampshire audience in October 2007 that his 'green energy' program, the one that he promised would help America achieve energy independence in a short time, would obligate Americans to replace inefficient light bulbs with more efficient lighting:

> … *we know that if every home in America replaced just 5 incandescent light bulbs with 5 compact fluorescent bulbs, it would eliminate the need for 21 power plants. We'll do one better. I will immediately sign a law that begins to phase out all incandescent light bulbs — a measure that will save American consumers $6 billion a year on their electric bills.*[122]

Obama could have spared us his empty promises about signing such a law. A bill obligating that phase-out had already passed the Senate four months earlier.[123] It had cleared the House five months before that.[124] Of course, Senator Obama knew this to be so. But he was counting on his audience not knowing it. The bill was signed into law by President Bush just ten weeks after his Portsmouth speech.[125]

As every American knows, Thomas Alva Edison is credited with inventing the incandescent light bulb. His invention revolutionized life in America and the world. A filament inside the bulb composed of a semiconducting material like tungsten actively resists the flow of electricity passed through it. The heat-producing resistance causes the filament to glow, which then gives off light. Incandescent bulbs are relatively energy-intensive, relying upon a change of energy from one form into another and then into a third — converting electric energy into heat energy and then into light.

Fluorescent lamps work on a different principle. An electric current passes through a material called a phosphor which readily undergoes electron activation. An electron from the current strikes a phosphor atom transferring some electron energy to a phosphor atom, knocking its electrons temporarily into higher, more energetic orbital states. The excited electrons of the phosphor then return to their original lower energy state by ejecting the excitation energy in miniscule packets of visible light photons. Fluorescent lamps require much less energy per unit of light produced than incandescent lamps. Phosphorescent materials used in most energy-efficient lighting devices such as compact fluorescent light bulbs rely upon rare earth elements like terbium and europium, produced almost exclusively in China.

The Energy Independence and Security Act of 2007 (EISA), the law Obama pretended didn't exist when he spoke in Portsmouth, contained provisions that established minimum efficiency standards for various wattage ratings on incandescent light bulbs sold in the country that must be in place by certain effective dates.[126] EISA imposed regulations establishing a phase-out schedule for incandescent light bulbs with the highest wattage bulbs being outlawed beginning on January 1, 2012.[127] Thereafter, lower wattage bulbs would be outlawed over the course of the next several years. These provisions necessitate transition to more energy efficient light bulbs such as compact fluorescent lighting (CFL) and light emitting diodes.

If America is to achieve energy independence in accordance with Obama's vision that relies upon domestic control of all sources of 'green energy' gadgetry, it will certainly need to be able to satisfy 100% of the country's demand for energy efficient lighting from domestic supply sources. American will need to produce all or at least most of its own CFLs. How likely is this to occur?

In September 2010, General Electric announced it would close the last incandescent light bulb factory in the U.S. located in Winchester, Virginia and fire all of the plant's 200 workers.[128] The operation would be relocated to China. In conformance with 'green energy' mandates enacted by the EISA 2007 law, GE phased out sale of incandescent bulbs in the U.S. replacing them with CFLs, which are made exclusively in China. Obama is a proponent of these and other jobs destroying 'green energy' mandates. So, whether phase-out of incandescent light bulbs in favor of more energy-efficient CFLs amounts to good public policy, one fact is indisputable. Mandating usage of energy-efficient lighting puts the country deeper at the mercy of foreign supply sources, making 'green energy' independence an even more remote likelihood.

ENERGY BONDAGE THROUGH 'GREEN ENERGY'

The last refuge of 'green energy' promoters is their contention that we need to make wholesale changes in our way of life to free us from foreign sources of supply.[129] Adoption of their 'green energy' program would put the U.S. at the mercy of a single unreliable trading partner for nearly the entirety of our energy security. And it would require us to rely upon critical materials whose economically recoverable supply is probably far more finite than are hydrocarbons.[130]

Promoters of 'green energy' tell us not to worry, that the rare earth metals industry is relatively small. Rare earth mining accounts for only about $3 billion per year, around one percent of the iron ore market.[131] But size is not the overriding concern. Criticality is. Just ask a motorist stranded on a deserted rural road on a freezing night whose car broke down after a ten dollar part in his car failed. The cost of the part is inconsequential. Mission criticality is what matters.

'Green energy' promoters might be cheered by DoE's 2011 DoE Wind *Technologies Market Report* that found that "a growing percentage of the equipment used in U.S. wind power projects has been sourced domestically in recent years."[132] The report notes that "installed wind power capacity has outpaced the growth in imports" recently. DoE notes that excess assembly capacity has resulted as volume dropped in recent years simultaneously with increases in domestic capacity. But DoE's focus is solely upon final assembly of wind towers and turbines rather than critical, long lead-time components made from strategic materials. Had DoE included America's trade position relative to this essential aspect of supply chain security, it would have resulted in a very different assessment.

A quote from Bart Gordon, the Chairman of the House Science Committee, sums up the situation well:

> *It would be foolish to stake our national defense and economic security on China's good will, or hope that it will choose to compete in a fair and open global marketplace for rare earths. The stakes are simply too high.*[133]

'Green energy' proponents are willing to wager the future national defense and economic security of the country on China, a nation that props up and supports a genocidal regime in North Korea. They don't think the risk is very great. Are you willing to go along with their idea and place all our marbles into a basket that obligates us to rely upon China's good will for 100% of our energy security? A pair of MIT researchers concluded a peer-reviewed study in 2012 estimating that if Obama's 25-year 'green energy' plan is to come into fruition, the U.S. will need to secure a 700% increase in neodymium supply and a 2,600% increase in dysprosium.[134] Given current production trends, there is virtually no hope that demand could ever be met even if China was willing to loosen the reins of its supply chokehold.[135]

America will be producing well over 86% of its energy needs from domestic supply sources by 2016.[136] And that estimate is probably too conservative given continued slack energy consumption from America's lackluster economy, rapidly increasing domestic oil and gas supply potential, and EIA's unbroken track record of overestimating future consumption while undershooting future domestic output.[137] That represents a remarkable improvement from 2007 when the country produced only about 70% of its requirements.[138] America is on a solid path toward authentic energy independence without a sizeable assist from taxpayer-subsidized 'green energy.'

If the country were to adopt a crash program built around Obama's 'green energy' plan, instead of achieving energy independence, we would find ourselves in complete bondage, relying upon China for every last vestige of supply.[139] And we would spend anxious years waiting for that inevitable day when economically recoverable supplies of dysprosium, terbium, neodymium, yttrium, and all the rest will become too expensive to recover in large enough quantities to meet our needs in an affordable manner — as they certainly will. We would then achieve the realization of Obama's real vision of transforming America into a wholly dependent, poverty-stricken, Third World economic basket-case unable to project its planet-stabilizing power. All of America could become Detroit through Obama's 'green energy' program. The next time you hear a 'green energy' minstrel like Obama or Gore promoting their vision on the basis of energy independence, simply cue the laugh track. All their ideas deserve is derisive laughter.

CHAPTER 11

THE EXTERNAL COSTS
OF 'GREEN ENERGY'

"The cold reality is that honest, scientific, accurate mortality studies in the Altamont Pass area would result in [migratory bird] death tolls that would shock Americans. They would also raise serious questions about wind turbines throughout the United States, especially in major bird habitats like Oregon's Shepherds Flat wind facility and the whooping cranes' migratory corridor from Alberta, Canada, to Texas."[1]

JIM WIEGAND, WILDLIFE RESEARCHER
U.S. REGION VP, SAVE THE EAGLES INTERNATIONAL

This toxic lake poisons Chinese farmers, their children and their land. It is what's left behind after making the magnets for Britain's latest wind turbines ... one of a multitude of environmental sins committed in the name of our new green Jerusalem.[2]

SIMON PARRY AND ED DOUGLAS
THE DAILY MAIL

Any honest appraisal of 'green energy' will readily acknowledge that wind, solar and biofuels are indisputably more expensive than fossil fuels. Proponents of 'green energy' counter by arguing that competitive analysis doesn't adequately account for the cost of "external" impacts that result from fossil fuels.[3] So, they contend, if these "externalities" are included in the fully-allocated cost of fossil fuels, then 'green energy' will suddenly become competitive by comparison, or even cheaper.

Economists refer to externalities as the costs imposed upon society that are not paid by the purchaser, but are borne by others not involved in the transaction. It is absolutely correct that fossil fuels impose external costs that are rarely or never factored into comparative analysis. Fossil fuel combustion is polluting, environmental damages occur in the extractive process, the fallout from major spills can be horrendous even if temporary, there are environmentally damaging impacts from transport, refining and distribution, etc. The now discredited *Stern Review* described this situation as the single largest market failure in history, a wildly overblown contention.[4]

External costs of coal usage are acute. Coal extraction is often performed by stripping away an entire mountain top, which imposes serious environmental damage. Scouring a hilltop uncovers partially soluble mineral deposits that run off into streams and rivers, leaching heavy metal poisons and acidity into drinking water reservoirs and fisheries. Coal mining liberates heat-trapping methane into the atmosphere. Coal combustion leaves behind piles of fly ash that contain heavy metal residues and even radioactive elements. It also liberates neurotoxins like lead and mercury compounds into the air, which can persist for long periods in the environment, are biologically concentrated in nature, and which severely damage human health when breathed or ingested.

All fossil fuels liberate carbon dioxide, a compound that stimulates green plant growth but also traps heat in the atmosphere. The environmentally conscious progressive refueling her *Prius* does not pay for all carbon and other pollution that results from her car's operation or throughout the fuel supply chain. It is appropriate to impute the costs of all these externalities when making a cost comparison to other energy sources.

So these 'green energy' proponents advocate a heavy government role to assess and collect for these external costs. Yet they rarely reason through where the funds should go, why they should go there, and how it would help if they did. In addition, their calculus fails to account properly for the immense externalities that their preferred options would impose. This chapter is devoted to discussing some of these. Unfortunately, the 'green energy' case is usually motivated far less by a desire for economic efficiency and far more by a desire to exert greater control, to choose future technologies. These advocates are central planners at heart. Most of them are unabashed about admitting as much.[5] This gives rise to a number of very problematic questions:

1. *Do the funds collected go toward mitigating the cost of externalities, or something else?* The mechanism for distributing the proceeds collected for mitigation of fossil fuel externalities will, in all likelihood, resemble the crony slush funds of the 2009 economic "stimulus" plan that shoveled mountains of cash to every rent-seeking, Democrat-aligned, special interest group under the sun. The Obama "stimulus" plan included subsidies and payments to public employee unions, ethanol producers, AIG executives, steel producers, inner-city school districts, hog farmers, vintners, citrus growers, high technology companies, artists, lithium-ion car battery makers, Indian tribes, rural abortion clinics, plug-in electric car makers, wildlife enthusiasts, 'green energy' purchasing electric utilities, pharmaceutical companies, ship builders, and thousands of others.[6] The act even included $2.4 million in a futile attempt to resurrect the reputation of infamous Penn State climate campaigner Michael Mann whose paleoclimatology "hokey schtick" had been thoroughly discredited.[7] It became a mud-wrestling contest between K Street lobbyists, public-funding dependent wards of the Democratic Party, rent-seeking corporate special interests, and campaign contribution-hungry legislators — with nothing left over for fossil-fuel mitigation.

2. *Is there a solid justification for collecting extra levies?* Like many assessments imposed by government to fund a specific purpose, the funding quickly becomes detached from the putative justification for which it was imposed. The federal tax you pay for phone service was a "temporary" levy enacted to cover expenses related to the Spanish-American War that ended in 1898. The tax remained. *The Washington Post* profiled a raisin farmer in 2013 who owes the federal government $650,000 in fines for failure to comply with a law adopted during the Truman administration, a law enacted to solve an emergency raisin shortage that genius government bureaucrats fretted over during the 1940s.[8] Fuel excise taxes collected for road and bridge building become a private piggy bank for money-grubbing federal and state politicians. The revenues collected will be devoted to offsetting negative impacts from fossil fuel use — just like the phone tax collected today is desperately needed to ameliorate the lingering negative fallout from the Spanish-American War.

3. *Are the external costs of fossil fuels being properly assessed?* Much mischief is afoot among 'green energy' proponents who are hoping to build a case that fossil fuel use is far more expensive than reality would suggest. For instance, a pair of EPA staffers published a study claiming, in typical EPA fashion, that the adverse health costs from coal use in electricity are so high that "on average, U.S. consumers of electricity should be willing to pay $0.24–$0.45/kWh for alternatives such as energy efficiency investments or emission-free renewable sources that avoid fossil fuel combustion."[9] I'll go out on a limb here and wager they won't. The all-sector cost of electricity in 2012 was only 9.87 cents per kWh.[10] Let's have a show of hands: how many ratepayers out there want to pay a price 2.4 to 4.6 times more than today for electricity? These authors wildly claim that their estimate of $885.5 billion of fossil fuel external costs in the U.S. is likely an underestimate.[11] This amounts to a $2,820.84 per capita cost, a staggeringly absurd number. There's a rule in football against piling on. It should apply to federal rulemaking. EPA has a long track record of vastly overestimating the negative costs of pollution as a method to justify ever more stringent environmental regulations. A pair of university researchers published a peer-reviewed paper in the *Journal of Economic Research* in 2013 contending that the U.S. economy would be generating $53.9 trillion in GDP in 2011 instead of the $15.1 trillion it actually recorded if federal regulatory impact had remained at 1949 levels.[12] Whether regulations are worthy of the costs society bears is an open question. But there is indisputable evidence that they are excessively costly.

A competing study to the EPA's farcical effort published by a European advocacy group which measured the adverse health-related costs of coal usage concluded the impact in more populous Europe was only €42.8 billion across the entire continent.[13] Since Europe hosts 2.4 times more people than does the U.S., the adverse per-capita health cost in Europe is only $75.66 per person. In other words, a more reasonable assessment of per capita adverse health impact from fossil fuel use is only about 2.7% of the value that EPA staffers wildly assert. Another estimate of external costs from fossil-fuel usage in electricity generation performed by the National Academy of Sciences puts the cost at 3.2¢ per kilowatt-hour for coal[14] and 0.16¢ per kWh for natural gas.[15] At least these studies were conducted down here on Earth.

The preferred path of 'green energy' enthusiasts is to wildly overstate external costs of fossil fuels while ignoring dangerous health- and environmental-related externalities of 'green energy' usage. They also fail to allocate cost shifting from large 'green energy' public subsidies, understate or ignore the fully allocated costs of backup generation required to overcome intermittency, and are putting in place mechanisms to spread the large capital costs for 'green energy' transmission infrastructure investment onto the backs of ratepayers who will not even directly benefit from those investments.

4. *Are 'green energy' mitigation costs appropriately matched to the true economic costs of CO_2 emissions?* There is little relationship between the putative costs of fossil fuel use and the "solutions" that have been put forth by 'green energy' central planners or are already in place today. The largest meta-study in human history combining 311 economic estimates of the social cost of CO_2 emissions arrives at an average of $5 per metric ton. So CO_2 abatement measures that impose costs above this level would be wasteful and economically damaging.[16] But every 'green energy' example cited imposes abatement costs from dozens to even thousands of times more than this value. California imposes a charge of $88 per metric ton to abate CO_2 under the most generous set of assumptions. Professor Gordon Hughes of University of Edinburgh demonstrates how the UK's master plan to solve global warming will impose a charge of £270 per metric ton to abate CO_2, which, in all likelihood, will actually lead to higher greenhouse gas emissions than a program built around natural gas generation.[17] The massive wind energy complex at Shepherds Flat in Oregon, constructed with $1.2 billion in public subsidies, will abate CO_2 at a cost of $130 per metric ton.[18] Obama's carbon tax would impose a cost of $261 per metric ton of CO_2 abated.[19] Since American taxpayers will foot 100% of the bill on these measures while reaping only 4.4% of the climate-related benefits based upon their proportion of the global population, the real cost is actually 22.7 times higher than these numbers suggest.

5. *Are the externalities of favored 'green energy' alternatives being properly assessed and charged?* We have seen in these pages how the heavy hand of federal government has been used to disrupt, impede, criminally prosecute, fine, and stigmatize oil producers in North Dakota and elsewhere because a handful of dead birds were found floating in waste discharge ponds. But wind turbines chop hundreds of thousands or even millions of fragile migrating avian species into fish bait each year without fear of prosecution. Solar thermal plants routinely barbeque them. Rare earth mining pollutes waterways and agriculture leading to as many as a million premature human cancer deaths from toxicities caused by heavy metal contamination in poor, rural parts of China. Fertilizer runoff from crops grown for biofuels results in widespread eutrophication and "dead zone" anoxia in the Gulf of Mexico that renders thousands of square miles each year useless for fishing. 'Green energy' enthusiasts, self-described champions of environmental justice, look the other way. Wind farms require vast areas of natural scenery to be destroyed for turbine towers and long-distance transmission lines. Energy storage systems required to balance 'green energy' intermittency will destroy countless more square miles of priceless natural beauty.

Based upon the evidence collected thus far, the prognosis is not good. Instead of leveling the playing field to achieve desired social, economic, and environmental goals, we are likely to erect a permanent bureaucratic drag on our way of life that imposes economic costs far in excess of any tangible benefits. That will retard the most promising path that could improve the largest number of lives and livelihoods. Central planning has a lousy track record, a fact that presents absolutely no impediment to its most vocal proponents. Devotees of central planning suffer from what Friedrich Hayck called "the fatal conceit."[20] All we are ever likely to do by following their advice is impair economic growth, incomes, and living standards. This is not a future we should desire.

As Professor Severin Borenstein correctly observes, it is a terrible idea to promote renewable energy technologies to address supposed ancillary benefits like energy security, job creation, or energy cost reduction. As he states it, "it's a bad idea and likely to backfire."[21] Borenstein has researched and written extensively on the topic. But like most energy researchers, he often ignores the external costs imposed by renewable energy.[22] It is clear that overwhelming numbers of academic researchers who study energy economics are focused solely upon the externalities of fossil fuels while ignoring the externalities of renewable sources. This is a debate from which fossil fuel producers must not flinch because any fully allocated cost comparison between 'green energy' and fossil fuel energy would almost certainly improve the relative competitiveness of fossil energy.

PERSECUTING ENERGY PRODUCERS

News media outlets triumphantly announced in August 2009 that Exxon Mobil, the nation's largest oil company, had pleaded guilty in federal court to killing eighty five migratory birds at its drill sites in five states during the previous five years.[23] The birds had either ingested oily waste or had become trapped after their wings had been coated in hydrocarbons from waste ponds.[24] The federal prosecutor in the case, John Cruden, lauded the stiff $600,000 fine levied against the company, proclaiming that it would serve "as a useful example to other companies charged with violating the Migratory Bird Treaty Act of 1918 (MBTA)."[25] While none of the bids included in the federal filing appears on the endangered species list, the judgment served as a potent reminder to energy producers that they could face fines of up to $7,000 per bird killed if their operations resulted in loss of fragile avian species.[26] But those numbers were chump change compared to the $10 million fine paid by PacifiCorp for electrocuting birds at their substation power lines in 2009 or the $100 million paid by BP for harming migratory birds after the Gulf oil spill.[27]

A few months after his 2009 inauguration, Obama traveled out to Newton, Iowa to visit a manufacturing plant that builds towers upon which sit the electricity-generating wind turbines that would be largely responsible for powering his new energy economy. Obama had promised on innumerable occasions that environmentally benign 'green energy' innovations like wind turbines would solve the pressing problem of environmental degradation being wrought by fossil fuels. Even if he had also promised to increase domestic production of oil and natural gas, it would, in his words, only be a "short term" measure as more wind turbines were deployed and more of America's electricity generation needs were satisfied by those marvelous inventions with their spinning turbine blades. This was the source of electricity that wasn't likely to trap fragile migrating birds in oily waste pools. Migratory birds could celebrate Obama's 'green energy' expansion.

During his run for office, Obama had claimed that America was "running out of places to drill."[28] Accordingly, we needed to begin building wind turbines immediately, and in large numbers. The real truth is, American oil producers were being run out of places — by federal prohibitions and regulatory impediments. Despite his wildly erroneous claims, reliable estimates by the *International Energy Agency* show that by the year 2020, America will become the largest producer of oil and gas on the planet, surpassing Russia and even Saudi Arabia.[29] That claim was way too conservative.[30] The country had become the world's largest producer by mid-2013.[31]

America didn't really need a heavy dose of wind turbines. A small dose of honesty would have sufficed. A good example of how America had obviously not run out of places to drill is North Dakota. In the last few years, North Dakota became the country's second largest producer of oil.[32] In January 2006, North Dakota produced fewer than 100,000 barrels per day (bpd). But by October of 2013, oil production had shot up to 941,843 bpd, more than a 9-fold increase.[33] The state is projected to be producing a million bpd in 2014, leaving traditional oil producing powerhouses Alaska and California in the dust.[34]

So it would be an especially difficult challenge for an energy policy visionary like Obama to kick-start an energy revolution for wind energy when facing the headwinds of a rejuvenated oil and gas sector. How was the man who confidently proclaimed that America was running out of places to drill ignite his 'green energy' program when oil was gushing out of holes in places like North Dakota where oil had never previously figured into America's energy equation? Only a special breed of politician could get the job done. Enter Timothy Purdon, stage left.

Purdon's selection as U.S. Attorney for North Dakota was a transparently political choice. Purdon boasted zero prosecutorial experience. Having no experience fit squarely with Obama's other energy policy choices. His main qualification was that he had been a large campaign-contributing member of the Democratic National Committee who was married to a woman who had worked as a lobbyist for the National Environmental Trust, an organization that has led malign public relations campaigns designed to disrupt U.S. oil drilling.[35]. It was an appointment that even the *Los Angeles Times*, a normally reliable Obama-supporting media outlet, found room to criticize.[36]

Purdon promptly enclosed his thanks by initiating dubious prosecutions against seven energy drilling companies in North Dakota for supposedly killing twenty eight migratory birds.[37] In all likelihood, the drilling activities had nothing to do with killing the birds. It was clearly designed to disrupt and intimidate oil producers in the state.[38] Purdon eventually succeeded in obtaining guilty pleas against some of the companies, collecting $1,000 fines for each dead bird, a pittance compared to the $7,000 that Cruden chiseled out of Exxon Mobil.[39] Nevertheless, the message was clear. An Obama administration was intent on protecting migratory birds from ravenous energy producers. Obama also wanted to add $35 billion in new taxes to try and cripple domestic oil and gas drilling, adding an additional layer of security for birds.[40]

The malicious nature of the prosecution is readily apparent. The Migratory Bird Treaty Act had never been successfully used against companies accused of incidental takings of migratory birds. Lumber companies successfully defended themselves when their logging activities, unrelated to poaching or hunting, had destroyed nesting habitats of migrating birds.[41] Even more salient was a New Mexico case from 2002 in which the court declined to permit any action to be taken against an oil company that had negligently allowed a storage pit to overflow, which ensnared thirty four migrating birds covered by the MBTA.[42] Despite the negligent actions of the company, its intent was not to "take" birds but to produce oil. The taking was purely incidental.

Whatever Exxon Mobil's motives in pleading guilty, the company would have likely been fully exonerated had it contested the malicious prosecutions. When Purdon pursued three other companies, U.S. District Judge David Hovland dismissed the claims in January 2012, writing that:

> ... *it is highly unlikely that Congress ever intended to impose criminal liability on the acts or omissions of persons involved in lawful commercial activity which may indirectly cause the death of birds protected under the Migratory Bird Treaty Act ... the conduct of [defendants] is insufficient as a matter of law to trigger criminal liability.*[43]

One of the defendants, Continental Resources, had been maliciously accused of killing a single Say's Phoebe, one of North America's most common birds, a species found in great numbers in dozens of states.[44]

CUISINART ENVIRONMENTALISM

Of course, like with every aspect of Obama's 'green energy' vision, the lens is distorted. In actuality, the landscape in the U.S. is being overrun with wind farms whose rotating blades act like giant bird and bat blenders. Nevertheless, and not surprisingly, as of October 2013, no prosecutions had been lodged against wind turbine electricity generators.[45]

A wind turbine mortality estimate published in a peer-reviewed journal in 2013 derived an annual estimate of 880,000 bat and 573,000 bird fatalities, of which 88,000 were raptors.[46] This is considerably more than the American Bird Conservancy estimate of 440,000 migratory birds killed each year.[47] If these operators were fined like oil drillers in Denver, taxpayers would collect $10.2 billion in fines each year to help offset the countless billions they squander on subsidies to erect, operate, and maintain these rotating bird killers.

But consider for a moment how badly understated these numbers may be. The

California Energy Commission published a report in 2002 on avian collisions with wind turbines. The authors cited research work by a Dutch team that examined bird fatalities from wind turbine collisions in Europe. The key passage was that "In a summary of avian impacts at wind turbines by Benner et. al. (1993)[48] bird deaths per turbine per year were as high as 309 in Germany and 895 in Sweden."[49] Suppose one accepts a low-range average of 365 fatalities per turbine per year as a representative number. There were 45,100 wind turbines installed across the U.S. at the end of 2012.[50] That would equate to 16.5 million bird deaths per year. That is twenty nine times more than the 573,000 death toll figure supplied above. A recent estimate of turbine-caused bird and bat mortality in Spain places the toll at anywhere between 6 and 18 million fatalities per year.[51] Spain has only about a third of the installed wind power capacity as does the U.S.[52] Had Cruden been on the turbine operator case, we could have recouped $115.2 billion in bird death fines.

Consider the plight of one of the rarest avian species on the planet, the Tasmanian wedge tailed eagle. Wildlife experts estimate there are only 130 successful breeding pairs in the wild.[53] Yet these fragile birds are slowly being wiped out of existence by the increasing number of wind turbines being deployed on Australia's largest outer island.[54]

The estimates of the avian holocaust from wind turbines are consistently underestimated by the U.S. Fish and Wildlife Service (FWS).[55] FWS is not alone. Wind farm operators are also guilty of vastly understating their counts of bird kills by restricting search areas, under-reporting, excluding mortally-wounded birds, failing to account for removals, etc. A 50-meter turbine blade will fling a raptor an average of 372 feet.[56] But wind farm operators restrict their searches to 165 foot diameters from the base of the tower. If carcass distances are normally distributed, the searches will miss 67% of the fatalities. This is a deliberate process designed to miss a majority of bird kills, permitting the operator to report "acceptable" losses.[57]

The Obama administration is an active participant in the underreporting, as AP reporter Dina Cappiello makes clear:

> *When companies voluntarily report deaths, the Obama administration in many cases refuses to make the information public, saying it belongs to the energy companies or that revealing it would expose trade secrets or implicate ongoing enforcement investigations.*[58]

According to FWS, "the combined effects of direct annual mortality from wind turbines may, for some species, be causing impacts at the population level."[59] That means whole populations of endangered species are being driven to extinction by wind towers. The federal government gave fast-track approval to a $6 billion wind farm project in Carbon County, Wyoming that will sell its 3,000 megawatts of power to Southern California.[60] The site requires construction of a 725 mile high-voltage transmission line that would cost ratepayers another $3 billion to construct.[61] This project is slated to move forward even though the Bureau of Land Management estimates the turbine complex would kill at least sixty four endangered golden eagles each year.[62] A large wind energy complex in Solano County, California was the first wind project to be granted a permit to kill golden eagles.[63] A deputy assistant regional director of external affairs for FWS was quoted in press reports saying "the bottom line is a permit will help preserve eagles."[64]

So, in the upside-down world of Obama-style 'green energy' logic, if we permit wind farm operators to kill thousands of golden eagles each year, that will help preserve the species. The FWS published a notice in the *Federal Register* inviting public comment on their plan, claiming it was designed to "avoid, minimize, and mitigate adverse effects on eagles, birds, and bats."[65] If they really wanted to do that, they would shut down that and all other wind farms immediately.

One noted environmental advocacy group, the National Audubon Society, claimed in news reports that they are "taking a hard look" at proposals for more wind farms. The Audubon Society was named after James Audubon, a naturalist and authority on birds. Jane Graham from Audubon's Florida chapter was quoted saying, "We think alternative energy is absolutely necessary. You see what's happening with coal plants and climate change."[66]

Actually, we can't see what's happening with coal plants and climate change. Neither can Jane Graham. She just pretends like she can. However, everyone can clearly see what's occurring with *Cuisinart Environmentalism*, although environmentalists feel obligated to pretend like they can't. If Jane Graham really wanted to see what her beloved "alternative energy" was doing to avian species, she could dial up a cringe-inducing video on *YouTube* showing an endangered Griffon Vulture being maimed by a wind turbine on the island of Crete.[67] Griffon vultures are listed as endangered — 400 were killed at the wind farms of Navarre in the Pyrenees region of Spain in a single year.[68] Or she could travel to the hills of West Virginia and discover the carcasses of 59 birds killed in a single night by a wind turbine at the Mount Storm Wind Energy complex.[69]

Audubon Society's "hard look" at wind turbines didn't seem too hard after it decided that its initial opposition to the Cape Wind project off Nantucket would be easily overcome.[70] The project is located squarely within the migratory flyway of numerous threatened aquatic avian species.

Such is the moral conundrum in which deep environmentalism finds itself. They must maintain a dogmatic adherence to a faith-based explanation of changes to the earth's geology, climate, and ecosystem that have been occurring naturally and without human influence for 4.6 billion years while ignoring the undeniably obvious human causality of rampant species extinction of migrating birds in the vicinity of wind farms. That is the energy source environmental activists claim is necessary to avoid upsetting the delicate balance of the planet's climate and its equally delicate species. So the Audubon Society, an environmental group dedicated to preserving and enhancing habitats for birds, must struggle to make up its mind about whether shredding millions of migrating birds amounts to good public policy.

Like their Audubon Society counterparts in the U.S., the Royal Society for the Protection of Birds (RSPB) in the UK laughingly proclaimed that:

We know that with the right planning, design and location, wind turbines have little or no impact on wildlife.[71]

Eleven months later, when a rare white-throated needletail showed up in the country, the first one spotted in the country for twenty two years, dozens of bird-watching enthusiasts flocked to the Isle of Harris off the coast of Scotland for the rare event. But as they stood observing their unusual visitor, they were horrified as the hapless needletail flew into a spinning wind turbine blade and was killed instantly.[72] Interestingly, it wasn't one in a massive wind farm but a solitary turbine that provides power to a small community.[73] As Clive Hambler, a senior lecturer in Biological and Human Sciences at Oxford University points out, this event would have been exceedingly unlikely unless something about the turbine itself was responsible for attracting the bird.[74]

The rare species of bird that inhabits Asia and Australia had only been spotted eight times in the UK in all the years back to 1846.[75] Yet, when it was killed in front of spectators, RSPB went silent.[76] That might be due to the fact that RSPB has accepted over £1 million in hush money from wind farm operators over the past ten years.[77] Instead, RSPB assured themselves that their own wind turbine which they proclaim will reduce their carbon footprint 80% by 2050 will enable the planet to solve global warming.[78] So by 2050, wind turbines like the one on the RSPB estate will presumably enable the planet to avoid global warming. The problem is that by then, there won't be any more migrating birds left to protect.

RSPB is typical of "big green" outfits that bloviate *ad nauseum* about how climate change poses the biggest threat to avian species. Consider the Royal Society's claim:

We believe that renewable energy is an essential tool in the fight against climate change, which poses the single biggest threat to the long-term survival of birds and wildlife.[79]

This is simply a preposterous conceit given that every species of bird on earth today has managed to survive anywhere from ten to twenty ice ages along with sea-level rises that were far more severe than anything forecasted to occur in the next several centuries.[80] It's obvious these advocates don't really do science. Environmentalism, which began its existence as a branch of biology, has been transmuted into a strange pagan religion.

In California, where zealous adherence to faith-based environmental creeds is imprinted into the genetic code of most of the state's residents, wind farms have long been linked to catastrophic avian species destruction, especially among vulnerable birds of prey. Included on the list of victimized species from the churning rotary blades are red tailed hawks, bald eagles, golden eagles, kestrels, various species of owls, and other endangered raptors. Estimates range as high as 5,000 birds per year among these threatened species that are chopped into fish bait by the rotating blades of 'clean energy' wind farms in the Altamont Pass Wind Resource Area (APWRA) alone.

The APWRA is endowed with steady winds as warm air masses over the adjacent

San Joaquin Valley collide with the cooler air of the San Francisco Bay. But it is those very wind conditions that make the area attractive to raptors that soar on the upland air currents that the turbines hope to harvest. An effort was announced to reduce the frequency of raptor deaths by 50% in the APWRA.[81] After three years of investigation, the result was a staggering increase in raptor fatalities. There is direct evidence that the Obama administration is deliberately hiding the fearful toll of endangered golden eagle deaths caused by wind turbines.[82]

In a hilarious passage in a *USA Today* article from 2005, the paper claimed that "Scientists don't know whether the kills reduce overall bird populations."[83] Needless to say, they do know. It is axiomatic that birds killed by rotating blades do "reduce overall bird populations." What other realistic option is available? What scientists don't know is how many research grants and speaking invitations they would suddenly lose if they admitted the truth.

Interestingly, FWS imposed an indefinite ban on permitting for wind farms until the situation surrounding bald eagle deaths was better understood.[84] To the environmental movement, the most pressing item on the agenda is stoking irrational public fears about catastrophic planetary warming, which they claim is caused solely by human activities. To the extent that the planet is warming, the causes are not well understood, the degree to which human influence is to blame is largely unknown, and the resulting impact is pure guesswork. Their conclusions about runaway climate warming are based solely upon a set of deeply flawed climate models that they built themselves, models which contain fudge factors and parametric estimates they inserted themselves, models that are incapable of replicating past climate behavior, and have already been shown to be inadequate to explain current climatic conditions.[85] Global warming hysterics can't pretend some ill-defined 97% consensus can negate these truths. Furthermore, as far as anyone knows, slight planetary warming may amount to a net positive for the environment. Either way, remediation efforts by building wind farms would be wholly inconsequential and may be counterproductive relative to more feasible alternatives.

Birds are not the only victims. Bats are suffering an even more grievous toll than birds. There is something about a whirling turbine blade that appears to attract bats.[86] Researchers in Germany have discovered bats migrate more than 1,000 miles only to be shred into carrion by wind turbines.[87] Scandinavian researchers "recorded 11 species (of a community of 18 species) flying over the ocean up to 14 kilometers from the shore."[88] Their peer-reviewed research helped explain "why and how bats might be exposed to additional mortality by offshore wind power."[89]

A fascinating sidelight on the situation has been playing out in Kern County, California over wind farm projects already deployed or slated to be built in the Tehachapi Range. Of all the endangered species restoration projects ever undertaken by mankind, no single species has received a greater amount of attention and resources than the California condor. The species became badly depleted due to hazards like wire fences, land use changes, and environmental threats. At one point, there were only an estimated nine or ten individual birds in the wild.[90] The total wild population had dwindled to an estimated five breeding pairs.[91] A decision was made by FWS to capture every living condor in an effort to captive breed and eventually restore them to their natural habitat.

By 1992, California condors began being released back into the wild. In October 2010, a key milestone of 100 wild condors was announced.[92] But deployment of wind turbine farms in the Tehachapi Range poses a substantial threat to condors. Kern County granted a permit to the 300 mW Manzana project, claiming the threat was low. The FWS objected to Kern County's characterization of this project and an adjacent 350 mW Catalina project.[93] The slow-moving condor, with its nine-foot wingspan, is especially susceptible to turbine blade collision.[94]

But in spite of the threat to this rarest of rare species, environmentalists are conflicted about the environmentally correct stance to take. Whatever objections FWS might have had, they were overcome as the service notified wind farm operators that they would not face prosecution if their wind turbines killed endangered condors.[95] This decision came in the face of a survey published in March 2013 showing that 65 of the 132 free-flying condors inhabit the Tehachapi Range.[96] Telemetry data from implanted tracking devices show many of these birds fly directly into the turbine area.[97]

FWS seems to be able to get around these kinds of problems that would land other landowners and businesses in jail, facing heavy fines. When a crony-connected company named Bright Source decided to build a solar ranch in the California desert, the company surveyed the site for the presence of endangered desert tortoises. Bright Source claimed to have found only 25 turtles on the plot earmarked for the Ivanpah solar plant. But when FWS performed its own survey, they discovered 2,862 adult or juvenile tortoises and tortoise eggs of the endangered species.[98]

Interestingly, the land upon which the Ivanpah solar ranch sits has a curious history. The Wildlands Conservancy raised $45 million in the 1990s to acquire 1,000 square miles of privately-owned desert land which they donated to the federal government.[99] The gift prompted President Bill Clinton to write a May 2000 letter of thanks, assuring the group that the donated land would remain forever out of the hands of rapacious developers.[100] But the Obama administration decided to grant access to Bright Source to build its Ivanpah plant on the same donated land, outraging members of the Conservancy who had wrongly assumed the land would remain inviolate into perpetuity.[101]

Because highly dispersed 'green energy' projects like wind towers are located in regions far from population centers where the power will be consumed, massive transmission projects will be required to harvest the power and transmit it to where it is needed. New transmission lines are also needed to balance intermittency of unpredictable load flows caused by highly variable wind and solar power. Obama and Ron Binz, his deservedly rejected pick to head the Federal Energy Regulatory Commission, believe 'green energy' is so important, we need to throw all the rules out the window and create new rules to "socialize" the costs of these dreadfully expensive, technically unworkable, problematically intermittent, low density power sources that would otherwise be unaffordable.[102]

So not only will thousands of miles of poorly utilized transmission lines be necessary to accommodate 'green energy' investments. But the private investor-owned projects whose benefits will flow to wealthy investors will see a large portion of their primary cost structure offloaded onto the backs of middle- and lower-income ratepayers. The transmission lines will take an ever-increasing toll on migrating birds. Transmission line cost shifting, the toll exacted upon fragile avian and bat populations, and the administration policy to excuse wind farm operators from culpability amounts to a massive taxpayer subsidy to wind farm operators never enacted into law.[103]

Wind farms wreak widespread environmental damage by causing massive bird deaths to fragile avian species. The bird deaths are incontestably taking place and their impact is devastating to any number of threatened species. Moreover, wind turbine production requires mining of rare earth heavy metals to fabricate permanent magnets. Rare earth metals mining causes substantial water pollution resulting in rampant cancer deaths in poor rural regions where the activity takes place. These effects are provable and beyond dispute. This *Cuisinart Environmentalism* is destroying some of the most fragile species of life on the planet in the name of environmentalism.

And what is the Obama administration's response to the widespread environmental devastation being wrought by this program? It was to continue waging specious prosecutions against oil and natural gas drilling companies, slowing down the rate of permitting for domestic oil and gas drilling while bypassing the Bureau of Land Management to speed up the permitting approval process for migratory bird *Cuisinart* projects.[104]

Wind enthusiasts counter these realities by claiming that house cats kill more birds each year than wind turbines do. That may be true. But how often has your house cat brought home a Tasmanian wedge tailed eagle, a California condor, an American bald eagle, a whooping crane, a white-throated needletail, an American kestrel, a golden eagle, a Griffon Vulture, or any of a thousand species of endangered birds that are being driven to extinction by wind turbines?

Apparently the Obama administration's Fish and Wildlife Service feels flush enough with resources to issue a $535 citation against the mother of an 11 year old Virginia girl who saved a baby woodpecker from being devoured by the family cat.[105] Possessing a woodpecker is a violation of the MBTA. Eradicating infestations of bats nesting in your attic can get you fined thousands of dollars. Possessing a bald eagle feather, even one taken from an eagle chopped to pieces by a wind turbine, can land you in jail, facing a $100,000 fine.[106] But the FWS is in no hurry to issue citations to wind farm operators that destroy millions of environmentally sensitive, endangered migratory birds. Just before departing on his endless 2013 Christmas holiday, Obama issued a thirty year waiver to wind farm operators, allowing them to slaughter eagles and other endangered species without fear of prosecution.[107] It was history's most undeserved Christmas gift.

GREEN ENERGY CANCER DEATHS

As a candidate, Barack Obama spelled out in great detail his vision for America's energy future at a speech in Portsmouth, New Hampshire in 2007. He boasted that "my plan isn't just about making dirty energy expensive; it's about making clean energy affordable."[108] The 'clean energy' that Obama was describing included wind turbines, renewable fuels, hybrid-electric cars, and other low-carbon sources while the 'dirty energy' involved fossil fuels like coal, oil and natural gas. Obama's plan was to rid the Earth of sources of energy that spewed carbon dioxide into the atmosphere, substituting that unbearable menace for 'clean energy' that emitted no trace of CO_2. Carbon dioxide is the compound used by plants for respiration and plant tissue growth during photosynthesis. It has no known deleterious health effects upon humanity at normal atmospheric concentrations.[109] Without it, all life on the planet's surface would perish. Naturally therefore, Obama wants it banned.

Just how clean is Obama's 'clean energy' anyway? On September 30, 2011, Energy Secretary Steven Chu announced the award of $1.46 billion in loan guarantees to Desert Sunlight 250, LLC and Desert Sunlight 300, LLC to construct a facility with 550 megawatts of solar power.[110] The station would utilize 8.8 million cadmium telluride photovoltaic modules. Chu proclaimed that:

> *To win the clean energy race we must invest in projects like this that fund jobs and increase the generation of clean, renewable power in the U.S. Deployment of utility-scale solar power will help bring down the cost of solar and strengthen our position as a global clean energy leader.*[111]

Chu mentioned the word 'clean' three times in two sentences. Anybody who does that is serious about cleanliness. You get the idea that Chu would be out there scrubbing and polishing the energy until it shined. The Desert Sunlight project was similar to dozens of other 'clean' solar energy projects that utilize cadmium telluride thin film photovoltaic panels, the ones Obama and Chu had poured billions of taxpayer dollars into over the course of the previous three years.[112]

There were several problems with Secretary Chu's claim, but the most glaring was his contention that cadmium telluride thin layer photovoltaic solar panels were in any sense of the word 'clean.' Cadmium is an element that is a highly toxic carcinogen, considered the sixth most toxic heavy metal element on the planet.[113] The U.S. Occupational Safety and Health Administration identifies the binary compound cadmium telluride as a carcinogen, exposure to which can lead to lung and kidney damage, fragile bones and, depending upon exposure levels, even death.[114] Tellurium, while a relatively common element throughout the observable universe, is rare on the surface of the Earth. Virtually all of this metalloid is mined in China.[115]

The majority of the world's cadmium telluride solar panels are manufactured in

China.[116] China mines all of the tellurium and cadmium used in its cadmium telluride thin film photovoltaic panel manufacturing at its world-scale metallic ore mines located in rural areas of the country. These mines are notorious as generators of massive toxic pollution from heavy metal runoff that leaches into waterways and fresh water aquifers. The situation at Baotou in Mongolia is an example of what has been accurately described as environmentalism's "dirty little secret."[117]

The world-scale rare earth element processing plant at Baotou uses a vast array of toxic chemicals like ammonia, acids, and sulfates to separate and extract the desired metallic elements from the ores mined nearby. Workers at the plant experience high levels of toxic exposure as they are afforded little of no protection.[118] A report filed by British journalists from *The Daily Mail* tells a grisly tale of how life changed as more rare earth mining occurred around Baotou:

> *As more factories sprang up, the banks grew higher, the [discharge] lake grew larger and the stench and fumes grew more overwhelming. People too began to suffer. Dalahai villagers say their teeth began to fall out, their hair turned white at unusually young ages, and they suffered from severe skin and respiratory diseases. Children were born with soft bones and cancer rates rocketed. Official studies carried out five years ago in Dalahai village confirmed there were unusually high rates of cancer along with high rates of osteoporosis and skin and respiratory diseases. The lake's radiation levels are ten times higher than in the surrounding countryside, the studies found.[119]*

Of course, these shocking realities would never be allowed to intrude upon the festive atmosphere among well-heeled, jet-setting, environmentally conscious delegates celebrating their ecological sensitivity at climate summits in fabulous places like Kyoto, Rio de Janeiro, Copenhagen, Bali, and elsewhere. But villages like Baotou become the ultimate price tag of their policies. You can draw a straight line between their political conceits and the indefensible situation in Baotou.[120]

The heavy metal pollution from mining ore used to fabricate 'clean energy' technology has created what researchers refer to as China's "cancer villages."[121] The village of Shangba in Southern China is an example of one of these cancer villages. In a single year, six villagers in their 30s and 40s died from cancers. In a 20-year period from 1987 to 2007, an estimated 250 people in a village of only 3,000 people died from cancer.[122] This is many times the expected cancer death rate in the U.S.[123] Estimates of premature deaths from cancer in China range from a half million to a million people per year.[124] Given that these estimates rely on official Chinese government data, the number is likely many times higher. For years, Chinese environmental officials denied the country even had a pollution problem.[125] But a visit to Shangba would prove otherwise. Acceding to the undeniable, China's environment ministry finally acknowledged in early 2013 the existence of what the rest of the world had known but few, including 'green energy' campaigners, were willing to admit.[126]

Drinking water in Shangba comes from contaminated wells that contain high levels of cadmium, the element used to manufacture the photovoltaic solar panels that Secretary Chu claimed repeatedly were "clean."[127] The contaminated water also finds its way into the food chain through rice paddy irrigation.[128] Nanjing Agricultural University researchers discovered that 10% of China's rice output is contaminated with cadmium.[129] The Chinese government classifies these findings a state secret, disclosure of which can result in prison sentences.[130]

Consumption of contaminated food and drinking water has led to high rates of digestive tract cancers in rural villagers. While press reports typically focus upon lung cancer associated with atmospheric contamination from coal-burning power plants, it is clear that digestive tract cancer problems are actually a far worse calamity. Eighty five percent of cancers detected among the Chinese people are those affecting stomach, liver, kidney and colon.[131] All across China, there are hundreds and perhaps even thousands of cancer villages like Shangba where digestive tract cancer is the primary cause of death.

Cancer is now the leading cause of death in China thanks, at least in part, to production of minerals essential to 'clean energy.'[132] As many as a half a billion people in China lack access to safe drinking water according to World Bank data. Environmental remediation and site restoration in China often involves measures like painting the landscape with green paint at sites where metals mining had previously occurred rather than undertaking effective containment of toxic materials that would be far more expensive.[133]

Environmentalists like Barack Obama style themselves champions of environmental justice for their opposition to "dirty" fossil fuels. But these environmental justice champions must avert their gaze from this appalling situation that their favored public policies are, in part, to blame lest they be confronted with the incongruities that they have unleashed on poor villagers in a far away land. It is indefensible to pretend that they don't know what is happening, or that the problems are not severe. Real climate justice would involve obligating them to hold their next climate summit in Shangba where only well water would be served to the delegates.

Cadmium telluride solar panels are not the only source of China's cancer epidemic stemming from 'clean energy' manufacturing. Other rare earth metals are key ingredients in things like wind turbines, electric car batteries, hybrid cars, and so forth. Manufacturing processes to produce these elements liberate substantial amounts of sulfur and fluorine compounds into the atmosphere.

Each ton of rare earth metal output produces 2,000 tons of mine tailings, the toxicity-laden materials left behind after metals are extracted.[134] The tailings often contain substantial amounts of radioactive thorium.[135] Waste water runoff is highly toxic containing dangerous levels of heavy metals, asbestos, acidic compounds, poisons, and even radioactive isotopes that flow into rivers and pollute aquifers and groundwater. Collection reservoirs have destroyed vast areas of farmland from seepage due to inadequate containment. Crops grown in the vicinity of major metallic mining and smelting operations like Baotou can no longer be safely consumed.

Cindy Hurst, an analyst with the U.S. Army Foreign Military Studies Office at Fort Leavenworth, Kansas, is an expert in China's rare earth mining industry.[136] She cites a report from the Chinese Society of Rare Earths showing that China's rare earth mining industry is plagued by an unprecedented level of pollution and environmental lawlessness:

> *Every ton of rare earth produced generates approximately 8.5 kilograms of fluorine and 13 kilograms of dust; and using concentrated sulfuric acid high temperature calcination techniques to produce approximately one ton of calcined rare earth ore generates 9,600 to 12,000 cubic meters of waste gas containing dust concentrate, hydrofluoric acid, sulfur dioxide, and sulfuric acid, approximately 75 cubic meters of acidic wastewater, and about one ton of radioactive waste residue.*[137]

When the raw ore is further refined into rare earth metallic oxide, each ton of finished product produces 1.4 tons of radioactive industrial waste, 200 cubic meters of acid-laden sewage, and 63,000 cubic meters of waste gas containing deadly hydrofluoric and sulfuric acids.[138] Hydrofluoric acid is powerful enough to dissolve glass.

The Bayan Obo mine in Baotou is the world's largest rare earth mine. Over the previous decade, the mine supplied about 80 percent of the world's rare earth oxides.[139] More than 5,000 residents of Baotou suffer from pneumoconiosis, better known as black lung.[140] That amounts to half of the cases throughout the entire Inner Mongolia autonomous region. The mine generates ten million metric tons of wastewater each year, all of it untreated.[141] The wastewater is discharged into the Yellow River which flows another 1,300 miles through both rural and densely-populated urban areas of China before emptying into the Yellow Sea. About 180 million Chinese people obtain their drinking water from the highly contaminated Yellow River.

Tom McGregor, the Chinese government's Lord Haw Haw, dishonestly attempts to dismiss water contamination claims by attributing them to the aforementioned U.S. Army analyst Cindy Hurst. Yet he certainly knew that Hurst's report actually originated with the Chinese Society of Rare Earths. Nevertheless, like the blind squirrel that occasionally finds the acorn, McGregor correctly acknowledges the staggering hypocrisy inherent in the position of environmentalists, who advocate for 'clean energy' in the U.S. which relegates hundreds of millions of poor Chinese to endure horrific pollution exposure.[142]

In Portsmouth and everywhere else, Obama promised to lessen America's usage of 'dirty energy' in favor of 'clean energy.' To Obama, 'clean energy' was the kind that fouled groundwater with cancer-causing toxic heavy metal elements and compounds, while 'dirty energy' was the kind that liberated CO_2, a benign compound that accelerates planetary greening.

Obama warned his listeners in Portsmouth that "all polluters will have to pay based on the amount of pollution they release into the sky."[143] It's fine if you poison the streams, rivers, oceans, and ground water with toxic pollution that causes millions of premature cancer deaths. Those industries are not labeled "polluters" in Obama's 'clean energy' lexicon. But industries that emit the same essential life ingredient required by plants and exhaled by humans and all mammalian and animal life forms would be obligated to pay fines for enhancing green growth.

Obama cannot be blamed for lax environmental standards in China, a lawless country afflicted by deep-seated corruption. But he can be blamed for averting his gaze from the consequences of his energy policies. And he can be held accountable for supporting a program whose direct consequence is substantial increases in heavy metal mining and smelting that causes rampant cancer deaths in poverty-stricken rural areas of China.

SOCIAL COST OF CARBON

In May 2013, the Obama administration decided to update its 2010 estimate of what climate change economists call "the social cost of carbon."[144] The 2010 estimate was prepared in an effort to justify the administration's Corporate Average Fuel Economy (CAFE) regulation. The putative benefits from reduced traffic congestion, fuel usage, and air pollution were calculated by White House economists to be $73 billion less than the economic costs the rule would impose.[145] So they needed to invent something to plug the hole. Claiming that society will benefit enormously if we eliminate carbon dioxide emissions, suddenly the $73 billion deficit would become a $108 billion benefit by virtue of regulatory magic.[146] Never mind that the administration's CAFE plan will remove as many as fifteen million households from the new car market by the year 2025.[147] Those are real, measureable costs that were easily ignored. Meanwhile, carbon dioxide emission costs are subject to far greater uncertainty. Prior to 2010, CO_2 emissions rightly bore no regulatory cost.

The social cost of carbon (SCC) measure refers to the cumulative cost, expressed in today's dollars, of future impacts our progeny would bear by the release of one metric ton of CO_2 today. Since the negative impact would presumably be felt in the far distant future, we attempt to place a present value on the delayed impact by expressing it in today's dollars. SCC refers to a point at which society would be exactly indifferent between paying that cost today or paying the accumulated future cost from negative effects caused by that emission release when and if those impacts ultimately occur many years in the future.

Let's face it, there is no real present cost of a metric ton of carbon dioxide emissions. One metric ton of CO_2 is about the amount that a 150 pound man would exhale during three and a third years of life.[148] Despite the hysterics emitted by global warming evangelists, this really doesn't impose a burden on the planet or its ecosystem today. But hysterical climate modelers, with help from their economist fellow-travelers, have devised forecasts that purport to show that sometime in the future, bad things will begin to happen as humanity releases more CO_2 from fossil fuel burning.

One concept exceptionally important to this line of analysis is what some economists refer to as the *rate of time preference of money*. That's a fancy way of saying money has a *time value.* Economists and financial analysts utilize a computation method called *discounting* to determine how much we would be willing to pay today in exchange for some delayed future benefit. While it may not be intuitively obvious to those not steeped in the arcane computational intricacies of economic and financial analysis, the plain fact is that the discounting concept is one of the key drivers in future valuation. It is the proverbial straw that stirs the SCC drink. We would rather accelerate a receipt and postpone a payment because, in both cases, we would have use of the extra money in the interim. But there is a limit to how much we would pay next year to avoid paying $1,000 today. The number that allows us to equate next year's payment limit to this year's avoided $1,000 payment is called the *discount rate.*

Economists have attempted to develop a present value cost of CO_2 emissions to understand how much equivalent discounted cost we would bear today that just equals the forecasted unsavory future impacts they say will be caused by CO_2 emissions. Such thinking underlies the claimed justification for a carbon tax, which is based upon a belief that present generations care about the welfare of their descendants. So if that we liberate a metric ton of CO_2 today that damages a future generation, it results in a discounted reduction in present utility.[149]

What climate hysterics don't bother mentioning is that, long before these bad things happen, a lot of good things will occur. This is not just idle, speculative musing. An incontestable pattern of expected net economic benefit resulting from a temperature increase of up to two degrees Celsius and even beyond has been documented extensively in the academic literature.[150] In addition, there is a long period of sustained wealth-induced economic benefit we derive from the energy we use today. This is especially true when alternative energy sources are considerably more expensive and technically more problematic than conventional sources. Wealth-creation and induced income-growth considerations are never factored into assessments of the social cost of carbon. They have very high utility also, and yet are ignored.

For a long time to come, the good things in a gradually warming planet will provide net benefits that will far outweigh any offsetting costs that will occur simultaneously. For instance, crop yields will gradually increase in a warmer climate because growing seasons will be longer. Crop yields will also benefit from a net increase in rainfall despite all the lurid fables being peddled about droughts and famines. The IPCC's Summary for Policymakers document, the only one that media outlets ever bother reading, deliberately falsified this impact in 2007. It listed the amount of land area forecasted to suffer lower rainfall without bothering to mention that a much larger land area would see enhanced precipitation.[151] In addition, higher CO_2 concentrations will cause a fertilization effect which will boost agricultural yields.[152] Farms and fields will become more productive. There will also be many fewer temperature-related deaths since many more people die from hypothermia than from heat-related causes.[153] Yes, people die from heat-related causes. But deaths from cold far exceed heat-related mortalities. All of these factors work to significantly reduce the present value cost of CO_2 emissions.

In addition to the above, there is also the issue about selection of the appropriate discount rate. It needs to be realistic so that we don't place too high or too low a present value on a future impact. The most common method people use to select a discount rate is to figure out what their alternative financial opportunities are at any point in time. If you had an extra $1,000 now, what debt reduction or investment benefit could you achieve? When you sandbag the discount rate, you completely warp all the results. That is what the Obama administration has chosen to do with its application of a paltry 3% discount rate in its "social cost of carbon" executive order.[154]

How many people pay a 3% interest rate on their credit card debt? How about on student loan debt, or on a car loan, or on outstanding mortgage debt over a long term? These rates are essentially unheard of on consumer debt. Our discount rate, the number we would implicitly use to equate a present cost with something postponed, is much higher than 3%.

But how about the federal government? Is it accustomed to paying a 3% rate on outstanding federal debt? The federal government borrows money today to achieve a societal benefit for which it will pay more at a later time when repaying the loan. That's the theory anyway. The U.S. Treasury paid an average annual rate of just 1.5% during the fiscal years from 2009 to 2012.[155] But those years are not good examples. The Federal Reserve has monetized a rapidly increasing level of federal debt, purchasing a substantial portion of Treasury issuances and remitting the interest payments back to the Treasury.[156]

Interest rate exposure on federal debt in prior years shows much higher payout levels. Interest rates on 30-year Treasury bond issuances between 1990 and 2002 show an average payout of 6.77%.[157] The average payout rate on federal debt from 1975 to 2005 was 5.07%.[158] The running 30-year average payout rate has been above 4% in every fiscal year going back 29 years.[159] Fourteen of those 30-year averages were above 5%.[160] And in 1984, the average interest rate on federal debt reached 7.22% in a year when the Treasury sold 30-year bonds carrying a 16% coupon rate.[161] There is little in the way of empirical support for a 3% discount rate based upon federal debt.

On top of that, the issue is "the social cost of carbon" not "the federal government cost of carbon." So we need to look at a broader measure of interest and discount rate measures than just federal debt payouts, since society at large will supposedly bear the cost. All of those alternative discount rates would be far higher than 3% or even the 4.25% average interest rate paid on federal debt over the past 30 years up to fiscal year 2012. The compound annual return on the S&P 500 stock index over the past 30 years up to the end of 2012 is 10.8%, which includes the steep sell-off that occurred in 2007-2009.[162] Why isn't that a better estimate since many American workers park a large portion of their 401(k) savings into index funds that aim to mirror the performance of the S&P 500? Likewise, the Congressional Budget Office uses a 10% discount rate to understand the tradeoffs between paying higher up-front costs for an electric or hybrid car that consumers would be willing to bear in exchange for lower operating costs that result from reduced gasoline consumption.[163]

Office of Management and Budget Circular No. A-94 establishes rules that federal agencies must employ in developing cost-benefit analysis of regulations to determine the social impact they will have. The circular directs agencies to employ a 7% discount rate when the timing of costs society bears differs from the benefits society will derive from the proposed rule-making:

Constant-dollar benefit-cost analyses of proposed investments and regulations should report net present value and other outcomes determined using a real discount rate of 7 percent.[164]

Lest one be inclined to dismiss this regulatory directive due to its age, OMB updated its guidance 11 years later, reiterating its earlier finding. The new guidance in Circular No A-4 states clearly that, for federal agency rulemaking:

A real discount rate of 7 percent should be used as a base-case for regulatory analysis. The 7 percent rate is an estimate of the average before-tax rate of return to private capital in the U.S. economy. It is a broad measure that reflects the returns to real estate and small business capital as well as corporate capital. It approximates the opportunity cost of capital, and it is the appropriate discount rate whenever the main effect of a regulation is to displace or alter the use of capital in the private sector.[165]

Of course, Obama ignored his own regulatory guidance. Why is this important? The Obama White House Interagency Working Group that fictionalized this whole issue noted in May 2013 that, when it developed its 2010 estimate of $11 per metric ton of CO_2 emission based upon a 5% discount rate, the SCC number would balloon to $52 per ton if it applied a 2.5% rate.[166] In other words, when you cut the discount rate in half, the SCC result more than quadruples.

Amazingly, the Obama administration increased its earlier estimate of the social cost of carbon in 2013 even though every known development we could cite since 2010 that would impact the equation served to lower its estimated valuation. And it did so by burying the announcement in an obscure regulation covering microwave oven efficiency standards without inviting public comment, a cynical move that engendered widespread criticism even from a variety of Obama-friendly media.[167] Interest rates are likely to climb, not drop.[168] That would reduce, not increase, the valuation we place on future streams of income or expense. The planet's temperature has not increased in more than seventeen years.[169] Even leading climate hysterics among the IPCC community are questioning previously modeled outcomes, which now appear will be less severe and substantially postponed.[170]

The practical effect of this can't be underestimated. Because the climate appears not to be as sensitive to CO_2 emissions as the climate "consensus" believed just a few years ago, the cost of future impacts will likely be far lower than previously feared. The apparent effect of the slowdown in global warming will be to prolong the period over which net favorable impacts will be enjoyed, postpone the period when net negative impacts finally begin to be felt, and reduce the severity of the net negative impacts when and if they do occur. In addition, because there is such a high degree of uncertainty in the estimates, the valuations that market dynamics typically places on highly fluctuating future patterns is far less than on patterns that exhibit higher degrees of certainty. Under any transparent analysis, all of these factors should serve to reduce "the social cost of carbon."

Lastly, usage of carbon-based fuels to support economic growth and development generates a self-sustaining wealth-effect benefit. Because energy is such an essential enabling input to economic growth, efforts to suppress its usage will impair growth today. That will leave humanity less equipped to handle the malign effects of global warming through adaptation strategies later on. When we impair economic growth, we reduce present and future generations' ability to deal with the negative effects of climate change. By curtailing fossil fuel usage which curtails economic growth, we raise the social cost of carbon by reducing the *social benefit of carbon*. This concept is utterly absent in the administration's analysis — or anywhere else for that matter.

We are being slowly conditioned to believe mistakenly that carbon-based fuels impose only negative consequences. Go to your favorite internet search engine and enter the text string "Planet Mongo." You will get millions of hits. But enter the text string "social benefit of carbon." You'll get close to zero. You get nothing searching for the beneficial impacts from the source that provides more than 80% of the world's energy, the stuff that powers humanity's modern way of life.

Carbon-based fuels deliver substantial, sustained economic benefits. Economic growth is essentially impossible without copious inputs of energy. And we get over 80% of our primary energy from fossil fuels that emit CO_2. Naturally therefore, in the face of these considerations, the Obama administration, the one that bills itself as the most transparent administration in history, effectively doubled its cost estimate, doing so in secret.[171] Don't be terribly shocked if, before it's all done, the number will be boosted again and again in response to hectoring from the climate hysteric community that wants to transmute energy policy into a regulatory freak show.[172]

Suppose there were an economist of unparalleled credentials — maybe someone who has been a professor at a leading university for more than 30 years — who believed wholeheartedly that there was little or no credible debate that CO_2 emissions from fossil fuels are driving climate change. Imagine such a person contended that the human-induced climate change will result in future damages that will impact future generations, that proposals for carbon tax schemes among world governments have merit, and that those programs should be pursued as national policy.[173] Such a person would be expected to be a strong supporter of Obama administration efforts to use a social cost of carbon measurement approach to shape federal regulatory activity.

Meet Robert S. Pindyck, a Professor of Economics and Finance at the MIT Sloan School of Management. As his lengthy CV attests, Pindyck has published dozens of books, book chapters, scholarly journal peer-reviewed articles, and a wealth of material on environmental and climate change economics.[174] So the Professor is no easy foil for raving climate change zealots who spend every waking hour labeling anyone who criticizes Obama climate change policy as a rabid anti-science Holocaust "denier."[175]

Nevertheless, here is what Pindyck says in a peer-reviewed study that was published in the *Journal of Economic Literature* in September 2013 about Obama's social cost of carbon that is based upon what economists refer to as an *integrated assessment model* (IAM):

> *A plethora of integrated assessment models have been constructed and used to estimate the social cost of carbon and evaluate alternative abatement policies. These models have crucial flaws that make them close to useless as tools for policy analysis: certain inputs (e.g. the discount rate) are arbitrary, but have huge effects on the SCC estimates the models produce; the models' descriptions of the impact of climate change are completely ad hoc, with no theoretical or empirical foundation; and the models can tell us nothing about the most important driver of the SCC, the possibility of a catastrophic climate outcome.*[176]

This is the academic equivalent of blunt force trauma delivered to the glass-jaw conceits of policymakers at the White House who are trying desperately to make us believe that the "science is settled" on their worthless models, that we must accept every pronouncement lest we be compared to a bigoted Holocaust denier, and that every aspect of the policy has been carefully scrutinized and is above reproach. As Pindyck says, the SCC models the administration is relying upon "create a perception of knowledge and precision, but that perception is illusory and misleading."[177]

Even more startling is the method used by IAM creators to estimate the amount of damage or GDP loss that will supposedly occur with any temperature change:

> *... developers of IAMs can do little more than make up functional forms and corresponding parameter values. And that is pretty much what they have done ... The choice of values for these parameters is essentially guesswork ... Sometimes these numbers are justified by referring to the IPCC or related summary studies. But where did the IPCC get those numbers? From its own survey of several IAMs ... The bottom line here is that the damage functions used in most IAMs are completely made up, with no theoretical or empirical foundation.*[178]

If you're following closely here, IAM authors just make up values for damage without a shred of empirical support. And if they get stymied, the go to the IPCC for reference. And where did the IPCC get its supposedly authoritative findings? From those same IAMs, of course. It's an academic daisy-chain tarted up to appear like precision science.

Here's something else the IAM confabulators are hiding. They claim that GDP will shrink if global temperatures increase. That faith-based belief resides at the very core of their catechism. Needless to say, since we don't have empirical data to support that assumption because we've never measured GDP impact of a warmer planet, the belief rests entirely upon faith.[179] But is the belief sound? Consider that since 1880, the earth has undergone an atmospheric temperature increase of about 0.8° Celsius.[180] Did GDP decline as a result as IAMs assume? Actually, per capital GDP increased by about 1,700% globally.[181]

It appears increasingly likely that fudge numbers like his "social cost of carbon" could and would be used to throw a monkey wrench into plans for economic growth and energy self-sufficiency that projects like the Keystone XL pipeline could help boost.[182] In that case, it wouldn't be about the social cost of carbon but the social cost of politics that poses the real threat.

Famed climate change economist Richard S.J. Tol has probably forgotten more in a week about assessing the social cost of carbon than the Obama administration brain-trust will ever know in a hundred lifetimes. Tol and his colleagues sum up the issue well in a 2009 paper, saying that because the uncertainties about future impacts are so large and the selection of low discount rates makes the analytical result purely arbitrary, you can essentially get any result you want:

> As there are a number of crucial but uncertain parameters, it is no surprise that one can obtain almost any estimate of the social cost of carbon. We even show that, for a low pure rate of time preference, the estimate of the social cost of carbon is indeed arbitrary — as one can exclude neither large positive nor large negative impacts in the very long run.[183]

Getting any result you want by arbitrarily making it up as you go is exactly how Obama has approached every aspect of energy policy. It is the same whether it concerns warping the economics of 'green energy' projects through subsidies and mandates, hiding the truth about the domestic supply implications of 'green energy' whose critical componentry originates from offshore sources, wildly overestimating the negative societal impacts from clean coal-burning power plants, hyping the potential of creating 'green jobs' that will never materialize, overestimating the risks of offshore oil drilling to curtail production on federal lands, circulating fairy stories alleging minimal beneficial economic effects of increased domestic oil and natural gas supply, lying about the immense economic costs of shutting down a fourth of America's electricity generation capacity through onerous regulations, disrupting hydraulic fracking on private lands with phony "studies" alleging ground water contamination, broadcasting ludicrous estimates about CO_2 abatement potential of biofuels, pretending that solar and wind power can supply a large portion of our energy requirements, warping long-standing regulatory approaches to allocating the costs of long-distance electrical power transmission infrastructure, ignoring the societal damages that result from 15% volume formulations of ethanol, enacting tax credits for purchase of plug-in electric cars at levels far in excess of any societal benefit we could ever derive, vastly overestimating the net beneficial carbon reduction effects from energy conservation measures, filing dishonest assessments of carbon sequestration economic feasibility — or sandbagging an estimate of the social cost of carbon.

CHAPTER 12

THE 'GREEN JOBS' TIDAL WAVE THAT WASN'T

"My plan ... will create millions of new jobs and entire new industries right here in America ... my plan is to invest $150 billion over the next decade to ensure the development and deployment of clean, affordable energy."[1]

BARACK OBAMA
PORTSMOUTH, NEW HAMPSHIRE, OCTOBER 8, 2007

"The idea of government 'job creation' is a classic example of the broken window fallacy, which was explained by French economist Frédéric Bastiat way back in 1850. Obama's 'green jobs' plan would indeed create jobs, but it would do so by killing other jobs."[2]

KENNETH P. GREEN
ECONOMIST, AMERICAN ENTERPRISE INSTITUTE

"Since Obama has been in office ... $150 billion will [have been] spent by the government on new alternative energy sources, according to the Brookings Institution."[3]

INVESTORS BUSINESS DAILY, JULY 24, 2013

"The jobless nature of the recovery is particularly unsettling ... An estimated 22 million Americans are unemployed or underemployed ... Americans by the millions are in part-time work because there are no other employment opportunities ... a third of the currently unemployed have been out of work for more than six months ... the number of people leaving the workforce during this economic recovery has actually outpaced the number of people finding a new job by a factor of nearly three."[4]

THE WALL STREET JOURNAL, JULY 15, 2013

Few falsehoods are subscribed to more deeply than the one purporting that a public-ly-mandated transition to a 'green energy' economy will provide a bountiful net surplus of good, high-paying jobs. Those job gains will presumably usher in improved labor market conditions along with higher economic growth, enhanced economic competitiveness, and rapid gains in real personal and business income.[5] As an article of faith among 'green energy' religionists, the myth is firmly embedded so deeply in popular "wisdom" that efforts by leading economists and public policy experts to challenge it are routinely met with angry rebuttals. But the series of quotations above demonstrate that the "wisdom" is based on fallacy. As G.K. Chesterton observed in 1930, a fallacy doesn't cease being a false simply because it becomes fashionable.

Barack Obama is a guardian of the 'green jobs' faith. He based his candidacy around a plan for a radical, expensive, centrally-planned economic transition away from fossil fuels that account for over 80% of America's primary energy. He assured his followers that con-verting from affordable to costly sources of energy would deliver millions of high-paying jobs. Obama reiterated that promise in Denver in August 2008:

> *I'll invest 150 billion dollars over the next decade in affordable, renewable sources of energy — wind power and solar power and the next generation of biofuels; an investment that will lead to new industries and five million new jobs that pay well and can't ever be outsourced.*[6]

With his frequent psycho-dramatic, cult-of-personality overuse of the first-person sin-gular, the man made it sound like he'd be reaching into his own pocket. This was his iron-clad promise — the speech itself was entitled "The American Promise." It doesn't get more succinct than that. With $150 billion of your money, America would be well on the road to reaping the environmental fruits of his 'green energy' transition while enjoying the economic benefits of five million permanent jobs that "can't ever be outsourced." He assured us those sources were "affordable" but we already knew in 2008 that claim was wildly in error.

Obama is not alone in his 'green energy' job-creating delusion. The U.S. Conference of Mayors articulated its dogmatic adherence to this belief in a 2008 'green jobs' report:

> *The economic advantages of the Green Economy include the macroeconomic benefits of investment in new technologies, greater productivity, improvements in the U.S. balance of trade, and increased real disposable income across the nation. They also include the microeconomic benefits of lower costs of doing business and reduced household energy expenditures. These advantages are manifested in job growth, income growth, and of course, a cleaner environment.*[7]

It takes strenuous effort to articulate a broad, multi-faceted statement of principles that is exactly wrong on every single point. But the Conference of Mayors — or its consultant Global Insight — managed to do it. There will be no net advantage of a 'green economy.' Sensible Germans and Californians can explain it to you. The government-mandated investment in green technologies will not bring macroeconomic benefits, but will impair growth. There will be a substantial reduction in productivity as resources and labor are squandered on reduced, low-value output. The balance of trade will suffer as imported wind turbines and solar panels act to offset domestically produced fossil fuel. Real disposable income will decline as consumers are forced to pay for higher priced energy. Households and businesses will see their energy bills skyrocket. Countless authoritative studies demonstrate that many more jobs will be destroyed than will be created. Those findings are confirmed by labor force statistics already in our rear view mirror. And claims about a "cleaner environment" are unproven, highly dubious, marginal at best, and most likely false. Former GM chief Bob Lutz observes that squandering resources on a project with a negative payback is "like a car company spending hundreds of millions on a vehicle that either fails to sell, or sells at less than it costs to produce."[8] Lutz should know. He did exactly that with his ridiculous Chevy *Volt*.

Proponents of 'green jobs' acknowledge that a transition to the 'green economy' will entail crippling costs. For instance, the UN Environment Programme observes that:

No one knows how much a full-fledged green transition will cost, but needed investments will likely be in the hundreds of billions, and possibly trillions, of dollars.[9]

Is that all? We were afraid it would be expensive. Despite the astronomical costs, in every instance in the hagiographic literature, the 'green economy' transition cost is described as a net societal benefit. The 'green jobs' faith contends that the required spending provides a contribution to GDP, the publicly-funded "investment" creates a net gain in jobs, and the advertised environmental benefits are always accepted at face value.

The faith-based belief in promised beneficial effects of government 'green energy' spending is the point where faith-based environmentalism collides with a discredited macroeconomic theory authored by John Maynard Keynes in 1936.[10] Keynesian enthusiasts and 'green energy' promoters are joined at the hip. They both adhere to delusions that massive government borrowing to support deficit spending is always beneficial to the economy, that it won't result in a "crowding out" impact to more economically rewarding private sector activity, and it won't impose a fiscal drag later when taxes increase to repay the debt. And they both fancy statist industrial policy. Each group possesses limitless faith in the Delphic capability of federal government central planners to faultlessly forecast which applications will succeed in the marketplace among a set of nascent technologies.

Keynesianism has never worked as intended. In most instances when it has been tried, it has produced contrary results.[11] But to know that requires a long-distance detour to Planet Reality. Empirical evidence is the last thing that affects the thinking of technocratic social science geniuses like the 'green energy' cohort.

As Figure 12-1 shows, federal spending averaged a manageable 19.4% of real GDP in the ten years from 1999 to 2008.[12] During this period of time, the economy showed a semblance of a pulse as measured by the 4-year compound average real GDP growth rate. But when federal spending as a percentage of the economy exploded, economic growth evaporated. With the arrival of Obama's Keynesian 'green energy' experiment, economic growth disappeared at the same time as federal spending as a percentage of the economy soared to levels not witnessed since World War II. In other words, there was an inverse relationship between long-run real economic growth and federal spending. The more you have of one, the less you get of the other. Who do you believe? Obama, or your lying eyes?

Federal spending as a percentage of GDP leaped from a 10-year average of 19.4% to 25.4% in fiscal 2009 to provide a "temporary" stimulus in the face of recession. But those spending levels became permanent as the higher outlay levels were embedded in budgetary baselines. As spending soared, job creation and economic growth went south.

FIGURE 12-1. **Federal Spending % of GDP vs. GDP Growth**

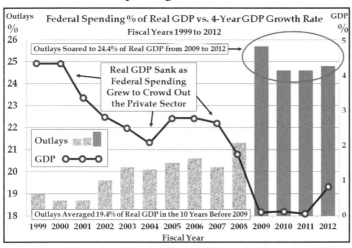

Sources: 'The President's Budget for Fiscal Year 2013,' Historical Tables, *Office of Management and Budget*, Table 1.2—Summary of Receipts, Outlays, and Surpluses or Deficits (-) as Percentages of GDP: 1930–2017; National Income and Product Accounts, *Bureau of Economic Analysis*, Table 1.1.6 Real Gross Domestic Product

Candidate Obama promoted carbon cap-and-trade and other aspects of his *New Energy Economy* like taxpayer subsidized 'green energy' as a job creating mechanism.[13] Obama claimed his proposals "will create millions of new jobs and entire new industries right here in America."[14] He assured the country that this glorious future was already happening in Europe and elsewhere. Sadly for America, Obama was not alone in this view as his opponent in the 2008 Presidential race, Senator John McCain, subscribed to the same delusion.[15]

'GREEN JOBS' IN SPAIN

Obama frequently cited the example of Spain, which he claimed had already leaped ahead of the U.S. in the jobs-creating 'green energy' race. In August 2008, he unveiled his *New Energy for America* blueprint,[16] a speech offering a collection of ideas built upon the numerous promises about the jobs-creating 'green energy' bounty awaiting America's struggling unemployed workers by "investing" a small amount of government seed capital coughed up by America's lenders, all of whom would need to be repaid with interest.

He praised Spain's example of leadership in 'green energy' investment, asking rhetorically:

Will America watch as the clean energy jobs and industries of the future flourish in countries like Spain, Japan, or Germany? Or will we create them here, in the greatest country on Earth, with the most talented, productive workers in the world?[17]

He left out the part about all of the required capital expenditure outlays by the most indebted nation on Earth. And he neglected to mention the part about the bone-crushing government-imposed mandates, regulatory burden, and feed-in tariffs required to effect it. There was no mention of the crippling cost increases that struggling American electric utility rate-payers and motorists would be obligated to shoulder, or the loss of disposable income, or the reduction in purchasing power, or the higher taxes, etc. Those highlights are never mentioned.

And, like a lot of aspects relating to Obama's 'green energy' paradise, he had inadvertently neglected to mention a few other details. For instance, a March 2009 study undertaken at King Juan Carlos University in Spain provided irrefutable evidence that, with respect to that country's experience, Spain had lost 2.2 jobs for every 'green job' created.[18] Industries and businesses voted with their feet, leaving for other locales where the climate was more favorable than Spain's with its high energy costs and onerous mandates.

The total labor market loss from the 'green energy' opportunity up to that point amounted to almost 110,500 jobs lost.[19] The introductory passage in the report explains it well:

Europe's current policy and strategy for supporting the so-called 'green jobs' or renewable energy dates back to 1997, and has become one of the principal justifications for U.S. 'green jobs' proposals. Yet an examination of Europe's experience reveals these policies to be terribly economically counterproductive.[20]

By 2009, the ruinous 'green energy' program in Spain, the one Obama wanted to install in America, had helped propel that vulnerable nation's headline unemployment rate to over 18% as of the date of the report.[21] By October 2012, it had soared to a new record at 26.2%.[22] Six million Spanish workers, more than one in four, were out of work.[23]

As London's left-wing bible *The Guardian* was forced to admit about life in Spain's leftist utopia, "… crowds scavenge the streets at night for food."[24] Dumpster diving had become the price tag for Spain's 'green energy' folly.

When asked about the King Juan Carlos University study, White House press secretary Robert Gibbs dismissed the findings saying "it seems weird that we're importing wind-turbine parts from Spain in order to build — to meet renewable-energy demand here if that were even remotely the case."[25] But that was before we learned about Solyndra, and cellulosic biofuel swindles, and a laundry list of other 'green energy' failures. It is impossible for a leftist to imagine that companies might pursue economically damaging activities incentivized by federal spending.

Spain had enjoyed thirteen years of steadily declining unemployment that saw its headline rate drop from nearly 20% in 1994 all the way down to 7.9% in May of 2007.[26] That was when Spain began kicking its Obama-style 'green energy' program into overdrive. Within 65 months, the country was looking at a jobless rate that had soared to over 26%.[27] That was more than twice the rate for the EU and 10.3 points above any other EU nation.[28] By the end of the first quarter of 2013, Spain's official unemployment rate had climbed to 27.2%.[29]

Fewer than 50,200 'green jobs' had been created as of 2009.[30] Yet Spain had squandered €571,138 or $759,614 for each job created. The price tag for a wind energy job was about $1.4 million. Each megawatt of installed 'green energy' capacity in Spain destroyed 5.28 jobs elsewhere in the economy. Job destruction varied by the specific source of 'green energy' power.[31] Solar power destroyed almost nine jobs for each megawatt deployed.[32]

The Andasol solar thermal power plant in the Andalucía region of Southern Spain offered an example of the job-destroying success stories that Obama was promoting in his speech. The Andasol 1 station was a highly innovative design opened in 2008.[33] What set Andasol 1 apart from other solar generating stations was the fact that light gathered from 510,000 square meters of parabolic solar collecting panels would be used to heat 28,500 tons of molten sodium and potassium nitrate that would power the grid by day while being stored for generation after sundown.[34]

As with wind power that only works when the wind is blowing, solar power only works when the sun is shining. But now, with the help of German design engineers,[35] an additional eight hours of electrical energy from the plant's fifty megawatt steam turbine could be unleashed.

Press reports glowingly reported that the generation cost of electricity would be 11% lower than conventional solar systems that don't use heat capture and storage. Another solar capture and storage plant was scheduled for opening the next year and a third would follow shortly thereafter.[36] Andasol II opened in 2009 and Andasol III began operation in September 2011.[37] The final project cost was estimated at €900 million.[38] A feed-in tariff showering sponsors with generous compensation for providing Spain with expensive solar thermal energy provided the foreign capital investment incentive.

Even though the cost of solar capture and storage technology was lower than the cost of solar photovoltaic energy, it was still several times higher than traditional fossil fuel or nuclear generation sources. Andasol produced electrical power that was 3.3 times more expensive than advanced combined-cycle natural gas generation, 2.8 times more expensive than conventional coal and 2.5 times more expensive than nuclear power based upon the DoE data.[39] And those ratios are vastly understated because they fail to account for massive renewable energy cost shifting.

To fair-minded members of the press, these were inconsequential details. Like its press counterparts, *Wikipedia* helpfully avoids any mention of relative cost differentials also. Long recognized for its propagandist orientation promoting catastrophic, human-induced global warming, *Wikipedia* doesn't trouble readers with trivial details like economic efficiency, competitiveness, or cost of "environmentally friendly solar electricity" power as they describe it.[40]

Spain provided a "feed-in tariff" of about €0.27 per kilowatt-hour for concentrated solar power (CSP) of the type like Andasol.[41] That was 3.8 times more expensive than U.S. ratepayers paid in 2009. The heavy feed-in tariff cost burden from projects like these — Spain had 11 CSP plants in operation by 2010[42] — was thrown onto the backs of its utilities since Spanish law forbids them from passing on these payments to consumers. By early 2012, Spanish utilities had piled up government-backed debt — €520 per man, woman and child — to cover the increased cost.[43]

Not surprisingly, as the debt load soared and Spain's credit rating plunged, Parliament curtailed feed-in tariff payments to these hideously expensive solar thermal projects like Andasol.[44] So many of these solar thermal projects are likely to be forced into bankruptcy.[45] Project sponsors from all over the world who were suckered into believing the 'green energy' gravy train could last into perpetuity were lining up lawyers to sue the government for breach of contract in the wake of reduced payment flows necessary for Spain to salvage its solvency.[46]

So, at least in one respect, Andasol and other thermal solar projects like it were bona fide 'green energy' job-creating success stories. Hundreds of trial lawyers will be required to argue these cases in courts all across the planet for the next umpteen gazillion years. If there was a shortcoming in Professor Calzada's study, it was his failure to anticipate the legions of liability lawyer jobs created by the program. Obama's political party is a beneficiary of massive campaign contributions from the Association of Trial Lawyers of America. He argues strenuously that this is the model for America to follow. What a surprise.

The 'green energy' program has rapidly transformed Spain into an economically uncompetitive landscape, fueling the flight of industry and jobs to more favorable climates, even as leftist jet-setting glitterati flock into Spain for its warm, sunny climate. It is a metaphor for an all too familiar pattern. Call it the Fidel Castro model — leftism flocks in while entrepreneurial spirit, capital, talent, jobs, and prosperity stampede out.

Spain's introduction to 'green energy' followed the same path as Germany's and

California's. A "visionary" leader, Socialist Prime Minister Jose Luis Rodriguez Zapatero, identified renewable energy as humanity's salvation, the program was sold to voters as a 'green jobs' bonanza, the government established a lucrative feed-in tariff many times the market value of the power produced to promote investment, central planners badly miscalculated the degree to which the public would respond to wildly misplaced incentives, and rapid build-out of uncompetitive sources, fueled by a deluge of global investment capital, flooded onto the grid.

Within a few years, trade deficits worsened as hastily-organized solar projects procured components from foreign producers in Germany and China, the only available sources with the necessary scale to meet rapidly growing demand. Subsidy payments to power producers soared, feed-in tariff costs borne by utilities increased, electricity system deficits piled higher, staggering deficit loads were covered with Spanish-backed debt issuance, public budgets became strained, subsidy levels to distributed producers had to be drastically cut to rein in runaway deficits, renewable energy companies collapsed, producers who had mortgaged properties to invest in power production under the old subsidy payout rates defaulted after reduced payout schedules were introduced, unemployment soared as renewable energy projects collapsed, capital availability dried up, sovereign credit ratings were cut, coupon rates and borrowings on sovereign debt spiked higher, and energy poverty, hitherto a condition experienced only by the poorest, spread rapidly to middle-class households and pensioners.[47]

When Zapatero came to power, he unveiled a "sustainable economy" program based around the three pillars of 'green energy' catechism: (1) rapid expansion of renewable energy funding, (2) massive infrastructure spending on high-speed rail transport, and (3) payments up to €20,000 in subsidies for buyers of electric vehicles.[48] The feed-in tariff rate established by the Spanish Parliament in 2007 was ten times the wholesale rate for electricity.[49] This program closely resembles California's "sustainable economy" blueprint.

The bounty of 'green jobs' in Spain never materialized. But all of the other things like massive subsidy payouts, budget deficits, impaired economic growth, record unemployment, mortgage defaults, trade and payment deficits, higher energy prices, staggering debt levels, and credit downgrades all came to pass. Finally in January 2012, the Spanish government halted subsidy payments to solar photovoltaic projects[50] and, a year later, to a list of others.[51]

Not surprisingly, the welfare-dependent industry collapsed.[52] Spain now requires massive bailout-style loans from the European Central Bank,[53] its unemployment rate soared to more than twice that of the rest of the EU,[54] and middle-class families dine out on dumpster food.[55] Investors, who had relied upon worthless subsidy promises are filing suit against the government for trying to assert sovereignty correcting the horrendous mistake that leftist visionaries have bequeathed to future generations.[56] To one degree or another, this is what already is, or will soon be, occurring in Germany and California as an outgrowth of their own 'green energy' programs.

SPAIN'S NEIGHBORS GET SIMILAR RESULTS

Spain's dreadful experience is not unique. A study of the 'green energy' experience in Scotland found that each 'green energy' job came with a hefty price tag borne by more productive sectors of the economy. Economic consulting firm Verso Economics discovered that the renewable energy sector in Scotland survived solely because of massive subsidies that extracted hundreds of millions of pounds from consumers throughout the UK.[57] The net impact was that, for every 'green energy' job created, 3.7 jobs in more productive sectors of the economy were lost.[58] Each wind energy job in the UK is subsidized by at least £100,000 which, under circumstances, can rise to £1.3 million.[59] With its 230 wind turbines, Scotland's subsidy is £154,000 per job.[60] The London Array, the UK's largest wind farm, predicts its renewable obligation subsidy will amount to £160 million in its first year of operation, which amounts to £1.77million per job.[61] This is the affordable future Obama wants for America. Create one job, destroy two to four other jobs, and drive up the cost of energy.

Another study in Italy with remarkably similar results was released in May 2010. The study's authors found that for the investment required to create one job in the 'green energy' sector, anywhere from 4.8 to 6.9 jobs could have been created if the capital had been invested elsewhere.[62] The authors noted that, irrespective of whatever other merits there were, if the policy is aimed at 'green jobs' creation, "it is a wrong policy choice."[63] A survey by *American Enterprise Institute* of the experience in Germany, the Netherlands, Denmark and elsewhere produces the same result.[64]

In February 2011, the government of the Netherlands announced that it would abandon its commitments under the European Union's 2009 Renewable Energy Directive[65] obligating member nations to generate 20% of their energy from renewables by 2020.[66] The Netherlands will curtail its subsidies of renewable fuels by a factor of 75%. It is difficult to see how the country will meet its 20% mandate without subsidies. The private sector will surely not volunteer to bankrupt itself to satisfy 'green energy' conceits running rampant in Europe.

The Dutch have had a significant head start over the U.S. in harnessing wind energy as a practical source of motive power. About 1,100 years would be a fairly good estimate. Windmills have been used for centuries to drain low-lying areas, the 30-40% of the country's land mass that sits below sea level. Of all places on Earth, implementing a broad-based wind energy exploitation strategy in the Netherlands would seem to be the best place to launch a 'green energy' future.

But the Dutch government, composed far more practical souls than those found among Obama political appointees, has discovered that the renewables mandate is too costly. Instead, they have decided to launch a major program built around nuclear energy.[67] Interestingly, given a substantial expansion of Dutch nuclear capacity, it is well situated to reduce CO_2 emissions greatly, which was the original goal of the EU's fetish with renewable energy.

The Dutch decision may have been prompted by reports issued the previous summer demonstrating that the EU's 2009 Renewable Energy Directive was based upon flawed reasoning, faulty assumptions, and misrepresentations of fact. A study by famed climate-change economist Richard Tol entitled *The Costs and Benefits of EU Climate Policy for 2020* found that, in spite of the EU's claim that the cost of instituting the policy would "only" be €48 billion per year, the actual cost would be €210 billion annually, more than four times more.[68] And despite the EU's wild estimates of benefits from its draconian policy, Tol found that these would be just €7 billion per year.[69] So for each euro spent on the EU's Renewable Directive, there would be just 3 euro cents of benefit.

A country that appears to have already achieved its 20% renewable energy mandate is Denmark, at least on paper. Since 1980, the country has been relentlessly deploying both onshore and offshore wind power to supplement its fossil fuel electricity. The renewable power is heavily subsidized. As a result, Danish residential ratepayers pay the highest electricity rates in the European Union, more than 3.5 times the average U.S. electricity price.[70] More than 34% of total generation in Denmark is derived from wind power.[71] Nevertheless, as little as 5% of Danish electricity demand can actually be satisfied by wind.[72]

Most of the renewable power can't be used in Denmark because it is generated during inopportune periods when demand is low. So excess power is exported to Sweden and Norway where it can be stored or used to meet current demand. Denmark exported 84% of its total wind energy production in 2003.[73] By 2012, exports had reached 96%.[74] Norway derives all of its electricity needs from hydro power. Exports from Germany and Denmark can be pumped uphill into hydroelectric reservoirs in Norway for later power generation. Accordingly, since Norway and Sweden derive most of their electricity from non-carbon sources, there is no CO_2 offset from wind power exports. But reducing CO_2 was the original goal of the exercise.

In addition to the exorbitant costs borne by Danish ratepayers for expensive wind power, all of that power exported to Sweden and Norway is sold back to Denmark at a profit, driving Danish power costs even higher.[75] Denmark exported 96% of its wind generation in 2012 only to re-import 155% of it in the same year.[76] But the most salient aspect is the labor impact.

CEPOS, a Danish think tank, completed an exhaustive study in late 2009 on the effect that Denmark's wind energy has had upon employment. CEPOS observes that:

> *The effect of the government subsidy has been to shift employment from more productive employment in other sectors to less productive employment in the wind industry. As a consequence, Danish GDP is approximately 1.8 billion DKK ($270 million) lower than it would have been if the wind sector work force was employed elsewhere.[77]*

Most sources acknowledge that the Danish wind industry employs many people building, deploying, and maintaining wind turbines. But authoritative studies indicate that if the country had never pursued its 'green energy' program, there would be far higher levels of employment. 'Green energy' is a net job killer in Denmark, just as it is in Spain, the UK and everywhere else.

Germany's labor impact experience with 'green energy' replicates what has been observed in Spain, Scotland, and Denmark. A study published by an economic consultancy Rhenish-Westphalia Institute (RWI) challenges the boastful claims by the German Environmental Ministry. Like Obama's optimistic forecasts, the Ministry's estimates:

> ... obscure the broader implications for economic welfare by omitting any accounting of off-setting impacts. The most immediate of these impacts are job losses that result from the crowding out of cheaper forms of conventional energy generation along with indirect impacts on upstream industries. Additional job losses will arise from the drain on economic activity precipitated by higher electricity prices.[78]

The RWI study notes that "the private consumers' overall loss of purchasing power due to higher electricity prices adds up to billions of Euros." Accordingly:

> ... increased prices ultimately divert funds from alternative, possibly more beneficial, investments. The resulting loss in purchasing power and investment capital causes negative employment effects in other sectors.[79]

The authors examined claims that higher labor inputs per unit of output are beneficial. Not surprisingly, the labor inefficiency and reduced productivity cited as a putative benefit "lowers the output potential of the economy and is hence counterproductive to net job creation."[80] As Frédéric Bastiat convincingly showed decades ago, it's like the benefit to society by breaking windows. It results in a big increase in labor-intensive jobs in the window replacement trades.[81] But sensible people avoid doing these counter-productive things. It drains resources better used elsewhere.

PRODUCTIVITY STOOD ON ITS HEAD

Preposterous claims about supposed economic benefits from a large decrease in worker productivity commonly appear in propaganda pieces published in the U.S. RWI demolishes these claims. In studies that the American Solar Energy Society (ASES) has performed for a number of states, the rent-seeking trade group regularly boasts about:

> ... the broad economic benefits that could accrue if regulators and policymakers support aggressive growth in these (renewable energy and energy efficiency) sectors ... By 2030, under an aggressive deployment forecast scenario, there could be more than 40 million Americans employed in these industries — about one in every four working Americans.[82]

Given their generous job counting methodology, ASES observes that these industries employed 8 million workers in 2007, the year of the report. But with a massive commitment of borrowed taxpayer money, the U.S. could be employing 40 million workers by 2030.

Looking at total energy forecasts in DoE's *Annual Energy Outlook 2012*, American primary energy demand is projected to grow from 94.71 quadrillion BTUs in 2009 to 104.32 quadrillion BTUs in the year 2030.[83] If the ASES "dream" scenario comes to pass, America will go from requiring 84.5 workers per trillion BTUs in 2009 to 383.4 workers for the same output by 2030. ASES claims that it will be beneficial if 4.5 times more workers are required to produce a unit of energy in 2030 as in 2009, a 78% productivity erosion.

It is difficult to understate the degree of intellectual dissonance required to believe that a 78% productivity reduction could be beneficial to the economy. Any sober economist will acknowledge that the main driver of economic growth in a dynamic economy is productivity improvement — the ability to wring more value out of the employment of a fixed amount of resource. That is how wealth is produced. If we are to accept the inane 'green energy' logic, we should be adopting policies to greatly expand agricultural employment such that by 2030, the U.S. could employ 7-8% of the American workforce producing the same food supply that 1.5% of the workforce produces today.[84]

Economists Jerry Taylor and Peter Van Doren observe that "one does not go about creating wealth by maximizing the inputs associated with production."[85] Would we be better served if mechanized power equipment were prohibited and only hand tools were used on road building projects? That would certainly boost employment. The ideas that animate 'green jobs' enthusiasts are breathtaking for their astounding degree of absurdity.

FIGURE 12-2. **Productivity for Energy Industry Workers**

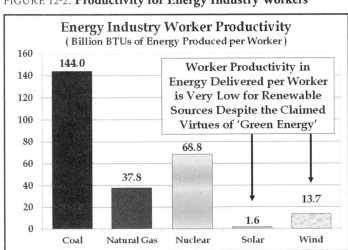

Sources: Annual Energy Review 2012, Total Energy, Table 1.2 Primary Energy Production by Source, EIA; Employment data for competing energy sources is supplied by NaturalGas.org

It is instructive that 'green jobs' enthusiasts tout the supposed job creation potential of green energy investments but shy away from acknowledging any discussion about productivity. For instance, 'green jobs' promoters have widely circulated claims that $1 million invested in solar energy will provide three times more jobs than an equivalent amount invested in natural gas.[86] The context missing is that the U.S. derived more than 148 times more energy from natural gas than it derived from solar energy.[87]

When actual worker productivity statistics are compiled for various sources of primary energy, a different story emerges. The amount of energy per worker employed in each source industry is shown in Figure 12-2.[88] A worker employed in the natural gas industry is able to deliver about 24 times more energy to American consumers than a worker in the solar energy business. A coal industry worker generates 91.2 times more than a solar worker. When measured against wind energy, a natural gas worker delivers 2.8 times more and a coal industry delivers 10 times more.

Navigant Consulting is one of the world's leading promoters of this faulty productivity reduction logic. The firm advanced some analysis in 2010 claiming nearly twenty times more jobs would be created per megawatt of installed capacity from photovoltaic energy than for natural gas combined cycle.[89] Navigant's source for this was a bit fuzzy, derived as it was from "annual staffing surveys, benchmarking services, plant staffing databases and discussions with industry experts."[90] And tarot cards and deciphered texts from unearthed ancient scrolls. Arguing against the absurd Navigant logic, the American Energy Alliance suggests the country should never base decisions:

> … on which source of electricity generation creates the most jobs per megawatt of installed capacity. Goals such as economic efficiency, productivity, and grid reliability are all arguably much more important considerations."[91]

This is exactly right in all respects. There is no argument. Economic growth occurs through productivity enhancements, getting more out of an amount of resources. It does not result from a contest based upon creating the largest number of make-work jobs for a given amount of taxpayer money. The American economy, like Japan's during and after its "lost decade," has suffered a decline to less than half of its historic post-War productivity growth since Obama has been in office. The result is a GDP that will remain below trend for years to come. While the causes are varied and deeply rooted in a wide range of Obama policy failures, 'green energy' expansion is partly responsible. Should we covet India's agricultural performance that employs much more labor per bushel of output? Enthusiasts like Obama and Navigant want to do more — and cause even greater impairment.

America should be following a path that advances economic growth through productivity improvements and investment which enhances reliability of the grid. Otherwise, it would be analogous to prohibiting power equipment and requiring only hand tools for road building because doing so creates a need for many more workers.

THE 'GREEN JOBS' PRICE TAG

German government subsidies to the photovoltaic solar panel industry amount to $240,000 per worker, a level that far exceeds average worker wages.[92] To compensate, German ratepayers were obligated to fork over an extra 2.2 Euro cents per kilowatt-hour in 2010.[93] Those subsidies soared to 5.5 Euro cents per kWh in 2013.[94] That would boost American electricity bills by 60%.

Subsidies for wind and solar power in Germany had surpassed $101 billion by 2010. If transplanted onto a much larger U.S. economy, it would exceed half a trillion dollars.[95] That amount would depress real GDP by a staggering 3.7% in an economy that generated only 1.7% real GDP in 2012.[96] The cost of German wind and solar power generation is now three times the cost of other sources of power generation.[97] Lastly, and most important, any jobs created by 'green energy' investment by the German government disappear the moment subsidies are removed.[98]

Green jobs proponents like the ASES are fond of contending that "renewable energy jobs are often well-paying, skilled positions that cannot easily be outsourced to other countries."[99] But is it true that these jobs can't be outsourced? Germany is a good test case as it is so far down this path. The country embarked upon its renewables program in 1991, greatly boosting it in 2000 under the EEG law. That led to a massive expansion of photovoltaic solar energy financed by subsidies.[100] By the end of 2011, solar subsidies surpassed €100 billion.[101] German industry accounted for the single largest share of the world's solar panel manufacturing.[102] At one point, a German company Q-Cells was the world's largest solar panel manufacturer with a market capitalization of over $10.7 billion.[103] That was then. In April 2012, Q-Cells filed bankruptcy claiming it was insolvent.[104]

Virtually all of those solar panel manufacturing jobs were shifted to China, and most of the other German solar companies have gone bankrupt.[105] Despite a 12-digit mountain of German government subsidies — costs borne by ratepayers — nearly all of these jobs have been outsourced to China or other Asian competitors.[106] To rub salt into the wound, Chinese solar panel manufacturers are the principal sponsors of two of Germany's professional soccer teams.[107]

The EU retaliated by announcing punitive tariffs on Chinese solar panel manufacturers.[108] This initiated yet another 'green energy' trade war as the Chinese government responded by imposing punitive tariffs on European wine exported to China. This was a deliciously well-aimed tit-for-tat retaliation since the EU's trade commissioner, Karel de Gucht, also happens to be a vintner in his spare time.[109] This was enough to force the EU to cave into Chinese panel makers. The EU signed a deal establishing a floor price of €0.56 per watt on solar panels.[110] Winemaker de Gucht, who stood the most to lose, hailed the agreement as "an amicable solution ... that will lead to a new market equilibrium at sustainable prices."[111] It's not entirely clear if he was talking about solar panels — or European wine exports.

European workers have long since given up believing in the 'green jobs' fairy tale.[112]

But blue-collar workers protests are routinely ignored.[113] The same job-shifting situation occurs in the U.S. Take the case of Evergreen Solar. Many other examples can be cited. The White House website crowed loudly about $219.2 million in stimulus money shoveled to the State of Massachusetts to implement energy efficiency and 'green energy' investments.[114] An April 2009 stimulus plan *Progress Report* for the State of Massachusetts on the website struck a self-congratulatory note:

> *Thanks to the Obama Administration's American Recovery and Reinvestment Act, real impact is already being felt across the state. Because of the stimulus bill and new contracts, green energy companies are looking to hire many new employees.*[115]

Evergreen Solar was cited as a model of America's government-industry transformation that would spark revolutionary energy technologies, boost industrial activity, and create jobs.[116] The White House cited a *Boston Globe* report claiming that:

> *Evergreen Solar, the Marlborough-based maker of solar panels, also is hoping to hire 90 to 100 people at a manufacturing plant in Devens … The plant, which opened last summer, is expected to employ more than 800 when it reaches full capacity.*[117]

After receiving the $219.2 million in federal stimulus funds, Massachusetts governor Deval Patrick shoveled $58.6 million of that handout to Evergreen for its planned expansion. Governor Patrick cut the ribbon for the Devens plant opening.[118] After pocketing the money, Evergreen Solar announced it would shift production of solar panels to China and lay off hundreds of company and contract workers.[119] There would be no solar panels built in Devens. In August 2011, Evergreen Solar declared bankruptcy listing $485.6 million in debts that would never be repaid, including the $58.6 million taxpayer loan.[120] This was Obama's affordable 'green energy' future producing jobs "that can't be outsourced."[121] Taxpayers spent tens of millions to create jobs for Chinese workers.

A study undertaken at the Investigative Reporting Workshop at American University found that overseas firms were collecting most of the 2009 "stimulus" plan subsidies.[122] The researchers found that eleven wind farms received $3 billion in handouts under Section 1603 of the act. Of the 982 wind turbines installed with these funds, 695 of these had come from foreign suppliers.[123] A House Energy and Commerce Committee report notes that "nine of the top-ten global wind turbine suppliers were headquartered outside the U.S."[124] Even with respect to small-scale government loans under the Treasury Department Section 1603 program — the median size of the 8,705 loans was less than $71,000[125] — a fourth of the money went for overseas job creation.[126] The "stimulus" plan was providing jobs — benefitting foreign workers. This shouldn't be surprising. Chinese-made wind turbines and solar panels cost less than those produced in Germany, Spain, or the U.S.[127]

Researchers at the Center for Energy Economics at the University of Texas published a study in December 2008 that looked in detail at four earlier studies issued by left wing advocacy groups whose work heavily influenced Obama-style thinking about the 'green energy' economy.[128] Their review found the four previous studies were polluted by mistakes due to lack of analytical rigor, flawed assumptions, methodological errors, wide variances in basic definitions, and a host of other problems. The *Longhorn* authors show that the four previous studies could all be rejected because:

> *There is no effort to balance the potential positive impacts with potential negative impacts of job destruction and higher energy costs. In a sense, these studies are cost-benefit analyses without any cost considerations.*[129]

In other words, these one-sided left-wing "studies" amount to junk-science. Other authoritative critiques of these same discredited studies cite precisely the same shortcomings.[130]

An example among the four leftist 'green jobs' cheerleading studies was one issued in 2008 by the University of Massachusetts and the Soros-funded Obama-mouthpiece outfit Center for American Progress. Robert Pollin, the principal author of this report, promised that if the country were to invest $100 billion in 'green energy' projects, there would be 2 million jobs created within two years.[131] Obama's economic "stimulus" plan took its cue from this, appropriating $103.5 billion for three 'green energy' investment programs[132] along with another $17.2 billion from the Treasury Department's Section 1603 program.[133] The private sector portion of these projects added many more billions of dollars in 'green energy' investments. It is difficult to overstate the cartoonish nature of Pollin's report, and its boundless faith in Keynesianism. He assumes that federal "investments" can materialize out of nowhere, as if we could simply shake the money tree and funds would appear, projects would begin, and the flood of jobs would arrive without offsetting negative impacts.

Perhaps we would have been better advised to pay attention to press remarks from Professor Pollin when he claimed that he was "in favor of investing in things that will promote a clean environment, fight global warming and those investments will all create jobs, and I don't really care what color they are."[134] He didn't care what color they were, he didn't care if they destroyed more jobs than they created, he didn't care how much it cost, he didn't care about technical integration feasibility, he didn't care how much we had to pay for each dollar of net benefit, he didn't care if the deluge of spending degraded productivity, he didn't care if we had to suffer increased deficit and debt burdens to make it happen, he didn't care if doing a lot of this stunted real economic growth, he didn't care if the result was to drive up energy prices for middle- and lower-income households, and he didn't care if these "investments" left the economy at more of a disadvantage relative to global competitors.[135]

WHERE ARE THE GREEN JOBS?

Despite the $120.7 billion in 'green jobs' investment, by the end of August 2012 — more than three and a half years after Obama's inauguration — instead of 2 million new jobs, the Bureau of Labor Statistics' Household Survey reported that the entire U.S. economy had added only 11,000 jobs, green, brown, and every other color.[136] Even worse, that 11,000 increase in jobs was composed of a gain in 1,360,000 part-time jobs and a loss of 1,328,000 full-time jobs.[137] The BLS Household Survey was nowhere to go looking for evidence of the job-producing power of 'green energy.'

In the BLS Payroll Survey, the economy had seen an increase of 296,000 jobs.[138] Instead of shaving 1.3 percentage points from the headline unemployment rate, we saw an increase of 0.3 percent. Using a constant labor force participation rate back to January 2009, the unemployment rate would have been 11.1%, an increase of 3 percentage points. Needless to say, the money had been spent but Pollin's multi-colored jobs went missing.

The author of the *Longhorn* study, Gürcan Gülen, produced an updated review of his study for the Copenhagen Consensus Center (CCC). Released in February 2011, Gülen shows that (1) job creation claims are based upon a dubious set of assumptions, (2) any measured job creation is far outweighed by job destruction elsewhere, (3) the investment required for 'green' job creation would result in far greater levels of employment had it been deployed elsewhere, and (4) the evidence does not support claims by proponents about productivity improvement.[139] As CCC head Bjørn Lomborg observes, "You can create jobs in clean energies but unfortunately it ends up at the cost of competitiveness elsewhere."[140] He might have added that it ends up at the cost of many more jobs elsewhere also. He might also have said that you can create a lot of jobs replacing windows that you deliberately broke, but it comes at the cost of resources that could have been efficiently deployed elsewhere. The cost in lost jobs and competitiveness far exceeds any benefit.

Another 'green jobs' study was released in April 2009 by the Energy Modeling Forum at Stanford University. The author Hilliard Huntington blindly accepts without a shred of doubt the twin popular and false theses that increasing the proportion of renewable energy will help combat catastrophic global warming, and that government should expand investments in renewable energy because it would stimulate the economy. Nevertheless, the conclusion of the report is damning.[141]

Huntington conducted a review of other supposed cost-benefit economic studies that had been performed by advocates of 'green energy.' His analysis relied heavily on the *Longhorn* study and even examined the very same reports that the *Longhorn* researchers reviewed, finding that:

> *The advantages of increased jobs from renewable energy are vastly overstated at costs prevailing today. It will require dramatic break-through in costs if renewable energy is to become a job generator.*[142]

Would that Huntington had been equally alert to recognize that the advantages of reduced CO_2 emissions and economic stimulus are also vastly overstated at costs prevailing today. Instead, as most 'green jobs' enthusiasts do, Huntington contends inaccurately that greatly reduced productivity of 'green energy' would amount to an economic benefit rather than an economic drag:

> *If green energy power projects provide more new jobs than conventional energy projects, they may stimulate more additional jobs as incomes expand. This possibility provides green energy with a "two-for-one" possibility. Governments should advance these technologies, because they stimulate the economy as well as protect against global climate change and energy insecurity.*[143]

Huntington's statement here is wrong in every material respect. If 'green energy' projects provide more jobs than conventional sources, that will reduce productivity. Lost productivity will reduce income, degrading net economic benefit. The experience in Spain, Germany, and elsewhere demonstrates that the lost economic benefit destroys more jobs than can be created. Government should not advance these projects because they won't stimulate the economy, but will damage it by draining resources that could be more efficiently devoted elsewhere. And the evidence from Germany, Colorado, Texas, and elsewhere shows that claims that renewable energy will reduce CO_2 emissions — the cause of dreaded "global climate change" that keeps authors like Huntington shaking in terror — is wildly overstated, or even opposite of what he posits.

Germany's contribution to global climate change will be increasing, not decreasing, as its usage of fossil fuels expands to plug holes in unreliable renewable sources.[144] Rapid on-off cycling of conventional base-load power generation stations to overcome wind and solar intermittency has led to vastly increased fossil fuel inefficiency, which has resulted in an increased level of CO_2 emissions per unit of energy produced.[145] Germany's contribution to global climate change will be increasing, not decreasing, as its usage of fossil fuels expands to plug holes in unreliable renewable sources.[146] Lastly, Germany's expanded usage of renewable energy is increasing rather than decreasing its energy insecurity, as the country is also increasingly reliant upon 'green energy' component imports from an array of offshore suppliers. The "two-for-one" that the arithmetic-challenged Huntington promises would actually result in (1) degraded economic performance, (2) an overall increase in atmospheric CO_2 emissions, (3) fewer jobs, and (4) a decrease in energy security.

Huntington actually alludes to these exact impacts later in his study:

> *When governments provide additional incentives (subsidies) or funds to expand more expensive conventional or renewable electricity generation, resources need to shift away from other sectors in the economy. On average, a decline in these sectors will lose 9.78 jobs for every million dollars. Electricity generation across all sources creates far fewer jobs than other activities in the economy … These net job losses mean that subsidies to either green or conventional sources will detract rather than expand the economy's job base, because they will shift investments from other sectors that will create more employment.*[147]

This is an accurate statement, directly contradicting all his earlier assertions. So why does he need to genuflect toward all the 'green energy' pieties and CO_2 abatement nonsense? The absence of 'green job' creation potential was alluded to by former Obama White House economic advisor Jared Bernstein, co-author of the economic "stimulus" report that promised an unemployment rate of 5.2% by 2012.[148] U3 averaged 8.1% during all of 2012.[149] Bernstein, in a rare moment of candor, admitted that 'green energy' really doesn't create very many jobs.[150] Now they tell us.

Huntington's dramatic job-generating cost breakthrough, if it ever occurs, is decades away. The U.S. has been squandering public funds on renewable energy schemes trying to achieve that cost breakthrough since Nixon administration days and has not come close to the goal. Why do we elect politicians who offer worthless promises claiming they can solve the riddle?

An exhaustive economic analysis of claims about the promise of 'green energy' jobs was published in 2009 by the University of Illinois School of Law.[151] This study went much further than those cited above in that the scope was broader, entailing a review of dozens of advocacy group claims, all of which were dubious. The lengthy list of studies each claimed a surplus of high-paying jobs would result if nations would merely undertake a commitment to do just a few simple things. The list included "investing" trillions of scarce dollars, reordering entire societies, restructuring pertinent aspects of global trade, imposing massive cost increases on businesses and consumers, retooling energy infrastructure, and greatly limiting individual freedom by devolving sovereignty to the UN, non-governmental groups and cooperating government entities.

As Professor of Law Andrew Morriss and his colleagues note:

> *Our review convinces us that the real purpose of the green jobs initiative is not to create jobs but to remake society. The sweeping changes advocated in these reports under the guise of greening our economy are intended to shift the American and world economies away from decentralized decision making, in favor of centralized planning. Therefore, instead of allowing individuals to voluntarily trade in free markets in pursuit of their own ends, green jobs advocates would instead discourage trade and allow technologies to be chosen by central planners and politicians, who would determine the choices faced by consumers and workers. By wrapping these policy shifts in the green jobs mantle, those advocating the reorganization of much of life hope to avoid a debate over the massive costly changes they want to impose.[152]*

Studies by advocacy groups make numerous errors in basic economic analysis that involve mistakes in understanding the doctrine of comparative advantage in global trade, mistakes in calculating consumer surplus, errors in modeling consumer response to mandates, failure to consider opportunity costs of resources siphoned away to 'green energy' programs, and ignoring the effects of market incentives regarding energy efficiency. Most disturbingly, the Illinois College of Law authors show that these errors are not accidental but represent "a thinly concealed hostility to market ordered societies, a hostility which strongly influences its policy recommendations."[153]

So the wakeup call to voters who had hailed Obama's promises about a deluge of 'green jobs' was that they were predicated upon economic studies that were deeply flawed and erroneous. Even worse was that those studies had deliberately misrepresented economic realities for the most disreputable reasons possible, hostility to free market dynamics and opposition to personal freedom.

Even the high priests of 'green energy' catechism were forced to accept the inherent job-killing realities of their program. A well-hidden labor market dislocation provision in the Waxman-Markey cap-and-trade bill provided a three-year unemployment benefit package, relocation allowances of $1,500, and a substantial subsidy for health care insurance premium payments to assist the countless millions of workers that the drafters of the bill knew would lose their jobs.[154] Obama has never addressed the incongruity of how his program would supposedly create five million new jobs, yet it would also be necessary to authorize disbursement of tens of billions of dollars to ameliorate the long-term job-killing damage it would cause.

The Teamsters and the Laborers International Union of North America commissioned a report in 2009 in conjunction with the Sierra Club to study the quality of Obama's 'green jobs.' Remember, those are the "jobs that pay well and can't be outsourced."[155] Their report found that (1) 'green jobs' are often low paying, (2) wage rates at solar and wind assembly plants are below national averages for manufacturing workers, (3) in some locations the wage rates are below "income levels needed to support a single adult with one child," (4) many 'green' manufacturers have been busy off-shoring assembly operations to lower-wage countries, and (5) most workers surveyed were not covered by collective bargaining agreements.[156]

The 'green energy' economy touted by Obama has fallen drastically short of projections.[157] In the eight years up to 2011, the 'green energy' sector actually shed jobs even as Obama threw billions of dollars at trying to help it achieve escape velocity.[158] That finding was based upon an assessment performed by left-of-center Brookings Institution, which bent over backward to reclassify every job it could possibly find as a 'green' job. For instance, Brookings included "wastewater and mass transit" into their definition of 'green jobs.'[159]

Bus drivers are classified as 'green jobs' workers. Never mind that passenger buses used in urban mass transit burn, on average, 2.6 times more energy and liberate 2.7 times more CO_2 per passenger-mile than a Toyota *Prius*.[160] Yet, according to Brookings, we must genuflect and call it a 'green job.' to inflate the count. Hilariously, the *Associated Press* filed an editorial masquerading as a news story during the 2012 campaign labeling the Gabriel Calzada Alvarez study in Spain "controversial," the study that discovered that each 'green job' created destroys 2.2 other jobs, a finding that has been replicated dozens of times in numerous other countries.[161] But *AP* treated the Brookings study, the one that got laughed out of polite company, that counted antiques dealers, bus drivers, and trash collectors as 'green jobs' workers, as indisputable, quoting its author as if his absurd pronouncements were the final, authoritative word.

Sensible 'green energy' promoters are vocal in tempering optimism about the potential for a 'green jobs' explosion. An example comes from Sunil Sharan, director of GE's Smart Grid Initiative. He explains that smart meter conversion might create as many as 1,600 meter installation jobs.[162] But once installed, smart meters will destroy 28,000 meter reader jobs.[163] Of course, installer jobs are temporary. They will mostly terminate or be greatly reduced when installations near completion. Meanwhile, meter reader jobs were permanent. So, for every 175 permanent jobs destroyed, 10 temporary jobs will be created. This does not suggest that smart meters are bad. They will boost productivity, enable better grid management, and improve overall performance. But don't expect a gusher of 'green jobs.'

Obama's "stimulus" program allocated $90 billion to create 'green jobs.'[164] The White House assured Americans that the program would create 200,000 new jobs each year.[165] The Bureau of Labor Statistics began measuring quarterly state-wide 'green jobs' gains (and losses) in 2011. Following the example of Brookings, BLS adopted exceedingly broad definitions.[166] Bicycle repairmen, farmers, hybrid bus drivers, museum curators, antique dealers, sanitation workers, and janitors in solar panel factories were all 'green collar' workers.[167] BLS established a fourth quarter 2010 baseline so subsequent progress could be measured and reported.[168]

As of the third quarter of 2011, Obama's $90 billion in 'green energy' outlays had produced a grand total of 9,245 jobs.[169] That amounts to $9,734,992 per 'green job' created, an achievement that rivals anything the Germans have accomplished with their more ambitious program. BLS published three quarterly reports in 2011 and then discontinued the practice. In an economy that had more than 140 million working-age adults employed during those same reporting periods, Obama's $150 billion outlay could only measure 9,245 jobs created.[170] Maybe when Obama promised "countless well-paying jobs," he had meant it would be impossible for BLS to actually count them.[171]

The $9.7 million cost per job figure was by no means a fluke. Veronique de Rugy, a senior research fellow at George Mason University, performed a detailed study of three DoE 'green energy' loan programs, Section 1703, Section 1705 and Advanced Technology Vehicles Manufacturing (ATVM) loans. In testimony before the House Committee on Oversight and Government Reform, de Rugy reported that a total of $16 billion was shelled out to fund 26 Section 1705 loans. Among these projects, DoE claimed to have created 2,378 permanent jobs. That equated to $6,731,034 per job.[172]

Compare the 9,245 'green jobs' created in the U.S. in 2011 with an estimate produced by economist Timothy Considine of the number of fracking jobs created in a single state of Pennsylvania in the same year. Considine used a model similar to that used by the Pennsylvania Department of Labor, estimating that 111,000 jobs in hydraulic fracking would be created in 2011. That total dwarfs the entire U.S. total for 'green jobs' by a 12-to-1 margin.[173] It had happened in just a single state that hosts only 4% of the nation's workforce. No borrowed public funds were required to achieve it.

A better example came out of testimony before the House Committee on Oversight and Government Reform on June 19, 2012.[174] During the hearings, Congressional

Research Service (CRS) 'green jobs' expert Molly Sherlock was asked repeatedly to provide a figure for the number of 'green jobs' produced under the Section 1703 loan guarantee program. After hemming and hawing, Sherlock admitted that only 355 permanent jobs had been created.[175] Based upon the $10 billion spent in the Section 1703 program, this amounted to $28,169,014 per 'green job' created. At this rate, we would only need $140.8 trillion to get to five million jobs.

The Department of Energy cited figures in late 2012 showing $34.5 billion expended under the Treasury Department Section 1603 program and a remarkable 60,000 'green jobs' had been created.[176] If you believe the jobs part, you believe in the Tooth Fairy. Nevertheless, it equated to a more palatable $575,000 per job created. Still, even with DoE's generous job counting,[177] there are still 4,940,000 jobs to go to reach the five million that Obama promised.[178] We would need $2.9 trillion to get to five million jobs at this pace.

No discussion of 'green anything' is complete without hearing from the useless National Renewable Energy Laboratory (NREL). That agency published a typically one-sided report admitting that Treasury Section 1603 grant program "also had 'the near term goal of creating and retaining jobs' in the renewable energy sector."[179] Of the $9 billion in funds allocated under the program, NREL counted "between 5,100 and 5,500 direct and indirect jobs per year on an ongoing basis over the 20- to 30-year estimated life of the systems."[180] That equates to $1.7 million per 'green job' created. It's obvious that no matter which set of numbers is accepted, the 'green jobs' tidal wave we were promised only produced a flood of red ink.[181]

The DoE revised its site in May 2013 to provide updated numbers of 'green jobs' created under its Section 1703 and 1705 programs. The site showed 2,308 permanent jobs were created for $25.96 billion in public outlays.[182] That comes to $11.25 million per job.[183] It's immensely fortunate that Obama failed in his promise to create 5 million 'green jobs' as he claimed he would. At this expenditure rate, had he made good on his vow, it would have cost the American taxpayer $56.2 trillion. It's unlikely this amount of Treasury paper could have been sold to cover the borrowing.

Obama made good on his promise to spend billions of taxpayer dollars on 'green energy' projects.[184] He also promised that oceans of deficit spending would create "five million jobs that can't be outsourced." That part of it came up woefully short, as the House Committee on the Budget observes:

> By seeking to pick winners and losers in a dynamic and diverse economy, the government-as-investor model distorts markets, weakens the rule of law, wastes taxpayer dollars, and fails to spur sustainable job creation.[185]

Someone should pass the news along to 'green jobs' ideologue Robert Pollin — if they can pry him away from his new full time occupation of trashing the reputations of Harvard economists Carmen Reinhart and Kenneth Rogoff. Pollin was an architect of the fairy tale that helped Obama kick off this wasteful train of events.[186]

CHAPTER 13

THE FALSE PROMISE OF
WIND ENERGY

"Extraordinary claims require extraordinary evidence."[1]

CARL SAGAN, 1980

"The whole aim of practical politics is to keep the populace alarmed — and hence clamorous to be led to safety — by menacing it with an endless series of hobgoblins, all of them imaginary."

H.L. MENCKEN

Proponents of 'green energy' think the U.S. and other industrialized societies can completely convert from fossil fuels to 'green energy' sources like wind, solar, and biomass for electricity generation within a relatively short amount of time. Al Gore says this must be accomplished by 2018.[2] The absurdity of his position is scarcely describable. The U.S. derived 87% of its primary energy from fossil fuels during the past decade.[3] Biomass is used chiefly to produce biofuels. Solar power accounted for less than 0.2% of our energy needs in 2011.[4] Because solar energy is so diffuse, and therefore it requires such a large amount of resources to harness, and therefore is so expensive, wind power is the source upon which 'green energy' enthusiasts are most hopeful.

Wind power has grown quite rapidly in the U.S. and around the world in recent years. Relying upon a set of generous subsidies that increase proportionately with the amount of wind power sold, turbines are springing up on mountain tops, on open prairies, in desert wind corridors and, within a few years, in offshore areas adjacent to scenic coastlines.

Texas enjoys the distinction — or suffers the ignominy — of having the largest amount of installed wind power in the U.S. By the end of the 4th quarter of 2012, the American Wind Energy Association (AWEA) showed there was an installed capacity of 12,212 megawatts (mW) in Texas, more than double the 5,549 mW in California, the next largest wind power state.[5] During the afternoon of February 26, 2008, the winds that had been blowing across the Texas prairie suddenly dropped precipitously. Within a three-hour period, thousands of wind towers reduced output 75%.[6]

The sudden loss of 1,500 mW coincided with a demand spike that caused a dangerous fluctuation in the alternating current profile across the grid.[7] With the entire Texas grid nearing collapse, operators shut off power to industrial customers and went scrambling for backup. A catastrophe was narrowly avoided by diverting an estimated 1,100 mW from electricity customers who were suddenly blacked out.[8] As *Reuters* gently phrased it during a similar incident, "The grid operator said its plan for the week takes into account current outages and the possibility of losing additional resources."[9] Translated into English, it reads "This week, we fully expect wind power to contribute nothing and cause the grid instability." Grid managers know they cannot rely upon wind power during peak demand periods.

If Texas were to harvest all 12,212 mW of its installed wind capacity, it would have amounted to 18.5% of peak electric generation demand for the summer 2012 period in areas administered by the Electric Reliability Council of Texas (ERCOT), which is responsible for 85% of the Texas grid.[10] But what AWEA does not mention is that ERCOT can only rely upon 8.7% of the installed wind capacity at summer peak periods.[11] ERCOT would only be counting on 874 mW of wind power. That's because the wind is unreliable, especially in peak usage periods. So instead of 18.5% of demand, it would only supply 1.3% during the hot summer of 2012.

But that won't daunt wind promoters. AWEA claimed in early 2012 that there was an additional 847 mW of wind generation capacity under construction and a breathtaking 63,504 mW in the queue.[12] Using their numbers, if all of that capacity were to become usable, it could displace more than 100% of generation requirements in the state. Wind alone would amount to 116% of peak requirements, allowing Texas to become a major electricity exporter to other states or Mexico.

However, because the effective load carrying capacity (ELCC) during summer peak months is a mere 8.7% of nameplate capacity, all of that additional wind installation will contribute only about 10.1%, rather than 116%, of the state's generation requirements. That's a lot of investment for a trifling amount of power.

Reliability is low, especially at extreme periods of excessive heat or cold like the cold snap in early February 2011, when ERCOT staged a series of blackouts to conserve power.[13] On August 24, 2011, Texas experienced triple-digit temperatures. But of the 10,135 mW of nameplate wind capacity on that date, ERCOT was able to wring just 880 mW to keep the air conditioners running.[14] That was exactly in line with the 8.7% ELCC figure used to plan for peak demand.

As a result, Texas imports electricity from Mexico rather than the other way around.[15] The problem occurs every summer with 2012 being no exception. ERCOT planned for peak power generation requirements to exceed all previous records and activated previously mothballed power facilities to help overcome the shortfalls from wind.[16] ERCOT activated 1,984 mW of mothballed fossil fuel capacity to get through the summer.[17]

CAPACITY AND INTERMITTENCY

The effective load carrying capacity, or ELCC, refers to the actual amount of power you can usually rely upon as a fraction of the total capacity that could conceivably be delivered if every wind turbine was spinning at its optimal rate 100% of the time. It's an important concept since wind promoters often cite nameplate capacity potential of wind power to displace conventional capacity. While wind promoters blow incessantly, wind doesn't. And when it does, it rarely blows at the optimum speed for power generation. This is referred to as the "intermittency problem."

The American Wind Energy Association (AWEA) claims that the average name-plate-rated capacity of wind turbines installed during 2008 was 1.67 mW and that it should generate 5,000 mWh of energy during the year. That means the turbine will actually harvest 34.2% of its nameplate capacity once installed.[18] In other words, for a 1.67 mW turbine, AWEA says the ELCC is 34.2%.

The most common approach for comparing costs of competing generation sources is the "levelized cost" method where the present value of total life-cycle costs of building and operating a generation plant are converted to a single factor based upon a flow of equal periodic amounts of energy output.[19] A check of the Levelized Costs of New Generation Resources in DoE's Annual Energy Outlook 2013 (AEO2013) shows they assume a capacity factor of 34% for onshore wind.[20] This is the number DoE used to compute wind energy costs. But how realistic is that figure?

DoE has assembled capacity and generation data from most of the wind farms in the country going back to 1990 up to 2012, the last complete year of data compiled. It is readily apparent that DoE's database is not comprehensive as the nameplate capacity statistics compiled for each state and for the U.S. are well below the industry-wide totals reported by AWEA. Nevertheless, DoE data is highly detailed and not believed to be biased.

Between 1990 and 2011, the U.S. experienced rapid growth in wind generation, logging a 19.6% compound annual growth rate.[21] During that twenty two-year period, wind contributed 503.2 terawatt-hours of energy.[22] That's more than you need at home — unless you're Al Gore or some carbon-belching Hollywood gasbag with fifteen palaces scattered around the globe. Yet that represented only 28.8% of rated capacity. As marginally more efficient, higher capacity turbines were deployed in later years, the period between 2002 and 2011 witnessed a slightly larger 29.7% capacity realization.[23] Between 2006 and 2011, wind yield increased slightly to 30.2% of capacity.[24] Despite claims by DoE and AWEA that we can achieve 34% or more of capacity, the U.S. managed to achieve a number above 31% only once in twenty two years. In 2004, the U.S. squeezed only 25.9% of the nameplate capacity out of wind turbines.

This is important because DoE uses its 34% figure to determine wind energy cost estimates. If DoE computes a cost per megawatt-hour figure for wind energy based upon a 34% capacity factor but the actual number is closer to 25.9%, DoE will have understated the true cost of wind energy. In this limited case, cost would be one-third higher. The true divergence is far higher as we will see.

It's clear there is confusion, even among supposedly authoritative sources. A good example is contained in a report from the International Energy Agency (IEA) for the year 2011. IEA triumphantly proclaims that the average capacity factor for wind turbines in the U.S. was 33%.[25] Where does it get that figure? It was sourced to a report from the Lawrence Berkeley National Laboratory (LBNL). And what is the source for LBNL's 33% number? It is merely an idle assumption provided in an obscure Market Report for 2011, not actual data compiled by the DoE.[26] IEA's statistic in their own report shows a computed yield figure of only 31%.[27]

Another example concerns the Regional Transmission Operator (RTO) PJM Interconnection that serves a large power consuming region in the U.S. East Coast and Midwest states. The RTO publishes their capacity and output data. For the 13-month period from November 1, 2011 to November 30, 2012, PJM reported average ELCC of only 27%.[28] But the RTO also acknowledges its reported measure of wind yield doesn't include outages. So the real ELCC is even lower because equipment failures and planned maintenance outages are ignored.

A look at California's wind energy deployment tells a similar story, widely diverging from AWEA and DOE claims about a 34% capacity yield. California was the first state in the country to deploy wind turbines in any large measure, installing a vast array in the Altamont Pass east of San Francisco beginning in the 1960s.[29] There is mounting evidence suggesting that wind investments in California are increasingly unwarranted. In a 2003 study prepared by the California Wind Energy Collaborative, the actual realization for the state's three major wind farms were measured to be 26.0% of capacity for the Altamont Pass, 23.9% for the San Gorgonio station, and 22.0% for the Tehachapi plant.[30] Those figures are in close alignment with DoE data for 2003 which shows a state-wide 24.6% utilization figure.[31] Compare that to an available capacity rating of close to 100% for gas generation power plants.

But even those slender measures are misleading when they were really put to the test. During the summer of 2006 for instance, California suffered a sizeable heat storm. Grid operators had to scale up every available increment of power while businesses were told to curtail or shut down. On the peak day of August 24th when every spare kilowatt was needed, wind contributed only 254.6 mW of its 2,500 mW nameplate capacity, an ELCC of 10.2%.[32] During the previous seven-day period, wind generated an average of only 99.1 mW, just 4% of rated capacity.[33]

In November 2012, wind essentially disappeared all across California. Wind promoters had deployed more than 5,000 megawatts of capacity across the state. Yet actual output from all of these far-flung locations dropped to a mere 33 megawatts.[34] That amounted to less than 0.8% of rated capacity. Nearly every electron in the grid came from fossil fuel, hydroelectric, or nuclear generation.

Another obvious problem concerns the timing of the wind's intermittency. California had 4,287 mW of nameplate capacity in the 1st quarter of 2012.[35] But on August 9, 2012, as output scaled up to meet peak daytime demand, wind production plummeted.[36] During the hours between 8:30 AM and 5:00 PM when statewide demand peaked at 45,000 mW, wind power declined, never even reaching 400 mW.[37] That was substantially less than 1% of peak requirements. Between 10:00 AM and 2:00 PM, wind output never reached above 200 mW. At 2:00 PM, when customers were drawing 44,000 mW, wind was providing 275 mW despite its 4,287 mW capacity.[38] Californians were getting just 6.4% of wind's capacity.

A report from North American Electric Reliability Corporation shows an even more disturbing picture. The authors depict a typical daily power output chart from California's five largest wind farm projects, Altamont, San Gorgonio, Tehachapi, Solano, and Pacheco. Between 10:00 AM and 2:00 PM, the total output from all five of these stations drops almost to zero for the entire four hour period.[39] Despite the sub-optimal production realities of California wind power, the onerous nature of the state's renewable portfolio standard requires the state to purchase 33% of its electricity from renewable sources by 2020. This actually permits wind power producers to extract a much higher price than they can in other markets given their stronger negotiating position.[40]

FIGURE 13-1. **California Wind Energy Percentage of Nameplate Capacity**

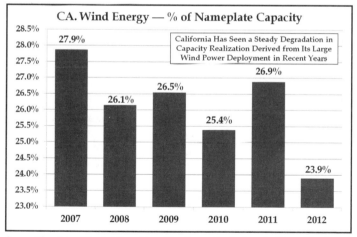

Source: Electricity: Detailed State Data, Net Generation by State by Type of Producer by Energy Source 2001-Present, *Energy Information Administration*

Despite these obvious shortcomings, California continues to deploy more wind capacity. But is it a worthwhile investment? DoE figures show an uneven pattern over the previous five years in actual energy yield from the state's considerable investment in wind power as Figure 13-1 shows. The state has been unable to improve yield despite continually replacing older turbines with more efficient, higher yielding units. This may indicate that the state is gradually exploiting its most productive locations. Each new addition locates in increasingly less optimal wind resource locations.

During the 22-year period for which DoE maintains detailed wind energy data, California managed to harvest only 23.8% of its rated capacity. Based upon a cost factor supplied by DoE that assumes a 34% ELCC, California wind power is 43.1% more costly than DoE assumes. But the truth is far worse.

WIND POWER ELSEWHERE

The International Energy Agency publishes an annual global wind energy report that enables one to calculate the yield on wind projects. During 2012, the entire planet began the year with 203 gigawatts (GW) of capacity and ended with 239.6 GW.[41] Throughout 2012, those wind turbines generated an estimated 449.4 terawatt-hours of wind energy.[42] That means the entire world's wind fleet generated only 23.2% of capacity.[43] During the previous 10 years, capacity factors ranged between a low of 21.7% in 2003 and a high of 26.5% in 2008.[44] Actual wind energy costs on a global basis would be 43.3% higher than assumed by DoE in its costing model.[45]

Another classic example of the wind energy yield problem concerns the experience with wind power curtailments in the UK. That country is embarked upon a path of significant wind energy deployment to meet its 20% renewables mandate. By December 2010, the UK had deployed nameplate wind generating capacity of 5,891 mW to serve a grid whose peak capacity is estimated at 60,000 mW.[46] Using rated wind energy capacity, wind should be contributing 9% of peak demand.

The country appears intent on installing much more wind energy in future years as it adopts stringent policies designed to eliminate fossil fuel power. In 2013, as the UK shivered through the coldest March since 1963, two thirds of the country's electricity came from fossil fuel generation.[47] But it had also enacted a tax that, by the year 2020, will add £30 per metric ton of CO_2 emitted and £70 per ton by 2030.[48] Those crippling levies will essentially eliminate fossil fuel from consideration, leaving only wind or nuclear power as realistic choices. How is this likely to work out in practice?

On December 20, 2010, a severe cold front swept across the region. Temperatures plunged to 22 degrees Fahrenheit, the coldest day up to that point in 2010. When consumers needed every watt of electrical power to heat homes and offices, wind was able to supply only 140 mW.[49] That amounts to just 2.4% of rated capacity and a laughable 0.2% of overall power needs. On the evening of December 20, power yield from wind dropped to 59 mW.[50] That amounted to one out of every 1,000 watts required at peak demand. At the hour when temperatures hit their lowest, wind supplied just 20 mW.[51] This is not unique to winter time. At one point in the first week of August 2012, wind was delivering only 12 mW of the 38,000 mW being used, one electron out of every 3,167 needed.[52] Despite billions of pounds wasted, wind power was able to supply not one in ten but only one of every 429 units of demand. During the day, yield dropped to one watt of every 3,000 demanded.

BBC meteorologist Paul Hudson[53] cites peer-reviewed research in the journal

Environmental Research Letters authored by Mike Lockwood, a professor of space environment physics at the University of Reading.[54] Lockwood claims that if there is a return to minimum solar sunspot activity similar to the icy cold Maunder Minimum conditions between 1650 and 1700, the UK and much of northern Europe would experience even more severe cold weather winters in the coming decades.[55] Those weather patterns would be marked by the same anomalous low-wind conditions.[56] That would devastate the electrical grid if reliance on wind power were to grow appreciably.

The same unreliability problem during severe weather conditions has been observed in Minnesota. Wind turbines regularly fail in the severe cold weather in that unforgiving northern climate, one of the last places in the U.S. where you'd want to experience a blackout due to power failure.[57] Wind farms are euphemistically referred to as "no spin zones" in Minnesota.[58]

Another case is the Province of Ontario. There are thirteen wind farms with an installed capacity of about 1,512 mW. Nevertheless, the Province only averages about 8% of that amount throughout the year.[59] On one of the hottest days in the summer of 2012, the combined power output was only 77 mW, or 5% of installed capacity.[60] On the evening of August 13, 2012, the system operator showed total power output from all thirteen stations at 58 mW, just 3.8% of capacity.[61]

Proponents of the Cape Wind offshore wind project in Nantucket Sound claim their project will enjoy yields as high as 48%, but sheepishly admit down in the fine print that real day-in, day-out yield will be closer to 21%.[62] Even reputable media outlets like *The Wall Street Journal* display a basic ignorance about the distinction between nameplate capacity vs. ELCC.[63]

In another example, a study of small-scale wind turbines in Massachusetts found that, of the 21 in operation, only 4.9% of rated capacity was being realized.[64] That was less than one-third of the amount project promoters and contractors had promised. Whether the reliable ELCC estimate from wind power generation is 26%, or 21%, or 10.2%, or 8.7%, or below 5%, it doesn't appear to be 34% and it sure isn't 100%. Thus, the real cost burden becomes much higher than proponents claim.

And the story gets worse. In arguing for the expiration of the wind energy tax credit, the *Kansas City Star* notes that "Like solar, wind isn't readily scalable. It uses enormous amounts of land to produce relatively small amounts of energy from an intermittent source at very high capital costs. Wind power must be backed up by conventional power, which means it does little to reduce carbon emissions."[65]

The newspaper zeroes in on the CO_2 emission aspect in its observation about wind power and its need to be backed up by conventional generation. But failure to reduce CO_2 substantially is hardly the story. Massive quantities of investment are being squandered in countries all over the planet on wind power in the mistaken belief that it will reduce CO_2 emissions. But the most salient aspect of this situation is not about CO_2, but with economics. We are siphoning away oceans of public funds toward a form of energy that is unreliable, expensive, unpredictable, and would not exist without costly subsidies.

The Minnesota Rural Electric Association was obligated to pay an extra $70 million in 2010 to purchase renewable wind energy due the 2007 Renewable Portfolio Standard (RPS) law that obligates every operator in the state to generate 25% of its power from renewable sources by the year 2025.[66] Most RPS programs exempt rural co-operatives. But not in progressive Minnesota. Co-ops were sent scrambling to lock in long term supply contracts on a take-or-pay basis at above-market rates. When the economy went south in 2008-2009, electricity demand plummeted. Rural co-ops had contracted to purchase fixed quantities of high-priced wind power that was spread over a smaller base of competitively-priced "normal" power.[67] Their appeals for relief fell on deaf ears. The Minnesota Division of Energy Resources ignored the complaints, claiming "that complying with the Renewable Energy Standards, to date, has been cost-effective."[68] The term "cost effective" carries a different meaning in Minnesota than everywhere else.

Wind energy also tends to be resource intensive for the paltry amount of power derived. Author Robert Bryce tells a story about resource requirements to construct a wind complex. The Milford Wind Corridor is a sprawling 306 mW wind energy project completed in May 2011 in Utah. The 2-phase project deploys 165 wind turbines across Millard and Beaver Counties,[69] spreading out over forty square miles of the Utah desert.[70] Total project cost will be $400 million.[71] Anomalously, the power produced by the Milford Wind Corridor project will all be transported 500 miles from Utah to Los Angeles.[72] That will help enable that city to meet its obligations under AB32, otherwise known as the California Assisted Suicide Act.[73]

A concrete plant needed to be built to supply the emplacement anchors for each of the 165 towers. A total of 44,344 cubic meters of concrete was consumed.[74] That equates to a single cube of concrete with each side the height of a 10-storey building. The project required 145 cubic meters of concrete for each megawatt of nameplate capacity. According to a document filed by the Los Angeles Department of Water and Power, the wind project will have a capacity factor of 29%.[75] That means that for every mW of delivered power, the project will actually consume 500 cubic meters of concrete. The 500 cubic meter figure compares favorably with estimates by Per Peterson, Professor of Nuclear Engineering at the University of California at Berkeley, who figures that each mW of wind power requires 870 cubic meters of concrete and 460 tons of steel.[76]

But compare 500 cubic meters of concrete and 460 tons of steel per delivered mW of wind power with just 27 cubic meters of concrete and 3.3 tons of steel per mW for a combined-cycle natural gas plant. This is "clean energy"?

ATTEMPTS TO MEASURE REAL COSTS OF WIND

Researchers must scour the known universe looking for economic studies that provide an accurate measure of true, fully allocated cost of wind power. In DoE's levelized cost tables,[77] the model includes only capital, operating and maintenance costs of wind generation and transmission.[78] Among the numerous cost categories DoE ignores in its model is the enormous capital expenditures required to maintain backup power for those periods when wind isn't producing. Because those investments need to be maintained solely to accommodate wind unpredictability, it is appropriate to allocate a portion of backup facility capital cost to the wind energy cost equation. It is also appropriate to include any additional operating costs of inefficiency that results from the increased stop-start cycling of backup power caused by wind intermittency.

Engineering consultancy Mott MacDonald was retained by the Department of Environment and Climate Change in the UK in 2010 to perform a levelized cost analysis similar to DoE's.[79] Like the DoE, Mott MacDonald significantly understated the true cost of wind generation by ignoring the cost of backup capacity needed to cover intermittency. Nobody wants to address the subject forthrightly. It's not difficult to understand why.

A study on the exorbitant costs of wind power prepared by Professor Gordon Hughes at University of Edinburgh notes that:

> *Any large scale investment in wind power will have to be backed up by an equivalent investment in gas-fired open cycle plants. These are quite cheap to build but they operate at relatively low levels of thermal efficiency, so they emit considerably more CO_2 per mWh of electricity than combined cycle gas plants.*[80]

Hughes observes that, for the UK to meet its 20% renewable generation target by 2020, the country will need to deploy 36,000 mW of wind power that would be backed up with 13,000 mW of open cycle gas plants. The investment cost to achieve this target is estimated to be £120 billion.[81] The same power requirements could be met by deploying 21,500 mW of combined-cycle gas plants at an investment cost of just £13 billion. The £120 billion wind and open cycle gas plants proposal would deliver £0.5 billion per year in reduced operating costs for the additional £107 billion investment capital required.[82] That plan offers a 214 year payback period and a negative real rate of return.[83]

Even more interestingly, the report observes that, under certain circumstances, CO_2 emissions could actually be higher by using the £120 billion wind plan than simply following the £13 billion combined cycle gas generation option.[84] But even under the most favorable set of circumstances, only 23 million metric tons of CO_2 would be abated by 2020 at a cost of £270 per metric ton at 2009 constant prices.[85] Compare that to the price for carbon offsets trading on the ETS in early April 2012 of £5.10 per metric ton.[86] The December price of £4.61 was so low that it prompted Australian firms to begin buying carbon offsets in anticipation of a cap-and-trade law.[87] They didn't know that the Labour government of Kevin Rudd would soon be thrown out office. So the chances for that law would go down the toilet along with Rudd and his disgraced predecessor Julia Gillard.

Take your pick. Shell out an extra £107 billion in taxpayer capital to reduce CO_2 at a net cost of £270 per metric ton. Or save all that money and buy carbon offsets at £5.00 per metric ton if CO_2 emissions even increase at all. Naturally, since the choice is being dictated by the UK government, the climate change law prohibits buying carbon offsets.

Professor Hughes' findings about the exorbitant CO_2 abatement costs are borne out by a earlier report on Ireland's wind energy experience. A study published in February 2004 by the transmission service operator in Ireland, ESB National Grid, examined the cost of CO_2 abatement provided by wind power relative to other alternatives:

It can be estimated that, in the long term, using wind power generation to comply with the EU target will increase electricity generation costs by 15% … This translates to a CO_2 abatement cost in excess of €120/tonne. The cost of CO_2 abatement arising from using large levels of wind energy penetration appears high relative to other alternatives.[88]

That's putting the case a bit mildly. Ireland can abate CO_2 with wind power at €120 per metric ton at 2004 prices or buy carbon credits on the exchange at levels below €4 per metric ton at 2012 price levels. Can anyone seriously demonstrate that one additional metric ton of atmospheric CO_2 would impose harm on the global economy greater than even the lower of those two numbers?

Those results were also replicated in a comprehensive study undertaken by Bentek Energy.[89] Colorado imposed an RPS program that included a "must take" provision requiring utilities to absorb 100% of the electricity generated by wind farms. This causes utilities to cycle back-up generators on and off abruptly to accommodate wind intermittency. Between 2003 and 2011, Colorado wind farms generated only about 32% of nameplate capacity.[90] That means backup stations were cycling more than two-thirds of the time.

Studying hourly wind energy operational data over a four year period, Bentek discovered that, because of the high degree of cycling, coal-fired backup operates at much lower efficiency levels than if coal units were allowed to operate continuously without interruption. As a result, wind actually results in more, not less dangerous, smog-inducing sulfur oxides, nitrogen oxides, and CO_2 emissions than if Colorado had not imposed its expensive, technically unworkable, climate damaging, counter-productive RPS program.[91]

A lengthy but very hard-hitting passage from Bentek sums up the disastrous situation that 'green energy' proponents have unleashed:

Integrating erratic and unpredictable wind resources with established coal and natural gas generation resources requires [the Public Service Company of Colorado] to cycle its coal and natural gas-fired plants. Cycling coal plants to accommodate wind generation makes the plants operate inefficiently, which drives up emissions. Moreover, when they are not operated consistently at their designed temperatures, the variability causes problems with the way they interact with their associated emission control technologies, frequently causing erratic emission behavior that can last for hours before control is regained. Ironically, using wind to a degree that forces utilities to temporarily reduce their coal generation results in greater SO_2, NO_X and CO_2 than would have occurred if less wind energy were generated and coal generation were not impacted.[92]

This is a devastating indictment of wind power in particular and RPS programs in general. As if additional evidence were required at this point given the foregoing, RPS programs designed to reduce harmful emissions, produce cleaner air, and lower a state's carbon footprint are effecting precisely the opposite outcomes.

Wind proponents go to inordinate lengths to hide the true costs of wind power. An example comes from Synapse Energy Economics of Cambridge, Massachusetts.[93] They studied wind power penetration scenarios in the PJM Interconnection region out to the year 2026.[94] More wind power is forecasted to be brought on line in the "deep-blue" states of Pennsylvania, New Jersey, and Maryland served by PJM in coming years. That will enable those already high cost-of-living states to meet RPS obligations.

Synapse triumphantly points out that "wind output displaces coal, gas and oil-fired generation" but, of course, not coal or gas generation *capacity*.[95] Those baseload plants will still need to be kept in spinning reserve — and their very high capital costs will still need to be borne — when wind power disappears. It often does, especially in the summer months when air conditioners are running. For example, PJM only derived 13.8% and 10.4% of its wind power nameplate capacity in the stifling months of July and August 2012 respectively.[96] When PJM power consumers were roasting in the unbearable heat wave of the first two weeks of July, 86% of PJM's wind capacity went on holiday. A damaging "derecho" super-storm struck the region on June 29th.[97] In the several days following that event, temperatures across the region soared into triple digits. Wind power essentially collapsed in the PJM service area dropping to midday levels below 2% of capacity.[98] Not a scintilla of peak baseload capacity was able to be displaced by wind power, as every baseload plant needed to be brought on line to meet peak power demand. Synapse completely ignores this capital degradation impact of wind power.

Synapse also claims that its analyses of future generation scenarios for high wind penetration in the PJM region "lead to a production cost savings on the order of $14.5 to $14.9 billion dollars per year."[99] But Synapse only gets to this wildly generous conclusion after allocating a staggering $30 per metric ton cost of CO_2 emissions against sensible, reliable, low-cost, baseload power generation.[100] This is the kind of dubious "social cost of carbon" accounting magic that the Obama administration employs to justify his unwarranted expansion of 'green energy.'

In its comparison, Synapse fails to allocate the $23 per mWh cost of the federal wind energy Production Tax Credit (PTC) that gets shifted onto the backs of federal taxpayers. If you don't think it amounts to very much, consider that the $23 cost is an after-tax figure. The pre-tax equivalent is $41.13 per megawatt-hour.[101] That was equivalent to 131.5% of the pre-tax electricity price for wholesale power traded on the ten largest electricity hubs during 2012.[102] Wind proponents imagine this PTC cost just goes away, sort of like the garbage someone throws out into the street during a heavy downpour that gets washed down into the storm drain. It just goes away.

Synapse might reply that the same cost-shifting issue arises with respect to CO_2 emissions from coal and gas generation. But we're still waiting for those onerous social costs to manifest themselves anywhere other than in the anger-wracked minds of 'green energy' junk science promoters.[103] Al Gore told us in 2006 that the ocean would rise 20 feet within the next 100 years because of CO_2 emissions. That is 24 inches per decade or 2.4 inches per year.[104] So we should have already seen 19.2 inches of sea level rise in the eight-year interim. The increase, if there has been one, is almost too small to measure.

Here are a few other interesting comparisons highlighting the unreliability embedded in Synapse's analysis. Because they are buried deep in the detailed assumptions, they escaped notice of green-left media evangelists. To find it, you actually need to read the report instead of just the press release. Synapse assumes PJM's peak generating capacity requirements will be 190.9 gigawatts in year 2026. But in all scenarios, they have only assumed 140.5 gigawatts of baseload coal and natural gas capacity.[105] There was another 33.7 gigawatts of nuclear power in the PJM system in 2013.[106] That still leaves a sizeable gap, which means all of the capacity odds and ends in place today will need to remain in the system until 2026. Otherwise there will not be enough reliable capacity to meet peak requirements on those days when temperatures soar and wind disappears. So higher capital costs for baseload generation will need to be either retained or installed to close the gap. That will drive the wind cost case higher than Synapse assumes.

Next, Synapse laughingly assumes wind will generate an ELCC of 38% in all its scenarios.[107] Yet wind only achieved about 27% ELCC in the PJM service territory during the 13-month period from November 2011 to November 2012.[108] DoE data show that nationwide wind power only achieved about 30.2% ELCC in the previous five year period up to 2011 and barely squeezed past the 30% threshold just three times in 22 years.[109] So the actual costs of wind are at least 26% more — and likely 41% higher — than Synapse assumes from its ELCC distortion.

Synapse also assumed a turbine price to be $936 per kW capacity.[110] But during 2012, turbine contracts observed by the Lawrence Berkeley National Laboratory's annual *Wind Technologies Market Report* indicated that prices had reached as high as $1,300 per kW.[111] The report observed that prices reached as high as $1,500 per kW in 2009.[112] So Synapse underestimates wind capital costs.

Synapse then assumes a natural gas price in 2026 of $6.67 per million BTUs.[113] Who knows? Maybe it will be and maybe it won't. But in the 44 month period beginning in January 2010, the average price for natural gas at the Henry Hub was only about $3.71 per million BTUs.[114] So, predicated upon recent spot price levels, Synapse could be overstating natural gas fuel costs by as much as 80%. It was operating savings of avoided natural gas that partly compelled Synapse to boast of the marvelous value ratepayers would receive by deploying wind.

Synapse might ask themselves, if wind power is so affordable, why is it driving up the cost of electricity in states where it is being deployed. The ten states with the highest wind penetration levels have seen electricity rates advance nearly four times faster between 2008 and 2012 than the other forty states.[115] They might ask themselves why, if it so economic, is it causing electric utility risk profiles to be upended and capital costs to soar in countries where there are high levels of wind penetration.[116] And they might want to ask who is paying the tab for the billions in federal tax credits that get funneled to wind farm operators. We can easily identify, locate, and measure the wind energy costs they ignore. Can they locate their "social cost of carbon" anywhere other than in the fever swamps of their imagination?

There is much public misunderstanding on this vital topic for which we can thank a clueless 'green energy' promoting mass media culture for instilling. With side-splitting hilarity, green bloviating media preposterously claim that PJM "could double the amount of planned wind and would still save ratepayers money."[117] They shout in the headline that "Doubling Wind Will Cut Rates for PJM Customers." Yeah, sure. If you're offered an "over-under" wager, take the "over." PJM customers can expect to see the same "savings" that German and Danish ratepayers enjoy for power priced more than three times the amount the average U.S. consumer pays.[118] These ridiculous claims arise because shallow media ideologues swallow the discredited Synapse press release without bothering to read the report to understand how the calculations were derived. Can PJM customers expect to see a "savings" on their monthly bills because the $30 per ton "social cost of carbon" is being pocketed with wind energy? Try not to fall out of your armchair laughing at that inanity.

Another hilarious case is provided courtesy of the *Los Angeles Times*. The paper recites typical 'green energy' catechism in a December 2012 editorial telling its gullible audience that wind farms are "helping to wean the country off fossil fuels."[119] But evidently the *Los Angeles Times* doesn't read the *Los Angeles Times*. Just two and a half weeks earlier, the very same paper advised its readership in a carefully-researched column that a "Rise in Renewable Energy Will Require More Use of Fossil Fuel."[120] So which is it? Do wind farms help wean us from fossil fuel, or do they require us to use more? Only one version could possibly be accurate. Not surprisingly, it was the earlier, thoroughly documented column written by reporter Ralph Vartabedian, someone who actually knew what he was talking about, that had gotten the story right. The editorialists, like Synapse and countless other 'green energy' confabulators, were peddling counter-factual eco-religion.

FULLY-ALLOCATED COST OF WIND ENERGY

The foregoing examples are useful to understanding the difficulties encountered when comparing of the costs of intermittent sources like wind with dispatchable technology. They also illustrate the wild imbalance between costs to abate CO_2 emissions using wind energy compared to claims from proponents about the necessity of undertaking these measures. It's a certainty that if voters understood the actual costs they must bear to eliminate CO_2 emissions, particularly when those costs are compared to the social costs of not doing so, support for 'green energy' would collapse even among many ardent proponents.

The Levelized Cost of New Generation Resources contained in the *Annual Energy Outlook 2013* provides what DoE claims are the typical costs to add additional generation resources in the year 2018.[121] Chief among those is that baseload power like coal, natural gas and nuclear are dispatchable sources which can deliver power whenever we need it. Wind, on the other hand, blows only when it wants to. Therefore, intermittent sources can never be directly compared to baseload sources unless all of their spillover effects are taken into consideration.

There are a number of very costly impacts that DoE does not take into consideration when attempting to derive an estimate of long-run marginal cost. Only when all of these substantial cost impacts are included can a realistic comparison with other sources be made. Let's examine some of those impacts:

Effective Load Carrying Capacity — America's investment in wind turbines have not produced anywhere close to the 34% ELCC figure supplied by DoE. The most recent 10-year period has shown something closer to 30.2%.[122] That means the actual cost of wind power is at least 25.8% higher than DoE claims. We'll use that ratio to measure the real cost of wind energy.

Renewable Energy Tax Credits — The costs provided by DoE don't include the 2.3¢ per kWh PTC that taxpayers fork over for wind energy that generators produce and sell. Based upon AWEA's estimate of 60,007 megawatts of wind power installed at the end of the fourth quarter of 2012,[123] U.S. taxpayers will fork over about $3.5 billion in PTC in 2013.[124] But the PTC is an after-tax credit. So it must be converted to a pre-tax basis to be comparable with other cost categories. The after-tax PTC is equivalent to a pre-tax 3.5 to 4.5¢ per kWh. So the actual cost from this impact relative to on-shore wind power is at least 40.9% higher than DoE's 8.66¢ per kWh figure.[125] We must likewise add back at least 3.5¢ per kilowatt-hour to the 22.15¢ per kWh figure DoE supplies for offshore wind.

Capital Cost of Underutilized Backup Capacity — Wind can never serve as a substitute for baseload power but only as a supplement. Despite 45,100 turbines installed in the U.S. at the end of 2012,[126] wind has never displaced a single baseload power plant.[127] Not one — anywhere. DoE numbers do not consider the impact of excess dispatchable generation capacity that needs to be maintained as a backup when wind disappears or declines below levels that grid managers anticipate. A study performed by George Taylor and Thomas Tanton for the American Tradition Institute examined this question. They derived a set of parameters that can be used to estimate the impact that this factor exerts.[128] We'll rely upon their work in our analysis.

Operating Efficiency Degradation of Backup Generation — In Colorado, Bentek Energy discovered that coal utility plant efficiency declined significantly due to rapid stop-start cycling as wind power waxed and waned.[129] The UK is considering a plan to use less efficient, lower capital cost open cycle gas turbines (OCGT) to backup wind intermittency. This plan would pose far higher costs — £107 billion additional — than one devoted to avoiding wind power altogether and relying upon efficient combined-cycle gas turbines (CCGT), estimated to cost just £13 billion.[130] OGCT turbines are less efficient per cubic foot of natural gas than CCGT units. The additional costs that arise solely from the presence of wind must be added back to DoE's underestimate. Fortunately, Taylor and Tanton estimated these impacts also.[131]

Wind Turbine Output Degradation Over Time — DoE assumes that a turbine placed in service will have a 20-year useful life.[132] But they fail to account for gradual output degradation over time. They assume that the turbine produces the same amount of power on the 20th year as when it rolled off the dealer showroom floor. Machinery efficiency degrades over time from accumulated wear and tear of constant usage. As equipment ages, progressively more maintenance is required, making it less available to produce output. Virtually every wind power study ever undertaken by man or beast ignores this impact. But a groundbreaking examination of output from thousands of Danish and UK wind turbines by Professor Gordon Hughes shows that turbines degrade appreciably.[133] In addition, turbines exhaust their serviceable lives sooner than DoE forecasts. For purposes of estimating the present value of this impact, the wind turbine output degradation curve derived by Hughes for on-shore turbines in the UK will be used to adjust DoE factors.[134]

Longer Distance Transmission Infrastructure — Wind energy is produced in places far from consuming centers. Unlike most dispatchable baseload capacity that locates close to consumers, a network of long distance high-voltage transmission lines need to be installed to distribute wind power. Also, because of wind's low yield that is often only a third of baseload capability, transmission build-out for wind will be three times higher per mile than it would be for dispatchable sources of equivalent rated capacity.[135] But a typical wind farm is only a small fraction of capacity as is a dispatchable plant. So wind power distribution means longer distances with much lower current densities. Germany's expansion of wind towers far out into the Baltic and North Seas has necessitated construction of hugely complex converter stations and a high-voltage transmission network to get power from sparsely-populated northern to densely-populated southern regions. The buildout will require at least €42.5 billion in extra investment.[136] DoE includes some additional transmission infrastructure impact, but it is woefully understated. Taylor and Tanton provide a better estimate of these additional impacts.

Power Loss in Transmission — Needless to say, the longer current is transported, the more power in the circuit is lost due to impedance caused by capacitive reactance. These losses will be far more pronounced for wind energy since it needs to travel far longer distances than conventional sources. Also, there are incremental transmission grid build-outs necessitated because wind surges in one area need to be balanced with wind shortages in other areas. The typical wind energy electron travels much farther on average than a conventionally-produced cousin. These transmission losses can be reduced by boosting voltages through the network. But higher voltages carry their own set of offsetting negative impacts like 50- or 60-cycle interference with radio signals, increased frequency of avian electrocutions, higher risk to human populations, higher intensity magnetic fields in the vicinity of the lines, more costly materials, etc. Taylor and Tanton estimated these transmission loss and mitigation costs.

When the impacts cited above are factored into a fully-allocated cost model, DoE's cost of Onshore Wind increases from $86.60 per mWh to $198.70 as Figure 13-2 depicts. That is 2.3 times higher than current EIA estimates. Wind farm operators may deride this exercise, claiming their costs are nowhere near this level.

FIGURE 13-2. **Fully Allocated Cost of Wind in DoE's Levelized Cost Table**

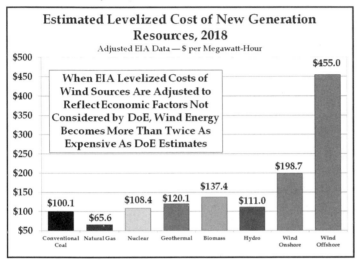

Sources: Analysis based upon DoE's Annual Energy Outlook 2013 levelized cost data adjusted for economic factors not included by DoE.

True enough as far as it goes. But many of these impacts do not fall onto their shoulders. Wind farm operators don't pay to keep standby power in reserve and held at degraded utilization rates. Utility investors and ratepayers do. They don't pay the 2.3¢ per kWh production tax credit, you do. They pocket it. They don't bear the cost of efficiency degradation of standby generation capacity from frequent stop-start cycling caused by wind power's intermittency. System ratepayers do. They will not bear the burden of large transmission build out. You will. And so forth. You can eat cheaply at an expensive restaurant when the other patrons pay most of your tab. But cost shifting stops at the border. You can ask Danes and Germans paying a rate three and a half times what the average American pays about that.

Offshore wind, already a dicey proposition under favorable DoE assumptions, increases to the point where it almost slides clear off the chart, soaring by 220% to $455.00 per mWh. That makes it nearly seven times more expensive than natural gas. It is not difficult to understand why Danish ratepayers, who must absorb all of these costs, pay the highest electricity rates in the EU.

Consider an example of the soaring and largely understated transmission costs that arise from wind power in Texas. Most Texans live in the eastern part of the state while the heaviest winds blow across the central prairie and western panhandle. That means that if the wind resources are to be harvested, a massive network of transmission lines needs to be built to connect remote producing areas with far-flung consuming regions. So in

2005, the Texas legislature authorized the Competitive Renewable Energy Zones (CREZ) transmission project.[137]

The CREZ transmission project was originally forecast to cost less than $5 billion.[138] But that number increased to nearly $7 billion by 2011.[139] As opposition mounted and state wind promoters were obligated to reroute around towns and housing developments, the project cost leaped by $2 billion.[140] The cost burden upon each Texan will be at least $300.[141]

The state's electricity grid is straining under the loads required during peak summer months when parts of the state experience more that 80 days of triple-digit temperatures. So the state will dump at least $7 billion down a rat hole to build 3,500 miles of high-voltage transmission lines for the purpose of complementing peak demand with an additional 1.3% of power production. Does this sound like a good deal?

Need more evidence? Consider the fact that the Cape Wind project off Nantucket will deliver offshore wind energy into the National Grid at an initial rate of 18.7¢ per kWh, which will increase by 3½% each year over a 15-year life of the contract.[142] By the end of the contract, utilities will be paying more than 30¢ per kWh. The governor of Massachusetts calls this "cost-effective" for the state's ratepayers.[143] Meanwhile, during 2012, wholesale power contracts traded in the NEPOOL Mass Hub that serves the New England region maintained a weighted average price of 4.4¢ per kWh.[144]

An even worse prospect is facing Cape Wind ratepayers. The complex may only be able to sell half the output expected from the initially planned 130 offshore turbines. Fewer turbines will drive up the cost to the top end of the contracted range of 19.3¢ per kWh.[145] How "cost effective" is it when consumers pay 425% the price of competitive options in the region, and maybe more?

Based upon total wind usage in 2011, there was an additional cost of $16.9 billion imposed on the U.S. economy over what would have been incurred had advanced combined-cycle natural gas had been used.[146] That means wind power caused a drain of 0.11% against 2011 GDP.[147] And yet wind only supplied about 1.2% of U.S. primary energy needs during the year.[148] 'Green energy' enthusiasts contend we need to do much more of this. Ramp up wind to 20% of our power needs and you almost completely eliminate economic growth in the U.S. How much more can an economy, crawling at real GDP growth rates half of that we typically achieve, really afford?

News reports and analyses focus on higher electricity rates that arise from feed-in tariffs, mandates, subsidies and all the rest. Often overlooked is the burden of cost-shifting. When the fully-allocated cost impacts are attributed to each competing source, wind power and especially offshore wind power becomes unaffordable.

At the risk of piling on, there are additional costs imposed on system ratepayers from wind power that have not been estimated in the analysis above, but which certainly occur in actual experience. Intermittent sources are granted a priority position on the grid in markets where renewables are accorded a "must-take" preference. There is an implied higher capital impairment cost imposed by markets against utilities whose once-predictable cost, revenue, and earnings patterns have been degraded in this way. German utilities have seen their credit ratings diminished as renewable energy pours into the grid, displacing traditional sources.[149] This adverse selection impact raises utility borrowing costs as high renewables penetration levels upend risk profiles of traditional electric utility operation that once relied upon merit-order portfolio selection. The German government's response was to propose an increase in public subsidies to be paid to utilities whose generation asset values have been undercut.[150] Those costs will be borne by ratepayers.

There may ultimately be additional costs imposed by energy storage scenarios required to balance intermittency. While there are no pumped-storage or battery storage investments in the U.S. thus far, such scenarios have been proposed. They are already in operation in Europe. An example is Danish and German excess wind power that is produced during inopportune periods that gets shipped to pumped-storage facilities in Norway and Sweden. Since 1980, Denmark has been relentlessly deploying onshore and offshore wind power to supplement fossil fuel electricity. Anomalously, while about 34% of total electricity generation in Denmark is now derived from wind power, less than 5% of Danish electricity demand can be satisfied by wind.[151] Most of the wind power can't be used in Denmark because it is generated during inopportune periods when demand is low. As a result, the excess power is exported to Sweden and Norway where the portion not lost in transmission and multiple conversions can either be used or stored. In addition to the exorbitant costs borne by Danish ratepayers for expensive wind power, some of that power is sold back to Denmark at a profit, driving Danish power costs higher.[152] As a result, Danish ratepayers suffer the highest electricity rates in the EU.[153]

Likewise, Germany is proposing to invest mountains of funds for undersea cabling to offload more excess electricity onto Norway's pumped-storage facilities.[154] It is also experimenting with hydrogen-conversion storage, a monumentally wasteful program that highlights the extreme absurdity of Germany's mad dash into renewable energy oblivion.[155]

There is also the cost of grid instability of severe intermittency imposed by wind power that exhibits extreme surges and power losses in very short periods of time. Examples are documented in the Appendix. The amount of wind energy derived by a turbine is proportional to the cube of the wind speed.[156] In a very brief period, wind power can increase by 800% from a mere doubling of wind speed. But if wind speeds get too high, turbines need to be shut down completely. This current flow instability imposes substantial grid management costs not borne by wind farm operators.

These impacts are alluded to by DoE in its renewable energy modeling assumptions. They acknowledge that "as wind or solar constitutes more of the system capacity, the variability of its peak-load operation will have a decreasingly beneficial effect on system reliability."[157] The degradation in system reliability will need to be increasingly supplemented by more poorly-utilized dispatchable power capacity, which drives up the cost of power to ratepayers.

THE "VALUE" OF WIND ENERGY

Levelized cost comparisons focus solely upon capital investment, public subsidies, and operating expense outlays. They disregard what economists refer to as "opportunity costs." An opportunity cost is the one you bear when you take off work to go fishing. In addition to the cost of gas, bait, beer, and junk food, there is also the "opportunity cost" of not earning the wages you chose to forego. Examining the operating profiles of wind and solar power provides a good illustration of why this opportunity cost concept is so critical.

In most markets, wind energy output is higher during off-peak hours than during peak daytime periods, particularly in summer peak periods. Recall that the five largest wind plants in California are scattered over a very large area. Nevertheless, during certain meteorological conditions typical of summer months, all five plants act in unison during peak demand periods, producing practically zero power.[158] Wind power production often disappears at just the time when power becomes most valuable.

Most economic evaluations of competing electricity sources attempt to compare life-cycle generation cost. We examined how levelized cost model supported by DoE is wholly inadequate for understanding the true economic costs of wind power. But that analysis focuses solely on generation cost rather than value. Professor Paul Joskow, a former chair of the Economics Department at MIT, writes persuasively that the levelized cost "metric is inappropriate for comparing intermittent generating technologies like wind and solar with dispatchable generating technologies like nuclear, gas combined cycle, and coal."[159] Instead of levelized cost comparisons, we need to consider the actual value of intermittent sources based upon their production profiles.

Professor Joskow has been analyzing the economics of electricity markets for decades. Following introduction of wholesale competition, the proportion of the non-utility electricity power supply market grew from 7.2% in 1990[160] to over 40% by 2010.[161] Joskow notes that wholesale market mechanisms have matured over this time, and the imperfections that exist in the marketplace are political rather than market-based.[162]

Joskow demonstrates that levelized cost comparisons are inappropriate methodology for comparing baseload sources vs. intermittent sources like wind and solar power because:

> ... they fail to take into account differences in the production profiles of intermittent and dispatchable generating technologies and the associated large variations in the market value of the electricity they supply. Levelized cost comparisons overvalue intermittent generating technologies compared to dispatchable base load generating technologies. They also overvalue wind generating technologies compared to solar generating technologies.

So not only do typical levelized cost comparisons woefully understate system-wide cost impacts of intermittent generation. In addition, levelized comparisons are flawed because they treat all generation output as a homogenous product governed by a single pricing structure. But electricity prices vary greatly throughout the year and even throughout the day. Every megawatt-hour is not the same. Professor Joskow shows that the price of electrical energy produced during daylight peak periods can be three to four orders of magnitude greater than for megawatt-hours generated during low-demand nighttime periods.[163]

High cost and low value. These are the principal defining characteristics of wind energy, the source expected to contribute by far the largest share of Obama's 'green energy' portfolio.

THE BIOFUEL BOONDOGGLE

CHAPTER 14

BIOFUEL OVERDOSE

"By 2030, the administration aims to increase the production [of biofuels] to 60 billion gallons per year … If projected future increases in use of corn for ethanol production do occur, the increase in harm to water quality could be considerable. In addition, expansion of corn production on fragile soils can increase loads of both nutrients and sediments."[1]

NATIONAL ACADEMY OF SCIENCES

"The harm done to consumers and the environment by the federal biofuels mandate is destined to grow worse as a result of the recent decision to once again increase the amount of corn ethanol that must be added to the nation's gasoline supply."[2]

ENVIRONMENTAL WORKING GROUP, AUGUST 2013

America's fetish with biofuels has brought a dreadful harvest. In addition to higher food prices, we have achieved devastating environmental degradation, a boatload of perverse economics, contamination of fresh water supplies, widespread hunger and starvation in some of the most vulnerable places on earth, and no meaningful reduction in CO_2 emissions.

The U.S. began promoting biofuels in a small way after passage of the Energy Tax Act of 1978, which established an excise tax exemption for ethanol equating to 40 cents per blended gallon of fuel.[3] Ten years later, the Alternative Motor Fuels Act of 1988 offered auto manufacturers a set of incentives to produce flexible fueled vehicles through a system of credits on corporate average fuel economy standards.[4] Two years later, the federal government ramped up its involvement in the biofuels market as a result of provisions in the 1990 Clean Air Act that were designed to reduce atmospheric ozone and carbon monoxide, requiring gasoline to contain additives equaling 2.7% oxygen by weight.[5]

Although there were a number of potential oxygenates able to fulfill the role of 2.7% by weight, the two alternatives that emerged to capture the market were ethanol, produced in a grain distillery, and a volatile organic compound called methyl tertiary butyl ether, or MTBE, produced in an oil refinery. While MTBE initially captured the lion's share of the gasoline oxygenate market, it was recognized within a few years that it was a powerful carcinogen when inhaled.[6] And due to high volatility, it easily leaked out of underground storage tanks, causing widespread toxic groundwater contamination in many areas of the country.[7] So the federal government's first foray into saving the planet and improving the health of mankind by mandating oxygenated fuels resulted in widespread poisoning of fresh water aquifers.[8]

FIGURE 14-1. **EISA Renewable Fuels Mandate 2008-2022**

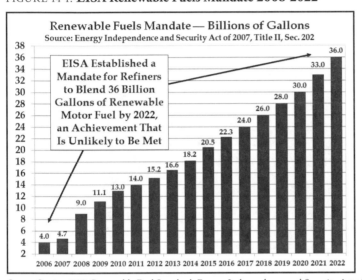

Source: Section 202, Renewable Fuel Standard, Energy Independence and Security Act of 2007

During the George W. Bush administration, the federal government jumped into biofuels with both feet, first by passing the Energy Policy Act (EPAct) in 2005[9] and the Energy Independence and Security Act (EISA) of 2007 two years later.[10] EPAct established the Renewable Fuel Standard (RFS)[11] that required 7.5 billion gallons of renewable fuel to be blended into gasoline by the year 2012.[12] Under EISA, the scope and ambitions of the RFS were substantially expanded in several key respects.[13] Sections 201 and 202 of EISA added biodiesel to the list of renewable fuels under the mandate. Rather than promoting production of domestic oil resources, EISA sought to displace foreign supply by mandating renewable fuels. The obligated thresholds would grow from 9 billion gallons in 2008 to 36 billion gallons by 2022 as depicted in Figure 14-1.

EISA established new categories for renewable fuels and a schedule of ever-increasing mandated volumes for each category. The act included cellulosic biofuels as a designated category, mandating 100 million gallons in 2010, rising to 16 billion gallons by 2022.[14] EISA also directed the EPA to establish life-cycle greenhouse gas reduction thresholds to assure that each incremental gallon of renewable fuel in each category achieved a targeted CO_2 reduction.[15]

FIGURE 14-2. **EISA Mandate vs. DoE's Long-Term Biofuel Forecast**

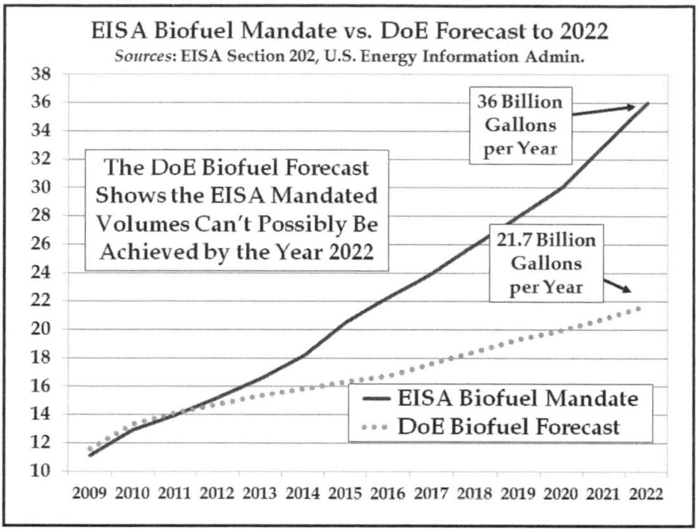

Sources: EISA Sec. 202 Biofuel Mandates vs. Energy Information Administration U.S. Gasoline Consumption in Annual Energy Outlook 2011 Reference Case

Even as EISA was being debated, knowledgeable sources predicted that these aggressive biofuel mandates were unlikely ever to be achieved.[16] Chief among the skeptics was the U.S. Energy Information Administration (EIA).[17] EIA predicted in 2008 that the country would only be able to use a maximum of 21.7 billion gallons of biofuel by 2022, with shortfalls from mandated levels beginning almost from the outset of the new legislation as depicted in Figure 14-2. EIA figured it would take producers until 2030 to meet the 36 billion gallon target. Most of that volume would be corn ethanol. The most glaring deficiency in EIA's estimation was the shortfall in cellulosic ethanol, a fuel made from corn stover, grasses, wood chips and other non-food biomass.

Amazingly, in the months prior to passage of EISA, there were vocal comments from sources claiming the act suffered from a lack of ambition. A junior Senator from a Midwest farm state declared that the measure did not go nearly far enough to suit his ambitions. In an angry Senate speech, that legislator claimed the nation could produce double the amount of biofuel mandated by the 2007 act:

First, we should ramp up the renewable fuel standard and create an alternative diesel standard in this country so that by 2025, 65 billion gallons of alternative fuels per year will be blended into the petroleum supply.[18]

So the unattainably large volume of 36 billion gallons of biofuels would be insufficient. We'd need 65 billion gallons. But even that enumerated goal was not really good enough. Less than two months later, the same Senator visited Chicago where he claimed that America should produce 187.8 billion gallons of biofuels per year by the year 2025 — triple his previous target:[19]

> *With technology we have on the shelves right now and fuels we can grow right here in America, by 2025 we can reduce our oil imports by over 7.5 million barrels per day — an amount greater than all the oil we are expected to import from the entire Middle East.*[20]

The freshman legislator who uttered these comments was Barack Obama, the first term Senator from Illinois, a self-styled energy policy expert. Obama had been blathering for years in front of every audience that could endure it about the magic quality of renewable fuels.

CAN WE EVEN CONSUME IT ALL?

EISA's aggressive mandate for cellulosic ethanol was based upon an unshakeable belief that, simply by enacting something into law, it would naturally come into fruition. Would that such certitudes underlined the approach taken by industrial policy enthusiasts in Congress to lowering crime rates, reducing budget deficits, boosting jobs and economic growth, or improving student performance on standardized tests? Why can't we have a Cancer Elimination Act of 2014 that mandates its eradication? How about an Affordable Care Act?

Further complicating the situation was America's inability to consume mandated ethanol levels, even if supplies were actually available. EPA had been studying the so-called "blend wall" problem that their policy faced. Ethanol is blended into gasoline at a 10% level by volume. The blend wall is the maximum amount of ethanol that could be blended into gasoline given current fuel demand. Figure 14-3 provides a depiction of EIA's forecast of blend proportions that result from EISA 2007 mandated biofuel volumes. Some of the volume is biodiesel which can drop directly into diesel fuel supply. And a few stations are selling E85, a blend of 85% ethanol and 15% gasoline. But it won't be long before the U.S. will have exceeded its maximum blending capacity. After that, things become problematic.

The only way these higher levels could be attained is if there are significant increases in the amount of ethanol that is blended into gasoline — if the blend ratios are boosted above the 10% level. The obvious solution for EPA was to advocate for gasoline containing 15% ethanol (called E15) and E85. Most vehicle warranties would be voided if owners use fuels exceeding 10%.[21] Vehicle makers contend that E15 or E85 damages engine components and catalytic converters.[22]

EPA had a ready-made response. In October 2010, the agency simply decreed that E15 would be permissible in all cars from model year 2007 and later.[23] The agency ignored the voided vehicle warranty problem.[24] It was a stunning expansion of EPA's legislative charter. EPA, now branded as the Ethanol Promotion Agency,[25] had decided that its regulatory mandate was not just limited to regulation of exhaust emissions under the Clean Air Act.[26] It now had the power to determine appropriate automotive operations and maintenance practices, override vehicle manufacturer guidelines on fueling, and restructure private contracts between car makers and buyers by modifying warranties. The following January, EPA extended its E15 waiver to model years 2001-2006 cars.[27] And in April 2012, EPA announced approval of the first applications for E15 registration, the first step toward widespread distribution.[28]

FIGURE 14-3. **Biofuel Blend Percentages under EISA 2007**

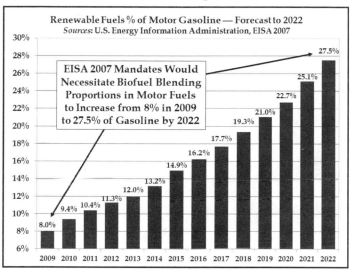

Sources: EISA 2007 Sec. 202 Biofuel Mandates vs. Energy Information Administration U.S. Gasoline Consumption in Annual Energy Outlook 2011 Reference Case

Obama's nomination of Gina McCarthy to succeed Lisa Jackson — or Richard Windsor as she calls herself when she's lawlessly hiding her e-mail exchanges from Freedom of Information Act (FOIA) requests[29] — was a clear indication that the administration would step up its ethanol promotion program.[30] As for Richard Windsor, it was her illegal use of pseudonymous email that prompted her hurriedly forced "resignation" as EPA administrator.[31]

EPA received counsel from numerous sources to delay its E15 decision to allow for more thorough testing. Experience in Australia where E15 is already in use showed that car engine problems are widespread.[32] Identical findings have been reported by authoritative studies in the U.S., even by consultancies hired by EPA to study the issue.[33]

The 53 million member American Automobile Association (AAA) urged EPA to reverse its ruling.[34] AAA released a study in November 2012 showing there were inherent dangers posed by E15 such as "potential corrosive damage to fuel lines, gaskets and other engine components."[35] AAA determined that 95% of consumers had never even heard of

E15.[36] Despite the fact that ethanol consumes 41% of corn production in America, EPA was determined to boost consumption by 50%.[37]

In addition, manufacturers of gas-powered equipment indicate that many of these equipment types will be damaged and may pose significant safety hazards to users if E15 is used. Naturally, EPA's response was to ignore the advice and order E15 into use. Power equipment product safety is some other agency's job.

Who were automakers that had designed, built, tested and warrantied these automobiles to tell the Ethanol Promotion Agency what fuel was best for their cars?[38] It wasn't like all automakers were unanimous. The list of automakers opposing EPA only included Ford, Chrysler, Toyota, Mazda, Nissan, Volkswagen, Daimler Mercedes-Benz, BMW, Honda, Subaru, Suzuki, Kia, Aston Martin, Hyundai, Ferrari, Maserati, McLaren, and Volvo.[39] Missing from the list was General Motors, or Government Motors as it was better known by then. Naturally, America's government-owned automobile company sat on the sidelines cheering on its fellow government agency's power grab.

EPA's credibility wasn't bolstered when we learned the agency had issued its ruling on E15 just one day after a raft of new test data allegedly attesting to E15's safety had been submitted to the agency's public rulemaking docket.[40] It would have taken a typical government agency a month just to verify that it had actually received safety data rather than coloring books. There was no possible way EPA could have examined any safety data in the space of 24 hours. It didn't need to. They had already made up their minds years earlier.

It didn't take long for responsible adults to begin filing lawsuits to prevent EPA from overstepping its authority. Scarcely a month after EPA's controversial ruling, farm groups filed suit to block EPA's power grab.[41] In December 2010, a group of automakers did likewise.[42] In March 2011, petroleum refiners joined the fight.[43] To demonstrate that the agency was handling the matter in a responsible manner, giving due credence to the public's objections, EPA sent senior agency officials to testify before Congress under oath that automakers were a pack of liars.[44] It was a fight that was destined to be decided by the Supreme Court.[45]

Automakers countered that the government's tests of E15 were inadequate since they had not studied the impact on engine damage after 100,000 miles of using E15.[46] For instance, a study of eight distinct engine types undertaken by consultancy FEV for the Coordinating Research Council over a two year period used a 100,000 mile test standard. FEV discovered that engines using E15 "suffered lower performance, misfiring, reduced fuel economy, damaged valves and valve seats."[47] Automakers insist that E15 will damage engine components and invalidate vehicle warranties. Toyota added a sticker to gas caps on model year 2012 and later vehicles saying "Up to E10 gasoline only."[48] Others followed suit.

Another obvious problem concerns misfueling. EPA's idea is to place orange labels on E15 pumps alerting consumers. The label reads "E15 Up to 15% Ethanol: Use Only in 2001 and Newer Passenger Vehicles and Flex Fuel Vehicles."[49] Nothing about the potential to void vehicle warranties or anything. But then, why should they issue any warning? EPA is not on the hook to indemnify vehicle owners who damage their engines running dangerous fuel. For the average motorist who only looks at price, this approach will further muddy the waters.

In an effort to boost E15 market penetration while shielding automakers from warranty repair liability exposure caused by misfueling, a group of lawmakers dominated by farm-state Representatives proposed HR.4345 called the Domestic Fuels Protection Act of 2012. The purpose of the proposed act is "To provide liability protection for claims based on the design, manufacture, sale, offer for sale, introduction into commerce, or use of certain fuels and fuel additives, and for other purposes."[50] In other words, the act would put taxpayers on the hook for cleaning up monetary damage caused by Congress and the EPA. It was reintroduced in 2013 as H.R. 1214. GovTrack gives it a 1% chance of passage, which is 1 percent more than it deserves.[51]

E15 is not what the U.S. gasoline market needs: an additional gasoline blend to add to the list of anywhere from 45 to 70 specialized blends already in use.[52] It likely won't be *one* additional blend but dozens as E15 formulations are fed into the miasma of what are called "boutique fuels" in use across the country. The crazy quilt of boutique fuels has been mandated into use by the Clean Air Act and EPA. Nevertheless, as studies show, the effect on air quality is minimal or nonexistent. But the impact upon price is substantial as a retail fuel oligopoly has resulted.

The GAO studied this problem in 2005 and found that the proliferation of gasoline blends caused by regulatory excess has boosted prices and increased refiner margins:

> *The proliferation of special gasoline blends has put stress on the gasoline supply system and raised costs, affecting operations at refineries, pipelines, and storage terminals. Once produced, different blends must be kept separate throughout shipping and delivery, reducing the capacity of pipelines and storage terminal facilities, which were originally designed to handle fewer products. This reduces efficiency and raises costs.*[53]

Author Steven Hayward provides an example of the impact this has upon retail fuel market complexity in the St. Louis area. One blend type is required for St. Louis, Missouri, another type is required for the surrounding Missouri suburbs and a third is used in East St. Louis, Illinois just across the Mississippi River.[54] East St. Louis is only a few miles from the Missouri suburbs. So there is no possible atmospheric or terrain-related justification for these variations. A supply disruption in Tucson cannot be alleviated with diversion of product destined to Phoenix.[55] EPA can't even demonstrate that there is any air quality improvement from its dense thicket of regulations.[56] One thing is certain: consumers pay a higher price. Even the Dallas Federal Reserve Bank observes that imported fuels are prohibited since foreign refineries don't produce the specialized blends required in the U.S.[57]

EPA's absurd policies have spawned a new eco-criminal class. A well publicized case involved a Baltimore company called Clean Green Fuel. The company was formed to collect waste oil from restaurants to be converted into biofuel. As of February 2012,

Clean Green had sold credits on EPA's Moderated Transaction System representing 21 million gallons.[58] The company's owner converted $9 million in proceeds into luxury cars including a Bentley, a Rolls Royce, a Lamborghini, a Maserati, and two Ferraris.[59] He also chartered private jets for lavish vacations. At his criminal trial, the defense stated that everyone knew the credits were fake, but they were purchased anyway because the activity was mandated by law.[60] He was telling the truth.

But the best part concerns EPA's handling of the case. EPA estimates that 12% of the Renewable Identification Numbers (RINs), the identifier tags the agency assigns to each qualifying unit of biofuel production, are fraudulent.[61] That amounts to 140 million fraudulent RINs in the biodiesel market alone.[62] That doesn't include the immensely larger ethanol scam, er, market. The EPA waited 15 months after its raid on Clean Green to notify victimized companies they had purchased phony RINs and were not in compliance. EPA allowed victims just 14 days to replace their defective RINs with new, potentially fraudulent replacement RINs.[63] Better still, EPA levied fines against 24 victim purchasers for due diligence failures. The total price tag for the government-manufactured fiasco came to $40 million. Imagine if SEC had fined Bernie Madoff's victims for being defrauded. Those extra enforcement costs get passed along to motorists in higher fuel prices.

Clean Green's owner Rodney Hailey was convicted on all counts.[64] He should have been given a public service medal for highlighting the absurdity at the core of the nation's reckless biofuel policies. Following the conviction, the National Biodiesel Board sniffed to the press that:

> *Mr. Hailey's greed has caused immeasurable damage to an industry and a government policy that are working for the public good.*[65]

This is working for the public good? Naturally, just a week later, the National Biodiesel Board convened a group of 120 biodiesel producers in Washington to urge lawmakers to expand the biodiesel volumes under the Renewable Fuel Standard, the one working for the public good, the one backed up with 140 million fraudulent RINs.[66]

The American Fuel & Petrochemical Manufacturers used the occasion to urge EPA to abandon its indefensible program of levying fines against refiners for not buying fuels that don't exist, and levying even more fines when purchased RINs turn out to be fraudulent.[67] EPA's Windsor replied: "We thank you for your interest in these programs," but go pound sand.[68] Richard (Milhous) Windsor's lawless agency routinely denies FOIA requests filed by "unhelpful" groups like the Competitive Enterprise Institute or the Institute for Energy Research.[69] But it replies promptly and even waives filing fees for eco-hysterical groups like the odious Natural Resources Defense Council and other politically-aligned outfits. EPA is the agency that Richard Milhous Obama will use to administer his lawless CO_2 cap-and-trade program in an impartial, non-partisan manner.

BIOFUELS AND THE ENVIRONMENT

Each year, rainfall in the giant Midwest drainage basin causes runoff of nitrogen fertilizers from fields of row crops grown for human and animal consumption, and for biofuels. The 2013 Spring saw the heaviest rains in decades, which means that the amount of fertilizer runoff may have exceeded records.[70] When nitrogen fertilizers flow into fresh water estuaries, it causes an algae bloom as single-celled organisms go mad consuming nutrient-rich fertilizers. Once these organisms die, it results in a condition called anoxia, better known as a "dead zone."

The National Research Council (NRC) noted in 2007 that the primary cause of the dead zone in the Gulf of Mexico is discharge of fertilizer from row crops in the Mississippi River basin:

> *The nutrients of major concern with respect to the water quality of the Mississippi River and the Gulf of Mexico are nitrogen and phosphorus, especially from agricultural lands used for row crop production.*[71]

By far, the most important row crop grown in the giant Midwest basin is corn, more than 40% of which is diverted to ethanol production.[72] Corn substantially depletes nutrients from the soil. Without regular crop rotation, farmers are required to use nitrogen and phosphate fertilizers to maintain sufficient yields. But much of this fertilizer runs off into streams and rivers that flow into the Mississippi River system.

These fertilizers not only promote plant growth in fields. They are also a source of food for algae. A large accumulation of algae in a body of water due to presence of nutrients is called eutrophication. As concentrations increase, algae at the top layers die and fall to the bottom where bacteria decompose them. Decomposition requires oxygen, which it gets from occluded and dissolved oxygen in the water. As water becomes oxygen depleted, hypoxia from low-oxygen concentrations or anoxia from oxygen-free conditions, results. It's usually called "river death." It occurs in the Gulf of Mexico each summer, turning a vibrant ecosystem into an aquatic desert. The dead zone in 2010 measured 7,722 square miles, the size of New Jersey. That was twice the level observed the previous year.[73] The dead zone has reached up to 10,000 square miles in recent years.[74]

In the wake of the Gulf oil spill, media coverage rightly focused exclusively on potential damage upon marine life in the Gulf.[75] But media reports opportunistically used the occasion to falsely attribute the Gulf dead zone to the oil spill.[76] The dead zone damage wasn't due to oil. It was due to fertilizers used to grow corn and soybeans, much of which is for biofuel. Corn and soybean cultivation contributes 3.7 times as much fertilizer runoff as all other crops combined according to a report by the Environmental Working Group.[77] It has been well known for decades that the majority of the nitrogen pollution emanates from the middle-Mississippi area around Iowa and Illinois, the corn and soybean bread-basket of the world.[78] The Bureau of Labor Statistics descends into bureaucratic dementia, labeling a farmer who grows corn for ethanol a 'green job' worker while his counterpart on an adjacent farm who grows corn for human or animal consumption is not.[79] Both contribute to the dead zone, which makes them both 'brown jobs' workers.

NRC authors cite substantial shortcomings in the EPA's efforts in exercising its regulatory authority to reduce the impact caused by nutrient runoff. There should be no surprise that EPA is unwilling to undertake aggressive regulatory actions to minimize Gulf of Mexico dead zone.[80] How could it? On the one hand, EPA's Clean Air Act regulators are parading biofuel as the penultimate salvation of the planet. How could the other side of the house charged with enforcing the Clean Water Act co-exist at EPA, undertaking strong enforcement actions against biofuel crop farmers whose output goes into biofuel production, especially when the administrator is a biofuel fanatic?

For its part, EPA is content at the moment to hold field trips, wring its hands, lament about the complexity of the issue … and double-down on its quixotic biofuels mandates that are the source of the problem.[81] Some environmental groups have filed suit to force EPA to act.[82] All of which would be great if it weren't for the fact that many of the very environmental groups that filed suit, including the Natural Resources Defense Council, are the same outfits that have been most vocal flogging climate hysteria and the 'clean energy' scam that brought us biofuels in the first place.[83] Their sudden conversion to "clean" clean energy rings hollow.

Critics are correct in observing that market-distorting mechanisms like ethanol subsidies have the pernicious effect of retarding development of more promising technologies. But the solutions they often prefer involve imposition of other market-distorting mechanisms like carbon cap-and-trade, imported oil floor prices, renewable fuel mandates, carbon taxes, and carbon credits.[84] That amounts to a substitution of one set of bad public policy approaches for another.

It should seem clear by now that these ridiculous market-distorting outcomes can never be corrected through more government intervention. No amount of legislative or administrative correctives will fix the problems government created in the first place. Only when governments exit fuel markets and reduce the impact of their regulatory straightjacket will the situation eventually return to normalcy. And fuel prices can then begin to drop. But don't hold your breath waiting for that to happen.

CHAPTER 15

CAN BIOFUELS HELP REDUCE CO$_2$?

"Global warming is not a someday problem, it is now. We are already breaking records with the intensity of our storms, the number of forest fires, the periods of drought ... The polar ice caps are now melting faster than science had ever predicted. The first step ... is to phase out a carbon-based economy that's causing our changing climate ... That starts with the next generation of biofuels ... We know that corn ethanol has been the most successful alternative fuel we have ever developed. I've been a champion for ethanol. In just two years, the Renewable Fuel Standard I helped pass has sparked an historic expansion of ethanol production ... we must invest in the next generation of advanced biofuels like cellulosic ethanol that can be made from things like switchgrass and woodchips."[1]

BARACK OBAMA
REAL LEADERSHIP FOR A CLEAN ENERGY FUTURE
PORTSMOUTH, NEW HAMPSHIRE, 2007

"... anticipated biofuels will actually exacerbate global warming. Emerging calculations now indicate that over a reasonable time frame and within a broad, reasonable set of assumptions, the increased emissions of greenhouse gasses from direct and indirect land use changes are likely to exceed the greenhouse gas savings of most biofuels whether these land use changes occur directly or indirectly."[2]

LETTER FROM 10 PROMINENT CLIMATE
SCIENTISTS TO THE PRESIDENT
FEBRUARY 7, 2008

In the latter part of the Cenozoic era during the Miocene epoch about seven million years ago, the Earth evolved a variety of hardy grasses capable of assimilating heat-trapping gases more efficiently than their Oligocene and Eocene ancestral cousins that had preceded them tens of millions of years earlier.[3] In a very short period of time geologically speaking, new varieties of grasslands spread across every continent except Antarctica.[4] The newly evolved Miocene strains were not only adept at sequestering carbon dioxide, but also methane and water vapor.[5] All of these atmospheric compounds act at varying degrees of efficiency as atmospheric greenhouse gases.[6]

The ability of these greenhouse gas-assimilating strains led to very sudden changes in the Earth's climate and geology.[7] Forests were quickly displaced by grasslands.[8] Grazing animals that thrive on vast expanses of grass replaced earlier species of forest-dwelling mammals.[9] A cooler and drier planet caused by a sharp reduction in atmospheric greenhouse gas concentrations came into being. A more pronounced seasonality also manifested itself as a consequence of a cooler climate. Large expanses of grasslands that supported a variety of grazing mammals able to grind and digest these hardy grass strains became, in turn, a steady diet for predatory carnivores that evolved alongside of the grassland grazers.[10] The Earth had largely evolved into its present form with its highly unstable climate undergoing relatively brief inter-glacial periods of mild conditions similar to today that change rapidly into prolonged ice ages.[11]

In addition to their carbon-sequestering ability, grasslands are beneficial to our present way of life.[12] Grass is efficient at holding onto moisture. As summer and autumn give way to winter, most perennial grass plants go dormant, producing a thick layer of nutrient-rich organic surface material. Grass cover is effective in preventing erosion, allowing the soil to hold essential nutrients. Grasslands are efficient at exporting carbon-based compounds and metallic ions that chemically combine to produce long-lived, low-soluble calcite materials that bury carbon in the deep oceans.

Grass is also more efficient at enhancing atmospheric drying due to its higher surface reflectivity, and because grass transpires moisture back into the atmosphere at much lower rates than equivalently sized forests do. This atmospheric humidity-reducing feature of grass is crucial because, notwithstanding all of the politicized hype and junk-science you've been accustomed to hearing in the media, water vapor is actually a far more vigorous greenhouse gas than carbon dioxide. This fact has been known for a very long time by scientists but is kept well-hidden in media reports aimed at the general public.[13]

The point of all this paleoclimatology and natural history recitation is to establish that, on most of the Earth's surface, grasslands are present acting as extremely efficient carbon sinks. They capture and store huge amounts of heat-trapping greenhouse gases. The carbon is converted by grass to a chemical form that prevents its ready return to the atmosphere. The rapid spread of Miocene grasslands removed large amounts of greenhouse gas from the atmosphere which caused a substantial change in the global climate, greatly reducing planetary temperatures. With the exception of the driest deserts, permanent ice fields, thick forests, or permafrost, nearly every square inch of Earth's land surface is covered with these hardly plants performing their vital climate-balancing work.

Why is this relevant to a discussion about biofuels? Simply stated, proponents of biofuels claim that using them in place of fossil fuels will cause large reductions in the atmospheric accumulation of CO_2 which, they contend, is leading to catastrophic global warming. The theory they promote is that using biomass for fuel involves a continuous loop where crops that remove CO_2 during their growth cycle are converted to fuel that liberates that same CO_2 back into the atmosphere during combustion. So there is no net gain in atmospheric CO_2. It is a simplistic idea, it sounds very appealing on the surface, millions of people believe in it, and as with nearly every doctrinaire belief in the 'green energy' catechism, it collapses when we examine the details.

THE BIOFUEL CONCEIT

Travelers taking a daylight ride from the Kuala Lumpur International Airport to the central city are immediately struck by the immensity of tropical rainforest acreage that has been cleared away to establish palm oil plantations. The tropical old growth rainforests that have been destroyed were, at one time, impenetrable thickets containing millions of unique plant and animal species spreading over vast areas of the Kra peninsula. High biodiversity, high carbon stock rainforests have been replaced by monotypic rows of low density palm trees. Each tree is separated by a sizeable distance to permit trucks and equipment to move between rows. The output from these plantations is palm oil whose principal use is as a feedstock for biofuels primarily destined to Europe.

The amount of carbon dioxide sequestered by these slow-growing single species palm trees is a fraction of what occurred in old growth tropical rainforests before they were clear-cut and burned away. In addition, many of these rainforests were located on what are called peatlands which once contained high levels of carbon-rich biomass below the surface. Much of the sequestered peatland carbon was released back into the atmosphere when the rainforests were destroyed.

A central plank in every leftist's religion is a reliance on biofuels. They assume that biofuel can compete with fossil fuel without massive offsetting societal costs like mandates, subsidies, or other market-distorting mechanisms. All those beliefs are false. They also believe in the absolute necessity of biofuels which is predicated upon an unassailable faith that their use necessarily results in a net reduction in atmospheric CO_2 that will mitigate or forestall climate change. The theory that biofuels reduce atmospheric CO_2 also disintegrates when one examines changes in land use required to produce them. We need to understand what degree of carbon sequestering took place on the land prior to biofuel conversion and what is the net change in the atmospheric carbon dioxide balance sheet once conversion is complete and biofuels are burned.

Since its inception, the European Union has proudly boasted of its self-anointed role as the world's moral exemplar. Nowhere is the moral preening better displayed than with respect to energy policy. The EU has imposed punitive tariffs on air flights into and out of the continent, has proposed a tariff regime designed to lessen the competitive disadvantage suffered by its domestic producers harmed by its climate policies, regularly hectors the U.S. over global climate treaties, and urges adoption of a variety of other measures designed to extend its climate dogmatism onto the rest of the world. Playing a leading role in the EU's climate program is its biofuels policy, particularly in the transport sector.

In 2003, the EU adopted a mandated threshold target for biofuel usage for both petroleum and diesel fuel of 5.75% of total transport fuel energy. The goal was to be fully implemented by December 31, 2010.[14] That level will increase to 10% by the year 2020.[15] But this directive came under substantial scrutiny as people learned about the severe ecological damage that had been wrought in the name of planetary salvation.[16] The European Commission's April 2009 progress report showed that Germany was alone among twenty seven EU nations that had met its goal for renewable transport fuel.[17] By 2010, Austria, Slovakia and Sweden had also reached their biofuel goal.

The European Commission soothes its anxiety about the widespread irreparable ecological devastation brought about by its climate change policy, assuring the world that its directive will not have any negative effects on the climate:

> *The Directive also aims to ensure that as we expand the use of biofuels in the EU we use only sustainable biofuels, which generate a clear and net greenhouse gas saving and have no negative impact on biodiversity and land use.*[18]

But that statement is ridiculous on its face as travelers to Kuala Lumpur or Sumatra or dozens of other clear cut tropical rainforests now hosting palm oil plantations can readily attest. Sheryl Crow brags about powering the trucks and buses of her concert tour with biodiesel derived from palm oil that originated on lands where high carbon-stock, high biodiversity tropical peat-bog jungle had been destroyed. Does she really deserve the glowing adulation she receives for it?

Visitors to Singapore will notice persistent hazy skies on most days that take on a grayish color even after heavy downpours that would ordinarily be followed with clear skies.[19] The grey sky in Singapore is caused by smoke emitted from fires of drained and clear cut peatland rainforest on the nearby Indonesian island of Sumatra. The island is fast being converted to palm plantations.

Biofuel production has enabled Indonesia to become the world's third largest emitter of carbon dioxide.[20] And yet the country only ranks 17th in primary energy consumption.[21] As the headline in *The New York Times* makes clear, "Once a Dream Fuel, Palm Oil May Be an Eco-Nightmare."[22] There is no "May Be" about it. The story describes how "the production of biofuels, long a cornerstone of the quest for greener energy, may sometimes create more harmful emissions than fossil fuels, scientific studies are finding."

An authoritative scientific study undertaken by Wetlands International and Delft Hydraulics on the degradation of peatlands in Southeast Asia paints a devastating portrait of the indiscriminate damage being wrought by the EU's environmental policies:

> *One important crop in drained peatlands is palm oil, which is increasingly used as a biofuel in Europe. It was found that current likely CO_2 emissions caused by decomposition of drained peatlands amounts to 632 Megatonnes per year. The current total peatland CO_2 emission of 2,000 Mt/y equals almost 8% of global emissions from fossil fuel burning.*

Over 90% of this emission originates from Indonesia, which puts the country in 3rd place (after the USA and China) in the global CO$_2$ emission ranking. It is concluded that deforested and drained peatlands in SE Asia are a globally significant source of CO$_2$ emissions and a major obstacle to meeting the aim of stabilizing greenhouse gas emissions.[23]

Europe's policies designed to stabilize greenhouse gas emissions present "a major obstacle to meeting the aim of stabilizing greenhouse gas emissions." For each ton of palm oil, Indonesia releases 33 tons of CO$_2$ into the atmosphere.[24] This is referred to as a "carbon debt" that must be repaid with CO$_2$ reductions from burning biofuels. But that debt won't be repaid for decades if ever. When that one ton of palm oil is used as fuel, it only displaces three tons of CO$_2$ relative to fossil fuel. It will take decades to restore the fossil fuel emissions equilibrium.

The Delft Hydraulics report also aims misdirected fire at a policy prescription, stating that "This emission will increase in coming decades unless land management practices and peatland development plans are changed, and will continue well beyond the 21st century."[25] In reality, what the authors should have stated is that this emission will increase in coming decades because irreparable damage to highly efficient carbon-sinks in tropical old growth forests that will last for centuries has already occurred. Unless the European Union radically alters its indefensible, thoroughly discredited policies about the primacy of biofuels, the problem will be compounded.

Environmental groups have taken notice. As *The New York Times* observed, "Friends of the Earth estimates that 87 percent of the deforestation in Malaysia from 1985 to 2000 was caused by new palm oil plantations. In Indonesia, the amount of land devoted to palm oil has increased 118 percent in the last eight years."[26] During the autumn of 1997 alone, Indonesia experienced devastation from 176 fires that claimed 12 million hectares of virgin old growth forest.[27] More CO$_2$ was liberated from these illegal fires in just three months than from the United States in an entire year.[28] Indonesia contributed more atmospheric CO$_2$ in 1997 than the entire Earth's biosphere can remove during a single year.[29] Europe's desire for moral self-approval as expressed through its demand for biofuels has caused irreparable destruction that has depleted the planet's ability to sequester greenhouse gases.

It has also resulted in widespread species destruction. Villagers and plantation owners on Sumatra are systematically destroying critically endangered Sumatran elephant populations to prevent the dwindling herds from straying onto plantations.[30] The World Wildlife Fund (WWF) changed the status of these majestic animals from "endangered" to "critically endangered" in January 2012 due to severe habitat loss primarily as a result of the vast growth of palm plantation acreage.[31] Conservationists are making valiant efforts to save other species including the Sumatran tiger,[32] the rare Sumatran orangutan,[33] and the Sumatran rhinoceros from almost certain extinction.[34]

Peninsular Malaysia has limited room for new plantations. So most of the expansion is taking place in East Malaysia. Wetlands International estimates that, at the present rate of depletion, Sarawak on the island of Borneo will experience complete destruction of its peatswamp forests by the end of the decade.[35] These forests are home to some of the world's most exotic species including the Borneo pygmy elephant and the Borneo clouded leopard.

WWF estimates there are only 2,400 to 2,800 Sumatran elephants surviving in the wild, a 50% reduction in their numbers since 1985.[36] Over that time, the giant tropical island has lost more than two thirds of its tropical rainforest habitat, primarily to palm plantations.[37] WWF has been one of the planet's most vocal organizations sounding the alarm about catastrophic global warming.[38]

To salve its collective conscience, the European Commission issued further directives that established criteria on sustainability hoping to convince the world that their policy would not have negative knock-on effects:[39]

These criteria aim at preventing the conversion of areas of high carbon stock and high biodiversity for the production of raw materials for biofuels.[40]

So the European Commission wants biodiesel fuels that only come from somewhere where large tracts of "high biodiversity" land containing millions of unique species in "high carbon stock" formation are not clear cut to install low-density plantations of one single species of plant. We can help the Commission locate such a place. It would be in their dreams. That's really the only place for them to look. Anywhere biofuel crops are grown, you need to make substantial land use changes.

It is way too late to lament the species destruction and negative carbon sequestration that has taken place in Malaysia and Indonesia and a hundred other places as a result of the EU's commitment to saving the planet.[41] Lands that previously hosted millions of species have been converted to zero species diversity with low sequestration potential.

THE SCIENTIFIC EVIDENCE ABOUT BIOFUELS AND CO_2

The European Union has been at the forefront of promoting biofuel use as a pathway for reducing the carbon footprint of motor fuels. This belief was based upon the mistaken notion that biofuel usage would merely emit the carbon that had been sequestered during the growth phase. But in 2011, the EU issued a highly embarrassing recantation, announcing that it had made a "serious accounting error."[42] It had failed to account for the fact that lands where the biofuel crops are grown were already sequestering CO_2 before the lands were plowed up to grow feedstock crops.

There is a large question mark about *direct* land use changes that take place since the land to be cultivated for biofuel feedstock was already sequestering carbon either in forests or grasslands. So biofuel use is, at best, only marginally more effective than the vegetation it replaced, if there is any improvement at all. In many instances there is actually a degradation in carbon capture occurring when high carbon-stock old growth tropical forests are burned or even productive grasslands are plowed up to establish low-productivity biofuel croplands.

But there are also substantial *indirect* land use changes taking place as a result of biofuel policies that are counter-productive to reducing atmospheric CO_2. *Time* magazine provides an example of how Midwest soybean farmers switch to lucrative corn cultivation used for ethanol production which led Brazilian farmers to increase soybean cultivation on lands which displaced sugar cane farmers who in turn displaced ranchers who clear-cut and burned highly productive Amazon rain forest to maintain their grazing lands.[43] You can draw a direct line — more biofuels in the U.S., less Amazon rainforest.

Lastly, as many researchers have known for decades, a substantial amount of fossil fuel is used to produce seeds and fertilizer, cultivate fields, irrigate and harvest crops, produce yeast for fermentation, dry grain, store and deliver feedstock to refiners, ferment and distill biofuels, and then transport them to blend terminals. Earlier studies of this impact for corn ethanol indicated that six times more energy was used in corn ethanol production than was actually delivered in fuel combustion.[44] Later studies incorporating newer data indicate that there may be a small net energy contribution.[45] But not all studies agree. Either way, the net *energy return on energy investment* for biofuels is very low. Biofuels, under any set of circumstances, offer no realistic route to energy independence. If that was our hope, we'll need to look elsewhere.

Proponents of biofuels attempt to argue that land use changes can be ignored because there is disagreement about the amount of impact.[46] When a farmer plows up a field of carbon-sequestering grass to grow corn for biofuel, there is uncertainty about the net balance of carbon sinking that results. Does the corn sequester more or less carbon dioxide than the grass that was plowed? Since there are varying estimates on the precise amount of net CO_2 sequestered, should we ignore the impact from land use changes? Biofuel proponents say yes.

Likewise, when U.S. farmers switch from soybeans to corn for ethanol which prompts Brazilian soybean farmers to fill the market void by expanding their range into cattle grazing areas which causes destruction of high carbon-density Amazon rainforests, should we ignore the indirect land use displacement effects because there is uncertainty about the magnitude of the CO_2 net sequestration? Most biofuel promoters say yes.[47]

But by the same token, there is enormous controversy over the role of human-generated CO_2 in contributing to planetary warming, and the magnitude of the warming that is taking place. We have strong evidence that the planet's temperature has increased in recent centuries. But we are highly uncertain how much was caused by the increase in atmospheric CO_2 concentrations resulting from human activities. Should we ignore pleas to switch to 'green energy' because there are divergences in the amount of measured impact caused by human contribution to atmospheric CO_2? 'Green energy' zealots would, of course, say no.

There is a wealth of peer-reviewed science that suggests biofuels make only miniscule contributions to CO_2 reduction relative to competing alternatives. Many studies claim biofuels actually increase CO_2. A study by researchers at Oregon State University found that attempts to produce biofuel from West Coast forest biomass would actually lead to at least a 14% increase in CO_2 even if the biofuel production process was optimal.[48] They were not the first to make this claim. In every scenario the team examined, there was a net increase in CO_2 emission.[49] Utilizing a record of CO_2 storage capability of Pacific Northwest forests that they had published previously,[50] the team's lead researcher Tara Hudiburg reported that:

> On the West Coast, we found that projected forest biomass removal and use for bioenergy in any form will release more carbon dioxide to the atmosphere than current forest.[51]

Another Oregon State University researcher William Jaeger and his colleague Thorsten Egelkraut released a study one month later that challenged the whole premise of U.S. and EU biofuel policy. The authors examined the difficulties posed by a policy with multiple objectives — reducing fossil fuels *and* limiting CO_2 emissions. Nevertheless, the pair examined whether the biofuel policy compared favorably with other leading options and whether it was actually possible for biofuels to be produced at sufficient scale to make a meaningful contribution to stated policy goals. The current policy fails on both points because it was:

> ... 14–31 times as costly as alternatives like raising the gas tax or promoting energy efficiency improvements. The analysis also finds the scale of the potential contributions of biofuels to be extremely small in both the U.S. and EU. Mandated U.S. corn ethanol production for 2025 reduces U.S. petroleum input use by 1.75% and would have negligible net effects on CO_2 emissions.[52]

Professor Jaeger summed up the situation succinctly, saying "Our results suggest that existing biofuel policies have been very costly, produce negligible reductions in fossil fuel use and increase, rather than decrease, greenhouse gas."[53] This study confirmed longstanding suspicions that ethanol usage made no meaningful contribution to CO_2 reduction and barely reduced gasoline use — only 1.75% according to the team.

Consider the impact from this finding. In DoE's *Annual Energy Outlook 2012* reference case forecast, 18.2 billion gallons of ethanol will be supplied in the year 2025.[54] But that volume will only effect a 1.75% reduction in petroleum use according to the research. DoE estimates that total ethanol-blended gasoline volume in 2025 will be 127.1 billion gallons.[55] On a thermodynamic basis, ethanol is only 66% as energetic as gasoline. So 18.2 billion gallons of ethanol *should* be expected to displace twelve billion gallons of gasoline. But according to Jaeger and Egelkraut, the actual offset will only be 1.75%, a mere 1.9 billion gallons. In effect, 10.1 billion gallons of gasoline will be wasted producing ethanol that will actually increase atmospheric CO_2.

Worse still, even when researchers contend that the U.S. ethanol program abates a measure of CO_2 as the International Institute for Sustainable Development does, "buying greenhouse gas reductions by subsidizing U.S. corn-based ethanol production is not very efficient, costing well over $500 per metric ton of CO_2-equivalent removed."[56] And that finding is produced for the most advantageous set of assumptions possible. How do promoters of a carbon cap-and-trade program that might see emission permits trade in the $10-30 per metric ton range justify their parallel support for a program that costs $500 per metric ton under the most generous rendering?

The results obtained by Oregon State researchers have been replicated elsewhere. An international team headed by Danish researcher Finn Danielsen discovered that biofuel plantations established on forest land require 75 years and, if located on peatlands, require 600 years, to deliver any net carbon benefits.[57] Danielsen claims that biofuels "hasten climate change by removing one of the world's most efficient carbon storage tools, intact tropical rain forests."[58]

It may be naive in the extreme to hope that these findings would ever alter public policy embedded in the Energy Independence and Security Act (EISA) of 2007 which obligates the country to blend 16 billion gallons of cellulosic ethanol and 36 billion gallons of all types of biofuels by 2022. But it is worth noting that a gas tax increase would be 21 times more effective at achieving the policy goal than the nation's absurd biofuel policy. The editors of the British peer-reviewed scientific journal *Nature* characterize biofuel policies, observing:

> *... that they are expensive and ineffective at reducing fossil-fuel consumption, that they intensify farming needlessly, that they dress up discredited farm subsidies in new green clothes, and that they push up the price of food. All these things are true to some extent of corn-based ethanol, America's biofuel of choice, and many are also true of Europe's favoured biodiesel plans.[59]*

This is what happens when Soviet-style central planners rather than market forces manage complex market outcomes.

CAN THE PLANET SURVIVE OUR BIOFUEL POLICY?

Jerry Melillo, a researcher at the Marine Biological Laboratory at Woods Hole in Massachusetts discovered that indirect land use changes could contribute as much as twice the carbon-loss impact as direct land use changes.[60] Far more disturbingly, Melillo and his team announced that nitrous oxide emissions from the use of fertilizers used to grow biofuel crops could potentially overtake the greenhouse effect of CO_2 in the 21st century, and that biofuel cultivation will account for more than half of all nitrous oxide emissions.[61] As Melillo reports:

> *Europe and the U.S. have mandated significant use of biofuels in part because they are seen as reducing greenhouse gas emissions. Unfortunately, such technological-based policies often go awry because they fail to account for unintended environmental consequences.[62]*

Thomas Hertel and a team at Perdue University confirmed this finding. Hertel analyzed market-mediated responses to the corn ethanol biofuel program in the U.S.[63] His conclusion was that indirect land use changes completely cancel out any CO_2 emission benefits.[64]

The International Council on Clean Transportation (ICCT) undertook a study of EU biofuel policies and found they were far more damaging to the environment than previously thought.[65] European drivers account for far larger proportions of diesel usage than their American counterparts. ICCT published a whitepaper in 2011 concluding that "the cost of carbon abatement with biofuels in the absence of measures to address indirect land use changes could be around €2,500 per tonne of carbon dioxide abated."[66] ICCT contends that with an effective policy, the EU could cut this figure by a factor of five.[67] But that would still mean carbon abatement costs using biofuels would be a hundred times more expensive than alternatives. Carbon emission permits traded on the Emission Trading System (ETS) priced at about €6 per metric ton during the month of December 2012.[68]

In response to the growing body of evidence demonstrating that the EU biofuel policy was destroying the environment, the European Commission announced they would consider adopting draft legislation limiting subsidies after 2020 for biofuels unless they generate substantial greenhouse gas reductions.[69] The announcement amounted to a humiliating climb down and a clear demonstration that the entire European biofuel policy had become little more than a cesspool for parasitic, rent-seeking, biofuel-peddling corporate interests.[70] So the EU might eliminate some subsidies, but they will still keep their mandates.

Media reports claimed the EU ruling would boost the appeal for ethanol since indirect land use changes for biodiesel are so damaging. But 60% of the European car fleet burns diesel.[71] So the ethanol impact will be limited. Ethanol itself is problematic if CO_2 emission reduction is the goal.

It was a position the EU was certainly averse to adopting. But it was forced into it after its internal modeling research data on land use changes had been leaked to leading media outlets.[72] The results of the EU analysis showed that ordinary diesel fuel made from crude oil was far less CO_2-intensive than biodiesel made from palm oil, soybeans and rapeseed, the three leading feedstocks for EU biofuels.[73] To add insult to injury, yet another study published in *Nature Climate Change* contended that the EU biofuel policy could cause an additional 1,400 premature deaths in Europe and cost society more than $7 billion per year due to air quality degradation from atmospheric release of isoprene emitted by cellulosic biofuel feedstock.[74]

Physical chemists had long believed that, at 22.59 grams per cubic centimeter, the element osmium was the densest substance on the planet's surface. But that was before creation of the European Union. We now understand that osmium's density pales in comparison to bureaucratic brain matter, large deposits of which are found in Brussels. Yet even the hysterical old women of Brussels have been reluctantly forced to confront the incontestably negative consequences of their policy.

The UK hasn't been paying attention. Under the terms of its Renewable Fuels Transport Obligation (RFTO), the country requires biofuel usage for any supplier that provides more than 450,000 liters per year of motor fuel.[75] The UK enacted the RFTO to enable it to comply with two EU directives. One requires each member country to reduce carbon dioxide emission intensity of transport fuels 6% by the year 2020.[76] Given the foregoing, there is zero hope that biofuels can help the country achieve that outcome. The other directive obligates signatories to satisfy 10% of transport demand with renewable fuels by 2020. This obligation makes no sense whatsoever since the objective was supposed to be about reducing CO_2 emissions. As Jaeger and Egelkraut show, renewable fuel usage and CO_2 reduction are not the same thing. Acceptance of one does not automatically entail adoption of the other. Given the lower energy density of biofuels, the UK would need to increase its volumetric contribution of biofuel to about 14% to meet its 10% target.[77]

The UK used biofuels for about 5% of its motor fuel requirements in 2013, the highest penetration level heretofore ever achieved. But, to meet the twin obligations, this level would need to rise many times over by 2020. Without regard to indirect land use changes, the abatement cost is estimated to be in the range of $165 to $1,100 per metric ton according to a report from Chatham House, a highly respected UK think tank.[78] When indirect land use changes are factored into the equation, the abatement cost rises to between $330 and $8,500 per metric ton depending upon the specific feedstock pathway chosen.[79] The program in 2013 will cost UK motorists £460 million, a needless penalty that is expected to rise to £1.3 billion by 2020.[80] This is ecological and economic suicide wrapped up in one elegant package.

Chatham House report author Rob Bailey offers a devastating indictment of the policy:

> *Current biofuels are at best an expensive way of reducing emissions. At worst they produce more emissions than the fossil fuels they replace and contribute to high and unstable food prices.*[81]

Not surprisingly, this wake-up call makes clear the policy is damaging the environment, increasing fuel prices, destroying economic growth, and driving up food prices. It came just weeks after the EU reiterated its plea for member countries to use more biofuels. Against all evidence and in keeping with their counterparts at the Ethanol Promotion Agency in the U.S., the European Commission justified its ruinous policy saying "EU expanding bioethanol use has contributed only little to the historical cereal price increases in 2008 to 2010."[82] If this is even true in the EU, it is certainly not the case in the U.S.

Bailey makes clear that "policy making needs to catch up with the evidence base."[83] As he patiently explains to the Brussels-based slow-learners:

> *… the weight of expert opinion identifies biofuels as an important contributing factor to recent food market instability. This is not to say that biofuel policies have been the single*

most important factor, but they are among the most troubling because they are politically created and maintained.[84]

Politically created and maintained — a deliberate program that exacerbates CO_2 emissions, creates widespread harm to sensitive tropical rainforests, drives species to extinction, harms consumers by making fuel more costly, reduces economic growth, and contributes to human suffering by driving up prices of agricultural commodities like corn, wheat, sugar, milo, and edible oils. It's hard to find a comparably harmful program.

Of course, Bailey's plea will fall on deaf ears. The UK, and depressingly even the Tory Party, appears hell bent on destroying every last vestige of economic competitiveness. The Cameron government instituted a floor price of £16 per ton for carbon emissions, a policy that took effect on April 1, 2013.[85] On the day that carbon emissions permits on the ETS plunged to €2.55 per ton, businesses in the UK were obligated to pay a price 7.3 times higher.[86] The floor price, which will rise to £20 per ton in 2020 and £70 in 2030, is expected to double the cost of electricity for UK households.[87] These cost differentials will only serve to drive away prospective job-creating capital investment, making the country an increasingly unattractive place for business. It is clear that the UK government has not been honest with British subjects about the ultimate cost of its disastrous policy.[88] Thankfully, there are a few honest people like Rob Bailey left in the world.

The sheer scale of devastation caused by the EU biofuel program is nothing short of mind-boggling but is worth reiterating. Wetlands International provides an estimate that if present trends continue, Malaysia's Sarawak Province on the island of Borneo will see all of its irreplaceable peatswamp forests completely destroyed by 2020.[89] These forests are home to some unique endangered species like the Borneo pygmy elephant and the Borneo clouded leopard.

The destruction on Borneo is not confined to Sarawak. Borneo is shared by three countries and about 70% of the land area of the island comprises the Indonesian province of Kalimantan. A survey published in April 2012 in the *Proceedings of the National Academy of Sciences* undertaken by a pair of researchers discovered that half of the existing Kalimantan palm plantations were established on drained peatland.[90] Researchers Kimberly Carlson of Yale and Lisa Curran at Stanford professed to be "surprised" at these findings. Evidently the pair hadn't been paying much attention over the past twenty years.

They had obviously not read the 2007 report in *The New York Times* that provided an estimate from Friends of the Earth claiming that establishment of monotypic palm stands had caused 87% of the deforestation in Malaysia from 1985 to 2000.[91] Academic reports estimated that 176 massive Indonesian fires observed during the autumn of 1997 had destroyed tropical peat forests equal in size to Pennsylvania.[92] During the first decade of the century, palm oil plantation land area more than doubled in Indonesia.[93]

Nevertheless, the Yale-Stanford team reported that unless major changes are undertaken, an unlikely outcome, 90% of CO_2 emissions from palm plantations in Kalimantan in 2020 will originate on peatlands.[94] The researchers expanded their research findings and published another report in *Nature Climate Change* in October 2012 claiming that the palm plantation expansion expected to occur on Kalimantan alone would account for 18-22% of all of Indonesia's CO_2 emissions by the year 2020.[95] Emissions from these plantations are forecast to be 558 million metric tons, greater than for all of Canada.[96] Tropical deforestation contributes 20% of the world's human-generated atmospheric CO_2 emissions.[97]

THE DAY THE BIOFUEL SCAM COLLAPSED

Few researchers on the topic possess the credentials of Timothy Searchinger, an Associate Research Scholar and Lecturer in Public and International Affairs at Princeton University's Woodrow Wilson School. Almost none can surpass the notoriety he has gained. For 17 years, Searchinger was a lawyer for the Environmental Defense Fund working on wetland protection programs. After moving to Princeton, Searchinger and his team published a widely cited paper in the journal *Science* in early February of 2008 about the impact of U.S. biofuel production upon CO_2 emissions. The title of the paper sums up perfectly the nature of the biofuel swindle. In their three-page report, his team concluded that:

> ... *corn-based ethanol, instead of producing a 20% savings, nearly doubles greenhouse emissions over 30 years and increases greenhouse gases for 167 years. Biofuels from switch-grass, if grown on U.S. corn lands, increase emissions by 50%.*[98]

Another paper published on the same day in the same journal from a team headed by Dr. Joseph Fargione of The Nature Conservancy looked at biofuel production not only in the U.S. but also in Brazil and Southeast Asia. They reached a substantially similar conclusion as Searchinger:

> *Converting rainforests, peatlands, savannas, or grasslands to produce food crop–based biofuels in Brazil, Southeast Asia, and the United States creates a "biofuel carbon debt" by releasing 17 to 420 times more CO_2 than the annual greenhouse gas (GHG) reductions that these biofuels would provide by displacing fossil fuels.*[99]

Biofuel promoters contend that Earth's salvation can only be achieved through fossil fuel elimination that will be partly achieved by vigorous adoption of biofuels. It is difficult to locate a more damaging indictment of such a sweeping claim as these twin findings published on the same day by two unrelated research teams pursuing the same subject independently of one another. Even *The New York Times* was forced to admit to its faithful congregation that:

The destruction of natural ecosystems — whether rain forest in the tropics or grasslands in South America — not only releases greenhouse gases into the atmosphere when they are burned and plowed, but also deprives the planet of natural sponges to absorb carbon emissions. Cropland also absorbs far less carbon than the rain forests or even scrubland that it replaces.[100]

Most vociferous in the criticism of Searchinger's findings has been a researcher named Michael Wang at the U.S. government's Argonne National Laboratory. Wang is the primary developer of Argonne's GREET model (Greenhouse gases, Regulated Emissions, and Energy use in Transportation) which purports to be able to measure the amount of CO_2 that can be removed from the atmosphere from combustion of a given amount of ethanol.[101] Over the years, GREET has taken into account *direct* land use changes — those that occur when you replace one type of plant growing on a field with another. But until recently, the model ignored *indirect* changes — those that occur when unanticipated "knock on" effects occur as with the ethanol-soybean-sugar cane-Amazon rainforest example. Wang and his colleague Zia Haq attempted to justify their methodology:

There seems to be no indication that U.S. corn ethanol production so far has caused indirect land-use changes in other countries, since U.S. corn exports have remained at about 2 billion bushels a year.[102]

Dr. Searchinger had a ready response to Wang and Haq's empty rebuttal. He noted that it was misleading and hardly dispositive to focus on a single crop export statistic, particularly when Wang and Haq had not examined changes in crop inventories or the amount of land under cultivation. Searchinger might have also added annual variations in crop yield to his list of considerations as well. Searchinger replied:

… to maintain these corn exports in 2007, the U.S. planted 16 million more acres of corn in 2007 than it did in 2006, a 22% increase.[103] *Those acres came mainly out of soybeans, but also some out of cotton. That resulted in decreases in soybean and wheat production, which maintained exports only by decreasing stocks. Meanwhile, diversion of corn to ethanol and higher crop prices reduced the rate of growth in meat production.*[104] *At the same time, data is showing increased deforestation in the Amazon as crop prices rise, after years of decreases when crop prices declined.*[105]

On the very day that the two papers were published in *Science*, a group of 10 prominent environmental biologists and ecologists wrote a letter to President Bush and Congressional leaders urging them to adopt a new policy in place of the disastrous one set in train by EISA 2007.[106] The 10 environmental scientists, which included four members of the National Academy of Sciences, explained how the nation's biofuel policy was doing exactly the opposite of what was intended. The scientists proclaimed that "biofuels are contributing to the loss of some of the world's most valuable habitats, such as the Amazon and Cerrado in Brazil, and the rainforests of Southeast Asia."[107] So who are the anti-science deniers in the climate mitigation debate?

Section 201 of EISA redefined the term "lifecycle greenhouse gas emissions" in the Clean Air Act to include "direct emissions and significant indirect emissions such as significant emissions from land use changes."[108] To comply, EPA developed its renewable fuel standard (RFS2) incorporating both direct and indirect land use changes into a single variable. In keeping with its culture of Soviet-style lawlessness and institutional secrecy — the administrator was accustomed to using an alias named after her dog for internal agency communication to hide her email from subpoenas[109] — EPA considers its model to be proprietary. So researchers are unable to understand the magnitude of *direct* versus *indirect* land use changes in their calculation logic.[110] Satisfied that it had accounted sufficiently for the damage it was inflicting upon the planet, the federal government charged ahead with its reckless biofuels policy — and the prestige media went back to sleep.

Dr. Fargione's colleague Jason Hill noted that conversion of an Indonesian peat bog to a palm oil plantation would require biofuel cultivation for 423 years before the first molecule of CO_2 reduction would even occur.[111] The EISA 2007 law that obligates the U.S. to utilize 16 billion gallons of grain-based ethanol by 2022, of which 14.2 billion gallons were already being used by 2012,[112] actually results in a 93% increase in CO_2 rather than a 20% decrease as Wang and his colleagues contend — or is it pretend?[113] EPA's biofuel policy designed to reduce CO_2 emissions by use of ethanol will emit nearly twice as much carbon as using an equivalent amount of gasoline. A farmer would need to farm a plot of land for 167 years before there was a net carbon savings.[114]

The 2008 Searchinger and Fargione findings, together with the high profile intercession of four members of the National Academy of Sciences, was more than the mass media could casually ignore. Having been willfully complicit for years in promoting lurid, apocalyptic stories of impending planetary catastrophe for which biofuels could offer at least a partial solution, these revelations were hugely embarrassing. It also served as a significant repudiation of the Department of Energy which had funded and supported the work of the Argonne National Laboratory team which had produced and continues to support the GREET model. While initially attempting to deflect and deny the effects of indirect land use changes — who are the science denialists again? — Wang and Haq announced that Argonne might reassess their prior position:

> Argonne, and several other organizations, have begun to address both direct and indirect land-use changes associated with future expanded U.S. biofuels production.[115]

Following this pronouncement, the latest version of GREET available as these pages went to press was released in September 2013. That came more than five and a half years after the February 2008 Searchinger and Fargione publication. The model that had hitherto made specious claims about greenhouse gas savings and had ignored indirect land use changes finally made an attempt to quantify indirect changes.[116] Needless to say, Wang's re-assessment was based upon his previously discredited work which found land use change impacts that were less than one-third of EPA's own sand-bagged estimate, given his heroic assumptions about magical crop yields, stupendous resources availabilities, imaginary refining efficiencies, and land use conversion impact modeling.[117] Even worse, EPA's measured impact itself assumed land use change impacts only about one-third as severe as the more realistic estimates published by knowledgeable academic researchers like Timothy Searchinger. As a CBO report points out, most federal agencies over the years simply adopted the discredited GREET findings rather than internalize thoroughly indigestible reality that challenges the very justification for a society-transforming national policy enshrined in EISA 2007.[118] So based upon volumes of scholarly work, GREET had been useless for modeling CO_2 emissions of biofuels for decades, and may still be. This is your taxpayer dollars hard at work.

Biofuel promoters have attempted to hide behind various academic studies that purport to prove that there have been no indirect land use changes that occurred as a result of biofuel policies in the U.S. or the EU. One example is a paper published in *Biomass and Bioenergy* in July 2011 by a pair of Michigan State University researchers. The authors Seungdo Kim and Bruce E. Dale attempted to identify a statistical correlation between U.S. biofuel policy and global land use changes between 2002 and 2007. Kim and Dale reported there was no correlation using what they described as their "bottoms up, data driven statistical approach."[119] But they also admitted there may be two possible explanations for their conclusion. Either there were no indirect land use changes ... or ... the method they used was not capable of actually locating it.

The latter explanation was more persuasive. A group of researchers including Wallace Tyner at Perdue and Jason Hill from the University of Minnesota, a collaborator with the aforementioned Joseph Fargione in the pivotal 2008 paper, wrote in response that the Kim and Dale paper:

> ... presents a principal inference not supported by its results, that rests on a fundamental conceptual error, and that has no place in the current discussion of biofuels' climate effects. The paper takes correlation between two variables in a system with many interacting factors to indicate (or contraindicate) causation, and draws a completely incorrect inference from observed sample statistics and their significance levels.[120]

To put it politely, Kim and Dale published garbage better suited for the recycling bin than for policy guidance. As Professor Jason Hill observed, "It's difficult to distinguish the signal from the noise."[121] In order to do that, you actually need to know what you're doing. Professor Tyner observed that between 2006 and 2011, an additional 27 million hectares of land was placed under cultivation worldwide, mostly for rapeseed, corn, and soybeans.[122] That is a land area larger than the entire state of Colorado. Those crops are all major feedstock for biofuels. Kim and Dale's "data driven" approach failed to locate this data.

What credence should be given to a spurious finding from researchers like Kim and Dale and their assorted biofuel boosters who claim to be unable to discover a direct link between biofuels and tropical deforestation? After all, Professor Holly Gibbs of the University of Wisconsin and her research team[123] point to numerous studies incontestably demonstrating that: (1) biofuel demand will likely quadruple over the next 20 years,[124] (2) large industrialized nations don't have sufficient land to produce biofuel volumes sufficient to satisfy their climate conceits,[125] (3) U.S. and especially EU biofuel mandates have spurred feedstock expansion into tropical countries,[126] (4) biofuel feedstock production is one of the fastest growing markets for global agricultural produce,[127] (5) increasing biofuel feedstock demand has come primarily at the expense of fragile, irreplaceable tropical rainforests,[128] (6) massive rainforest clearing can be readily observed in numerous countries like Brazil, Indonesia, and Malaysia that already supply large amounts of biofuel feedstocks,[129] and (7) recent evidence is mounting that potentially dangerous tropical deforestation is rapidly accelerating.[130] All of these facts are incontestable.

Where is the mystery? Why would Kim and Dale publicize that they lack the academic skill to demonstrate statistical causation between biofuel demand and indirect land use changes when the evidence for its existence is overwhelming and impossible for reasonable people to deny? And why should the U.S., the world's largest consumer of motor fuels, proceed with its EISA 2007 biofuel mandates designed to reduce global CO_2 emissions when it is obvious that the program is effecting precisely the opposite outcome?

The U.S. Department of Agriculture attempts to justify their continued malfeasance in their review of the academic literature on indirect land use change, saying "no single model currently exists that can address all of the questions related to this (indirect land-use change) issue."[131] Because no model has yet been produced to replicate precisely the multivariate behavioral response to complex agricultural market signals affecting seven billion persons living in 192 countries is hardly a reason to postpone undertaking meaningful public policy actions that would reverse the immense damage our current approach has unleashed. After all, no single climate model can accurately address all of the questions related to the countless interrelated natural phenomena impacting the planet's climate. Does the Obama administration therefore reject energy policy approaches predicated upon climate models as a result? Not a snowball's chance in hell. The hypocrisy is breathtaking.

Professor Holly Gibbs observes that:

> ... the expansion of biofuels into productive tropical ecosystems will always lead to net carbon emissions for decades to centuries, while expanding into degraded or already cultivated land will provide almost immediate carbon savings ... No foreseeable changes in agricultural or energy technology will be able to achieve meaningful carbon benefits if crop-based biofuels are produced at the expense of tropical forests.[132]

So when biofuel production destroys tropical rainforest, the planet sustains serious, irreversible harm. But when cultivation occurs on unproductive, depleted, or eroded farmland or non-arable wasteland, biofuels can actually play a role in sequestering CO_2 or even offsetting some fossil fuel demand. Whether it is economically sensible to do so is entirely another question.

Daemon Fairless provides an example in India with cultivation of a weed called *Jatropha curcas* in places where conversion of low-productivity land to high-productivity biofuel production can actually occur.[133] But cultivation of the plant has spread to China, Burma, the Philippines, various African countries, and other places where it could well displace more productive land uses. Of course, the prospect of higher yields attainable in lands better suited to agriculture will always provide an economic incentive to shift from barren soil to more arable regions. And if there is an institutional mechanism like the UN's Clean Development Mechanism (CDM) that provides an economic incentive to expand these environmentally ruinous practices, you can count on it happening at ever greater scale.

China has learned how to "game" the CDM system, collecting more than 61% of all the Certified Emission Reduction certificates as of September 2013.[134] The CDM program has been described as a corrupt shell game loaded down with fund transfers to climate mitigation projects that either would have occurred anyway,[135] or could have never met a threshold for financial viability without the CDM carbon credit payments.[136] It is clear that current global due diligence efforts to assure that non-threatening conditions apply in biofuel cultivation are woefully inadequate. At present, biofuels are merely destroying the planet.

In a case that can only be appreciated by those possessing a deep sense of cynical humor, EPA issued a waiver to ethanol producers against compliance with greenhouse gas emission rules in 2011. Initially EPA was determined to include biomass producers in the rule in the same manner as any other emitter.[137] After all, the atmosphere can't distinguish between a molecule of CO_2 emitted when biofuel is burned vs. one emitted by fossil-fuel combustion. But under pressure from the Obama White House, EPA was directed to issue a waiver to biofuel producers and other biomass energy emitters.[138] Obama simply didn't want the rules that govern everyone else's conduct applying to his cherished biofuel industry.

EPA was sued by an assortment of environmental advocacy groups on the grounds that biomass emissions are indistinguishable from fossil-fuel emissions once CO_2 is liberated.[139] A decision was handed down by the 2nd Circuit Court of Appeals for the District of Columbia in July 2013. The court reversed EPA's exemption — or Obama's exemption to be more precise — ordering the agency to include biomass energy producers, including ethanol producers, in its rulemaking. The agency's logic was "Do a good job, cellulosic fuel producers. If you fail, we'll fine your customers," according to the panel of judges.[140] When the Obama administration's genuflecting water-carriers at *The New York Times* take to calling EPA's policies "wishful thinking," you have serious PR problems.[141] The majority opinion was written by justice David Tatel, who admitted that:

> *We simply have no idea what EPA believes constitutes 'full compliance' with the statute. In other words, the deferral rule is one step towards ... what?*[142]

We can help clarify this for the court. For the benefit of the mystified justices, full compliance in the minds of EPA central planners means only those industries it doesn't like must comply with emission rules. All others get a free pass. For EPA, the deferral was one step toward ... another deferral, which would be one step toward ... another deferral, and so on. EPA announced it would "review the decision to determine any next steps."[143] That means they'll huddle together and figure a way to evade the court's ruling. Then the prestige media can go back to sleep.

DO WE REALLY NEED BIOFUELS?

One might be justified in wondering why anyone would even bother attempting to make fuel from plants in the first place. Is it not appropriate to consider CO_2 sequestration and fuel production as two distinct, wholly severable considerations? As long as we use fuel that liberates CO_2, does it make any difference where the CO_2 comes from?

Biofuel promoters boast that biofuels are one potential response to human-induced global warming because they provide energy derived from biomass that sequestered CO_2 during its growth cycle. But as we've seen, there is a wrong way and a right way to go about doing that. By undertaking a vigorous biofuel cultivation program on lands that are more productive at sequestering carbon than the biomass to be used in fuel-making, humanity will increase overall CO_2 emissions. Likewise, expanding biofuel agriculture that causes indirect knock-on effects that degrade productive carbon sequestering elsewhere will also be counterproductive.

But carbon sequestration through expanded agriculture on unproductive, depleted, degraded or marginal lands might result in a net improvement in CO_2 retention if it can be accomplished without degrading carbon-rich or highly productive grasslands. But by the same token, highly productive plant strains that increase the overall carbon-fixing potential of marginal lands can be cultivated without subsequent biomass harvesting. On balance, increasing the overall carbon-sequestering potential of Earth's land masses appears to be a worthwhile endeavor even if we acknowledge that by doing so, we will change the environment in subtle ways that are difficult to forecast.

Humanity has expended countless trillions deploying fossil fuel exploration, recovery, transportation, refining, finished product distribution, and delivery infrastructure. Al Gore pretends these are "stranded assets." I'll wager they're not. If you want to see what a "stranded asset" looks like, go to Fremont, California where the bankrupt, taxpayer-funded Solyndra plant sits. Or go to Soperton, Georgia where the rusting hulk of bankrupt, taxpayer-funded Range Fuels sits.

Oil is produced all over the world — more than 100 countries produced more than 1 million barrels of it in 2011.[144] It is uniquely capable of enabling production of a wide range of organic compounds that fulfill millions of varied requirements of modern society including motor and heating fuels. Fossil fuels are capable of delivering an astonishing amount of energy for an affordable price.

It still marvels an author that, with a fill up of about 16 gallons of gasoline, a weight of material that can easily be lifted and carried, enough work can be derived to power an unsightly hunk of metal, glass, plastic, rubber, fabric, fuel and other materials loaded down with people, ski equipment, food, beverages and other assorted detritus from the foot of Hunter Mountain in the Catskills all the way to Baltimore, more than 331 miles away, and still leave enough energy to drive around for the next two days before requiring a refill. That equates to more than two man-years of energy content.[145] These fuels are easily produced, relatively safe with proper handling, convenient to store and transport, quick to refuel, contain copious amounts of energy, integrate well with our way of life, and enable a freedom of movement our ancestors could scarcely imagine.

Meanwhile, biofuels lack many of these important properties. Current infrastructure to produce a sizeable fraction of U.S. motor fuel requirements does not exist and would need to be deployed at staggering expense. Production of biofuels is an energy-intensive activity relative to production of fossil fuels — a much higher expenditure of energy is required to produce a given quantity of biofuel energy compared to that of motor gasoline. Biofuel production also emits a far higher proportion of CO_2 than fossil fuels per unit of energy delivered. Biofuels lack energy density because the feedstock from which they are produced suffers the same shortcoming. Ethanol (C_2H_5OH), with its high oxygen content of 34.8% by weight, contains only two-thirds the amount of energy as an equivalent volume of gasoline, which is primarily a blend of paraffins (C_nH_{2n+2}) like octane (C_8H_{18}), nonane (C_9H_{20}) and decane ($C_{10}H_{22}$) and aromatics like benzene (C_6H_6), toluene (C_7H_8) and xylene (C_8H_{10}), none of which contain oxygen. Lastly, biofuels like ethanol are hygroscopic — they have a very high affinity for water contamination. As such, ethanol travels only by rail tank car, barge, or tank truck, which are more expensive transport modes than finished product pipelines used to replenish gasoline depots.

The point of all this lengthy digression is that we can potentially scale up our efficiency at sequestering CO_2 through an expansion of hardy perennial plant species on vast expanses of low-productivity land masses to remove carbon from the atmosphere without wasting enormous resources trying to harvest, dry, transport, catalyze, ferment, distill, and deliver the resulting poorly-performing fuel. And we can continue leveraging our supposedly "stranded" investment in producing liquid fuels that are cheap, affordable, sensible, powerful, energetic, and well-matched for the job for decades to come. We can achieve both goals without trying to destroy our environment attempting to disprove the laws of thermodynamics in a futile quest to make biofuels work.

Such proposals to reshape landscapes with carbon-sequestering planting would likely be met with howls of indignation by environmentalists. They would claim that we had embarked upon a dangerous path of "geo-engineering," of trying to alter the planet's eco-system in an effort to stave off damaging effects of climate change.[146] The same environmentalists who cheered when the EU adopted biofuel programs that irreparably destroyed irreplaceable tropical peatlands and emitted countless millions of tons of CO_2 into the atmosphere would condemn responsible efforts to "green" the planet. Leftist "progressives" who oppose human progress have already done exactly that.[147]

For instance, an American business executive named Russ George organized an experiment in July 2012 where 120 tons of iron sulfate were dumped into the Pacific Ocean off the coast of British Columbia in an effort to stimulate phytoplankton growth.[148] The Canadian government cooperated in the endeavor.[149] The phytoplankton would become a meal for zooplankton which, in turn, would offer a seafood buffet for salmon and other depleted species. In doing this, the plankton bloom would absorb tons of CO_2 from the atmosphere in the formation of calcium carbonate shells. The portion of phytoplankton that did not become a meal for aquatic species would sink to the ocean floor along with its bounty of fixed carbon intact.[150]

Environmentalists immediately condemned the experiment.[151] The same people who spend every waking hour opposing fossil fuel usage because of its climate-altering potential were in violent opposition to undertaking any efforts to reverse the damage that they contend is taking place. They described Russ George as a "rogue" geo-engineering experimenter who sought to "hijack" the world's climate.[152] They claimed it opened a Pandora's Box for dangerous planet-altering environmental changes and violated two UN agreements.[153]

But that was a subterfuge. The game was given away by an anti-technology activist group called ETC Group[154] whose spokesperson announced the real motive behind vocal opposition:

> *It is now more urgent than ever that governments unequivocally ban such open-air geo-engineering experiments. They are a dangerous distraction providing governments and industry with an excuse to avoid reducing fossil fuel emissions.*[155]

In other words, environmentalists don't really care if the risks of climate change are reduced. Their approval of biofuel programs makes that realization crystal clear. What they fear is any attempt by organized groups or individuals to undertake any actions that would reduce the stated justification for trans-national government's minute supervision over the lives of ordinary people. Leftists flinch from a geo-engineering experiment, fretting whether "we are capable of actively, co-operatively and equitably managing the global commons."[156] But they are authors of their own geo-engineering program, a biofuel policy that has wrought indiscriminate damage across some of the most sensitive carbon-fixing tropical biomass locations on the planet. They appear unwilling to draw the obvious comparison. Why aren't the geo-engineers of the European Commission or EPA ever properly labeled geo-engineers? Where are the sanctimonious, hypocritical leftist ideologues like David Roberts of *Grist* urging Nuremberg tribunals for biofuel promoters?[157]

Consider sworn testimony from a Senior Vice President of the Environmental Working Group to a House Committee in July 2013 on the geo-engineering caused by the horribly misguided Renewable Fuel Standard (RFS2) under the Energy Independence and Security Act of 2007:

> *Since it was expanded in 2007, the corn ethanol mandate has contributed to plowing up more than 23 million acres of U.S. wetlands and grasslands to plant crops — an area the size of Indiana … By accelerating conversion of wetlands and grasslands to grow crops, the RFS has driven up greenhouse gas emissions by releasing carbon stored in the soil[158] and by increasing fertilizer applications.[159] Although the RFS was promoted in 2005 and 2007 as a tool to address climate change, the Environmental Protection Agency's own analysis[160] has since shown that the lifecycle greenhouse gas emissions of corn ethanol were higher than gasoline last year (2012) and will be higher in 2017 … The rapid expansion of corn ethanol production has increased greenhouse gas emissions, worsened air and water pollution, and driven up the price of food and feed.[161]*

Proving that truth is stranger than fiction, a German marine biologist named Victor Smetacek was one of the most vocal in condemning the marine fertilization experiment undertaken by Russ George.[162] Never mind that, following George's experiment, the resulting salmon catch in the Northeast and the Fraser River quadrupled over the largest volume ever previously recorded. Smetacek has arrogated to himself the coveted role of gatekeeper for proper geo-engineering experimentation as his comments to *The New York Times* make clear.[163] Incredibly, Smetacek was lead author of a study by a team of 30 researchers published in the respected British peer-reviewed journal *Nature* in the very same month as the Russ George experiment was conducted. The Smetacek study involved dumping iron sulfate into the ocean to determine if carbon could be removed and sequestered at the bottom of the ocean, exactly the same process undertaken by Russ George:

> *Fertilization of the ocean by adding iron compounds has induced diatom-dominated phytoplankton blooms accompanied by considerable carbon dioxide drawdown in the ocean surface layer … multiple lines of evidence … lead us to conclude that at least half the bloom biomass sank far below a depth of 1,000 metres and that a substantial portion is likely to have reached the sea floor. Thus, iron-fertilized diatom blooms may sequester carbon for timescales of centuries in ocean bottom water and for longer in the sediments.[164]*

In other words, half of the phytoplankton bloom created by Smetacek's own iron sulfate dump permanently sequestered tons of carbon dioxide and buried it on the deep ocean floor. But Smetacek's work was presumably virtuous while Russ George's was somehow flawed.

The very same UK leftist rag that first alerted the world to the horrors of the Russ George experiment, and then condemned it for weeks on end, wrote a glowing tribute to the vegetarian Smetacek and his experiment. *The Guardian* proudly boasted in its reverential paean that "dumping iron into the sea can bury carbon dioxide for centuries, potentially helping reduce the impact of climate change."[165] But when someone else who wasn't a vegetarian did precisely the same thing, they launched into an angry, indignant public rampage. You can't even make this stuff up.

It seems clear that efforts to facilitate carbon removal from the atmosphere by "greening" the planet will be met with deep disapproval by those who purport to be most alarmed by carbon accretion in the atmosphere. Carbon sequestration efforts would cut the legs from under the multi-billion dollar fossil fuel vilification industry. That's all the more reason to get started now. The first step is to understand the staggering hypocrisy espoused by the anti-carbon zealots. The rest will then be easy.

DOES BIOMASS HAVE A FUTURE?

If you're intent on saving the planet by using oodles of biomass, it is madness to use it for production of transportation fuels. It would be far more energy efficient just to just burn the material to produce electricity rather than consuming vast quantities of the BTU potential of biomass for processes like thermal depolymerization, gasification, pyrolysis, fermentation, and distillation, processes that consume inordinate amounts of the potential energy producing a biomass fuel that contains only a small fraction of the original latent energy potential. Indeed, the heat required to kick-start cellulosic pyrolysis is usually derived from fossil fuels which, as industry analyst Robert Rapier notes, is a form of thermodynamic "theft" by energy exchange from fossil fuel to biomass.[166] Promoters of biofuels never mention that part of it.

Paradoxically, as a clear demonstration of Earth's self-healing ability — scientists call it a "negative feedback mechanism" — increased atmospheric CO_2 concentration partly as a result of fossil fuel combustion actually assists in greening the planet. The productivity of plants, their innate ability to suck CO_2 out of the atmosphere, improves with increased concentration of atmospheric CO_2. That doesn't suggest we should simply dump more CO_2 into the air. But NASA satellite data indicates that since 1958, a 19% increase in CO_2 concentration has been accompanied by a 14% increase in global plant growth.[167] A further 37% increase in atmospheric CO_2 concentration to 550 parts per million will lead to an additional 24% increase in photosynthesis activity according to studies undertaken at Oak Ridge National Laboratory.[168]

Other studies have confirmed these findings. Examining the driest areas of the Middle East, North America, Africa and the Australian Outback, a research team from Australia discovered that between 1982 and 2010 when atmospheric CO_2 concentration increased by 14%, plant growth over arid regions increased by 11% on average.[169] The report appearing in the authoritative peer-reviewed journal *Geophysical Research Letters* was able to distinguish between rainfall- and temperature-related effects to isolate changes solely related to CO_2 fertilization.[170] Lead author of the report Randall J. Donahue expresses the study team's conclusions thusly:

> *Trees are re-invading grass lands … Long lived woody plants are deep rooted and are likely to benefit more than grasses from an increase in CO_2. The effect of higher carbon dioxide levels on plant function is an important process that needs greater consideration. Even if nothing else in the climate changes as global CO_2 levels rise, we will still see significant environmental changes because of the CO_2 fertilization effect.*[171]

Higher-productivity growth conditions from atmospheric CO_2 fertilization permits further penetration of non-food biofuel feedstock growth into previously marginal or non-arable lands. It also results in a net increase in the amount of latent moisture and rainfall that will occur, which helps support an expansion of agriculture.

Clearly the best policy prescription for biofuels like ethanol is to produce them only for human consumption, limit intake to moderate amounts, restrict distribution to adults, share them among friends and relatives on celebratory occasions, and remember: never drive or operate heavy machinery immediately afterwards. It's a tragedy this sensible logic never found its way into the thinking that produced the Energy Policy Act of 2005, the Energy Independence and Security Act of 2007, or the EU 2020 directives.

CHAPTER 16

THE "RACE" TO PRODUCE CELLULOSIC ETHANOL

"Large stocks of [cellulosic ethanol] could be distilled in years of abundant crops and thus serve as a sort of balance wheel to maintain an equilibrium in the price of the materials used ... the time is not far distant when the price of gasoline even for automobile use will be prohibitive."[1]

THE NEW YORK TIMES
AUGUST 5, 1906

"The fuel of the future is going to come from ... apples, weeds, sawdust — almost anything. There is fuel in every bit of vegetable matter that can be fermented. There's enough [cellulosic] alcohol in one year's yield of an acre of potatoes to drive the machinery necessary to cultivate the fields for a hundred years."[2]

THE NEW YORK TIMES
SEPTEMBER 20, 1925

"Until recently, the only ethanol anyone had heard about was corn-based ethanol ... What the experts are talking about now, however, is cellulosic ethanol, derived from a range of crops, native grasses like switchgrass and even the waste components of farming and forestry — in short, anything rich in cellulose."[3]

THE NEW YORK TIMES
MAY 1, 2006

Cellulosic ethanol is "right around the corner." Cellulosic ethanol is "what the experts are talking about now" says *The New York Times*. The experts were also talking about it in the *Times* one hundred years earlier. But apparently the *Times* was unaware of it in 2006. Too bad the editors at *The New York Times* don't read *The New York Times*. They would have heard about cellulosic ethanol sometime before 2006, like I dunno, maybe 1906.

So it's time to stop fiddling around and just make it happen. Perhaps you're wondering why we don't just legislate it into existence. If that's what you're thinking, you're too late. The Energy Independence and Security Act of 2007 did exactly that, mandating billions of gallons of cellulosic ethanol into existence starting in 2010. Of course, it was no impediment that cellulosic ethanol didn't exist in commercial-scale quantities. Nor did anyone know how to do it at the time. Realities like that never impede our central planners when enacting wildly optimistic pieces of legislative folly. We can just vote and it will happen. What's to worry? Is this a great country or what?

It wasn't exactly like potential cellulosic ethanol producers had been abandoned in their efforts to achieve the mandates. At least a dozen companies had been "racing" to build refineries with oceans of public money. And they had a guaranteed market.[4] But if it was a race, it would be among snails and we'd need to wait around for years — maybe decades — to see if anyone wins.

In February 2007, DoE proudly boasted that they had awarded $385 million to six cellulosic biofuel refiners to build demonstration plants.[5] Once the plants became operational, the total output was estimated to be 133 million gallons per year (mmgy).[6] Problem solved. Those plants, even if 100% successful, would only be able to satisfy one out of every 1,535 gallons of annual gasoline usage needs on a BTU basis. This is a 'green energy' proponent's idea of money well spent.

Three of the grantees would utilize traditional fermentation technology while the other three would develop enzymatic gasification processes.[7] A month later, DOE announced the award of another $23 million to five additional recipients for development of high-efficiency fermentation enzymes to convert cellulosic biomass into biofuels, an amount that could increase to $37 million over time.[8] Let's have a look at how each of the six cellulosic start-up plants awarded $385 million by DOE had fared as of 2013.

The first on the list is Abengoa Bioenergy, a company based in Madrid, Spain, that was awarded $76 million for constructing an 11.4 mmgy facility in Hugoton, Kansas.[9] In September 2011, the highly influential, widely read *Hay & Forage Grower* magazine reported that construction was underway on the Hugoton facility, which would use 315,000 tons of biomass like corn stover, wheat straw, and 20,000 acres of switchgrass.[10] Total cost of the plant would be $350 million.[11] Other estimates place the cost at north of $400 million.[12] That amounts to $15 to $17 of investment per gallon of annual capacity. Compare that number to about $2.00 to $2.25 per gallon of capacity that DoE reported in 2010 for construction of a corn ethanol plant.[13]

Despite the high investment, Abengoa exudes optimism about its Hugoton plant scheduled to open in 2014.[14] The company also announced that it may open a second plant on the site of its York, Nebraska pilot.[15] That plant could cost as much as $500 million.[16] Nevertheless, the company also announced the closure of two of its existing corn ethanol plants.[17] The company cited weak market conditions as the cause for the closures. So weak market conditions for a product that forced closure of two existing plants using proven technology would be no impediment to the company to invest another half a billion dollars for a plant using unproven technology that would supply an identical product that bore seven to nine times the capital cost burden.

The second company on the list of six DoE beneficiaries was a 109-year old land management company called ALICO.[18] The company was awarded $33 million to construct a 13.9 mmgy cellulosic ethanol plant in La Belle, Florida.[19] Construction on the thermo-chemical gasification–fermentation plant was slated to begin in 2008 and be completed by 2010. ALICO planned to utilize a gasification technology developed and piloted by an Arkansas company called Bioengineering Resources Inc.[20]

A year after DoE's award program introduction, ALICO announced that it would abandon its cellulosic ethanol plans.[21] ALICO claimed that the project risks "outweighed any reasonably anticipated benefits."[22] The technology that had been developed together with assumptions of all grants and awards for the proposed project would be turned over to a company called INEOS New Planet Bioenergy.[23] That company, flush with a $50 million DoE grant, would construct an eight mmgy agricultural waste-to-ethanol facility in South Florida scheduled for completion in 2012.[24] In actuality, the company announced production commencement on July 31, 2013.[25] With its $130 million construction cost and 8 mmgy capacity, that amounted to an initial investment of $16.25 per gallon of annual capacity.[26]

The next recipient on DoE's list was BlueFire Ethanol. DoE's press announcement in early 2007 promised to shovel $40 million towards a 19 mmgy facility to be built atop a landfill in Lancaster, California.[27] But in an SEC 10-K filing in April of 2011, BlueFire admitted that construction cost had escalated to $100 to $125 million while throughput volume would be only 3.9 mmgy.[28] That was $25 to $32 per gallon of annual capacity. BlueFire disclosed that definitive agreements for financing hadn't been completed.[29] It's $5 million in revenues in the prior two years had come exclusively from DoE grants.[30] BlueFire's SEC 10-Q filing in May 2012 indicated that "The Company is evaluating whether or not it's prudent to extend the project's permits an additional year while we await potential financing."[31] In other words, we're moving on from cellulosic biofuel.

The next company on the DoE's list of grantees was Broin Companies of Sioux Falls, South Dakota. Privately held Broin was named after its entrepreneur founder Jeff Broin who, together with his brothers, founded the company when Jeff was still in college.[32] Three months prior to the February 2007 DoE award announcement, Broin promised the Governor of Iowa that the company would be producing cellulosic ethanol at an existing corn ethanol plant in Iowa before the end of 2009.[33] Then DoE announced that Broin would be awarded $80 million to expand its Emmetsburg, Iowa plant to produce about 30 mmgy of cellulosic ethanol.[34] In 2007, Broin Companies changed its name to Poet. It was Poet's announced goal to produce cellulosic ethanol in a commercially viable production plant by 2011.[35] Poet is today the world's largest ethanol producer, capturing about 13% of the total U.S. corn ethanol market share at its twenty seven production plants.[36]

Poet's revised plan was to begin construction on its commercial-scale $260 million Emmetsburg plant in late 2011 using a $105 million loan guarantee from DoE.[37] The plant would produce 25 mmgy using 700 tons of corn cobs, stover, and other farm waste each day. But in early 2012, Poet announced plans to scrap the DoE loan and instead partner with a Dutch company that has expertise in enzyme technology.[38] Enzymes are used in large quantity in cellulosic ethanol production. To reduce cost, enzyme production would be co-located alongside the Emmetsburg plant. A key portion of the economic justification for the construction will be maintenance of the $1.01 per gallon producer tax credit[39] since Poet's production costs are about fifty cents to a dollar per gallon higher than for corn ethanol.[40] But, in March 2012, the Senate refused to extend the $1.01 per gallon producer tax credit for cellulosic ethanol.[41] Despite that reversal, the plant expects to finally begin production in 2014.[42]

The fifth company on the DoE $385 million award list is Iogen Corporation. Iogen is a Canadian company that bills itself as "a world leading biotechnology firm specializing in cellulosic ethanol."[43] Iogen has been touting cellulosic ethanol as a reality today, not some ethereal promise far off in the distance.

Iogen executive Maurice Hladik made a presentation to the Emerging Energies Conference at the University of California Santa Barbara in February 2006 proclaiming "Cellulose Ethanol Is Ready to Go."[44] In May of that year, Iogen invited a gullible reporter from *National Public Radio* to its demonstration plant in Ottawa to view the technology and hype the promise to *NPR*'s liberal, urban, upper income listeners.[45] These are the urbane sophisticates who assure us that catastrophic global warming is "ready to go," for which cellulosic biofuel would be a solution.[46]

Favorable media hyped the fact that Royal Dutch Shell PLC and Goldman Sachs had taken equity stakes in the company.[47] Nevertheless, Iogen cancelled plans to build a cellulosic ethanol plant in Idaho in 2008 to concentrate efforts on a Saskatchewan plant.[48] In 2010, Iogen and Shell announced plans to build a commercial-scale plant in Manitoba using funds from Shell.[49] This came just two years after Shell had increased its stake in Iogen to 50 percent.[50]

But that news coincided with other news reports describing the company at the center of an "ethanol boom, minus the boom."[51] Iogen officials cited the financial crisis, unfavorable oil prices, and high capital demands as reasons why its proven technology was slow to be implemented in commercial-scale deployment. Other accounts were a bit more forthright, observing that Iogen's "enzymes simply don't break down the cellulose into ethanol efficiently enough." In other words, the technology is not quite "ready to go."

Finally, in April 2012, Iogen and Shell cancelled their plans to build a cellulosic ethanol plant.[52] While company officials put on a brave face, sheepishly describing the action as an effort to "refocus" its strategy, observers recognized it as a major defeat for the company's technology.[53] Scratch another one off DoE's list.

The last of the six companies was Range Fuels of Soperton, Georgia, the epic train wreck of government industrial planning. Range, backed by cellulosic ethanol flim-flam artist Vinod Khosla, was the recipient of over $162 million in taxpayer loans and grants. After making countless empty promises, Range filed bankruptcy in 2011, laid off all its staff, and shut down the plant.[54] It never produced a drop of cellulosic ethanol. So, out of the list of six planned recipients with an announced target of 134 mmgy capacity slated for realization by 2011, it will be a miracle if we even see 52 mmgy from three producers by sometime in 2014. When Las Vegas odds makers establish an "over-under" wagering line, take the "under."

But DoE did not plan to put all of its eggs in six baskets. In May 2007, the department announced it had awarded $200 million for small-scale cellulosic biorefineries.[55] The list of intended recipients for the first $114 million was announced in January of 2008 and included some household names that readers will instantly recognize like ICM Incorporated, Lignol Innovations, Pacific Ethanol, and Stora Enso Oyj.[56] Three months later, DoE announced recipients for the remaining $86 million in federal funding.[57] Those funds were earmarked for other well-known names like RSE Pulp & Chemical, Mascoma Corp., and Ecofin LLC.[58] Then, in July 2008, DoE added two more names to the list, kicking in another $40 million in funding for recipient companies Flambeau River Biofuels LLC and Verenium Biofuels Corp.[59] DoE also shoveled hundreds of millions for three biomass research facilities, tens of millions to universities for biomass genomic research, tens of millions for projects designed to demonstrate biomass-to-biofuels, millions for enzyme research, and so forth.[60] DoE could not spend taxpayer money fast enough. As of April 2013, the total qualifying production of cellulosic ethanol from all these recipients had been zero.

A Department of Energy Inspector General audit report released in September 2013 concluded that DoE was not on target to meet its own internal goal to have 100 million gallons of annual capacity of "advanced biofuels" fully operational by 2014.[61] No kidding. Half of the projects on DoE's wish list had been terminated. The legislative goal under the EISA 2007 law required 1.75 billion gallons of cellulosic biofuels for 2014. So 100 million gallons represented a 94.3% reduction from the mandated goal. And yet there was zero hope that this greatly reduced goal could be met. There was zero probability of even one million gallons of product in 2013. The IG makes clear that all these projects were to have been completed and producing between 2008 and 2011 at the latest.[62]

KIOR MIGHT SUCCEED — OR MAYBE NOT

The company that cellulosic boosters proclaim is closest to commercial realization of cellulosic biofuel is a publicly-traded company called KiOR. Like Range Fuels and a bunch of other cellulosic start-up companies, KiOR received much of its early round funding from Khosla Ventures. KiOR went public in June 2011 with an initial price of $15 per share.[63] That was well below the anticipated price range of $19 to $21 that promoters wanted.[64] By the end of September 2011, KiOR stock had traded up to an intra-day high of $23.85 per share.[65] The share price spike coincided with some hype delivered by Vinod Khosla at a fireside chat during an industry conference in San Francisco. Khosla told audience members that his biofuels portfolio contained $1 billion in liquid profits which he described as tradable public shares thanks to several ventures that had gone public in the previous two years.[66] After the euphoria wore off, the stock quickly returned to earth.

Well into 2012, KiOR had yet to report any revenues, a not uncommon situation in the world of speculative start-ups.[67] KiOR planned to commence operations in Columbus, Mississippi in September 2012.[68] Actual production began in early November. The company expected to produce 454 metric tons per day of cellulose-based diesel and gasoline using catalytic pyrolysis, a pathway notorious for developing tons of residual coke and carbon-based char.[69] KiOR's CEO actively promoted the catalyst platform, making wild production promises.[70] The company's 4th quarter 2012 results were highlighted by only $87,000 in revenues.[71] Analysts had been expecting $1.5 million in revenue.

The company had been planning to open a second location in Natchez, Mississippi.[72] But those plans never came to fruition. Shares of KiOR hit a six-week high after EPA granted Part 79 registration for its cellulosic blendstock, a regulatory hurdle required for any company to sell fuel or additives.[73] KiOR became the first applicant to be granted that status, which was certainly no surprise given that EPA would have granted it to a six year old kid's lemonade stand by that point.[74] But getting EPA's permission to compete does not mean KiOR had obtained the market's seal of approval.[75] Analysis by respected oil industry observer Robert Rapier indicates that half of the energy content of the final cellulosic fuel product from KiOR's process is derived from the latent heat energy of the natural gas used to heat the biomass that initiates pyrolysis, a form of thermodynamic theft.[76]

And then the bottom fell out. KiOR stock crashed. By September 2013, KiOR's IPO investors had surrendered more than 90% of their investment. But that was better than the 100% loss that Khosla had engineered for his investment partners in his Range Fuels fiasco. By the way, if you didn't know already, as a taxpayer, you were one of Khosla's Range Fuels partners. That sparked what is called a "race to the courtroom steps" as parasitic class-action trial attorneys began filing class-action lawsuits against the dwindling remnants of shareholder value.[77]

Just a month earlier, EPA issued its final RFS2 forecast for 2013 claiming that six million gallons of cellulosic biofuel would be produced.[78] KiOR accounted for the largest share of volume.[79] The company had announced forward plans to produce 300,000 to 500,000 gallons of fuel in the second quarter of 2013 but, actual production was only 75,000 gallons.[80] And then the Columbus plant was shut down for an undetermined period.

The American Petroleum Institute had taken EPA to federal court to force the agency to back off its ridiculous cellulosic biofuel mandates.[81] The court agreed with the plaintiff.[82] EPA turned right around and thumbed its nose at the court, raising its initial 2013 estimate to 14 million gallons.[83] And where did EPA get that estimate from? A report in *The Washington Post* claimed that EPA accepted assurances from Vinod Khosla published in an interview the previous October that his KiOR plant would produce most of that 14 million gallons.[84] According to EPA Administrator Lisa Jackson's sworn deposition to Congress, KiOR would produce 8 million gallons while INEOS Bio would produce 6 million.[85]

"If you believe in Santa Claus and the Easter Bunny, you believe in 14 million gallons," quipped an oil industry executive.[86] Most of us know doorknobs that are smarter than the brain trust at EPA for believing that load of cellulosic waste from biofuel flim-flam man Vinod Khosla. How many triumphant forecasts that turn out disastrously wrong does one get to make in life?

Khosla proclaimed in 2006 that producing cellulosic ethanol was "brain dead simple" and yet seven years later, there still were no commercial-scale plants operating.[87] Khosla was keynote speaker at the 2007 World Congress on Industrial Biotechnology and Bioprocessing held at Walt Disney's World Swan and Dolphin Resort in Orlando. He recited the usual litany of cellulosic fairy tales, claiming that DoE grants were an acknowledgement that progress on development was moving faster than expected, that cellulosic fuel would completely displace gasoline in the U.S., that cellulosic ethanol would be competitive with corn ethanol by 2009, and that cellulosic ethanol was a viable pathway to reduce CO_2 emissions.[88] All of these claims were ridiculous. It was appropriate that he spoke at Walt Disney World, the land of fairy princesses and pixie dust.

We've heard these wildly optimistic forecasts before. They have all come up short. Bush administration Agriculture Secretary Ed Schafer claimed in early 2009 that cellulosic ethanol production would "explode" by 2012.[89] Given actual production volume of 20,069 gallons as of May 2013, the only thing that exploded was USDA's credibility.

If you're dozing off at this point, here's something sure to revive you. The 20,069 gallon achievement was produced by Western Biomass Energy.[90] The output occurred in 2011[91] but the registration number wasn't issued by EPA until April 2012.[92] Western Biomass Energy produced the product at a technology demonstration plant in Upton, Wyoming that had been constructed with grant money under USDA's Biofuel Crop Assistance Program.[93] After the 20,069 gallon batch, the company never produced another drop.[94] Western Biomass Energy declared bankruptcy in 2012 and shut down the plant.[95]

So the delicious aspect of the story was that the few drops of cellulosic ethanol ever produced under the Energy Independence and Security Act to qualify for a cellulosic biofuel credit in the five years after the law's passage, the fuel that politicians assured the country was essential for the energy independence and the planet's survival, ended up being exported to Brazil to be used for a publicity stunt at the Rio+20 climate conference.[96] Brazil is the place Obama had asserted falsely on a thousand occasions had achieved energy independence by making boatloads of the stuff from sugar cane. They are the world's second largest producer behind the U.S. What did Brazil need with U.S. produced ethanol?

By the end of May 2013, EISA had mandated cumulative production of 1.3 billion gallons of cellulosic ethanol.[97] After countless billions of taxpayer dollars had been squandered, there had been not 1.3 billion gallons produced, nor 1.3 million gallons — not even

130 thousand gallons. All of the 20,069 gallons of qualifying production that did occur was exported to Brazil, a country that exports shiploads of ethanol to the U.S. You need a sense of humor to appreciate the irony.

WE'VE BEEN DOWN THIS ROAD BEFORE

Cellulosic biofuel hype has been occurring for 200 years. A French biochemist named Henri Braconnot published an account in 1815 in the journal *Annales de Chemie* about his work on plant decomposition using acids on biomass to produce sugars.[98] This is the first step toward breaking down cellulose from woody biomass for alcohol fermentation and distillation.

The first commercial-scale cellulosic biofuel process was developed in Germany in 1898. The method used by the Germans was based upon using dilute sulfuric acid to decompose wood into sugar in the same manner as Braconnot had demonstrated seventy years earlier.[99] The German government established an office in 1899 to promote alcohol sales supported by a subsidy paid to producers, a mandated price parity with petroleum products, and a tariff on oil imports.[100] With these and other incentives, fuel alcohol production soared to 26 million gallons by 1904.[101] So the U.S. was unable to do in 2013 what the Germans had mastered in 1904.

Methods similar to the German process were adapted in the U.S. during World War I at two large-scale plants in the Southeast where feedstock is plentiful.[102] Each plant had an annual capacity of about 1.8 million gallons per year.[103] Both plants discontinued operations shortly after the war ended when lumber production declined.[104]

Consider the following claim:

> *The fuel of the future is going to come from fruit like that sumach out by the road, or from apples, weeds, sawdust — almost anything. There is fuel in every bit of vegetable matter that can be fermented. There's enough alcohol in one year's yield of an acre of potatoes to drive the machinery necessary to cultivate the fields for a hundred years.*[105]

It sounds like it came from an administration ethanol flak at DoE's National Renewable Energy Laboratory running interference for cellulosic biofuel promoters. Nope, actually it was Henry Ford speaking to *The New York Times* in 1925, long before the invention of man-made global warming. Ford called ethanol "the fuel of the future." This is a line *The New York Times* had been peddling long before Ford made his meritless prediction — and long after.

In November 1906, the *Times* effused about "a great new industry" which was launched after Congress removed a $2.09 per gallon tax on alcohol fuel that had been around since the Civil War. The newspaper heaped praise upon Kaiser Wilhelm II — the guy America would declare war against 11 years later — saying "To Emperor William, it seems, we are really indebted for the new, great industry which is to revolutionize things

American."[106] The Kaiser is long gone, we got the war — two wars if you're counting — but we're still waiting for his revolution.

A few months earlier in May 1906, the *Times* had urged immediate passage of the Free Alcohol bill that would drive down the price of fuel for consumers in the Northwest "where kerosene oil costs 18 cents a gallon and gasoline 22 cents."[107] The bill, claimed the *Times*, would enable use of "denatured alcohol for light and fuel … at a cost of 14.2 cents a gallon" which "will utilize completely an important class of agricultural crops and by-products."[108] Since ethyl alcohol has only two thirds the heat content of kerosene or gasoline, there was no price advantage.

Three months later in August 1906, the paper was acting as a sales agent for the nascent alcohol fuels industry. "Large stocks of it could be distilled in years of abundant crops and thus serve as a sort of balance wheel to maintain an equilibrium in the price of the materials used," the paper promised.[109] The *Times* quoted an ex-President of the Automobile Club of America who claimed that "the time is not far distant when the price of gasoline even for automobile use will be prohibitive."[110] Since we seem to be able to afford it today, does one hundred and eight years qualify as "not far distant?" This pattern of boosterism has continued unabated for over one hundred years without success, though it never seems to embarrass "the newspaper of record."[111]

Rudolf Diesel, inventor of the diesel engine, claimed in 1912 that vegetable oil would become a good substitute for fossil fuels, the world supply of which he expected to be completely exhausted soon:

> *The fact that fat oils from vegetable sources can be used may seem insignificant today, but such oils may perhaps become in course of time of the same importance as some natural mineral oils and the tar products are now.[112] In any case, they make it certain that motor power can still be produced from the heat of the sun, which is always available for agricultural purposes, even when all our natural stores of solid and liquid fuels are exhausted.[113]*

Diesel used peanut oil to demonstrate his revolutionary engine design at the 1900 Paris World's Fair. Diesel's engine and its successive improvements would transform motor transport. But nearly all of the fuel used to power it would be petroleum-based.[114] Consider this promise:

> *From our cellulose waste products on the farm such as straw, corn-stalks, corn cobs and all similar sorts of material we throw away, we can get, by present known methods, enough alcohol to run our automotive equipment in the United States.[115]*

Does that quote come from a global warming hysterical biofuel policy zealot at a left-leaning environmental advocacy office in Washington? Nope. It came from a presentation by Thomas Midgley to the Society of Automotive Engineers at a meeting in October 1921.[116]

The Germans improved their acid-decomposition preparation in 1932 using a dilute sulfuric acid percolation method called the Schöller process.[117] During World War II, the U.S. War Production Board funded a cellulosic demonstration plant in Springfield, Oregon that was based upon an improved Schöller process.[118]

In 1944, the Synthetic Liquid Fuels Act was signed into law.[119] It was aimed at creating fuels derived from a variety of sources including coal, natural gas and cellulosic materials. A total of $87.6 million was spent between 1944 and the mid-1950s before the project was abandoned.[120] A forecast was published in the peer-reviewed journal *Science* in 1991 assuring us that "in light of past progress and future prospects for research-driven improvements, a cost-competitive process [for cellulosic ethanol production] appears possible in a decade."[121] It hasn't been possible in two decades. Anyone want to wager on three?

The National Renewable Energy Laboratory (NREL) holds the cellulosic ethanol promotion portfolio today and claims it is now ready to be competitive with other transport fuels.[122] They said that in 2011. Not surprisingly, they made the same claim in 2010.[123] And in 2009.[124] And in 2008.[125] And in 2007.[126] And in 2005.[127] And 2002.[128] And in 1999.[129] And so on. One or another agency of the U.S. government has been fiddling around hoping for commercialization of cellulosic ethanol, this "great new industry" as *The New York Times* called it in 1906, since well before World War I.

Every prior attempt to commercialize cellulosic ethanol failed because its cost could not compete with the leading alternative, gasoline. That brutal fact of market reality is not likely to change anytime soon despite the mountain of taxpayer "investment" trying to reverse the tide of history. BP announced in late October 2012 that it was cancelling plans to spend $300 million for a 36 million gallons per year cellulosic ethanol plant in Florida.[130] BP decided it had better things to do with shareholder funds. The U.S. government under Obama leadership feels no similar constraint since it plays with taxpayer money and can extract it a gunpoint by an agency that will audit you if you espouse opposing political beliefs.

While cellulosic ethanol mandates were established based upon an assumption that biomass feedstocks could be produced and delivered to plants at $30 per ton, more recent estimates place that cost at $80 to $130 per ton.[131] That means that feedstock cost amounts to $1.30 to $1.48 per gallon before the expensive production processes involving copious heat and enzyme inputs even get underway.[132] Professor Wallace Tyner at Perdue observes that since commercial-scale cellulosic plant economics are largely unknown — every available estimate is based upon pilot- scale plant sizes — the eventual cost could be 10 times higher than for a conventional corn ethanol plant.[133] Unlike biofuel promoters at NREL who have been repeating a worthless, century-old promise, Professor Tyner actually knows what he's talking about. We have already seen examples where the capital cost component of DoE-funded cellulosic start-up ventures is seven or eight times more than for corn ethanol plants. And corn ethanol output is about 40% more expensive than gasoline on a thermodynamic basis.[134]

The CEO of Poet optimistically proclaims he can get his cellulosic ethanol plant at Emmetsburg, Iowa to produce product in 2014 at about $3.00 per gallon.[135] Wonderful news. Even if it's true, with an average nationwide distribution cost of $0.21 per gallon, that amounts to a delivered cost to the blend terminal of $3.21 per gallon. Given that ethanol has less than two thirds the energy content of gasoline, that means cellulosic ethanol carries a gasoline mileage-equivalent delivered cost of $4.93 per gallon. This is Obama's plan to lower gas prices.

PHYSICS IS THE REAL ENEMY

The real problem with pinning such a large portion of America's energy-related public policy on cellulosic biofuels is physics. Maybe the IRS should start auditing physicists. Biomass is not energy dense. There's not a lot of BTUs per unit of cubic volume. It's a fact, it can't be legislated away, mandates won't help improve it, the EPA can't issue new guidelines to change the situation, intrusive IRS audits won't work, and all the wishful thinking in the universe can't alter the basic equations of science. There just aren't many BTUs in a ton of biomass compared to coal or oil.

For instance, a 100 mmgy corn ethanol plant requires about 2,500 tons per day of corn feedstock throughput to maintain production. That's about 125 truckloads per day, or one every eleven and a half minutes during a 24 hour day. A cellulosic plant of the same throughput volume would require somewhere in the neighborhood of 7,000 tons each day.[136] That requires a truckload delivery of biomass material every three minutes around the clock every day.[137]

DoE has a number of programs underway designed to reduce the volume of material by increasing density. One idea involves pelletizing material at the source.[138] But all of these approaches only add to biomass gathering and processing cost. And think of all the high-density diesel fuel energy consumed in delivering low energy-density biomass to refineries.

A related problem concerns physical logistics. Because biomass is not energy dense, there are practical limits on how much material is available and how far it can transported before one consumes more energy in transportation than is returned in biofuel production. Forget about running unit trains of wood chips out of the Powder River Basin in Wyoming to cellulosic ethanol plants scattered all over the country in the way coal is delivered to power plants. Oh, that's right, they're doing exactly that in Europe. European utility companies are pellitizing wood chips in the U.S., moving them in rail cars to ports, shipping them across the ocean to ports in Europe, loading back onto rail cars, and dragging them to power plants.[139]

Notwithstanding the madness in the European Union, coal still has seven to ten times the BTU density per volume as the most energy-dense biomass.[140] Therefore, to get the same energy return as a trainload of coal, you would need to run seven to ten trains of biomass. Likewise, you would need to source the material from one seventh to a tenth the distance to achieve the same distance-related economics. NREL even acknowledges that the governing constraint on cellulosic plant size is mean feedstock distance.[141]

Another problem concerns cellulosic resistance to decomposition. Here we're not talking about plants' well-placed political opposition to Obama's policy agenda but rather their inherent, genetically-evolved resistance to biochemical assault on their organic cellular structures. This is referred to as *lignocellulosic recalcitrance to saccharification*, a stiff aversion of plant material to being broken down into sugars for eventual conversion to ethanol. It's why most animals can't digest grass, why so much wasteful energy input is required in the cellulosic ethanol production pathway, and why its economic feasibility is so improbable.

Another problem is scale. In 2011, Americans used almost 134 billion gallons of gasoline according to the EIA.[142] If the United States were to reduce its gasoline consumption by just 10% through substitution, it would require 20.4 billion gallons of cellulosic ethanol since ethanol supplies only 66% of the energy of gasoline by volume.[143] If the average cellulosic plant capacity to be built equals the 22.3 mmgy average capacity of the six proposed startups that DoE funded, the nation would need to build 916 plants to meet the demand. Given the $15 capital cost per gallon of annual capacity, it would require almost $306 billion to bring into fruition. For full gasoline displacement, the country would require nearly 9,200 plants and $3.1 trillion of investment.

Consider the issue about actual energy content of cellulosic material. Plants obtain their energy from the sun as everyone knows. The sun pours forth about 3.84×10^{26} watts per second and will continue to shine brightly for billions of years into the future. The problem is that the sun's energy is radiated outwards in all directions and we only inhabit our tiny portion of space, relatively speaking. Another problem is that the sun is 93 million miles away from Earth. So by the time the photon energy arrives here on Earth, most of it ended up going elsewhere — to solar power ranches and cellulosic biofuel feedstock plantations on other planets. Only about one out of every 1.1 billion photons emitted actually gets here.[144]

The solar power delivery that occurs is only about 1,364 watts per square meter.[145] That's not too much on any specific spot especially when you have cloudy days, steep angles of incidence in the far northern and southern latitudes, over 70% of the planet's surface covered by water, and extended night time periods. Trees and plants have evolved mechanisms to extend their reach by branching out and producing broad leafy vegetation that soaks up more solar radiation. Still, it's just not a lot of energy. Biomass suffers by comparison to coal, oil, and natural gas that achieved higher energy density from geological compression and chemical conversion over hundreds of millions of years.

Each year USDA's Forest Service provides an inventory of the amount of timber biomass within each state. We're not talking just about waste. They are considering living trees. Bill McKibben, the country's second most prominent climate hysteric behind Al "Jazeera" Gore, says we need to "do the math" about renewable fuels. So let's do the math.

USDA estimates that there are 15.9 million acres of timberland in Minnesota.[146]

That resource base contains an estimated 12.6 billion trees of 1-inch or greater diameter totaling 442.4 million tons of biomass.[147] USDA also reports on the progress of cellulosic ethanol demonstration plant development, which shows that yield expectations are about 75 gallons of fuel per ton of biomass.[148] So, if every tree and sapling in Minnesota's timberlands is clear cut for cellulosic ethanol production — assuming there was sufficient capacity to harvest, deliver, process, and refine it all — we could expect to derive 33.2 billion gallons of cellulosic ethanol product. But ethanol only contains about 66% of the energy on a thermodynamic basis as gasoline. All of Minnesota's timberlands, if clear cut and converted to cellulosic ethanol, would displace only 21.9 billion gallons of gasoline. And it also assumes we can do all that cutting, pelletizing, delivery, and refining without incurring any incremental fuel usage, which is obviously absurd. All of these steps are energy-intensive.[149]

The U.S. consumed 133.9 billion gallons of motor gasoline in 2011.[150] So Minnesotans, should they be willing to donate all of their timberlands to our "climate emergency" requiring immediate replacement of fossil fuels with biofuels, can only displace 16.4% of our motor gasoline needs, and can only do so once.[151] It would require another 30 to 40 years to replant the acreage and await a complete growth cycle before we would call upon Minnesota to clear cut the state again to meet just one sixth of our motor fuel needs in one single year.

If you wanted to meet the country's gasoline demand for a whole year, in addition to clear cutting Minnesota, you would also need to clear cut Wisconsin (617.2 million tons),[152] Iowa (118.3 million tons),[153] Illinois (237.5 million tons),[154] Indiana (260.5 million tons),[155] North Dakota (14.8 million tons),[156] South Dakota (43.4 million tons),[157] Missouri (623.4 million tons),[158] Kansas (81.7 million tons),[159] Nebraska (44.0 million tons)[160] and Vermont (275.9 million tons).[161] After clearing all the timberland in all of those eleven states and converting it to cellulosic ethanol, you would finally have enough motor fuel to meet the nation's gasoline demand for one year. So let's get started with the sweet music of chain saws.

Of course, we need to recognize that the Northern Forest timberlands of the U.S. capture and store an estimated 75 million tons per year in atmospheric carbon.[162] If we clear cut them, the carbon sequestering activity would cease. Remember, it was the net carbon emissions into the atmosphere that propelled us into this policy cul-de-sac in the first place. I dunno, maybe we shouldn't do it.

Sarcasm aside, clear-minded observers, and perhaps even a few die-hard climate hysterics, can readily see the problem. The sun, for all its ferocious power, only delivers scant amounts of energy per square unit of area. Earth's various species of plants have evolved mechanisms to harvest and store a portion of it. But it is woefully inadequate. Even using the proven, higher-yielding method of ethanol from corn, the U.S. would require cultivation acreage equal to twice the amount of the total land area of the U.S. just to meet annual requirements.[163] I'll wager the needed land area won't be found.

A former Chief Executive Officer of the Tennessee Valley Authority named S. David

Freeman wrote in his 2007 book *Winning Our Energy Independence: An Energy Insider Shows How* that America could generate 18.4 billion gallons of cellulosic ethanol each year by converting 368 million tons of forest wastes.[164] That would displace only 9% of gasoline demand without considering any offsetting fuel consumption from energy-intensive production activities. All the living trees in the timberlands for the entire state of Illinois only provide 238 million tons.

Energy "experts" like Freeman quote these numbers supposing that all 368 million tons of biomass, if that's the right number, could just magically appear dried and pellitized on the doorstep of cellulosic ethanol refineries, assuming there were any, without a single drop of fuel being consumed to cut, process, dry, and deliver it. They also assume it can be refined into ethanol without using any energy or water. And don't sustainable forest lands depend upon those cellulosic wastes as a source of nutrients to maintain a healthy biome? If biomass is continually removed from an ecosystem, nutrients in the form of nitrogen-based fertilizer need to be added back to restore soil vitality.[165]

There are a few other issues to consider. Fertilizer production is very energy intensive. Production of it consumes about 2% of global energy.[166] You can drive a car 600 miles with the energy required to produce the amount of fertilizer needed for a single acre of corn.[167] In addition to that, nitrogen fertilizers also release nitrous oxide or N_2O, which has a 310 times higher global warming potency than CO_2.[168] Are we to ignore these inconvenient realities?

Maybe we should look at a feedstock like switchgrass instead of clear-cutting timberlands. The list of switchgrass ethanol boosters like Vinod Khosla could fill an encyclopedia. An acre of switchgrass can produce 11.5 tons of biomass each year.[169] If we can get 75 gallons of ethanol from a ton of switchgrass, that would give us 862.5 gallons of cellulosic ethanol per acre of land without considering offsetting fuel use in production. To displace our annual requirement of 133.9 billion gallons of gasoline, we would need 203 billion gallons of cellulosic ethanol. Therefore, we would need to devote 235.2 million acres of land for switchgrass cultivation, which is 367,534 square miles. That is an amount of land larger than the combined area in the states of Massachusetts, Rhode Island, Connecticut, New Jersey, Pennsylvania, Maryland, Delaware, Virginia, West Virginia, North Carolina, South Carolina, Georgia, Florida, and the District of Columbia. Where would ethanol boosters likely to find this much arable real estate that is not already busy sequestering CO_2 and doesn't need biomass to restore soil nutrients? You guessed it: in their dreams.

Americans are not going to win their energy self-sufficiency following the advice of S. David Freeman or Vinod Khosla.[170] The scale of biomass needed to meet even a fraction of our requirements and the immense costs it would impose upon our industrial and natural landscapes make it unlikely to compete. Despite claims to the contrary, cellulosic biomass is no free lunch and will never meet even a modest proportion of our needs.[171] Yet it is always ready "to blast off."[172] We've been hearing the same story for more than a century.

CHAPTER 17

BIOFUELS AND OUR FOOD SUPPLY

"An increase in oil price would reduce global food supply through direct impacts as well as through diversion of food commodities and cropland toward the production of biofuels."[1]

WORLD BANK REPORT, 2011

"Expanding biofuel production to meet various national targets in the next decade would have a limited impact on the global economy, but poor people in some developing countries would find it harder to afford an adequate diet."[2]

WORLD BANK REPORT, 2011

Among the lengthening list of imponderables regarding U.S. biofuel policy concerns its impact on food prices, food supply, and human diets in the world's poorest regions. Barack Obama has been slobbering all over his tie for years about the wonders of ethanol. Consider his Portsmouth, New Hampshire speech in October 2007:

We know that corn ethanol has been the most successful alternative fuel we have ever developed. I've been a champion for ethanol. In just two years, the Renewable Fuel Standard I helped pass has sparked an historic expansion of ethanol production. It has helped displace foreign oil and strengthen our rural economy.[3]

There has been considerable public debate about whether diversion of massive quantities of food to produce biofuel exacerbates hunger around the world. Acreage devoted to corn planting shot skyward following passage of the Energy Policy Act in 2005 and again in 2007 after passage of the Energy Independence and Security Act.[4] Between 1996 and 2006, corn averaged $2.15 per bushel.[5] But since late 2005, prices have trended upwards.[6] A bushed of corn averaged above $7.00 during the first few months of 2013.[7] Corn accounts for an estimated 30% of all acreage planted in the U.S.[8] An estimated 40% of that crop in normal growing years is diverted to ethanol production.[9] That is enough grain to feed 350 million people.[10] The amount of corn in a single SUV fill-up of ethanol can feed one adult for an entire year.[11]

Corn is perhaps the most important food crop on the planet. Some 75% of food items in a typical American grocery store contain corn.[12] A smaller but not insignificant percentage of soybeans are diverted to produce biodiesel. But during years of poor harvest, as in drought-ravaged 2012, the percentage of the total grain harvest diverted to fuel production expands well above years when yields are bountiful. Amazingly, because fuel blenders are *obligated* to use ethanol to blend with gasoline at 10% of volume, ethanol production takes a higher priority than human or animal consumption. Ethanol producers deny this contributes to global hunger.[13] The facts say otherwise.

The 2012 corn harvest was expected to establish a record size due to a 5% increase in acreage planted over the previous year.[14] But during the summer months, poor weather sent corn and soybeans prices to record highs, easily surpassing their 2008 all-time highs.[15] A rally in grain pits followed on the heels of a Department of Agriculture (USDA) report showing that forecasted corn production would be 1.8 billion bushels lower than originally believed with per acre yields plunging more than 12% below earlier estimates.[16] While the harvest declined by 12%, corn for ethanol declined by just 2%.[17] That rally would continue on almost uninterrupted throughout the summer months with new high prices being established nearly every week.[18]

Ethanol production in the U.S. utilizes 4.9 billion bushels.[19] Season-end inventories for the 2012 growing season were 37% below forecast.[20] Global corn inventories plummeted to only 15% of global demand as a consequence of the shortfall.[21] U.S. corn exports for the 2011-2012 season sank to a 9-year low due in large measure to the increasing volume of supply being siphoned away for ethanol production.[22]

The U.S. normally supplies 50% of the world's corn exports.[23] In early August 2012, USDA announced it would open more forage land and permit farmers to stagger their crop payments.[24] But suspension of the biofuel mandate, the one thing that would have had immediate and lasting benefit in driving down corn and soybean prices, was not part of the plan.

The rally in the grain pits wasn't a one-time event. The same thing had happened in 2011, in 2008 and in 2007. Biofuels today consume 6.5% of global grain supply and 8% of the world's vegetable oil.[25] Those astounding levels are up from only 2% of grain supply and essentially zero vegetable oil in 2004.[26] The proximate cause for much higher grain and soybean prices in 2012 may have been unfavorable weather in the grain belt.[27] But it is axiomatic that without the massive diversion of grain and soybean harvests, prices would have been far lower. By July 2012, corn had topped $8.24 per bushel.[28] Smithfield Foods, the nation's largest pork producer, was forced to take the unprecedented step of importing corn from Brazil due to the scarcity of domestic supplies.[29] Obama and his allies love to talk about America's "addiction to foreign oil."[30] Far more indefensible is environmentalists' addiction to biofuels and the knock-on effect that has upon global trade and food prices.

In years prior to 2012, crop diversion for biofuel production had driven grain prices much higher than they otherwise would have been. The spike in food prices led to food riots and hunger around the world that claimed thousands of lives.[31] The death toll from starvation caused by crop diversion for ethanol production may exceed 200,000 people per year.[32]

Here is a classic example of the biofuel policy impact on food prices. The RFS is estimated to have caused Guatemalan food import costs to have risen by $28 million during 2011.[33] But that was the amount of U.S. food aid extended to Guatemala during that same year. So, in essence, the RFS did not just incinerate 42% of the U.S. corn crop. It also incinerated all of our food aid to a developing nation in Central America.

The International Food Policy Research Institute analyzed the global food crisis of 2007-08. They rejected contentions that the crisis was caused by increased meat production in China and India, or reduced yields in major grain exporting countries, or even market speculators, the usual villains cited by leftists who don't understand market dynamics. Instead, study authors cited diversion of food supply to biofuel production as the culprit.[34] A World Bank study in 2011 reiterated those findings, showing that the run up in food prices in the 2008-09 period was partly due to rapid expansion in biofuel production.[35] A companion study contends that increased taxes on fossil fuels such as carbon taxes or cap-and-trade schemes could substantially worsen the crisis, sending a market signal to producers to divert even larger shares of food stocks to biofuels. World Bank authors contend that biofuel substitution is so sensitive to oil prices that if petroleum prices were to double by 2020, it would lead to a four-fold increase in global biofuel production.[36]

Corn prices set all time highs near $9.00 per bushel during 2012.[37] In the wake of a dreadful USDA corn harvest forecast in August 2012 showing U.S. corn harvest would be 13% below the year earlier,[38] UN Food & Agricultural Organization director José Graziano da Silva called for "an immediate, temporary suspension of the mandate."[39] Why not an immediate permanent suspension? For its part, the Renewable Fuels Association (RFA) rushed out a press release after the USDA report to assure agitated gasoline blenders not to worry, "obligated parties under the Renewable Fuel Standards (RFS) will have every opportunity to demonstrate compliance this year."[40] No need to entertain talk about ethanol waivers. No doubt blenders were sweating that one.

Higher corn prices were also sparking negative ripple effects through the economy. Livestock growers were negatively impacted by high feed prices.[41] Many hog and cattle farmers were forced to send their herds to slaughter earlier than expected, causing meat prices to spike.[42] Milk and dairy prices climbed in the wake of thinning herds.[43] Higher food prices at the grocery market crimped consumer budgets, reducing discretionary spending in the slow-growing economy.[44] While many farmers' incomes were shielded by higher crop prices and insurance coverage, crop insurers suffered their first losses in decades because of record insurance payouts.[45] Grocery manufacturers' earnings wilted alongside shriveling corn stalks as margins were squeezed by higher input prices.[46] Restaurant chains felt the pinch with the American Restaurant Association voicing optimism that the EPA would soon issue an ethanol waiver that would drive down corn prices.[47] What planet do those guys live on?

Higher corn prices also drove up the price of ethanol-blended gasoline as blendstock prices soared.[48] Ethanol was supposed to be salvation for American motorists. Instead, it had become their albatross. But EPA was sleeping soundly, confident that they were saving the planet from … lower food and fuel prices? The Obama White House claimed the matter was being looked at carefully over at Ethanol Promotion Agency.[49] EPA staffers could scarcely contain their laughter at that brazen whopper.[50]

Having ignored calls from grocery industry groups, livestock growers, fuel blenders, poultry producers, dairy farmers, starving indigents in developing countries, restaurant operators, and American consumers to change the nation's damaging ethanol policy, the only thing likely to get White House attention was waiver requests from influential Democratic governors in key swing states.[51] The Energy Independence and Security Act of 2007 granted EPA administrator Lisa Jackson authority to waive blending mandates if the mandate "would severely harm the economy or environment of a State, a region, or the United States."[52] Obviously when the price of the world's most important food crop soars from $2.00 to $8.38 a bushel, it didn't qualify as economic harm.[53]

With reelection in hand and swing state concerns no longer a consideration, EPA announced its decision in mid-November 2012 that there was no justification for entertaining any waiver.[54] Long-time EPA observers were never in any doubt which way EPA would rule on waiver petitions. In the agency's request for comments, the administrator had clearly signaled EPA's intent to deny the petitions filed by a host of state governors even before she considered them.[55] EPA had denied a similar waiver request in 2008 filed by the governor of Texas who sought relief from only 50% of the blending mandate:[56]

Artificial demand for grain-derived ethanol is devastating the livestock industry in Texas and needlessly creating a negative impact on our state's otherwise strong economy while driving up food prices around the world.[57]

It was incontestable. But truth and logic don't hold sway in Obama's Washington. EPA claimed that the state had not demonstrated that the RFS "itself" was the cause of the harm.[58] EPA openly acknowledged that it "interpreted the waiver provision as providing only narrow waiver authority."[59] Thus, in the agency's tortured reasoning, "it is not enough to determine that implementation of RFS would contribute to such harm."[60] The RFS "itself" must constitute the entirety of the harm and not just be a major contributing factor. In addition, the agency obligated petitioners to demonstrate that "the relief requested will remedy the harm."[61] These amounted to impossible hurdles. Thus, the negative outcome was a foregone conclusion.

EPA claimed that advocates of waiving the ethanol blending mandate were unable to demonstrate a sufficient economic justification for their waiver request. In 2012, EPA resurrected a discredited analytical model it had used in 2008 to deny the Texas governor's waiver petition.[62] The agency stated there would only be a minimal impact on corn prices — less than a 1% price reduction they claimed — if 42% of the nation's corn crop did not need to be diverted to ethanol production.[63] As EPA gently put it, "our extensive analysis makes clear that congressional requirements for a waiver have not been met and that waiving the RFS will have little, if any, impact."[64] Apparently the agency's "extensive analysis" didn't include economic considerations like supply and demand.

The National Council of Chain Restaurants (NCCR) commissioned its own study of the impact of the RFS on food prices. Not surprisingly, the results were far more reliable than the slipshod paste-up that EPA pretended to perform. NCCR hired PricewaterhouseCoopers to undertake the analysis.[65] PwC observed that the RFS mandate consumed 5.3 billion bushels of corn each year and would cause corn prices to increase by 27% by the time the 2015 mandated 15 billion gallon ethanol ceiling are produced.[66] In addition, the RFS mandate would boost prices across an entire range of other food commodities like pork, which would rise by 14%, soybeans that would increase by 16% and poultry that will be 8% higher as a direct result of the mandate.[67]

The approach EPA adopts for waiver requests — the burden upon petitioners to prove the regulation "itself" causes the harm — is precisely the opposite of the agency's approach for imposing additional regulatory burdens.[68] As an example, EPA and the Department of Transportation issued regulations in December 2010 seeking to boost fuel efficiency on medium- and heavy-duty trucks for model years 2014 and after.[69] The agency estimated the impact of the new rule would be a global reduction in atmospheric CO_2 concentration amounting to only 0.732 parts per million.[70] The effect of this infinitesimally small decrease would "avert an estimated 0.002 to 0.004 degrees Celsius of global warming and 0.012 to 0.048 centimeters of sea-level rise by the year 2100."[71] These values are so inconsequential it would be impossible to measure the impact, to distinguish the contributory signal of the regulations from the entire range of climatological noise.

An even more egregious example of the hypocritical posture that EPA takes regarding its rulemaking as opposed to rule waiver authority concerns the so-called "new source emission standards" imposed upon coal-fired generating plants. EPA attracted widespread attention in April 2012 when it published rules governing CO_2 emission limits on new coal-fired electricity generation plants.[72] Lacking a shred of embarrassment, the agency noted that in return for the immense burden its rule will place upon the electricity generation market — it will effectively destroy use of coal as a source of electricity generation in the U.S. into the foreseeable future — the country will derive no measureable benefits." There are no direct monetized climate benefits in terms of CO_2 emission reductions associated with this rulemaking," claimed EPA.[73] So why impose the rule?

A bushel of corn requires 65% less land to produce than fifty years ago.[74] Corn output quintupled between 1940 and 2010 and yet acreage under cultivation actually declined.[75] Author Indur Goklany, a science and technology policy analyst with USDA, noted that one of the great achievements of recent decades is the stabilization of humanity's agricultural footprint. Between 1990 and 2003, the planet only expanded agricultural acreage by about two percent while the population grew by 20% during those same years.[76] But all that progress could be undermined by biofuel policy:

> *Ironically, much of the hysteria over global warming is itself fueled by concerns that it may drive numerous species to extinction and increase hunger worldwide, especially in developing countries. Yet the biofuel solution would only make bad matters worse on both counts.*[77]

In other words, biofuel policy is actually worsening both of the problems it was established to help remediate. The policy is driving up the price of food, it is driving species into extinction, and as we'll see shortly, it is driving up fuel prices. And higher fuel prices will spur more biofuel output.

History is replete with examples of armies destroying the food supply of enemies for strategic reasons. But the U.S. is the first known example of a country that burned up its own food supply to placate an angry climate-campaigning mob. We can argue until the next ice age about whether or how much human fossil fuel consumption is causing catastrophic global warming. But it is undeniable that biofuel use to ameliorate planetary warming from an increase in atmospheric CO_2 is resulting in higher food prices and food shortages in the world's poorest places.[78]

The Interior Department policy expert Indur Goklany summarizes the situation well:

> *Biofuel policies motivated, in part, by the desire to mitigate global warming may be responsible for more death and disease than climate change itself.*[79]

Maintenance and even significant expansion of biofuel production is the brilliant policy vision of the Nobel Peace Prize-winning champion of environmental justice Barack Obama and his like-minded leftists. Widespread starvation among hundreds of thousands or even millions of the poorest people each year in the most impoverished regions of the world is the butcher's bill humanity must pay for Obama and his crowd to satisfy their environmental conceits.[80]

SECTION 6

THE 'GREEN ENERGY' ECONOMY

CHAPTER 18

AFFORDABILITY OF 'GREEN ENERGY'

"To prohibit a great people, however, from making all that they can of every part of their own produce, or from employing their stock and industry in the way that they judge most advantageous to themselves, is a manifest violation of the most sacred rights of mankind."

ADAM SMITH
BOOK I, PART II, SECTION I
THE WEALTH OF NATIONS, 1776

Occasionally in life we encounter a salesman, or a cynical politician or a flam-flam artist — or maybe someone who is all three — peddling a modern equivalent of snake oil, something we all understand is outlandish. But because the case is put forward in a manner that appeals to our emotions rather than our intellects, a case that tugs at our heartstrings rather than our better judgment, a case articulated in terms that summon us to a higher calling, to perform some duty in service to all mankind, millions of otherwise practical people are lulled into suspending their innate disbelief. Barack Obama is a man who has perfected the art of making the ridiculous appear plausible to tens of millions of seemingly intelligent people.

Over the years, Obama has peddled the notion that 'green energy' can be made affordable, or that it already is. Listeners to this storyline are asked to believe that there are market imperfections or nefarious conduct among vested interests or paralyzing political dysfunction that prevents widespread adoption of renewable energy. We're assured that if only these obstacles could be removed, the cost of energy would drop.

Most 'green energy' proponents have the good sense to avoid the question of affordability altogether, preferring instead to argue some other justification like imminent planetary climate doom or a need for energy independence or ending our "addiction to foreign oil" or promising a flood of 'green jobs' or a need to deny funding to Middle East terror-supporting states or its putative ability to eliminate extreme weather or whatever. But rarely do they bother trying to claim that 'green energy' is affordable.

But Barack Obama is not among those more practical souls. He is one of the few who can stand in front of an audience and claim with a straight face that 'green energy' already is driving down energy prices. Consider the claims he made in Lansing Michigan in August 2008 when he told listeners that he would put a million pug-in hybrid cars on the road by 2015 with the help of a $7,500 tax credit for electric car buyers.[1] So we have the exquisitely ridiculous Chevy *Volt* that has a range of less than 40 miles on a charge and carries a sticker price of about $41,000. That price tag was more than the median income of 42% of American households in 2011.[2] The deal offered a $7,500 tax credit as an inducement, which was more than the tax liability of 83.4% of American families.[3] The median income of a *Volt* buyer is $170,000.[4] The tax credit gets paid by American taxpayers, an income transfer from middle-income taxpayers to upper-income buyers.

The indefensible nature of this wealth transfer is highlighted in a report from the Congressional Budget Office:

> *Because the credits are not refundable, however, people with a small income tax liability may be eligible to receive only a fraction of the credit available to them. In practice however, most purchases of new vehicles — especially fairly expensive vehicles — are made by people in higher income households who are more likely to have enough federal income tax liability to apply the full value of the credit.*[5]

Obama also told his audience how biofuels were already affordable. But biofuels are driving pump prices up substantially. He also assured his audience that continuation of the federal Production Tax Credit (PTC) for wind and solar energy would help displace fossil energy and make those sources competitive. The most common refrain heard from 'green energy' proponents is that we can't afford not to adopt a robust program of wind and solar power deployment. These claims are supported by very few facts and loads of rhetorical excess. Obama has often made that case, as he did in Portsmouth, New Hampshire in October 2007:

> *The global market is already moving away from fossil fuels. The question is not if a renewable energy economy will thrive in the future, it's where. And if we want that place to be the United States of America, we can't afford to wait any longer.*[6]

Let's examine the contention that Americans can't afford to postpone the supposedly affordable 'green energy' future that Obama advocates.

THE ECONOMIC IMPACT OF 'GREEN ENERGY'

Among the many costly successes that 'green energy' supporters have celebrated is their ability to convince states to adopt Renewable Portfolio Standards (RPS) that require electric utilities to purchase ever-increasing amounts of renewable energy. The additional cost of purchasing power from these higher-cost sources is passed along to electricity ratepayers in the form of higher utility bills. Most of these programs were adopted during the previous decade and were based upon the usual litany of problematic or false assumptions: (1) impending climate change driven solely by human influences was humanity's most urgent priority, (2) a finite supply of hydrocarbons was being rapidly exhausted, (3) renewable energy would have a measureable impact upon reversing the impact of climate change, (4) renewable energy was free because wind and sunlight were free, (5) increasing proportions of renewable energy overlaid upon an existing portfolio of low-cost baseload energy would not have significant impact upon the cost of energy to consumers, and (6) states that mandated renewable energy would reap significant economic benefits and job growth from "clean" energy deployment that other states would not enjoy.[7]

RPS programs have been enacted in twenty nine states and the District of Columbia as of 2013.[8] Based upon 2010 Census data, 71.9% of Americans live in states where these measures have become law. Because higher cost renewable power in these states is overlaid onto a portfolio of lower cost power, RPS programs push electricity prices higher than they otherwise would be in the absence of the program. But do electricity ratepayers in RPS states pay measurably higher rates than in states that have not enacted RPS mandates?

An examination of all-sector electricity rates in RPS states shows they were 25.3% higher on average than for all sector ratepayers in non-RPS states between December 2008 and November 2012.[9] Figure 18-1 shows that electricity in RPS states is always higher in cost. The two curves never come close to one another. In addition, RPS states saw more price volatility during the peak-use months, when prices rose in far higher proportion in RPS states relative to the price spikes felt in non-RPS states. So not only is electricity more expensive on a consistent basis in RPS states. But the differentials become more exaggerated during periods of price spiking — at times when consumers can least afford it.

The premium paid by all-sector ratepayers in RPS states averaged $7.6 billion per month in extra cost over the four-year period.[10] Renewable portfolio standards have imposed serious additional costs upon electricity consumers in the states where they have been enacted, forcing electricity ratepayers to expend a portion of the disposable income for expensive renewable energy. This disadvantage has contributed to a relatively unfavorable economic climate in RPS states compared to those states that have not imposed these burdensome costs. They have also contributed greatly to a deterioration in nominal after-tax income of American households across all income groups but especially low-income households. Energy costs consumed 36% of nominal after-tax household income for those making less than $10,000 per year in 2001.[11] But by 2013, the percentage of income these households paid for energy had soared to 77% of after-tax income, adding nearly $1,000 per year to the costs they must bear.

FIGURE 18-1. **All Sectors Electricity Rates in RPS vs. Non-RPS States**

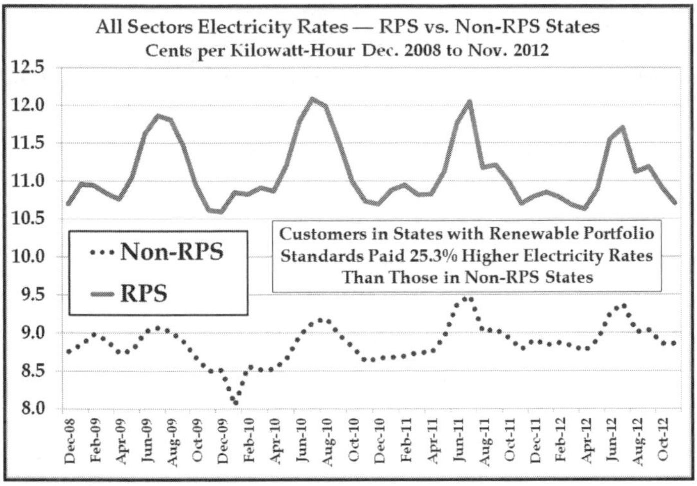

Sources: Energy Information Administration, Electric Power Monthly, Table 5.6.A. Average Retail Price of Electricity to Ultimate Customers by End-Use Sector by State (Cents per Kilowatt-Hour); U.S. Census Bureau, Population Data from 2010 Census

A comparison of residential electricity rates between December 2008 and November 2012 shows an identical pattern. Residential ratepayers paid an average of 22% more for electricity in RPS states than in non-RPS states.[12]

The effect of unloading higher cost renewable energy onto electricity ratepayers has had a profound and immediate impact upon the rates that consumers paid for power over recent years. While proponents of RPS mandates claim these programs lead to an improvement in the environment, that is wholly unproven. But there is no debate that they have resulted in a degraded economic environment.

And the negative impact is not relegated only to electricity rates. It is also impacting labor market competition. There was no readily apparent difference some years ago in unemployment rates between states that had begun enacting RPS programs vs. those that had not. But over time as the higher costs for energy began to take their toll on disposable incomes of the rate-paying public, a substantial unemployment gap opened up between the two groups of states. As Figure 18-2 shows, there is now a pronounced gap in the unemployment rate that averages about 0.7%.[13]

If the fossil fuel 'brown energy' producing state of Texas is counted among the tally of non-RPS states, the headline unemployment rate difference between the two groups of states widens to a full percentage point. This is not some esoteric statistical mumbo-jumbo with little attachment to reality. The impact of RPS programs results in real differences in disposable income and real job losses. Households are forced to pay more for electricity than their neighbors in non-RPS states. Based upon a 0.7% unemployment gap observed in November 2012, RPS mandates had helped destroy more than 807,800 jobs in those states where they were in place.[14] Higher-priced electricity has contributed to a competitive disadvantage as employers and job-holders voted with their feet, moving to more favorable economic environments.

FIGURE 18-2. **Impact on Unemployment Rates in RPS vs. Non-RPS States**

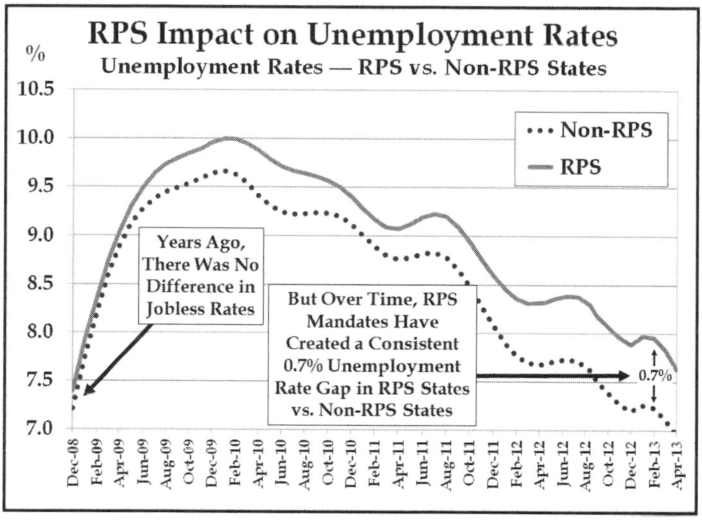

Sources: BLS Local Area Unemployment Statistics; EIA Renewable Portfolio Standards Map

RPS boosters actually claim that their policies were imposed to create jobs.[15] In a sense they're correct. There was job creation. It all took place in states that did not impose RPS mandates. Job growth claims arising from 'green energy' policies are predicated upon a mountain of economic fallacies.

Indeed, economic growth and migration patterns have tracked implementation of RPS programs with a very high degree of correlation. While by no means the sole criterion, it is obvious that access to low-cost energy is one of the principal considerations that is accelerating the shift in high-technology manufacturing and other job creation from moribund blue states to dynamic RPS-free red states.[16] All of the states that lost seats in the 2000 and 2010 apportionments were high-cost blue states like Illinois, Massachusetts, California, and Michigan. The biggest gainers were non-RPS states like Utah, Georgia, South Carolina, and Florida that have not signed on to the delusions of climatism.

Consider the composite economic growth logged by the two groups of states. Prior to 2007, the composite growth rate achieved by the group of RPS states minus oil-producing Texas was about equal to the rate achieved by the group of non-RPS states plus Texas. Just as we observed with unemployment rates, a permanent gap has opened up between the two groups with an average of 0.7% real GDP growth rate advantage for low-cost non-RPS states as Figure 18-3 indicates.

Professor Robert J. Michaels observes that while RPS programs may have been sold to the public as an economic free lunch, it has been an exorbitantly costly lunch, one that has caused an employment and economic growth disadvantage that RPS states must endure every day.[17] There is little evidence that any cost-benefit analysis has ever been performed prior to states' enactment.[18]

FIGURE 18-3. **RPS Impact on State-Level Real Economic Growth**

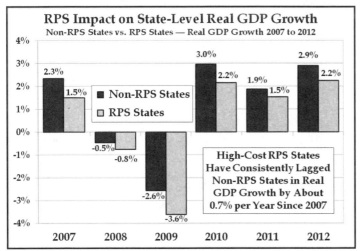

Sources: Bureau of Economic Analysis Real Gross Domestic Product by State; EIA Renewable Portfolio Standards Map

During the 12-month period from December 2011 to November 2012, price differentials caused ratepayers in RPS states to pay about $83 billion more for electricity than their cousins in non-RPS states.[19] The rate surcharge alone acts like a climate tax amounting to $368.00 per man, woman and child in each of those states. It amounts to more than a half a percent of gross domestic product.[20] In a moribund economy presided over by a President that logged only a 1.48% compound annual real GDP growth over his first four years in office — the lowest sustained GDP growth of any President in post-War history[21] — a half percent is nothing to sneeze at.

Curiously, the Energy Information Administration (EIA) prepared an estimate of the impact that a federally mandated 25% renewable portfolio standard would have on electricity prices. EIA wrote in 2009 to Rep. Edward Markey, Massachusetts co-author of the cap-and-trade bill that was narrowly defeated in the Senate, telling him that the 25% renewable energy standard that went into his cap-and-trade bill "is not expected to affect national average electricity prices until after 2020."[22] This was a preposterous finding given that virtually all of the data in the above analysis showing large price increase impacts from RPS programs in 29 states and DC comes from EIA.

Just three months after EIA wrote to Rep. Markey, DoE's Oak Ridge National Laboratory published a study of the impact that RPS programs have upon electricity prices and low-income consumers. The report noted that most of these RPS "mandates are adopted without any analysis of the impact of increasing electricity bills."[23] Noting that the lowest income households had seen their proportion of total household income spent on energy soar from 10% to over 25% during the previous decade, the report demonstrated that state-level assistance programs to afford these price increases were wholly inadequate to meet the cost of rapidly rising electricity in RPS states.[24] It's good to know DoE has its story straight on RPS impact.

LEFTIES SAY "ONLY 'DIMWITS' OPPOSE RPS"

Liberals who promote RPS programs do so using shoddy 'green energy' style economic analysis methodologies that we observed in the chapter on 'green jobs' — cost-benefit analysis using all benefits and no costs. A typical example is the propaganda from an unhinged staff writer David Roberts at the ultra-leftist rag *Grist*.[25] Using lurid language to defame RPS opponents, calling them "dimwits and "dim bulbs" of the Tea Party, the magazine extols the supposed economic benefits of an RPS program enacted in Kansas in 2009 as part of a grand compromise.[26] State politicians agreed to mandate a gradually increasing renewable energy threshold in exchange for an expansion of a coal-fired power plant. After the coal proposal became mired in procedural and legislative complications, RPS opponents sought to roll back the mandates since the terms of the grand bargain were never fulfilled. It was like a Capitol Hill budget negotiation during the Obama years — tax increases now for promised budget cuts sometime later that never materialize.

To meet its 10% renewable energy threshold, Kansas has deployed a sizeable amount of wind power and generates nearly all of its renewable energy from wind farms. *Grist* cites a study prepared by the propagandizing National Renewable Energy Laboratory (NREL) that compiles a list of all the wondrous economic benefits that will be achieved from deploying 1,000 megawatts of wind power.[27] Among those are both annual and one-time direct and indirect benefits. But needless to say, NREL never bothers to list the offsetting costs that such a program will impose upon taxpayers in Kansas and elsewhere. So let's fill in the other side of the ledger and determine who the real dim bulbs are.

Kansas underwent a rapid build-out of wind power in recent years. Between 2003 and 2011, wind power grew at a compound annual growth rate of 35.2%.[28] EIA data shows that by the end of 2011, the state had deployed 1,272 mW of wind power.[29] But EIA is not fully up-to-date. Other authoritative sources show the amount as of November 2012 was closer to 2,346 mW.[30] That is more nameplate-rated output than two typical light-water nuclear reactors.

By 2012, Kansas boasted the sixth highest level of wind penetration — the amount of wind energy as percentage of total all-source generation — among states in the country, accounting for almost 12% of the electricity generated.[31] Not surprisingly, residential electricity rates paid by customers had correspondingly seen the fifth fastest rate of growth among states between 2008 and 2012, climbing more than 26%.[32] This was a growth rate that was nearly five times higher than for the U.S. in total.[33] As Figure 18-4 shows, the top 10 states by degree of wind penetration collectively saw residential rates climb almost four times faster than the other 40 states did.

It won't matter that EIA data is not up to date with respect to Kansas wind power build-out since all the numbers in our analysis will be scaled as a ratio of NREL's 1,000 mW example. We would reach the same relative conclusion about wind costs using a higher or lower capacity figure.

Among "direct" benefits, NREL shows that royalty payments to local landowners will be $2.667 million per year, property tax payments from wind farm operators to state and local government will be $2.9 million annually, and permanent wind farm operator jobs would provide $21.2 million per year in benefits. In addition, construction jobs would provide $188.5 million in one-time benefits. Indirect benefits would include annual job-related gains of $16.7 million and a one-time indirect construction benefit of $137.5 million. Over the expected 20-year life of the project, NREL boasts a $1.08 billion economic gain from deployment of 1,000 mW of wind power.

FIGURE 18-4. **Residential Electricity Rate Growth in High-Wind States**

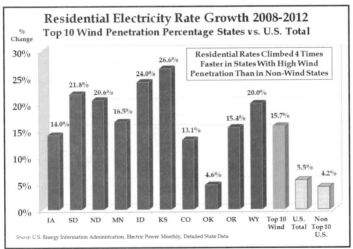

Sources: Electric Power Monthly, February 2013, Electric Power Monthly, March 2009 and Electricity: Detailed State Data, *Energy Information Administration*

Needless to say, renewable energy-promoting NREL never bothered to factor in any offsetting costs of wind power. First, wind power qualifies for federal wind energy Production Tax Credits of 2.3¢ per kWh.[34] Given that Kansas derived nearly 4.78 million mWh of wind energy in 2011 from its wind capacity, a cost of $86.4 million per 1,000 mW in tax credits was imposed upon taxpayers each year, money that flowed into the pockets of heavily subsidized wind farm operators.[35] These costs are real and must be included even if they were shifted onto the backs of taxpayers, most of whom reside outside of Kansas. Even worse, the benefits are not taxable.

Also, wind power is more expensive than conventional energy. There is some considerable debate about the magnitude of this extra cost. But a low-ball figure comes from the Kansas Corporation Commission which claims wind power caused electricity rates in Kansas to rise by "only" 1.7% in the state during 2012.[36] Let's use that number in our example. Wind accounted for just 10.7% of all electricity production in Kansas and yet, at that modest penetration level, it still boosted electricity rates by 1.7%.

Even with that 1.7% rate increase, wind energy still cost Kansas ratepayers $53.4 million per 1,000 megawatts each year in extra electricity costs.[37] With the 1.7% rate increase, wind power resulted in a cost difference of at least 1.42¢ per kilowatt-hour over conventional electricity (8.97¢ per kWh for conventional sources vs. 10.39¢ for wind power) in the 12-month period from December 2011 to November 2012.[38] So wind power is at least 15.8% more expensive than conventional power sources in Kansas, a number which fails to account for cost shifting and is obviously too low.

Let's examine the economic picture for 1,000 mW of wind power using all these factors. To understand the impact, assume all factors are purely linear and can be scaled up to adjust for the actual wind capacity whether it is 1,272 mW shown by EIA or 2,346 mW compiled by other sources. The composite picture of annual and one-time benefits and costs is shown in Figure 18-5.

FIGURE 18-5. **Real Costs and Benefits of 1,000 Megawatts of Wind Power in Kansas**

Impact	Cost - Benefit Category	Annual Flows	One-Time Flows
Direct Impacts	Landowner Royalties	$2,667,000	$0
	Property Tax Benefit	$2,900,000	$0
	Operational Jobs	$21,200,000	$0
	Construction Jobs	$0	$188,500,000
	Production Tax Credit	-$86,401,656	$0
	Wind Power Surcharge	-$53,383,611	$0
Indirect Impacts	Operational Jobs	$16,700,000	$0
	Construction Jobs	$0	$137,500,000
Total Project Summary	TOTALS	-$96,318,266	$326,000,000
	20-Year Flow Values	-$1,926,365,328	$326,000,000
	20-Year Combined Flow	-$1,600,365,328	

Sources: Benefits from 1,000 Megawatts (mW) of New Wind Power in Kansas,' *National Renewable Energy Laboratory*; 'Electricity: Detailed State Data,' Net Generation by State by Type of Producer by Energy Source, 2001-Present, *Energy Information Administration*

The four annual benefit categories from royalties, property taxes and jobs totaling $43.5 million per year are shown on the left column of figures. A one-time benefit of $326.0 million from the initial construction phase is shown in the right column. But both one-time and annual benefit flows are quickly overwhelmed by annual net outflows of $86.4 million per year cost for PTC and $53.4 million in higher electricity costs borne by

Kansas ratepayers, as shown also in the left-hand column. Those are the outflows NREL forgot to include in its lopsided portrayal.

'Green energy' proponents ignore the federal tax credit cost because it doesn't show up on monthly electricity bills of Kansas ratepayers. But it is entirely proper to allocate it since it is a cost that gets shifted to American taxpayers. So over the 20-year life of the project, the economic picture will not result in a positive $1.08 billion for 1,000 megawatts as the ridiculous analysis from NREL contends but will actually cost taxpayers and consumers nearly $1.6 billion in total. This is no small discrepancy. And truth be told, you can more than double all these numbers since Kansas actually had at least 2.35 times more wind power in 2012 than NREL's example depicts.[39] And since it doesn't include the negative impact of depressed GDP as we saw above, the numbers are far worse.

Recognize that the analysis assumes that additional cost of wind power in Kansas results in "only" a 1.7% increase in electricity rates. That underestimate ignores the large incremental capital cost of underutilized standby generation capacity required to supplement wind energy, a cost estimated by George Taylor and Thomas Tanton in their study of *The Hidden Costs of Wind Electricity*.[40] Nor does it include efficiency degradation costs that occur when backup generation is forced to cycle on and off to accommodate intermittent wind power as described by Bentek Energy in their analysis of generation performance in Texas and Colorado.[41] Nor does it include actual costs from output degradation over the useful life of a turbine, a significant factor documented by Professor Gordon Hughes in his seminal study of Danish and UK wind turbines in 2012.[42] Nor does it account for the fact that the wind energy PTC shown above are more expensive after-tax costs while all the other factors expressed in the analysis are on a pre-tax basis.

To get a handle on the total costs of wind generation that arise from these other issues that are routinely ignored by 'green energy' boosters as well as by DoE in its levelized cost comparisons, a recalculation of fully-allocated wind energy costs was provided in Chapter 13. Even in this highly limited context, wind power costs far exceed benefits claimed by NREL. There is a large net cost.

There is plenty of evidence from other states that the extra cost of wind energy is far higher than the modest rate differential used in our Kansas analysis. For instance, residents in Bismarck, North Dakota pay a wind power surcharge equal to 3.69¢ per kWh. The power provider, Otter Tail Power, sought to increase it to 5.72¢ per kWh in 2010.[43] If the analysis is redone using a 3.69¢ per kWh surcharge, the net 20-year project cost for Kansas wind would balloon to $3.3 billion. And if the higher 5.72¢ premium for wind energy is used, the 20-year net cost expands to a staggering $4.8 billion. That would be $1,687 for every man, woman, and child in Kansas.

An even more in depth study of the RPS program in Kansas performed by the Beacon Hill Institute arrived at remarkably similar results as those shown above. The Beacon Hill economists found that the RPS program will inflict substantial harm on the Kansas economy, reducing disposable income by nearly $1.5 billion.[44] That is a figure very much in line with the analysis shown in Figure 20-5. In addition, Beacon Hill contends the

Kansas RPS program will drive electricity rates 45% higher and will boost average household electricity bills by $660 per year by 2020, will destroy 12,000 more jobs than it will create, and will cost Kansas ratepayers $644 million by the year 2020.[45] The unfriendly climate that the Kansas RPS program creates will also lead to a large reduction in business investment in the state.[46]

Defenders like Kansas Governor Sam Brownback support wind energy tax credits to maintain these untenable arrangements which punish their constituents by pretending that credits "are not cash handouts; they are reductions in taxes that help cover the cost of doing business."[47] But this is sophistry, a distinction without any difference. They claim they only need a temporary extension of tax credits.[48] They've been saying that for three decades. As with ethanol subsidies that were finally phased out but replaced with a gradually increasing schedule of mandated blending volumes, their idea is to implement a national RPS program which forces utilities to purchase ever greater amounts of expensive wind and solar power no matter the price. The costs, of course, will be passed along to rate-paying customers. It would be a green wolf in sheep's clothing.

Another example concerns wind power purchase agreements that Louisville Gas & Electric and its sister company Kentucky Utilities were negotiating in 2009. During that year, the House passed the Waxman-Markey bill which contained a 25% RPS provision obligating all power providers to comply. LG&E petitioned the Kentucky Public Service Commission for permission to impose a surcharge to cover wind power that would have cost the utility twice as much as it did to produce power at its own generating stations.[49] That means that LG&E customers would have been paying a surcharge of around five to seven cents per kWh for wind power.

Notwithstanding all the assurances from liberal 'green energy' triumphalists like *Grist*'s David Roberts, the one who calls RPS opponents "dim bulbs" and "dimwits," opponents of RPS mandates in Kansas had very good reason to oppose the program. They don't want to shell out $3.8 billion dollars more than they needed to over a 20 year period to purchase expensive, intermittent, unreliable wind power.[50] They're tired of seeing their residential electricity rates climb faster than those paid by 93% of the other ratepayers in the country. These were the economic benefits that "dimwits" as leftists call them oppose. Who exactly are the dim bulbs?

THE FINAL TALLY ISN'T IN YET

A deeply disturbing aspect of Obama's 'green energy' program concerns the requirement to construct extensive transmission lines to gather wind and solar power from far-flung producing locations to distant consuming markets. Historically, electricity ratepayers were charged for the transmission lines that carried power from utility plants to customers under a "user pays" framework.[51] But conventional sources are typically located close to consuming markets. So the cost of constructing transmission lines was modest. Not so for 'green energy' like wind farms located in America's prairie state wind corridor or solar ranches out in remote locations like the Mojave Desert. DoE figures for levelized costs of new generation capacity placed in service in 2017 in the Annual Energy Outlook 2012 report show that transmission investment costs for wind energy were 3.2 times higher, and for solar photovoltaic ranches 3.6 times higher, than for natural gas or coal plants.[52]

If states that have chosen to adopt RPS mandates are forced to bear the entirety of 'green energy' transmission line costs, as they certainly should since they are the sole beneficiaries of the power produced, the cost differentials and economic disadvantage between RPS and non-RPS states will be magnified. Naturally, this would help drive another nail into Obama's 'green energy' coffin. So the Obama's ideological appointees at the Federal Energy Regulatory Commission (FERC) needed to effect a daring rescue.

FERC issued Order No. 1000 in 2011 specifying that Regional Transmission Operators "must consider transmission needs driven by public policy requirements established by state or federal laws or regulations."[53] That is a euphemism for RPS programs mandated by state laws. The fact that FERC lacks authority under the Federal Power Act to regulate public utility transmission planning was absolutely no impediment.[54] FERC decided it possessed authority to decide that the long-standing practice would be inadequate to enable Obama's 'green energy' vision.[55] FERC applied a vague formula whereby cost allocations to rate-paying customers from transmission build-outs would need to be "roughly commensurate" with benefits received.[56] So now FERC was free to require that ratepayers in Kentucky could be charged for transmission build-outs necessary to connect far-flung wind farms in Texas, because those renewable energy assets would presumably deliver "roughly commensurate" climate benefits that would be bestowed upon residents of non-RPS states even if not a single ampere of current ever found its way from Texas wind farms into Kentucky homes and businesses.[57]

Indeed, a report by Edison Electric Institute found that, of the $51.1 billion in transmission grid build-out projects on the planning books between 2013 and 2023, fully 76% of the amount will be devoted to connecting far-flung renewable energy projects.[58] Those costs will be socialized by all ratepayers, not just those in the affected regions.[59] In the Obama era, external costs of unaffordable 'green energy' projects are offloaded on all ratepayers to make it appear that they are less economically unpalatable than they really are.[60]

Utility operators are not standing still. Interstate Power and Light Co. (IPL) filed a complaint with FERC that the Midwest Transmission System Operator will charge its customers $170 million between 2008 and 2016 for grid system build-out and upgrades that will not offer any benefit to IPL's 500,000 customers.[61] But they'll be getting "roughly commensurate" climate benefits, right? In all likelihood, given the FERC chairman's past pronouncements and unilateral actions to unfairly distribute the enormous costs of supplying wind and solar power onto the shoulders of an unwilling public, IPL stands little chance with its complaint.[62] Its first attempt to get a hearing was rejected out of hand by FERC, which lamely claimed IPL lacked sufficient data to substantiate its case.[63]

Obama promised that oceans of taxpayer funds for 'green energy' projects were vital to restore American competitiveness and create lots of green energy "jobs that pay well and can't be outsourced."[64] An example was a solar energy project that received administration fast-track backing.[65] In September 2011, DoE awarded a $737 million Section 1705 taxpayer loan to Tonopah Solar Energy, LLC. Once complete, the project will create a 110 megawatt solar thermal power plant in the Nevada desert called Crescent Dunes Solar Energy.[66] The project received expedited review and approval from the administration.[67] According to project sponsor Solar Reserve's website,[68] one of its primary investment backers is a San Francisco outfit called PCG Clean Energy & Technology Fund (East) LLC. The number two guy at PCG is Ronald Pelosi.[69] As you can guess, Ronald Pelosi is the brother-in-law of former Speaker of the House Nancy Pelosi.[70]

Another investment partner at Solar Reserve is Argonaut Private Equity. Argonaut was the primary investor in Solyndra, the infamous recipient of a $535 million fast-track loan guarantee that ended up a total loss for taxpayers after Solyndra declared bankruptcy and defaulted.[71] Argonaut is the investment fund owned by George Kaiser, the Obama campaign "bundler" at the center of the Solyndra scandal.[72] Argonaut Private Equity firm would now get a second trip to the well.[73]

The crony-connected Solar Reserve plans to sell 100% of the output from Crescent Dunes to NV Energy over a 25-year period.[74] The stated price is 13.5 cents per kWh, a rate which grows 1 percent per year over the 25-year project life.[75] 'Green energy' cheerleading media were quick to point out that the 13.5 cent price was not much different from prices paid by Nevada ratepayers.[76] Residential ratepayers in Nevada paid an average of 11.83¢ per kWh in 2012. But Crescent Dunes will supply power to *all* ratepayers, and the average all-sector rate paid throughout the state in 2012 was only 8.95¢ per kWh.[77]

'Green energy' boosters also note approvingly that the annual increase of 1% paid to Solar Reserve over the 25-year project life compares favorably to the average retail price increase over the previous ten years of about 3% a year.[78] Extrapolating into the future using these growth rates, Crescent Dunes will be able to deliver power at a lower cost in just six years, they contend. And it will be able to do that for years to come. "This isn't a bad deal for NV Energy" they claim.[79] It all sounds convincing, it's a wonderfully welcome 'green energy' success story in a landscape littered with epic failure, and not surprisingly to those paying attention, it's completely bogus.

First, all-sector electricity rates in Nevada over a 10-year period from 2003 to 2012 had only increased about 0.8% a year.[80] It was only residential rates that had seen annual increases in the 3% range.[81] It was homeowners who have been taking it on the chin. To soften the impact on industry, the extra generation costs in states like Nevada are mostly being paid by residential consumers.

Looking over the portfolio of 'green energy' projects that will sell power to NV Energy, the Crescent Dunes project is the most expensive by a wide margin.[82] Even Ormat's McGinness Hills geothermal project in Lander County, which will cost NV Energy 8.6¢ per kWh, is priced substantially lower than Crescent Dunes.[83] That modest 8.6¢ price compares to an average wholesale power price of 4¢ per kWh that NV Energy had been paying for sensible, affordable power.[84]

Another thing to consider when you hear 'green energy' is that retail electricity prices are growing much more quickly in states that have imposed Renewable Portfolio Standards mandates than in those that have not. A Manhattan Institute study of electricity rate increases found that electricity prices in states like Nevada that have imposed RPS programs obligating them to buy expensive power from projects like Crescent Dunes were growing at about twice the rate of adjacent states that had imposed no mandates.[85] It is these 'green energy' projects themselves, the ones that media boosters are telling us are so affordable, that are causing retail electricity prices to grow far faster than they had grown in years prior to their widespread introduction.

NV Energy paid $89.6 million in 2008 for renewable energy at rates that were more than twice the wholesale price it paid for fossil-fuel power.[86] Those added costs are shifted onto the backs of Nevada residential ratepayers. They're the ones who voted in favor of it. Nevertheless, the utility still rejects three quarters of 'green energy' proposals because their costs are simply too high.[87]

This is not rocket science here. If you overlay a bunch of 8.6 and 13.5 cent power onto a portfolio of 4 cent wholesale power, it won't come as a big surprise that retail prices start increasing at a faster growth rate than before introduction of RPS mandates. But 'green energy' boosters have the *cojones* to proclaim that differential growth rates between the two payment streams amounts to a putative selling point for even more expansion of ruinously expensive 'green energy.'

"Look," they say, "our 'green energy' project cost will only grow 1% a year while retail electricity prices are growing 3% a year. You should be thanking us." But it was their increasingly onerous 'green energy' projects that caused the 3% growth rate in the first place. You should accord the same appreciation for this as you do to the guy who steals your wallet and car but then expects appreciation for returning to you a couple of bucks for bus fare. Ratepayers are fully justified if they don't show gratitude.

The same justification is being advanced by military branches that are busy deepening their involvement in purchasing expensive renewable energy over long periods of time into the future. As *The Wall Street Journal* points out, the Navy thinks it would be a good idea to buy up a whole bunch of really expensive energy that costs many times more than competitively-priced alternatives. The Navy "expects the project will save money because the agreed-upon price for the solar power will rise more slowly than market electricity rates."[88] Long-term growth rates are immaterial as to whether one option is better than the other. What matters is which option involves the higher net present cost. Memo to Navy Secretary Ray Mabus: It won't be solar power or algae fuels.[89] It is the high-cost of these renewable energy projects that are being overlaid upon a portfolio of lower-priced energy that is causing electricity rates to rise faster than the taxpayer-subsidized 'green energy' contracts.

The almost manic nature of RPS mythology is readily observable in media coverage of the issue. The renewable energy-cheerleading *Associated Press* cites an example of New England states — all of them except Vermont have RPS programs in place — attempting to collaborate to lower the cost of renewable energy. The self-evident implication is that it is too expensive. *AP* offers its obligatory genuflection, claiming pursuit of more renewable energy is a "laudable goal" which it justifies by its putative benefit of "reducing the region's reliance on fossil fuels."[90] But *AP* readily acknowledges that fossil fuel energy costs four to six cents per kWh while renewable energy is priced at 8.5 cents.[91]

So to the brain trust at *AP*, it's a "laudable goal" for the region to free itself from "reliance" upon four cent power so it can enjoy the benefits of power that costs twice as much. Mere words can scarcely express how delicious it is to long-time observers of wholly unbalanced media coverage like this. The cheerleading *AP*, which reverentially genuflected to every Obama utterance in the early days, found itself ruminating in 2013 over the damage to the integrity of its news gathering process caused by intrusive wiretapping surveillance of its reporters by Obama's Department of Justice?[92] 'Clean energy' can sure be a dirty business.

The Obama administration wants to "improve" funding for 'green energy' by packaging numerous smaller-scale projects serving state RPS programs into asset-backed securities that could then be sold to an unwitting public.[93] Without citing evidence, they claim that securitization using private-sector funds would drive down 'green energy' project financing costs that currently enjoy unlimited funding of free or low-interest money from taxpayers. Presumably securitizing 'green energy' projects would be an attempt to replicate the success of mortgage-backed securities that caused a global economic meltdown in 2008.

One obvious problem with securitizing 'green energy' projects that doesn't plague mortgage-backed securities is that 'green energy' survives upon political willingness to institute lucrative mandated feed-in tariffs to provide a project funding mechanism. Without them, there would be no 'green energy' because it's simply too expensive. Maintenance of those feed-in provisions is based solely upon political will to keep them in place at originally agreed-upon levels. But as we have seen in Spain,[94] Germany,[95] Italy,[96] Poland,[97] Czech Republic,[98] France,[99] the UK,[100] South Africa,[101] and Japan,[102] when political will foundered, feed-in payment streams were reduced or eliminated. Almost certainly, the same action will need to be taken in California at some point in the future.

By contrast, mortgage-backed securities are pools of individual mortgage contracts that are governed by inviolable contract law between private parties. As such, even the most desperate politicians are incapable of altering or abrogating them. And yet they caused a near collapse of the world's financial system. By contrast, securitized pools of 'green energy' projects depend solely upon the forbearance of the political class not to amend or alter the public funding spigot. Good luck there. This should make these securities far riskier than the lowest rated junk bonds. It seems entirely fitting; junk bond ratings for junk energy.

At least sixteen of the 29 states that have enacted RPS programs are considering legislative or other measures to pare back the scope and damaging impact they are now having.[103] This impact becomes especially salient as cheap, abundant natural gas renders economic comparisons between wind power and baseload natural gas increasingly problematic. Only the most unbalanced, disingenuous studies can render a verdict in favor of wind power.[104] According to the law firm Keyes, Fox & Wiedman, legislatures in those 16 states are considering at least 35 separate measures to curtail renewable obligations.[105] It seems likely that at least some of these states will begin to scale back their zeal for self-inflicted injury.

THE COST OF REDUCING CO_2

The stated justification for RPS programs is to reduce CO_2 emissions. Taxpayers are assured by RPS program proponents that this objective can be accomplished at a reasonable price. But is there any truth to this claim? An analysis of the cost of CO_2 abatement provided by wind energy in California is provided below for the year 2011.

California generated 7.75 million mWh of energy from wind turbines in 2011, which amounted to 3.9% of the 200.8 million mWh of electricity generated in-state from all sources.[106] While no doubt a significant understatement of the true costs as discussed in Chapter 13, wind power imposed a 51% cost premium over the composite costs of all generation sources in California during 2011 based on EIA data with pre-tax PTC impacts included.[107]

Meanwhile, California all-sector electricity consumers paid a 2.51 cents per kWh premium in 2011 over all-sector consumers in non-RPS states that used conventional generation sources.[108] Californians paid a volume-weighted average of 13.38 cents per kilowatt-hour for all-sector electricity in 2011 vs. 10.86 cents per kilowatt-hour paid by all-sector consumers in non-RPS states.[109]

The British Wind Energy Association (BWEA) estimates that CO_2 abatement potential from wind energy is about 430 grams of CO_2 per kWh of electrical energy.[110] As with the EIA levelized cost of wind energy, this is probably a grotesquely overstated number based upon other available work. But, for sake of argument, let's borrow their over-generous estimate.

Thus, wind energy imposed additional costs upon all-sector consumers in California of $293.7 million over the cost of conventional power purchased by all-sector consumers in non-RPS states.[111] The use of wind power abated 3.3 million metric tons of CO_2 using the wildly inflated metric from BWEA. Therefore, California electricity consumers paid at least $88.10 per metric ton to abate CO_2 using wind power.

Did that represent good value? Consider that California held its first carbon emissions auction under its AB-32 Global Warming Solutions Act in November 2012.[112] The state established a floor price of $10.00 per metric ton, which was close to the $10.09 per ton amount that auction participants paid on average for emission certificates. Under its RPS program, California has been abating CO_2 using wind energy at a cost that is at least 8.7 times what emitters were willing to pay in California's first cap-and-trade auction.

But the $10.09 auction price reflected the fact that the "market" price was not permitted to go below $10.00 per metric ton under the rigged rules. The Europeans have been playing this carbon-pricing game for far longer. The Emissions Trading System does not establish a floor price. At about the same time that California emitters were being mugged for $10.09 per metric ton, emitters in the EU were paying something close to €3.00 or about $4.00 per ton.[113] So, based upon the ETS market price signal, wind energy in California was abating carbon dioxide emissions with wind energy under the most favorable assumptions imaginable at a cost that was 22.1 times more expensive than market prices.[114] As carbon emissions prices are "inching ever closer to zero" in Europe, Americans who have the misfortune to live in RPS states are being hectored by politicians who think it's acceptable to abate CO_2 at cost levels that are dozens of times more than comparable world prices.[115]

A study of the impact of California's RPS program by Professor Timothy Considine and his research associate Edward Manderson from the University of Wyoming calculated that "carbon dioxide emission reductions cost between $150 and $160 per ton. While these costs decline to about $62 per ton by 2035, they remain well above market prices for carbon permits."[116] Does RPS sound like good value to California taxpayers?

Consider the case of New York, which adopted an RPS program in 2004 obligating the state's utilities to acquire 25% of their electricity from renewable sources by 2013.[117] The target was later boosted to 30% by 2015.[118] To achieve that goal, New York will be required to boost its deployment of wind power capacity to 8,000 megawatts. What will New York residents pay and what do they receive for it? New York will reduce its CO_2 emissions by 8.5% at a cost of $331 per metric ton.[119]

Another example concerns the cost of CO_2 abatement embedded in the EIA's *Annual Energy Outlook 2013* document. Each year, EIA provides a forecast of energy demand, supply, and prices for the next 30 years. EIA also provides variations to what they call the "reference case," the picture they forecast would emerge if we maintain our current path of "business as usual."[120] EIA includes another case for what they call the "No Sunset" approach. That case describes their forecast of the future if the current renewable energy subsidies scheduled to expire at the end of 2013, the subsidies America is currently spending borrowed money to maintain, would continue into perpetuity. The overwhelming majority of those subsidies are for the wind energy PTC, which pays producers 2.3 cents per kWh for energy they produce and sell.

Under the "No Sunset" case, there would be substantially more renewable energy produced vs. the "Reference Case" since producers would be paid an exorbitant subsidy to furnish us ever more expensive power. EIA forecasts that between 2011 and 2040, there will be an extra 3.2 trillion kWh of extra renewable energy produced under "No Sunset."[121] If we follow that path, the extra renewable energy would result in a cumulative reduction of 1.7 billion metric tons of CO_2. Green cheerleading media reflexively praise this approach because it will avoid release of 1.7 billion tons of CO_2 over the next twenty nine years.[122] They pretend that if the U.S. generates 3.2 trillion kWh more of renewable energy, the risk of "climate change catastrophe" will be reduced or avoided.[123] The reduction will amount to only 0.15% of forecasted global emissions.

So the U.S. could potentially eliminate a lot of CO_2 emissions. But how much would we have to pay? EIA doesn't say and neither do green cheerleading media.[124] So let's do the math for them. First, if the 2.3 cents per kilowatt-hour PTC is extended out to 2040, U.S. taxpayers would need to fork over a back-breaking $73.5 billion to subsidize the extra renewable energy assuming that wind will account for 98.5% of the combined total of wind and solar as it did in 2011.[125] But the pre-tax equivalent of the subsidy is actually $113.1 billion. That would equate to a real subsidy cost of $66.52 per metric ton.

But renewable energy is more expensive than natural gas and coal generation. So there is an additional abatement cost imposed onto the backs of ratepayers. Using cost assumptions in the levelized cost figures supplied in EIA's *Annual Energy Outlook 2013*,[126] the extra renewable energy generation cost to electricity consumers would equal $72.7 billion more than natural gas usage between 2011 and 2040. This would impose an additional cost of $42.74 per ton. So the total abatement cost comes to $109.26 per ton. And these estimates don't include the additional wind power costs that EIA ignores in its levelized cost analysis, costs that are examined and quantified in Chapter 13. Nevertheless, compare this $109.26 figure to a probable social cost of climate change of around $5 per metric ton calculated by a consensus of climate change economists as compiled by the Copenhagen Consensus Center.[127]

Thus, under the "No Sunset" approach, the U.S. would embark upon a path that would burden U.S. consumers by $155.8 billion to achieve only $8.5 billion in climate benefits, a 18.3-to-1 cost-benefit ratio. Moreover, the putative benefits, such as they are, would be spread among everyone on the planet. The U.S. accounts for only about 4.4% of the planet's population but would pick up 100% of this inflated tab for the abatement. So the real cost-benefit ratio becomes 417-to-1. Do green nags who tell us we need to "do the math" ever bother doing the math themselves?

Consider the value that U.S. taxpayers derive by forking over a $7,500 tax credit to upper-income buyers of electric vehicles. The median annual income of a $41,000 Chevy *Volt* buyer is $170,000. Lower- and medium-income taxpayers are forced to subsidize this wealth transfer because the social benefit of greenhouse gas emissions reduction is presumably so great that we should be on our knees thanking our far-sighted central planners. And how much do taxpayers shell out per ton of CO_2 abated under the electric vehicle tax credit program? From an analysis conducted by economists at the CBO:

> *The cost to the government of using the electric vehicle tax credits to achieve those reductions ranges from $300 to $1,200 per metric ton of CO_2 equivalent emissions reduced, depending on the battery size of the electric vehicle that is substituting for an average-fuel economy conventional vehicle.*[128]

Because so much of the public debate on energy policy is waged in the land of make-believe, there is an inexhaustible supply of people who argue — or pretend — that electric vehicles eliminate CO_2 emissions. In reality, these vehicles usually only relocate emissions from the tailpipe to the power plant. As the aforementioned CBO report makes clear, "compared with an average-fuel-economy conventional vehicle, an electric vehicle of similar size and performance will have about 35 percent lower life-cycle emissions."[129] So lower- and middle-income taxpayers, by and large, receive no benefit from this wealth-transfer subsidy arrangement. But they are obligated to pay anywhere from $300 to $1,200 to eliminate one metric ton of CO_2 which only imposes a present value cost of about five dollars. This is government hard at work improving the economy.

Another case concerns the master plan to erect a vast array of massive wind towers across the UK to enable it to achieve its EU2020 mandate which requires the country to derive 20% of its electricity from renewable sources by the year 2020. An analysis by Professor Gordon Hughes at the University of Edinburgh shows that, even under the most favorable set of assumptions, wind power will abate CO_2 at a cost of £270 per metric ton.[130] That compares to carbon offset permits on the Emission Trading System that had traded as low as €2.81 per metric ton in January 2013.[131] And under some completely reasonable scenarios, the wind energy experiment would actually result in higher emissions of CO_2 than a program built around efficient natural gas plants.[132]

Readers who have made it this far — God bless them all — know that Germany's dreadful experience with 'green energy' is no exception. Germany subsidizes solar electricity, paying solar producers more than eight times the rate that electricity can be purchased on the Leipzig wholesale power exchange.[133] That subsidy results in a cost to abate CO_2 of about $1,050 per metric ton according to economic consultancy RWI. Compare that to carbon offset prices on the ETS that, even at their highest levels, never reached much above €30 per metric ton.[134] Blessedly for Europe's over-stressed consumers, those days appear to be gone forever.

We also examined the case for biofuels programs and whether they even abate any CO_2 at all. Rather than revisit every instance, recall that Oregon State researchers William Jaeger and Thorsten Egelkraut found that biofuel programs "produce negligible reductions in fossil fuel use and increase, rather than decrease, greenhouse gas."[135] But even under the most generous set of assumptions, researchers like the International Institute for Sustainable Development show that "buying greenhouse gas emission reductions by subsidizing U.S. corn-based ethanol production is not very efficient, costing well over $500 per metric ton of CO_2-equivalent removed."[136] We also saw how the International Council on Clean Transportation measured the abatement cost of EU biofuel policies to be €2,500 per tonne of CO_2."[137]

Barack Obama's latest idea to juice revenue flows into the federal government to support his dreadful expansion of permanent government is to burden the economy with a carbon tax. CBO estimates that a carbon tax would raise $1.2 trillion in its first 10 years while reducing CO_2 emissions by 8% over that time.[138] EIA forecasts CO_2 emissions will average 5,752.99 million metric tons a year between 2014 to 2023.[139] So Obama's carbon tax would equate to an abatement cost of around $260.73 per metric ton if the carbon tax reduces emissions by 8% over the next ten years. But since emissions will likely decline as natural gas continues to displace coal in electricity generation and as autos become more fuel-efficient, the actual CO_2 abatement cost will be even higher.

Even if you accept every syllable of the IPCC's most frightful scenario — and you'd be a loon if you did — there is no remediation strategy yet dreamed up that is even remotely compensatory.[140] No matter how you slice it, our leftist central planning geniuses have yet to conjure up a scenario where CO_2 emissions from energy generation can be reduced at a price within even an order of magnitude of the external "cost" that CO_2 supposedly imposes on the global economy.

The now thoroughly discredited *Stern Review* published by the UK government in 2006 claimed that climate change represented the "greatest and widest-ranging market failure ever seen" in human history.[141] But the inconvenient truth is exactly the opposite. The incontestable fact, as shown above and in a thousand other examples, is that climate change remediation has become the single greatest and wide-ranging regulatory failure in human history as governments adopt climate change abatement solutions that bear a present value cost to taxpayers one to three orders of magnitude greater than the putative costs that climate change itself could ever hope to impose. Since the U.S. represents only about 4.4% of the Earth's population, it will enjoy only 4.4% of the benefits from its climate mitigation outlays. In effect, 'green energy' becomes a vast foreign aid scheme since the rest of the world will enjoy 95.6% of the benefits of America's climate remediation spending.

'Green energy' promoter Vinod Khosla is on record extolling *concentrating solar power* (CSP) technology similar in design to the Andasol solar thermal power plant in the Andalucía region of Southern Spain. Khosla told a reporter in 2007 that CSP was able to produce energy at $500 per kW, which would be $500 million for 1,000 megawatts of rated power output.[142] If true, this would make CSP very competitive with the most efficient energy sources. But Khosla is in the venture capital business. His success depends upon a steady flow of gullible investors with deep pockets who can be hoodwinked out of their trust funds with fantastic claims about the limitless potential for future 'green energy' riches. These are the same triumphant claims Khosla has made on countless occasions about the prospects for "brain dead simple" cellulosic ethanol, all of which were hollow.

Khosla had never bothered to avail himself of some wisdom delivered by a scientist named John Ericsson who wrote convincingly about concentrating solar thermal energy:

> ... *the fact is ... that although the heat is obtained for nothing, so extensive, costly, and complex is the concentration apparatus that solar steam is many times more costly than steam produced by burning coal.*[143]

Ericsson wrote those words in a letter in 1887. Yet it is as accurate today as it was 127 years ago. Recognizing the inescapable truth of these words, DoE naturally approved a Section 1705 loan in December 2010 to the Spanish company Abengoa Solar Inc. for construction of a $1.446 billion CSP plant at Gila Bend, Arizona.[144] Press reports indicate the final cost of the facility will come in at $2 billion.[145] DoE claims the Gila Bend plant will have a generating capacity of 250 megawatts. Assuming an interest rate of 8% and a 25 year project life, the annual capital cost alone without regard to operating or maintenance costs comes to $741 per kW of capacity.[146]

Because Arizona is one of the 29 states that has enacted an RPS program, it must get its 'green energy' from somewhere. So Arizona ratepayers will have the Gila Bend CSP plant to serve their needs. Gila Bend will sell all of its power to the Arizona Public Service Company (APS) at a price of 14 cents per kWh.[147] This is 3.7 times more than the wholesale rate that APS paid for power from the Palo Verde hub in 2010.[148] Overlaid onto existing electricity sources, Gila Bend will increase the cost of electricity to all-sector ratepayers in Arizona by about 7 percent.[149] This will add about $100 to the electricity bills of residential ratepayers in the state.

Even at that inflated 14-cent wholesale rate, press reports indicate that APS will spend $4 billion over a 30-year period for the power that the Gila Bend plant produces, or $133.3 million per year.[150] This figure seems low on a pro forma basis. Nevertheless, given the station's 85-person full time staff and other annual expenses, there would likely only be about $127 million or even less per year in free cash flow to fund its $2 billion construction debt. That means that the plant could not break even with an implied interest rate above 4.8% per year. This rate is low for a risky project like Gila Bend. But the federal government is providing taxpayer money to solar projects at levels half of what the private market would charge.[151] So no need to worry.

Nevertheless, based upon these back-of-the-envelope calculations, even with the tax-payer generosity, the Treasury-backed loan of $1.446 billion would seem to be in some substantial degree of jeopardy if press reports about the 30-year payments of $4 billion to be made by APS are accurate. But the payment streams to APS may be substantially higher than $4 billion over the life of the project, in which case the taxpayer-guaranteed lenders would be in better shape, but ratepayers would be the worse for it.

Either way, Vinod Khosla will have a challenge substantiating that he can do CSP projects for $500 per kW as he claimed back in 2007. EIA updated a 2010 study on capital costs for utility-scale electricity generating plants. The number EIA reported for CSP is $5,067 per kW, or 10.1 times higher than what Khosla claimed.[152] It was "brain dead simple" to check these numbers. And that was just the capital cost, which excludes operating and maintenance costs. All that would cost extra. This is the level of confidence we can ascribe to wild forecasts of economic viability made by 'green energy' flim-flam promoters.

We've been assured for decades that affordable solar energy is right around the corner. Peter Glasser, head of the Engineering Sciences division of the Arthur D. Little consultancy wrote an article in *Science* in 1965 claiming that a type of solar thermal energy could be produced for about 2 cents per kWh, and that space-based satellites could soon be built to transmit 10 megawatts of collected solar power back to earth, enough to power a city like New York.[153] Biologist Barry Commoner wrote an embarrassingly muddled book in 1976 entitled *The Poverty of Power* claiming that solar power would "become the most economical alternative in most parts of the United States within the next few years."[154]

Jimmy Carter assured the nation we needed to make an immediate switch to solar energy because global oil supplies would be fully exhausted by 1985.[155] He installed solar panels on the roof of the White House to underscore his claim. Management consultancy Booz-Allen & Hamilton testified to Congress in 1983 that solar energy would be commercially viable by 1990.[156] Energy policy gadfly Amory Lovins proclaimed in 1986 that solar energy economic viability was just one to three years from fruition.[157] A solar industry mouthpiece testified to Congress in 1987 forecasting that "after the year 2000, somewhere between 10 and 20 percent of our energy could come from solar technologies, quite easily."[158] In 2001, the country derived not 10-20% of its energy needs but just 0.067% from solar technologies.[159] That forecast was wrong by a factor of 150 to 300. *The New York Times* triumphantly announced in 1994 that a large natural gas company was planning to build a 100 megawatt photovoltaic plant in the Nevada desert that would provide power for a whole city of 100,000 people at the unimaginably low cost of just 5.5 cents per kWh.[160] There was not a syllable of doubt in that report. The name of the company was Enron. Needless to say, the plant was never built.[161]

As a candidate, Obama told an audience in Portsmouth, New Hampshire in October 2007 that he planned to drive up the cost of affordable energy so that expensive energy could be made more competitive by comparison:

Once we make dirty energy expensive, the second step in my plan is to invest $150 billion over the next decade to ensure the development and deployment of clean, affordable energy.[162]

Between Obama's inauguration day in January 2009 and the middle of 2013, America had already "invested" at least $139 billion of Obama's $150 billion in so-called "clean, affordable energy."[163] Did energy prices go down? Americans were paying higher tax bills to cover mounting deficits resulting in part from 'green energy' projects, workers in RPS states were experiencing the curse of higher unemployment and lower economic growth than surrounding states caused in part by higher energy prices, ratepayers in RPS states were paying higher electricity bills than their neighbors in non-RPS states to the tune of nearly $100 billion per year, motorists were paying higher pump prices caused by the country's biofuel program, consumers were paying higher food prices that resulted from a corn ethanol program incinerating more than 40% of the nation's crop, affordable energy-generating plants were being shut down by regulatory actions motivated by a desire to accelerate 'green energy' adoption, etc. As the tee-shirt might read, "Barack Obama Went to the White House and All I Got Was This Lousy Energy Bill."

Without a trace of equivocation, a former Clinton administration Energy Department official and RPS program enthusiast proclaimed in recent years that "There's no way we can create a better future without the price of energy going up."[164] For all those unlucky souls living in states that have enacted RPS programs, their energy prices are going up. Ask them if their futures are the better for it.

Like the Clinton administration official, we can pretend that adding $100 to residential electricity bills in Arizona means a better future for its residents. We can pretend that paying $88.10 per metric ton to abate CO_2 using wind power in California amounts to good public policy. We can pretend that adding $3.8 billion in costs over twenty years for wind power in Kansas is a good deal for ratepayers and taxpayers. What do you think?

We can pretend that higher energy prices can be justified on the basis of saving the planet from some impending climate doom, or appeasing an unforgiving Mother Gaia, or leading more fashionable lives, or acknowledging a necessity to lead less energy-intensive lifestyles, or earning indulgences from our moral exemplars in the environmentalist movement, or currying favor with leftist media, or winning plaudits from Fabian socialist central planners who have bankrupted Euro-sclerotic welfare states across the Atlantic, or whatever. But there's not a chance in the world that higher energy prices resulting from Obama 'green energy' policies will ever help us create a better future — no more than higher food prices would. But with his biofuel program that is driving up the price of basic food commodities, Obama is doing that also. At least on this score, he's consistent.

CHAPTER 19

OBAMA'S 'GREEN ENERGY' ECONOMY

"If ... people think that government spending projects are generally wasteful and add little to national wealth or productivity, then taxpayers may view increased government spending as simply increasing the burden of government debt that they must bear ... as a result, the net stimulative effect of fiscal actions will be reduced."[1]

BEN BERNANKE
SPEECH TO THE JAPAN SOCIETY OF MONETARY ECONOMICS
MAY 31, 2003

Readers at this point may be scratching their heads in befuddlement at what relevance the above quotation could have possibly have to a book devoted to 'green energy' public policy. It will be the author's burden in this chapter to demonstrate that government spending to promote 'green energy' cannot possibly be justified on any rational economic basis at this point in time, if ever.

Even if every triumphal claim advanced by 'green energy' boosters were to be true — that it is necessary to avoid climate catastrophe, that it will help the U.S. achieve energy independence, that it will result in a large net bounty of high-paying jobs that can't be outsourced, that it will readily integrate into existing portfolios of reliable energy, that it won't impose undue burdens on the environment, that it is environmentally pristine in all its contemplated manifestations, etc. — American simply can't afford to devote more resources to government spending programs that "are generally wasteful or add little to national wealth or productivity."

We need to begin our examination of this vital subject by establishing a basic principle of macroeconomics. Chapter 1 of Econ 101 teaches that there are four basic inputs to production; land, labor, entrepreneurship such as technical know-how or technology, and capital. Anyone who has seen a picture of a photovoltaic solar ranch generating station or seen an large array of wind towers spread across vast expanses of prairie or mountain ridges understands that these forms of 'green energy' require massive expanses of land. The energy they harvest is highly diffuse, not concentrated. To harvest usable quantities of solar or wind power, we need to dedicate huge amounts of land just to gather it.

To do that, we need to devote large amounts of capital to procure generating components, lease or purchase tracts of land, and chop up landscapes building solar collecting arrays or wind towers. Once we do all that, we need to connect the power to the grid, which is usually far away from the place where it is produced, requiring yet more land and capital for high-voltage transmission lines. So, in a financial sense, land can be considered a proxy for capital in that we need to expend lots of money to acquire or condemn remote lands, build roads, bulldoze and clear away forest or scrub brush, build solar or wind farm installations, construct perimeter fencing, erect transmission towers, and so forth. All of these considerations are important for understanding why 'green energy' is so expensive and impractical.

America derived 82% of its primary energy in 2011 from fossil fuels which liberate carbon dioxide during combustion.[2] The other sources were nuclear energy which accounted for 8.6% and renewable energy which accounted for the balance of 9.4%.[3] So less than one tenth of our needs are satisfied by renewables. Biomass like wood and biofuels accounts for half of the renewables portion.[4] Another third of the renewable energy comes from hydroelectric dams.[5] The balance of renewables comes from wind and solar, most of which is wind energy. In total, wind and solar provide only about 1.4% of our total energy requirements.

Let's examine a comparison between the only two competing routes to a low-carbon future that have the required scale to succeed. If we are serious about reducing our carbon footprint, and we want to maintain our modern way of life, we have only two possible routes. Option number one is to begin harvesting large amounts of wind and solar power backed up with a massive storage infrastructure to balance intermittency. The other option is to harvest the binding energy from the nuclei of readily available fissionable isotopes like thorium-233 and uranium-235 found in nature, or from plutonium-239 that can be produced in a nuclear reactor.

That's it. There are no other realistic low-carbon alternatives on the table today. As Barack Obama told his student audience at the University of Miami in February 2013, anybody who tells you otherwise "doesn't know what they're talking about, or just isn't telling you the truth."[6] Of course, there is a rampant belief among leftists that we shouldn't maintain our modern way of life. The authors of the UN Environment Programme,[7] or Pol Pot-wannabes Bill McKibben and Naomi Klein, and dozens of others all advocate a reversion to primitive, poverty-stricken, agrarian-based, communal-style, 14th century peasantry.

Serious authors like Robert Bryce have written compellingly that the first of these routes, harvesting wind and solar power, is wholly impractical.[8] Other serious authors like the Oxford Institute for Energy Studies (OIES) point out that substantial deployment of low-carbon technologies are not producing any measureable reductions in CO_2 in any of the countries where there is high-level penetration — Denmark and the Netherlands for example — while countries that actually have achieved a measure of CO_2 reductions have done so by deploying copious nuclear or natural gas baseload energy.[9] Denmark, the 'green' community's poster child of renewable energy virtue, has seen its CO_2 emissions as a percentage of energy produced rise substantially over recent years.[10] Danish CO_2 emissions per unit of energy were higher in 2011 than in any year since 2000. Bryce and OIES are completely correct in their assessments. But for the sake of illustrating an aspect that they often overlook, the economic impracticality of 'green energy' solutions, let's persist.

Among the numerous problems with renewable energy, the one that poses the greatest challenge is that it suffers from low energy and power density. You need a lot of space to produce a small amount of power. For instance, you only derive about 0.0049 watts of power from a single square meter (m²) of hydroelectric capacity in the U.S.[11] You can get nearly 10 times as much power per unit of area from corn ethanol production, but that still only provides 0.047 watts per square meter.[12] A wind farm might give you 1.2 watts per m² while a solar thermal station would yield 3.2 watts per m² and a solar photovoltaic ranch could deliver as much as 6.7 watts for each square meter utilized.[13] Compare those power outputs to a typical nuclear power plant that can generate 56 watts per m² of sprawl.[14]

To better illustrate the concept of capital efficiency and its impact upon the economic feasibility of competing options, let's compare what was the country's largest deployment of wind energy at the time of its commissioning with the largest nuclear power plant. Multinational electric utility company E.On operates one of the country's largest wind energy farms, the Roscoe Wind Energy Complex in central Texas.[15] The Roscoe complex comprises 627 wind turbines that boast a total nameplate capacity of 781.5 megawatts.[16] Roscoe stretches over 100,000 acres in four counties, a total of 156.25 square miles.[17] It required more than $1 billion in capital to deploy.

Between 1996 and 2011, wind turbines in Texas produced a combined 30.5% of their nameplate capacity.[18] So on average, it's reasonable to expect the Roscoe complex will actually produce only 238.4 mW of usable power capacity. This power output would be able to generate 2.1 million mWh of wind energy throughout a typical year. In addition to the high-priced revenue the plant derives selling this energy to Texas electric utilities and other spot market buyers, federal taxpayers fork over an additional $48 million per year in production tax credits. Either way, the Roscoe Wind Energy Complex required $1 billion in capital outlays to generate 2.1 million mWh of electrical energy, or about a $479 capital cost per mWh.

Two states to the west sits the Palo Verde Nuclear Generating Station, the nation's largest nuclear power complex.[19] Operated by Arizona Public Service, it boasts a capacity of 3,937 mW providing 31.2 million mWh of energy throughout the year.[20] The plant occupies 4,050 acres, or six and a third square miles.[21] The station required $5.6 billion to construct and place into operation.[22] This amounts to about $189 in capital outlays per mWh. Thus, the capital requirements for Roscoe wind are more than 2.5 times greater per mWh than for Arizona's Palo Verde nuclear plant.

Though not dispositive, one can readily see that the nuclear plant can wring 407 times more power output out of each acre of land than the wind plant. Needless to say, there are many other factors to consider. The Roscoe plant is more than 200 miles from Fort Worth, the nearest large consuming market whereas the Palo Verde plant is just 55 miles outside of Phoenix. Thus, high voltage transmission grid build-out is four times longer for the Roscoe wind complex but transmits only one fifteenth the energy as the Palo Verde transmission lines. A map of U.S. wind availability vs. power demand shows wind resources are far removed from major population centers.[23]

Due to intermittency, wind power needs to be supplemented with dispatchable backup. When the amount of wind power is small in relation to other sources, the negative impact of intermittency can be better mitigated and the extra capital cost is manageable. But at high wind penetration levels, the incremental capital cost of poorly utilized standby capacity becomes very problematic, and it is directly attributable to wind power.

The incremental economic costs of maintaining poorly utilized standby generation are not factored into EIA levelized cost calculations. The 'green energy' crowd proposes to solve its intermittency problem with massive infrastructure build-out of batteries, pumped water, or compressed air storage installations that would add directly to renewables cost exposure by significant degrees. Those nature-disruptive, capital-intensive costs are not factored in to the current 'green energy' cost calculation either. To solve the intermittency problem, one or the other is needed. And those costs are directly attributable to intermittent power generation.

Intermittency degrades the performance of standby generators causing wasteful use of fossil fuels and often more CO_2 liberation in total than if there had been no wind power in the first place.[24] The cost impacts from these effects are also attributable, but not included in EIA figures.

Wind and solar energy both qualify for generous subsidies that are funneled to project owners through tax credits, low-interest loans, grants, mandates, and other lucrative arrangements not available elsewhere in the economy. These economic costs, while shifted onto the backs of others, cannot be ignored. But they are not embedded into EIA calculations.

Lastly, recent work by a variety of authors suggests that turbine performance over time declines along a steep degradation curve, economic effects that are not factored into EIA's levelized cost estimate, or in the analysis above.[25] But an estimate of this impact in Chapter 13 indicates that, at a capital cost of 7.5%, wind costs about 72% higher than the assumptions provided by EIA.

The arc of human history is characterized by innovation and technology enabling people to derive more energy from ever more concentrated sources. Primitive humans discovered how to warm caves and cook meat using wood fires. During the Bronze Age, metallurgists discovered they could increase the temperature of wood fires using charcoal, which enabled them to smelt metallic oxide ores into base metals. The widespread use of coal with its equivalent or higher energy density allowed for even higher temperatures, greater versatility, and less deforestation. When petroleum was adopted in the nineteenth century, humans found a source of energy that delivered even more energy per unit of volume than coal as the higher latent energy in carbon-hydrogen chemical bonds became a substitute for pure carbon combustion. In the twentieth century, humans harnessed the power of nuclear fission which was millions of times more powerful than the most energetic chemical reaction. Just seven years later the first successful test of a nuclear fusion device — the form of energy that powers the stars, nearly a thousand times more powerful than nuclear fission — was demonstrated. 'Green energy' reverses this inexorable trend providing, in some manifestations like wind and solar, lower energy density — less energy per unit of mass or area — than cave men were able to generate. These are the energies of the future?

Leftists like Obama appear to be oblivious to the mania embodied in their energy policy conceits, something that is obvious to most of the rest of us. His advocacy for his twenty first century energy technology is a classic example of the dissonance that voters in the U.S. must endure. He enjoys using the lexicon of our psychobabble-infused, over-medicated cultural sensibilities to describe America's basic energy situation:

> *Each and every year we become more, not less, addicted to oil — a 19th century fossil fuel that is dirty, dwindling, and dangerously expensive. Why?*[26]

Why? Oh I dunno, maybe it's because it actually works. Using oil is an addiction and resort to energy fairy tales is the miracle cure of Doctor Obama, inventor of Obamacare. The good doctor might want to ask himself, if fossil fuels are really so "dangerously expensive" as he says they are, why people use them in such large amounts. He might want to ask why he doesn't flinch from filling up Air Force One to fly out to Hawaii for a seventeen day holiday or down to Miami to tell fairy stories to impressionable adolescents. And the doctor might also ask himself why he needs to shake taxpayers down for all these taxpayer subsidies if his cherished 'green energy' is so affordable.

Proponents of 'green energy' like recounting to us about the OPEC official who reminded his colleagues that "the Stone Age didn't end because they ran out of stones."[27] It's true. It ended because they found something better. The trouble with that disclaimer is that 'green energy' proponents don't have something better; they're pushing something much worse.

Obama advances the notion that we need to transition away from nineteenth century fossil fuels in favor of his twenty first century technology. His solution to twenty first century energy and transportation problems will be installing more rail lines, a nineteenth century technology that was first prototyped in England in the seventeenth century.[28] He is wildly enthusiastic about twenty first century technology embodied in electric cars. Those are the kind that first arrived on the market in the 1830s[29] and reached their full fruition in 1896 with the *Roberts* electric car, an example of which still participates in road races today — and hilariously gets the same mile range on a charge as a Chevy Volt.[30] He says the twenty first century solution to America's energy independence problem will be biomass, the very low-density energy source pioneered by Paleolithic cave dwellers hundreds of thousands of years ago. We'll convert it into ethanol, a fuel that has 66% of the thermodynamic content of gasoline and has been in use by humans for 9,000 years.[31] His cellulosic version was first introduced in commercial application in the 1800s.[32] He favors carpeting America's breathtaking landscapes with massive arrays of twenty first century windmills, the kind that made their first appearance 3,700 years ago in the ancient Babylonian empire.[33] Hammurabi should have been Obama's Energy Secretary. The first electricity-generating windmill was invented in 1887.[34] *Harper's New Monthly Magazine* ran advertisements from the Windmill Light & Power Company of Walpole, Massachusetts in the 1890s which offered a generation system and "a storage battery for periods of calm."[35] Naturally, with a 126-year old technology still struggling with teething pains, federal subsidies are required to see it over the hump. Just be patient.

GETTING MORE FROM LESS

Agriculture is characterized by the same trend of ever-increasing density of yield. Between 1968 and 2005, the world's cereal production doubled using the same cultivation area.[36] Had yield remained constant, the world would have required eight billion acres of agricultural land to feed the planet's population in 1998 rather than the 3.7 billion acres actually needed.[37] The grain output from 100 acres in 1961 could be produced on just thirty five acres in 2012.[38] The amount of land required to produce food stopped growing more than twenty years ago.[39] The sole reason why there is growth in area under cultivation is the spread of crops for biofuels.[40]

Malthusian quacks are fond of telling us that we need to adopt a very dangerous program of societal transformation that includes halting and reversing economic growth, foreswearing personal transportation, eliminating most of our energy usage, forcibly limiting family size, mandating dietary choices, adopting a communal social model built around small-scale subsistence organic farming, and a list of other highly disruptive measures. All of this is quackery. Yet for some peculiar reason, organic farming has gained a wholly unearned sanctity in 'green' mythology.

In 2010, the U.S. Agricultural Department undertook a comprehensive survey of more than 14,500 organic farmers in the U.S.[41] When agricultural researcher Steven Savage compared yield statistics on organic farms with those of traditional farms, he discovered that "national organic average yields are moderately to substantially below those of the overall, national average."[42] Savage noted that some organically-grown crops like squash, peaches and apples did modestly better in certain regions. But humanity won't survive on peaches and squash. For the bulk of its calories, humanity depends upon grain and vegetable crops grown in rows.[43] Organic yields on those crops were far worse than for traditional methods: organic corn yielded 29% less output than traditional methods, spring wheat was 53% lower, winter wheat was 40% lower, sorghum 58% lower, rice 41% lower, etc.[44] These results have been borne out in peer reviewed studies published in the world's most prestigious scientific journals.[45] Because organic farming requires one and a half to two times as much land to grow the same amount of food as conventional farming, it poses the threat of massive deforestation that would surely occur if these pseudoscientific methods were to be adopted on a widespread basis.[46]

Organic farming boosters regularly claim that their methods can adequately meet the needs of the planet's population growth.[47] They even erroneously claim science is on their side. But like 'green energy' promoters who make the same specious claims, they can't possibly meet humanity's needs.[48] Organic farming is the agricultural equivalent of 'green energy.' It grinds up more land, requires more resources, offers far lower yields, feeds fewer people, costs a lot more, tastes much worse, results in substantial amounts of waste, reverses the arc of human progress, threatens humanity's existence, relies upon pseudoscientific charlatanism for its perpetuation, is damaging to the planet, undermines prospects for economic growth, is trendy, it enjoys an eco-fuzzy appeal in popular culture it doesn't deserve — and "progressives" like the Obamas love it.

For some obscure reason, leftists labor under another delusion that food transportation is the height of ecological irresponsibility. Liberal ideologue Barbara Kingsolver actually wrote an entire book bragging about how she and her family strengthened their moral and ecological credentials by eating nothing but locally-grown food for an entire year.[49] Bill McKibben brags that he did the same thing in the Vermont valley where he lives. Kingsolver is one of those insufferably sanctimonious left-liberal moralizers who actually uses terms like "spiritual errors" to describe the consumption practices of others. You know the type, those ill-mannered folks who buy their food at the grocery store and don't possess the requisite enlightenment to inquire if it was trucked to market. But was all that local eating even worth her effort? What about the environmental impact?

Researchers at Carnegie-Mellon University published a study in 2008 finding that transportation from producer to retail outlet accounts for only 4% of total life-cycle greenhouse gas emissions in the "farm-to-fork" food production chain.[50] The researchers noted that shifting meal choice from red meat to poultry or fish just one day a week "achieves more greenhouse gas reduction than buying all locally sourced food."[51] The team's findings completely destroyed the myth that eating locally carries any measureable environmental benefit. The news hasn't reached our food theoreticians in the White House.

The "eating local" movement seems at first glance like just another entry on an endless list of harmless delusions that leftists beguile themselves into believing. It is built upon a fantasy that a small landholder will achieve the same life-cycle resource impact as a large-scale operation that can take advantage of economies of specialization, scale, scope, and trade. Liberal ideologists like Kingsolver, who studied piano in college, don't really do comparative life-cycle supply chain economic analysis. Idaho potato farmers can achieve yields of 38,300 lbs. per acre while Alabama potato farms produce only about 17,000 lbs.[52] Should Alabamans squander resources growing potatoes to avoid the slight amount of life-cycle energy usage shipping potatoes from Idaho? Supply chain economics pianist Kingsolver would say yes.

The popular delusion about "food miles" is widespread. Typical is a 2010 tome from New York organic food enthusiast Anna Lappé, author of *Diet for a Hot Planet: The Climate Crisis at the End of Your Fork and What You Can Do About It*.[53] Like other authors of the genre, Lappé deliberately conflates unrelated emission footprint issues, tortures a set of statistics she doesn't understand, ladles on a heavy dose of new-age spiritualism as a substitute for rational thinking, and predictably arrives at a solution that relies upon heavy-handed authoritarian control. Does your kid like Fruit Loops? Forget about it. In Lappé's future, you'll eat whatever the authorities decide and like it. Do you enjoy the versatility offered by packaged convenience foods? You can be cured of those defects.

So the real problem begins when organic farming and "eating local" advocacy, built as it is upon obvious falsehoods, strays into advocacy for coercive, centralized "redesign" of the food system. That's an idea that McKibben's fellow Vermonters Philip and Erin Ackerman-Leist promote in their 2013 book *Rebuilding the Foodshed: How to Create Local, Sustainable, and Secure Food Systems*.[54] What happens if we don't like the new design? What if we have acquired a taste for ham imported from Parma, bananas from Guatemala, or rambutan from Indonesia? To leftists, these are obvious "spiritual errors" that need to be corrected by force if necessary. The entire global shipping industry consumes only 8% of the world's oil and accounts for just 3% of global CO_2 emissions.[55] That includes shipping everything: cars, TVs, appliances, oil, iron ore, steel, and everything else in the world. Food is a miniscule fraction of that.

A Democratic Senator from Ohio drafted legislation that would propose to cure us of our "spiritual errors" by requiring federal taxpayers to fork over hundreds of millions or even billions of dollars each year to promote wasteful local farming and food markets.[56] And a federal regulation issued by the Department of Agriculture requires school boards to give preference to locally-grown food in school lunch procurement contracts.[57] That rule grew out of a 2010 bill signed into law by "eating local" theorist-in-chief Obama.[58] Alabama schools will now be coerced into buying Alabama potatoes so school children can be spared the 225% efficiency advantage offered by Idaho potato farming. This is your federal tax dollar hard at work pursuing wasteful, eco-fuzzy, feel-good programs that will have precisely the opposite of the intended outcome.

Obama is the world's largest booster of corn ethanol which can deliver about 0.05 watts of power per square meter of crop land.[59] Compare that to a small natural gas drill pad producing just 60,000 cubic feet of gas a day that can deliver 28 watts of power per square meter, 560 times the power density.[60] The American corn ethanol industry incinerated 4.9 billion bushels of corn in 2011, more than 42% of the country's total production of that vital food crop, enough output to feed 350 million people.[61] That's about 5% of the planet's population. We do that to produce a volume of motor fuel which satisfied only 0.7% of the world's petroleum consumption.[62] The amount of resources the U.S. squanders to accomplish such slender results is scarcely believable.

True environmentalists are conservationists. They believe in utilizing low-impact methods to satisfy needs. They advocate maintenance of pristine spaces in their natural condition. They shudder at the thought of churning up vast expanses of forest and grassland to grow food crops that aren't even used to feed people or livestock. They recoil at proposals to scour natural landscapes to erect solar ranches or wind farms. They detest proposals to grind apart our fruited plain constructing poorly utilized high-voltage transmission grids for the purpose of connecting remote, far-flung, low-productivity 'green energy' production to consuming centers in far distant places. They abhor the idea of shearing apart natural mountain vistas to construct highly inefficient pumped-storage plants to provide a mechanism to balance the problematic intermittency of already expensive, ecologically damaging 'green energy.' And they can't understand why anyone would consider squandering so much scarce capital doing these destructive things when there are so many far more justifiable, competing demands.

But why concentrate so much attention on capital costs when other resource costs like fuel and maintenance also play a role in the total cost to produce energy? Let's look more closely.

THE HIGH CAPITAL COSTS OF 'GREEN ENERGY'

A corollary of low energy and power density is the high capital requirements to produce a given amount of power. Because the energy being harvested from wind and solar sources is diffuse, a substantial amount of physical plant is required to capture and convert sizeable amounts of it. That unfortunate reality means that capital outlays become enormous per unit of energy produced.

A comparison of wind and solar capital costs per mWh from DoE data is provided in Figure 19-1.[63] Note how much more capital is required to deliver a given amount of energy for wind and solar than for combined cycle natural gas and conventional coal generation. Without equivocation, absent major advances in energy efficiency from these sources, the needle is unlikely to move very far in the future for these highly touted alternative energy sources.

When interest rates begin to rise, as surely as they will, capital costs will begin to rise also just as the monthly payment on a mortgage would rise if the interest rate on a home loan were to increase appreciably. For example, on a 30-year loan with a $100,000 principal at 4% per year, a monthly payment of $477.42 would soar to $733.76 if the interest rate doubled to 8%.

Within practical limits, power generation economics can be made to work if relatively high initial capital outlay requirements can be matched with low on-going operating costs. But debt service and capital depreciation can be considered part of the base of the on-going cost structure for a power generation entity like an electric utility or a fuel refinery. If power generation and fuel businesses are subjected to a series of crippling mandates that obligate them to bear very high capital outlays for 'green energy' projects that return very little revenue-generating power output, the economics and their ability to attract capital begin to head south in a hurry.

FIGURE 19-1. **Levelized Capital Cost of Electricity by Source**

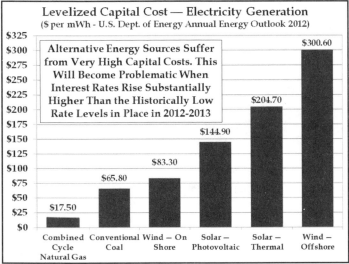

Source: Levelized Capital Cost of New Generation Sources, Energy Information Administration, Annual Energy Outlook 2012

A good example of this phenomenon can be seen with European electric utility companies that have been subject to crippling 'green energy' mandates for many years. According to Ernst & Young, nine of the top ten European utilities boasted credit ratings of AA+ to A+ in 2001. But after a decade of high capital outlays to meet renewable energy mandates, only one single company still retained that coveted investment-grade credit rating.[64] Between 2005 and 2009, capital-related expenses had jumped from 60% to 78% of the composite expense structure of these ten utilities.[65] Clearly they were reaching their limit on new debt loads.

Yet the EU will require them to invest an additional €1.1 trillion for storage, generation, and network-related capital spending by 2020, of which €350 billion would be devoted to renewable energy necessary to achieve compliance with mandates.[66] E&Y concludes that bond issuances and equity injections will not be able to raise the required capital. So non-recourse bank lending will needed to make up the difference. But E&Y also acknowledges that banks are unlikely to possess the credit-worthiness, lending capacity, or desire to do so. The EU has backed itself into a 'green energy' financial cul-de-sac of high capital requirements with no exit in sight.

The attractiveness of a capital outlay will vary with the interest rate prevailing at the time the outlays are required. During the Summer of 2012, Treasury borrowing rates were at all-time low levels. The yield on the 10-year Treasury note dropped below the unprecedented rate of 1.6% by the end of the May 2012.[67] The next day, as panic-stricken investors fleeing from a collapsing Eurozone poured into safe-haven U.S. Treasuries, the yield on the 10-year note crashed through 1.46%, the lowest level ever observed in over 200 years of record-keeping.[68] And just when it seemed like a bottom had been reached in 10-year yields, a new low was set seven weeks later, taking the yield below 1.4%.[69] Perhaps not coincidentally, the U.S. and even the whole world deployed the largest annual addition to high-capital cost wind power capacity during that very year.

FISCAL POLICY IMPACT ON 'GREEN ENERGY'

During the Obama years, capital had momentarily become absurdly cheap. The net interest expense on the U.S. federal debt dropped to only $359.8 billion in fiscal year 2012 from $454.4 billion in FY'2011[70] even while U.S. public debt soared by nearly $1.2 trillion over the same one-year period.[71] Part of the reason for the low interest payout exposure was the fact that the Federal Reserve had unleashed a tidal wave of Treasury bond buying in a futile effort to stimulate economic growth. In FY'2011 alone, the Federal Reserve purchased 77% of all Treasury-issued debt. Interest payments that were due on those Treasury holdings in the Fed's portfolio were remitted back to the Treasury.[72] So the real budget impact was far greater than the official numbers suggest. When the Fed finally ends its accommodative policy of throwing money out the window — perhaps timed to coincide with the next Republican President — debt service outlays will soar making today's 13-digit deficit even worse.

Equally problematic, the Fed is purchasing long-dated Treasuries using short-term obligations, shortening the maturity profile of the Treasury's debt portfolio. This will expose the federal budget to an increased risk of sudden interest rate reversal. Interest rates will begin to back up across the yield curve, and refinancing events will be increasingly exposed to higher coupon rates. This is going to get mighty ugly and we may not need to wait a lifetime for it to happen.

Because of the Fed's intervention, fiscal year 2012 saw a lower level of interest expense outlay in the federal budget in any year going all the way back to FY2005. The average interest rate paid on Treasury borrowings at the end of June 2012 was only 2.651%.[73] It is an absurdly low number that would not remain in place for very long.

Given the rapid accumulation in public debt over the previous few years — debt doubled from 2008 to 2012[74] — when the interest rate picture does change, all hell will break loose with respect to the federal budget which, during fiscal year 2012, saw the country borrow 35 cents of every dollar it spent.[75] Aided and abetted by reckless Federal Reserve policy that attempts to sustain an equally reckless fiscal policy, America has temporarily benefitted from the forces of competitive sovereign devaluation whose pace is unlikely to abate as the European Central Bank[76] and the Bank of England[77] unleash their own rounds of quantitative easing in a fruitless attempt to stave off Eurozone monetary collapse.

As investors flee a slowly disintegrating Europe, they see U.S. Treasuries and other debt obligations as an attractive momentary shelter. But that fact should afford little comfort. On that score as the numbers above demonstrate, the U.S. is merely the best house in a lousy neighborhood. The bill for fiscal prolificacy at the federal and state levels will be coming due. And when it does, interest rates will rise sharply. And with it, so will budget deficits, making the availability of capital all the more constrained.

A classic example of Obama's detachment from reality on fiscal matters was illustrated during a speech he delivered to employees at Argonne National Laboratory in March 2013.[78] Calling for yet more federal funding for 'green energy' programs, Obama decried the budget sequester that threatened to chop an unendurable 2% of a federal budget that had jumped 29% in two years between FY2007 and FY2009 and then grew another 8% over the next four years.[79] Practically sobbing into his handkerchief, Obama drew his line in the sand:

One of the reasons why I was opposed to these cuts was because they don't distinguish wasteful programs and vital investments. They don't trim the fat, they cut into muscle and into bone.[80]

Obama was the world's leading authority on "wasteful programs" since he had championed that cause more than any other President in history. Here was a guy who had staged a kabuki theatre during the previous two years, first over the debt ceiling, then over the fiscal cliff, and once again over the budget sequester, all because he couldn't endure relinquishing a dime of federal spending in a budget that was $1.3 trillion in the red. When he was forced to accept a token 2% budget cut under the sequester, he targeted programs to make the impact as painful as possible.[81] He directed his agencies to identify budget cuts that would inflict the maximum disruption on normal civilian life.[82] When the government shut down over Obamacare expenditures, he sent his uniformed goons into national monuments to rough up wheelchair-bound veterans.

He was the guy who defended a Senate controlled by his own political party that had not submitted a single budget in four years despite being obligated by law to produce one every year, whose federal budget had witnessed a 28% increase over four years and a tripling of the budget deficit in a single year, who had never uttered a syllable of regret or even introspection over the fact that countless billions of federal dollars had been squandered on bankrupt crony 'green energy' giveaway projects like Range Fuels, Solyndra, Abound Solar, and a hundred others. He was the guy who decried that the sequester had cut deep "into muscle, into bone" of his cherished 'green energy' program. Never mind that the government from 2009 to 2012 had shoveled more than $120 billion into 'green energy' projects.[83] Obama was crying that he might not be able to get $2 billion more to fund … wait for it … additional 'green energy' projects.

The sole reason why the federal government budget deficit was "only" $1.3 trillion for fiscal year 2012 is because the yield on Treasury obligations was so low and so much interest had been remitted back to Treasury by the Federal Reserve. For example, yields on Treasury paper ranged between 0.03% on 30-day T-bills to an astoundingly low 2.53% on a 30-year T-bond during the month of June 2012.[84] During the early years of the Reagan administration, 30-year Treasury paper carried a coupon rate north of 15%. These astonishingly low rate levels are unheard of in our experience and held down interest payouts.

The U.S. federal government ran 13-digit budget deficits, or nearly so, for five straight years. Since fiscal year 2009, the federal budget has been in the red by a cumulative $5.3 trillion.[85] Federal Spending as a percentage of GDP ballooned during the Obama years, averaging 24.4% during the 4-year period of Obama's Presidency compared with an average of only 19.4% in the prior 10 year period. The gravy train that relies upon the rest of the world's willingness to finance America's profligate spending habits to support unsustainable promises growing out of the country's burgeoning entitlement programs, transfer payments to states being strangled by the limitless appetites of bloated public sector pay, benefit and retirement packages for unionized workers, and government's unquenchable fetish for expanding the size and scope of dubious industrial policy programs like wasteful energy schemes, is fast approaching its terminus.

Shortly before the 2008 election, Al Gore delivered an address to his usual assembly of entranced 'green energy' groupies proclaiming in his usual overbearing manner that:

> … *we're borrowing money from China to buy oil from the Persian Gulf to burn it in ways that destroy the future of human civilization. Every bit of that has to change.*[86]

This couldn't be more dishonest. No one is borrowing a dime to buy oil from the Persian Gulf. The only borrowing from China that occurs is by the federal government. And it does so at a reckless pace to help fund 13-digit budget deficits that support an ever-expanding range of entitlements and 'green energy.' These are programs Gore and Obama support. And as to Persian Gulf oil, by the end of 2013, it represented less than 10% of U.S. requirements. Imports from Canada alone were 50% greater.[87]

It is a fact that economic growth can cure a lot of what ails you. It can produce jobs and income that generate increased income-based remittances to the government. It can stimulate consumer spending that helps fund state government through sales tax revenue and helps close budget deficits. It can also pump up asset prices that add to the wealth effect of household balance sheets leaving consumers more willing to spend, and thus reduce the urgency of correcting excessive fiscal recklessness. It would postpone the day of fiscal reckoning that is surely coming. All of which would be great if we had any economic growth to speak of. But sadly, we don't.

What we do have barrels of is red ink — at both the federal and state levels. There are enough publicly subsidized 'green energy' projects in various stages of realization to fill an encyclopedia, projects that require continuous infusions of taxpayer funds. We also have boatloads of rent-seeking vested interests intent upon maintaining a steady flow of subsidized funding aimed at hideously expensive renewable energy programs like wind, solar, biofuels and such. Gore himself manages a vast portfolio of them. We also live in an age where, judging by election results, a majority of voters wrongly believe that the country can continue to afford doing these counterproductive, economically damaging, fiscally ruinous things into perpetuity. There is little mystery why so many people delusionally think this way.

We shower ecological doomsayers with the highest honors, awards and accolades, acclaiming them as 'green energy' prophets. We are smothered by a cheerleading media that is accustomed to boosting the urgency of pursuing 'green energy' to assure our collective survival that they routinely claim is threatened with imminent catastrophic climate doom. We are immersed in a popular culture that has established 'green energy' as one of the noblest public virtues. Our singers and songwriters hold mega-concerts proclaiming a planetary emergency while maintaining high-impact, jet-setting, carbon-belching lifestyles. We indoctrinate our school children with lurid fables about the sanctity of 'green energy' and recycling. We append fuzzy, eco-friendly labels like "cleantech" on even the most technically dubious low power-density, low energy-density generation schemes that could never exist without massive public subsidies, and which have no hope of ever attaining economic feasibility. And we seem to possess an inexhaustible supply of widely-held public delusions about the fictitious promise of 'green energy' programs, delusions that are nurtured and sustained by widespread economic misunderstanding, scientific illiteracy, basic mathematical innumeracy, and endless multitudes of mass media-inspired material misrepresentation.

FIGURE 19-2. **Post-War Recoveries vs. Obama Recovery**

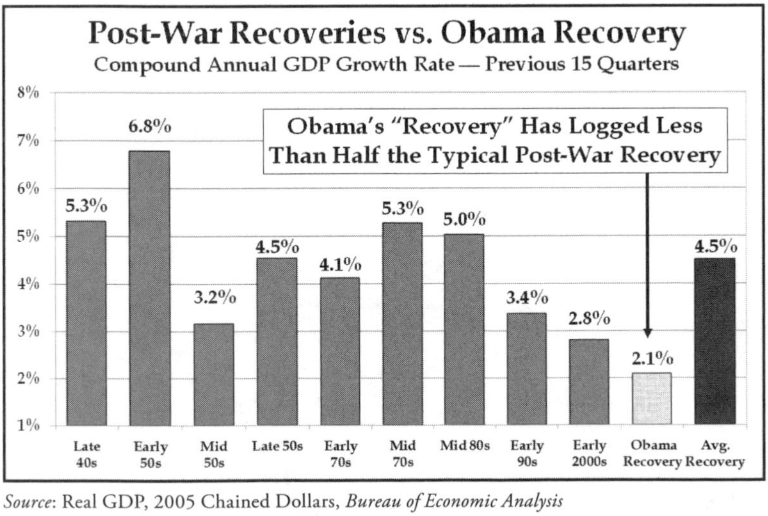

Source: Real GDP, 2005 Chained Dollars, *Bureau of Economic Analysis*

But we have precious little in the way of economic growth that could provide a steady flow of other peoples' money to keep this inanity on life support. From the third quarter of 2009 — that was the first quarter of positive real GDP after the previous recession — until the first quarter of 2013, America had experienced a compound average real GDP growth rate of less than 2.1% as Figure 19-2 shows.[88] That anemic level compares with a typical post-War economic recovery growth rate more than double that amount.

Not surprisingly, the Obama post-recession "recovery" has seen a steady downward progression of real GDP growth rates as Figure 19-3 demonstrates. By the end of 2012, economic growth had ground to a halt with only a miserable 0.4% annualized growth rate being posted in the fourth quarter.[89] It's not hard to understand why. Researchers have convincingly demonstrated that as a country's debt level approaches 90% of its annual real GDP, its economic growth rate declines markedly.[90] We've already blown well past 100%.[91] Remember all the media fanfare when that happened? Neither does anyone else.

FIGURE 19-3. **GDP Growth During Obama "Recovery"**

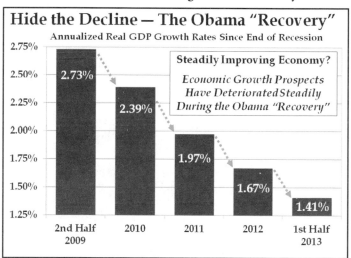

Source: Real GDP, Chained Dollars, *Bureau of Economic Analysis*

Some analysts posit that oil consumption is essential to economic growth. Chris Martenson, author of *Peak Prosperity* claims that "If you want to have economic growth you're going to need growth in oil consumption."[92] Martenson looks at the correlation between per capita oil consumption and per capita economic growth rates since 2005, finding the countries with the highest economic growth rates also had the fastest growth rates in oil consumption. Meanwhile, the U.S., Europe and Japan had the lowest oil consumption growth rates which correspondingly resulted in economic stagnation. He believes that oil consumption actually causes economic growth.

It's certainly too strong to assert that Martenson has it exactly backwards. Some economic activity directly results from energy use just as energy use is a direct consequence of unrelated economic activity. One impact feeds off the other in each case without doubt. But the stronger causative factor suggests that it is more likely that low economic growth resulted in increasingly lower oil consumption and not vice versa. The causes for moribund economies can most often be located elsewhere, not in reduced oil consumption. Nevertheless, there are certainly a range of beneficial knock-on effects from increased oil consumption even if such a prospect causes climate hysterics to shiver under their beds in panic.

Without a doubt, affordable oil prices are key to a healthy economy. Sharp increases in oil prices act like a sudden imposition of an unanticipated tax forcing consumers to pay a premium for oil, much of which flows out of the country to oil-supplying nations that export oil to the U.S.[93] Higher oil prices reduce disposable personal expenditures and worsen our balance of trade. Both factors cause a deterioration in relative economic performance.

Since the 1970s, every time there has been a spike in oil prices, economic decline followed shortly thereafter. The relationship works almost like clockwork. There is a very high correlation between oil prices and the unemployment rate that subsequently occurred. Notice in Figure 19-4 how each spike in oil prices was followed by an unemployment rate spike about 20 months later.

FIGURE 19-4. **Oil Prices vs. Unemployment**

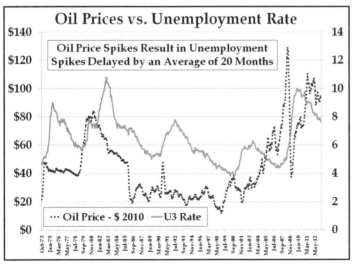

Sources: Bureau of Labor Statistics, Seasonally adjusted unemployment rate; Energy Information Administration, U.S. Landed Cost of Crude Oil; Bureau of Economic Analysis, Implicit GDP deflator

Whichever is closer to the truth, one thing is undeniable. Obama's 'green energy' economy has been a dismal failure from an economic growth standpoint. Since the end of the recession, we have seen a steady downward record of increasingly lower real economic growth. The Keynesian experiment has led to the worst post-war recovery in U.S. history.[94]

It goes without saying that the crowd pushing the 'green energy' future idea also happens to be the same people telling us we don't need to worry about rapidly increasing sovereign debt exposure. They say "the U.S. is the reserve currency and the rules are different and blah, blah, blah." Being voted the best-looking horse in the glue factory is not terribly reassuring when you're the horse. It doesn't require a Ph.D. in abnormal psychology to identify the motive for this view. The specious claim that heavy debt buildup is no problem is aimed squarely at loosening the purse strings to fund a continuous orgy of deficit spending. Since 'green energy' survives on a steady oxygen supply of federal and state subsidies, and would surely wither and die off in a heartbeat without it, these advocates need to convince the public that more deficit spending is not a problem.

If rising debt levels had been used for investments offering high economic rates of return — roads, bridges, telecommunications infrastructure, medical research, aerospace research, etc. — it might have been possible for the economy to wring enough future benefit from them to meet our interest obligations and eventually retire the outstanding principal. But this is not where federal deficit spending is going.

Instead, we are throwing the money out the window by the dump truck load into endeavors that have little or no sustainable value. And, to keep the ship from sinking, the Federal Reserve is simply monetizing the debt, temporarily hiding its true impact. The Fed's balance sheet was expanding by at least $85 billion each month throughout 2013, ballooning from $800 billion to almost $3.3 trillion in just six years.[95] Memo to the "sustainability" crowd: this is not sustainable. Neither is sustainable 'green energy' if it requires more deficit spending, which it obviously does, by the boatload.

Has deficit spending been beneficial to the U.S. economy? Have these spending programs that led to our massive debt buildup generated enough increased income to have made this a worthwhile endeavor? Businesses incur debt in hopes of growing earnings at a faster rate than debt accumulation. This allows them to repay bond holders and enhance shareholder value. How does the rate of federal debt accumulation over recent years compare to the rate of income growth it supposedly was incurred to produce? Figure 19-5 shows what has taken place during the Obama years. We are growing debt more than six times faster than we produce income that could be used to service it.[96] 'Green energy' proponents want to do more — lots more.

Financial analysts look at debt coverage ratios to determine what chances a borrower has to repay a loan. When you buy a house, the bank compares your income to the amount you want to borrow to determine if you qualify for the loan. If you only make 20% of the loan amount each year, you'll be denied. If you make 40%, you stand a better chance of being approved. But if we borrow the money when our annual income covers 40% of the loan and, in subsequent years, drive up borrowing at a rate faster than we increase income, we run the risk of default. The only realistic solution at that point is to stop spending and reduce deficits and debt. As economist Niall Ferguson points out, high sovereign debt levels end in only two ways: high inflation or default.[97] In reality, high inflation is just slow-motion default. So sovereign default of one or another flavor is the only option on offer. High debt levels have never resulted in high economic growth rates. Alas, 'green energy' proponents don't play by the rules that reality dictates.

FIGURE 19-5. **Obama Debt Growth Compared to Real Economic Growth**

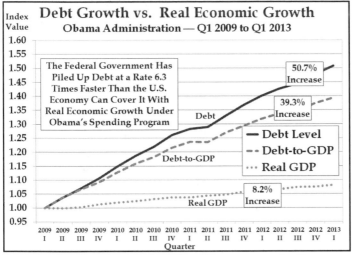

Sources: Debt-to-the-Penny, U.S. Treasury Direct, Real GDP Chained Dollars, Bureau of Economic Analysis

The fiscal and monetary prolificacy fiesta may continue for a while longer but it can't last forever. Financial analyst Michael Pento makes clear in his book *The Coming Bond Market Collapse: How to Survive the Demise of the U.S. Debt Market* that by 2015 or 2016, global lenders looking at the U.S. will see an ugly picture.[98] They'll see an economy that has piled up $20 trillion in debt, that has run six or seven consecutive budget deficits in or near the 13-digit range, that added trillion-dollar entitlement programs in recent years onto a heap of already unaffordable entitlement programs, that monetized $1 trillion per year of federal deficits in an environment of negative real interest rates, that has been issuing 10-year Treasury paper that trades at 550 basis points below its 40-year average, an economy whose fundamentals are far below the "prices" that have been artificially established for its debt issuances, an economy kept afloat by a central bank that will be sitting on a balance sheet loaded down with $5 to $6 trillion of Treasury debt which will need to be unwound eventually.[99] Global lenders will demand a far higher interest rate than those being paid in the 2012-2013 time frame. This will erupt in a bond market rout and fiscal train wreck.

And all the while, the 'green jobs' explosion we were promised, the robust job market of five million high-wage jobs that can't be outsourced, is nowhere in evidence. Instead, the Obama "recovery" looks far more like a recession from a labor force standpoint. The number of private sector payroll jobs only recovered to the levels achieved in November 2000 after Obama had been in office for 43 months, nearly a 12-year restoration delay.[100] Yet the working age population had grown by almost thirty million persons during those years. There were 2.3 million more people employed in March 2007 than in June 2013 despite the fact that the working-age adult population in the U.S. had grown by 14.5 million persons over that time.[101] Obama's economic "recovery" came equipped with a labor force participation (LFPR) rate that declined by a staggering 2.2 percentage points, a reading more in line with a deep recession than an economic recovery.

Correspondingly, the proportion of the working age adult population actually employed has sunk during Obama's economic stewardship to depths not observed since the early 1980s.[102] For the twenty three and a half years prior to Obama's inauguration, the employment-population ratio was above 60% averaging about 62.5% over that 282 month period. But under Obama policies, this crucial measure of labor market health had sunk to levels not witnessed since early 1983. Even as clueless media portray an improving U.S. job market, the exact opposite is true. The lowest ratio since October 1983 was posted with the release of the August 2013 Employment Situation Report.[103] If this is an improving job market, you'd hate to see what a lousy job market looks like.

The June 2013 BLS Employment Report is a perfect reflection of the deterioration in the quality of America's labor market. Stock traders and brainless media celebrated the fact that 195,000 non-farm payroll jobs were created over the previous month.[104] Almost in unison, Obama-friendly media outlets proclaimed the "U.S. labor market is on solid footing."[105] But a closer peek under the covers showed a much different picture.

A very large percentage of the payroll job gains in the June 2013 report — nearly 40% — were in the Leisure and Hospitality industry.[106] We have nothing against these hard-workers. But average weekly wages in this industry are only $351, less than 43% of the average for all private-sector industry groups.[107] While media celebrated the non-farm payrolls increase, the number of full-time workers actually declined by 240,000, continuing a disturbing trend.[108] The following month's BLS report deepened the trend showing that an astounding 97% of job growth that occurred over the prior six months was for part-time work.[109]

Every single job created during the Obama years up to June 2013, and even beyond, had been for part-time work.[110] There had actually been a decrease of 1.1 million full-time jobs since Obama took office up to that time.[111] From January to June 2013, the economy had created 753,000 jobs in the Household Survey of which 557,000 had been part-time workers. More than 80% of newly created workers were entering the labor force in 2013 as part-timers, the only work available. The number of people exiting the civilian workforce was three times higher than the number of people who actually found work.[112] And only one out of every ten working-age adult entrants to the civilian non-institutional population managed to find their way into the Obama workforce during his tenure.[113] This is the media's labor market on a "solid footing." As Mortimer Zuckerman says, "a jobless recovery is a phony recovery."[114] It's a perfect match: phony Obama energy is driving a phony Obama recovery.

Observers like Mohamed El-Erian, Niall Ferguson and others have warned repeatedly that there is no historical precedent for a country that succeeded in its attempt to borrow and deficit-spend its way to prosperity. This is especially true when the labor market is in such dismal straits. If he even had the foggiest clue how to do it, Obama could double the number of jobs that have been created during his tenure in office up to August 2013 and there would still be fewer working Americans than there had been in November 2007.[115]

We are in uncharted waters for which there are no maps, guide books, or compasses. The cautionary signposts that do exist all say the same thing: Turn Back, Wrong Way, or Do Not Enter. Our present era that favors debt-financed, redistributive welfare policy over economic dynamism is not sustainable. We can safely lay bets on whether this Obama-Krugman experiment will succeed. With zero or negative real interest rates, federal debt at 110% of GDP, a historically dismal labor market, real economic growth lower than anytime in post-War experience, and a Fed balance sheet north of $4 trillion, now is not the time to be pouring borrowed money down a rat hole on absurdly expensive 'green energy' boondoggles that retard economic growth.

CHAPTER 20

BIOFUELS AND THE COST OF FUEL

"Nothing is so firmly believed as that which least is known."

MICHEL DE MONTAIGNE, 1533-1592

"It is a curious fact about human nature that many people actually seem to want to believe in an approaching catastrophe. ... The ecological panic of our times is driven by exactly the same emotional needs. Indeed it is yet another example of how, during the twentieth century, the declining religious impulse has been replaced by ... secular substitutes, which are often far more irrational and destructive."[1]

HISTORIAN PAUL JOHNSON, 1984

Biofuel promoters are consistent in a number of things. They all claim that that biofuels emit lower CO_2 than comparable amounts of gasoline. They claim that biofuels reduce the country's dependence on foreign oil. They claim that biofuel mandates are good for the country economically because it creates lots of well-paying 'green jobs' that can't be outsourced. As we have seen, all these claims are either false or highly dubious. Another claim that fits squarely within this category of dubious biofuel benefits is that it lowers the price of gasoline at the pump. The opposite is true.

The Renewable Fuels Association (RFA) is the Washington-based lobby that promotes the use of ethanol use in everything except our mixed drinks where it actually belongs. RFA proudly unveiled the results of a study in May 2011 claiming that ethanol use in the U.S. drove down the price of retail gasoline by 89 cents a gallon in 2010.[2] A year later, RFA announced even better news that retail fuel consumers saved $1.09 per gallon in 2011.[3] At this rate, motor fuel was going to be free in a few years. According to RFA, had it not been for ethanol, the average per gallon retail price at the pump would have been $4.61 instead of the $3.52 we actually paid.[4] RFA ran a series of advertisements touting the achievement.[5]

The news was so good, it prompted Agriculture Secretary Tom Vilsack to rush back to his home town of Des Moines and deliver a speech to a receptive audience at agricultural equipment manufacturer John Deere proclaiming the fantastic benefits of ethanol.[6] Praising corn ethanol to a farm machinery company audience in Des Moines is not exactly a high-risk endeavor, especially for a man who, a few years earlier, had been Iowa's Governor. Vilsack proudly proclaimed that:

> We've gone from importing 60 percent of our oil to 52 percent. As a result of our biofuel industries, consumers across America are paying about $0.90, on average, less for gas than they would otherwise pay.[7]

RFA President Bob Dinneen boasted to friendly media that ethanol enabled the average consumer to save $340 per year over the previous decade.[8] Based upon the 2011 figure of $1.09 per gallon, the annual savings to the average household had soared to $1,200 according to RFA.[9] Because ethanol displaces some gasoline in our retail fuel blend, consumers demand fewer barrels of oil which drives down the price of oil, based upon RFA logic.[10] Of course, RFA never extends their logic to measure how much food prices increased from siphoning off 42% of the corn supply[11] to convert to motor fuel and how much that impact adversely impacted household budgets each year.[12]

This was not the first appearance of such claims. In 2008, the National Renewable Energy Laboratory (NREL)[13] hired McKinsey to look into the question of whether, and the degree to which, ethanol drives down the cost of gasoline. Based upon the market situation in the first three quarters of 2008, McKinsey concluded that ethanol reduced retail fuel costs by 14 cents per gallon without regard to the $0.51 per gallon ethanol blender tax credit then in place.[14] Of course, it was no fault of McKinsey that their NREL task order occurred in 2008 when crude oil prices spiked at $147 per barrel in July of that year.

RFA's fantastic claims about fuel price reduction from using ethanol came from a study performed at Iowa State University's Center for Agricultural and Rural Development (CARD). The CARD study was commissioned by RFA and undertaken by Xiaodong Du from the University of Wisconsin and Dermot J. Hayes of Iowa State.[15] Du and Hayes assumed that, without the ethanol that accounts for about 10% of fuel volume in the U.S., total fuel availability would only be 90% of the amount demanded by consumers, causing a steep price increase and even fuel rationing.[16]

There are numerous problems with these claims. The study authors ridiculously contend by implication that refiners would have been incapable of responding to a need for increased gasoline demand in the short run either through adjusting refinery crack fractions, increasing offshore crude sourcing, or reducing exports of petroleum. According to Robert Dinneen, "We make 13.5 billion gallons, 10 percent of the motor fuel supply. If you take that off the market, gas prices go through the roof."[17] Just like in 1978 when the U.S. used only a few drops of ethanol and gasoline sold for 65 cents a gallon.[18]

It's a little hard to swallow a claim that, were ethanol to disappear over the course of a year or ten years, it would have been impossible for refiners to respond in a country that exported a volume of petroleum products in 2011 equal to 27.7% of the volume of motor gasoline it consumed.[19] Stated differently, for every ten gallons of gasoline America consumed, it managed to export almost another three gallons of petroleum products. In 2011, motorists consumed 13.2 billion gallons of ethanol but exported 37.3 billion gallons of petroleum products.[20] Had ethanol disappeared, refiners would have only needed to supply an extra 8.7 billion gallons of gasoline into domestic commerce to make up for the 13.2 billion gallon displacement of ethanol since ethanol only provides 66% of the mileage equivalent as gasoline does. The U.S. exported a half a million barrels of gasoline per day in 2011, which would amount to 7.7 billion gallons on an annualized basis, or 88% of the 8.7 billion gallon gap without regard to other exported refined petroleum products.[21] So the Du and Hayes domestic gasoline production shortfall was really just a figment of their imagination.

Even if we make the entirely implausible assumption that existing refinery capacity in the U.S. is incapable of supplying the extra 8.7 billion gallons of gasoline needed to make up for the lost ethanol, a position we have already observed is inaccurate, Du and Hayes contend by implication that the capital markets would be unable to funnel enough capital to enable refiners to make up for the extra gasoline refinery capacity for all eternity.[22] Those were the same markets that were able to find enough risk capital to construct more than 218 biofuel refineries in use in 2012, or the dozens that had gone bankrupt and been shuttered.[23]

If this wasn't enough to refute RFA's and Secretary Vilsack's ethanol conceits, a pair of researchers completely dismantled whatever remained of the flimsy case, and they did so in a highly playful manner that rendered the Iowa State study a laughingstock. Economist Christopher Knittel of MIT and Aaron Smith of the University of California Davis critiqued the Du and Hayes boast about ethanol saving consumers $1.09 per gallon in 2011, concluding that:

> *Given the obvious importance of these estimates, we investigate their robustness. We show that they are driven by implausible economic assumptions and spurious statistical correlations.*[24]

Knittel and Smith note that the Iowa State study identified correlation between two unrelated trends and merely attributed causation between them. Where have we heard that before? Such a thing could never happen in real scientific research like, say, climate science. For example, as more Redskins games are played each year, the more leaves fall off the maple trees in your neighborhood. There is a very high correlation coefficient. Clearly the Redskin games are causing leaves to fall. Washington Nationals baseball brings the leaves back, a subject to be covered in later research reports. This is an example of "spurious correlation" where two unrelated trends lead researchers to conclude there is causation between them.

A great example of spurious correlation is provided by Steven F. Hayward at American

Enterprise Institute.[25] *Rolling Stone* magazine provides a listing of the 500 greatest rock songs of all time. A frequency distribution by year shows the greatest number of additions to the song list occurring in the years from 1964 to 1970, when the annual additions begin to drop off steadily. The plot of that curve very closely resembles the curve of U.S. crude oil field production, which peaked in November 1970 and dropped off steadily. As statisticians would say, there is a very high correlation coefficient. Therefore, the decline in rock music quality was obviously the cause of the decline in crude production. Or was it the other way around?

The MIT researchers utilized the identical model assumptions adopted by Du and Hayes to "prove" that increasing ethanol production resulted in a decrease in natural gas prices and an increase in unemployment. Obviously, there was no connection between these wholly unrelated variables. To underscore the absurdity, Knittel and Smith were able to demonstrate "proof" that increasing ethanol production caused an author's small child to age 26 days for each extra million gallons of ethanol produced.[26] That also showed a high correlation.

It is interesting to note that the Iowa State University CARD study utilized the same discredited modeling methodology[27] that EPA used in its "extensive analysis" to reject RFS waiver requests filed by the governor of Texas in 2008 and by various other state governors in 2012.[28] According to EPA, widespread usage of ethanol actually lowers the price of retail fuel. So naturally, it stands to reason that if a consumer were to use more ethanol in their fuel blend, the savings would be even higher than for consumers using only a 10% ethanol blend.

Not surprisingly, EPA can't seem to get its story straight. If one references the "Fuel Economy" website jointly maintained by EPA and DoE, one would readily observe that precisely the opposite is the case. Flexible fuel vehicles using E85 blends would cost motorists between $500 and $550 more per year than identical cars that use conventional gasoline.[29] Presumably EPA can't buffalo the numbers when it needs to go public with a numerical determination in conjunction with a sister agency. By all means, boost your usage of ethanol to see if it really lowers your fuel bills.

The next time you see a bus roll by bearing an ad from RFA proclaiming that ethanol saved consumers $1.09 a gallon on fuel costs in 2011, just laugh derisively.[30] Because the truth is that ethanol was actually causing gasoline prices to rise, not fall.[31]

ANOTHER METHOD TO TEST THE CLAIM

Non-academic researchers and even curious readers who endeavor to probe further might find the research papers described above to be confusing and even a bit beyond their range. Peer-reviewed papers tend to be steeped in complex statistical analysis and freighted with impenetrable academic jargon. The good news is that we don't need to take refresher courses in graduate-level mathematics to prove that ethanol actually drives fuel prices higher.

The New York Mercantile Exchange price for unleaded gasoline on August 13, 2012 was $2.99 per gallon.[32] During the same week, ethanol prices averaged $2.55 per gallon in major producing regions of the Midwest.[33] With an average $0.205 per gallon as a low-side estimate for the cost of rail tank car delivery to blending racks,[34] that amounts to a price of $2.755 per gallon of ethanol delivered to the blend rack. But ethanol is only 66% as energetic as gasoline — we can only drive 66 miles for the same volume that would get us 100 miles using gasoline. So, on a mileage-equivalent basis, the delivered rack price of ethanol equated to $4.17 per gallon vs. about $2.99 for the gasoline into which it was being blended. That brought the blended fuel price to $3.11 per gallon vs. $2.99 for pure gasoline. Ethanol was adding about twelve cents per gallon at the pump.

Eleven months later, the situation was little changed. DoE's "Today in Energy" web page for July 19, 2013 showed unleaded gasoline at $3.11 per gallon while ethanol cost $2.50 per gallon in the Midwest.[35] Adding ethanol delivery charges of $0.205 per gallon and factoring its 66% energy ratio, the delivered ethanol price was $4.10 to the blend rack. It was undeniable. Ethanol was driving up the cost of fuel.

But readers do not need to rely upon the author's analysis of the relative prices between ethanol and gasoline. They can just retrieve the quarterly Clean Cities Alternative Fuel Price Report from Obama's DoE. There they can find a comparison between the cost of gasoline vs. E85, a mixture of 85% ethanol and 15% gasoline. On an energy-equivalent basis, ethanol cost $1.19 per gallon more than gasoline in January 2013.[36] In April 2013, the premium was $1.07 per gallon.[37] In July 2013, ethanol cost $0.92 more per gallon than gasoline.[38]

POLICY DISASTER ON STEROIDS

Another factor driving fuel prices higher concerns the regulatory mechanism put in place by the Energy Independence and Security Act of 2007 (EISA). That law established absurdly high mandated levels of ethanol. Those levels steadily increase each year. By 2013, they had exceeded the nation's capacity to absorb them. The spillover effect has driven up prices — and consumers are picking up the tab.

Each ethanol producer applies to EPA and receives a unique 38-digit Renewable Identification Number (RIN) for each gallon of biofuel they produce. RINs are the fraud-plagued compliance mechanism examined earlier. Blenders are required to purchase one of these RINs for every gallon of renewable fuel they use in their 10% ethanol blend to certify that they are in compliance. RINs can be traded as though they had intrinsic worth. Throughout 2011, RIN prices for fuel ethanol traded at around three cents per gallon.[39] But because the mandated amount of ethanol had soared past the nation's appetite to burn it, the price of a RIN that cost about five cents per gallon in 2012 soared 1,400% by March 2013 to over one dollar a gallon.[40] By mid-July, RIN prices had climbed even further to 2,740% above the level at the beginning of the year.[41] This RINsanity had become an EPA-created backdoor tax aimed at the wallets of American motorists.

EISA was enacted in a year when the U.S. consumed 142.7 billion gallons of gasoline.[42] Gasoline demand had been rising 1.5% per year in the ten years prior to 2007.[43] Central planners forecasted the trend to continue. So they naturally believed that larger ethanol volumes could easily be absorbed into blend pools.

But history didn't turn out the way our central planners in Washington had mandated. Imagine that. Between 2007 and 2012, gasoline demand declined by about 6.2%.[44] The U.S. only used about 133.5 billion gallons of gasoline in 2012.[45] EIA forecasted that 2013 demand would be a hair shy of 136 billion gallons, of which 122.6 billion would be composed of gasoline derived from crude oil refineries and 13.4 billion would come from ethanol producers.[46] But EISA mandates that blenders use 13.8 billion gallons of ethanol in 2013 and 14.4 billion gallons in 2014.[47] They would be obligated to purchase this same number of RIN credits even if ethanol producers can't produce and sell this much product. It is more RIN volume than motor fuel demand can accommodate.

Steadily declining gasoline demand had met with rapidly increasing ethanol blending mandates.[48] Fuel blenders have collided with the "blend wall" or more accurately, with the phony compliance mechanism put in place by EPA to sustain its biofuel policy.[49] The consequences are far-reaching. There was an excess of 2.6 billion RINs at the end of 2012, and yet the year saw 400 million more consumed than were supplied.[50] The deficit would grow to more than 1.35 billion in 2013 according to an analysis by the University of Missouri's Food and Agricultural Policy Research Institute.[51] Unless a policy reversal occurs, RIN prices will likely rise further as more ethanol is mandated in subsequent years.[52] As of mid-2013, RIN prices had soared to $1.40 per gallon.[53]

By mid-March 2013, retail gasoline prices had risen an average of 41 cents per gallon nationwide, or 12.5%, while crude oil prices over that same period of time had increased only about 1 percent.[54] Not only was expensive ethanol driving up the price of retail gasoline. But the ethanol compliance mechanism itself was also costing consumers needlessly as blenders were being forced to purchase wildly inflated RINs. The situation prompted Congressional hearings, producing calls to scrap the phony "market-based" system, calls that will likely be ignored by ethanol-promoting EPA and the Obama administration.[55] Even Obama's Department of Energy forecasted that the RIN bank, like the RFS2 program itself, will be completely bankrupt by 2014.[56] Analysis by *The Wall Street Journal* suggests the RIN mechanism alone adds 10 cents to the price of a gallon of gasoline.[57]

Rare bipartisan support to reverse or modify the most damaging aspects of the country's reckless biofuels policy had formed.[58] Hearings were held in July 2013 as a first step to drafting revisions to RFS2 mandates.[59] Amazingly, petroleum refiners in their second quarter earnings calls with investment analysts cited soaring compliance costs — expected to rise to $20 billion by the end of 2013 — indicating that the cost of RINs had become one of their largest operating costs.[60] Given the penalty structures in place by the EPA Borg, resistance is futile.[61] Don't hold your breath waiting for any bi-partisan legislative reversal to get past the Obama Berlin Wall. The delicious irony is that as gasoline demand falls while renewable fuel obligations increase along with RIN purchase requirements, refiners are increasingly being forced to export fuel to maintain compliance.[62] Remember, EISA is the law intended to boost energy independence. You need a deep sense of humor to endure the Obama years.

Not surprisingly, the RIN cost situation prompted RFA's Dinneen to weigh in with preposterous, self-contradictory claims that the RIN policy was not driving prices higher, a claim he reiterated at House hearing in July 2013 citing the discredited Du and Hayes study.[63] The renewable fuels lobbyist admitted in an editorial placed in friendly media that "the price of RINs rose dramatically" in March 2013.[64] And yet, he went on to claim that the soaring cost of "RINs are not raising America's gas prices."[65] But then later, Dinneen acknowledged that if the country would only adopt E15 — a 15% ethanol blend — that would create an additional 6.5 billion RINs, driving RIN prices back down."[66] So according to Dinneen, RIN prices are not driving up fuel prices, but if we blend 50% more ethanol, RIN prices and retail fuel prices that he says hadn't increased would promptly come back down. On the day Dinneen posted his comments, RBOB gasoline cost $2.78 per gallon while the delivered price of ethanol destined to blend terminals where it would be blended was priced at $4.06 per gallon on a BTU basis.[67] Yet, Dinneen says ethanol is not driving up the price of retail fuel. As Malthusian global warming hysteric Bill McKibben says, "do the math."

An even more insane version of this lopsided math will play out when and if cellulosic ethanol ever reaches commercial-scale fruition. EISA requires both corn-based and cellulosic ethanol to be blended. Corn-based ethanol has nearly reached its maximum mandated blend volume of 15 billion gallons. The law requires ever increasing amounts of non-existent cellulosic ethanol to also be blended such that, by 2022, an additional 16 billion gallons of that output must also be blended.[68] The 2022 ethanol mandate will total 31 billion gallons. Never mind that with gasoline consumption declining and maximum blend percentages of 10% for most cars models, the market in 2012 could only reluctantly accept 13.4 billion gallons of ethanol.[69] And never mind that, with his mighty magic wand, Obama has also mandated greatly improved Corporate Average Fuel Efficiency standards so that by 2025, new car fleets will need to double their fuel efficiency from today.[70] Much of that attainment will need to occur through fleet sales of plug-in electric cars that don't even use fuel blends. This will drive down demand for gasoline further, and thus the amount of ethanol required. But don't worry. Our brilliant central planners will figure it all out.

According to renewable fuels market analyst Maxx Chatsko, cellulosic biofuel refiner KiOR may realize revenue of $5.24 per gallon of cellulosic biofuel if it gets its production problems fixed.[71] That would not be due to intrinsic value of the output, but solely because of the lopsided compliance mechanism. The company would be able to earn as much as $2.00 per gallon in profit.[72] Included in this windfall is an expected RIN price of $2.36 per gallon, a staggering market imperfection for which motorists would ultimately pay the tab.[73] Compare that $2.00 per gallon profit number under EISA rules to the profit of seven cents a gallon that Exxon Mobil earned in 2011 on gasoline sales.[74] Even federal, state, and local governments, which squeezed motorists for an average of fifty cents a gallon in fuel excise taxes, didn't come close to this windfall.[75] The situation reminds historians of the Stamp Act imposed by the Parliament during the colonial era where the enforcement powers of the sovereign were used to force consumers to use its product or face crippling sanctions.[76] The EPA's ethanol scam is our modern Stamp Act.

Every time we "do the math" the picture gets uglier. As we saw earlier, the biofuel policy drives up the price of food.[77] Researchers at Texas A&M University found that Americans pay $40 billion per year more for food than they would if the ethanol mandate didn't exist.[78] And what was humanity's bountiful benefit from this extravagant waste of irreplaceable resources? The policy reduced global CO_2 emissions by 0.08%.[79] If that estimate is applied to the IPCC's mid-range twenty first century modeled temperature increase of 2.96 degrees Celsius, it would reduce atmospheric temperatures by less than 0.0024 degrees. Surely now we can proclaim victory in the fight against the apocalyptic, runaway, human-induced global warming.

On top of that, when per gallon cost factors derived from DoE's quarterly Clean Cities Alternative Fuel Price Report are applied to actual biofuel production volumes, the biofuel program cost motoring consumers $19.2 billion extra in fuel cost during 2013.[80] So when food and fuel price increases are lumped together, Americans paid a combined $59.2 billion extra for biofuels, which amounts to a reduction of 0.4% of GDP.[81] Using the CO_2 emission reduction estimate above, the abatement cost comes to $2,169.69 per metric ton.[82] With just 4.4% of global population, U.S. consumers pay 100% of that cost but enjoy only 4.4% of the climate benefit, such as it is. So with a "social cost of carbon" estimate of $5.00 per metric ton, our biofuel program imposes a cost on consumers 9,862 times greater than any climate benefit they or their distant progeny will ever derive. This is government policy working hard to improve the economy. It is also the math that climate hysterics like Al Gore and Bill McKibben effortlessly ignore.

Luckily we can always rely on mass media to help straighten out our understanding of these often confusing issues. *The New York Times* helpfully sorts out the puzzling economics of fuel prices. In 2006, "the newspaper of record" observed that higher oil prices had improved the climate for "substitute fuels that could make us less vulnerable to market forces."[83] The *Times* assured us that domestically-produced biofuels would insulate the country from global market forces and high prices. Motor fuel market pricing is obviously not exposed to forces of global competition. Just six years later, the same newspaper acknowledged that motor fuel is traded globally and that "if the United States were to import little oil because of a homegrown energy boom, Americans would still be vulnerable to global events that raise the price of oil."[84] Motor fuel market pricing is obviously exposed to forces of global competition. Does that clarify the situation now?

SECTION 7

IT'S YOUR FUTURE

CHAPTER 21

WHAT IS REALLY DRIVING THE ECONOMY

"The economic and employment contributions from U.S. unconventional oil and gas production are now being felt throughout the U.S. economy, increasing household incomes, boosting trade and contributing to a new increase in U.S. competitiveness ... Unconventional oil and gas activity increased disposable income by an average of $1,200 per U.S. household in 2012 ... the trade deficit will be reduced by more than $164 billion in 2020 ... More than 460,000 combined manufacturing jobs will be supported in 2020."[1]

AMERICA'S NEW ENERGY FUTURE, IHS

From his earliest recorded pronouncements on the subject of energy policy, Barack Obama has advocated for the substitution of fossil fuels for what he describes as twenty first century 'green energy' solutions. As a freshman Senator, Obama never hid his hostility to oil and gas. At a Governor's Ethanol Coalition held in Washington, DC in February 2006, Obama lashed out at the soon-to-be enacted Energy Policy Act of 2005 (EPAct), claiming it was woefully short of the measures needed to reduce dependence on imported oil. He wondered aloud:

The President's energy proposal would reduce our oil imports by 4.5 million barrels per day by 2025. Not only can we do better than that, we must do better than that if we hope to make a real dent in our oil dependency.[2]

Obama was referring to the provision in EPAct to displace petroleum with ethanol. He claimed that if America were to rely upon that program rather than a more aggressive biofuel program, the country would only be able to reduce oil imports by 4.5 million barrels per day (bpd).

Obama's mistaken belief was that America could eliminate the need for crude oil by using corn-based and other types of ethanol as he falsely implied Brazil had done to achieve energy independence. He reiterated this philosophy to an audience in Chicago in April 2006, claiming that:

> ... *one of the biggest contributors to our climate troubles and our energy dependence is oil, and so any plan for the future must drastically reduce our addiction to this dirty, dangerous, and ultimately finite source of energy.*[3]

Make no mistake. Obama wanted to reduce fossil fuel imports. But his plan was to substitute imported crude oil with domestically grown and produced biofuels. The other part of his program involved an intrusive federal government program of mandating fuel efficiency standards, flexible fueled vehicles, plug-in hybrid cars and of course, deployment of wind and solar power on every square inch of the American landscape. In the same Chicago speech, he proclaimed that:

> *With technology we have on the shelves right now and fuels we can grow right here in America, by 2025 we can reduce our oil imports by over 7.5 million barrels per day — an amount greater than all the oil we are expected to import from the entire Middle East.*[4]

FIGURE 21-1. **U.S. Net Petroleum Imports 2005 to 2013**

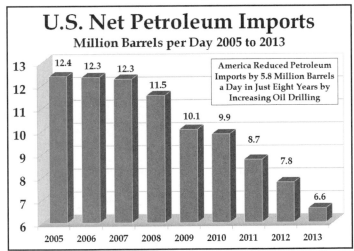

Source: Weekly U.S. Net Imports of Crude Oil and Petroleum Products (Thousand Barrels per Day), *Energy Information Administration*

Completely absent in the Obama remarks was any mention that America's oil and gas producers should utilize the "technology we have on the shelves right now" to boost production of the fossil fuels we actually need and use. No, the technology on the shelves that Obama was talking about was for things like cellulosic ethanol that was an epic failure even seven years after he promised us it was ready. And his plan called for more plug-in hybrid cars whose critical components are sourced exclusively from foreign suppliers. It also included wind turbines, 90% of which are produced by foreign-based companies and which have zero substitution impact upon oil supplies, as turbines are used exclusively for electricity generation, virtually 100% of which is derived in the U.S. from non-oil sources. These were the elements of the policy visionary's plan to achieve independence from foreign oil suppliers.

Rather than pinning their hopes on some hokey ethanol displacement program, America's oil companies stepped up their recovery of domestic oil and gas on private-ly-held lands. It would be domestic production of oil combined with a modest reduction in demand resulting from the economic recession instead of ethanol substitution and other 'green energy' deployments that would be responsible for driving down oil imports.

In Obama's view, it would take America twenty years, from 2005 to 2025, to reduce oil imports by 4.5 million barrels per day (bpd). But in truth, the country had already decreased its net imports of crude oil and petroleum products 5.8 million bpd by 2013 as Figure 21-1 indicates.[5] This chart shows the steady decline in net oil imports from 2005 to 2013. There were still twelve years to go to reach 2025 with every expectation that the country could achieve full oil independence long before 2025. America was on a path to achieve the outcome Obama envisioned but would be doing it without a shred of help from wind turbines, electric cars, solar panels, or cellulosic fuel ethanol, a far better outcome than the ridiculous Obama plan. By 2012, America had already achieved 77% of the goal of reducing oil imports of 7.5 million barrels a day by 2025. Oil and gas producers had drilled their way to this outcome.

AN UGLY PAGEANT OF BAD IDEAS

The likely collapse of the European Union in its original form is mostly due to the sovereign debt-driven insolvency of periphery countries — the PIIGS group of Portugal, Italy, Ireland, Greece and Spain. But without a shred of doubt, the high energy cost structures imposed upon EU countries by carbon capping, renewable energy portfolio standards, and the onerous feed-in tariffs upon which these mechanisms rely for their lifeblood have contributed greatly to the EU's overall economic deterioration. Those programs have driven away jobs, impaired economic growth, reduced disposable incomes, and destroyed prosperity. The deadweight that EU businesses and citizens must bear has helped to sap the region of its economic competitiveness, causing growth to slow to a crawl. The obvious knock-on effect is a lower level of income-based remittances to public treasuries, thereby exacerbating in a vicious cycle the sovereign debt problem.

Amazingly, the EU thinks it is only scratching the surface of the 'green energy' transition the region needs to make. Günther H. Oettinger, the European Commissioner for Energy is unequivocal. Two thirds of energy by 2050 "must" come from renewable sources and emissions "must" be reduced by 80% from today.[6] By 2050, this transition "must" be complete.[7] And how much will it cost? Investment just to build out the grid will require an estimated €1.5 to €2.2 trillion between 2011 and 2050.[8] That leaves aside construction of renewable energy production assets, standby capacity, energy storage infrastructure, and other essential components that will dwarf the amount required for grid build-out.

The Paris-based International Energy Agency (IEA) contends that the world would need to make $36 trillion in 'green energy' investments between today and 2050 if the we are to realize our goal of limiting atmospheric concentration of CO_2 to 450 parts per million.[9] But IEA triumphantly proclaims that these "investments" would return three dollars in fuel savings for every dollar invested in infrastructure, providing a positive rate of return even if future fuel savings are discounted at 10% per year.[10] This seems wildly optimistic given that there have been no net benefits thus far in any market where the 'green energy' future has been road-tested. A forecast prepared for the UK energy market indicates that generation costs would be 2.6 pence per kW higher and ratepayers would pay £320 billion more between 2012 and 2050 to meet the twin goals of decarbonization and renewable energy integration.[11] It is guaranteed that we would need to make the $36 trillion "investment" or something close to it. But the payoff at the back-end appears highly unlikely. Given our experience thus far, it is almost certainly unachievable.

The moral exhibitionist aspects of 'green energy' greatly appeal to European political sensibilities. EU officials assured their complacent populations enthralled with the idea of saving the planet through adoption of 'green energy' policies that the extra cost imposed by these programs would be minimal, no more than one latte per week they promised.[12] But an analysis by the economic consultancy Rhenish-Westphalia Institute (RWI) finds that the actual cost per kWh is closer to five Euro cents.[13] An increase of that magnitude in the U.S. would translate into a 56.3% surcharge on the average residential electricity bill.[14] That would drive the average household electricity bill in the U.S. higher by almost $744 per year.[15] At $14.31 a cup, that's some pricey latte.

The EU led the way for the world on renewable fuels mandates, with disastrous consequences. Likewise, the EU was the first political entity to impose a large-scale carbon cap-and-trade system.[16] The Emission Trading Scheme (ETS) began in 2005 and now encompasses 30 nations — the 27 member states of the EU plus Norway, Lichtenstein and Iceland.[17] The ETS is designed to put a price on CO_2 emissions by capping the amount that can be liberated into the atmosphere, which aims to drive up the price. The system thereby attempts to create an economic incentive to switch to non-carbon emitting energy sources.

But obviously, if that results in higher costs for lower-priced carbon-based energy, the ETS produces a kind of tax on energy usage. As a general rule, taxes are not usually considered to be inducements to economic growth except in extreme circles of opinion where appeals to reality are rigidly discouraged. Accordingly, cap-and-trade has never worked as intended. Instead of driving up the price of emission certificates, emissions prices have plummeted due to a severe decline in the economic activity that would otherwise promote energy use.

It is not difficult to understand why. During the year 2008, emission certificates were trading on the exchange for nearly €30 per metric ton.[18] But the global recession that began in 2009 along with the increased cost of energy from the EU's love affair with its 'green energy' schemes had reduced economic activity. Associated energy demand was driven down to such a low level that emission certificates regularly traded as low as €8 per metric ton in 2011, even reaching €7 by December of that year.[19] The downward spiral continued as the EU boosted the supply of certificates by selling an additional 300 million permits to raise more funds in order to subsidize — get ready for it — more 'green energy' programs.[20]

Hilariously, the declining cost of emission permits substantially boosted the economic appeal of emission-intensive coal power in Germany even while that country decommissioned eight emission-free nuclear power plants following the Fukushima disaster.[21] In 2012 alone, coal's share of total electricity generation in Germany had grown from 53% to 68% while in the UK, coal generation stations were operating at full capacity.[22] It was coal burning that the ETS was designed to eliminate. Instead, economic perversities resulted in precisely the opposite outcome.

The predictable response from the EU is to propose ever more Byzantine features in an effort to salvage its regulatory train wreck. Included in the list is a slowdown in the expansion of permit issuance and establishment of an ETS central bank to manage the "market."[23] The heroic efforts of EU climate policy apparatchiks to perfect the EU economic central planning reminds historians of the incongruities that Soviet central planners faced with their endless five-year plans as they attempted to perfect "scientific socialism."

Proponents of "carbon cap-and-trade" delude themselves that such a mechanism is a market-based system that aims to place a rational price on carbon emissions. In reality, cap-and-trade is merely a dense thicket of taxes and regulations tarted up to look like a market. To power providers and other emitters of CO_2, it looks a lot more like a tax than a market. Carbon emission "rights" can be auctioned to bidders, auctions of emission rights set the prices that are paid and these rights can subsequently be traded. Unelected monopsonistic bureaucratic mandarins control the supply of rights. Cronyism allows politicians to reward favored constituents at the expense of others, transmuting the system into a giant hyper-politicized cesspool of regulatory corruption. At its most basic, it is a costly, inefficient, hugely burdensome regulatory mechanism that results in a set of economic perversities that have become legendary.

Italian free-market think tank Istituto Bruno Leoni published a study in 2012 arguing in favor of a carbon tax as a replacement for the ridiculous, economically perverse ETS.[24] The study notes that the ETS system never worked as designed, allowed operators to capture windfall profits, resulted in a pass-through of costs onto the wallets of middle-class energy consumers, and had minimal impact on reducing carbon emissions.[25]

A carbon tax would merely slow the rate of descent into permanent competitive disadvantage rather than posing a real "solution" to the EU's economic woes. Carbon taxes would serve to drive up the price for energy. Since the extra cost would be collected by the government rather than by energy producers, it would offer no inducement to produce more supply. Higher energy prices would only serve to reduce consumption — and the economic activity that goes along with it. Ultimately, given the centrality of energy as the primary enabling input to economic growth, any scheme that imposes extra costs on energy will impair economic growth and retard its ability to compete. But a carbon tax would be far less destructive than a phony cap-and-trade scheme.

That should be small comfort to those who want the U.S. to succeed economically. Not surprisingly, rather than finding ways to reduce the federal government's disastrously bloated spending and budget deficit that is crowding out private sector economic activity, Obama favors imposition of a carbon tax.[26] Obama's solution to a situation that is depressing economic growth — deficits and spending that have produced the lowest period of sustained economic growth in U.S. post-war history[27] — is to enact a carbon tax that will impose even more damage on the fragile economy and further choke off America's potential to free itself from the economic stranglehold that his statist policies have caused.

The putative reason for imposing these schemes is to reduce CO_2 emissions that cause global warming. That's the warming that no one has been able to locate over the past seventeen years. But few Americans recognize the utter futility in this exercise. Carbon tax promoters claim that carbon taxes would provide an effective mechanism for controlling the amount of future global warming caused by atmospheric of greenhouse gases from fossil fuels.[28] That is a falsehood of the first order.[29] Even if the country were to completely eliminate every vestige of CO_2 emission for the rest of the twenty first century, it would only reduce the IPCC's mid-range temperature increase estimate of 2.96 degrees Celsius by a mere 0.17 degree.[30] There will be no meaningful global warming impact.

So all America will accomplish by imposing Obama's carbon taxes is to increase energy prices, fuel inflationary pressures, choke off economic growth, reduce industrial output, destroy jobs for American workers, transfer wealth from workers to an already bloated federal government, drive industry offshore, reduce the amount of personal income of American families, and lower our standard of living.[31] It is instructive to note that the two U.S. Senators pushing hardest for the scheme, Bernie Sanders of Vermont and Barbara Boxer of California, hail from the two states that have the lowest carbon intensity.[32] The carbon taxes they want to impose on the rest of the country would impact their states the least. It's also interesting that 18 of the 20 states worst hit by a carbon tax voted against Obama's reelection while 17 of the 20 states least impacted supported him.[33] As with proposals to bailout bankrupt blue states, this idea is merely a naked tax on vibrant red states designed to aid Obama-leaning economic basket-cases.

'Green energy' boosters pretend, as does Obama, that America must make a complete transition to 'green energy' sources over the next two decades, wildly contending that this can be done on the cheap.[34] Obama proclaims that "by 2035, 80% of America's electricity will come from clean energy sources."[35] They parade a study published in *Nature Climate Change* purporting to demonstrate that the average American would be willing to pay up to $162 per year to transition to 'green energy.'[36] That would entail devoting over $51 billion per year toward 'green energy' at the present U.S. population level.[37] Such an amount would have shaved almost one fourth of real economic growth off the anemic level logged in 2012.

But how enthusiastic would American taxpayers be to pay this staggering toll if they knew that the $48 billion in subsidies squandered mostly on 'green energy' investment since 2011 have had almost zero effect on CO_2 emissions?[38] One wonders how eager they would be to pay anything each year if the question were posed this way: How much extra money would you be willing to fork over each year on 'green energy' if those investments depressed economic growth, reduced job creation, impaired personal income and had practically no impact on the future trajectory of climate change? Because that is exactly what has taken place.

A National Academy of Sciences study was published in 2013 by a team of climate change economists headed by William Nordhaus of Yale University, the man who wrote the book on global warming economics. The team included some of the most prominent names in the field of academic research on climate change economics. Amazingly, they were unable to determine whether the mountain of 'green energy' subsidies shoveled out the door through U.S. tax policy thus far had even reduced greenhouse gases (GHG) by as much as a single CO_2 molecule.[39] According to the team, "the combined effect of current energy-sector tax expenditures on GHG emissions is very small and could be negative or positive."[40] In other words, for all the researchers could determine, it was entirely possible that 'green energy' subsidies may have actually led to an increase rather than a decrease in greenhouse gas emissions. Either way, the impact was so slight that the team essentially punted on trying to develop a measure. This is your federal tax dollar hard at work saving the planet from the depredations of job creation and economic growth.

More interestingly, the Nordhaus team concluded that federal subsidies forked over to the wind industry were, at best, able to reduce greenhouse gas emissions by only 0.3%.[41] That placed a price tag on CO_2 emission reduction at $250 per metric ton.[42] And that only included subsidies, not the massive extra system costs wind energy imposes. If the U.S. is to reduce emissions by 80% as the climate hysterics advocate, the annual tax subsidy cost alone would be $1.1 trillion.[43] That would reduce a moribund 2012 real GDP growth rate of positive 1.67% to a depression-level negative 6.7%. Remember, these are the hysterics who swear their 'green energy' ideas will be "cheap."[44] Does an annual net reduction of 8.4% in real GDP sound cheap? A reduction of that magnitude would drain $13,300 from median household income and throw twelve million workers out of their jobs. Never forget that the man Americans reelected in 2012 advocates getting started down this path post haste.

WHERE IS U.S. ECONOMIC GROWTH COMING FROM?

Few readers may be familiar with the minutiae of National Income and Product Accounts, the accounting methodology used by the U.S. Commerce Department's Bureau of Economic Analysis to compute gross domestic product and personal income statistics. But most understand implicitly that the economy benefits when it exports goods and services while it suffers when we import them. Each dollar of exports adds to GDP and each dollar of imports subtracts.

Sometime around 1943 as our wartime consumption of oil increased faster than domestic production, the U.S. became a net oil importer.[45] Net imports surpassed a billion barrels by 1973, the same year of the Arab oil embargo, growing steadily to hit a high point in 2005 of 3.68 billion barrels.[46] In 1958, the U.S. became a net importer of natural gas.[47] Consumption rapidly overtook production from that point forward by as much as 3.1 trillion cubic feet in 2002.[48] By 2007, the U.S. was net importing 3.8 trillion cubic feet of natural gas.[49] As oil and natural gas net imports grew, the U.S. economy suffered.

FIGURE 21-2. **U.S. Domestic Production Percentage of Oil and Gas Consumption**

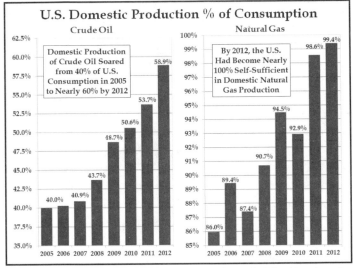

Source: Crude Oil Production, U.S. Product Supplied for Crude Oil and Petroleum Products, U.S. Natural Gas Marketed Production, Natural Gas Consumption by End Use, *Energy Information Administration*

But the trend of ever-increasing oil and natural gas net imports hit a peak in the middle of the last decade. American oil and gas producers expanded shale oil and natural gas recovery. Only 40% of crude oil consumption needs in 2005 were satisfied with domestic production.[50] By 2012, the U.S. produced 60% of its petroleum requirements as Figure 21-2 shows.[51] Based upon an average crude oil spot price during 2012 of $94.05 per barrel, imports displacement was worth $119.4 billion in aggregate economic benefit from improved global trade impact.

Likewise, U.S. production of natural gas rose from 86% of domestic consumption in 2005 to 99.4% by 2012.[52] This occurred even as natural gas consumption for energy increased, going from 21.7 trillion cubic feet (tcf) in 2006 to nearly 25.5 tcf in 2012.[53] Electric utilities were shutting coal-fired power plants and replacing the capacity with natural gas. Had domestic natural gas production held constant at the 2005 level of 18.9

tcf, the production shortage would have been more than 6.5 tcf in 2012. That shortage would have been covered by imports. Based upon average natural gas import prices of $2.86 per thousand cubic feet in 2012,[54] the value of avoided imports amounted to an $18.2 billion improvement in the trade balance.

The impact of more domestic production of oil and natural gas and its offsetting of imports had a pronounced positive effect on U.S. economic performance. Increased domestic crude oil production and natural gas yielded a trade balance improvement of $137.7 billion in 2012.[55] That contributed 0.9% to nominal GDP. Given that the Obama economy only managed to eke out a mere 1.67% real GDP during the year, enhanced oil and gas recovery accounted for far more than half of America's real economic growth.

By December of 2012, the U.S. Commerce Department reported an improvement in the nation's trade deficit to $38.5 billion, the lowest level in three years.[56] The quarterly trade balance improvement alone caused the preliminary estimate of fourth quarter real GDP to swing from a negative to a slight positive growth rate number.[57] Rarely do Americans get treated to a more hopeful sign — and a more stunning indictment of Obama policies — as it did with the posting of December 2012 trade balance data:

> *Petroleum exports rose 9% vs. November to a record $11.6 billion — up 1,056% from December 1999. Petroleum imports fell 11% to $30.3 billion and were down 21% from a year earlier, as greater U.S. energy output cut demand for foreign supplies. Hydraulic fracturing, or fracking, also has unlocked more natural gas, which is now more attractive to U.S. industry as a cheap energy source and chemical feedstock.*[58]

With the exception of one single month in 2006, America's trade deficit hit an all-time high in October of 2005 and has declined ever since.[59] Not coincidentally, October 2005 was the exact month when the country's net imports of oil hit an all-time high. By the end of 2013, net petroleum imports had fallen to 40% of their previous peak as domestic production soared.[60] Correspondingly, the country's overall balance of trade deficit had been cut almost in half.[61] These were the important economic achievements Obama was working overtime to reverse.

The foregoing numbers only reflect the favorable economic impact from trade balance improvement. They do not include the substantial domestic economic improvement resulting from increased discretionary spending resulting from lower oil and gas prices. Nor does it include the macroeconomic multiplier effect that results, where one extra dollar produced in the domestic economy becomes extra income to its recipient who spends a portion on something else, producing income to another recipient, who in turn creates income to other recipients, and so on. The effect magnifies the impact, producing much more economic growth than the initial dollar.

A good case for this is found in Texas which accounted for 734.8 million barrels of crude oil field production in 2012.[62] That was an 84% improvement from the 399 billion barrels produced as recently as 2009.[63] At $95 per barrel, the 2012 production generated about $80 billion in oil revenue to producers. The Texas oil industry employs as many as 400,000 workers at an average salary of $100,000 per worker, which totals $40 billion in wage-related earnings.[64] The majority of wages earned by those workers is spent in local communities, generating many times that amount of residual income.

If economic activity from domestic oil and gas production has a multiplier of only three — a low-ball estimate — you can multiply all of the numbers in the example above by a factor of at least three to arrive at a better estimate of the net beneficial impact from enhanced domestic oil and gas production. To illustrate the concept, labor market economist Timothy Considine estimates that each oil and gas job leads to the creation of at least four additional jobs elsewhere in the economy either in the energy industry supply chain or from the workers' wages being spent on goods and services.[65] There is good reason to believe the income multiplier may well be higher than three.

A 2011 study performed by PricewaterhouseCoopers (PwC) found that 4.18 jobs were created in the economy for each direct oil and gas job.[66] An earlier PwC study using 2004 data found the multiplier was 3.18.[67] A 2009 analysis prepared by IHS Global Insight found the multiplier was 4.54 jobs created for each direct oil and gas industry job.[68] A study performed by IHS CERA for the 2012 World Economic Forum found the employment multiplier for deepwater oil and gas drilling was 3.0 with $171,000 value added per direct worker employed.[69] For unconventional gas, the job multiplier was 3.2 with $218,000 of value added.[70] And for unconventional oil recovery, it was 4.1 jobs per direct job created with a value addition of $317,000 per direct oil industry worker.[71] Today we do lots more of the latter than in years previous.

An examination of the boom in economic activity taking place around Corpus Christi, Texas provides strong support for these claims. Corpus Christi serves as the focal point for activity from the nearby Eagle Ford shale play. Oil and gas production in the Eagle Ford alone generated an estimated $61 billion in economic activity supporting as many as 116,000 high-paying jobs.[72] But that is hardly the end of the story. Domestic and foreign direct investment funds are pouring into the region in the form of capital investment projects to take advantage of the raw material supply.

Austrian steelmaker Voestalpine abandoned expansion in the business-hostile 'green energy' paradise of the EU, deciding to open a $718 million iron ore reduction plant in the Corpus Christi area.[73] The company is unequivocal in its statement saying that low energy prices from abundant natural gas was the deciding factor in its decision.[74] The plant represents the largest foreign investment the $15 billion company has ever made. Company officials unapologetically admitted to reporters that "it would have been impossible to build a comparable plant in the European Union."[75] The finished product will be shipped back to Voeslalpine's European fabrication mill. The company's European and other global suppliers will follow since they will need to open or expand operations in the U.S. to remain competitive.[76]

Liquefied Natural Gas producer Cheniere Energy Partners will sink $10 billion of investment into a natural gas liquefaction plant on a 664 acre site in Corpus Christi.[77]

The LNG plant in Corpus Christi will join the plant at Sabine Pass as the second one of its kind to be built by Cheniere. Corpus Christi's export terminal will receive its natural gas volumes from the Eagle Ford shale deposits sixty miles away.[78] Another $10 billion LNG export terminal was approved by DoE at nearby Freeport on Quintana Island.[79]

Italian chemical company M&G Group is investing $900 million to build two chemical plants in Corpus Christi. One plant will produce a million tons per year of a plastic called polyethylene terephthalate (PET) used to make bottles.[80] The second plant will produce 1.2 million tons of purified terephthalic acid, a PET feedstock.[81] M&G will benefit from Corpus Christi's proximity to the Eagle Ford shale and will use a large flow of natural gas to produce ethylene, a main ingredient in PTA and PET.[82] The project will generate 800 new jobs.

China's Tianjin Pipe Company is building a $1 billion steel pipe plant in Corpus Christi that will be located next door to the Voestalpine iron reduction plant.[83] The steel pipe plant may purchase some of Voestalpine's output.[84] The plant will create hundreds of permanent jobs. Due to the upsurge in oil and gas drilling activity in the Eagle Ford, more steel pipe for wells and pipelines will be supplied by domestic production, offsetting demand for imported pipe. The plant will export some of its production adding additional economic benefit by improving the country's balance of trade and payments.

Occidental Chemical plans to construct an ethylene plant near Ingleside in San Patricio County, Texas. Once complete, the facility will be capable of producing 1.2 billion pounds of ethylene from natural gas feedstock delivered from the Eagle Ford wells.[85]

Linde North America, the U.S. subsidiary of German-based Linde AG, is pouring $200 million into a plant expansion project at its La Porte, Texas plant.[86] The company will add a gas separation unit to its synthetic gas plant located not far from the Eagle Ford mother lode. Company officials cite low prices for U.S. natural gas as the primary factor in the investment decision.[87]

While the value of oil produced in the Eagle Ford during 2012 was valued at about $15 billion, the actual economic impact is estimated to be more than four times this amount according to a study from the University of Texas at San Antonio.[88] The Eagle Ford will soon be producing more oil than OPEC member country Ecuador.[89] It is enjoying this bounty solely due to hydraulic fracturing, or fracking, an activity that the Obama administration did everything in his power to prevent by employing his overzealous "crucifiers" at EPA.[90] While the perpetually clueless Obama and his equally deluded leftist allies imagine that economic stimulus is something that emanates from deficit spending in Washington, the real economic stimulus is coming out of the ground in Texas, North Dakota, Pennsylvania, and dozens of other locations.[91]

Nearby Houston, the country's fourth largest city, is experiencing a similar bounty. Of the twenty largest metropolitan areas, Houston posted the fastest job growth in the twelve months prior to February 2013.[92] That's not surprising given Houston also had the fastest rate of economic growth in 2011.[93] Try to guess why. Was it Obama's 'green energy' that accounted for the boom — or the oil and gas business? If you thought Obama or his policies had anything to do with Houston's success, you've been on a holiday from reality for far too long.

In a stunning display of cynical opportunism, Obama made a series of highly publicized trips to the Lone Star State hoping to score a political payday on the back of robust job growth that has been attracted to the state as a result of its growing oil and gas production.[94] Rather than visiting the moribund, job-market wastelands of California, Illinois, Rhode Island, Nevada, and other failed "blue states" to tout his jobs-obliterating program, Obama chose Texas, the state best associated with the future he was doing everything in his power to destroy.[95] Texas Governor Rick Perry was on hand to greet the President's arrival and rub his nose in the 'brown energy' economic reality.[96] If you're thinking this is just idle polemics, consider the job market numbers. Between Obama's January 2009 inauguration day and July 2013, the Bureau of Labor Statistics (BLS) reported a nationwide increase of 2.1 million employed persons in the Household Survey.[97] Texas had accounted for 42.9% of those new jobs even though it comprised only 7.8% of total nationwide employment on Obama's inauguration day.[98] Texas had outpaced the rest of the nation in Household Survey job creation by a factor of better than eight-to-one.

FIGURE 21-3. **The Color of U.S. Employment Growth — 'Brown' vs. 'Green'**

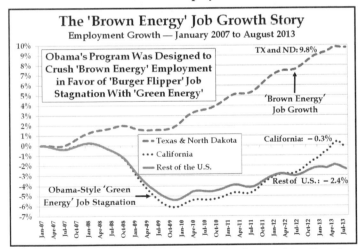

Source: Bureau of Labor Statistics, State employment data from Local Area Unemployment Data series

Another salient fact to consider is the quality of job creation that had occurred in Obama's 'green energy' graveyard compared to job creation in Texas. Between inauguration day 2009 and July 2013, the BLS Institutional Survey[99] showed a net increase of 1,705,000 jobs had been added to employers' payrolls throughout the entire country over that fifty four month period.[100] Texas accounted for the second-highest rate of job creation during that time with the highest rate being logged by the other oil and gas producing miracle state, North Dakota.[101] Nearly 56% of Obama's nationwide non-farm payroll job creation had occurred in the Leisure and Hospitality industries where the average weekly wage rate in July 2013 of $349.13 was just 42% of the national average.[102] Excluding the contribution from Texas, a total of only 1,107,500 non-farm payroll jobs had been created in the nation-wide Obama economy outside of Texas. Among those new jobs, an astounding 74.5% were in the low-wage Leisure and Hospitality industries.[103] Meanwhile, the tens of thousands of mining jobs that had been created in the Texas oil patch brought in weekly wages that were 56% higher than the national private-sector payroll average.[104] It was a clash between Rick Perry's high-wage 'brown energy' oil and gas drilling economy and Barack Obama's hourly-paid, starvation wage, burger-flipper economy brought to you with magic 'green energy.'

Figure 21-3 shows the undeniable pattern of employment growth in Texas and North Dakota compared to the job slump in the 'green energy' paradise state of California and in the rest of the nation. Employment grew 9.8% in Texas and North Dakota while declining in California and in the rest of the U.S. Put another way, the only reason the country has seen any net job creation since January 2007 can be explained solely by the employment activity in Texas and North Dakota.

If you want to understand how ideological pollution stunts normal cognitive function, examine the way the condescending liberal editors at the *USA Today* describe the Texas job growth story depicted in Figure 22-3. According to the towering intellects on the paper's editorial board:

> *Texas' economic performance is more of a mixed bag than a miracle. The state has seen nearly a million new jobs since the depths of the recession. But much of this growth is purely a function of its swelling population.*[105]

North Dakota's population had swelled also at nearly the same rate as in Texas. While it would never in a lifetime occur to the brain trust at the liberal paper, people were relocating to Texas and North Dakota to fill job openings. To the geniuses at *USA Today*, Texas population growth was just an accident, pure happenstance. Shucks, it could have happened to anybody. It's simply too difficult to wrap their heads around the concept of labor force mobility.

USA Today had probably taken its cue from Paul Krugman, chief commissar of ideological warfare at *The New York Times*, who had expressed a similar viewpoint a couple of years earlier. Krugman's goal by mischaracterizing the "Texas Unmiracle" as he called it was to short-circuit a challenge to Obama's reelection.[106] As with his less clever counterparts at *USA Today*, Krugman wildly claimed that jobs materialized after workers showed up rather than vice versa. "But what does population growth have to do with job growth? Well, the high rate of population growth translates into above-average job growth," claims the equally deluded columnist.

"The Texas miracle is a myth, and more broadly that Texan experience offers no useful lessons on how to restore national full employment," according to the polemicist who much prefers Obama's graveyard, job elimination story in California and elsewhere. Hilariously, Krugman concludes his farcical myth-making thusly: "So when Mr. Perry presents himself as the candidate who knows how to create jobs, don't believe him." That's right, believe Paul Krugman, not your lying eyes.

Consider the labor force dynamics of Texas and North Dakota collectively compared to that of the Obama "burger-flipper" economy at large. Between December 2008 and July 2013, North Dakota had seen a 7.7% increase in the number of employed workers while Texas had seen its own job rolls swell by 6.7%.[107] And how did the rest of the country do? The country had seen overall population growth of 10.7 million working-age adults, a 4.6% increase.[108] So, by Krugman-*USA Today* logic, it too should have seen robust job growth. Nevertheless, outside of North Dakota and Texas, the country saw employment growth of only 0.1%.[109] During this time, Texas and North Dakota had seen a combined increase in employed persons of 1,048,000.[110] But total job growth in the U.S. outside of Texas and North Dakota was only 132,600 in a labor force pool that was 10 times larger than the combined total of those two states.[111] Had the rest of the Obama 'burger flipper' economy kept pace with Texas and North Dakota, there would have been another 8.8 million jobs created in the U.S. You can think of the 8.8 million jobs that went missing as the opportunity cost of the Obama-Krugman-*USA Today* 'green energy' experiment. Supposedly all of this was just an accident. *USA Today* dismisses Rick Perry's self-promotion calling it "mildly amusing." The only thing amusing is how imbecilic liberals in the prestige media can be.

Obama's program involved massive economic "stimulus" spending on a vast array of dubious programs, subsidies to wind farm operators, fuel blending requirements benefitting ethanol producers, government contracts favoring crony 'green energy' entrepreneurs, warping markets to facilitate growth of solar power, cash payouts to buyers of electric cars, government "cash for clunkers" economic tinkering, wasteful tax credits, mandated levels of expensive 'green energy' production, taxpayer bailouts of electric car-building auto manufacturers, seed capital infusions to failing car battery makers, and a thousand other hands-on experiments in progressive industrial planning. The predictable result was a job market wasteland. Meanwhile, in Texas and North Dakota, they ignored the 'green energy' graveyard model and set about creating a high-growth economy built around producing oil and natural gas, a model that generated a million new jobs filled by a large migrating population of job seekers. The tragedy is that the last people on earth who will ever figure it out are big-government progressives like Barack Obama and their media enablers at *The New York Times* and *USA Today*.

Consider the relative rates of real economic growth that Texas and North Dakota have generated in recent years compared to the rest of the country. Between 2007 and 2012, Texas and North Dakota piled up much higher economic growth rates than the rest of the country. Growth has been higher in those two states in every year as Figure 21-4 clearly shows. Texas and North Dakota posted a compound annual growth rate of 3.1% compared to something less than 0.5% for the rest of the country.[112] Was this 6-to-1 economic growth rate advantage also a "mildly amusing" accident to the cognitively-impaired Obama water-carriers at *USA Today*?

It was way too much for the brain trust at *USA Today* and *The New York Times* to dial up income growth data at the Bureau of Economic Research. Had they done so, here's what they would have learned:

> *Midland, Texas was the fastest growing Municipal Statistical Area, in terms of personal income, for the third year in a row. Odessa, Texas, which grew 11.5 percent, was second fastest, as it was in 2011. For both MSAs, the mining industry, which includes oil and gas extraction, contributed more than any other industry to personal income growth. North Dakota's three MSAs were also among the fastest growing MSAs in the country in 2012.*[113]

FIGURE 21-4. **Real GDP Growth for Texas and North Dakota vs. the Rest of the U.S.**

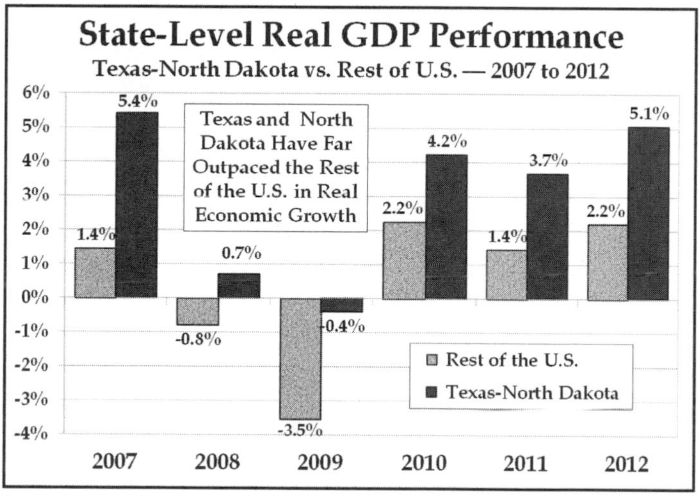

Source: Bureau of Economic Analysis, Regional Real GDP in 2005 Chained Dollars, 2007 to 2012

This "amusing" anecdote didn't come from some ill-mannered author. It came from BEA reporting on the economic benefits derived from the oil and gas industry, the one that Obama was trying to impede, the one *USA Today* says was an accident. It had been happening for years. And it was the news *USA Today* was trying to hide. Texas and North Dakota posted the highest rates of personal income growth among states in 2012.[114] Texas outpaced the national average by 38% and North Dakota by 254%. It was all just coincidence according to the Krugman-*USA Today* narrative.

Of course, Texas has its own share of market-distorting 'green energy' as evidenced by its massive physical plant of wind power. But that is largely for show, it contributes little in the way of usable energy, much of the real economic costs are shifted onto the backs of federal taxpayers all across the country through the Production Tax Credit and other distorting mechanisms, and its contribution to economic decline is overwhelmed by the oil and gas industry's beneficial impacts. In addition, Texas wind producers receive almost $400 million more per year in Production Tax Credit payments than the state's ratepayers are forced to fork over in 'green energy' subsidies.[115] If the disclaimer about Texas wind power sounds too harsh, don't take it from any book author. Take it from the Texas State Energy Conservation Office which proclaims that "For wind farms being installed today, the Production Tax Credit is still the main driver of economic viability."[116]

In other words, if it wasn't for your generosity as a federal taxpayer, there would be no wind power in Texas. Oil and gas consumers pay for Texas oil. Federal taxpayers all across the country — you and me — pay for their wind power. Nevertheless, with its solid "red state" sense of practicality, Texas won't voluntarily walk off California's suicidal 'green energy' economic gang plank.

So the comic aspect to this issue is that Barack Obama propounded a theory that America needed to embark upon a drastic program of replacing its main source of energy, fossil fuels, with 'green energy' sources that he claimed were not dirty or dangerous, were limitless in their abundance, and which would free the country from dependence upon foreign supplies. As we have seen, all of those contentions were completely unsupported. Obama based his entire political philosophy around doing everything in his power to delay, disrupt, forestall, impede, tax, and regulate out of existence domestic fossil fuel production. And yet it was that very domestic oil and gas production improvement that had provably accounted for every vestige — and probably a lot more — of the paltry amount of job-producing real economic growth that the U.S. economy had managed to achieve under his pitiful stewardship in 2012 and beyond.[117]

The Manhattan Institute estimates that the U.S. economy could capture as much as $5 trillion in economic benefit over the next two decades from enhanced oil and gas recovery.[118] At an annual rate of $250 billion of incremental economic activity, that would boost U.S. GDP by 1.6% per year.[119] This would effectively double U.S. economic growth from the dismal level compiled in 2012. Enhanced oil and gas recovery offered so much promise that some observers like Robert Levitt of Levitt Capital Management are actually forecasting an oil glut that will drive down Brent crude oil prices to $80 per barrel.[120] The average price for Brent North Sea crude was $111.63 per barrel in 2012.[121] So $80 Brent would entail a sizeable reduction.

Likewise, Citigroup forecasts that increased production could lead to a reduction in crude prices to between $70 to $90 per barrel by the end of the decade.[122] Citigroup compiled a list of more than thirty U.S. companies that are busy expanding domestic production operations in response to increasing oil and gas supply and lower domestic prices.[123] This factor provides strong anecdotal evidence that the U.S. economic benefit will extend far beyond trade balance improvement into generation of organic growth through macroeconomic multiplier effects. Citigroup also estimates that future oil demand and prices will be kept in check by a combination of fuel efficiency improvements and rapid switching in the U.S. and other countries from oil to natural gas.[124]

PwC estimates that shale oil could reduce oil prices by 25% to 40% by 2035.[125] The global advisory firm forecasts that shale oil and gas recovery will increase global GDP by 2.3% to 3.7% by 2035, an amount that equals $1.7 to $2.7 trillion of GDP at today's dollars. Interestingly, PwC's GDP forecasts are predicated solely upon the price reduction impact that enhanced oil and gas recovery will have. Their forecasts don't seem to account for the economic impact of offsetting energy imports or the induced income-multiplier impact, the effects of which are already being felt.

This view is also reflected in a report issued by the National Intelligence Council (NIC), a think tank that advises the U.S. Intelligence community:

A dramatic expansion of U.S. production could ... push global spare capacity to exceed 8 million barrels per day, at which point OPEC could lose price control and crude oil prices would drop, possibly sharply. Such a drop would take a heavy toll on many energy producers who are increasingly dependent on relatively high energy prices to balance their budgets.[126]

The NIC is not the only outfit forecasting rough sledding for OPEC. With the U.S. possessing resources equal to the entire world's proved reserves, with oil production levels soaring past every other global producer by mid-2013, and with the need for net oil imports forecasted to completely disappear in a few years, the time when OPEC could squeeze the economic genitalia of the U.S. is waning.[127] They'll need to look elsewhere.[128] As former Treasury official Roger Altman notes, the days of rogue regimes like Iran or Venezuela using oil as a weapon to destabilize the planet appear numbered.[129] Indeed, America had surpassed Saudi Arabia in total oil supply for three months in a row — November 2012 to January 2013 — becoming the world's largest oil supplier during that period.[130] The year 2013 saw the U.S. become the world's largest producer of oil and natural gas overtaking Russia and Saudi Arabia. This will continue for many years to come.

As a result, some observers forecast lower oil prices in the near future.[131] But these forecasts should be treated cautiously. China has already overcome the U.S. as the world's largest oil importing nation.[132] By the same token, China already consumes more coal than the combined total of all of the other nations in the world.[133] It also seeks to import ever larger amounts of natural gas. Press reports speak solely about soaring Chinese domestic petroleum demand growing out of new car sales to first-time car buyers in the country's rapidly expanding middle class.

China's substantial economic growth and its rapidly expanding middle class are boosting domestic demand for automobiles in a nation of 1.3 billion people, 95% of whom have never owned a car. China is already the largest producer of automobiles with a 16 million unit per year production output compared to only about 14.4 million units in the U.S. in 2012. While the U.S. production rate in the first half of 2013 jumped up to an annualized rate of 16 million units, it is unlikely to grow much beyond that level anytime soon if ever.[134] GM's Dan Akerson forecasts the Chinese market will reach 30 million units by the end of the decade.[135] Global auto sales may reach 100 million units by 2018 according to reliable forecasts.[136]

So petroleum demand could easily expand well beyond even the most bullish forecasts.

We may want to hold off popping champagne corks in celebration of anticipated oil price reductions. That may never come to pass. But we can begin celebrating the improvement in U.S. economic growth, nearly all of which will occur despite Obama's best efforts to prevent it. And no matter how you slice it, whether expanded U.S. oil production actually lowers oil prices or merely serves to forestall future price increases, the U.S. economy will benefit. This point is completely overlooked by most analysts.

Various observers point to the incontestable fact that increased domestic oil and gas production won't insulate the U.S. from oil price shocks.[137] Some obtuse observers even offer this fact as a lame excuse to avoid producing more of the essential product that, in its absence, we would be forced to import from global suppliers.[138] Most of these foreign oil suppliers are highly problematic to put it charitably. It is certainly accurate that oil prices are set by international supply and demand. But if oil prices spike globally, as we produce more output, the extra money U.S. consumers pay will flow to U.S. instead of foreign producers.

It is axiomatic. Money spent for domestic production has a much larger direct impact on gross domestic product than an equivalent spent on foreign supply. It also has a far more beneficial indirect income multiplier effect.[139] When we produce oil and gas, our money stays home where it belongs, benefitting American workers, savers, investors, and consumers.[140] And if global markets or political events cause prices to go higher, that will provide an incentive to domestic producers to supply even more domestic production. The effect of this will be to further lessen our dependence on foreign supply. Whether prices rise or fall is immaterial to the question of whether we should produce more domestic oil and natural gas. It goes without saying that higher production volumes will either lower prices or forestall higher prices that would otherwise have occurred in its absence. Only energy Luddites like Obama and his leftist allies who don't understand or believe in market dynamics attempt to argue otherwise.

Other observers point to the fact that the U.S. will still depend on large amounts of imported crude even if the country's domestic producers were able to supply volumes equivalent to 100% of domestic consumption.[141] This is because our domestic production cannot supply all of the various grades of crude required to match the specific needs of domestic refiners. This is likewise true but also completely beside the point. Again, some of these observers offer this as another lame excuse not to produce more domestic supply. Whether America supplies some, most, or all of specific grades of crude is again completely immaterial. It is total hydrocarbon supply and America's ability to satisfy its total BTU needs from domestic requirements that is the critical economic and national security concern.

CHAPTER 22

THE PHILOSOPHICAL BASIS
OF 'GREEN ENERGY'

"The environmental movement has lost its way, favoring political correctness over factual accuracy, stooping to scare tactics to garner support. Many campaigns now waged in the name of the environment would result in increased harm to both the environment and human welfare if they were to succeed.[1] The movement was captured by the left ... It's more about globalization and anti-capitalism than it is about science and ecology.[2] If we stopped using fossil fuel today, or by 2020 as Al Gore proposes, at least half the human population would perish and there wouldn't be a tree left on the planet within a year, as people struggled to find enough energy to stay alive ... By around the mid-1980s ... anti-establishment lifers adopt[ed] ever more extreme positions, eventually abandoning science and logic altogether in zero-tolerance policies ... I fear the irrational policies of extreme environmentalists far more than a warmer climate on this relatively cold planet.[3]

PATRICK MOORE
CO-FOUNDER, GREENPEACE

It is at least plausible — even probable — that the dreadful economic performance logged over the Obama years is no accident, that it represents a deliberate strategy borne out of a basic "deep green" hostility to economic growth itself. This view holds that resources are finite, air and water quality are bad and getting worse, rapacious cultivation is eroding irreplaceable fertile farmlands, species are going extinct at alarming rates, oceans are filling up with oil spills and garbage, forests are being clear-cut, the planet is heating up to dangerous levels, and pasture lands are being paved over. Unless we make an immediate about face they say, our inescapable fate is famine, resource wars, starvation, and death. To leftist doomsayers like Obama, the cause for this is economic growth.

This disreputable school of pessimistic thought can trace its origins back to British political theorist Thomas Malthus, whose six-volume tome entitled *An Essay on the Principle of Population* published in the late 1700s and early 1800s postulated the idea that population grows exponentially while food supply can only grow arithmetically. It is axiomatic from an computational standpoint. Given enough time, no matter the starting point, a geometric progression will always overtake an arithmetic growth curve. Sooner or later as Malthus taught, population outstrips the ability of man and land to keep the population fed, with widespread starvation the inevitable result.

Modern environmental philosophy is deeply influenced by these strains of belief, adapting and tarting it up in a new 'green' suit. Modern eco-Malthusian belief, to which Obama is a subscriber, contends that our present course is unsustainable, that the earth's resources will soon be exhausted, its ability to withstand environmental degradation has passed its physical limits, a changing climate will overwhelm our agricultural capabilities, billions will face starvation, and a breaking point will soon be reached.

For instance, we saw how improved farming methods produced higher crop yields without expanding area under cultivation. Improved methods and higher-density wheat strains allowed India to increase its harvest seven-fold from 1968 to 2006 using about the same amount of land.[4] Interestingly, 1968 was the year when Malthusian charlatan Paul Ehrlich, a Stanford University biologist, published his famous quackery *The Population Bomb* in which he professed to be "sickened" by the throngs of people crowded into New Delhi slums. He issued a doom-laden forecast contending that hundreds of millions would soon die from starvation:[5]

> *The battle to feed humanity is over. In the 1970s and 1980s hundreds of millions of people will starve to death in spite of any crash program embarked upon now. At this late date nothing can prevent a substantial increase in the world death rate.*[6]

Remember the Indian famine that claimed hundreds of millions of lives during the 1970s and 1980s? Neither does anyone else. In place of low-density farming that had often led to famine and malnourishment prior to the 1960s, Indian farmers applied modern techniques like improved wheat strains, pesticides, fertilizers and so forth to improve yields.

Ehrlich also forecast that his famine-induced mass die-off would be accompanied by a substantial collapse in living standards if population doubled by the year 2000. Author Robert Zubrin points out that Ehrlich might be forgiven for getting a future prediction wrong, but not for incorrectly predicting the past. If population growth leads to a decline in living standards, then the 1960s must have been poverty-stricken compared to the 1930s when the population was only half the amount in 1968.[7] But per capita income in the 1930s was only a fraction of what it would become in a more populous world three decades later:

> *It is this willingness to ignore readily available data, and continually make predictions on the basis of a theory that has been shown to be completely counterfactual, that defines Ehrlich and his fellow Malthusians as cranks.*[8]

That wasn't all that qualified Ehrlich to be considered a crank. He had advocated forced sterilization for poor women, putting contraceptives in the nation's water supply, luxury taxes on diapers and baby bottles to discourage births, outlawing internal combustion engines, eliminating long weekends to curtail holiday travel, and a variety of other bizarre measures.[9] Ehrlich supported expansionary government power to limit the number of children a family could have to control the population, saying "we must change public opinion in this country and through public opinion change the direction of government."[10]

To Ehrlich, more people meant more economic growth, more resource exploitation, more environmental damage and, a greater future ecological catastrophe. Ehrlich's ideal population was one billion. But given that there were 3.5 billion people on the planet in 1968 when he published his thoroughly discredited quackery, it was obvious the only possible paths to his target would be through draconian, coercive power over individuals or even global-scale genocide.

Ehrlich rejected proposals to put anti-fertility drugs into the water supply, not because it was monstrous to even consider but because, to his regret, he concluded it was impractical. Obama and his environmental leftists are deeply influenced by these absurdist views. His appointment of long-time Ehrlich co-author colleague and Malthusian charlatan John Holdren as administration science czar is proof positive.[11]

Of course, Ehrlich could have easily acquainted himself with the inexorable trends of history, incontestable facts readily available to researchers with even the mildest degree of intellectual curiosity. In a lengthy 1997 magazine column, author Ed Regis shows that:

In the United States, for example, between 1800 and 1980, the price of wheat plummeted while the population grew from 5 million to 226 million. According to Malthus, all those people should have been long dead, the country reduced to a handful of fur trappers on the brink of starvation. In fact, there was a booming and flourishing populace, one that was better-fed, taller, healthier, more disease-free, with far less infant mortality and longer life expectancy than ever before in human history. Obesity, not starvation, was the major American food problem in 1980. Those were the facts.[12]

Those were the facts in 1980 and they still are today. Yet they are inconsequential to doomsters like Ehrlich, or John Holdren, or Barack Obama. The first Earth Day in 1970 became a festival for eco-catastrophists proclaiming imminent societal collapse. In honor of this annual pagan ritual glorifying trees and insects with its obvious origins in ancient Druid culture, Paul Ehrlich was invited by *The Progressive* magazine to author some forecasts for the world. Ehrlich updated a 1969 article he had published entitled "Eco-Catastrophe" in which he forecasted that four billion people including 65 million Americans would soon die from starvation.[13] Surely you remember when that happened.

He outlined a comic book scenario where, in 1979, the Soviet government would release a dangerous pesticide into the ocean that would cause a massive algae bloom resulting in widespread toxic contamination and death to coastal communities, propelling

China to invade Russia leading to thermonuclear World War III. Though the man had taken complete leave of his sanity, it never interfered with his celebrity.

Using his typical wrist-slitting, fear-mongering monotony, Ehrlich wrote that:

Most of the people who are going to die in the greatest cataclysm in the history of man have already been born. More than three and a half billion people already populate our moribund globe, and about half of them are hungry. Some 10 to 20 million will starve to death this year.[14]

Ehrlich offered to his readership plague, thermonuclear war and famine as "death rate solutions to the population problem." Eco-Malthusian pessimists cheered. President Jimmy Carter eagerly sought out his sage advice. Despite having made a laughingstock of himself over the years, Ehrlich never altered his views. After having been spectacularly wrong about impending human catastrophe in his 1968 book, Ehrlich and his charlatan wife updated their screed in 1990 with *The Population Explosion* which predictably recycled the same discredited nonsense.[15]

Centuries of evidence demonstrates unequivocally that human population growth has led to a substantial improvement in living standards along with gradual reductions in the prices paid for basic resources that they claim would soon be depleted.[16] In essence, population growth itself is a victory over early mortality as human longevity has doubled since the dawn of the Industrial Age. It is astonishing how much currency Malthusian pessimism has gained among "enlightened" thinkers of the intelligentsia who, out of cognitive limitations, intellectual dishonesty, laziness, or dreadful ignorance, are able to turn a blind eye to the incontestable verdict of history.[17] Like some sort of reverse Cassandra curse, the Greek goddess who was fated always to being right but never heeded, Malthusians like the foregoing are seemingly always heeded but are never right.[18]

"The ultimate resource — the one thing we'll never run out of is imbeciles" intoned Paul Ehrlich, speaking in his typically vicious manner in Washington, DC on Earth Day 1990 about economist Julian Simon who had authored a book years earlier entitled *The Ultimate Resource*.[19] Simon's work completely debunked Ehrlich's Malthusian thesis.[20] Who should know better about a surplus of imbeciles than Ehrlich? He was leader of the pack. Simon was the University of Maryland economist who, more than any individual, had by his indisputable academic research and highly public wager, discredited Ehrlich in the eyes of history for all time.[21] Or at least he should have.

Ehrlich was asked by a hagiographical British interviewer in 1971 if there was anything in the world that could shake him from his bombastic pessimism. Hilariously, Ehrlich replied that "I'll be only too happy to switch to optimism when somebody shows me the numbers that can make me optimistic. Until then, I'll go on saying that, at the moment, things look very pessimistic."[22] Simon showed him the numbers. In 1980, the two men even placed a ten year wager about future resource prices.[23] Ten years later, despite the world's population having grown 28% over the previous decade, the shamed and disgraced Ehrlich was forced to pay off the bet. That was in 1990, the same year Ehrlich was sliming the man who had humiliated him. History long ago rendered its verdict. And yet Ehrlich continued being an ever more spiteful pessimist right up to the present day.

The thin-skinned sore loser Ehrlich developed a life-long hatred for Simon, who he labeled "a fringe character," refusing to meet him in public or even shake his hand.[24] Ehrlich snidely remarked to a *Wall Street Journal* reporter in 1995 that "If Simon disappeared from the face of the Earth, that would be great for humanity."[25] Simon passed away in 1998 so Ehrlich would live to see his graceless wish granted. The wrong man passed and humanity was the worse for it.

Amazingly, when Ehrlich told his Earth Day 1990 audience of over 200,000 worshipers that their grandchildren would suffer from starvation and food riots, they applauded respectfully. Ehrlich's appearance had come 22 years after his ridiculous 1968 forecast that a billion people were supposedly to have already died from famine and starvation. By 1990, that mendacious imbecility was — or at least should have been — laughed out of polite company. Given that many more than half of those Earth Day 1990 adult attendees are grandparents today, the real danger to their grandchildren is obesity from over-abundance, not famine and food riots. You could ask Michelle Obama, if you can catch her in between her fabulous, self-indulgent foreign vacations.[26]

Yale University historian Paul Sabin wrote a 304 page book chronicling the Ehrlich-Simon wager.[27] Yet, in all those pages, Sabin never answers why such a discredited crackpot like Paul Ehrlich could continue to enjoy a stature among media and popular culture long after his sorry track record and easily debunked pronouncements should have served to disqualify him. That most of semi-literate media and popular culture were ideologically aligned with Ehrlich's worshipful Earth Day 1990 audience helps answer the unasked question.

As a tenured Stanford professor safely ensconced within the towering, impenetrable, hermetically sealed walls of academia where oxygen concentrations are dangerously low, brain wave flux densities are barely detectable, viewpoint diversity is punished, and reality is prohibited from intruding, Ehrlich fashioned a long career out of making bombastic predictions, each and every one of which has been discredited. Naturally therefore, within left wing circles, he is celebrated as a true visionary, showered with lucrative awards and honors, sought out repeatedly by shallow media for his advice, feted as a cultural icon, and lionized as an environmentalist hero of the ages.

London School of Economics author Kenneth Minogue eruditely described the mindset of those who push this strain of belief.[28] Minogue believed the academic environment made it "possible to combine theoretical pretension with comprehensive ineptitude" transforming the university into "a kind of adventure playground, carefully insulated from reality" which allowed it to "become the institutional base for civilizational self-hatred."[29] Clearly he had Ehrlich in mind. Tragically, Minogue passed away on a flight from the Galápagos Islands to Guayaquil in June 2013. Once again, the wrong man was taken from us.

If his Earth Day 1990 pronouncements sounded bizarre, consider Ehrlich's comments at Earth Day 1970. To a crowd of thousands of worshipers, he fearlessly predicted that "In ten years, all important animal life in the sea will be extinct. Large areas of coastline will have to be evacuated because of the stench of dead fish."[30] One year later at a speech to the British Institute for Biology, he insultingly predicted that "By the year 2000 the United Kingdom will be simply a small group of impoverished islands, inhabited by some 70 million hungry people of little or no concern to the other five to seven billion inhabitants of a sick world ... If I were a gambler, I would take even money that England will not exist in the year 2000."[31]

Ehrlich was or would soon be a gambler, and his only real wager humiliated him, discrediting his odious philosophy unto eternity. Yet his pronouncements were lauded with effusive praise by the editor of *New Scientist*, the wacky leftist rag that pretends to cover science issues forthrightly from a public policy standpoint.[32] Just two years earlier, Ehrlich had told a London audience that the country would soon suffer thermonuclear war, ecological catastrophe, global plague, crippling levels of pollution, overwhelming population growth, and the collapse of the country.[33] People like these are the architects of our gloomy, eco-pessimistic, Malthusian future that adherents like Obama tell us we're supposed to follow obediently.

Such Malthusian fear-mongering was a staple of the 1960s and 70s. A group of Nobel laureates and other population control freaks calling themselves the Campaign to Check the Population Explosion ran full-page advertisements in *The New York Times* during the Johnson administration days telling readers that "the population bomb threatens the peace of the world," hectoring readers to cut out the ad and mail it to Washington.

The *Times* ran a page one feature in 1977 entitled "World's Deserts Are Growing By 14 Million Acres a Year."[34] The claim turned out to be based upon a book written by Erik Eckholm from a Washington-based outfit called Worldwatch Institute, a crackpot non-profit group founded by a notorious doom-peddling crank named Lester Brown. Eckholm's claim was later debunked.

Newsweek reported in August 1977 that "more than 100,000 West Africans had perished of hunger" in the Sahel region.[35] That phony report was sourced back to a flim-flam broadcast by a former Nazi SS officer, the disgraced UN Secretary General Kurt Waldheim.[36]

Just two years earlier, *Newsweek* had assured its readership that:

There are ominous signs that the earth's weather patterns have begun to change dramatically and that these changes may portend a drastic decline in food production — with serious political implications for just about every nation on earth.[37]

While these lines closely resemble the global warming eco-catastrophe rhetoric of today, this *Newsweek* report was warning readers about a global cooling that would endanger the planet and its food supply. The cause of *Newsweek*'s impending catastrophe was human fossil fuel burning.

Interior Department science analyst Indur Goklany noted in a 2007 column in *The New York Times* that the percentage of people in the developing world suffering from chronic hunger declined from 37% to 17% between 1970 and 2001.[38] But over those years, the world's population had increased by 83%.[39] This is a devastating indictment of Malthusian belief. And yet a few years later, *The New York Times* warned readers that "the rapid growth in farm output … has slowed to the point that it is failing to keep up with the demand for food, driven by population increases and rising affluence in once-poor countries."[40] The problem was that this last report came from a doom-laden series authored by staff reporter Justin Gillis in June of 2011. Obviously Gillis, the *Times*' resident Malthusian crank, doesn't bother reading *The New York Times*.

With a nod to Ehrlich's laughable 1990 book, a University of Michigan researcher claimed to be surprised at findings in a 2011 peer-reviewed paper in the scholarly journal *Demography*, noting:

> *… the world really did have a population explosion, that we are well through the worst of it, and that we have made it through in remarkably good shape, with increased per capita food production, declines in commodity prices during the period of most rapid growth, and declining rates of poverty.*[41]

Academic researchers assailing the canonical left-liberal orthodoxy with incontestable truths are obligated to affect surprise — or was it regret? — for publishing such revelations. All of these achievements would have been impossible if there was a shred of credibility in the doom-laden eco-Malthusian hysteria driving today's 'green energy' mindset.

PROGRESSIVE NIGHTMARES: POPULATION AND GROWTH

To progressives, humanity is merely a blight to be scrubbed from the face of the planet. Consider a quote from biologist David Graber with the U.S. Park Service, who said: "Until such time as *homo sapiens* should decide to return to nature, some of us can only hope for the right virus to come along."[42] He longs for the day when hundreds of millions or even billions of people die from horrific illness.

Former chief scientist for the Environmental Defense Fund Charles Wurster was asked if he believed that the ban on DDT he championed had caused tens of millions of people in poor countries to die from the malaria that DDT helped prevent. He replied, "Probably. So what? People are the cause of all the problems. We have too many of them. We need to get rid of some of them, and (malaria) is as good a way as any."[43]

William Aiken, writing in a 1984 book of essays called *Earthbound*, claimed that "massive human diebacks would be good. It is our duty to cause them. It is our species' duty, relative to the whole, to eliminate 90 percent of our numbers."[44] Jacques Cousteau told a UNESCO interviewer in 1991 that 350,000 people needed to die every day.[45] Writing from Landsberg Prison in 1924, an obscure Austrian author during the previous century had advanced similar ideas — he called it *lebensraum*, the German word for living space. Graber, Wurster, Aiken, Cousteau and their ilk find themselves in peculiar company.

Greenpeace founder Patrick Moore reflected upon his own mindset in the early days of his organization, recollecting that "I got the impression that instead of going out to shoot birds, I should go out and shoot kids who shoot birds."[46] Moore claims that, by the middle of the 1980s, the environmental movement had accomplished the majority of its earlier goals. To maintain relevance, environmentalism needed to go off the deep end, adopting ever more extreme tactics and viewpoints. "What happened is environmental extremism. They've abandoned science and logic altogether," explains Moore.[47]

Eco-Malthusian charlatan Paul Ehrlich flew all over the world making speeches, proclaiming that "Giving society cheap, abundant energy … would be the equivalent of giving an idiot child a machine gun."[48] Maurice Strong, who delivered the opening address at The United Nations Conference on Environment and Development in 1992 — the Rio Earth Summit as it is often called — proudly posed a rhetorical question during a *BBC* interview in 1990, asking an interviewer "Isn't the only hope for the planet that the industrialized civilizations collapse? Isn't it our responsibility to bring that about?"[49]

In the late 1980s, leftist eco-agitprop outfit Greenpeace enlisted actress Meredith Baxter-Birney to appear in a public service TV spot warning of the threat of impending planetary resource exhaustion that could be averted by recycling. The camera panned to her TV family happily sorting garbage on their living room floor.[50] To environmentalists, humanity is a cancer, economic growth itself is the cause of our problems, garbage is an object of veneration, and its preservation is a celebratory environmental ritual. They are unabashed about saying so.

Leftist rag *New Scientist* proclaims that "personal carbon virtue and collective environmentalism are futile as long as our economic system is built on the assumption of growth."[51] Let's have a quick show of hands: how many of us think deeply about our personal carbon virtue?

In the same issue of *New Scientist*, the editors invited a list of eco-extremists to bolster the magazine's editorial viewpoint. Tim Jackson, advisor to the UK Sustainable Development Commission, tells us the very logic of the free-market is warped. He says "it is time to stop pretending that mindlessly chasing economic growth is compatible with sustainability."[52] In those same pages, Canadian environmental extremist David Suzuki, who advocates jailing politicians who don't share his climate hysteria,[53] argued that we can achieve more preferable negative economic growth rates by reducing our standard of living. To Suzuki, personal virtue involves emulating poverty-stricken Third World villagers by pursuing low-productivity agrarian lifestyles characterized by poverty, disease, hunger, suffering, destitution, and early death.[54]

Without acknowledging that it was economic growth itself that enabled a cleaner planet with healthier inhabitants, long-time environmental doomster Herman Daly claims that "as long as an economic system is based on chasing economic growth above all else, we are heading for environmental and economic disaster."[55] This is stunning for its degree of manic incomprehensibility. We should avoid economic growth because it might lead to economic decline. Daly speaks about the inevitable crash, the same one Malthus forecasted in 1786 would shortly arrive, the same one Ebenezer Scrooge parroted in the 1820s when he angrily refused pleas to help hungry Londoners "so as to reduce the surplus population,"[56] the same one Paul Ehrlich warned us in 1968 would shortly be on our doorstep, the one the insufferable nag Jimmy Carter scolded us about during the 1970s.

Claiming that the economy is "rapacious," James Gustave Speth, a co-founder of the infamous Natural Resources Defense Council, posits that it is "capitalism, with its overwhelming commitment to growth at all costs, its devolution of tremendous power to the corporate sector, and its blind faith in a market riddled with externalities" that is the real problem.[57] He scolds us for "our own pathetic capitulation to consumerism." In his book *The Bridge at the Edge of the World: Capitalism, the Environment, and Crossing from Crisis to Sustainability*, Speth wildly claims that the environment is far worse than decades ago, a blatantly counter-factual claim.[58] Every potential indicator tracked by EPA shows marked improvement in air and water quality.[59]

Of course, Speth and his clueless brethren have the story exactly backwards. It is 'green energy' and its support structure that is riddled with ruinous subsidies, cost shifting, and externalities. And it is poverty that is ecologically devastating while it is economic growth that results in a halt to rapacious exploitation. Don't think so? Go to the internet and dial up aerial images of the island of Hispaniola. The contrast is stunning. Haiti, mired in grinding poverty, is wholly denuded. The Dominican Republic, with a GDP eight times larger, is lush and green. As *The New York Times* columnist John Tierney observes, "the richer everyone gets, the greener the planet will be in the long run."[60] Peer-reviewed research verifies this. Findings published in the *Proceedings of the National Academy of Sciences* in 2006 show that when a country reaches a per capita GDP of $4,600, deforestation completely ceases.[61] Those findings, from Jesse Ausubel and his team at Rockefeller University, have never been refuted. The eco-hysterics crying about economic growth causing a collapse of living standards are delusional and have it exactly backwards.

Reading these inane, eco-extremist tomes is like being forced to attend a Calvinist convention where a steady succession of bible-thumping preachers admonish us in bitter vitriol to mend our ways or face the everlasting hellfire and damnation that surely awaits sinners like us who stray outside of the stringent environmentalist confines. Most sensible readers would prefer to be waterboarded than endure another page of the angry, negative, pessimistic drivel these authors spew forth.

In his book *The Shadows of Consumption: Consequences for the Global Environment*, author Peter Aauvergne points the finger of blame at cars, boats, refrigerators, meat, and fuel as proof of the ruinous economic growth that he says is destroying the planet.[62] All of these things need to be eliminated he argues. Ready to surrender your fridge? That's the thing that prevents food spoilage, the appliance that helps billions around the world avoid illness and death from food-borne pathogens, the device that allows doctors to keep on hand a ready supply of life-sustaining blood plasma, antibiotics, and insulin. Aauvergne says they're a nuisance and we need to get rid of them.

Perhaps best known in this genre of doom-and-gloom evangelizing is Al "Jazeera" Gore's *Earth in the Balance*, his laughable 1992 tome that heavily influenced Unabom perpetrator Ted Kaczynski. He was the madman who carried out an appalling yet all too predictable mail bombing rampage against university professors, research scientists, and others. Both he and Gore, in nearly verbatim prose, blamed these victims for despoiling the planet. A dog-eared, heavily underlined copy of Gore's insane manifesto was recovered in Kaczynski's mountain hovel.[63]

Economist Jeffrey Sachs argues in *Common Wealth: Economics for a Crowded Planet* that one of the primary dangers humanity faces is extreme poverty. He claims poverty can be solved through "sustainable development" which, of course, would mean limiting the very economic growth that could lift billions out of poverty.[64] Here we encounter Daly's manic theme, imagining we can improve economic growth by limiting economic growth. Eventually, we can all enjoy the fruits of grinding poverty the way Haitians do.

Kate Soper, a researcher at London Metropolitan University, is best known for her penetrating analysis of "alternative hedonism." Soper tells us that impending environmental catastrophe will require us to redefine our understanding of pleasure. She claims that "the good life" as she calls it — the one stuffed to the brim with personal carbon virtue — will require us to do away with "dull" creature comforts like "regular steaks, hot tubs, luxury cosmetics and easy foreign travel."[65] We need to train our minds to reject the sensory appeal of a juicy, sizzling sirloin steak. Soper mines a rich vein of eco-guilt with her attack on foreign travel.

There was a time in the recent past when fabulous leftist jet-setting glitterati would endlessly boast about their luxurious foreign trips. But no more. It has become unfashionable to cross a foreign frontier in an airplane, unless you're headed to a climate change conference, in which case it's okay. Image-conscious celebrities now sneak out of town to avoid the limelight. To maintain their air of respectability, the travel industry has created something called "eco-tourism" which permits affluent eco-hysterics — and those who wish to avoid receiving mail bombs from them — to go to all the world's most fabulous travel destinations and still brag to neighbors and friends without engendering the stigmatism attached to it.

Malthusian doomster Richard Heinberg is unabashed about predicting when economic growth will come to an end. It already has in his laughably absurd analysis. His 2011 tome *The End of Growth: Adapting to Our New Economic Reality* claimed that economic growth was impossible from 2010 onward because the planet had reached its physical resource limits:

The central assertion of this book is both simple and startling: Economic growth as we have known it is over and done with. *The "growth" we are talking about consists of the expansion of the overall size of the economy and of the quantities of energy and material things flowing through it ... There are now fundamental barriers to ongoing economic expansion, and the world is colliding with those barriers ... From now on, only* relative growth *is possible; the global economy is playing a zero-sum game, with an ever-shrinking pot to be divided among winners* [emphasis in original].[66]

Ignore Heinberg's dreadful innumeracy. An "ever shrinking pot" would make it a negative-sum, not a zero-sum game. Unlike his smarter colleagues who are at least clever enough to avoid enumerating a precise timetable for the impending apocalypse, we didn't need to wait long to see Heinberg's thesis disproven.[67] It was wrong before the manuscript ink even dried based upon IMF and World Bank global GDP data. Observers like Heinberg view people merely as "consumers," which undoubtedly they are. But he never acknowledges that they are also "producers" who can and do act in their own self-interest to improve their circumstances and those of their offspring. This fact supplies the other half of the economic growth equation which he is incapable of understanding. This essential reality of people acting freely to improve their basic condition, rather than some vague notion about physical resource limits, is what causes economic growth. The U.S. consumed more primary energy in the year 2000 than in 2013.[68] Yet real GDP expanded by nearly 26% over that time.[69] That would have been impossible if Heinberg's thesis were even remotely accurate. These are the indisputable elements that are absent in Heinberg's Malthusian gloom as well as those of his cloistered, like-minded ideologues.

Like Heinberg, an angry and uncompromising environmental activist named David Brower took out a full-page ad in *The New York Times* in 1993 proclaiming that "Economics is a form of brain damage."[70] Brower was proudly repeating a call to arms issued by a progressive theorist named Hazel Henderson who had advocated at the 1992 Rio Earth Summit for all of the economists in the world to be rounded up and put in political reeducation camps once her glorious environmental revolution, just over the horizon, was complete.[71] The coercive strain of anti-intellectualism of the progressive left has clearly not budged an inch beyond the infantile days of its earliest founders.

One of the most disturbing recent installments of the illiberal trend among eco-Malthusian cranks is the movement to force university endowments to divest their holdings in fossil fuel companies. The effort is spearheaded by Bill McKibben, America's second most prominent global warming hysteric. It is clear that divestment is merely a tactical approach to his much more basic objective, de-legitimizing our free enterprise system with oil companies the most visible symbols.[72] The ultimate goal is to bring about an end to individual freedom and economic growth. There is much McKibben doesn't tell his student audiences lest they recognize the intense strain of quackery in his eco-doom philosophy. But his writings, and those of his ideological soul mate Naomi Klein with whom he is in league in their divestment campaign, explain in unmistakable detail exactly what it is they are advocating.

McKibben, a scholar at Middlebury College, believes the entirety of modern industrial society can ultimately be transformed to resemble the quaint, leafy, tree-lined Vermont college town where he lives. All of the food consumed and everything used in daily life would need to be produced locally using manual labor rather than mechanization. Klein and McKibben advocate reversion of modern, fossil fuel-based industrial society into primitive, manual-laboring, communal, agrarian village life of pre-industrial peasantry reminiscent of life in the 1400s.[73] McKibben doesn't advertise this in his campus appearances. But his writings make it clear this is his plan.

In the instances where the McKibben-Klein plan has been put into action, the results have not been encouraging. The Soviets attempted a forced collectivization along the McKibben-Klein lines in the early 1930s. The result was starvation death of 30 million people. In the late 1950s, Mao Zedong launched his Great Leap Forward where bizarre Maoist agricultural theories were forcibly put into place. Klein's agriculture ideas remind the careful historian of Mao's theories that predated hers by six decades. Famine was so severe that widespread cannibalism in rural areas of the country became commonplace. The Mao-McKibben-Klein plan left 30 million Chinese people dead of starvation within just a few years.[74]

Two decades later, Pol Pot advocated a program similar to the one advanced by McKibben and Klein. Following the fall of the Lon Nol government in 1975, Khmer Rouge forces were able to put their plan into action.[75] Naomi Klein and McKibben, like the Khmer Rouge before them, want private transportation to be confiscated and all food to be produced locally. Cities would need to be de-populated with citizens force-marched into rural agricultural collectives, exactly as advocated by Pol Pot's intellectual mentor Khieu Samphan in his blueprint *Cambodia's Economy and Industrial Development*, which he authored as a student radical in Paris in 1959.[76]

Within weeks of seizing power, the Khmer Rouge force-marched the residents of Phnom Penh out of the city at gun point into hastily organized rural agrarian collectives and political reeducation camps. Those who failed to comply were summarily executed. Three years later, three million Cambodians in a country of only eight million people had been starved, brutalized, and systematically slaughtered.[77] This is exactly how McKibben's and Klein's vision for post-industrial America would end. Authoritarian utopias always end in bloodshed and genocide. It's a tragedy that the college students who have rallied to McKibben's side are so detached from reality, so alienated from actually reading the books authored by those whose ideology they claim to support, that they fail to understand what motivates these doom-laden, apocalyptic ideologies.

Like Stalin, Mao, or Pol Pot, McKibben and Klein don't really care about oil, energy, food, communal life, rural collectives, or even the climate. Klein brazenly admits as much.[78] Climate change remediation is just a convenient means to their ultimate objective. Her provocative 2011 essay "Capitalism vs. Climate" in *The Nation* clearly articulates that global warming is just a stalking horse for seizing control of the levers of political power.[79] As with the Khmer Rouge, they want control over your lives and livelihoods. And exactly like the Khmer Rouge, they favor coercive means by heavy-handed government to achieve it. As the joke goes, progressives don't really care what the policy is as long it's mandatory.

Klein pretends that with respect to her forced agrarian collectivist utopia, "We are not talking about a return to authoritarian socialism, after all, but a turn toward real democracy."[80] It is the same concept of democracy championed by Mao Zedong whose bizarre theories closely resemble those of Klein. Massive starvation that piled up sixty or seventy million corpses during the twentieth century was the bitter harvest of Klein's "real democracy." Columnist H.L. Mencken observed long ago that "the urge to save humanity is almost always a false front for the urge to rule."[81] Mencken would have needed no introduction to McKibben or Klein.

CLIMATISM AS RELIGION

French philosopher Pascal Bruckner finds interesting parallels between the religious zealotry of an earlier age and today's apocalyptic environmental neo-asceticism that attempts to frighten us into submission. His 2011 French language book entitled *The Fanaticism of the Apocalypse: Save the Earth, Punish Human Beings* was translated into English in 2013.[82] According to Bruckner, at the turn of the twenty first century following the collapse of Soviet-style collectivism, the era of perpetual revolution gave way to an era of doom-laden apocalypse.[83] Disappointed elite opinion leaders that had long fancied the inevitable triumph of the Soviet model were reluctantly forced to switch focus after the collapse of the Soviet system. In response, they fashioned a spiritualistic, quasi-religious philosophy of pessimism. It was one where its supposedly clear-headed exponents are able to envision the undeniable cataclysmic future that the rest of us, incomprehensibly vegetating in our darkened ignorance, lack the intellectual prowess to understand. The root of that imagined cataclysm is humanity, with its rapacious impact upon the planet.

The parallels between eco-doom and fundamentalist religiosity are striking. The quasi-religious nature of climatism is manifest across a broad spectrum of practices and beliefs.[84] There is a fervent sack-cloth-and-ashes set of pessimistic warnings about impending doom. The faithful are required to adopt a doctrinaire adherence to an enforced orthodoxy of unchallengeable revelation. They insist upon an ecclesiastical conformity. Practitioners can attain grace through observance of holy rituals like recycling. There is even a calendar designation of an annual Earth Day of reverential worship. Guilt is attached to those leading resource-abundant lifestyles marked by big houses, SUVs, foreign travel, meat-eating and other sinful practices. Worshippers are obliged to genuflect toward an infallible epistemology built around resource sustainability. A supreme deity, Gaia, has been invented. The faithful lustily engage in hellfire-and-damnation demonizing of heretics as Holocaust "deniers." There is a preposterous industry devoted to selling indulgences called "carbon offsets" reminiscent of the Medieval practice that prompted

Martin Luther's protest against the Vatican. The faithful have erected a set of rigid strictures requiring adherents to maintain their core dogmatic acceptance in the increasingly
doubtful catechism despite accumulating contrary scientific evidence. They have elevated
climate "scientists" as the unassailable high priests of the faith. A popular cultural zeit-
geist of "climatism" has evolved as a penance to assuage guilt for leading privileged lives
marked by material abundance. Congregations of the faithful are encouraged to venerate
sacred idolatry like wind turbines and solar panels. There is coercive pressure exacted in
Galileo-style upon deviant researchers to recant their scientific heresies that undercut the
canonical basis of the sacred creed. And so on. For all their empty rhetoric about science,
it certainly seems like thirteenth century religious fundamentalism.

There is an inherent self-contradiction in the apocalyptic narrative according to
Bruckner. If there is a truth in the sheer scale of devastation from this impending cataclysm, how could such inconsequential activities like switching off air conditioners,
replacing a few light bulbs, keeping tires inflated, sorting through garbage on the living
room floor, bicycling to work or any of the other trivial "little rituals of a post-technolog-
ical animism" ever help us avert the cosmic catastrophe?[85] Clearly if this was all that was
required, it mustn't have been very serious to begin with. So the warnings offered by the
Cassandras of disaster are not meant "to prepare us so much as to condemn us."[86] Anger
and bitterness are the mother's milk that animates and sustains the gloom merchants.

Christian religion at least offers followers the forgiveness of sin and the promise of
eternal redemption. Eco-hysterical catastrophism is a one-way street offering only damnation. The West, inhabited by a cultural elite that is unapologetically disdainful of its
own material way of life, serves as no model for developing nations striving to achieve
economic growth and abundance that Western nations take for granted. Unless and
until this mindset is purged, we are unlikely ever to influence the course of events. All
of these deluded visionaries suffer from F.A. Hayek's "fatal conceit" which supposes that
the entire arc of human evolution, which proceeded along purely natural lines, can be
supplanted by unnatural central planning.[87] They imagine that humans accustomed to
making the endless minutiae of individual decisions that determine the course of their
own lives would willingly concede control to some morose, pessimistic, doctrinaire, central planning authority whose collective decision-making claims to have the wisdom to
produce superior outcomes. But history shows that utopian central planning leads to only
one possible outcome: mass murder. Graber, Wurster, Aiken, Cousteau, and their ilk are
only too happy to get it started.

The point of all this is that Obama finds himself in easy company with apostles of
the doom-laden apocalypse, the gospel of eco-pessimism that sustains their faith. There's
a much better than even chance that the dreadful economic growth we have experienced
during his reign, in perfect alignment with his eco-extremist fellow travelers, is precisely
the outcome he intended all along. As columnist Fred Barnes notes, Obama and his press
flaks may proclaim endlessly that their ultimate goal is robust economic growth, yet his
policies are designed to thwart it.[88]

From maintaining ruinous levels of government spending, to piling up soaring deficits and debt, to imposing a lengthening array of crippling mandates, to penalizing job creators, to imposing regulatory roadblocks against economically beneficial energy production and distribution, to subsidizing economic inefficiency by supporting inefficient sources of energy, to driving up the price of energy — everything he is doing is designed to win favor with the Malthusian left while undermining prospects for economic growth.

The aforementioned Herman Daly claims that:

After 200 years in a growth economy, it is hard to imagine what a steady-state economy might look like, but it does not have to mean freezing in the dark under a communist tyranny.[89]

This is exactly what it must look like if his vision is to be realized. Though it will never in a thousand lifetimes occur to eco-hysterical lefties like Daly, there is no deliberate strategy of "chasing economic growth above all else" as he describes it. Growth is not a deliberate, planned, pre-ordained product of an "economic system" as he mindlessly imagines it. Instead, growth results from the collective efforts of billions of individuals pursuing their own enlightened self-interest. To change that would require a deeply repressive regulatory regime that would resemble the former East Germany. It would be a place where economic activity is directed by the state, where travel requires a permit, where career choices are determined by a Party committee, where major purchases must be approved by a local apparatchik, where private property and capital accumulation are strictly *verboten*, where housing is assigned by government officials, where basic health and living conditions are a function of Party rank, where admission to choice schools and careers is decided by Party functionaries based upon family connections or ideological suitability, where food is scarce, and most importantly, where countervailing viewpoints about policies that maintain the orderly structure of the system are answered with a soft-nosed bullet to the brain pan.

We might not freeze to death in our homes the way nearly 8,000 Britons who can't afford to heat their flats do each year. But as with the multitudes in Erich Honecker's tyrannical East Germany, we will certainly be required to shiver in silence. And with the environmentalists in firm control of the *Vopos*, we can count on receiving a call from a jackboot-wearing leftist thug like Markus Wolfe if we should step out of line.

Are you thinking this is a stretch, just a wild exaggeration from an over-active imagination? Then take it from Tom Steyer, an ultra-wealthy California hedge fund manager who plans to spend his $1.4 billion fortune promoting the cause of climate alarmism. And how does he plan to overcome his opposition? In his own words, he says "the goal here is not to win. The goal here is to destroy these people. We want a smashing victory … they will be punished"[90] Amazingly, such is the tenor of the leftist smashmouth jihad against sensible energy that Steyer has even obliquely threatened Obama himself.[91] Just like the Soviet-enforced system with their bullet to the brain pan, the violence-prone environmental left seeks to "destroy these people" who counsel a sober approach. Whether it is mail bombs, Nuremberg-style show trials, or just social and career ostracism, you will be punished for your deviations from the approved orthodoxy.

Most well-meaning people think of deep environmentalists as just harmless, slightly eccentric people who care a little more about butterflies and squirrels than others do. The foregoing demonstrates this is a misconception. Nevertheless, regardless how effective their PR campaign, deep environmentalism is destined to remain marginalized among the broad swath of the public because its strictures of sack cloth and ashes are simply untenable to most people. These elites demand we eschew our acquisitive lifestyles, reduce our consumption to subsistence levels, surrender hopes that our children will enjoy more fruitful lives than our own, adopt their morose pessimism, move into densely-packed cities or rural collectives, forsake the convenience of our cars to crowd into public transport, discontinue using affordable, easily-obtainable energy, avoid the pleasure of travel in favor of vacationing at home, shiver quietly in the dark, eat only a small range of locally-grown, low-protein organic fruits and vegetables, relinquish national prerogatives to unelected trans-national bureaucrats — and of course, indoctrinate our rigidly-enforced single offspring in the dogmatic asceticism of green orthodoxy. Who's ready for that?

While campaigning for Barry Goldwater in 1964, Ronald Reagan gave a speech called "A Time for Change." He told a compelling story worth recounting:

> *Not too long ago, two friends of mine were talking to a Cuban refugee, a businessman who had escaped from Castro, and in the midst of his story one of my friends turned to the other and said, "We don't know how lucky we are." And the Cuban stopped and said, "How lucky you are? I had someplace to escape to." And in that sentence he told us the entire story. If we lose freedom here, there's no place to escape to. This is the last stand on earth.*[92]

Those lines sum up our dilemma — and our choice. If we choose to surrender our future and our liberty to the doom-laden, pessimistic 'green energy' social planners with their limitless conceits, boundless faith in government competence, hatred for humanity, ideological aversion to economic growth, and penchant for heavy-handed interventionist approaches, there will be nowhere to which we can escape. America is the world's last stand, Lincoln's last, best hope on Earth. We must not surrender to their utopian vision. We already know how it will end.

CONCLUSION

A BETTER PATH FORWARD

"Failure in the management of practical affairs seems to be a qualification for success in the management of public affairs."

ERIC HOFFER

"We have found it of paramount importance that in order to progress we must recognize our ignorance and leave room for doubt. Scientific knowledge is a body of statements of varying degrees of certainty — some most unsure, some nearly sure, but none absolutely certain."[1]

RICHARD P. FEYNMANN
ADDRESS TO THE NATIONAL ACADEMY OF SCIENCES, 1955

"The nations of the world may yet pay a dreadful price for the public behavior of scientists who depart from ... fact to indulge ... in hyperbole"[2]

PHILLIP HANDLER
PRESIDENT, NATIONAL ACADEMY OF SCIENCES
TESTIMONY TO CONGRESS, 1970

"Today's debate about global warming is essentially a debate about freedom. The environmentalists would like to mastermind each and every possible — and impossible — aspect of our lives."[3]

VACLAV KLAUS

Clearly the biggest challenge facing the country in its quest to adopt a rational approach toward energy policy is the degree of deference we seem obligated to accord to concerns about climate change. The earth's atmosphere has been gradually warming since about 1680.[4] Prior to this, the planet has undergone an incalculable number of warming and cooling climate cycles, all of which had causes rooted in natural physical events. For various reasons, a large body of thought posits a claim, usually expressed as an unshakeable certitude, that this gradual and completely ordinary atmospheric warming that began prior to the 1700s is solely due to increasing atmospheric emissions of CO_2 from fossil fuel burning, more than 80% of which were released after 1957.[5]

The UN Intergovernmental Panel on Climate Change (IPCC) is routinely invoked in press accounts and elsewhere as the final, authoritative voice for scientific certitudes regarding climate science in general, and humanity's influence on the climate in particular. Interestingly, the IPCC claimed in 2007 that it was about 90% certain that humanity is the chief culprit behind the 0.4°C planetary warming that took place since the mid-twentieth century. But they acknowledged that humanity did not cause the equivalent 0.4°C planetary warming that took place between 1910 and 1940.[6] It is difficult to deny that a certain amount of mania is required to maintain this position. It's like contending that the circumstances behind a man's carefree fall from the 80th to the 40th floor was unrelated to the events connected with his tragic descent from the 40th floor to the sidewalk.

There appears to be something of a popular psychosis among a large segment of the public that imagines the earth to be some sort of nature museum, a place that remains cemented into perpetual stasis except under malign influence of humanity. In this view, the planet's natural state is for Mother Earth, its species, its climate, and every other natural condition to be permanently locked into a perpetually unvarying state, delicately perched in absolute optimum conditions until everything gets irreparably upset by the evil influence of human industrialization.

Science can prove that CO_2 molecules in the atmosphere trap heat. But so do water vapor molecules, and atmospheric humidity traps far more heat than CO_2 because each molecule of water vapor traps heat more effectively than CO_2 and it comes in concentrations 50 to 200 times larger than CO_2 at any given moment. Virtually all of the atmospheric water vapor gets there through natural evaporation.[7]

The IPCC relies upon *global circulation models* to forecast the earth's climate changes over the next several centuries that will result from increasing concentrations of CO_2 as a result of deposition from fossil fuel combustion. All of the climate models the IPCC examines share a uniformity in at least one major respect. They posit what scientists refer to as "positive feedbacks" between CO_2 and water vapor.[8] What that means is that if some extra CO_2 enters the atmosphere, it traps extra heat. Most sensible people accept that proposition. It can be demonstrated experimentally in a laboratory and explained at a molecular level by reference to absorption and emission spectra of the CO_2 molecule. The climate models contend that extra heat in the atmosphere causes an increase in the evaporation of surface water, which increases the amount of atmospheric water vapor. This also seems reasonable even if the empirical data is contradictory and largely fails to validate that part of the theory.[9]

For instance, a 2012 study in the *Journal of Applied Meteorology and Climatology* of absolute humidity and dew point readings at 145 monitoring stations in the U.S. between 1930 and 2010 found a gradual increase in temperature over the period but absolutely no measureable change in humidity.[10] That finding coincided with an increase in observed

CO_2 concentration from about 310 parts per million (ppm) in 1930[11] to 386 parts ppm in 2010.[12] Such findings cast a shadow over the robustness of climate models at replicating climate dynamics. Irrespective of how that debate will ultimately be settled, IPCC's modelers contend that the extra water vapor can only act in one direction, increasing the overall heat trapping potential of the atmosphere primarily through significant, measureable, and permanent increases in atmospheric humidity. The IPCC contends that it is actually water vapor and not CO_2 that does the heavy lifting when it comes to greenhouse warming of the atmosphere.[13] That's the vast increase in the amount of heat-trapping water vapor that no one is able to locate.

According to the IPCC models, there is a "positive feedback" between CO_2 and H_2O, with one reinforcing the other.[14] They contend that the extra CO_2 captures heat which results in extra water vapor, which captures extra heat which evaporates more water, which captures more heat and so on in a spiraling manner. But many leading researchers like climatologists Roy Spencer and John Christy contend that increasing water vapor actually results in a "negative feedback" that reduces heat trapping properties of water vapor by increasing the amount of low elevation cloud cover.[15] It is well understood that low clouds reflect sunlight back into space, thus reducing the amount of atmospheric heat content.[16] There is a large and growing body of scientific evidence to support this contention.[17] In other words, the planet, just like the human body, has a self-correcting mechanism to balance and restore temperature equilibrium. Clearly the science is not settled.

INTELLECTUAL PARALYSIS

While the science may seem confusing, there is one aspect that is easy to understand. The IPCC, the organized climate science community, the mass media, and every segment of elite opinion has coalesced around consideration of only a single narrow viewpoint. This has occurred despite the presence of highly authoritative research that demonstrates very strong evidence that the IPCC models are unreliable and wrong in significant respects. Don't take that from me. You can refer to comments from the IPCC's lead climate science author Hans von Storch who spoke to the German periodical *Der Spiegel* in June 2013 about the then 16 year pause in global temperature increases:

> *If things continue as they have been, in five years at the latest, we will need to acknowledge that something is fundamentally wrong with our climate models. There are two conceivable explanations — and neither is very pleasant for us. The first possibility is that less global warming is occurring than expected. The other possibility is that, in our simulations, we have underestimated how much the climate fluctuates owing to natural causes.[18]*

Von Storch noted that only 2% of modeled outcomes permitted a 16-year hiatus in temperature increases and none permit a 20-year pause.[19] Put another way, there is more than a 98% certainty that the climate models are wrong. Those who hold to a singular explanation positing that we are in the midst of an unprecedented, runaway climate catastrophe have adopted an increasingly intolerant view toward any legitimate scientist who strays from the approved viewpoint. They routinely ignore science that does not support their preferred theory.[20] Outlandish claims by catastrophe purveyors within the climate science discipline have become commonplace.[21] They often earn rebukes from other climate catastrophists.[22] Psychotic ranting from media luminaries, the kind that would have resulted in instant dismissal in an earlier, more sensible era, are glossed over without a moment's notice or even welcomed as vital additions to our body of understanding.[23]

Whichever path the scientific debate about human-induced climate change takes, there is one undeniable aspect about the present situation that makes it almost impossible to imagine the day will ever arrive when a widespread political consensus will emerge on exactly what to do about it. The reason for saying that is that the political climate presents a much more dangerous threat to humanity than the atmospheric climate does. The most disturbing trend we face is not related to higher temperatures, rising ocean levels, disappearing glaciers, wilting crops, increasing ferocity of storms, prolonged droughts, melting ice caps, threats to wildlife, malarial outbreaks, or any other factor. The trend that poses the greatest threat to humanity is the increasing toxicity of our political discourse due to the intolerance expressed by leftists toward those with whom they disagree.[24]

A passage that perfectly exemplifies this toxic atmosphere can be found in the writings of liberal professor of psychology Drew Westen at Emory University in Atlanta. Westen has carved out a second career as a sort of progressive svengali of Democratic Party thought, helping to solidify the party's core doctrine as one of elite, dismissive condescension. Hoping to explain why university professors overwhelmingly lean left, Westen helpfully explains that:

> *Math professors are just as pro-Democratic as sociologists. That suggests that people who think logically and have been selected for intellect are more convinced by Democrats than Republicans. Perhaps that's not a surprise when you take into consideration that Republicans defy basic math by arguing that you can cut deficits by throwing public employees out of work, which cuts the number of taxpayers, and hence reduces tax revenue. Democrats tend to believe in science.*"[25]

If leftists believe in this, then they also believe in magic. Needless to say, 100% of the cost of a public employee is borne by taxpayers. Public employees remit only a portion of their salaries back to the Treasury but get to keep the rest. In effect, taxpayers pay public employee taxes in the first place. Reduce public employees and you reduce the cost of government.

But you knew that. Westen didn't. It really doesn't take rocket science to figure this out. Westen's thesis also requires us to maintain that government employees who lose their public sector jobs could never find a job in the private sector and become net contributors to the public purse.

Of course, one is inclined to laugh uncontrollably at Westen's narcissistic display. With liberalism relying on the likes of Westen, conservatives can rest easy. As George Orwell said, "some ideas are so absurd, only an intellectual could believe them." He had Westen in mind.

Remember, Westen was the guy who proudly took to the pages of *The New York Times* in 2011 to inform its readers that Obama's main political problem was that he had not told enough bedtime stories to his American audience.[26] Intellectuals like Drew Westen invest their faith in a self-reinforcing notion of a cognitive meritocracy where he is obviously one of its leading lights. The rest of us, with our inferior capabilities and bovine instincts — he calls us "ignorant" if we disagree with him[27] — are obligated to follow the light or, if not, remain silent. The trouble, as we see above, is that his bulb is so dim that we bump into solid structures when we try to follow.

And Westen and fellow leftists like him also hold equally unshakeable certitudes not only that humans are the sole cause of the planet's atmospheric temperature change but that everyone who doesn't agree with him are cretins. He and his ilk see anyone who is skeptical about the most problematic aspects of the IPCC's thesis or even the indefensible economic incongruities of climate mitigation as half-witted, inbred morons running around their trailer-park neighborhoods waving confederate flags and burning crosses on their neighbors' lawns.[28]

The drinking water down in Atlanta should be tested to see if there is something inducing this sort of intellectual paralysis and dementia. As many reliable studies suggest, the real reason university professors are overwhelmingly leftist is because respondents in surveys of academic professionals openly admit that they deliberately discriminate against conservatives in hiring and promotion.[29] They certainly wouldn't want anyone challenging the confirmation bias at work on campus, the tendency to seek out only those viewpoints that support one's own.[30]

Our basic problem is that, in the debate, one side is composed of "logical scientific" geniuses like Westen who know they are incapable of error, who have acquired a monopoly on the correct interpretations of even the most rarified matters ranging far beyond their chosen fields of expertise, who think conservatism is evidence of a character defect, whose preferred method of discourse with ideas with which they disagree is condescension, who wage public debate by demonization and ostracism of their opponents rather than by a defensible intellectual refutation of their ideas. In other words, they are people who are a perfect fit for modern liberalism.

As the sole guardians of proper scientific thought, they needn't be inconvenienced by the scientific method that requires a healthy degree of skepticism, multiple lines of evidence, and numerous substantiations of provable assertions that are, by their very nature, falsifiable. The cornerstone of science is skepticism. We do not merely accept anyone's word for it — *nullius in verba* or "take no one's word for it" is the motto of the Royal Society — we must demonstrate scientific truth through careful observation, repeatable experimentation, ready access to the data and records of previous research, and multiple lines of evidence that are derived from adjacent scientific fields. Assertions that are not falsifiable do not reside within the realm of science, but of religion.

Nevertheless, intellectuals like Westen permit no skepticism of their increasingly narrow interpretations about imminent, catastrophic human-induced global warming, which is neither provable nor falsifiable. They dismiss devout followers of organized religion as buffoons while hewing to a faith-based belief in pseudo-intellectual junk science, every vestige of which they consider infallible, unchallengeable, and unable to withstand skepticism. We must simply take their word for it. Uncertainty is a hallmark of every branch of science except climate science. There we must traffic in absolute certitudes.

No one questions when a psychologist like Westen pronounces upon rarefied matters involving climatology, the nuances of which he is as knowledgeable as he is with quantum chromodynamics. Westen is hardly alone. The world-renowned *New England Journal of Medicine* turned its pages over to Dr. Emily K. Shuman, M.D. in 2010 to author an opinion piece about global warming wherein the medical professional recited a lengthy list of certitudes about climatology, many of which were clearly in error.[31] Imagine if the learned journal *Geophysical Research Letters* had allowed a climatologist to submit a paper instructing heart surgeons on proper methods in cardiovascular surgery. No one questions the former example while the latter would provoke an avalanche of angry opposition.

Consider another example of this elite condescension over climate policies presented in an error-riddled, hyper-politicized, pseudo-intellectual screed published in early 2013 by a Harvard professor of sociology named Theda Skocpol.[32] Pretending to be purely a dispassionate analyst — an "empirical, big-picture political scientist" she laughingly describes herself[33] — Skocpol effortlessly labels opponents of the Waxman-Markey cap-and-trade bill as "bomb-throwing"[34] and "extreme right-wingers"[35] while labeling supporters of the measure as "Democrats." Does that sound empirical to you? All throughout 145 pages of laborious text, Skocpol misrepresents the opposition's point of view while never questioning the scientific, and even worse, the economic rationale behind climate mitigation measures. These cheap tricks are the tools of polemicists, not empiricists.

Skocpol attributes failure of the Waxman-Markey bill to Republicans. It had escaped the big-picture political scientist's notice that the GOP labored under a filibuster-proof 40-60 disadvantage in the Senate during the Congressional term when the measure was defeated. Republicans were powerless to affect the outcome in any material way. As with the Obamacare law that dramatically improved health care markets — pause for audience laughter — Democrats could have passed the measure entirely on their own. Skocpol views the public's low priority ranking of climate change as a "crisis" rather than what it really is, an indication of political maturity.[36]

There is not even a syllable devoted in her essay to dissecting the Waxman-Markey bill — she actually calls it the "holy grail"[37] — to determine whether it represented good public policy. Waxman-Markey, the ugly 1,000-plus page behemoth that mercifully died in the Senate when it failed to garner enough *Democrat* support, contained a CO_2 cap-and-trade arrangement like the corruption-plagued, special interest cesspool in the

European Union that has spectacularly collapsed in miserable failure. The bill would also have imposed a 25% Renewable Portfolio Standard (RPS) on the entire country similar to but more draconian in scope than most of the programs enacted in twenty nine states, mandates that have helped destroy economic growth while driving up electricity rates and unemployment. In addition, the bill would have imposed so-called "border carbon adjustments" on foreign trade against nations that had not enacted similar economically ruinous measures, a unlawful provision that violates WTO obligations and would have almost certainly launched a devastating global trade war.

Former Secretary of Energy Steven Chu espoused the philosophy in early 2009 at a Congressional hearing. "If other countries don't impose a cost on carbon, then we will be at a disadvantage... we would look at considering perhaps duties that would offset that cost."[38] Skocpol's "holy grail" entailed all the niceties of a global trade war. Thus, you can think of Waxman-Markey as a tarted up version of the devastating Smoot-Hawley tariff act dressed in a new green suit. Skocpol labels Waxman-Markey "wise policy and effective politics," in the same way that the Smoot-Hawley tariff that deepened and prolonged the depression of the 1930s was "wise policy."[39]

Like Drew Westen, whose disdain for anyone philosophically opposed to his politics borders on irrational, Skocpol attempts to delegitimize opposition to her climate agenda by ill-tempered labeling rather than rational analysis. Speaking about environmentalists who she claims "are highly educated, who think about problems scientifically", Skocpol posits "they find it impossible to believe that the climate issue is ideologically polarizing. It's hard to accept the fact that there are trade-offs here."[40] It's hard because, like Westen, she has never attempted to understand the opposition — or even learn any climate change economics for that matter. She, like Westen, is comfortable to label it condescendingly and then dismiss it.

One could accept every vestige of the anthropogenic climate change explanation but still bitterly oppose climate mitigation measures like biofuels, wind farms, RPS programs, Waxman-Markey, border carbon adjustments, carbon taxes, and all the rest. To Skocpol and other narrow-minded leftists, there are no economic tradeoffs between spending mountains of resources today for climate-related benefits that won't even be measureable in the twenty first century and would have, at best, a minimal impact in the twenty second century. To Skocpol, there are no tradeoffs when the government imposes trillions of dollars of extra costs on the economy to effect carbon dioxide abatement measures, money that could have been used for other, more pressing human needs including climate change adaptation measures. For Skocpol and "scientifically" inclined leftists, there are no tradeoffs at work with legislative proposals to spend $100 to $7,500 for each metric ton of CO_2 emissions avoided when those emissions impose a present value cost of only about $5 per metric ton if even that much.[41] Leftists like Skocpol can't fathom why anyone would oppose spending up to $300 to derive a net benefit of only a single dollar.

Skocpol proclaims that the climate issue is so urgent it can't wait another 15 years even though global temperatures haven't increased in the past 17 years.[42] It looks like waiting paid off. And Skocpol never bothers to question whether climate policies like cap-and-trade would even have any substantive impact on the climate. As we will soon see, they won't.

The empirical, big-picture political scientist Skocpol, like her ideological soul mate Drew Westen, can't be burdened to do any of the actual empirical research she claims to do so well into CO_2 emissions history and forecasts. Had she bothered, she would learn that DoE forecasts that, even without cap-and-trade or carbon taxes, the U.S. economy will emit lower amounts of CO_2 each year through the year 2040 than it did in 2005. Climate change mitigation is already well underway. But she and her close-minded "scientific" colleagues haven't been paying attention, as DoE explains about greenhouse gas emission reductions:

> *Reasons for the decline include: an expected slow and extended recovery from the recession of 2007-2009; growing use of renewable technologies and fuels; automobile efficiency improvements; slower growth in electricity demand; and more use of natural gas, which is less carbon-intensive than other fossil fuels.*[43]

The U.S. is addressing its emissions footprint and, by implication, global climate change without imposing suicidal measures like Waxman-Markey. This research finding wasn't hard to locate. It only required two minutes of time and an honest empirical mindset driven by intellectual curiosity as opposed to a desire to propagate ideological drivel.

Skocpol might have also put forth some effort to see if CO_2 abatement measures would have any meaningful impact at slowing climate change. The CBO estimates that the carbon tax Obama proposed would cost $1.2 trillion over ten years while reducing CO_2 emissions in the U.S. by 8%.[44] And what impact would that have on global emissions? Over the ten year period, according to the most recent forecast numbers from the EIA, it would reduce global CO_2 emissions by 1.3%.[45] Based upon the UN IPCC's modeled midrange twenty first century atmospheric temperature increase forecast of 2.96 degrees Celsius, this would reduce global temperatures by 0.038 degrees.[46] That's an impact that is simply too small to even distinguish from other climate impacts.

And yet the abatement cost of Obama's carbon tax would be about $261 per metric ton compared to a social cost of carbon of about $5 per ton, a 52-to-1 cost-benefit ratio.[47] Furthermore, since the U.S. only comprises 4.4% of the global population, it would enjoy only 4.4% of the climate remediation benefit, but would be required to pay 100% of the cost. Therefore, the real cost-benefit ratio rises to 1,172-to-1. One only wonders if the empirical, big-picture intellects like Skocpol or Westen, had they bothered to spend five minutes doing the empirical research, would conclude this represents money well spent. If so, they would be the only ones on the planet who think so. Authors like Peter Glover and the late Michael Economides rightly describe this line of advocacy where massively destabilizing policies are advocated that would impose enormous costs for no apparent environmental benefit as a clear-cut case of "anti-intellectualism."[48]

Skocpol might have also invested fifteen minutes researching the fact that global temperatures have undergone a standstill over the past 17 years. As we saw with IPCC lead author Hans von Storch, fewer than 2% of modeled outcomes even permit a complete halt in atmospheric temperature increases over that length of time.[49] As noted earlier, it means that there is better than a 98% chance the infallible climate models are wrong. Given that one-third of human-generated global CO_2 emissions from fossil fuels usage since 1751 occurred in the period since global warming stopped, the empirical data strongly calls into question the integrity of these IPCC climate models upon which their climate religious extremism is based.[50] But detailed research is too much to ask of shallow academic polemicists who masquerade as empirical researchers. If Waxman-Markey is the climate zealot's "holy grail" as Skocpol contends, they pray in a very strange church.

Much time and attention is expended by opinion leaders decrying the current polarized political atmosphere, wondering how Americans can ever hope to find a national consensus on contentious issues of national policy. These observers long for the quiet, peaceful days of our founders. They yearn for those kinder, gentler days when Federalists backing John Adams in the election of 1800 accused Thomas Jefferson of wanting to install the guillotine and French Jacobin terror while their Republican opponents who backed Jefferson accused Adams of treasonously trying to restore the British monarchy.[51] These same people dream wistfully of our forefathers, who worked to forge a consensus amicably, statesmen like Aaron Burr and Andrew Jackson, both of whom killed men in duels.[52] They yearn for those somnolent days of political quietude that remind us of pre-Civil War days in May 1856 when slavery-supporting South Carolina Democrat Preston Brooks brutally beat abolitionist Republican Senator Charles Sumner of Massachusetts into a bloody pulp in the Senate antechambers with a metal-topped wooden cane.[53]

Perhaps the issue about political consensus should be inverted. Maybe the clear-headed question to ask is: Why should we bother trying to forge a consensus about highly divisive aspects of national energy and climate policy? One side of the debate has built its entire philosophical foundation around an unshakeable belief that their intellectual opponents are morally unfit — "bomb-throwers" they are called by polemicists like Skocpol — their ideas considered to be products of obviously inferior minds, their viewpoints just primitive superstitions held by sad, mutated, knuckle-dragging remnants of stunted evolutionary progress. Why should we seek to achieve political compromise with an increasingly intolerant political philosophy whose preferred method of discourse, in the tradition of slavery-supporting Congressman Preston Brooks, is the metal-topped wooden bludgeon of Westen- and Skocpol-style bigoted, spiteful, divisive, condescending, hyper-politicized rhetoric?[54]

Jonathan Haidt, a politically liberal social psychologist at New York University, helps explain why liberals tend to be so bigoted in their intolerance toward viewpoints with which they disagree. Haidt interviewed hundreds of subjects about their political views and published his findings in a 2012 book entitled *The Righteous Mind: Why Good People are Divided by Politics and Religion*.[55] Haidt discovered that conservatives are far more likely to understand liberals' world views than liberals are to understand those of conservatives. Haidt discovered this was due to limitations in liberal cognitive capability, the truth of which these foregoing pages convincingly demonstrate. Despite Westen's contrary assurances, liberals themselves are the ones who lack the intellectual horsepower to comprehend the utter futility of climate mitigation. The obvious implication from Haidt's research is that there is no point trying to reach a consensus since conservatives believe liberals are decent people who happen to be mistaken while liberals believe conservatives are evil so their views, even if they could be understood, need never be considered. Thus there is no possible middle ground.

TIME TO GET ON HUMANITY'S SIDE

Supporters of America's real energy future need not cede the moral high ground to 'green energy' religionists like these. Environmentalist doom-and-gloom advocates, guided by the likes of Malthusian extremists who view humanity as a cancer, do not enjoy and should never be accorded the presumption of moral superiority. Fossil fuel producers and electric utilities have done a terrible job of arguing their own case, even lending moral legitimacy to their tormenters. The author marvels at a company like BP that spent more than a decade demonizing its own core business,[56] proclaiming the dangers of human-induced global warming,[57] pretending that the future value of the company was predicated upon going "Beyond Petroleum",[58] promoting alternative energy as humanity's salvation,[59] investing countless billions of its investors' funds on solar and other renewable energy follies,[60] building alliances with environmental groups dedicated to the company's demise,[61] burnishing its 'green' credentials in media placements, and undertaking a wide variety of other initiatives in a horribly misguided attempt to purchase indulgences — it was actually called "public affection" by some observers[62] — from the green-left and their media cheerleaders.[63] BP redesigned its logo, replacing the previously robust green color scheme with a sunny pastel to soften its image.[64]

Sensible companies carefully examined the economics of 'green energy' and, to their shareholders relief, predictably said, "No thanks."[65] If there was an aspect to the otherwise horribly tragic Deepwater Horizon disaster that spoke of a higher justice, it was seeing all of BP's prior efforts disintegrate in a single instant when the drilling platform exploded in 2010.[66] Today, BP is among the most vilified brands on the planet.[67] In the time it takes to read these words, BP went "Beyond Petroleum" to "Bumbling Pariah." What exactly did the company's shareholders receive for all the self-flagellatory, counterproductive efforts?

In its monthly customer billing, Commonwealth Edison attaches a Home Energy Report that compares each customer's electricity usage to that of their neighbors.[68] If a customer has used more electricity than the neighborhood average, the offending customer is unpleasantly reminded about his shortcomings. Prior to its redesign, ComEd's website included a section with a cartoon character shaped like a fiery demon that hectored customers to "Beat the Power Bandit and learn lots of ways to save energy, save money and help save the planet!"[69] Residential electricity accounted for less than 5% of the nation's consumption of primary energy in 2012.[70] So if anyone thinks we're going to save the planet by changing a few light bulbs or upgrading a couple of appliances, they need to book return passage back to the Milky Way galaxy. Power companies and their customers have succumbed to a decades-long campaign equating energy usage to committing a moral outrage. Imagine how ridiculous it would seem if Microsoft warned its customers they were using too much software or if Del Monte sent advisories warning grocery shoppers that they were buying too many cans of vegetables. Only in the energy business does consumption carry with it a stigma of guilt.

Chesapeake Energy, one of the country's largest natural gas producers, thought it would be clever to make a $26 million contribution to the Sierra Club to enable that eco-extremist group to maintain its war against coal-fired electric utilities.[71] By doing so, Chesapeake's CEO Aubrey McClendon believed that this would hasten the day when regulators would prohibit the use of coal in power generation and drive up the demand for natural gas — and also its price. That would make Chesapeake more profitable. But after Cornell University activist pseudo-scientists Robert Howarth and Anthony Ingraffea published their ridiculous "study" alleging that natural gas fracking was exacerbating global warming by releasing large quantities of heat-trapping methane into the atmosphere,[72] work that is now thoroughly discredited,[73] the Sierra Club turned the tables on Chesapeake. It reversed course and began advocating for regulatory curtailment of this promising technology that is revolutionizing America's energy future.[74]

What mode of thought would compel a fossil fuel company to fund an outfit dedicated to elimination of fossil fuels and companies that produce them? And yet, by doing so, Chesapeake had surrendered its own moral standing, in essence conceding Sierra Club's ridiculous contention that Chesapeake was on the wrong side of the issue, that using the fossil fuel the company produces, the product customers use to avoid freezing inside their homes and with which they cook their meals to avoid food-borne pathogens, was somehow worse for humanity than going without. Winston Churchill described the forlorn belief motivating this appeasement-oriented behavior as feeding the crocodile hoping it will eat you last. It comes as precious little comfort to Chesapeake's shareholders that McClendon was forced to resign in disgrace.[75] The company can always find a new chief. But as former Labor Secretary Ray Donovan asked, where does it go to get its reputation back?[76]

Activists have been waging a relentless campaign of vilification on college campuses all across America against fossil fuel companies, attempting to pressure university endowments to divest shares of fossil fuel companies.[77] Harvard students voted overwhelmingly in favor of a measure urging the university to divest all of its fossil fuel company holdings in its $32 billion endowment portfolio.[78] Amazingly, the Harvard vote in favor of divestment produced a higher majority of support than students' vote two decades earlier to divest from companies associated with the odious racial apartheid in South Africa.[79] The fact that, on the blustery cold November day the vote was held, virtually every single Harvard student had arrived on campus in a vehicle powered by fossil fuels and lived comfortably in a warm accommodation that used fossil fuel heating was absolutely no impediment to a full-throated expression of the student body's logical inconsistency. They claim we need to switch immediately from fossil fuels to wind and solar power. Sensible minds have difficulty comprehending this astonishing level of intellectual dissonance.

Harvard's 'green energy' proponents blindly led by global warming hysteric Bill McKibben contend we need to "do the math" in relation to the world's use of fossil fuels. Here's some problematic math that these arithmetic-challenged advocates should consider. According to the reference case in EIA's International Energy Outlook 2013, in the five years from 2014 onwards, the world is projected to increase its usage of electricity each year by an average of about 707 terawatt-hours.[80] As of the end of 2012, the world's entire fleet of wind turbines generated an annual output of only about 449 terawatt-hours.[81] So forget about replacing fossil fuels. For the planet simply to hold its fossil fuel use for electricity constant, it would need to increase wind turbine deployment each year by 157% of the total amount of wind power in use today.

Using the wind farm land sprawl example cited in Chapter 19, to wring 707 terawatt-hours out of wind farms spaced like the Roscoe Wind Energy Complex in Texas, you would need to churn up more than 52,900 square miles of land for turbine towers every single year. An area greater than the size of Arkansas would need to be torn apart each year to erect wind towers and turbines.[82] And substantially more land would need to be devoured to accommodate high-voltage transmission lines needed to distribute wind power from its far-flung producing areas to distant demand centers. That result is in line with deliberately understated survey estimates from the wind promoting National Renewable Energy Laboratory.[83]

Renewable fuel zealots like McKibben tell us we need to switch to renewable fuels to end our addiction to oil. If all of the heavily-forested timberlands in all six New England states plus New York and Pennsylvania were clear cut and converted to cellulosic ethanol, would we be able to declare victory over oil?[84] In actuality, if all of that biomass were converted to cellulosic biofuel, it would displace only nine months of a single year's consumption of gasoline, diesel, and aviation fuel.[85] We would need twice as much land area as the entire U.S. for corn cultivation just to meet our annual gasoline needs with corn-based ethanol.[86] So how does that terrible math sound? It is McKibben and his adolescent audience at Harvard that flunked their math tests.[87]

Like Obama's student audience at the University of Miami, Harvard students are not obligated to live in the real world. As trust-funded sons and daughters of America's richest, they can continue pretending since they'll never be required to endure the economic hardships that 'green energy' programs impose upon the country's lower- and middle-income groups who need to work for a living.

But wind turbines and solar panels are not going to be able to rush an injured child to the emergency room. Nor will they be of any use in getting a rural medical staff to remote villagers who have fallen ill from a bacterial infection in a destitute, Third World nation. And they will be utterly useless in helping to get emergency relief supplies to victims of an earthquake or a tsunami. Biofuels that incinerate food supplies or displace food cultivation acreage aren't going to be much help to starving, poverty-stricken villagers.

We inhabit an age where cynical politicians can demonize "Big Oil" and caterwaul about the virtues of alternative fuels — then throw tantrums at Congressional show-trials when fuel prices go up. Our mass media pretends not to notice the incongruity. Much of our popular culture seeks to delegitimize capitalism itself, with oil companies being merely its most visible symbols. And worst of all, we have elected and then reelected a man who espouses an odious political philosophy that seeks to supplant the free enterprise system that has produced our material abundance in preference for a collectivist "you didn't build that" ideology, the kind that piled up 100 million corpses in the last century.

The hard reality is that, even if 'green energy' could be made technically workable and deployed on necessary scales to meet all our needs, which the terrible math above shows it obviously cannot, its deployment has brought about conditions that are indefensible, a situation that robs any remaining vestige of moral legitimacy from its most ardent proponents.

'Green energy' has driven up energy prices in countries that have embraced these policies to unaffordable levels, hastening their economic decline. It is estimated that 7,800 Britons freeze to death in their flats every year because they cannot afford their heating bills.[88] A million poor, rural Chinese villagers die in unspeakable circumstances each year from premature cancer deaths caused by toxic pollution that originates mostly from the heavy metal mining operations that produce materials required for 'green energy' gadgets like wind turbine magnets, hybrid car batteries, energy efficient lighting phosphors, and solar photovoltaic semiconductors.[89] Wind turbines destroy millions of endangered migrating birds and bats each year, rapidly depleting some of the world's most endangered avian species.[90] Many of those species feed on mosquito larvae and are essential to controlling the spread of mosquito-borne diseases like malaria that claim millions of lives each year. High levels of renewable energy penetration cause backup coal-fired generators to operate far less efficiently than if they were to be operated steadily, resulting in worse NO_x, SO_x and CO_2 pollution than would be the case without intermittent wind and solar power.[91] And in most of the major countries of the world, the vaunted electric cars that cause 'green energy' promoters to swoon in apoplectic delight actually cause a higher degree of particulate soot and polluting emissions than internal combustion engines do over their life-cycles because the electricity used to recharge their batteries comes from coal-fired power plants that aren't properly outfitted with the same types of pollution control equipment used in the U.S.[92]

Biofuel programs have unleashed an unimaginable toll on the planet. Vast, irreplaceable tracts of fragile ecosystems in the tropics have been destroyed to establish monotypic stands of palm trees for use in biofuels.[93] This rapacious conduct has degraded biodiversity, stressed the carbon-sequestering capacity of the planet, destroyed irreplaceable tropical old growth peatland rainforests, and put some of the world's most majestic mammalian species, and thousands of others, on the verge of extinction.[94] Biofuels have driven up the price of fuel and food. Food crops that should be used to feed people and maintain affordable market prices are being siphoned away for biofuel production to placate an unhinged climate campaigning mob. Hundreds of thousands of the world's poorest are facing starvation due to indefensible biofuel policies enacted in the U.S. and the EU.[95]

Renewable Portfolio Standards in twenty nine states negatively impact middle- and lower-income ratepayers far more than they do upper-income households, costing tens of billions of dollars each year. Renewable energy project funding often goes exclusively to crony-connected corporate and high-income investors. Consumers in the bottom house-hold income quintile pay almost one fourth of their disposable income on energy while those in the top quintile pay less than 5%.[96] There are few examples of more regressive policies available than 'green energy' programs. And yet politicians like Obama, who pretend to be on the side of the poor, support them.

RPS programs damage economic growth prospects and are destroying the jobs upon which modest-income families depend for their livelihoods. As residential electricity and heating costs soar, families often must choose between energy and other essentials like food and health care. Why does the environmental left that promotes these indefensible policies enjoy the presumption of moral superiority? 'Green energy' proponents must be held to account for this dreadful toll.

Fossil fuels provide 80% of the world's energy. That is energy that powers hospitals, ambulances, schools, day-care centers, art museums, fire trucks, theatres, rape crisis hotlines, famine relief organizations, and even environmental activist group headquarters buildings. What possible justification exists for ceding moral superiority to 'green' activists whose real agenda is de-population, de-development, de-industrialization, centrally-planned economies, and authoritarian trans-national government that they claim is required to establish the rigid control that could bring their insane future into reality?

You don't need to take my word for it. Take it from James Lovelock, environmentalist extraordinaire, the originator of the Gaia hypothesis, who tells us "I have a feeling that climate change may be an issue as severe as war. It may be necessary to put democracy on hold for a while."[97] Just a while, maybe 250 or 300 years. Then you can have it back. The last time humanity surrendered its freedom to visionaries like these, it took almost 75 years and more than 100 million corpses to wrestle a portion of it back.

OBAMA DECLARES WAR ON THE WORLD'S POOR

Speaking to a largely sympathetic audience at Georgetown University in June 2013, President Obama proclaimed that he would use the immense power of his office to prohibit public financing for expansion of coal-fired power in poor countries of the world:

> *I'm calling for an end of public financing for new coal plants overseas unless they deploy carbon capture technologies or there's no other viable way for the poorest countries to generate electricity. And I urge other countries to join this effort.*[98]

This line drew applause from the audience of comfortable, well-heeled attendees who take their energy-abundant affluence for granted, a crowd that had been carefully selected for their ideological suitability. Of course there are always other alternatives so, in essence, Obama was prohibiting public monies for expansion of coal-fired power not just in the U.S. but everywhere in the world where the U.S. could exert influence.

One such place where that influence can be felt is with the World Bank, which describes how Obama's 'green energy' priorities can shape its own agenda:

> As the only World Bank shareholder that retains veto power over changes in the Bank's structure, the United States plays a unique role in influencing and shaping development priorities.[99]

It took the World Bank leadership only a month from the date of Obama's speech to snap to attention. In July 2013, the bank's leadership announced a policy change, saying that coal-fired electrification projects would receive development assistance "only in rare circumstances."[100] That's Washington-speak for "never."

The World Bank had been considering extending a loan guarantee to Kosovo to permit construction of a 600 megawatt coal-fired power plant.[101] The last time the bank provided financing for a coal plant was in 2010 in South Africa, a nation with copious quantities of indigenous coal reserves. That loan was not supported by the Obama although he chose to abstain rather than veto it.[102] The U.S. had hitherto vetoed fewer than 2.6% of World Bank funding proposals, and nearly half of those vetoes were because beneficiary countries had been lax in apprehending war criminals.[103]

Months before Obama's Georgetown speech, World Bank President Jim Yong Kim, a scientist who has voiced concerns over human-induced climate change in the past, sensibly enumerated the real-world choices facing developing nations. In April 2013, Kim addressed a panel discussion in Washington over the topic of coal-fired power development assistance:

> I don't think it's fair to tell the people in Kosovo, 'While the rich countries continue to burn coal, you're going to have to freeze to death because it's against our political ideology to support you.'[104]

He was exactly right. Kim had correctly identified the green-left's opposition to coal power development assistance in poor countries, and its indifference to the plight of the world's poorest, as rooted purely in ideology. Yet goaded by a powerful politician who lives in the White House, a building that is comfortably heated by coal-fired steam and powered by coal-fired electricity, the World Bank leadership decided that it would now be okay for people who live in poverty-stricken places like Kosovo to "freeze to death" rather than receive development assistance for expansion of coal-fired power.

Self-promoting 'green energy' entrepreneurs pretend that coal-fired power represents a false choice between coal-fired generation vs. no electricity since Kosovo has adequate solar, biomass, and wind resources together with a sufficient supply of development capital to bring a low-carbon generation capacity into existence.[105] But green-bleating promoters like these never mention cost. There's an infinite supply of people willing to sell you something at a price three to six times higher than competing alternatives, particularly in instances where consumers are forced to pay for it. The question is not one of supply but of supply-demand equilibrium at a particular price.

No one is likely to freeze to death in Vietnam. Nevertheless, like people everywhere, the Vietnamese find electricity to be useful. It keeps the lights on in the hospitals, schools, workplaces, homes, offices and everywhere else. They even use it at *Apocalypse Now*, Saigon's best known nightclub.[106] Like many poor countries, Vietnam has been planning to build a 1,200 megawatt coal-fired power plant at Thai Binh to assure adequate supply of electricity to its grid and help boost economic growth.[107] The proposed plant was a critical part of a World Bank initiative to transform Vietnam's power sector which, in the Bank's words, would help to "deliver reliable and good quality electricity supply to support economic growth."[108] Once complete, the country would be able "to attract a broader range of participants to invest in the power industry."[109] Attracting seed capital is considered crucial to a successful launch of Vietnam's power sector transformation.

Given that Vietnam is blessed with domestic supplies of coal, the Thai Binh plant would rank high on the World Bank's list of programs that would enable the country to help meet the Bank's goals for lending support.[110] But following Obama's announcement, Vietnam has zero chance of seeing its power plant proposal financed by the World Bank. Laughably, the U.S. Export-Import Bank joined in announcing that it would not finance U.S. exports for the project after a "careful environmental review."[111] That careful environmental review took five minutes to complete given that the Ex-Im Bank's announcement came exactly one day after the World Bank's announcement. Vietnam's underclass, which is to say nearly the entire populace, can forget about receiving any help from social justice champion Barack Obama.

Consider how expansion of access to the grid benefits poor countries. Rwanda has experienced an astounding 14.3% compound real GDP growth rate over recent years according to World Bank figures.[112] This has been brought about by expanding access to grid-based electricity. In 2008, only about 6% of the population had access to grid-based electrification.[113] Among those who do have power, it usually comes from expensive, polluting diesel-fired generators. But with expansion of coal-fired utility-scale capacity and World Bank-financed interconnections, millions of schools, hospitals, businesses, rural clinics, and homes are now being connected to the grid.

Each ton of carbon-based energy creates a $6,700 increase in global gross domestic product on average.[114] That is enough to "sustain" the livelihoods of more than eleven Rwandans using World Bank per capita GDP data for 2012.[115] This is the real "sustainable" energy the World Bank needs to be looking at for rapid economic development in poor nations. Grid-based electricity from CO_2-generating sources together with increasing scale of access will help drive down the cost of electricity to consumers in Rwanda from over 25 cents per kWh in 2012 to around ten cents by 2018.[116] This will bring enormous benefits to some of the neediest people on the planet.

The World Bank's primary mission is to eradicate poverty which is best accomplished through access to affordable energy.[117] A report from the World Economic Forum outlines the dilemma faced by trans-national development bodies like the World Bank:

> *Though little recognized, in terms of energy generated the biggest growth since the beginning of the century has been, by far, in coal — nearly twice that of natural gas, nearly three times that of oil, and almost ten times that of renewables. This is the result of high economic growth rates in emerging market countries and the rapidly rising need for power.*[118]

Coal-fired power is usually the lowest-cost, and in many cases, the only realistic alternative available to developing nations. It is difficult to understate the importance this aspect of modern life that Americans take for granted has at immeasurably improving the quality of lives in poor countries like Rwanda, Kosovo, or Vietnam. And now Obama, champion of the world's underclass, will thumb his nose at them, insisting this process must stop dead in its tracks. He prefers to pretend that these countries can install hideously expensive, technically unworkable wind turbines and solar panels instead of utility-scale coal-fired generation. Good luck with that.

HUMANITY'S REAL-WORLD TRADEOFFS

Between 1998 and 2012, the countries of the world grew global GDP from $30 trillion to $71 trillion, a compound annual rate of 6.3%.[119] During that time, humanity pumped 120.2 billion metric tons of carbon into the atmosphere.[120] During those years, the concentration of CO_2 in the atmosphere increased by about 7.4%.[121] While that may seem significant, in reality, this addition only led to a 0.0027% increase in overall atmospheric CO_2 trace gas concentration. Not surprisingly, given the vanishingly small overall contribution to the earth's atmosphere in those 15-years, the planet's observed atmospheric temperature did not increase by any measureable degree.[122] Why should it? Do we really imagine the climate is so sensitive that a 0.0027% increase in a weakly-interacting trace gas would cause temperatures to go careening upwards at unprecedented rates?

But the world economy certainly heated up during those years. In effect, each metric ton of carbon emitted into the atmosphere over that 15-year period generated a weighted average of $6,075 of additional real income for humanity.[123] That income helped to produce hospitals, schools, roads, libraries, medicine, food crops, jobs, homes, and a thousand other basic necessities of life.

No matter how the debate about the theory of human-induced global warming is finally settled, and it likely won't ever be finally settled, we should never delude ourselves into believing it is the most pressing human problem. We should not allow the weight of corrupt UN panels, discredited government-funded junk-science, rent-seeking corporate interests hoping to cash in on the deluge of taxpayer-funded lucre, ideologically-inspired mass media cheerleading, or Nobel Peace Prize-winning con artists stampede us away from the proper course. Instead, we should concentrate on improving the lot of humanity by advancing economic growth and prosperity for the world's poorest people.

Consider the counsel from James Lovelock, a founding father of the Green movement, the originator of the "Gaia Hypothesis," who laments that the movement he helped found has completely forsaken the plight of humanity in its reckless anti-energy, anti-human quest. In a letter to a local planning authority intent on deploying wind turbines in a rural area of his beloved home in Devon, Lovelock writes:

> *I am an environmentalist and founder member of the Greens but I bow my head in shame at the thought that our original good intentions should have been so misunderstood. We never intended a fundamentalist Green movement that rejected all energy sources other than renewable, nor did we expect the Greens to cast aside our priceless ecological heritage because of their failure to understand that the needs of the Earth are not separable from human needs. We need to take care that the spinning windmills do not become like the statues on Easter Island — monuments of a failed civilisation.*[124]

Monuments to a failed civilizational model is precisely what they are. Environmentalist Bjørn Lomborg observes that even if every death that occurs in the world today from weather-related disasters like flood, drought, heat wave or severe storm were to be attributed to human-caused global warming — a completely ridiculous supposition — it would still amount to only 0.06% of deaths in the developing world. Lomborg is no easy foil for climate hysterics, believing as he does that global warming is both a major threat and due solely to human influences.[125] By contrast, air and water pollution cause 13% of the mortalities in those countries.[126] But the world's globe-trotting elites would rather squander countless billions flying all over the planet holding climate conferences in the most fabulous places while ignoring some of humanity's closest, most easily addressable problems that are often right outside the conference hall doors.

Virtually every one of these intractable human problems in the developing world could be solved through enhancing economic growth. That will only occur if poor people in developing nations have access to affordable energy. While it will come as a shock to some, the poor don't need solar panels.[127] Unaffordable wind turbines won't keep the refrigerator that stores vaccines, antibiotics, insulin, and blood plasma running 24 hours a day. Biofuel plants that consume foodstuffs won't cut it when people nearby are malnourished or starving. The poor need clean burning stoves to prevent inhalation of cancer-causing smoke from wood and dung fires, refrigeration to prevent food spoilage, adequate sanitation to prevent the spread of infectious disease, nutrient-enriched diets from infancy to prevent stunted physical and cognitive growth, and clean water to prevent a wide range of debilitating illnesses.[128] We enjoy all of those things. We consider them part of our birthright. Why can't the world's poorest enjoy the same basic dignities we take for granted?

Not only are Obama's 'green energy' schemes helping to destroy the planet from toxicities, pollution, deforestation, and starvation. They are also siphoning precious resources away from worthwhile endeavors that could have substantially beneficial impact upon humanity. Every proposal involves an economic tradeoff. Every available public dollar presents us with a choice to spend it on one thing over every other competing opportunity. How do Obama's 'green energy' tradeoffs stack up against a range of real-world opportunities? Consider some of these tradeoffs:

- ✓ For $300 million, far less than Obama wasted on a failed and bankrupt Colorado company called Abound Solar, a crony solar boondoggle that was backed by a major Obama campaign contributor, the people of the U.S. could have helped prevent 300,000 childhood deaths from malaria.[129]

- ✓ For $122 million, about the amount of money that Obama squandered on a wind turbine project in Hawaii that created 10 permanent jobs, the world could have achieved complete Hepatitis B vaccine coverage that would avert 150,000 deaths each year.[130]

- ✓ As many as a half a million children in the world go blind each year from a deficiency of vitamin-A.[131] For about $250 million, the same amount Obama threw away on a bankrupt electric car battery maker called A123 Systems,[132] as many as 80% of these children could avoid this eventuality[133] through a micro-nutrient supplement program that would also reduce childhood mortality rates by more than 20%.[134]

- ✓ For $3 billion, the amount of money the Obama administration squandered on a flailing company called First Solar,[135] the world could have invested in a program of micronutrient provision, diarrheal disease prevention and other measures that would have helped more than 100 million children in poor countries avoid early childhood malnutrition and stunted growth, benefits that would have lasted an entire lifetime.[136]

- ✓ For $200 million, far less than half of the amount Obama shoveled over to his crony campaign contributing bundlers at bankrupt Solyndra, the country could have supplied low-cost heart attack medications to poor countries that would have prevented 300,000 deaths.[137]

- ✓ Two million people die each year from the effects of burning solid fuel on stoves according to the World Health Organization.[138] Half of those people could be furnished with improved equipment for $2.3 billion, the amount Obama squandered on just three crony-connected solar companies.[139]

- ✓ For half the amount of taxpayer money given by Obama, champion of the 99%, to a Finnish car maker to build electric cars that cost $100,000 apiece, we could have supplied iodized salt to 80% of the poorest people on earth to help them avoid developmental and cognitive problems associated with low-iodine diets.[140]

✓ Iron deficiency in the developing world is one of the most easily preventable health problems. As many as 3.5 billion people, half the world's population, suffer from an iron deficient diet. Iron deficiency stunts normal growth, reducing a person's manual labor output by as much as 17%. It also reduces cognitive development, stealing as many as 15 points of IQ from a person's true potential. For about $90 million, far less than government agencies wasted on Obama billionaire crony Vinod Khosla's bankrupt and shuttered Range Fuels cellulosic ethanol plant that never produced a drop of product, every iron deficient diet in the world could be overcome with the simple expedient of supplying iron cooking pots.[141]

The UN IPCC estimates that global warming will produce a warmer, wetter climate that will expose an additional 3% of humanity to the threat of malaria by the year 2100, a claim based solely upon some questionable, highly controversial academic studies.[142] Maybe it's true, but almost certainly it's not.[143] The panel's recommended solution is to spend anywhere from $40 trillion to as much as $553 trillion[144] between now and the end of the century on CO_2 abatement measures. The cost estimates are wide-ranging but there's no debate about the implications.

For just $3 billion a year, humanity could provide environmentally safe DDT indoor sprays, mosquito netting and combination therapies that could reduce the number of mosquito-borne deaths by half within ten years.[145] That would spare 524,000 lives each year according to mortality figures supplied by the World Health Organization (WHO).[146]

The UN World Food Programme estimates that almost half of the world's deaths each year in children under five result from poor nutrition.[147] That 3.1 million annual death toll[148] could be completely alleviated with just $3.2 billion in food aid.[149] That's about the amount of money federal taxpayers squandered in 2012 on Production Tax Credits subsidizing wind farms owned by billionaire wind farm operators.[150]

Respiratory illness resulting from indoor air pollution caused by wood and dung fires places an undue burden on the world's poor. These poor ventilation conditions result in an increased risk of acute lower respiratory infections (ALRI), especially pneumonia, during childhood.[151] ALRI is the second most important cause of death in children under the age of five, resulting in as many as two million deaths per year.[152] That death toll is easily preventable with improved cooking equipment. Just $2.3 billion per year could eradicate these tragic human losses. Compared to the Congressional Research Service's estimate of $68.4 billion[153] that the U.S. squandered between FY'2008 and FY'2012 on worthless climate change initiatives that had zero impact on improving either the climate or humanity's basic condition, a mere $5.5 billion for food aid and ventilation improvement doesn't really seem like much.[154] Remember, these are the real world tradeoffs that empirical social science genius Theda Skocpol of Harvard brags she was unable to detect.

The WHO estimates that 45% of all illnesses in poor countries are a result of poverty and are treatable with existing medicines or are entirely preventable through intervention measures.[155] Economic growth would enable poor countries to eliminate most of this human suffering and death. The surest path to that future is through access to affordable energy. For each human life that the IPCC's carbon-cutting measures claims to be able to save, humanity could preserve 78,000 lives through a more rational approach of steering funding to where it's really needed supplemented by some desperately needed sobriety regarding the highly speculative, supposedly catastrophic impacts of atmospheric trace gases.[156]

How much credence should we give to IPCC claims about the spread of malaria after the planet's atmosphere warms by two degrees Celsius? Incidence of malaria is weakly correlated to warm temperatures.[157] How many people in Florida die from it each year even as the average temperature in Miami throughout the year is 17 degrees Celsius warmer than in Minneapolis?

Amazingly, the IPCC gives prominence to highly problematic forecasts of malaria's rampant spread with a two degree change in global temperature while ignoring the incontestable evidence that malaria's incidence has been reduced by orders of magnitude since 1900 when the planet was about one degree colder than today. As the far more authoritative studies on the transmission of vector-borne diseases like malaria demonstrate:

> ... combined natural and anthropogenic forces acting on the disease throughout the twentieth century have resulted in the great majority of locations undergoing a net reduction in [malarial] transmission between one and three orders of magnitude larger than the maximum future increases proposed under temperature-based climate change scenarios.[158]

In layman's terms, history shows that human-induced malaria eradication measures will far outweigh any climate-related spread. Or in even simpler terms, the IPCC is blowing smoke on the fact-free fairytale it tells about climate-related malaria hysteria. Malaria is strongly correlated to poverty, a vestige of an energy-starved lifestyle. Authoritative research demonstrates that the incidence of malaria effectively disappears when per capita income reaches $3,100 per year.[159] We need to be working toward improving economic circumstances for the world's poorest along with climate change adaptation measures, not utterly useless CO_2 abatement.

To reiterate, the planet's temperature has warmed over the past several hundred years by a few degrees Celsius. And yet, in the face of that, malaria has been completely eradicated in many areas of the world where it once thrived and has been reduced in virtually all others by anywhere from a ten to a one thousand-fold degree.[160] Malaria was a common malady in St. Louis in the early 1800s. How many cases are reported today? And yet, in the face of this, the IPCC is peddling the notion that, with a small increase in global temperatures over the next century, all of humanity's adaptation strategies and all of the economic growth that is sure to occur in coming decades will simply be overwhelmed. This is a profoundly ignorant forecast we are being asked to swallow. And if the IPCC is that far outside of the mainstream about its forecast on the transmission of vector-borne diseases like malaria, why should we be obligated to genuflect to the rest of their discredited catechism?[161] Is it not at least reasonable to suspect that that body of research work has been greatly exaggerated also?

It's time to stop playing make-believe. Americans can no longer afford to pretend that we can fix the weather or that every time there is a hurricane or a tornado or a drought, it is our fault. We need to stop paying attention to people who say otherwise. The best antidote to the climate hysteria madness is well-earned, derisive laughter. Obama has spent his years in office pretending that when something went awry, he had no prior knowledge. It was all the fault of someone else, that evil guy in charge of the government. With the 'green energy' chaos he is planning, we can spare him the trouble and defeat it before it results in epic Obamacare-style wreckage.

WHAT KIND OF FUTURE FOR HUMANITY?

All of the sensible outcomes cited above can be achieved with economic progress which requires access to low-cost energy — fossil fuel energy. There is much work left to do. Though the African continent has the fastest per capita energy growth rate of any of the world's continents, 84% of Kenyans and 81% of Ugandans still do not have access to grid-based electricity.[162] Three quarters of the inhabitants of Sub-Saharan Africa are off the grid. That means that, if they have any rural electrification at all, it comes from highly localized, very inefficient, very expensive sources like diesel generators that emit far more harmful emissions per unit of energy than centralized power generation stations do.

How does a globe-trotting climate campaigner recommending to the world that it needs to spend trillions of dollars now to avert some imagined catastrophe far off in the future look a destitute villager in the eyes who just lost his child due to malnutrition or malaria, a death that could have been easily prevented with a miniscule amount of useful intervention? How long will this deadly climate charade last?

Global governments, leftist advocates and media cheerleaders were in unanimous agreement hailing the wonderful achievement of the Kyoto Protocol. At long last, they said, Kyoto will usher in mankind's salvation. Global warming will be eliminated as a planetary threat, right? Guess again. No serious person disputes the fact that Kyoto's impact upon the climate will not even be measureable in the twenty first century and, at best, would only postpone twenty second century warming by five years.[163] Leftist Bolivian dictator Evo Morales suggests we need Nuremberg-style show trials for nations that fail to comply with Kyoto, saying that "Those who do not fulfill the terms of the Kyoto Protocol should also be judged. And for those ends, we have to organize a tribunal for climate justice in the United Nations."[164]

Beside a perversion of justice, what is the price tag that would be placed upon that utterly useless Kyoto compliance outcome? By some estimates, it is $180 billion per year.[165] Just half that amount would provide adequate sanitation, clean drinking water, health care, nutrition, and education for every person on the planet according to UN estimates.[166] Essentially every preventable human death on the planet could be avoided. Kyoto is what leftist thugs like Morales call climate justice? How much human suffering and death must be blithely ignored by climate campaigners to advocate squandering this amount of precious resources on such an utterly worthless exercise when glaringly obvious, immediate human needs are in direct competition with it?

EU leaders and salivating media effused over the EU's agreement in 2008 to implement their EU 2020 mandate obligating signatory countries to derive 20% of their energy needs from renewable sources by the year 2020. Environmental agitators amazingly condemned the agreement as being too timid.[167] But European Commission President Manuel Barroso disagreed, proudly claiming it was a model for the rest of the world to follow. Gushing to sympathetic media, Barroso claimed that "Europe has today passed its credibility test."[168] And what is the cost for such moral exhibitionism? How credible is Europe now that it needs to incur annual costs of €210 billion for its agreement according to estimates by famed climate change economist Richard S.J. Tol?[169] Once EU 2020 is fully implemented and the irreplaceable mountain of resources is squandered, will the agreement eliminate the threat of global warming forever? Actually, it will postpone it by just two years.[170]

The sensible part of the world ignored EU President Barroso's conceits in favor of meaningful development programs. As Tol pointed out in a detailed study of climate change mitigation, "very stringent abatement does not pass the cost-benefit test."[171] Given the examples cited throughout this volume, Tol's disclaimer ranks as the understatement of the century. The cost of climate mitigation is anywhere from one to three orders of magnitude higher than the cost of climate change it seeks to avoid.

We saw how solar energy in Germany soaks up 56% of all energy subsidies but produces only about 4% of the country's electricity.[172] Annual subsidy payments have doubled in just three years since 2010, climbing north of €20 billion per year.[173] No matter the political direction in the country, these subsidy payouts cannot possibly decline until after 2030. So solar panels will cost ratepayers at least $280 billion in subsidy payments between 2012 and 2030, a figure that is no doubt woefully understated. And what will the planet achieve for that staggering investment? Is the planet saved from impending climate doom? Actually, twenty second century global warming will be postponed by just thirty seven hours.[174] Has Europe passed its credibility test knowing that incalculable amounts of human suffering throughout the world could have been alleviated with a fraction of the amount of irreplaceable capital it will squander on solar panels, for no practical benefit?

Given the seventeen year hiatus in atmospheric warming, it is increasingly clear that the atmosphere is far less sensitive to slight changes in atmospheric CO_2 concentrations than the supposed "settled science" posited just a few years earlier.[175] A slight warming will lengthen growing seasons, allow for more rainfall in arid regions, improve biomass growth in forests and fields, extend the northward range of cultivation, reduce the amount of energy required to heat homes in winter, and reduce cold-related deaths in milder winters that far outnumber heat-related mortalities that would occur in slightly warmer summers. There is better than a 50-50 chance that these net beneficial impacts from climate change will still be occurring after the year 2083.[176] What level of delusion could induce nations of the Earth to squander trillions now on climate remediation whose net negative effects probably won't even be occurring seventy years from now — if ever?

Which side of humanity's most pressing needs will we find ourselves on? Which future will we help create? Will we join the globe-trotting, jet-setting climate campaigners who are busy siphoning countless billions of our resources on useless carbon counting exercises, resources that could lift the world's poorest out of the indescribable misery, suffering and deprivation they face? Will we line up behind climate zealots supporting actions that will condemn millions to an unworthy future characterized by horrible deaths due to disease, cancers, unsafe drinking water, deforestation, and starvation caused or exacerbated by dubious 'green energy' schemes? Will we cede moral authority to angry, violence-prone, barely sentient campus mobs demanding college endowments divest holdings in companies that produce the fossil fuels which can dramatically improve lives and livelihoods of the world's poorest and most vulnerable, the very fuels those same agitators consume in massive quantities, the kind they rely upon to power their modern way of life?[177] Will we acquiesce to corrupt media myth makers pushing a malign agenda that seeks to replace affordable, reliable energy essential to our way of life, the energy the media's loudest and shrillest members consume in vast quantities, in favor of expensive, unreliable and un-workable 'green energy' that will condemn billions to fuel poverty and will exacerbate the gap between haves and have-nots?

Or will we help lift humankind out of poverty, disease, deprivation and ignorance. Will we assist the world's most vulnerable to achieve a worthy future of healthy, vibrant, dignified lifestyles filled with opportunity and assisted by a more equitable distribution of resources, lives and livelihoods that are powered by affordable, reliable energy? The choice is entirely ours.

"Nature never deceives us; it is always we who deceive ourselves."

Jean Jacques Rousseau, 1762

APPENDIX

WHAT IF THE WEATHER DOESN'T COOPERATE?

Proponents of 'green energy' pin their hopes for humanity's salvation on a form of energy that will require excellent cooperation from the weather if it is to offer even a shred of practicality. Experience indicates that cooperation may be lacking.

German and Dutch grid operator TenneT provides researchers a wealth of detailed data on the actual power yield it derives from its network of wind and solar assets. On its website, the grid operator provides readings of wind power fed into the grid based upon 15-minute intervals throughout the year.

FIGURE A-1. **On-Shore Average Monthly Wind Power — TenneT Grid Operator**

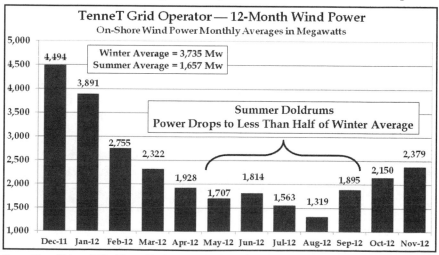

Source: TenneT Actual Wind Power Feed-In Data for December 2011 to November 2012

Needless to say, given prevailing weather conditions in Germany as elsewhere, some months are windier and thus, the amount of power that can be fed into the grid from the TenneT's fleet of wind turbines will change each month. Depicted nearby in Figure A-1. are the monthly averages of 15-minute interval power readings that TenneT fed into the grid over a one year period.[1]

Looking at monthly averages shows a fairly smooth transition from a relatively active winter period to a less active summer doldrums. During the months from the beginning of December 2011 to the end of February 2012, power readings averaged 3,735 megawatts. But beginning in May and lasting through to the end of September, winds power declines to less than half of winter months' output, averaging only 1,657 mW.

But there is no smoothness to wind activity and thus the resulting wind power fed into the grid. The pattern is highly variable throughout the year. A depiction of wind power conditions over a 12 month period is provided nearby in Figure A-2.

FIGURE A-2. **On-Shore 12-Month Wind Power — TenneT Grid Operator**

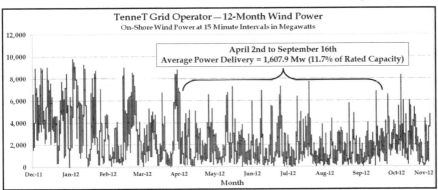

Source: TenneT Actual Wind Power Feed-In Data for December 2011 to November 2012

Figure A-2 shows that there were dozens of occasions throughout the year when power dropped to levels below 10% of rated capacity.[2] More than 40% of wind power observations captured by the grid operator during the 12-month period between December 1, 2011 and November 30, 2012 were delivering power at or below 10% of rated capacity for the fleet of wind turbines.

There were also dozens of occasions when power surges or drops of significant magnitude occurred over very short time intervals. There were at least 78 instances during the 12-month period when power dropped by more than 1,000 mW within a one-hour period. One thousand mW is the amount of power output from a typical light-water nuclear reactor. Grid operators at TenneT were left to manage a situation where, within a 60 minute time period, they had experienced a loss of power equivalent to an entire nuclear power station suddenly and unexpectedly being taken offline. Figure A-3 shows sixteen instances where wind power flow dropped by more than 1,000 mW within one-hour.[3]

In addition to the 78 instances when power suddenly dropped by more than 1,000 mW within one hour, there were 128 instances during the year when power surged by more than 1,000 mW within the space of one hour.[4]

FIGURE A-3. **Sudden Power Drops of 1,000 mW or Greater Within 1 Hour — TenneT Wind Power**

Initial Reading Date - Time	Initial Reading (mW)	Second Reading Date - Time	Second Reading (mW)	Change (mW)
24-May-12 10:15 AM	2,156	24-May-12 11:15 AM	0	-2,156
05-Jul-12 11:45 PM	1,758	05-Jul-12 12:45 AM	0	-1,758
31-Mar-12 6:30 PM	5,522	31-Mar-12 7:30 PM	4,148	-1,374
24-Sep-12 9:30 PM	5,976	24-Sep-12 10:30 PM	4,640	-1,336
31-Mar-12 9:30 PM	6,018	19-Jan-12 10:30 PM	4,683	-1,335
31-Dec-11 6:15 PM	5,590	31-Mar-12 7:15 PM	4,280	-1,310
31-Dec-11 4:45 PM	7,899	05-Oct-12 5:45 PM	6,601	-1,298
31-Dec-11 5:30 PM	5,188	18-Jun-12 6:30 PM	3,914	-1,274
05-Jul-12 5:00 PM	7,627	05-Oct-12 6:00 PM	6,357	-1,270
05-Jul-12 5:30 PM	3,318	08-Jun-12 6:30 PM	2,058	-1,260
05-Jul-12 6:00 PM	4,578	18-Jun-12 7:00 PM	3,338	-1,240
05-Jul-12 9:45 PM	5,707	19-Jan-12 10:45 PM	4,475	-1,232
24-May-12 6:15 PM	4,217	18-Jun-12 7:15 PM	3,001	-1,216
01-Dec-11 1:30 AM	4,391	21-Dec-11 2:30 AM	3,176	-1,215
01-Dec-11 5:30 PM	3,000	22-Sep-12 6:30 PM	1,789	-1,211
01-Dec-11 4:45 PM	3,782	09-Oct-12 5:45 PM	2,572	-1,210

Source: TenneT Actual Wind Power Feed-In Data for December 2011 to November 2012

Likewise, there were 1,009 instances when power dropped by more than a nuclear power station equivalent during a two hour period. On an astonishing 19 of those instances, power dropped by over 2,000 mW in a two hour period. There were also 1,086 instances when power surged by more than 1,000 mW over a two hour period and, on 60 of those occasions, power surged by more than 2,000 mW, the equivalent of two nuclear power plants. Grid managers were left scrambling with a way to offload more than two nuclear power stations of power that had flooded onto the grid within the space of 120 minutes.

It's also interesting to note how frequently wind power was delivering very low or essentially no power over sustained periods of time. During these instances, power levels being fed into the grid dropped below 10% of rated capacity and remained at these levels for well in excess of 24 hours.

Figure A-4. shows 16 instances during the year when wind power fell below 10% of rated capacity for the entire period lasting more than 40 hours in duration. In the first example, power dropped below 10% of rated capacity at 7:45 PM on May 5th and, for the next 57 ½ hours until May 8th at 5:30 AM, remained at levels below the 10% level. During the entire duration, power averaged only 558 mW. The lowest reading during this extended duration occurred at 8:45 AM on May 7th when only 153 mW of power flow was recorded.[5]

As the reader can readily observe, most of these instances occurred during the summer months of June, July and August when power requirements are substantial to run air conditioners inside stores, office buildings and homes. Note the duration beginning in the early morning of July 24th when power dropped and remained in the doldrums for the next 89¾ hours. That amounted to three days, 17 hours and 45 minutes. Were Germany to rely upon renewable energy for 80% of its power requirements as it aims to do under its EEG plan, large portions of the country would have been deprived of domestically-produced power for more than three and a half days. If power supply constraints materialize elsewhere within the European Union, Germans will need to learn how to live without electricity for extended periods of time.

FIGURE A-4. **Sustained Very Low Wind Power Periods — TenneT Wind Power**

Start Date - Time	End Date - Time	Duration (Hours)	Average Reading (mW)	Low Reading Date - Time	Low Power Reading (mW)
05-May-12 7:45 PM	08-May-12 5:30 AM	57.7	558	07-May-12 8:45 AM	153
02-Jun-12 9:00 PM	04-Jun-12 7:00 PM	46.0	832	03-Jun-12 8:15 AM	284
10-Jun-12 3:00 PM	12-Jun-12 5:00 PM	50.0	494	11-Jun-12 9:15 AM	124
13-Jun-12 6:30 PM	12-Jun-12 5:00 PM	40.7	584	14-Jun-12 7:45 PM	125
18-Jun-12 9:00 PM	21-Jun-12 8:30 AM	59.5	668	19-Jun-12 8:30 AM	92
26-Jun-12 10:00 PM	28-Jun-12 8:00 PM	46.0	544	28-Jun-12 8:00 AM	31
29-Jun-12 8:15 AM	01-Jul-12 4:15 AM	44.0	850	30-Jun-12 8:45 PM	149
02-Jul-12 5:45 AM	04-Jul-12 9:45 PM	64.0	458	03-Jul-12 8:30 AM	114
06-Jul-12 1:45 AM	08-Jul-12 11:00 AM	57.2	646	07-Jul-12 9:30 AM	106
24-Jul-12 2:30 AM	27-Jul-12 8:15 PM	89.7	642	25-Jul-12 9:00 AM	64
02-Aug-12 6:30 PM	06-Aug-12 2:30 AM	80.0	499	04-Aug-12 7:30 PM	119
16-Aug-12 7:30 AM	18-Aug-12 12:15 AM	40.7	468	16-Aug-12 8:15 PM	113
28-Aug-12 8:45 AM	31-Aug-12 10:45 AM	74.0	559	30-Aug-12 10:45 PM	151
02-Sep-12 1:15 PM	05-Sep-12 1:45 PM	72.5	616	03-Sep-12 9:30 AM	86
22-Oct-12 12:30 PM	25-Oct-12 9:15 AM	68.7	464	24-Oct-12 2:15 PM	64
13-Nov-12 7:15 PM	17-Nov-12 6:15 AM	83.0	463	15-Nov-12 12:15 PM	84

Source: TenneT Actual Wind Power Feed-In Data for December 2011 to November 2012

Another highly problematic aspect of wind power intermittency concerns the startling abruptness with which massive power flow changes take place. Such rapid changes of large magnitude are the cause of grid management nightmares and much premature graying for grid operators. They must scramble either to find replacement power when wind power disappears or find a power offset mechanism or storage outlet when sudden surges occur.

Over the 12-month period of time from December 1, 2011 to November 30, 2012, German and Dutch grid operator TenneT recorded numerous sudden drops in power. Figure A-5. shows 16 instances when the power flow dropped by more than 85% in a period of less than 24 hours. In the first example, wind power was feeding 7,039 mW into the grid on January 26 at 6:15 PM. But 20.7 hours later, the power level had dropped to only 915 mW, an 87% drop in less than a single day's time.[6] That was equivalent to six nuclear stations going off line suddenly and unexpectedly.

Note for instance the problems encountered by grid operators on April 2nd. In the 12-hour period up to 12:30 AM, wind was feeding in an average of 6,452 mW on a fairly steady basis with relatively low variability in intensity. But in less than 20 hours, the power flow had dropped from 6,719 mW observed at 12:30 AM to only 303 mW at 8:15 PM, wiping out more than 95% of the power flow rate observed just after midnight. Unlike the typical summer doldrums noted above, sudden power surges and abrupt drops occur throughout the entire year as Figure A-2. above demonstrates.

Northern European weather patterns have not signed the Kyoto Protocol nor agreed to cooperate with the EU's leading 'green energy' social engineers. So weather cooperation will be problematic and resistant to enforcement measures. Such was the case in the period of time from September 23 to the middle of November 2011 when a sustained frontal system descended over the northern region of Germany with each windless period lasting for many days on end.

FIGURE A-5. **TenneT Sudden Large Drops in Wind Power in Less Than 24 Hours**

Initial Reading Date - Time	Initial Reading (mW)	Second Reading Date - Time	Second Reading (mW)	Time Interval (Hours)	Percent Power Change
26-Jan-12 6:15 PM	7,039	27-Jan-12 3:00 PM	915	20.7	-87.0%
15-Feb-12 5:15 PM	6,336	16-Feb-12 10:15 AM	684	17.0	-89.2%
25-Feb-12 3:45 PM	5,611	26-Feb-12 2:15 PM	559	22.5	-90.0%
02-Apr-12 12:30 AM	6,719	02-Apr-12 8:15 PM	303	19.7	-95.5%
10-Apr-12 7:45 AM	5,119	10-Apr-12 8:30 PM	739	12.7	-85.6%
29-Apr-12 8:30 AM	5,026	30-Apr-12 5:00 AM	299	20.5	-94.1%
12-May-12 1:45 PM	6,709	13-May-12 7:45 AM	663	18.0	-90.1%
16-May-12 6:15 PM	6,425	17-May-12 6:15 PM	433	24.0	-93.3%
18-May-12 3:45 PM	4,311	19-May-12 10:15 AM	276	18.5	-93.6%
17-Jun-12 9:45 AM	5,534	17-Jun-12 11:15 PM	274	13.5	-95.0%
26-Jun-12 3:00 PM	4,228	27-Jun-12 3:45 AM	616	12.7	-85.4%
12-Jul-12 4:15 PM	4,927	13-Jul-12 9:00 AM	636	16.7	-87.1%
09-Oct-12 2:00 PM	4,613	10-Oct-12 10:45 AM	559	20.7	-87.9%
25-Oct-12 11:30 PM	4,092	26-Oct-12 11:00 AM	543	11.5	-86.7%
23-Nov-12 7:30 AM	5,064	24-Nov-12 5:30 AM	334	22.0	-93.4%
25-Nov-12 8:45 PM	8,508	26-Nov-12 8:15 PM	941	23.5	-88.9%

Source: TenneT Actual Wind Power Feed-In Data for December 2011 to November 2012

Figure A-6. shows a depiction of TenneT wind power fed into the grid over that 68-day period of time. A front descended over Northern Germany on September 23rd that dropped wind power to below 1,000 mW and, for the next nine days and 18 hours, power averaged only 391 mW.[7] That amounts to only 2.8% of system rated capacity. Instead of 16.7 million households being served as were promised by wind promoters, the physical plant could provide service to only 474,000 households. More than 16.2 million households would receive none of the promised wind power.[8]

An even longer-duration extreme event occurred several weeks later. A frontal pattern beginning on October 28 lasted throughout most of the next 26½ days. During that period of time, wind power fed into the grid averaged only 1,154 mW, which was 8.4% of rated capacity. Over this extended period, 15.3 million households would need to be served with power supplied from elsewhere.[9]

These long-duration periods of low or no wind activity are not unique to October and November 2011. Holger Gassner, who heads the Markets, Political Affairs and Corporate Responsibility at RWE Innogy, notes that there has been at least one sustained 10-day period in each of the past several years where wind power declined to below 10% of rated capacity.[10]

An almost identical pattern was exhibited by another grid operator managing a much smaller fleet of wind power turbines but very far removed from the area served by TenneT. Transnet BW operates Germany's grid situated largely in the southwestern state of Baden-Wurttemberg.[11] The Transnet BW wind pattern in Figure A-7 shows the same periods of inactivity between September 23rd and November 30th as was exhibited by TenneT hundreds of kilometers to the north.

FIGURE A-6. **TenneT Wind Power Over 68 Days — Sep. 23 to Nov. 30, 2011**

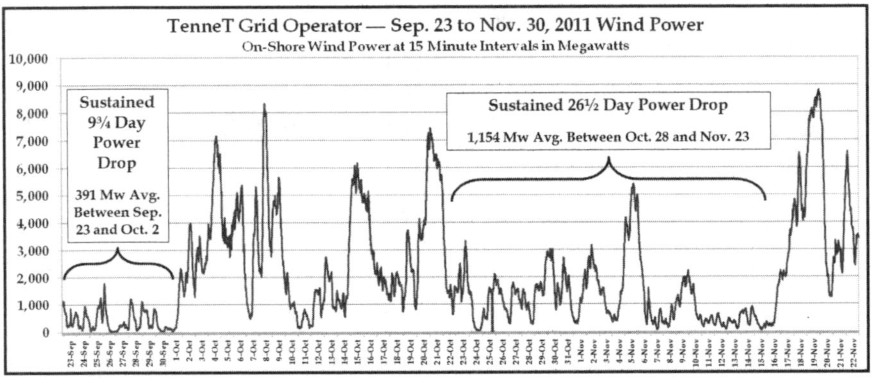

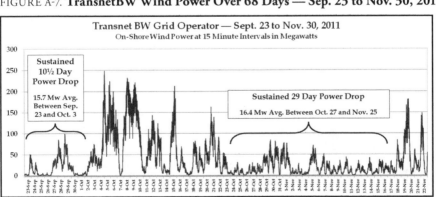

Source: TenneT Actual Wind Power Feed-In Data for September 23, 2011 to November, 30, 2011

As observed with TenneT, the turbine fleet of Transnet BW experienced a substantial drop in power on September 20th that continued almost continuously, with brief power surges, for the next 12 to 15 days. The grid operator fed only an average of 15.7 mW into the grid between September 23rd and October 3rd. Likewise, Transnet BW also suffered a long period of inactivity between October 27th and November 25th when wind power averaged only 16.4 mW.[12] These long-duration power flow readings represented a small fraction of the operator's rated capacity.

FIGURE A-7. **TransnetBW Wind Power Over 68 Days — Sep. 23 to Nov. 30, 2011**

Source: Transnet BW Actual Wind Energy Feed-In Data for September 23, 2011 to November, 30, 2011

Despite assurances in press reports and a sizeable body of belief that night time power flow in Germany from wind turbines is far higher than during daylight hours, there is little in the way of empirical evidence to substantiate that claim. Examining 12 months of power flow data for grid operator TenneT, there were actually eight months when daylight power flow showed averages that were higher than corresponding night time flow rates.

Figure A-8 shows night time and daylight average power readings by month over a 12-month period for wind power fed into the grid. As the graph shows, eight of the months experienced average daylight wind power readings higher than their corresponding night time readings. Night time readings were higher in only four of the months. Nevertheless, the differences throughout the year are relatively insubstantial.

While wind energy proponents contend that the problems of intermittency marked by extreme power drops and surges can be mitigated by increasing the scale of deployment, it is abundantly apparent that this contention lacks a factual basis. There is convincing academic support that refutes wind power promoters who claim more deployments will smooth out load variability.[13] But one does not need to consult academic journals for an accurate picture. Just examine the charts above. Or go to the wind operator databases and retrieve the data.

FIGURE A-8. **TenneT Monthly Wind Power by Night vs. Day — Dec. 2011 to Nov. 2012**

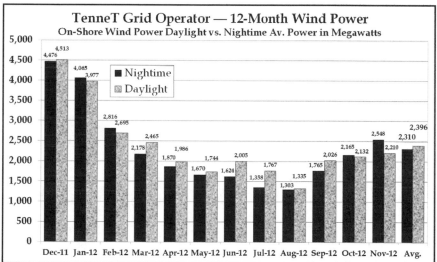

Source: TenneT Average Night Time and Daylight Wind Energy Feed-In Monthly Averages for December 2011 to November 2012

Increasing the scale of wind deployment has merely increased the scale of problems associated with intermittency. With wind tower deployed all over the German landscape and even out in the Baltic and North Seas, extreme intermittency is still clearly exhibited in the data provided by grid operator TenneT which has an impressive 13,775 mW of deployed nameplate capacity. That is more wind capacity than is deployed in any state in the U.S.[14]

ENDNOTES

INTRODUCTION

1   Ed Lasky, 'The World Turned Upside Down,' *American Thinker*, May 9, 2010

2   Mark Steyn, 'American Twilight,' *National Review*, July 7, 2012

3   Mona Charen, 'Obama and the Future Fallacy,' *Real Clear Politics*, March 20, 2012

4   John W. Schoen, 'Energy Boom Ripples Through U.S. Economy,' *CNBC*, March 26, 2013

5   Martin Zimmerman, 'RV Maker Fleetwood Files for Bankruptcy,' *Los Angeles Times*, March 11, 2009

6   Kelly Johnson, 'Manufactured Home Company Buys Closed Fleetwood Plant,' *Sacramento Business Journal*, August 16, 2009

7   Russell Gold, 'Oil and Gas Boom Lifts U.S. Economy,' *The Wall Street Journal*, February 8, 2012

8   Matthew Stone, 'Natural Gas Companies in Race to Connect Kennebec Valley,' *Bangor Daily News*, December 21, 2012

9   *op. cit.*, Russell Gold, 'Oil and Gas Boom Lifts U.S. Economy,' *The Wall Street Journal*

10   Mario Moretto, 'Natural Gas Poised to Expand to Communities Far Removed from Pipeline,' *Bangor Daily News*, December 21, 2012

11   Nick McCrea, 'Maine Needs to Catch Up, Take Advantage of Natural Gas, Officials Say,' *Bangor Daily News*, April 30, 2013

12   'Widespread Economic Growth in 2012,' *Bureau of Economic Analysis*, June 6, 2012

13   Keith Edwards, 'Natural Gas Firm Draws Hundreds to Job Fair,' *Kennebec Journal*, April 3, 2013

14   Ben Casselman and Russell Gold, 'Cheap Natural Gas Gives New Hope to the Rust Belt,' *The Wall Street Journal*, October 24, 2012

15   'Study Shows Manufacturing Renaissance from U.S. Shale Oil and Gas Development,' *Penn Energy*, September 6, 2013

16   Len Boselovic, 'CEO Says ATI Plant is "Game Changing",' *The Pittsburgh Post-Gazette*, May 12, 2013

17   Charles C.W. Cooke, 'The Quiet Gold Rush,' *National Review*, May 28, 2013

18   *ibid*

19   Tyler Hamilton, 'Canada's Oil Sands on the Verge of a Boom, Again,' *Technology Review*, April 8, 2011

20   Jack Gerard, 'Unwelcome Milestone for Keystone XL,' *Energy Tribune*, September 25, 2013

21   Jeff Bennett, 'Tire Makers' New Home,' *The Wall Street Journal*, April 16, 2012

22   'Michelin S.C. Expansion Now on Stream,' *Tire Business*, October 12, 2012

23   'Michelin Produces First Tire Plant at Expanded Lexington Plant,' *GSA Business*, October 15, 2012

24   Mike Obel, 'Michelin Spending $750M on U.S. Expansion, Job Creation,' *International Business Times*, April 10, 2012

25   Roddie Burris, 'Michelin Creating 500 Jobs in Lexington, Anderson As It Expands Tire Production in SC,' *The State*, April 11, 2012

26   Roel Landingin, 'Manufacturing Underpins Philippines' Surge in GDP,' *Financial Times*, May 31, 2013, Page 2

27   FMT Staff, 'Louisiana Foundry Makes Historic Cast,' *Foundry Management & Technology*, October 2, 2003

28   Michael Warren, 'Frack to the Future,' *The Weekly Standard*, Volume 18, No. 39, June 24, 2013

29   Joel Kurtzman, 'How Adam Smith Revived America's Oil Patch,' *The Wall Street Journal*, June 19, 2013

30   Michael Barone, 'Booming North Dakota,' *National Review*, July 23, 2012

31   ND Monthly Production Statistics, *North Dakota Department of Mineral Resources*, Bismarck, North Dakota

32   *op. cit.*, Michael Warren, 'Frack to the Future,' *The Weekly Standard*

33   A.G. Sulzberger, 'A Great Divide Over Oil Riches,' *The New York Times*, December 27, 2011

34   Noreen Malone, 'A.G. Sulzberger Writes Note to Dad Asking If He Can Come Home Yet,' *New York Magazine*, January 11, 2012

35   *op. cit.*, A.G. Sulzberger, 'A Great Divide Over Oil Riches,' *The New York Times*

36   *op. cit.*, 'Widespread Economic Growth in 2012,' *Bureau of Economic Analysis*

37   *ibid*

38   *ibid*

39   'Regional and State Employment and Unemployment — December 2011,' *Bureau of Labor Statistics*, January 24, 2012

40   *ibid*

41   'State Personal Income 2012,' *Bureau of Economic Analysis*, March 27, 2013

42   State Occupational Employment and Wage Estimates, New York vs. North Dakota, *Bureau of Labor Statistics*

43   *op. cit.*, Michael Warren, 'Frack to the Future,' *The Weekly Standard*

44   Jay Nordlinger, 'North Dakota Journal, Part II,' *National Review*, April 17, 2012

45   Barack Obama, 'Remarks in Columbus, Ohio,' *American Presidency Project*, November 2, 2008

46   Felicity Lawrence, 'Guatemala Pays High Price for Global Food System Failings,' *The Guardian*, May 31, 2011

47   Elisabeth Rosenthal, 'Once a Dream Fuel, Palm Oil May Be an Eco-Nightmare,' *The New York Times*, January 31, 2007

48   Tim Searchinger, 'How Biofuels Contribute to the Food Crisis,' *The Washington Post*, February 11, 2011

49   Govinda Timilsina, 'How Global Biofuel Expansion Could Affect the Economy, Environment and Food Supply,' *The World Bank*, June 27, 2011; see also Derek Headey and Shenggen Fan, 'Reflections on the Global Crisis,' *International Food Policy Research Institute*, 2010

50   Ethanol demand of 4.5 billion bushels of corn at Mario Parker, 'Ethanol Drops on USDA Corn Estimate,' *Bloomberg*, August 10, 2012; total corn production of 10.8 billion bushels at Mark Peters and Owen Fletcher, 'Prices Surge as Drought Stunts Corn Crop,' *The Wall Street Journal*, August 10, 2012

51   Bryan Walsh, 'Why Biofuels Help Push Up World Food Prices,' *Time*, February 14, 2011

52   Kristin Sundell, 'Ethanol Mandates Impairing Food Aid,' *Financial Times*, May 28, 2013, Page 8

53   'International Food Assistance: U.S. Nonemergency Food Aid Programs Have Similar Objectives but Some Planning Helps Limit Overlap,' *U.S. Government Accountability Office*, December 12, 2012

54   Barack Obama, 'Remarks in Portsmouth, New Hampshire: "Real Leadership for a Clean Energy Future",' *The American Presidency Project*, October 8, 2007

55   'Heating or Eating: Gloucestershire Pensioner Faces Tough Choice,' *Gloucestershire Echo*, October 31, 2011

56   'Woman, 32, Dies of Hypothermia in Cold Flat,' *Gloucestershire Echo*, March 20, 2009

57   John Bingham, 'Britain's Cold Weather: Tragedy of the Lonely Deaths of Jean and Derrick Randall,' *The Telegraph*, January 16, 2010

58   Stephen Adams, 'Cold Homes "Kill Over 5,000 a Year",' *The Telegraph*, May 12, 2011

59   'Chris Huhne at Wind Week in Leicester Square,' *YouTube*, June 17, 2010

60   Chris Semple, 'Is This the Man to Save Our Planet?,' *Southern Daily Echo*, October 21, 2007

61   Christopher Booker, 'The Climate Change Scare is Dying, But Do Our MPs Notice?,' *The Telegraph*, November 13, 2010

62   Christopher Booker, 'Chris Huhne Will Ensure the Coalition is Soon Out of Power,' *The Telegraph*, May 15, 2010

63   International Energy Statistics, CO_2 Emissions, Total Carbon Dioxide Emissions from the Consumption of Energy, Million Metric Tons, *Energy Information Administration*

64   Colin Brown and Ben Russell, 'Huhne: "We Must Be Radical But Rational - You Won't See Me Streaking Down the Street",' *The Independent*, October 10, 2007

65   'Chris Huhne Quits Cabinet Over Speeding Claims Charge,' *BBC*, February 3, 2012

66   Simon Walters, 'Chris Huhne 'Asked Others to Take Speeding Points': Climate Change Secretary Denies He Pressurised Others to Admit Motoring Offences So He Could Keep his Driving Licence,' *The Daily Mail*, May 8, 2011

67   Daniel Martin, 'More Than 25,000 Elderly Die of Cold as Fuel Poverty Hits One in Four Pensioner Households,' *The Daily Mail*, November 28, 2008

68   Nathan Rao, 'Heating Bills to Soar As You Shiver,' *The Daily Express*, January 19, 2013

69   'Fuel Poverty Is a Scandal,' *The Daily Express*, January 14, 2013

70   James Delingpole, ' "I Want to be Remembered for the Science" Says Phil "Climategate" Jones to Chorus of Titters,' *The Telegraph*, November 16, 2010

71   Phillip Sherwell, 'War of Words Over Global Warming as Nobel Laureate Resigns in Protest,' *The Telegraph*, September 25, 2011

72   Graham Hiscott, 'Price Hikes and Power Cuts: Regulator's Bleak Warning of Future Energy Crisis,' *The Daily Mirror*, February 19, 2013

73   Simon Read, 'Fuel Poverty Deaths Three Times Higher Than Government Estimates,' *The Independent*, February 28, 2012

74   James Hall, 'At Least 2,700 a Year Die in Freezing Homes,' *The Telegraph*, October 20, 2011

75   Daniel Martin and James Clayton, 'Frozen to Death as Fuel Bills Soar" Hypothermia Cases Among the Elderly Double in Five Years,' *The Daily Mail*, February 13, 2012

76   *ibid*

77   Michael D. Lemonick, 'Freeman Dyson Takes on the Climate Establishment,' *Yale Environment 360*, June 4, 2009

78   Felicity Lawrence, 'Fuel Poverty Affects a Quarter of UK's Households as Bills Soar and Pay Freezes,' *The Guardian*, December 1, 2011

79   Matt Chorley, 'Up to 9 Million Families "Will Be in Fuel Poverty by 2016" Without Action to Insulate Homes, Campaigners Warn PM,' *The Daily Mail*, January 21, 2013

80   Rowena Mason, 'Britain "On the Brink" of Energy Crisis, Warns Regulator,' *The Telegraph*, February 19, 2013

81   'Osborne Backs Fracking with Tax Breaks to Reduce U.K. Bills,' *Bloomberg New Energy Finance*, December 5, 2012

82   Tom McGhie, 'Customers Face Huge Bill for Wind Farms that Don't Work in the Cold,' *The Daily Mail*, January 8, 2011

83   'Era of Constant Electricity at Home Is Endings, Says Power Chief,' *The Daily Telegraph*, March 2, 2011

84   Steve Holliday, Part 1 - Speech to the "Power to the People" Conference, *Royal Academy of Engineering*, March 1, 2011 at the 7:27 mark

85   *ibid*, at the 16:46 mark

86   Simon Parry and Ed Douglas, 'In China, the True Cost of Britain's Clean, Green Wind Power Experiment: Pollution on a Disastrous Scale,' *The Daily Mail*, January 26,

87   Mark Kinver, 'Low Solar Activity Link to Cold UK Winters,' *BBC*, April 14, 2010

88   James Chapman and Matt Chorley, 'The Lights Will Go Out Over Britain: Shares in Energy Firms Drop 5% Amid Warnings of Blackouts from Miliband's Plan to Freeze Bills,' *The Daily Mail*, September 24, 2013

89   Richard Evans, 'Miliband's Energy Price Cap Hits Centrica and SSE Shares,' *The Daily Telegraph*, September 25, 2013

90   Tim Webb, 'Energy Bosses Vent Their Fury as Miliband Plan Hammers Shares,' *The Times*, September 25, 2013

91   'PG&E Seeks Bankruptcy,' *CNN*, April 6, 2001

92   'California Narrowly Escapes Power Cuts,' *BBC*, January 12, 2001; see also 'Energy Crisis Overview: How We Got Here,' *San Francisco Chronicle*, May 8, 2001

93   James Chapman, et. al., 'Miliband's Bid to Fix Fuel Price Blows Up in His Face As Critics Accuse Him of Pure "Economic Vandalism" and £2.bn Wiped Off Value of Energy Giants,' *The Daily Mail*, September 25, 2013

94   'Tougher Climate Target Unveiled,' *BBC*, October 16, 2008

95   *ibid*

96   'Gas: UK "Was Six Hours From Running Out",' *Sky News*, May 24, 2013

97   Louise Barnett, 'Gas Supplies Running Out as Britain Shivers,' *The Daily Express*, January 5, 2010

98   Padraic Flanagan, 'UK's Coldest Spring Since 1963 Claims 5,000 Lives: Pensioners Worst Affected — and Experts Say Final Toll Could Be "Horrendous",' *The Daily Mail*, March 23, 2013

99   *ibid*

100 Nigel Lawson, 'Let's Get Fracking,' *The House Magazine*, September 26, 2013

101 Peter Campbell, 'Britain "Was Just Six Hours Away from Running Out of Gas": And Experts Say a New Power Crisis Looms,' *The Daily Mail*, May 24, 2013

102 Louise Gray, 'Shale Gas "Could Heat All Homes for 100 Years",' *The Telegraph*, April 5, 2013

103 Tim Webb, Britain Has Shale Gas for 1,500 Years, But Bills Won't Be Lower,' *The Times*, February 9, 2013

104 Geoffrey Lean, 'Which Side Will You Take in Britain's Frack Wars?,' *The Telegraph*, May 10, 2013

105 Peter C. Glover, 'UK Government Still Dithering on "New North Sea" of Shale Gas,' *Energy Tribune*, June 18, 2013

106 CBC News, 'Northern B.C. Fracking License Concerns Critics,' *Canadian Broadcasting Company*, July 29, 2011; see also Stephen Ewart, 'Canadian Fracking Firms Join Big Debate,' *Calgary Herald*, February 23, 2013

107 'Fracking in Australia: Gas Goes Boom,' *The Economist*, June 2, 2012

108 Avital Lahav, 'Natural Gas Begins to Flow from Tamar Gas Field,' *YNet News*, March 30, 2013

109 Tim Daiss, 'Indonesia Tries to Jump-Start its Own Shale Revolution,' *Energy Tribune*, June 26, 2013

110 Jaime Kammerzell, 'China Looks to Emulate U.S. Shale Success,' *Rigzone*, November 15, 2012

111 Peter C. Glover, 'Europe's Fracking Energy Mess,' *Energy Tribune*, May 31, 2013

112 Karina Grazina, 'Chevron Says Argentina Has World's No. 2 Shale Oil Resources,' *The Globe and Mail*, May 16, 2013

113 Raphael Minder, 'Spain Stings Argentina Over Oil Company Nationalization,' *The New York Times*, April 20,

2012; Hilariously, investment capital to tap the country's bountiful supplies of natural gas resources would be pouring into Argentina today to take advantage of very high gas prices in the market had it not been for global producers' fear that their assets would be nationalized. The country could have used the foreign exchange earnings to help stave off sovereign default that appears to be a certainty. See Benedict Mander, 'Risk of Default Adds to Woes for Argentina's Fernandez,' *Financial Times*, September 16, 2013

114 Jens Thurau, 'Fracking Evokes "Angst" in Germany,' *Deutsche Welle*, January 8, 2013

115 'Technically Recoverable Shale Oil and Shale Gas Resources: An Assessment of 137 Shale Formations in 41 Countries Outside the United States,' *Energy Information Administration*, June 2013, Page 13

116 *op. cit.*, Geoffrey Lean, 'Which Side Will You Take in Britain's Frack Wars?,' *The Telegraph*

117 Richard North, 'United in Lunacy,' *EU Referendum*, April 19, 2013

118 James Delingpole, 'Lilley Sticks It to "Trougher" Yeo,' *The Telegraph*, April 22, 2013

119 *ibid*

120 UN Framework Convention on Climate Change,' *UK Parliament*, Westminster Hall, April 18, 2013

121 Christopher Booker, 'The Mercury is Falling, But Our MPs Are Full of Hot Air,' *The Telegraph*, April 27, 2013

122 Hayley Dixon, 'Trust in EU Falls to Record Low,' *The Telegraph*, April 24, 2013

123 Steve Goreham, 'The Tragedy of Climatism: Resource Misuse on a Global Scale,' *The Washington Times*, May 2, 2013

124 Christopher Booker, 'Saturday Essay: Eco Madness and How Our Future Is Going Up in Smoke As We Pay Billions to Switch from Burning Coal to Wood Chips at Britain's Biggest Power Station,' *The Daily Mail*, March 8, 2013

125 Jeremy Lovell, 'Biofuels: Europe's 2nd Biggest Coal-Fired Plant Will Turn to Wood from North America,' *Environment & Energy Daily*, April 8, 2013

126 Thomas K. Grose, 'As Coal Plants Shut Down, United Kingdom Faces a Power Crunch,' *National Geographic*, August 29, 2013

127 Review & Outlook, 'Burn the Forests, Save the Planet?,' *The Wall Street Journal*, May 29, 2013

128 Christopher Booker, 'Saturday Essay: Eco Madness and How Our Future is Going Up in Smoke as We Pay Billions to Switch from Burning Coal to Wood Chips at Britain's Biggest Power Station,' *The Daily Mail*, March 8, 2013

129 Justin Scheck and Ianthe Jeanne Dugan, 'Europe's Green-Fuel Search Turns to America's Forests,' *The Wall Street Journal*, May 28, 2013, Page A1

130 Anna Austin, 'Shaping Up to Ship Out,' *Biomass Magazine*, September 23, 2013

131 'Wood: The Fuel of the Future,' *The Economist*, April 6, 2013

132 Electricity: Wholesale Market Data, Wholesale Day Ahead Prices at Selected Hubs, Peak 2012, *Energy Information Administration*, May 2, 2013

133 Terry Macalister, James Ball and Damian Carrington, 'Big Six Energy Firms Face Fresh Accusations of Profiteering,' *The Guardian*, December 2, 2011

134 Damian Carrington, 'Cuadrilla Breached Fracking Conditions, Court Told,' *The Guardian*, September 10, 2012

135 'Climate Change Madness: Do the Europeans Know What They Are Doing?,' *Institute for Energy Research*, April 30, 2013

136 'Economic Affairs — Fourth Report: The Economics of Renewable Energy,' *House of Lords*, Chapter 3. Technologies for Renewable Electricity Generation, November 12, 2008

137 'UK Electricity Prices Almost Twice as Expensive as Germany Within Three Years,' *The Telegraph*, June 19, 2013

138 'Household Electricity Prices in the EU27 Rose by 6.6% and Gas Prices by 10.3%,' *Eurostat*, May 27, 2013

139 'Electric Power Monthly with Data for December 2012,' *Energy Information Administration*, February 2013, Table 5.3. Average Retail Price of Electricity to Ultimate Customers, Total by End-Use Sector, 2003 - December 2012 in Cents per Kilowatt-Hour

140 *op. cit.*, 'Wood: The Fuel of the Future,' *The Economist*

141 *ibid*

142 'Funding Shortfall: Germany Forced to Cancel Programs,' *Der Spiegel*, March 18, 2013

143 Gerard Wynn, 'Britain's Carbon Tax: Unfair and Ineffective,' *Reuters*, March 19, 2013

144 'Evidence of "Earliest Fire Use",' *BBC*, April 3, 2012

145 Ilan Brat and Christopher Bjork, 'Spain Said to Be Poised to Cut Renewable Subsidies,' *The Wall Street Journal*, June 6, 2013

146 'Zapatero Pins Faith in Renewable Energy Amid Nuclear Debate,' *Energy Daily*, January 17, 2007

147 Barack Obama, 'New Energy for America Speech,' *American Presidency Project*, Lansing, Michigan, August 4, 2008

148 Barack Obama, 'Closing Argument Speech: 'One Week,' Canton, Ohio, *The American Presidency Project*, October 27, 2008

149   Gabriel Calzada Alvarez, et. al., 'Study of the Effects on Employment of Public Aid to Renewable Energy Sources,' *Universidad Rey Juan Carlos*, Volumen VII, Número 1, Primavera 2010. ISSN: 1697-6797-13, March 2009, Page 28

150   Peter Altman, 'Spain Rejects Calzada "Spanish Jobs" Study,' *Switchboard*, May 20, 2009

151   Angel Gonzalez and Keith Johnson, 'Spain's Solar-Power Collapse Dims Subsidy Model,' *The Wall Street Journal*, September 8, 2009

152   *ibid*

153   Terry McAlister, 'Uncertainty Over Spanish Economy Hits Green Energy Firms' Ambitions to Float,' *The Guardian*, May 13, 2010

154   Ben Sills, 'Spain Halts Renewable Subsidies to Curb $31 Billion of Debts,' *Bloomberg*, January 27, 2012

155   'Voters Punish Zapatero: Spain's "Lost Generation" Vows to Fight On,' *Der Spiegel*, May 23, 2011

156   Andrés González and Tracy Rucinski, 'Update 2 - Spain Unveils Fresh Energy Reforms that Hit Renewables,' *Reuters*, February 1, 2013

157   Andrés González, 'Spain's Public Debt to Approach 100 Percent of GDP End-2014,' *Reuters*, September 30, 2013

158   International Energy Statistics, Solar Generation as a Percentage of Total Net Generation in 2012, *Energy Information Administration*

159   Bjørn Lomborg, 'Green Energy Is the Real Subsidy Hog,' *The Wall Street Journal*, November 11, 2013

160   AFP, 'Spanish Unemployment Rate at Record 27.16%,' *France24*, April 25, 2013

161   Harmonised Unemployment Rate by Sex, *Eurostat*

162   Giles Tremlett, 'Spain: The Pain of Austerity Deepens,' *The Guardian*, December 31, 2012

163   Barack Obama, 'Remarks at a Town Hall in Elkhart, Indiana,' *The American Presidency Project*, August 6, 2008

164   'Edison Mission Group Begins Commercial Operation of Cedro Hill Wind Farm in Texas,' *Reuters*, December 23, 2010

165   'Wind Farm Up in Oilton, But Not Many Local Jobs Offered,' *KGNS-TV*, June 10, 2010

166   Ianthe Jeanne Dugan and Justin Scheck, 'Cost of $10 Billion Stimulus Easier to Tally Than New Jobs,' *The Wall Street Journal*, February 24, 2012

167   *ibid*

168   *ibid*

169   Laylan Copelin, 'Combs Report Says Texas Overpays in Tax Breaks to Wind Farms Based on Job Creation,' *The Dallas Morning News*, December 20, 2010

170   Based upon 375 terawatt-hours of anticipated annual production at 'Cedro Hill Windfarm,' *The Wind Power Database*

171   Gary Scharrer, 'Teacher Pay Threatens Student Achievement, Expert Testifies,' *The Houston Chronicle*, December 4, 2012

172   'AWAE U.S. Wind Industry Third Quarter 2013 Market Report,' *American Wind Energy Association*, October 31, 2013, Page 5

173   'Rankings & Estimates: Rankings of the States 2010 and Estimates of School Statistics 2011,' *National Education Association*, December 2010, Table H-9 Expenditures for Public K-12 Schools per Student in Fall Enrollment, Page 54

174   'Statistical Abstract of the United States: 2012,' Table 233. Education Attainment by State 1990 to 2009, *U.S. Census Bureau*, 2012, Page 153

175   *op. cit.*, Ianthe Jeanne Dugan and Justin Scheck, 'Cost of $10 Billion Stimulus Easier to Tally Than New Jobs,' *The Wall Street Journal*

176   Jan M. Olsen, Associated Press, 'Denmark's First Female Prime Minister Presents New Coalition,' *1310 News*, October 3, 2011

177   'Danish PM Presents New Cabinet,' *Xinhua*, October 3, 2011

178   'Bicycles to Visit the Queen,' *Copenhagenize*, October 3, 2011

179   Bjørn Lomborg, 'Environmental Hypocrisy in Current Politics Runs Deeper than Photo Opportunities,' *The Economic Times*, November 22, 2011

180   Vincent Moss, 'We Find and Return Conservative Leader David Cameron's Stolen Bicycle,' *The Daily Mirror*, July 26, 2008

181   'Hypocrisy Claim Over Cameron Bike,' *BBC*, April 28, 2006

182   'Cameron Reveals Weekly Bike Ride,' *BBC*, August 8, 2006

183   Drew Ryun, CEO Surge Data Tech, *LinkedIn*

184   Josh Hicks, 'IRS Released Confidential Info on Conservative Groups to ProPublica,' *The Washington Post*, May 14, 2013

185   Glenn Harlan Reynolds, 'Tax Audits Are No Laughing Matter,' *The Wall Street Journal*, May 18, 2009

186   Mark Steyn, 'The Autocrat Accountants,' *National Review*, May 17, 2013

187   Ashley Southall, 'Obama Vows to Push Immigration Changes,' *The New York Times*, October 25, 2011

188 See for instance Marc A. Thiessen, 'Richard Milhous Obama?,' *The Washington Post*, May 23, 2011; see also Carl M. Cannon, 'Richard Milhous Obama,' *Real Clear Politics*, May 20, 2013

189 Michael Barone, 'The Coming Liberal Thugocracy,' *The Washington Times*, October 13, 2008

190 Primary energy data from 'Annual Energy Review 2011,' Table 1.1 Primary Energy Overview, *Energy Information Administration*, September 2012; population estimates from *U.S. Census Bureau*, Historical Data

191 See for instance Conor Dougherty, 'Income Slides to 1996 Levels,' *The Wall Street Journal*, September 14, 2011; see also Sabrina Tavernise, 'U.S. Income Gap Rose, Sign of Uneven Recovery,' *The New York Times*, September 12, 2012; see also Annie Lowrey, 'Household Incomes Remain Flat Despite Improving Economy,' *The New York Times*, September 17, 2013

192 Dennis Cauchon and Barbara Hansen, 'Typical U.S. Family Got Poorer During the Past 10 Years,' *USA Today*, September 14, 2011

193 Survey of Income and Program Participation, *U.S. Census Bureau*, Table 7. Number and Percent of Households Receiving Benefits from Selected Means-Tested Noncash Benefit Programs, August 2008 to End of 2011

194 *ibid*

195 Labor Force Participation Rate, Seasonally Adjusted, Labor Force Statistics from the Current Population Survey, *Bureau of Labor Statistics*

196 Unemployed, Seasonally Adjusted, Labor Force Statistics from the Current Population Survey, *Bureau of Labor Statistics*

197 See Labor Force Statistics from the Current Population Survey, ratio of change in Civilian Non-institutional Population December 2008 to September 2013 of 11,133,000 persons vs. change in Civilian Labor Force of 904,000 persons available at *Bureau of Labor Statistics*

198 See for instance 'Overlap and Duplication in Food and Nutrition Service's Nutrition Programs,' *Office of Inspector General*, U.S. Department of Agriculture, June 2013; see also Elizabeth Harrington, '101M Get Food Aid from Federal Gov't: Outnumber Full-Time Private Sector Workers,' *CNS News*, July 8, 2013

199 Current Employment Statistics, Total Private Payrolls, *Bureau of Labor Statistics*

200 See 2011 joint Census-BLS data from the Current Population Survey at '2011 Person Income Tables,' Annual Social and Economic Supplement, *U.S. Census Bureau*, Both Sexes, Worked Full-Time, Year-Round

201 'Supplemental Nutrition Assistance Program: Number of Persons Participation — January 2009 vs. 'Supplemental Nutrition Assistance Program: Number of Persons Participation — April 2013,' *U.S. Department of Agriculture* compared to Employment Level — Seasonally Adjusted, *Bureau of Labor Statistics*

202 Employed, Usually Work Full Time - Seasonally Adjusted of 116,053,000 for April 2013 vs. 115,820,000 for January 2009, *Bureau of Labor Statistics*

203 Hope Yen, 'Exclusive: 4 in 5 in U.S. Face Near-Poverty, No Work,' *Associated Press*, July 28, 2013

204 International Energy Statistics, CO_2 Emissions in Million Metric Tons, *Energy Information Administration*

205 Matt McGrath, 'Can Germany Afford Its "Energy Bender" Shift to Green Power?,' *BBC*, July 9, 2013

206 'Germany's Green Energy Destabilizing Electric Grids,' *Institute for Energy Research*, January 23, 2013

207 'Germany's Energy Poverty: How Electricity Became a Luxury Good,' *Der Spiegel*, September 4, 2013

208 Gunnar Beck, 'Germany the Euro Winner? Hardly,' *The New York Times*, June 26, 2012

209 'Tilting at Windmills,' *The Economist*, June 15, 2013

210 *ibid*

211 Spiegel Staff, 'The Price of Green Energy: Is Germany Killing the Environment to Save It?,' *Der Spiegel*, March 12, 2013

212 *op. cit.*, 'Germany's Energy Poverty: How Electricity Became a Luxury Good,' *Der Spiegel*

213 *op. cit.*, Matt McGrath, 'Can Germany Afford Its "Energy Bender" Shift to Green Power?,' *BBC*

214 See President's Fiscal Year 2013 Budget, Historical Tables, *U.S. Office of Management and Budget*, Table 1.1— Summary of Receipts, Outlays, and Surpluses or Deficits 1789–2017

215 Daniel Henninger, 'Enviromania,' *The Wall Street Journal*, August 7, 2008

216 *op. cit.*, Barack Obama, 'New Energy for America Speech,' *American Presidency Project*, Lansing, Michigan, August 4, 2008

217 *ibid*

CHAPTER 1

1 Friedrich Hayek, *The Fatal Conceit: Errors of Socialism*, Volume 1 of *The Collected Works of Friedrich August Hayek*, W.W. Bartley III, Editor, London: Routledge, 1988, Page 76

2 David Sout, 'Gore Calls for Carbon-Free Electric Power,' *The New York Times*, July 18, 2008

3 Murray Wardrop, 'Copenhagen Climate Summit: Al Gore Condemned Over Arctic Ice Melting Prediction,' *The Telegraph*, December 15, 2009

4   Zoe Brennan and Annette Witheridge, 'A Very Inconvenient Masseuse: How Saint Al Gore, the Sanctimonious Eco-Crusader, Lost His Halo (and His Wife),' *The Daily Mail*, July 2, 2010

5   Thomas R. Malthus, *An Essay on the Principle of Population, or a View of its Past and Present Effects on Human Happiness*, London: J. Johnson Publishers, 1803

6   William L. Laurence, 'Population Outgrows Food, Scientists Warn the World,' *The New York Times*, September 15, 1948, Page 1

7   As a graduate student in the late 1970s, Holdren co-authored a 1977 tract with Ehrlich and Ehrlich that advocated forced sterilizations, contamination of the nation's water supply with contraceptives, and other monstrous measures. See Paul R. Ehrlich, Anne H. Ehrlich, and John P. Holdren, *Ecoscience: Population, Resources Environment*, San Francisco: W. H. Freeman and Co., 1977

8   John Tierney, 'Betting on the Planet,' *The New York Times*, December 2, 1990

9   Indur M. Goklany, *The Improving State of the World: Why We're Living Longer, Healthier, More Comfortable Lives on a Cleaner Planet*, Washington, DC: Cato Institute Press, 2007

10   George F. Will, 'As the Oceans Rise,' *The Daily Beast*, June 7, 2008

11   Office of the White House Press Secretary,' Weekly Address: President Obama Calls Energy Bill Passage Critical to Stronger American Economy,' June 27, 2009

12   See for instance a poll by a Democratic Party-aligned firm testing partisan attitudes to "conspiracy theories" of which climate change is supposedly one at Ben Geman, 'Poll: Majority of Republicans Believe Global Warming a Hoax,' *The Hill*, April 3, 2013

13   See for instance Dorthe Dahl-Jensen, et. al., 'Eemian Interglacial Reconstructed from a Greenland Folded Ice Core,' *Nature*, Volume 493, January 23, 2013, Pages 489-494; see also 'Greenland Ice Cores Reveal Warm Climate of the Past,' *Niels Bohr Institute*, University of Copenhagen, January 22, 2013

14   See for instance Richard B. Alley, et. al., 'Abrupt Increase in Greenland Snow Accumulation at the End of the Younger Dryas Event,' *Nature*, Volume 362, April 8, 1993, Pages 527-529; see also the temperature data set at Alley, R.B.. 2004, 'GISP2 Ice Core Temperature and Accumulation Data,' *NOAA Paleoclimatology Program and World Data Center for Paleoclimatology*, Boulder, Colorado

15   *op. cit.*, 'Greenland Ice Cores Reveal Warm Climate of the Past,' *Niels Bohr Institute*, University of Copenhagen

16   International Energy Statistics, Total Carbon Dioxide Emissions from the Consumption of Energy (Million Metric Tons), *Energy Information Administration*

17   'Global CO2 Emissions Rise 3 Percent in 2011: Report,' *Reuters*, July 19, 2012

18   Alexis Madrigal, 'China's 2030 CO2 Emissions Could Equal the Entire World's Today,' *Wired*, February 8, 2008

19   Annual Energy Outlook 2013 with Projections to 2040, World Carbon Dioxide Emissions by Region, Reference Case, *Energy Information Administration*, April 2013

20   *ibid*

21   Ailun Yang and Yiyun Cui, 'Global Coal Risk Assessment: Data Analysis and Market Research,' *World Resources Institute*, November 2012, Page 1

22   'Countries Worldwide Propose to Build 1,200 New Coal Plants,' *Institute for Energy Research*, November 29, 2012

23   'Monthly Energy Review, November 2013,' Table 7.1 Electricity Overview (Billion Kilowatt-Hours), *Energy Information Administration*, Page 93

24   Coal Consumption (Million Tons of Oil Equivalent), *BP Statistical Review of World Energy 2013*

25   *ibid*

26   *ibid*

27   Roger Altman, 'Prepare to Celebrate OPEC's Demise,' *Financial Times*, May 21, 2012

28   Max Schulz, 'Media Blows Climate Change Story,' *Townhall*, December 11, 2009

29   Geoff Dyer, 'China Sets Target for 2020 Carbon Cuts,' *Financial Times*, November 26, 2009

30   'BP Energy Outlook 2030,' January 2013, Page 43

31   Ryan Tracy, 'China, India to Drive World's Growing Energy Use,' *The Wall Street Journal*, July 25, 2013

32   *op. cit.*, Geoff Dyer, 'China Sets Target for 2020 Carbon Cuts,' *Financial Times*

33   Chip Knappenberger, 'Carbon Tax: Climatically Useless,' *Master Resource*, December 3, 2012

34   Roger Pielke Jr., Tom Wigley and Christopher Green, 'Dangerous Assumptions,' *Nature*, Volume 452, April 3, 2008, Pages 531-2

35   Lee Kuan Yew, 'Warning Bell for Developed Countries: Declining Birth Rates,' *Forbes*, October 16, 2012

36   *op. cit.*, 'BP Energy Outlook 2030,' January 2013, Page 9

37   A silly 1979 book authored by a Harvard egghead helped kickoff a decade of delusional hysteria that Japan would soon eclipse America. The author offered helpful lessons on how Americans could accustom themselves to becoming junior partners to their Japanese masters. See Ezra F. Vogel, *Japan as No. 1: Lessons for America*, Lincoln, Nebraska: iUniverse, 1979

38   AFP, 'Population Clock Shows Japan Faces Extinction in 1000 Years,' *The Sydney Morning Herald*, May 13, 2012

39   Jonathan V. Last, 'America's Baby Bust,' *The Wall Street Journal*, February 12, 2013

40   Simon Mundy, 'Low South Korean Birth Rates Raises Fears,' *Financial Times*, January 2, 2013

41   *op. cit.*, Jonathan V. Last, 'America's Baby Bust,' *The Wall Street Journal*

42   Alex Greig, 'Baby Bust? National Birthrate Hits an All-Time Low Due to Weak Economic Recovery,' *The Daily Mail*, July 9, 2013

43   Jeevan Vasagar, 'Angela Merkel Wins Historic Third Term in German Elections,' *The Telegraph*, September 22, 2013

44   Patricia Kowsmann, 'Slowing Birthrates Weigh on Europe's Weak Economies,' *The Wall Street Journal*, January 7, 2013

45   Holly Ellyatt, 'Baby Blues in Europe as Birth Rate Declines,' *CNBC*, May 21, 2013

46   World Economic Outlook Database, *International Monetary Fund*, April 2013

47   *op. cit.*, 'BP Energy Outlook 2030,' January 2013, Page 9

48   *op. cit.*, World Economic Outlook Database, *International Monetary Fund*, April 2013; 'BP Energy Outlook 2030,' January 2013

49   *ibid*

50   See Figure 5-3 Per Capita Energy Consumption 2000-2012 chart in Chapter 5

51   Annual Energy Review 2011, *Energy Information Administration*, September 27, 2012, Page 5 vs. Historical National Population Estimates, 1900 to 1999, *U.S. Census Bureau*

52   Roger Pielke, Jr., *The Climate Fix: What Politicians Won't Tell You About Global Warming*, New York: Basic Books, 2010; see also Roger Pielke Jr., 'Decelerating Decarbonization of the Global Economy,' *Roger Pielke Jr. Blog*, July 1, 2010; see also J.G.J. Olivier and J.A.H.W. Peters, 'No Growth in Total CO_2 Emissions in 2009,' *Netherlands Environmental Assessment Agency*, June 2010

53   Ning Zeng, et. al., 'Climate Change — the Chinese Challenge,' *Science*, Volume 319,February 8, 2008, Pages 730-1

54   International Energy Outlook 2013, Table A1. World Total Primary Energy Consumption by Region vs. Table F1. Total World Delivered Energy Consumption by End-Use Sector and Fuel, *Energy Information Administration*, July 25, 2013

55   *ibid*

56   *ibid*

57   *ibid*

58   William D. Nordhaus, *A Question of Balance: Weighing the Options on Global Warming Policies*, New Haven, Connecticut: Yale University Press, 2008, Page 19

59   Walter Russell Mead, 'Another EU Greenfail as Poland Vetoes Carbon Targets,' *The American Interest*, March 10, 2012

60   *op. cit.*, 'BP Energy Outlook 2030,' January 2013, Page 11

61   'International Energy Outlook 2011,' Table A10 World Carbon Dioxide Emissions by Region, Reference Case, 2006-2035, *Energy Information Administration*, September 19, 2011

62   Annual Energy Review 2011, Table 1.1 Primary Energy Overview, *Energy Information Administration*, September 2012

63   Annual Energy Outlook 2013 Reference Case, Table A1 Total Energy Supply and Disposition Demand, *Energy Information Administration*

64   Vaclav Smil, 'Energy Transitions' in 'Energy Vision 2013 — Energy Transitions: Past and Future,' *World Economic Future*, January 2013, Page 10

65   'Key World Energy Statistics 2013,' *International Energy Agency*, 2013, Page 6

66   Primary Energy Consumption (Million Tons of Oil Equivalent) vs. Coal Consumption (Million Tons of Oil Equivalent), *BP Statistical Review of World Energy 2013*

67   Florence Tan, et. al., 'Coal to Surpass Oil as Top Global Fuel by 2020 — Woodmac,' *Reuters*, October 15, 2013

68   *op. cit.*, Vaclav Smil, 'Energy Transitions' in 'Energy Vision 2013 — Energy Transitions: Past and Future,' *World Economic Future*

69   *ibid*

70   *ibid*

71   Amory B. Lovins, 'Energy Strategy: The Road Not Taken?,' *Foreign Affairs*, Volume 55, No. 4, October 1976, Page 90

72   Lovins followed up this theme one year after his *Foreign Affairs* article was published, writing a book-length manuscript positing that his "soft energy path" would lead to a "durable peace." See Amory B. Lovins, *Soft Energy Paths: Toward a Durable Peace*, Cambridge, Massachusetts: Ballinger Press, 1977

73   Review & Outlook, 'The Coming Nuclear Breakout,' *The Wall Street Journal*, April 7, 2013

74   For a discussion of how the UN IPCC has deliberately exaggerated climate response to atmospheric CO_2, see

Matt Ridley, 'Cooling Down the Fears of Climate Change,' *The Wall Street Journal*, December 18, 2012; for a less forthright discussion that strives to save face for the climate hysterics at *The Economist*, see 'A Sensitive Matter, *The Economist*, March 30, 2013

75   Graham Lloyd, 'Twenty Year Hiatus in Rising Temperatures Has Climate Scientists Puzzled,' *The Australian*, March 30, 2013

76   Alistair Doyle, 'Climate Scientists Struggle to Explain Warming Slowdown,' *Reuters*, April 16, 2013

77   See for instance the gross overestimate of future warming in Figure 1 offered by global warming hysteric James Hansen in a 1981 paper at James Hansen, et. al., 'Climate Impact of Increasing Atmospheric Carbon Dioxide,' *Science*, Volume 213, No. 4511, August 28, 1981, Page 960

78   Rupert Darwell, 'The Climate-Change Circus,' *National Review*, September 22, 2013

79   Maxim Lott, 'Draft UN Climate Report Shows 20 Years of Overestimated Global Warming, Skeptics Warn,' *Fox News*, January 28, 2013

80   Michael Batasch, 'Top MIT Scientist. Newest UN Climate Report is "Hilariously" Flawed,' *The Daily Caller*, September 29, 2013

81   Sarah Griffiths, 'Why Has Global Warming Slowed? Scientists Admit They Don't Know Why — But Are "95% Sure" Humans Are to Blame for Climate Change,' *The Daily Mail*, August 21, 2013

82   Alex Morales, 'Global Warming Slowdown Data Sought in UN Climate Report,' *Bloomberg*, August 29, 2013

83   Rich Lowry, 'The New Climate Deniers,' *National Review*, April 2, 2013

84   Annual Energy Review 2011, Table 8.2a Electricity Net Generation: Total (All Sectors), 1949–2011, *Energy Information Administration*

85   Natural Gas Prices, U.S. Natural Gas Citygate Price, Dollars per Thousand Cubic Feet, *Energy Information Administration*

86   Spot Prices, Crude Oil in Dollars per Barrel, WTI-Cushing, Oklahoma, *Energy Information Administration*

87   *op. cit.*, Annual Energy Outlook 2013 Reference Case, Table A1 Total Energy Supply and Disposition Demand, *Energy Information Administration*

88   'Monthly Energy Review, October 2013,' Table 3.1 Petroleum Overview, *Energy Information Administration*

89   *ibid*; Spot Prices, Cushing, OK WTI Spot Price FOB (Dollars per Barrel), *Energy Information Administration*

90   Bryan Walsh, 'Carbon Regulations and Keystone Silence: Previewing Obama's Climate Speech,' *Time*, June 25, 2013

91   'Annual Energy Outlook 2013 with Projections to 2040,' *Energy Information Administration*, Table A18. Energy-Related Carbon Dioxide Emissions by Sector and Source, Page 155

92   'Annual Energy Review 2011,' *Energy Information Administration*, Table 11.1 Carbon Dioxide Emissions From Energy Consumption by Source, Selected Years, 1949-2011, Page 303

93   Kerry Picket, 'Picket: EPA Imposes Obama's Cap and Trade Regs — Energy Prices 'Skyrocket',' *The Washington Times*, August 20, 2011

94   *op. cit.*, Annual Energy Outlook 2013 with Projections to 2040, *EIA*

95   Ashley Killough, 'Obama Wants Limits on Coal Plants, Says Keystone Can't Boost Pollution,' *CNN*, June 26, 2013

96   *op. cit.*, 'International Energy Outlook 2011,' *EIA*, Table A10 World Carbon Dioxide Emissions by Region

97   Benjamin Zycher, 'Carbon Pollution and Wealth Redistribution,' *The American*, June 26, 2013

98   Steve Connor, 'Letters to a Heretic: An Email Conversation with Climate Change Sceptic Professor Freeman Dyson,' *The Independent*, February 25, 2011

99   Petroleum & Other Liquids, Crude Oil Production, *Energy Information Administration*

100   Annual Energy Review, Table 5.1b Petroleum Overview, 1949-2010, *Energy Information Administration*, October 19, 2011

101   Annual Energy Review, Table 5.19 Landed Costs of Crude Oil Imports From Selected Countries, 1973-2010, *Energy Information Administration*, October 19, 2011

102   William. D. Smith, 'Price Quadruples for Iranian Crude Oil at Auction,' *The New York Times*, December 12, 1973

103   'Environment: The Energy Crisis: Time for Action, *Time*, May 7, 1973

104   'President Nixon Imposes Wage and Price Controls,' *The Econ Review*, August 15, 1971

105   Editorial, 'How Gas Price Controls Sparked '70s Shortages,' *The Washington Times*, May 15, 2006

106   'Shortages: Gas Fever: Happiness Is a Full Tank,' *Time*, February 18, 1974

107   Joseph Kalt authored an insightful, book-length dissertation of the policy disaster that plagued the 1970s. See Joseph Kalt, *The Economic and Politics of Oil Price Regulation: Federal Policy in the Post-Embargo Era*, Cambridge, Massachusetts: MIT Press, 1981

108   An excellent recounting of government interventionism in energy markets during the 1970s is at Jerry Taylor and Peter Van Doren, 'Economic Amnesia: The Case Against Oil Price Controls and Windfall Profit Taxes,' *Cato Institute*, January 12, 2006, Pages 8-13. It took years to learn that Soviet-style economic interventionism is doomed to fail. In the Obama era, Americans have been forced to re-learn that lesson.

109 op. cit., Annual Energy Review, Table 5.19 Landed Costs of Crude Oil Imports, *EIA*

110 Robert D. Hershey, Jr., 'How the Oil Glut Is Changing Business,' *The New York Times*, June 21, 1981

111 James L. Williams, 'Oil Price History and Analysis,' *WTRG Economics*

112 op. cit., 'Shortages: Gas Fever: Happiness Is a Full Tank,' *Time*

113 Maryland adopted a scheme where motorists were allowed to refuel on certain days depending on whether their tags ended in an even or odd number. See 'Laws of the State of Maryland,' Volume 2, *Maryland General Assembly*, State Dept. of Legislative Reference, Page 3235

114 David Biello, 'Jimmy Carter Urges Energy Reform Again,' *Scientific American*, May 12, 2009

115 'Synthetic Fuels Corporation,' *Federal Register*

116 For a masterful recitation of the catastrophe resulting from creation of the Great Plains Coal Gasification project in North Dakota under Synfuels Corporation funding, see Ronald Bailey, 'Burning Money to Turn Coal Into Gas,' *Reason Foundation*, September 17, 2010

117 David Hogberg, 'Obama Refuses to Learn Government's Clean Energy Failures,' *Investors Business Daily*, January 25, 2011

118 Table 1.1.6 Real Gross Domestic Product, 2005 Chained Dollars, *Bureau of Economic Analysis*, All NIPA Tables

119 Obama told his faithful congregation that global warming was already curtailing New Hampshire's ski seasons resulting in a loss of jobs and income. See Barack Obama, 'Remarks in Portsmouth, New Hampshire: "Real Leadership for a Clean Energy Future",' *The American Presidency Project*, October 8, 2007. In the 2007-2008 winter that followed, New Hampshire recorded its most successful ski season in history with a record number of patron visits. See 'New Hampshire Resorts Announce Record Ski Season,' *Ski Magazine*, July 13, 2008

120 *ibid*

121 The Climategate revelations garnered significantly more press attention in the UK than in the U.S. press. The pilfered email treasure trove originated from the Climate Research Unit at East Anglia University in the UK. That outfit, headed by the notorious Phil Jones, had been at the forefront of the scandal. See for instance Christopher Booker, 'Climate Change: This Is the Worst Scientific Scandal of Our Generation,' *The Telegraph*, November 28, 2009; see also James Delingpole, 'Climategate: The Final Nail in the Coffin of "Anthropogenic Global Warming"?,' *The Telegraph*, November 20, 2009. In the U.S., the press largely ignored or papered over the story, calling it a "distraction" from the important public policy issue at hand. See for instance Brian Winter, 'Scientist: Leaked Climate E-mails a Distraction,' *USA Today*, November 25, 2009.

122 Office of the White House Press Secretary, Remarks by the President in State of the Union Address, United States Capitol, Washington, DC, January 21, 2011

123 Review & Outlook, 'Solar Flare-Out,' *The Wall Street Journal*, April 4, 2012

124 *ibid*

CHAPTER 2

1 Phillip Weiss, 'President Obama Talks SC Topics with Live 5's Debi Chard,' *Live 5 WCSC*, February 20, 2013

2 'Fossil Fuel Production on Federal Lands at 9 Year Low,' *Institute for Energy Research*, March 15, 2012

3 'Oil and Gas Production Decline on Federal Lands ... Again,' Institute for Energy Research, February 28, 2013

4 'Fossil Fuel Production on Federal Lands at a Ten Year Low,' *Institute for Energy Research*, June 10, 2013

5 Charles Krauthammer, 'Seaweed in Your Gas Tank,' *National Review*, March 16, 2012

6 Office of the White House Press Secretary, Remarks by the President on Energy, University of Miami, Miami, Florida, February 23, 2012

7 Petroleum and Other Liquids: U.S. Field Production of Crude Oil (Thousand Barrels), *Energy Information Administration*

8 Petroleum and Other Liquids: U.S. Product Supplied of Finished Motor Gasoline (Thousand Barrels per Day), *Energy Information Administration*

9 Petroleum and Other Liquids: Weekly U.S. All Grades All Formulations Retail Gasoline Prices, *Energy Information Administration*

10 op. cit., U.S. Field Production of Crude Oil, *EIA*

11 *ibid*

12 op. cit., Weekly U.S. All Grades All Formulations Retail Gasoline Prices, *EIA*

13 Petroleum and Other Liquids, Spot Prices for Crude Oil Dollars per Barrel, *Energy Information Administration*

14 *ibid*

15 Daniel Yergin, *The Prize: The Epic Quest for Oil, Money and Power*, New York: Simon & Schuster, 1991

16 Julia Cauble Smith, 'East Texas Oilfield,' *Texas State Historical Association*, June 12, 2010

17 Geoffrey Styles, 'Could U.S. Oil Trends Alter How Oil Prices Are Set?,' *Energy Tribune*, June 14, 2013

18 Jerry A. Dicolo, 'U.S. Crude Discount Narrows as Pipeline Problems Fade,' *The Wall Street Journal*, March 19, 2013

19   Alison Sider, Dan Strumpf and Ben Lefebvre, 'Texas' Next Big Oil Rush,' *The Wall Street Journal*, June 25, 2013

20   Jim Efstathiou Jr. and Jim Snyder, 'Americans Consider Exporting More Oil for First Time Since '70s,' *Business Week*, June 18, 2013

21   Keith Johnson and Cassell Bryan-Low, 'U.S., U.K. Discuss Tapping Oil Stocks,' *The Wall Street Journal*, March 15, 2012

22   *ibid*

23   Phil Kerpen, 'Here Comes Team Obama's Carbon Tax,' *Fox News*, March 21, 2013

24   See YouTube Video, 'Obama: My Plan Makes Electricity Rates Skyrocket,' *You Tube*, January 18, 2008; See also Obama interview with *San Francisco Chronicle* on January 18, 2008 posted at Ed Morrissey, 'Get Ready for Electricity Prices to "Necessarily Skyrocket",' *Hot Air*, June 12, 2011

25   Steve Hargreaves, 'Falling Gas Prices Could Boost Economy,' *CNN Money*, April 24, 2013

26   To see how obsolete mandates on gasoline formulations have driven up gasoline prices nationwide, see Steven F. Hayward, 'Bureaucratic Gas: To Lower Prices at the Pump, Abolish the Boutique Fuel Regime,' *The Weekly Standard*, Volume 17, No. 28, April 2, 2012; see also 'Editorial: Carbon-Cutback Debate Heating Up,' *The Orange County Register*, March 5, 2012 for how carbon cap mandates are driving up energy costs nationwide; see also Garance Burke and Jason Dearen, *Associated Press*, 'Analyst: Bills Rising Due to Overpriced Renewables,' *The Houston Chronicle*, November 12, 2011 on how renewable energy mandates have boosted costs for energy consumers in California

27   Pete Du Pont, 'The Anti-Energy President,' *The Wall Street Journal*, March 29, 2012

28   Jason Morgan, 'Comparing Energy Costs of Nuclear, Coal, Gas, Wind and Solar,' *Nuclear Fissionary*, April 2, 2010

29   *ibid*

30   'Clean Cities Alternative Fuel Price Report,' *U.S. Department of Energy*, January, July, October 2013

31   Rory Cooper, '10 Things You Need to Know About High Gas Prices and Obama's Oil Policy,' *The Foundry*, The Heritage Foundation, February 23, 2012

32   Electric Power Annual 2010, *Energy Information Administration*, Released November 2011

33   'How Much Do Wind Turbines Cost?,' *Windustry*

34   Electric Sales, Revenue, and Average Price, Table 5.A Residential Average Monthly Bill by Census Division, and State, *Energy Information Administration*, 2011

35   Table 5A. Residential Average Monthly Bill by Census Division, and State 2010, *Energy Information Administration*

36   Kevin D. Williamson, 'Deval-ued Wind Power,' *National Review*, December 3, 2012

37   James A. Johnson, 'Group to Study Errors Behind "$2 Million Mistake",' *The Westerly Sun*, September 29, 2012

38   *op. cit.*, Remarks by the President on Energy, Miami, Florida, February 23, 2012

39   Review & Outlook, ' "Stupid" and Oil Prices,' *The Wall Street Journal*, February 24, 2011

40   Christopher Goins and Michael W. Chapman, 'Number of New Oil Wells and New Leases Have Decreased Under Obama, Data from BLM Show,' *CNS News*, April 5, 2012

41   Nick Snow, 'White House Retains Oil Tax Increases in Proposed 2013 Budget,' *Oil & Gas Journal*, February 20, 2012

42   Office of the White House Press Secretary, Weekly Address: Taking Control of America's Energy Future, November 16, 2013

43   Mark Hemingway, 'Fossil Fuel Production on Federal Lands at a Nine-Year Low,' *The Weekly Standard*, March 15, 2012

44   'Sales of Fossil Fuels Produced from Federal and Indian Lands, FY 2003 through FY 2011,' *Energy Information Administration*, March 2012, Table 1, Page 2

45   Nick Snow, 'Industry Groups Dispute White House Energy Progress Report,' *Oil & Gas Journal*, March 13, 2012

46   Marc Humphries, 'U.S. Crude Oil Production in Federal and Non-Federal Areas,' *Congressional Research Service*, March 20, 2012

47   'Sales of Fossil Fuels Produced from Federal and Indian Lands, FY 2003 through FY 2012,' *Energy Information Administration*, May 2013, Pages 1-2

48   'Short Term Energy Outlook - February 2013,' Table 4a. U.S. Crude Oil and Liquid Fuels Supply, Consumption, and Inventories, *Energy Information Administration*

49   *ibid*

50   'U.S. Oil Production Up, But On Whose Lands?,' *Institute for Energy Research*, September 24, 2012

51   Lauren Ashburn, 'Candy Crowley Injects Herself Into the Presidential Debate,' *The Daily Beast*, October 17, 2012; see also Louise Boyle and Hugo Gye, 'Romney Was RIGHT! Crowley Admits Mitt Was Correct to Attack Obama Over Libya Killings After Siding with President … As Cameras Catch Michelle Breaking Rules by Clapping Husband,' *The Daily Mail*, October 17, 2012

52   Review & Outlook, 'Drill, Barack, Drill,' *The Wall Street Journal*, March 12, 2013

53   Michael Bastasch, 'Report: Oil Production on Federal Lands Falls Again in 2012,' *The Daily Beast*, March 5, 2013

54   Marc Humphries, 'U.S. Crude Oil and Natural Gas Production in Federal and Non-Federal Areas,' *Congressional Research Service*, February 28, 2013, Page 1

55   *ibid*, Page 2

56   Statistical Information, *Office of Natural Resources Revenue*, U.S. Department of Interior

57   Table 1.1.6 Real Gross Domestic Product, 2005 Chained Dollars, *Bureau of Economic Analysis*, All NIPA Tables

58   Typical is a muddled post at NRDC's blog from a zealot claiming to be a lawyer but who knows nothing about NAFTA, Foreign Trade Zones, or foreign trade law. The author ridiculously argues that duty elimination on oil exports is the sole economic justification for building the pipeline. Under NAFTA, there are no duties on Canadian oil imports. Even if there were, they could be recouped with duty drawback upon export. FTZ status is immaterial. He also offers the excuse about decades of deferral due to pipeline construction delay as a reason to oppose at Anthony Swift, 'Keystone XL Is a Tar Sands Pipeline to Export Oil Out of the United States,' *Switchboard*, December 20, 2011; see also Emilee Pierce, '*WSJ* Distorts Facts to Promote Keystone XL Pipeline,' *Media Matters for America*, November 9, 2011

59   Simone Sebastian, 'Oil and Gas Leaders Slam Obama,' *The Houston Chronicle*, February 22, 2012

60   *op. cit.*, Review & Outlook, ' "Stupid" and Oil Prices,' *The Wall Street Journal*

61   *op. cit.*, Review & Outlook, 'Drill, Barack, Drill,' *The Wall Street Journal*

62   Juliet Eilperin, 'Obama Administration Reimposes Offshore Oil Drilling Ban,' December 1, 2010

63   Nicolas Loris, 'Seven Years of Bad Policy: Government Maintains Offshore Drilling Ban,' *The Foundry*, The Heritage Institute, December 1, 2010

64   Jennifer Dlouhy, 'Obama Aims to Open More Areas to Drilling,' *The Houston Chronicle*, March 31, 2010

65   'Obama Administration Lifts Deepwater Drilling Moratorium,' *Fox News*, October 12, 2011

66   Peter Baker and John M. Broder, 'White House Lifts Ban on Deepwater Drilling,' *The New York Times*, October 12, 2012

67   Rob Bluey, 'Permitorium: 103 Gulf of Mexico Drilling Plans Await Government Approval,' *The Foundry*, The Heritage Foundation, February 4, 2012

68   *ibid*

69   *op. cit.*, Rory Cooper, '10 Things You Need to Know About High Gas Prices,' *The Foundry*

70   *op. cit.*, Rob Bluey, 'Permitorium: 103 Gulf of Mexico Drilling Plans,' *The Foundry*

71   'Update 1 – Fact Box – Deepwater Rigs Moved Out of the Gulf of Mexico,' *Reuters*, January 27, 2011

72   Nick Snow, 'Slower Gulf Permitting Pace Costs Jobs, API-Funded Study Finds,' *Oil & Gas Journal*, January 10, 2012

73   Paul Hillegeist, et. al., 'The State of the Offshore U.S. Oil and Gas Industry: An In-Depth Study of the Outlook of the Industry Investment Flows Offshore,' *Quest Offshore Resources* for the American Petroleum Institute, December 2011

74   'Do Higher Oil and Gas Taxes Pose a Threat to U.S. Energy Security?,' *Energy Policy Research Foundation*, August 4, 2009, Page 4

75   *ibid*

76   Paul Davidson, 'Obama's Budget Plan Targets Oil, Gas Tax Breaks,' *USA Today*, February 27, 2009

77   *ibid*

78   'Obama Signs Sweeping Public Land Reform Legislation,' *CNN*, March 30, 2009

79   Jennifer A. Dlouhy, 'Energy Industry Would Pay Higher Fees, Royalty Rates Under Obama Budget,' *The Houston Chronicle*, February 14, 2011

80   'Obama Administration FY 2012 Budget Proposal,' *Environmental and Energy Study Institute*, February 2012

81   *op. cit.*, 'Do Higher Oil and Gas Taxes Pose a Threat,' *Energy Policy Research Foundation*

82   Robert Pirog, 'Oil and Natural Gas Industry Tax Issues in the FY2012 Budget Proposal,' *Congressional Research Service*, March 3, 2011, Page 4

83   *ibid*, Page 4

84   *ibid*, Page 4

85   *ibid*, Page 5

86   *ibid*, Page 6

87   *Associated Press*, 'Salazar Announces Stricter Drilling Policies,' *The Boston Globe*, January 7, 2010

88   *Associated Press*, 'Salazar Announces Tougher Rules on Drilling,' *The Guardian*, January 6, 2010

89   Jeffrey Wright, 'President's Budget Proposes Substantial Changes for Business Taxation,' *Basin Oil & Gas*, Issue No. 19, July 2009

90   Nicholas Riccardi and Jim Tankersley, 'Salazar Cancels Bush-Era Leases in Utah,' *Los Angeles Times*, February 5, 2009

91   Tennille Tracy, 'U.S. Officials to Propose Changes to Oil Royalties,' *Marketwatch*, January 10, 2010

92   'Obama Administration Stops 2011 Chukchi & Beaufort Sea Exploration Programs - Alaska Rig Count Lowest Of Major,' *Alaska Business Monthly*, January 4, 2011

93   Rotary Rig Count, Baker Hughes, December 30, 2010

94   Keith Johnson, 'Obama Budget Spurs New Battle Over Energy,' *The Wall Street Journal*, February 13, 2012

95   Fred Barnes, 'No Energy from This Executive,' *The Weekly Standard*, Volume 14, No. 37, June 15, 2009

96   'Draft Proposed Outer Continental Shelf (OCS) Oil and Gas Leasing Program 2010-2015,' *Minerals Management Service*, U.S. Department of the Interior, January 2009

97   'Obama's Offshore Plan: One Giant Leap Backward,' *Institute for Energy Research*, May 8, 2012

98   Nick Snow, 'Latest Proposed 5-Year Plan Falls Short, API Official Says,' *Oil & Gas Journal*, November 21, 2011

99   Mike Cantrell, 'Obama's Energy Policy: Death By a Thousand Cuts,' *Forbes*, March 6, 2012

100   Phil Taylor, 'BLM to Suspend 61 Leases in Mont. to Review Climate Impacts,' *Environment & Energy News*, March 18, 2010

101   Daniel Gilbert and Russell Gold, 'EPA Backpedals on Fracking Contamination,' *The Wall Street Journal*, April 1, 2012

102   Neela Banerjee, 'Obama Administration Moves to Limit Diesel Use in Fracking,' *Los Angeles Times*, May 4, 2012

103   Press Release, 'Salazar Reforms U.S. Oil Shale Program: Offers New RD&D Leases; Asks IG to Investigate 11th Hour Lease Addenda,' *U.S. Department of the Interior*, October 19, 2009

104   Dan Joling, 'Chukchi Lease Sale Case Back in Federal Court,' *Associated Press*, Yahoo Finance, October 3, 2011

105   Nick Snow, 'White House Retains Oil Tax Increases in Proposed 2013 Budget,' *Oil & Gas Journal*, February 20, 2012

106   Margaret Kriz Hobson, 'Obama's Development Plans Gain Little Political Traction in Years Since Gulf Spill,' *Environment & Energy Daily*, April 18, 2012

107   Jonah Goldberg, 'All (Green) Thumbs,' *National Review*, June 1, 2012

108   Office of the White House Press Secretary, Remarks By the President on Clean Energy, Trinity Structural Towers Manufacturing Plant, Newton, Iowa, April 22, 2009

109   Office of the White House Press Secretary, Presidential Proclamation – Earth Day, April 20, 2012

110   Energy, Climate Change and Our Environment, The White House, June 1, 2012

111   *op. cit.*, Remarks By the President on Clean Energy, Newton, Iowa, April 22, 2009

112   *ibid*

113   John M. Broder and Clifford Krauss, 'U.S. in Accord With Mexico on Drilling,' *The New York Times*, February 20, 2012

114   Michael Barone, 'Obama's Sour Spot on Energy,' *The Washington Examiner*, February 22, 2012

115   Office of the White House Press Secretary, Remarks By the President at CEO Business Summit in Brasilia, Brazil, Tryp Convention Brasil 21 Center, Brasilia, Brazil, March 19, 2011

116   'Obama Underwrites Offshore Drilling,' *The Wall Street Journal*, August 18, 2009

117   Ángel González, 'The End of Deep-Water Drilling? Not in Brazil,' *The Wall Street Journal*, November 28, 2010

CHAPTER 3

1   Associated Press, 'High Oil Prices Threaten Global Economy, IEA Warns,' *The Guardian*, December 14, 2011

2   Barack Obama, 'Remarks in Portsmouth, New Hampshire: "Real Leadership for a Clean Energy Future",' *The American Presidency Project*, October 8, 2007

3   George Lobsenz, 'House Democrats to Obama: Tap SPR to Stop Speculators,' *The Energy Daily*, February 25, 2011, p. 1, Volume 39, Number 38

4   'Senators Ask Obama for Swift Action to Lower Gas Prices,' Senator Jeff Merkley, *U.S. Senate*, March 4, 2011

5   Jennifer A. Dlouhy, 'Feds Sell 30.6 Million Barrels of Emergency Crude to 15 Companies,' *Fuel Fix*, July 11, 2011

6   See SPRPMO Sales Offer Evaluation Program, Successful Awards Report, *U.S. Department of Energy*, July 11, 2011; Obama's *bête noire* BP was awarded a sale at $105.40 per barrel, one of the lowest prices awarded, well below the average price paid by participants.

7   Barack Obama, 'New Energy for America Speech,' Lansing, Michigan, August 4, 2008

8   Rebekah Kebede, 'Oil Hits Record Above $147,' *Reuters*, July 11, 2008

9   Mike Memoli, 'Obama for Tapping U.S. Oil Preserve,' *MSNBC*, August 4, 2008

10   'Competing Ideas?,' *The Washington Post*, August 5, 2008

11   Jim Geraghty, 'Does a Poll Drop Count As an Emergency?,' *National Review*, August 4, 2008

12   Dean Barnett, 'Required Reading, Part I,' *The Weekly Standard*, August 4, 2008

13   Jake Tapper, 'President Obama: Drill, Baby, Drill,' *ABC News*, March 31, 2010

14   Christine Jindra, 'Transcript of Barack Obama's Speech in Dayton,' *The Cleveland Plain Dealer*, July 11, 2008

15   'Annual Energy Review 2011,' *Energy Information Administration*, September 2012, Page 5

16   'Annual Energy Outlook 2013 Early Release Overview,' *Energy Information Administration*, December 5, 2012, Table A1 Total Energy Supply and Disposition Demand

17   *op. cit.*, 'Annual Energy Review 2011,' *Energy Information Administration*

18   *op. cit.*, 'Annual Energy Outlook 2013 Early Release Overview,' *Energy Information Administration*

19   *Associated Press*, 'Obama: Would Back Limited Offshore Drilling,' *MSNBC*, August 1, 2008

20   See prices for Cushing, Oklahoma Crude Oil Future Contract, Petroleum and Other Liquids, *Energy Information Administration*, July 11, 2011 of $95.16 per barrel vs. July 26, 2011 price of $99.61 per barrel

21   Amy Jaffe, 'America's Real Strategic Petroleum Reserve,' *Foreign Policy*, August 24, 2012

22   Carolyn Cui, 'Crude Bucks Efforts by the IEA to Tame Prices,' *The Wall Street Journal*, July 11, 2011

23   Editorial, 'The Wrong Reason for Depleting the Strategic Oil Reserve,' *The Washington Post*, June 23, 2011

24   Note the culture of paranoia afflicting Democrats who blamed evil speculators for the price spike. Note also Nancy Pelosi's hilarious, perpetual cluelessness as she errors by a factor of 2,000 on the size of the proposed release at John R. Parkinson, 'House Dems Applaud Obama for Tapping Strategic Petroleum Reserve, Boehner Says Move Threatens National Security,' *ABC News*, June 23, 2011

25   See quotations for Light Louisiana Sweet Crude Oil Spot Price, USCRLLSS:IND, *Bloomberg*, Ticker Symbol USCRLLSS:IND

26   Olga Belogolova, 'Insiders: Obama Will Tap Oil Reserve,' *National Journal*, February 28, 2012

27   Ross Kaminsky, 'Obamas Oily Desperation Redux,' *The American Spectator*,' March 16, 2012

28   EPCA 1975, PL 94-163

29   Anthony Andrews and Robert Pirog, 'The Strategic Petroleum Reserve and Refined Product Reserves: Authorization and Drawdown Policy,' *Congressional Research Service*, March 11, 2011, page 3

30   EPCA 1990, PL 101-383

31   *ibid*, page 3

32   *ibid*, page 8

33   Obama was fond of saying, "unlike some occupants of the White House, I actually believe in" the Constitution. See Barack Obama, Take Back America Conference, Center for American Priorities, Washington, DC, June 19, 2007, *American Presidency Project*

34   *op. cit.*, Olga Belogolova, 'Insiders: Obama Will Tap Oil Reserve,' *National Journal*

35   Austan Goolsbee, 'There's Too Much Crude in the Strategic Petroleum Reserve,' *The Wall Street Journal*, April 10, 2012

36   Darren Goode, ' Democrats to Obama: Tap Strategic Oil Reserve,' *Politico*, February 25, 2011

37   Seung Min Kim, 'Nancy Pelosi Endorses Tapping Oil Reserve,' *Politico*, March 1, 2012

38   Mark Whittington, 'Energy Secretary Chu Admits Administration OK with High Gas Prices,' *Yahoo News*, February 29, 2012

39   Neil King, Jr. and Stephen Power, 'Times Tough for Energy Overhaul,' *The Wall Street Journal*, December 12, 2008

40   See Europe's Energy Portal, Fuel Prices, Euros per One Liter With VAT

41   'WFTV's Greg Warmouth Tackles Tough Topics in One-on-One With President Obama,' *WFTV TV*, March 11, 2012

42   Keith Koffler, 'In 2008, Obama Seemed OK With High Gas Prices,' *White House Dossier*, February 23, 2012

43   See for instance Obama's unequivocal statement to *CNBC*'s John Harwood that he favors higher gasoline prices. But after three years, Obama claimed he favored lower prices. See 'Obama Wanted High Gas Prices ... Gradually (2008 Election Campaign),' *YouTube*

44   Review & Outlook, 'The Green Hornet,' *The Wall Street Journal*, August 6, 2008

45   Barack Obama, New Energy for America Speech, Lansing, Michigan, August 4, 2008

46   Ben Lieberman, '$6 a Gallon? Not Enough!,' The Heritage Foundation, *Frontpage Magazine*, March 29, 2007

47   'Transport and Environment: On the Way to a New Common Transport Policy,' *European Environment Agency*, Report No. 1, 2007, Page 14

48   See the EEA report 'Laying the Foundations for Greener Transport — TERM 2011: Transport Indicators Tracking Progress Towards Environmental Targets in Europe,' EEA Report No 7, 2011 Page 43; see also Eurostat, 2011b, 'Eurostat Transport Database'

49   *op. cit.*, Neil King, Jr. and Stephen Power, 'Times Tough for Energy Overhaul,' *The Wall Street Journal*

50   *ibid*

51   Ian Talley, 'Steven Chu: Americans Are Like 'Teenage Kids' When It Comes to Energy,' *The Wall Street Journal*, September 21, 2009

52   Noah Buhayer, 'Energy Department Fails its Own Energy Audit,' *The Wall Street Journal*, June 8, 2009

53   Keith Johnson, 'Energy Inefficiency: The Department of Energy Fails Another Audit,' *The Wall Street Journal*, July 23, 2009
54   'The Department of Energy's Energy Conservation Efforts,' OAS-L-11-02, *Office of the Inspector General*, U.S. Department of Energy, February 2011
55   *ibid*
56   Mike Brownfield, 'Morning Bell: White House Wants to Keep Gas Prices High,' *The Foundry*, The Heritage Institute, February 29, 2012
57   'Obama Energy Secretary Chu: I Don't Own a Car,' *Fox News*, March 8, 2012
58   John M. Broder, 'An Inconvenient Statement, Retracted,' *The New York Times*, March 13, 2012
59   David Shepardson, 'Chu Disavows '08 Comments on Gas Prices,' *The Detroit News*, March 13, 2012
60   Keith Koffler, 'Does Chu Really Want Cheaper Gasoline?,' *White House Dossier*, March 14, 2012
61   Andrew Restuccia, 'Obama Energy Chief Disavows 2008 Remark in Favor of Raising Gas Prices,' *The Hill*, March 12, 2012
62   Jimmy Carter, 'The President's Proposed Energy Policy.' *Public Broadcasting System*, April 18, 1977, Vital Speeches of the Day, Volume XXXXIII, No. 14, May 1, 1977, pp. 418-420

CHAPTER 4

1   The Editorial Board, 'What New Energy Landscape Means to USA: Our View,' *USA Today*, August 19, 2013
2   M.A. Adelman, 'The Real Oil Problem,' *Regulation*, Spring 2004, Pages 16-21
3   Nancy Benac, 'Who's Talking About Sasha, Malia? It's Dad, Again,' *Christian Science Monitor*, March 17, 2012
4   Jimmy Carter had once made a similar remark during a speech, offering Amy Carter as an authority on strategic nuclear policy. A firestorm of controversy resulted, permanently damaging Carter's political standing. In this instance, a far more partisan press let Obama off the hook.
5   Office of the White House Press Secretary, Remarks by the President on Energy, University of Miami, Miami, Florida, February 23, 2012
6   International Energy Statistics, All Regions by Country, 2009 Crude Oil Proved Reserves, (Billion Barrels), *Energy Information Administration*
7   International Energy Statistics, All Regions by Country, 2009 Total Petroleum Consumption (Thousand Barrels Per Day), *Energy Information Administration*
8   Neela Banerjee, 'U.S. Report: Oil Imports Down, Domestic Production Highest Since 2003,' *Los Angeles Times*, March 12, 2012
9   Nicolas Loris, 'High Gas Prices: Obama's Half-Truths vs. Reality,' *The Heritage Foundation*, February 23, 2012
10   'Technically Recoverable Oil in the United States,' *Institute for Energy Research*, May 1, 2012
11   'North American Energy Inventory: December 2011,' *Institute for Energy Research*, December 2011
12   Exposing the 2 Percent Oil Reserves Myth, *Institute for Energy Research*, March 13, 2012
13   U.S. Field Production of Crude Oil (Thousand Barrels), *Energy Information Administration*
14   George F. Will, 'Ever the Global Gloomster,' *The Washington Post*, November 18, 1999
15   M.A. Adelman, 'The Real Oil Problem,' *Regulation*, Spring 2004, Pages 16-21
16   'Establishment of the U.S. Geological Survey,' *U.S. Geological Survey*
17   Harold F. Williamson and Arnold R. Daum, *The American Petroleum Industry: The Age of Illumination, 1859—1899*,' Evanston, Illinois: Northwestern University Press, 1959
18   International Energy Statistics, All Regions by Country, Petroleum Production, (Thousand Barrels per Day), *Energy Information Administration*
19   Robert Bryce, *Gusher of Lies: The Dangerous Delusions of "Energy Independence"*, New York: Public Affairs, 2008, Page 37
20   'Prof. Bill Kovarik, The Oil Reserve Fallacy: Proven Reserves Are Not a Measure of Future Supply,' Radford University
21   Wallace B. Pratt, 'Our Oil and Natural Gas Reserves,' Chapter 5, of Leonard M. Fanning, Editor, *Our Oil Resources*, New York: McGraw Hill, 1945, Page 125
22   Harold Hibbert, 'The Role of the Chemist in Relation to the Future Supply of Liquid Fuel,' *Journal of Industrial and Chemical Engineering*, Volume 13, No. 9, September 1921, Page 841
23   Hibbert worried "Does the average citizen understand what this means? In from 10 to 20 years this country will be dependent entirely upon outside sources for a supply of liquid fuels, paying out vast sums yearly in order to obtain supplies of crude oil from Mexico, Russia and Persia." Reprinted in Bill Kovarik, 'Henry Ford, Charles Kettering and the "Fuel of the Future",' *Radford University*, 1998
24   John Tierney, 'Betting on the Planet,' *The New York Times*, December 2, 1990

25   Richard Heinberg, *The Party's Over: Oil, War and the Fate of Industrial Societies*, Gabriola Island, British
     Columbia: New Society Publishers, 2003, Page 104

26   *ibid*, Page 106

27   'U.S. Warned Oil Shortage in 20 Years,' *Los Angeles Times*, August 18, 1946, Page 6

28   Steven Horwitz, 'Are We Running Out of Resources?,' *Learn Liberty*, February 28, 2011

29   Ronald Bailey, 'Science and Public Policy,' *Reason*, February 4, 2004

30   The Club of Rome was headed by environmental charlatans Dennis Meadows and his biologist wife Donella. Its
     Malthusian doomsday forecasts were widely embraced by leftist media and purveyors of politicized junk science.
     Most notable among that group was eco-charlatan Paul Ehrlich who enjoyed a period of notoriety in the wake
     of the Club of Rome. See Donella Meadows, *The Limits to Growth: A Report for the Club of Rome's Project on the
     Predicament of Mankind*, New York: Signet, 1972

31   'Statement of Dr. Paul R. Ehrlich, Professor of Biology and Director of Graduate Studies, Department of
     Biological Sciences, Stanford University, Domestic Supply Information Act: Joint Hearings before the Committee
     on Commerce and Committee on Government Operations, United States Senate, Ninety-Third Congress, Second
     Session, *U.S. Government Printing Office*, 1974, Page 265

32   'Science Picks Signal Global Warming Policy Shift,' *USA Today*, December 20, 2008

33   Paul Ehrlich, Anne Ehrlich, and John Holdren, *Ecoscience: Population, Resources, and Environment*, San Francisco:
     W. H. Freeman and Company, 1977

34   Jad Mouawad, 'Oil Innovations Pump New Life Into Old Wells,' *The New York Times*, March 5, 2007

35   'Thirty-Fifth Annual Report of the State Oil and Gas Supervisor: Summary of Operations of California Oil
     Fields,' *Department of Natural Resources*, Division of Oil and Gas, Volume 35, No. 2, July-December 1949, Page
     26

36   Charles C. Mann, 'What If We Never Run Out of Oil?,' *The Atlantic*, April 24, 2013

37   'Annual Reports of the State Oil & Gas Supervisor,' *California Department of Conservation*, Years 1949 to 1977

38   '63rd Annual Report of the State Oil & Gas Supervisor,' *California Department of Conservation*, Division of Oil &
     Gas, 1977, Page 20

39   '2009 Annual Report of the State Oil & Gas Supervisor,' *California Department of Conservation*, Division of Oil,
     Gas & Geothermal Resources, Page 65

40   George F. Will, 'Oil's Expanding Frontiers,' *Townhall*, November 22, 2009

41   Gerald O. Barney, 'The Global 2000 Report to the President: Entering the Twenty-First Century,' Volume One,
     Council on Environmental Quality and the *U.S. Department of State*, 1980, Page 2

42   *ibid*, Page 27

43   Gerald O. Barney, 'The Global 2000 Report to the President: Entering the Twenty-First Century,' Volume Two,
     Council on Environmental Quality and the *U.S. Department of State*, 1980, Page 353

44   EIA International Energy Statistics, Petroleum Production, Thousand Barrels per Day, *Energy Information
     Administration*

45   *ibid*

46   *op. cit.*, International Energy Statistics, All Regions by Country, 2009 Crude Oil Proved Reserves, *EIA*

47   *ibid*

48   International Energy Statistics, All Regions by Country, 2009 Total Petroleum Production (Thousand Barrels Per
     Day), *Energy Information Administration*

49   M. King Hubbert, 'Nuclear Energy and the Fossil Fuels,' *Shell Development Company*, Publication No. 95, March
     7, 1956

50   *ibid*, Page 24

51   U.S. Field Production of Crude Oil (Thousand Barrels), *Energy Information Administration*

52   *Long-Range Environmental Outlook: Proceedings of a Workshop*, Washington, DC: National Research Council,
     November 1979, Page 20

53   Eugene Gholz and Daryl G. Press, 'Energy Alarmism: The Myths That Make Americans Worry About Oil,' *Cato
     Institute*, April 5, 2007

54   Colin Campbell, *Oil Price Leap in the Early Nineties*, Noroil, Kingston-upon-Thames, UK, 1989

55   International Energy Statistics, Petroleum Production 1989-2011, *Energy Information Administration*, Thousand
     Barrels per Day; 1989 = 65,518.8; 2011 = 87,483.0

56   Colin Campbell, 'Myth of Spare Capacity Setting the Stage for Another Oil Shock,' *Oil & Gas Journal*, March 20,
     2000

57   Thomas Black and Grace Nirang, 'Mexico, Indonesia Spurn Oil Companies as Global Oil Prices Soar,' *Bloomberg*,
     April 5, 2005

58   Colin Campbell, 'The Imminent Peak of Global Oil Production,' *Feasta Review 1*, March 2000, Page 5

59   Michael C. Ruppert, 'Colin Campbell on Oil,' *From the Wilderness*, October 23, 2002

60   Kjell Alekett and Colin Campbell, 'The Peak and Decline of World Oil and Gas Production,' *Minerals & Energy*, Volume 18, Issue No. 1, 2003

61   Jeffrey Ball, 'Dire Prophesy: As Prices Soar, Doomsayers Provoke Debate on Oil's Future,' *The Wall Street Journal*, September 21, 2004

62   Richard Heinberg and Colin Campbell, *The Oil Depletion Protocol: A Plan to Avert Wars, Terrorism and Economic Collapse*, Gabriola Island, British Columbia: New Society Publishers, 2006

63   Daniel Howden, 'World Oil Supplies Are Set to Run Out Faster Than Expected, Warn Scientists,' *The Independent*, June 14, 2007

64   *op. cit.*, International Energy Statistics, Petroleum Production 2011-2012, *Energy Information Administration*

65   James Picerno, 'Who Moved My Peak Oil?,' *Seeking Alpha*, October 9, 2012

66   Kenneth Deffeyes, *Hubbert's Peak: The Impending World Oil Shortage*, Princeton, NJ: Princeton University Press, 2001

67   John R. Coyne, Jr., Book Review: Gauging How Much Oil There Is,' *The Washington Times*, December 10, 2010

68   George Monbiot, 'Is Life Without Fossil Fuel Possible?,' *The Guardian*, August 23, 2004

69   EV World, 'Boone Pickens Warns of Petroleum Peak,' *Association for the Study of Peak Oil & Gas*, May 3. 2005

70   WSJ Staff, 'T. Boone Pickens: Oil Production Has Peaked,' *The Wall Street Journal*, March 2, 2007

71   F. Jay Schempf, 'Simmons Hopes He's Wrong,' *Petroleum News*, Volume 9, No. 31, August 1, 2004

72   Derived by taking 3.5 million bpd times 365 days per year times 40 years = 51.1 billion barrels remaining

73   *op. cit.*, International Energy Statistics, All Regions by Country, Petroleum Production, *Energy Information Administration*

74   *op. cit.*, International Energy Statistics, 2012 Crude Oil Proved Reserves, *Energy Information Administration*

75   Benoit Faucon, Dow Jones Newswires, 'Venezuela Oil Reserves Surpassed Saudis in 2010 — OPEC,' *Rigzone*, July 18, 2011

76   *op. cit.*, F. Jay Schempf, 'Simmons Hopes He's Wrong,' *Petroleum News*

77   Matthew R. Simmons, *Twilight in the Desert: The Coming Saudi Oil Shock and the World Economy*, New York: John Wiley & Sons, 2005

78   *ibid*

79   *op. cit.*, International Energy Statistics, Petroleum Production 1989-2011, *Energy Information Administration*

80   *op. cit.*, George Monbiot, 'We Were Wrong on Peak Oil. There's Enough to Fry Us All,' *The Guardian*

81   Matthew R. Simmons, 'Revisiting The Limits to Growth: Could the Club of Rome Have Been Correct, After All?,' *Resilience*, September 30, 2000

82   Mike Ruppert, 'Interview with Matthew Simmons,' *Oil Crash*, August 18, 2003

83   *op. cit.*, International Energy Statistics, All Regions by Country, Petroleum Production, (Thousand Barrels per Day), *Energy Information Administration*

84   *ibid*

85   Ajay Makan, 'Record Saudi Arabia Oil Output Fills Supply Gap,' *Financial Times*, September 16, 2013

86   *op. cit.*, Mike Ruppert, 'Interview with Matthew Simmons,' *Oil Crash*

87   International Energy Statistics, Natural Gas Production and Consumption Data, *Energy Information Administration*

88   *ibid*

89   John Tierney, 'Betting on the Planet,' *The New York Times*, December 2, 1990

90   Petroleum & Other Liquids, Spot Prices, Crude Oil in Dollars per Barrel, *Energy Information Administration*

91   Tamsin Carlisle, 'Maverick of the Oil Industry,' *The National*, August 12, 2010

92   John Tierney, 'Economic Optimism? Yes, I'll Take That Bet,' *The New York Times*, December 27, 2010

93   Stanley Kurtz, 'Fossil-Fuel Divestment,' *National Review*, March 4, 2013

94   Bill McKibben, *Deep Economy: The Wealth of Communities and the Durable Future*, St. Martin's Press, 2008

95   Mason Inman, 'Has the World Already Passed "Peak Oil?,' *National Geographic*, November 10, 2010

96   John Collins Rudolf, 'Is "Peak Oil" Behind Us?,' *The New York Times*, November 14, 2010

97   International Energy Statistics, All Regions by Country, Petroleum Production, (Thousand Barrels per Day), *Energy Information Administration*

98   Stanley Kurtz, 'Fossil-Fuel Divestment — Part 2,' *National Review*, March 5, 2013

99   See for instance 'George Monbiot Meets … Fatih Birol,' *The Guardian*, December 14, 2008; see also Max Oakes, 'Let's Face It, There's Simply Not Enough Oil and Gas to Go Around,' *The Guardian*, August 6, 2008; see also Ruth Sunderland, 'BP's Find Won't Kill Off Peak Oil Theory,' *The Guardian*, September 2, 2009; see also Andrew Simms, 'Our Addiction to Oil is Draining Every Last Drop,' *The Guardian*, March 1, 2011; *The Guardian* maintains a digest of its contributors' previous embarrassingly mistaken pronouncements available at http://www.guardian.co.uk/environment/peak oil

100   George Monbiot, 'We Were Wrong on Peak Oil. There's Enough to Fry Us All,' *The Guardian*, July 2, 2012

101   *ibid*

102   David Frum, ' "Peak Oil" Doomsayers Proved Wrong,' *CNN*, March 4, 2013

103   Rob Wile, 'Peak Oil Is Dead,' *Business Insider*, March 29, 2013

104   *op. cit.*, John Tierney, 'Economic Optimism? Yes, I'll Take That Bet,' *The New York Times*. Imagine how much you could have won betting against Gail the Actuary at *The Oil Drum* who forecast global production by 2012 of only 20 million barrels per day at Gail the Actuary, 'Where We Are Headed: Peak Oil and the Financial Crisis,' *The Oil Drum*, March 25, 2009

105   John W. Schoen, '17 Years Until Earth is Tapped Dry?,' *CNBC*, September 23, 2013

106   'Mobilizing for Impact,' *Clinton Global Initiative*, 2013

107   Kimberly Strassel, 'Conservation Wastes Energy,' *The Wall Street Journal*, May 17, 2001

108   BP Statistical Review of World Energy, June 2013, Oil Consumption, Barrels from 1965

109   *ibid*

110   *op. cit.*, International Energy Statistics, All Regions by Country, 2009 Crude Oil Proved Reserves, *Energy Information Administration*

111   'International Energy Outlook 2011,' *Energy Information Administration*, September 2011, Page 38

112   Remarks by Abdallah S. Jum'ah, *Third OPEC International Seminar*, Vienna, September 12-13, 2006, Page 6

113   M.A. Adelman and Michael C. Lynch, 'Fixed View of Resource Limits Creates Undue Pessimism,' *Oil & Gas Journal*, April 7, 1997

114   Barack Obama, 'Energy Independence and the Safety of Our Planet Speech,' Chicago, Illinois, April 3, 2006

115   Everett G. Martin, 'Brazil Spends Millions to Put Alcohol in Cars to Save on Oil Imports,' *The Wall Street Journal*, July 12, 1978

116   *ibid*

117   See Brazilian Energy Balance Balanço Energético Nacional 2009, Ano Base 2008, *Ministério de Minas e Energia*, Brazilian Federal Government, Table 2.27 – Ethyl Alcohol, Page 62, Year 2000 production of 10,700 m³; see also See Brazilian Energy Balance Balanço Energético Nacional 2011, Ano Base 2010, Ministério de Minas e Energia, Brazilian Federal Government, Table 2.30 – Total Ethyl Alcohol, Page 63, Year 2010 production of 27,963 m³

118   David Zilberman, 'The Role of Biofuels in the Energy Future: Lessons from Brazil,' *UNICA Sugarcane Industry Association*, September 22, 2011

119   Joe Leahy and Ed Crooks, 'A Sustainable Sugar Rush,' *Financial Times*, May 10, 2012

120   *ibid*

121   Michael Grunwald, 'The Clean Energy Scam,' *Time*, March 27, 2008

122   Ian Sample, 'Amazon's Doomed Species Set to Pay Deforestation's "Extinction Debt",' *The Guardian*, July 12, 2012

123   Steven F. Hayward, 'The Secret to Brazil's Energy Success,' *The Wall Street Journal*, April 1, 2011

124   Brazilian Energy Balance - Balanço Energético Nacional 2011, Ano Base 2010, *Ministério de Minas e Energia*, Brazilian Federal Government, Table 3.6.1.a – Transportation Sectors – Highways, Page 76

125   'Transportation Energy Data Book, 30th Edition,' U.S. Department of Energy, Appendix B. Conversions, Table B.4, Heat Content for Various Fuels, Page B-5, Conventional Gasoline = 115,400 BTU per gallon vs. Ethanol = 75,700 BTU per gallon

126   Alan Clendenning, Associated Press, 'Offshore Discovery Could Make Brazil Major Oil Exporter,' *USA Today*, November 9, 2007; see also Barbara Kollmeyer, 'BG Group Announces Offshore Brazil Oil Discovery,' *Marketwatch*, February 16, 2011; see also Gwladys Foucje, 'Repsol, Sinopec Make Big Oil Find Offshore Brazil,' *Financial Post*, February 27, 2012; see also Pierre Bertrand, 'Brazil's Petrobras Finds New Offshore Oil Well,' *International Business Times*, March 20, 2012

127   *op. cit.*, Ángel González, 'The End of Deep-Water Drilling? Not in Brazil,' *The Wall Street Journal*

128   See for instance Curry L. Hagerty, 'Outer Continental Shelf Moratoria on Oil and Gas Development,' *Congressional Research Service*, Washington, DC, May 6, 2011; see also John M. Broder and Clifford Krauss, 'U.S. Halts Plan to Drill in Eastern Gulf,' *The New York Times*, December 1, 2010

129   Stone Phillips, 'A Simple Solution to Pain At the Pump,' *MSNBC*, May 7, 2006

130   *op. cit.*, Brazilian Energy Balance - Balanço Energético Nacional 2011, Page 76

131   *op. cit.*, 'Transportation Energy Data Book, 30th Edition,' U.S. DoE, Appendix B. Conversions

132   For instance, the Petrobras station at the intersection of Avenida Duque de Caxias and Rua Vinte e Quatro de Maio in Fortaleza shows ethanol at R$2.09 per liter and gasoline at R$2.49. That means ethanol is 24% more expensive on a mileage-adjusted basis.

133   Jeff Fick, 'Brazil's Petrobras, Sinopec to Study Refinery Joint Venture,' *The Wall Street Journal*, June 19, 2013

134   Mario Sergio Lima and Rodrigo Orihuela, 'Petrobras in Talks With Sinopec to Develop Brazil Refineries,' *Bloomberg*, February 28, 2013

135   'Update 1-Petrobras, Sinopec in Talks to Build $20 Bln Refinery,' *Reuters*, June 19, 2013

136   Claudio Angelo, 'Growth of Ethanol Stalls in Brazil,' *Nature*, Volume 491, November 27, 2012, Pages 646-647

137   Stephen Moore, 'What North Dakota Could Teach California,' *The Wall Street Journal*, March 11, 2012

138   Norm Alster, 'U.S. Oil Producers Ramp Up Bakken Shale Output,' *Investors Business Daily*, February 8, 2011

139   Press Release, 'USGS Releases New Oil and Gas Assessment for Bakken and Three Forks Formations,' *U.S. Geological Survey*, April 30, 2013

140   *ibid*

141   Mark J. Perry, 'Amazing Energy Fact of the Day: Recoverable Oil in the Bakken Formation is More Than Double the Previous Estimates,' *Competitive Enterprise Institute,* April 30, 2013

142   *op. cit.*, Stephen Moore, 'What North Dakota Could Teach California,' *The Wall Street Journal*

143   *op. cit.*, Norm Alster, 'U.S. Oil Producers Ramp Up Bakken Shale Output,' *Investors Business Daily*

144   Dan Gunderson, 'ND Oil Patch is Bigger Than Thought, New USGS Report Says,' *Minnesota Public Radio*, April 30, 2013

145   'Obama Claims He's Visited 57 States,' *YouTube* Video, May 9, 2008

146   James McPherson, Associated Press, 'Oilman: Bakken and Three Forks Hold 20 Billion Barrels of Recoverable Oil,' *Grand Forks Herald*, January 20, 2011

147   'Editorial: We Have More Oil Than the President Says,' *The Houston Chronicle*, April 18, 2012

148   'In-Place Oil Shale Resources Examined by Grade in the Major Basins of the Green River Formation, Colorado, Utah, and Wyoming,' *U.S. Geological Survey*, January

149   Jane Wells, 'California's Monterey Shale, the Next Oil Boom?,' *CNBC*, February 21, 2013

150   Brianna Panzica, 'Russia's Massive Shale Potential,' *Energy & Capital*, June 19, 2012

151   Jake Rudnitsky and Stephen Bierman, 'Exxon Fracking Siberia to Help Putin Maintain Oil Clout,' *Bloomberg*, June 14, 2012

152   Christopher Helman, 'Meet the Oil Shale Eighty Times Bigger Than the Bakken,' *Forbes*, June 4, 2012

153   Peter Huber and Mark P. Mills, *The Bottomless Well: The Twilight of Fuel, the Virtue of Waste, and Why We Will Never Run Out of Energy*, New York: Basic Books, 2005

154   'Oil and Gas Reserves: Oil Output Rise in 1996,' *Oil & Gas Journal*, Volume 94, No. 53, December 30, 1996, Page 37

155   Seth M. Kleinman, et. al., 'Resurging North American Oil Production and the Death of the Peak Oil Hypothesis,' *Citi Investment Research & Analysis*, February 15, 2012

156   Russell Gold, 'Oil Drillers Boost Efforts to Coax More from Shale,' *The Wall Street Journal*, March 13, 2013

157   *op. cit.*, Jad Mouawad, 'Oil Innovations Pump New Life Into Old Wells,' *The New York Times*

158   See David F. Morehouse, 'The Intricate Puzzle of Oil and Gas "Reserves Growth",' Natural Gas Monthly, *Energy Information Administration*, July 1997, Page 10

159   Subsequent to 2009, the SEC has permitted U.S.-based companies to report potential (P2) and possible (P3) reserves if they have been verified by an independent advisory opinion. Most companies do not report P2 and P3 reserves, using them only for internal planning purposes.

160   James G. Ross, 'Nonstandard Reserves Estimates Lead to Resource Underestimation,' *The Oil & Gas Journal*, March 2, 1998

161   BP Statistical Review of World Energy June 2013, Oil - Proved Reserves History

162   BP Statistical Review of World Energy June 2013, Oil Production - Barrels

163   *op. cit.*, BP Statistical Review of World Energy June 2013, Oil - Proved Reserves History

164   'Member Countries,' *Organization of Petroleum Exporting Countries*

165   Adam Porter, 'How Much Oil Do We Really Have?,' *BBC News*, July 15, 2005

166   *op. cit.*, International Energy Statistics, All Regions by Country, Crude Oil Proved Reserves, *Energy Information Administration*. Venezuela went from 99.4 billion barrels of oil reserves in 2010 to 211.2 billion in 2011 to 297.6 in 2012.

167   *op. cit.*, Benoit Faucon, Dow Jones Newswires, 'Venezuela Oil Reserves Surpassed Saudis in 2010 — OPEC,' *Rigzone*; see also *'BP Statistical Review of World Energy 2012,'* Page 6

168   'An Estimate of Recoverable Heavy Oil Resources of the Orinoco Oil Belt, Venezuela,' *U.S. Geological Survey*, January 11, 2010

169   James W. Schmoker and T.R. Klett, 'Estimating Potential Reserve Growth of Known (Discovered) Fields: A Components of the USGS World Petroleum Assessment 2000,' *U.S. Geological Survey of World Petroleum Assessment 2000 — Description and Results*, Chapter RG, *U.S. Geological Survey*, 2000, Page RG-2

170   *op. cit.*, International Energy Statistics, All Regions by Country, 2009 Crude Oil Proved Reserves, *Energy Information Administration*

171   *ibid*

172   Walter Russell Mead, 'Israel's Emergence As Energy Superpower Making Waves,' *The American Interest*, July 2, 2012

173   'Russians Move Into East Med Gas Fracas,' *UPI*, April 20, 2012

174   *ibid*

175   'Levant Basin Given 122 TCF, 1.7 Billion Bbl,' *Oil & Gas Journal*, April 8, 2010

176   Ibrahim Saif, et. al., 'Gas in the Levant Basin: Another Source of Regional Conflict?,' *Carnegie Endowment for International Peace*, October 20, 2011

177   Israel Shenker, 'Golda Meir: Peace and Arab Acceptance Were Goals of Her 5 Years as Premier,' *The New York Times*, December 9, 1978

178   John Reed, 'Israel Natural Gas Exports Worth $60Bn Over Next 20 Years,' *Financial Times*, June 19, 2013

179   'Israel to Export 40 Percent of its Natural Gas,' *Associated Press*, June 19, 2013

180   *ibid*

181   International Energy Statistics, All Regions by Country, 2009-2012 Natural Gas Proved Reserves, (Trillion Cubic Feet), *Energy Information Administration*

182   'France's Total Joins Cypress Energy Rush,' *The Energy Tribune*, February 6, 2013

183   AFP, 'France's Total Joins Cyprus Energy Rush,' *France 24*, February 6, 2013

184   Helena Smith, 'Cyprus Makes Frantic Effort to Prevent Run on its Banks,' *The Guardian*, March 21, 2013

185   Michele Kambas, 'Cyprus Seeks EU Bailout for Banks, Budget,' *Reuters*, June 25, 2012

186   Roger Harrabin, 'IEA Doubles Global Gas Reserves Estimates,' *BBC*, January 20, 2011

187   Michael Economides and Xiuli Wang, 'Natural Gas: The Future Premier Fuel of the World Economy,' *Energy Tribune*, July 16, 2013

188   Amy Myers Jaffe, 'Shale Gas Will Rock the World,' *The Wall Street Journal*, May 10, 2010

189   Christopher B. McGill, 'Potential Supply of Natural Gas in the United States,' *Report of the Potential Gas Committee*, July 18, 2011

190   Dr. John B. Curtis, 'Potential Gas Committee Reports Significant Increase in Magnitude of U.S. Natural Gas Resource Base,' *Potential Gas Committee*, April 9, 2013

191   'International Energy Statistics, Natural Gas Proved Reserves,' *Energy Information Administration*

192   *op. cit.*, Dr. John B. Curtis, *Potential Gas Committee*, Page 2

193   Annual Energy Outlook 2012, Table 14. Unproved Technically Recoverable Resource Assumptions by Basin, *Energy Information Administration*, December 5, 2012

194   *ibid*

195   'World Energy Outlook 2011,' *International Energy Agency*, 2011, Page 7

196   Tim Webb, Rachel Sylvester and Alice Thomson, 'Britain Has Shale Gas for 1,500 Years, But Bills Won't Be Lower,' *The Times*, February 9, 2013

197   Dan Byles, 'The UK Needs a Serious Debate on Shale Gas,' *The Spectator*, February 14, 2013

198   *ibid*

199   'Propylene Solution Goes Beyond the Cracker,' *ICIS*, February 24, 2011

200   International Energy Statistics, All Regions by Country, 2012 Total Oil Supply, (Thousand Barrels per Day), *Energy Information Administration*

201   International Energy Statistics, All Regions by Country, 2012 Crude Oil Proved Reserves, (Billion Barrels), *Energy Information Administration*

202   OGJ Editors, 'Partners Sought to Pursue Arckaringa Basin Shales,' *Oil & Gas Journal*, January 23, 2013

203   'Australian Shale Oil Discovery Could Be Larger Than Canada's Oilsands,' *CBC News*, January 24, 2013

204   Jonathan Pearlman, 'Trillions of Dollars Worth of Oil Found in Australian Outback,' *The Telegraph*, January 24, 2013

205   Brian Robins, 'Australia's Shale Reserves Among World's Biggest,' *The Sydney Morning Herald*, June 11, 2013

206   'Technically Recoverable Shale Oil and Shale Gas Resources: An Assessment of 137 Shale Formations in 41 Countries Outside the United States,' *Energy Information Administration*, June 2013, Table 1, Page 2

207   Mark P. Mills, 'Unleashing the North American Energy Colossus: Hydrocarbons Can Fuel Growth and Prosperity,' *Manhattan Institute*, July 9, 2012

208   Kenneth P. Green, 'North America's Energy Wealth,' *American Enterprise Institute*, July 9, 2012

209   Anu K. Mittal, 'Unconventional Oil and Gas Production: Opportunities and Challenges of Oil Shale Development,' *U.S. Government Accountability Office*, May 10, 2012, Page 3

210   *ibid*

211   International Energy Statistics, All Regions by Country, Natural Gas Production, (Billion Cubic Feet), *Energy Information Administration*

212   International Energy Statistics, All Regions by Country, Natural Gas Proved Reserves, (Trillion Cubic Feet), *Energy Information Administration*

213   Gary J. Schmitt, 'Our Government's Foolish View of U.S. Energy Revolution,' *American Enterprise Institute*, July 25, 2013

214 Edward Luce, *Time to Start Thinking: America in the Age of Descent*, New York: Atlantic Monthly Press, 2012

215 Edward Luce, 'Welcome to the New World of American Energy,' *Financial Times*, July 15, 2012. Luce highlights his ideologically-inspired incomprehensibility by noting that America has substantially reduced its carbon emissions "without meaning to." It has done this, he admits, by making a switch from coal-fired to natural gas electricity generation consciously driven by EPA regulations and the Clean Air Act of 1990. Courts have decreed that EPA possesses the authority to regulate CO_2 emissions under the Clean Air Act. In other words, America "meant to" reduce its carbon footprint.

216 Walter Russell Mead, 'Energy Revolution 2: A Post-Post American Post,' *The American Interest*, July 15, 2012

217 Richard Anderson, 'U.S. Oil Production "to Jump by a Quarter by 2014",' *BBC*, January 9, 2013

218 Patti Domm, 'Power Shift: Energy Boom Dawning in America,' *CNBC*, March 18, 2013

219 John M. Broder and Matthew L. Wald, 'Cabinet Picks Could Take On Climate Policy,' *The New York Times*, March 4, 2013

220 *op. cit.*, Seth M. Kleinman, et. al., 'Resurging North American Oil Production and the Death of the Peak Oil Hypothesis,' *Citi Investment Research & Analysis*

221 Andrew Orlowski, 'RIP: Peak Oil – We Won't Be Running Out Any Time Soon,' *The Register*, February 23, 2012

222 Fareed Zakaria, 'The New Oil and Gas Boom,' *Time*, October 29, 2012

223 Barbara Powell, 'U.S. Was Net Oil-Product Exporter for First Time Since 1949,' *Bloomberg*, February 29, 2012

224 *ibid*, see also 'Monthly Energy Review - July 2013,' Table 3.3b Petroleum Trade: Imports and Exports by Type (Thousand Barrels per Day), *Energy Information Administration*, July 26, 2013

225 *op. cit.*, Seth M. Kleinman. et. al., 'Resurging North American Oil Production,' *Citi*

226 Edward L. Morse, et. al., 'Energy 2020: Independence Day — Global Ripple Effects of the North American Energy Revolution,' *Citigroup*, February 2013

227 'U.S. Oil Imports in October Fell to Lowest Level Since 2000,' *The Wall Street Journal*, December 28, 2012

228 Joshua Schneyer, 'Update 1 – U.S. Crude Stocks Drop Modestly, Fuel Inventories Up — EIA,' *Reuters*, December 28, 2012

229 Monthly Energy Review, March 2014, *Energy Information Administration*

230 *ibid*

231 ND Monthly Production Statistics, *North Dakota Department of Mineral Resources*, Bismarck, North Dakota

232 *ibid*

233 *ibid*

234 *ibid*

235 *ibid* based upon analysis of ND Monthly Production data

236 'Crude Oil Production,' *Energy Information Administration*

237 Simone Sebastian, 'Texas Pumping More Oil Than Some OPEC Countries,' *The Fuel Fix*, July 10, 2013

238 Ajay Makan and Abeer Allam, 'Alwaleed Warns of U.S. Shale Danger to Saudi,' *Financial Times*, July 29, 2013

239 'Saudi Prince: Fracking Is Threat to Kingdom,' *Sky News*, July 29, 2013

240 Mark Drajem, 'U.S. Oil Production to Exceed Imports, a First Since 1995,' *Bloomberg*, March 20, 2013

241 Ed Crooks and Anna Fifield, 'U.S. Oil Imports to Fall to Lowest in 25 Years,' *CNN*, January 9, 2013

242 'U.S. Crude Oil Production on Track to Surpass Imports for First Time Since 1995,' *Energy Information Administration*, March 20, 2013

243 Michael Cohen, 'A Renaissance in U.S. Production: Light Tight Oil,' *IEA Energy*, Issue 3, Autumn 2012, Page 18

244 Ronald Bailey, 'Running Out of Evidence,' *Philanthropy Magazine*, November-December 1998

245 Petroleum & Other Liquids, Crude Oil Production (Thousands of Barrels), *Energy Information Administration*

246 Tom Fowler, 'U.S. Oil-Production Rise is Fastest Ever,' *The Wall Street Journal*, January 18, 2013

247 *ibid*

248 Monthly Energy Review 2013, Table 3.1 Petroleum Overview, *Energy Information Administration*, December 24, 2013

249 For production statistics, see U.S. Natural Gas Marketed Production (MMcf), *Energy Information Administration*; for consumption data, see U.S. Natural Gas Total Consumption (MMcf), *Energy Information Administration*

250 M.A. Adelman, 'The Real Oil Problem,' *Regulation*, Spring 2004, Pages 16-21

251 Alan Petzel, 'World Hydrocarbon Supply "Relatively Boundless," SEG Told,' *Oil & Gas Journal*, September 30, 2013

252 'U.S. Crude Oil and Natural Gas Proved Reserves,' *Energy Information Administration*, August 1, 2013

CHAPTER 5

1 'Schumpeter In His Own Words,' *Economic Insights*, Federal Reserve Bank of Dallas, Volume 6, No. 3, 2001

2 *op. cit.*, Remarks by the President on Energy, University of Miami, February 23, 2012

3　William Stanley Jevons, *The Coal Question: An Inquiry Concerning the Problem of the Nation and the Probable Exhaustion of Our Coal Mines*, London: MacMillan & Co., London, 1865

4　*ibid*

5　John M. Polimeni, Kozo Mayumi, Mario Giampietro and Blake Alcott, *The Jevons Paradox and the Myth of Resource Efficiency Improvements* (Earthscan Research Editions), Routledge, ISBN 844074625, December 2007

6　'Low Carbon Development for Mexico,' *The World Bank*, March 2010

7　Robert J. Michaels, 'The Hidden Flaw of "Energy Efficiency",' *The Wall Street Journal*, August 20, 2012

8　Lucas W. Davis, Alan Fuchs and Paul J. Gertler, 'Cash for Coolers,' *National Bureau of Economic Analysis*, NBER Working Paper No. 18044, May 2012

9　Jeffrey Y. Tsao and Paul Waide, 'The World's Appetite for Light: Empirical Data and Trends Spanning Three Centuries and Six Continents,' *Energy*, Volume 6, Issue 4, Pages 259-281

10　David Wogan, 'North Korea by Night,' *Scientific American*, December 19, 2011

11　'The World Factbook,' GDP – Official Exchange Rate, *Central Intelligence Agency*

12　See for instance Horace Herring and Robin Roy, 'Technological Innovation, Energy Efficient Design and the Rebound Effect,' *Technovation*, Volume 27, Issue 4, April 2007, Pages 194-203

13　Kenneth A. Small and Kurt Ven Dender, 'Fuel Efficiency and Motor Vehicle Travel: The Declining Rebound Effect,' *University of California, Irvine*, Working Paper 05-06-03, April 10, 2006

14　See for instance the faith-based homily delivered by eco-agitators at 'Fuel Efficiency is as American as Apple Pie and Baseball,' *EcoWatch*, August 24, 2012

15　Kenneth Smith and Jack Raso, M.S., R.D., 'An Unhappy Anniversary: The *Alar* "Scare" Ten Years Later,' *American Council on Science and Health*, February 1, 1999

16　Devra Bachrach,et. al., 'Energy Efficiency Leadership in California: Preventing the Next Crisis,' *Natural Resources Defense Council*, April 2004, Page iv

17　*ibid*

18　Electric Power Monthly, Detailed State Data, Net Generation by State by Type of Producer by Energy Source (EIA-906, EIA-920, and EIA-923) 1990 - 2011, *Energy Information Administration*

19　Based upon population estimates provided by the California Department of Finance available at 'Table E-7. California Population Estimates, with Components of Change and Crude Rates, July 1, 1900-2012,' *California Department of Finance*

20　Electric Power Monthly, Detailed State Data, Average Price by State by Provider (EIA-861) 1990-2011, *Energy Information Administration*

21　Analysis by author based upon Net Generation by State by Type of Producer by Energy Source (EIA-906, EIA-920, and EIA-923) 1990 – 2011 and Detailed State Data, Average Price by State by Provider (EIA-861) 1990-2011, *Energy Information Administration*

22　Sierra Martinez, 'California Restores Its Energy Efficiency Leadership,' *Switchboard*, March 8, 2010

23　Marc Lifisher, 'You Can Thank Arthur Rosenfeld for Energy Savings,' *Los Angeles Times*, January 11, 2010

24　Anant Sudarshan and James Sweeney, 'Deconstructing the "Rosenfeld Curve",' *Stanford University*, June 1, 2008

25　*ibid*

26　Anant Sudarshan, 'Deconstructing the Rosenfeld Curve: Structural Determinants of Energy Consumption,' *Stanford University*, March 2011

27　Thomas Tanton, 'California's Energy Policy,' *Competitive Enterprise Institute*, April 1, 2008

28　Arik Levinson, 'California Energy Efficiency: Lessons for the Rest of the World, or Not?,' *National Bureau of Economic Research*, July 29, 2013

29　*ibid*

30　Alex Fitzsimmmons, 'Obama-California Energy Efficiency Mandates Coming to a Town Near You,' *Institute for Energy Research*, July 29, 2013

31　*op. cit.*, Arik Levinson, 'California Energy Efficiency: Lessons for the Rest of the World, or Not?,' *NBER*, Page 18

32　Severin Borenstein, Michael Jaske and Arthur Rosenfeld, 'Dynamic Pricing, Advanced Metering and Demand Response in Electricity Markets,' *Center for the Study of Energy Markets*, University of California Energy Institute, October 2002

33　Howard G. Chong, 'Evaluating Claims of Energy Efficiency: The Interaction of Temperature Response, New Construction, and House Size,' *University of California Berkeley*, July 7, 2010, Page 2

34　*ibid*

35　*ibid*, Page 21

36　Max Schulz, 'California's Potemkin Environmentalism,' *City Journal*, Volume 18, No. 2, Spring 2008

37　Craig Canine, 'California Illuminates the World, *On Earth*, Natural Resources Defense Council, Spring 2006

38　*op. cit.*, Max Schulz, 'California's Potemkin Environmentalism,' *City Journal*

39   David Goldstein, 'Energy Efficiency and the "Rebound Effect",' *Natural Resources Defense Council*, February 11, 2011

40   *ibid*

41   'Worldwide Trends in Energy Use and Efficiency: Key Insights from IEA Indicator Analysis,' *International Energy Agency*, 2008, Page 15

42   Arthur H. Rosenfeld, et. al., "Efficiency of Energy Use", *The Macmillan Encyclopedia of Energy*, John Zumerchik, Editor, New York: Macmillan, 2001

43   Arthur H. Rosenfeld, 'Energy Efficiency in California, *California Energy Commission*, November 18, 2008, Page 6

44   Paul L. Joskow, 'Energy Policies and Their Consequences After 25 Years,' *The Energy Journal*, Volume 24, No. 4, October 2003, Page 35

45   *op. cit.*, William Stanley Jevons, *The Coal Question: Can Britain Survive?*, MacMillan & Co., London, 1906

46   Andrew Stuttaford, 'Our Climate-Change Cathedral,' *National Review*, July 27, 2013

47   S. David Freeman, et. al., *A Time to Choose*: *America's Energy Future*, Cambridge, Massachusetts: Ballinger Publishing, 1974

48   Annual Energy Outlook 2013 Early Release Overview, *Energy Information Administration*, December 5, 2012, Table A1 Total Energy Supply and Disposition Demand

49   Petroleum & Other Liquids, U.S. Product Supplied of Crude Oil and Petroleum Products, Thousand Barrels per Day, *Energy Information Administration*

50   Table A1. Total Energy Supply, Disposition, and Price in Quadrillion BTUs, 'Annual Energy Outlook 2003 With Projections to 2025,' *Energy Information Administration*, Page 119 vs. Annual Energy Outlook 2013 With Projections to 2040,' *Energy Information Administration*, Page 121

51   Primary energy data from 'Annual Energy Review 2011,' Table 1.1 Primary Energy Overview, *Energy Information Administration*, September 2012; population estimates from *U.S. Census Bureau*, Historical Data

52   'Aluminum,' U.S. Geological Survey, Mineral Commodity Summaries, January 2012

53   *ibid*

54   See for instance Table 1.1.6, Real Gross Domestic Product, Chained Dollars, National Income and Product Accounts Tables, Seasonally Adjusted at Annual Rates, *Bureau of Economic Analysis*, 2nd Quarter 2012

55   *ibid*, Table 1.1.5, Gross Domestic Product, Seasonally Adjusted at Annual Rates, *BEA*

56   David B. Goldstein, Sierra Martinez and Robin Roy, 'Are There Rebound Effects from Energy Efficiency?: An Analysis of Empirical Data, Internal Inconsistency, and Solutions,' *Energy Policy*, May 4, 2011

57   Harry Saunders and Jesse Jenkins, 'Rebound and Rigor: NRDC's Entry into Rebound Effect Debate Stuck in the Past,' *Breakthrough Institute*, June 6, 2011

58   'FAQ: Rebound Effects and the "Energy Emergence" Report,' *Breakthrough Institute*, February 25, 2011

59   B. Metz, et. al., 'Contribution of Working Group III to the Fourth Assessment Report of the Intergovernmental Panel on Climate Change, 2007,' *Cambridge University Press*, 2007

60   Sir Nicholas Stern, 'Stern Review on the Economics of Climate Change,' *HM Treasury*, National Archives, 2006

61   'Pathways to a Low-Carbon Economy,' *McKinsey & Company*, January 2009

62   David Goldstein, 'How Bad Ideas Keep Rebounding Into Public Discourse: The Rebound Effect and Its Refutation,' *Switchboard*, Natural Resources Defense Council, May 8, 2011

63   *ibid*

64   Jesse Jenkins, Michael Shellenberger and Ted Nordhaus, 'Energy Emergence: Rebound and Backfire as Emergent Phenomena – Report Overview,' *Breakthrough Institute*, February 17, 2011

65   *ibid*, Page 4

66   *ibid*, Page 55

67   *ibid*, Page 13

68   *ibid*, Page 9

69   *ibid*, Page 21

70   *ibid*, Page 9

71   *ibid*, Page 36

72   *ibid*, Page 22

73   Robert J. Michaels, 'Energy Efficiency and Climate Policy: The Rebound Dilemma,' *Institute for Energy* Research, July 2012, Page 8

74   *ibid*, Page 8

75   *op. cit.*, David Goldstein, 'How Bad Ideas Keep Rebounding,' *Switchboard*, NRDC

76   *op. cit.*, Jesse Jenkins, et. al., 'Energy Emergence,' *Breakthrough Institute*, Page 18

77   Amory B. Lovins, 'Energy Strategy: The Road Not Taken?,' *Foreign Affairs*, Volume 55, No. 4, October 1976, Pages 65-96

78   'Green Energy Advocate Lovins: Guru of Fakir?,' *Energy Tribune*, November 12, 2007

79   ibid, Page 69
80   *ibid*, Page 68
81   *op. cit.*, 'Annual Energy Review 2011,' Table 1.1 Primary Energy Overview, *Energy Information Administration*
82   *ibid*
83   *op. cit.*, Amory B. Lovins, 'Energy Strategy: The Road Not Taken?,' *Foreign Affairs*, Page 67
84   'How Many Nuclear Power Plants Are in the U.S. and Where Are They Located?,' *Energy Information Administration*
85   Based upon a heat conversion factor of 5.85 million BTUs for one barrel of domestic crude oil as reported in 'Annual Energy Outlook 2012,' Appendix G Conversion Factors, Table G1. Heat Rates, *Energy Information Administration*, June 2012, Page 239
86   *op. cit.*, Amory B. Lovins, 'Energy Strategy: The Road Not Taken?,' *Foreign Affairs*, Page 69
87   Analysis by author based upon capital cost of 2017 nuclear power available at Levelized Cost of New Generation Resources in the 'Annual Energy Outlook 2012,' Annual Energy Table 1. Estimated Levelized Cost of New Generation Resources, 2017, Capital Cost of Advanced Nuclear per Megawatt-Hour, *Energy Information Administration*; for GDP price deflator data, see National Income and Product Accounts, Table 1.2.4. Price Indexes for Gross Domestic Product by Major Type of Product, *Bureau of Economic Analysis*
88   *ibid*, Page 70
89   *op. cit.*, Amory B. Lovins, 'Energy Strategy: The Road Not Taken?,' *Foreign Affairs*, Page 71
90   For nominal electricity prices, see 'Annual Energy Review 2011,' Table 8.10 Average Retail Price of Electricity, 1960-2010, *Energy Information Administration*, September 27, 2012; for GDP price deflator data, see *op. cit.*, NIPA, Table 1.2.4., *Bureau of Economic Analysis*
91   *op. cit.*, Amory B. Lovins, 'Energy Strategy: The Road Not Taken?,' *Foreign Affairs*, Page 77
92   For total energy usage, see Table 1.1 Primary Energy Overview, 1949-2011; for renewable energy consumption, see Table 10.1 Renewable Energy Production and Consumption by Primary Energy Source, 1949-2011, Annual Energy Outlook 2011, *Energy Information Administration*
93   For total primary consumption in 2025, see Table 1. Total Energy Supply and Disposition Summary; for renewable energy forecast for 2025, see Table 17. Renewable Energy Consumption by Sector and Source, Annual Energy Outlook 2014, *Energy Information Administration*
94   *op. cit.*, Amory B. Lovins, 'Energy Strategy: The Road Not Taken?,' *Foreign Affairs*, Page 91-92
95   Robert L. Bradley, *Capitalism at Work*: *Business, Government, and Energy*, Salem, MA: M&M Scrivener Press, 2009, Page 252
96   'Amory Lovins in *Business Week*,' available at *Breakthrough Institute*, February 17, 2011
97   Annual Energy Review, *Energy Information Administration*, October 19, 2011, Table 8.1 Electricity Overview, 1949-2010
98   Annual Energy Review, *Energy Information Administration*, October 19, 2011, Table 8.2b Electricity Net Generation: Electric Power Sector, 1949-2010
99   *op. cit.*, 'Amory Lovins in *Business Week*,' available at *Breakthrough Institute*
100   Annual Energy Review, *Energy Information Administration*, October 19, 2011, Table 8.10 Average Retail Prices of Electricity, 1960-2010
101   Christopher Martin and Maureen S. Malik, 'NRG Skirts Utilities Taking Solar Panels to U.S. Rooftop,' *Bloomberg*, March 25, 2013
102   Chris Martin, Mark Chediak and Ken Wells, 'Why the U.S. Power Grid's Days Are Numbered,' *Bloomberg Business Week*, August 22, 2013
103   Noelle Straub and Peter Behr, 'Energy Regulatory Chief Says New Coal, Nuclear Plants May Be Unnecessary,' *The New York Times*, April 22, 2009
104   *ibid*
105   Dan Reicher and Jeffrey Greenblatt, 'Clean Energy 2030,' *Google Official Blog*, October 1, 2008
106   'Annual Report on Fuel Poverty Statistics 2012,' *Department of Energy & Climate Change*, Page 9
107   *ibid*, Page 3
108   Stanley Reed, 'Europe Faces a Crisis in Energy Costs,' *The New York Times*, April 17, 2013
109   Sean Poulter, 'Thousands Dying Because They Can't Afford Heating Bills … and Green Taxes are Adding to the Burden,' *The Daily Mail*, October 20, 2011
110   Simon Read, 'Fuel Poverty Deaths Three Times Higher Than Government Estimates,' *The Independent*, February 28, 2012
111   James Hall, 'At Least 2,700 a Year Die in Freezing Homes,' *The Telegraph*, October 20, 2011
112   Daniel Martin and James Clayton, 'Frozen to Death as Fuel Bills Soar: Hypothermia Cases Among the Elderly Double in Five Years,' *The Daily Mail*, February 13, 2012

113 '01.11.07: "Rebound Effects" Threaten Success of UK Climate Policy,' *UK Energy Research Centre*, November 1, 2007

114 Steve Sorrell, 'The Rebound Effect: An Assessment of the Evidence for Economy-Wide Energy Savings from Improved Energy Efficiency,' *UK Energy Research Centre*, October 2007

115 'Real Prospects for Energy Efficiency in the United States,' *National Academy of Sciences*, 2010, Page 5

116 Editorial, 'Cleaner Cars, a Safer Planet,' *The New York Times*, August 31, 2012

117 Wendy Koch, 'Environmentalists Cheer Obama's Fuel-Economy Hike,' *USA Today*, August 1, 2011

118 For a lengthy recital of energy efficiency legislation and other efficiency mandate programs, see Fred Sissine, 'Energy Efficiency: Budget, Oil Conservation and Electricity Conservation Issues,' *Congressional Research Service*, October 29, 2004

119 'Monthly Energy Review — August 2012,' *Energy Information Administration*, August 29, 2012, Page 17

120 *op. cit.*, Kimberly Strassel, 'Conservation Wastes Energy,' *The Wall Street Journal*

121 Holman Jenkins, 'Newt Is Right About Gas Prices,' *The Wall Street Journal*, March 10, 2012

122 'Newer U.S. Homes Are 30% Larger but Consume About as Much Energy as Older Homes,' *Energy Information Administration*, February 12, 2013

123 Andrew Potter, 'Planet-Friendly Design? Bah, Humbug,' *Macleans*, February 13, 2007

124 See for instance the authoritative scientifically peer-reviewed study conducted over a long period of time by University of California researchers at Kenneth Small and Kurt Van Dender, 'The Effect of Improved Fuel Economy on Vehicle Miles Traveled: Estimating the Rebound Effect Using U.S. State Data, 1966-2001,' *University of California Energy Institute*, September 2005

125 'Fuel Efficiency is as American as Apple Pie and Baseball,' *EcoWatch*, August 24, 2012

126 Andrew P. Morriss, et. al., *The False Promise of Green Energy*, Cato Institute, Washington, DC, 2011, Page 36

127 Indur M. Goklany, *The Improving State of the World: Why We're Living Longer, Healthier, More Comfortable Lives on a Cleaner Planet*, Washington, DC: Cato Institute Press, 2007, Page 144

128 *ibid*

129 Craig Guillot, 'Do Energy-Efficient Appliances Add Up?,' *Bankrate*, January 22, 2010

130 Scott Carson, 'How Boeing Fights Climate Change,' *The Wall Street Journal*, May 23, 2009

131 John Horst, 'Super Bowl City Leads on Energy Efficient Forefront,' *U.S. Department of Energy*, February 2, 2013

132 CNN Staff, 'Superdome Power Outage Halts Super Bowl XLVII,' *CNN*, February 3, 2013

133 National Residential Efficiency Measures Database, Retrofit Measures for Flood Light, *National Renewable Energy Laboratory*

134 *ibid*

135 Based upon an average residential electricity rate in the U.S. in 2012 of $0.1184 per kWh

136 Cindy Brauer and Clement Driscoll, 'Telematics: A Growing Tool for Efficient Fleets,' *Automotive Fleet*, February 2006, Page 21

137 'The New Paradigm: 1999 Annual Report,' *Federal Reserve Bank of Dallas*, 1999, Page 14

138 See for instance 'Stonyfield Farms Measures Carbon Footprint of All Products,' *Sustainable Business*, January 14, 2013; see also 'The World Resources Institute to Measure Carbon Footprint in Supply Chain,' *Industry Week*, October 6, 2009; Do dog food manufacturers have carbon paw prints?

139 Pierre Desrochers, 'Did the Invisible Hand Need a Regulatory Glove to Develop a Green Thumb? Some Historical Perspective on Market Incentives, Win-Win Innovations and the Porter Hypothesis,' *Environmental and Resource Economics*, Volume 41, Issue 4, December 2008, Pages 519-539

140 Frank Gottron, 'Energy Efficiency and the Rebound Effect: Does Increasing Efficiency Decrease Demand?,' *Congressional Research Service*, July 30, 2001

141 Aidas Palubinskas, 'EU Energy Efficiency: Investment Targets Not Achieved; Average Pay Back Period Exceeds 50 Years (in Extreme Cases 150 Years),' *European Court of Auditors*, January 14, 2013

142 Dave Keating, 'Energy Efficiency Investments Not Cost-Effective,' *European Voice*, January 14, 2013

143 Dave Keating, 'Energy-Saving Projects Paid Little Heed to Costs,' *European Voice*, January 17, 2013

144 'Cost-Effectiveness of Cohesion Policy Investments in Energy Efficiency,' *European Court of Auditors*, 2012

145 *ibid*

146 *op. cit.*, Remarks by the President on Energy, University of Miami, February 23, 2012

147 *op. cit.*, 'Worldwide Trends in Energy Use and Efficiency: Key Insights from IEA Indicator Analysis,' *International Energy Agency*, Page 15

148 'Monthly Energy Review March 2013,' Table 3.1 Petroleum Overview (Thousand Barrels per Day), *Energy Information Administration*, March 27, 2013, Page 37

149 Peter Huber and Mark P. Mills, *The Bottomless Well: The Twilight of Fuel, the Virtue of Waste, and Why We Will Never Run Out of Energy*, New York: Basic Books, 2005, Page 123

150 'S. 761: Energy Savings and Industrial Competitiveness Act of 2013,' *Gov Track*, April 18, 2013

151 Nate Aden, 'A Closer Look at the Shaheen-Portman Energy Efficiency Bill,' *WRI Insights*, July 25, 2013
152 Ben Geman, 'Gasoline Costs Take Biggest Share of Household Income in Three Decades,' *The Hill*, February 4, 2013
153 Jeffrey H. Anderson, 'Obama Recovery Is Worst in Post WWII History,' *Investors Business Daily*, August 6, 2012

CHAPTER 6

1 Christopher Flavin, 'Electricity's Future: The Shift to Efficiency and Small-Scale Power,' *Worldwatch Institute*, Paper 61, November 1984, Page 35
2 Michael Weber, 'The Way Forward for Renewable Energy Policy in the U.S.,' *Worldwatch Institute*, July 26, 2012
3 Joel Stonington, 'A Mere Breeze: Era of Fast Growth Ends for Wind Energy in Europe,' *Der Spiegel*, February 8, 2013
4 Office of the White House Press Secretary, Remarks by the President on Energy, University of Miami, Miami, Florida, February 23, 2012
5 'Carney Asked Why Obama Supported Tax Breaks for Oil Companies in 2005,' *Real Clear Politics*, March 29, 2012
6 'The Candidates on Energy Policy,' *Council on Foreign Relations*, September 11, 2008
7 'American Taxpayer Investment, Foreign Corporation Benefit,' *Energy and Commerce Committee*, U.S. House of Representatives, Volume 2, Issue 1, January 17, 2013
8 Ron Fournier, 'Obama: It's Kids Versus Corporate Jets on Debt-Ceiling Talks,' *National Journal*, June 30, 2011
9 Lachlan Markay, 'Obama Blasts Private Jet Tax Breaks Included in His Own Stimulus,' *The Foundry*, The Heritage Foundation, June 29, 2011; see also Abby Phillip, 'Fact Checking a Claim on Tax Breaks,' *Politico*, June 30, 2011
10 Office of the White House Press Secretary, 'Remarks by the President on Oil and Gas Subsidies,' Rose Garden, Washington, DC, March 29, 2012
11 Robert Murphy, 'The Obama Administration's Dishonest Claims on "Big Oil Tax Giveaways",' *Institute for Energy Research*, April 6, 2012
12 'Fiscal Year 2013 Budget of the U.S. Government,' Executive Office of the President, *Office of Management and Budget*, February 13, 2012, Page 236
13 Barack Obama, 'Remarks in Des Moines, Iowa,' *The American Presidency Project*, October 31, 2008
14 *op. cit.*, 'Fiscal Year 2013 Budget of the U.S. Government,' *OMB*, Page 222
15 *op. cit.*, Robert Murphy, 'The Obama Administration's Dishonest Claims,' *IER*
16 Jeremy Fugleberg, 'Obama Tax Changes Could Hit Small Oil and Gas Operators in Wyoming,' *Casper Star-Tribune*, March 30, 2012
17 Office of the White House Press Secretary, 'Obama Administration Releases Report Outlining Benefits of Expensing Proposal in Encouraging Business Expansion, Hiring Now,' *The White House*, Washington, DC, October 29, 2010
18 Nicolas Loris and Curtis S. Dubay, 'What's an Oil Subsidy?,' *The Heritage Foundation*, May 12, 2011
19 *op. cit.*, 'Fiscal Year 2013 Budget of the U.S. Government,' *OMB*, Page 221
20 Michael Economides, 'Let's Inaugurate a Term of Energy Realism,' *The Energy Tribune*, February 7, 2013
21 'Across U.S. Companies, Tax Rates Vary Greatly,' *The New York Times*, May 25, 2013
22 *ibid*
23 'Impacts of Delaying IDC Deductibility (2014-2025), *Wood Mackenzie Consulting*, July 2013, Page 3-4
24 Petroleum and Other Liquids, U.S. Field Production of Crude Oil, Thousand Barrels per Day, *Energy Information Administration*, March 2012
25 'IRS Clarifies When 100 Percent Bonus Depreciation Applies,' *McDermott, Will & Emery*, April 21, 2011
26 *ibid*
27 Jake Tapper and Sunlen Miller, 'President Obama to Democrats: It's Not Enough to Have a 'Purist Position' and Feel 'Sanctimonious' — We Need "Victories for the American People",' *ABC News*, December 7, 2010
28 *Associated Press*, 'U.S. Senate Thwarts Obama's Bid to End Oil Company Tax Breaks,' *Caspar Star-Tribune*, March 29, 2012
29 'How Much Does the Federal Government Support the Development and Production of Fuels and Energy Technologies?,' *The Congressional Budget Office*, March 6, 2012
30 Steve Hargreaves, 'Energy Subsidies Total $24 Billion, Most to Renewables,' *CNN Money*, March 7, 2012
31 'Renewable Energy Subsidies 6.4 Times Greater than Fossil Fuel Subsidies,' *Institute for Energy Research*, May 31, 2012
32 'Federal Financial Support for the Development and Production of Fuels and Energy Technologies,' *The Congressional Budget Office*, March 2012, Page 6, Figure 3.

33   'Direct Federal Financial Interventions and Subsidies in Energy in Fiscal Year 2010,' *Energy Information Administration*, August 1, 2011

34   'Direct Federal Financial Interventions and Subsidies in Energy in Fiscal Year 2010,' *Energy Information Administration*, July 2011, Page xiii

35   'Annual Energy Outlook 2012: With Projections to 2035,' *Energy Information Administration*, Page 131

36   Robert Bryce, 'America's Most Favored Industry,' *National Review*, December 13, 2012

37   'Residential Energy Survey Data Show Decreased Energy Consumption per Household,' *Energy Information Administration*, June 6, 2012

38   It's noteworthy that Obama chose to deliver these stylistic broadsides to impressionable students, who would not know enough to laugh him out of the arena. See Keith Koffler, 'Raise Oil Taxes! Does Obama Get Economics?,' *White House Dossier*, March 2, 2012

39   *op. cit.*, 'Fiscal Year 2013 Budget of the U.S. Government,' Page 150, *OMB*

40   *ibid*, Page 150

41   Tom Zeller Jr., 'Studies Say Natural Gas Has Its Own Environmental Problems,' *The New York Times*, April 11, 2011

42   James Montgomery, 'Obama Proposes Tax Reform, Making Renewables Credits Permanent,' *Renewable Energy World*, February 23, 2012

43   *op. cit.*, Remarks by the President on Energy, Miami, Florida, February 23, 2012

44   Hibah Yousuf, 'GE to Supply World's Largest Wind Farm,' *CNN Money*, December 10, 2009

45   Herman Trabish, 'World's Biggest Wind Farm Gets Backing,' *Green Tech Media*, December 17, 2010

46   *op. cit.*, Hibah Yousuf, 'GE to Supply World's Largest Wind Farm,' *CNN Money*

47   Pete Danko, 'Big Wind: 845 MW Shepherds Flat Wind Farm Marks Opening,' *Green Tech Media*, September 24, 2012

48   Chris Clarke, 'SoCal Edison Adds 845 Megawatts of Wind from Oregon,' *KCET*, September 24, 2012

49   Ted Sickinger, 'The Cost of Green: Huge Eastern Oregon Wind Farm Raises Big Questions about State, Federal Subsidies,' *The Oregonian*, March 15, 2011

50   Ted Sickinger, 'Shepherd Flat Wind Farm's $30 Million in Tax Credits Will Be Reviewed by Oregon Energy Department,' *The Oregonian*, February 23, 2013

51   'Shepherds Flat Still Feeding at the Public Trough,' *Institute for Energy Research*, July 25, 2013

52   Ted Sickinger, 'Oregon Energy Department Blows Past Facts in Review of Subsidies for Shepherds Flat Wind Farm,' *The Oregonian*, July 21, 2013

53   *ibid*

54   Daniel Simmons, 'Corporate Welfare Masquerading Under an Environmental Rainbow,' *Institute for Energy Research*, September 29, 2011

55   Steven Mufson and Carol D. Leonnig, 'Some Clean-Energy Firms Found Loan-Guarantee Program a Bad Bet,' *The Washington Post*, September 26, 2011

56   Stephen Power, 'U.S. Weighs Funding for Renewable Energy Projects,' *The Wall Street Journal*, November 3, 2010

57   Robert Bryce, 'America's Worst Wind-Energy Project,' *National Review*, October 12, 2011

58   Calculation performed by author

59   *ibid*

60   'Shepherds Flat Wind Farm Opens Saturday in Eastern Oregon,' *The Oregonian*, September 21, 2012

61   Erin Carlyle, 'Full List: U.S. Billionaires of 2013,' *Forbes*, March 6, 2013

62   *op. cit.*, Herman Trabish, 'World's Biggest Wind Farm Gets Backing,' *Green Tech Media*

63   *op. cit.*, Daniel Simmons, 'Corporate Welfare Masquerading Under an Environmental Rainbow,' *Institute for Energy Research*

64   See for instance the example of NRG that is building several massive solar energy generating projects in California that will provide the company a 25% return on equity throughout the 20-year life of the projects at Eric Lipton and Clifford Krauss, 'A Gold Rush of Subsidies in Clean Energy Search,' *The New York Times*, November 11, 2011

65   Julianne Pepitone, 'Warren Buffet's MidAmerican Buys First Solar Plant,' *CNN Money*, December 7, 2011

66   Dan McCrum and Ajay Makan, 'Buffet Utility Makes Solar Power Move,' *Financial Times*, December 7, 2011

67   Eric Boehm, 'Green-Energy Mandates Will Hit PA's Poorest Hardest,' *Upper Southampton Patch*, December 21, 2012

68   David Sneed, 'Calif. Utility Agrees to Buy Solar Power from Two Proposed Plants,' *The San Luis Obispo Tribune*, August 14, 2008

69   *op. cit.*, Eric Lipton and Clifford Krauss, 'A Gold Rush of Subsidies in Clean Energy Search,' *The New York Times*

70   Composite price in 2012 at the SP-15 EZ California and NP-15 California hubs at 'Wholesale Market Data 2012,' *Energy Information Administration*

71   *op. cit.*, Eric Lipton and Clifford Krauss, 'A Gold Rush of Subsidies in Clean Energy Search,' *The New York Times*

72   *ibid*

73   Jillian Ward, 'Google Invests $200 Million in 161-Megawatt Texas Wind Farm,' *Business Week*, January 9, 2013

74   See for instance John Voelcker, 'Tesla Makes Money on Model S: $35K per Car Selling ZEV Credits,' *Green Car Reports*, May 7, 2013; Megan Durisin and Alan Ohnsman, 'Tesla Rises After Posting Surprising Quarterly Earnings,' *Bloomberg*, August 8, 2013

75   'Solarcity Corporation Form S-1,' *Securities and Exchange Commission*, Washington, DC, October 5, 2012, Page 13

76   *ibid*, Page 13

77   *op. cit.*, Composite price in 2012 at the SP-15 EZ California and NP-15 California hubs at 'Wholesale Market Data 2012,' *Energy Information Administration*

78   Electric Power Monthly with Data for December 2012, *Energy Information Administration*, February 2013, Table 5.6.A. Average Retail Price of Electricity to Ultimate Customers by End-Use Sector by State, December 2012 and 2011

79   Diane Cardwell, 'Solar Panel Payments Set Off a Fairness Debate,' *The New York Times*, June 4, 2012

80   *op. cit.*, 'Solarcity Corporation Form S-1,' *Securities and Exchange Commission*, Page 14

81   *ibid*, Page 17

82   *ibid*, Page 18

83   *ibid*, Page 21

84   Allysia Finley, 'How Government Is Making Solar Billionaires,' *The Wall Street Journal*, October 21, 2013

85   *op. cit.*, Office of the White House Press Secretary, Remarks by the President on Energy

86   Joel Gehrke, 'Obama: Use "Algae" As Substitute for Oil,' *The Washington Examiner*, February 23, 2012

87   See for instance 'Jet Fuel-Gate Is Obama's New Solyndra,' *Investors Business Daily*, December 13, 2011; see also Andrew Stiles, 'Obama's Great Green Fleet,' *National Review*, December 19, 2011

88   James T. Bartis and Lawrence Van Bibber, 'Alternative Fuels for Military Applications,' *Rand Corporation*, 2011

89   'Against Innovation: Right-Wing Media Mock Obama for Promoting Algae-Based Fuels,' *Media Matters for America*, February 29, 2012

90   'Editorial: Navy Blue Goes Green,' *The Washington Times*, December 19, 2011

91   'Algal Biofuels,' *Biomass Program*, U.S. Department of Energy

92   *op. cit.*, Joel Gehrke, 'Obama: Use "Algae" As Substitute for Oil,' *The Washington Examiner*

93   *op. cit.*, Office of the White House Press Secretary, Remarks by the President on Energy

94   Ralph McGill, 'Algae As a Feedstock for Transportation Fuels – The Future of Biofuels?,' *IEA Advanced Motor Fuels Implementing Agreement*, Vienna, Austria, May 2008

95   Jennifer Epstein, 'Obama: "No Quick Fixes" on Gas Prices,' *Politico*, February 25, 2012

96   Daily Mail Reporter,' "Is There Anybody Here That Thinks That Makes a Lot of Sense?": Obama Fires Back at Reporter on Question About Gas Prices,' *The Daily Mail*, March 6, 2012

97   Meenal Vamburkar, 'Obama to *Fox* Reporter: Do You Think a President Seeking "Re-Election Wants Gas Prices to Go Up?",' *Mediaite*, March 6, 2012

98   *op. cit.*, Holman Jenkins, 'Newt Is Right About Gas Prices,' *The Wall Street Journal*

CHAPTER 7

1   Michael Birnbaum, 'European Industry Flocks to U.S. to Take Advantage of Cheaper Gas,' *The Washington Post*, April 1, 2013

2   Hardy Graupner, 'High Energy Costs May Drive German Firms to U.S.,' *Deutsche Welle*, May 22, 2013

3   *ibid*

4   Robin Emmott and Michelle Martin, 'Euro Zone Falls Into Second Recession Since 2009,' *Reuters*, November 15, 2012

5   See for instance 'Eurozone Unemployment Rate Hits New High in October,' *BBC*, November 30, 2012; see also John M. Curtis, 'Eurozone's Unemployment Soars in Debt Crisis,' *The Examiner*, November 1, 2012

6   Christopher Alessi, 'The Eurozone in Crisis,' *Council on Foreign Relations*, July 23, 2012

7   'Household Electricity Prices in the EU27 Rose by 6.6% and Gas Prices by 10.3%,' *Eurostat*, May 27, 2013

8   Marek Dabrowski, 'Fiscal and Monetary Policy Determinants of the Eurozone Crisis and Its Resolution,' *CASE Network Studies & Analyses*, 2012, Page 15

9   'Graph: Gross Domestic Product in Germany,' *Federal Reserve Bank of St. Louis*, January 1, 2008 to July 1, 2013

10   See the discussion at 'Germany's Energy Policy: Man-Made Crisis Now Costing Billions,' *Institute for Energy Research*, October 30, 2012

11   See for instance Alexander Neubacher and Catalina Schröder, 'Sunny Business: Germans Cough Up for Solar

Subsidies,' *Der Spiegel*, July 4, 2012; see also Juergen Baetz, AP, 'German Minister Warns of Rising Electricity Prices,' *The Boston Globe*, June 5, 2012

12   Frank Dohmen and Alexander Jung, 'Stress on the High Seas: Germany's Wind Power Revolution in the Doldrums,' *Der Spiegel*, December 30, 2011

13   'Germany's New Energy Policy,' *Federal Ministry of Economics and Technology*, Page 10

14   'Germans Willing to Pay for Green Power,' *Renewables International*, October 1, 2012

15   See for instance the preposterous, one-sided hymns sung by progressive crusader Osha Gray Davidson, whose e-Book entitled *Clean Break*, is serialized in a 6-part series at Osha Gray Davidson, 'Germany Has Built Clean Energy Economy U.S. Rejected in 80s,' *Bloomberg*, November 14, 2012. Davidson's previous work focused on coral reefs, sea turtles, agricultural demography, gun control, and race relations, material that obviously qualifies him to be *Bloomberg*'s resident authority on energy economics; see also Adam Scott, 'Reports of the Death of Renewable Energy in Europe are Greatly Exaggerated,' *The Huffington Post*, February 24, 2012

16   Damian Carrington, 'Germany's Renewable Energy Revolution Leaves UK in the Shade,' *The Guardian*, May 30, 2012

17   Stefan Nicola, 'Germany Plans Cap for Renewable Energy Subsidies,' *Bloomberg Business Week*, October 11, 2012

18   Reuters, 'Germany Pledges Nuclear Shutdown by 2022,' *The Guardian*, May 30, 2011

19   Christian Wüst, 'Fear of Fracking: Germany Balks on Natural Gas Bonanza,' *Der Spiegel*, October 5, 2012

20   See for instance Mathias Elspass, 'Uncertainty Still Surrounds Carbon Capture and Storage Legislation,' *International Law Office*, February 20, 2012; see also 'German Mediation Committee Agrees Carbon Capture Law,' *Reuters*, June 27, 2012

21   See Ulrika Lomas, 'Bundesrat Blocks Energy Saving Tax Incentives,' *Tax News*, July 14, 2011; see also Ulrika Lomas, 'Merkel Slams "Blockade" of Energy Efficiency Tax Breaks,' *Tax News*, November 23, 2012

22   Judy Dempsey and Jack Ewing, 'Germany, in Reversal, Will Close Nuclear Plants by 2022,' *The New York Times*, May 30, 2011

23   Luke Harding, 'Angela Merkel Switches Off Seven Nuclear Power Plants,' *The Guardian*, March 15, 2011

24   Veit Medick and Philipp Wittrock, 'Energy Revolution Stalls: Berlin Struggles to Realize Nuclear-Free Ambitions,' *Der Spiegel*, March 12, 2012

25   Mari Iwata 'Japan's Hunger for Fossil Fuels Poses Challenges,' *The Wall Street Journal*, January 24, 2013

26   Tsuyoshi Inajima and& Yuji Okada, 'Japan Axing Nuclear for Renewables Means Missing Carbon Goal,' *Bloomberg*, September 7, 2012

27   'Annual Report 2011 — Completing the Internal Electricity Market by 2014: The Challenges for Europe's Transmission System,' *European Network of Transmission System Operators for Electricity*, Page 42

28   *ibid*

29   Julia Mengewein, 'Germany Faces Lack of Winter Power Generation, TransnetBW Says,' *Bloomberg*, December 6, 2012

30   *ibid*

31   Ladka Bauerova and Carol Matlack, 'Nuke-Free Germany Isn't Exactly Nuke-Free,' *Bloomberg Business Week*, September 28, 2011

32   Laura Gitschier and Alexander Neubacher, 'Greenwashing After the Phase-Out: German "Energy Revolution" Depends on Nuclear Imports,' *Der Spiegel*, September 15, 2011

33   Stefan Nicola and Tino Andresen 'Debate Continues in Germany over Cost to Ratepayers for Renewable Energy Incentives,' *Renewable Energy World*, October 12, 2012

34   Associated Press, 'Germany: No Prospect of Shale Gas Fracking Soon,' *The Sacramento Bee*, February 11, 2013

35   Stefan Nicola and Tino Andresen, 'Merkel Curbs Renewables to Limit Voter Anger on Power Bills,' *Bloomberg*, October 12, 2012

36   Alexander Neubacher and Catalina Schröder, 'The Move to Renewables: Germany's Nuclear Phase-Out Brings Unexpected Costs,' *Der Spiegel*, June 6, 2012

37   *ibid*

38   'Aftermath of Election Defeat: Merkel Fires Environment Minister Röttgen,' *Der Spiegel*, May 16, 2012

39   'The World from Berlin: Merkel Faces "Herculean" Task on Green Energy,' *Der Spiegel*, May 24, 2012

40   'German Ministers Cast Doubt on Green Energy Targets,' *Reuters*, July 17, 2012

41   Spiegel Staff, 'German Energy Plan Plagued by Lack of Progress,' *Der Spiegel*, October 10, 2012

42   Stefan Nicola, 'Munich's Biggest Power Outage in Two Decades Brings City to Halt,' *Bloomberg*, November 15, 2012

43   Carsten Dierig, ,Stahlriese ächzt unter Kosten des Ökostrom-Ausbaus,' *Die Welt*, September 16, 2012

44   *op. cit.*, Spiegel Staff, 'German Energy Plan Plagued by Lack of Progress,' *Der Spiegel*

45   Christopher Booker, 'Germany's Wind Power Chaos Should be a Warning to the UK,' *The Telegraph*, September 22, 2012

46   Frank Dohmen and Alexander Neubacher, 'Merkel's Switch to Renewables: Rising Energy Prices Endanger German Industry,' *Der Spiegel*, February 24, 2012

47   *ibid*

48   *ibid*

49   *ibid*

50   Chris Bryant, 'High Energy Costs Conspire to Drive Europe's Industry Abroad,' *Financial Times*, May 28, 2013, Page 15

51   Review & Outlook Europe, 'German Energy Drain,' *The Wall Street Journal*, June 13, 2013

52   Michael Birnbaum, 'European Industry Flocks to U.S. to Take Advantage of Cheaper Gas,' *The Washington Post*, April 1, 2013

53   *op. cit.*, Review & Outlook Europe, 'German Energy Drain,' *The Wall Street Journal*

54   Adam Shull, 'Wacker Receives Incentives,' *The Paducah Sun*, July 30, 2011

55   Ellis Smith, 'Wacker Unveils Dalton Facility: German Chemical Giant Supplies Binding Products to Carpet Industry,' *Chattanooga Times Free Press*, March 27, 2013

56   Dave Flessner, 'Wacker Warns of Solar Trade War, But Still Confident about Charleston, Tenn., Investment,' *Chattanooga Times Free Press*, March 23, 2013

57   Emery P. Dalesio, Associated Press, 'Siemens Expanding in Charlotte, Adding 825 Jobs,' WCNC-Charlotte, March 11, 2010

58   Alex Webb, 'Siemens Said to Prepare 1,400 Job Cuts Amid Profit Push,' *Bloomberg*, March 19, 2013

59   Chris Bryant, 'Germany's Renewable Energy Experiment Comes at a Cost,' *Financial Times*, September 15, 2013

60   Edward Taylor, 'BASF CEO Says Electricity Grid Fees Put Jobs at Risk-Paper,' *Reuters*, November 10, 2013

61   Jack Kaskey, 'Dow Chemical to Eliminate 2,400 Jobs and Close Factories,' *Bloomberg*, October 24, 2012

62   Daniel Michaels, et. al., 'Airbus's New Push: Made in the U.S.A.,' *The Wall Street Journal*, July 2, 2012

63   Associated Press, 'Airbus Breaks Ground on Alabama Jet Plant,' *The Seattle Times*, April 8, 2013

64   'Battling Boeing: Airbus Plans to Open First Factory in America,' *Der Spiegel*, June 28, 2012

65   Jim Powell, 'How Europe's Economy Is Being Devastated by Global Warming Orthodoxy,' *Forbes*, September 19, 2013

66   *op. cit.*, Michael Birnbaum, 'European Industry Flocks to U.S. to Take Advantage of Cheaper Gas,' *The Washington Post*

67   *op. cit.*, Alex Webb, 'Siemens Said to Prepare 1,400 Job Cuts Amid Profit Push,' *Bloomberg*

68   Rachel Morison, 'German Vote Won't Cut 20 Billion Euro Renewables Bill, BNEF Says,' *Bloomberg*, September 17, 2013

69   Melissa Eddy and Stanley Reed, 'Germany's Effort at Clean Energy Proves Complex,' *The New York Times*, September 18, 2013

70   Catalina Schröder, 'Energy Revolution Hiccups: Grid Instability Has Industry Scrambling for Solutions,' *Der Spiegel*, August 16, 2012

71   'EU Energy Chief Urges "Speed Limit" on German Green Power Costs,' *Reuters*, September 25, 2012

72   'EU Energy Chief Oettinger Warns of Deindustrialization,' *Reuters*, July 16, 2012

73   Jeevan Vasagar, 'Angela Merkel's Advice for Europe's Unemployed: Move,' *The Telegraph*, June 14, 2014

74   *op. cit.*, 'Germany's New Energy Policy,' *Federal Ministry of Economics and Technology*, Page 30

75   Rainer Hinrichs-Rahlwes, 'The New German Renewable Energy Sources Act (EEG),' *Federal Ministry for the Environment, Nature Conservation and Nuclear Safety*, November 23, 2004

76   Anselm Waldermann, 'Offshore Wind Farms: A Green Revolution off Germany's Coast,' *Der Spiegel*, July 24, 2008

77   See Matthias Land and U. Mutschler, 'Bundestag Approves 3rd Amendment of German Energy Act – Offshore Liability, Shutdown Restrictions for Conventional Power Plants, and More,' *German Energy Blog*, November 30, 2012; see also *op. cit.*, Alexander Neubacher and Catalina Schröder, 'Sunny Business: Germans Cough Up for Solar Subsidies,' *Der Spiegel*

78   *op. cit.*, Spiegel Staff, 'Merkel's Blackout: German Energy Plan Plagued by Lack of Progress,' *Der Spiegel*

79   Stefan Nicola, 'German Power Grid Seen Needing $55 Billion to Absorb Renewables,' *Bloomberg Business Week*, December 11, 2012

80   'German Minister Calls for Power Grid Expansion,' *EurActiv*, January 19, 2011

81   'Energy Transition: Setting the Course Properly,' *BDI*, January 30, 2012

82   Stefan Nicola, 'German Power Grid Seen Needing $55 Billion on Renewables,' *Bloomberg*, December 11, 2012

83   'German Non-Nuclear Strategy Stumbles,' *Utility Week*, June 6, 2012

84   *ibid*

85   *op. cit.*, Spiegel Staff, 'Merkel's Blackout: German Energy Plan Plagued by Lack of Progress,' *Der Spiegel*

86   Stefan Nicola, Merkel Cabinet Backs Power-Line Plan to Absorb Renewables Growth,' *Bloomberg*, December 19, 2012

87   Frank Dohmen and Gerald Traufetter, 'Power Play: Politician Calls for Nationalization of Electricity Grid,' *Der Spiegel*, January 16, 2013

88   *ibid*

89   See for instance David Gow, 'E.On to Sell Off Electricity Grid to Placate European Commission,' *The Guardia*n, February 28, 2008; see also Peter Dinkloh, 'Update 1 – RWE Sells German Grid in 1 Bn Euro Deal – Source,' *Reuters*, July 14, 2011; see also Andrew Ward, 'Vattenfall Sells Off German Power Grid,' *Financial Times*, March 12, 2010

90   Gerrit Wiesman, 'RWE Delays €3Bn Wind Park Decision,' *Financial Times*, July 25, 2012

91   Stefan Nicola, 'German Offshore Wind-Energy Delays Threaten Energy Overhaul,' *Bloomberg*, February 21, 2012

92   Stefan Nicola, 'Germany's $263 Billion Renewables Shift Biggest Since War,' *Bloomberg*, March 19, 2012

93   'Off-Shore Wind Farm "Riffgat": Start of Construction 2012,' *ENOVA*

94   Benjamin Dürr, 'Wind Park in No Man's Land: Offshore Project Stirs Up German-Dutch Border Dispute,' *Der Spiegel*, July 9, 2012

95   See 'EWE, Enove Form JV to Develop Riffgat Wind Park Offshore Germany,' *Power Engineering*, May 11, 2008; see also *op. cit.*, 'Off-Shore Wind Farm "Riffgat": Start of Construction 2012,' *ENOVA*

96   *op. cit.*, Chris Bryant, 'Germany's Renewable Energy Experiment Comes at a Cost,' *Financial Times*

97   Ted Kennedy, Jr., 'Cape Wind: Don't Be Tricked,' *The Boston Herald*, October 30, 2010

98   'Levelized Cost of New Generation Resources in the Annual Energy Outlook 2011,' *Energy Information Administration*, November 2010

99   *ibid*

100   Richard Gray, 'Wind Farms May Pose Risk to Shipping,' *The Telegraph*, October 25, 2008

101   'Wind Farm Operation and Maintenance Costs Plummet,' *Bloomberg New Energy Finance*, November 1, 2012

102   'BTM Cuts Offshore Wind Forecast on German Grid, Sweden Incentive,' *Bloomberg New Energy Finance*, November 19, 2012

103   'Electricity Market Module,' *Energy Information Administration,*, April 2010, Table 8.2, Page 91

104   Matthias Schulz, 'Germany's Offshore Fiasco: North Sea Wind Offensive Plagued by Problems,' *Der Spiegel*, September 4, 2012

105   *ibid*

106   Stefan Nicola, 'RWE, E.On Offshore Wind Projects May Be Unlocked by German Accord,' *Bloomberg*, November 28, 2012

107   Stefan Nicola, 'Germany Seeks to Pass Offshore Wind Law Before Year-End,' *Bloomberg*, November 23, 2012

108   'Taking Power Further,' TenneT Company Fact Sheet, November 2010

109   'Actual and Forecast Wind Energy Feed-In,' TenneT Transparency, Publications, Network Figures, Actual and Forecast Wind Energy Feed-In, January 2012

110   *op. cit.*, Christopher Booker, 'Germany's Wind Power Chaos Should Be a Warning to the UK,' *The Telegraph*

111   Analysis by author of TenneT Actual Wind Energy Feed-In data for December 2011 to November 2012

112   Based upon assumption that Riffgat's 108 Mw would provide power to 116,000 homes at *op. cit.*, 'EWE, Enove Form JV to Develop Riffgat Wind Park Offshore Germany,' *Power Engineering* and *op. cit.*, 'Off-Shore Wind Farm "Riffgat": Start of Construction 2012,' *ENOVA*

113   Richard Fuchs, 'Wind Energy Surplus Threatens Eastern German Power Grid,' *Deutsche Welle*, March 26, 2011

114   'Germany's Energy Supply Transformation Has Already Failed,' *Europäisches Institut für Klima und Energie*, January 9, 2012, Page 9

115   Stefan Nicola, 'Merkel's Other Crisis Spurs German Quest for Energy Holy Grail,' *Bloomberg*, August 26, 2012

116   'Pumped Storage Power Plants to Integrate Wind and Solar Power,' *DENA*, May 23, 2012

117   Annette Weisbach, 'Roesler: Limit Legal Suits Against Expansion of Power Grid, FAZ,' *Bloomberg*, June 13, 2012

118   *op. cit.*, 'Germany's Energy Supply Transformation Has Already Failed,' *Europäisches Institut für Klima und Energie*, Page 17

119   Torsten Fagerholm, 'Proposed EU Rules May Thwart New Norway-Europe Power Cables,' *Bloomberg*, December 10, 2012

120   'Review of the ITC Annual Cross-Border Infrastructure Compensation Sum,' *EU Agency for the Cooperation of Energy Regulators*, October 16, 2012, Page 5

121   *op. cit.*, Torsten Fagerholm, 'Proposed EU Rules May Thwart New Norway-Europe Power Cables,' *Bloomberg*

122   *ibid*

123   'RWE Innogy Sets Up Joint Venture to Develop Hydropower in Serbia,' *Energy Central*, May 25, 2011

124   See for instance Sean Patrick Farrell, 'Farewell, Dams. Hello Salmon?,' *The New York Times*, September 20, 2011;

see also Bettina Boxall, 'Utility Agrees to Removal of 4 Klamath River Dams,' *Los Angeles Times*, September 30, 2009

125 Renee Cho, 'Removing Dams and Restoring Rivers,' *The Earth Institute at Columbia University*, August 29, 2011

126 'Open Rivers Initiative,' *National Oceanic and Atmospheric Administration*

127 *op. cit.*, 'Germany's Energy Supply Transformation Has Already Failed,' *Europäisches Institut für Klima und Energie*, Page 4

128 Holger Gassner, 'German Energy Transition — Opportunities and Challenges,' *IEEJ - Japan Energy Policy Debate*, Tokyo March 22, 2012, Page 19

129 Frank Dohmen, Alexander Jung and Christian Schwägerl, 'The Dirty Bridge to a Green Future: How Quickly Can Germany Abandon Nuclear Energy?,' *Der Spiegel*, March 22, 2011

130 Toby Price, 'A First as Hydrogen-Hybrid Power Station Commissioned,' *Renewable Energy Magazine*, November 4, 2011

131 Samuel R. Avro, 'Germany to Build World's First Hybrid Power Plant,' *Consumer Energy Report*, April 22, 2009

132 *op. cit.*, 'Germany's Energy Supply Transformation Has Already Failed,' *Europäisches Institut für Klima und Energie*, Page 18

133 John Daly, 'Germany's Rising Cost of Going Green,' *Oil Price*, February 25, 2012

134 Richard Fuchs, 'Wind Energy Surplus Threatens Eastern German Power Grid,' *Deutsche Welle*, March 26, 2011

135 Ladka Bauerova and Tino Andresen, 'Windmills Overload East Europe's Grid Risking Blackout: Energy,' *Bloomberg*, October 25, 2012

136 *ibid*

137 Marek Strzelecki, 'Germany, Poland Sign Deal to Boost Grid Security, Power Trade,' *Bloomberg*, December 21, 2012

138 Nick Ottens, 'Region: German Green-Energy Push Needs a Rethink,' *The Prague Post*, January 16, 2013

139 Daniel Wetzel, ‚Polnische Quittung für Deutsche Energiewende,‘ *Die Welt*, December 12, 2012

140 Willem Post, 'Energy from Wind Turbines Actually Less than Estimated,' *The Energy Collective*, January 10, 2013

141 *ibid*

142 *ibid*

143 Gerard Wynn, 'German Wind Power Irks Neighboring Grids,' *Reuters*, December 20, 2012

144 'Germany Faces Struggle to Balance Electricity System as Loop Flows Curbed,' *ICIS*, December 12, 2012; see also 'German Power Loop Flows Threaten EU's Internal Market: Regulators,' *Platts*, February 1, 2012

145 Gerard Wynn, 'Stray Power Threatens EU Regional Grid Project,' *Reuters*, December 12, 2012

146 *op. cit.*, James Murray, 'Moody's: Renewables Boom Poses Credit Risk,' *Business Green*

CHAPTER 8

1 Mark Helprin, 'Obama's Europa Complex,' *The Wall Street Journal*, March 26, 2012

1 Joel Stonington, 'Leading or Following? Merkel Speaks with Two Tongues on Climate,' *Der Spiegel*, May 7, 2013

2 Stanley Reed, 'Europe Faces a Crisis in Energy Costs,' *The New York Times*, April 17, 2013

3 Michael Graham, 'The Butterfield Effect,' *Jewish World Review*, December 2, 2004

4 Madeline Chambers and Vera Eckert, 'Ballooning Costs Threaten Merkel's Bold Energy Overhaul,' *Reuters*, August 28, 2013

5 Sally Bakewell and Marc Roca, 'Renewable Subsidies "Unaffordable" at $725 Billion, Bank Says,' *Bloomberg*, November 12, 2012

6 *ibid*

7 Ben Backwell, 'Green Street: Subsidies Are Biting Now, But Support for Renewables Must Be Maintained,' *Recharge News*, November 15, 2012

8 'Renewable Subsidies: A Double-Edged Sword,' *Trend Online*, November 15, 2012

9 Rachel Morison and Julia Mengewein, 'German Power-Price Swings Threaten Growth Engine: Energy Markets,' *Bloomberg*, October 16, 2013

10 Andrew Curry, 'Can You Have Too Much Solar Energy?,' *Slate*, March 29, 2013

11 'How to Lose Half a Trillion Euros,' *The Economist*, October 12, 2013

12 'Wind and Solar Power Will Continue to Erode Thermal Generators' Credit Quality,' *Moody's Investor Service*, November 6, 2012

13 Spiegel Staff, 'German Energy Plan Plagued by Lack of Progress,' *Der Spiegel*, October 10, 2012

14 'German Wind Turbine Market Enjoys Stable Growth - The Wind Industry Faces Major Challenges on the World Market,' *BWE German Wind Energy Association*, August 1, 2012

15 'Moody's Warns EU of Renewables Risk,' *Electricity Policy*, November 7, 2012

16 Tino Andresen, 'RWE Shuts Unprofitable Power Plants to Spur Generation Unit,' *Bloomberg*, August 14, 2013

17   Volker Heck, 'RWE Confirms Forecast for 2013,' *RWE Investor Relations*, August 14, 2013

18   'RWE to Close or Idle Power Plants,' *BBC*, August 14, 2013

19   Jan Hromadko, 'RWE to Close Plants as Profit Drops,' *The Wall Street Journal*, August 14, 2013

20   Sonal Patel, 'RWE to Close 3.1 GW of Conventional Generation Across Europe on Profit Woes,' *Power Magazine*, August 15, 2013

21   *ibid*

22   *op. cit.*, 'RWE to Close or Idle Power Plants,' *BBC*

23   See RWE.GR 5-year stock chart for December 6, 2012 at *Bloomberg*

24   See EOAN:GR 5-year stock chart for December 6, 2012 at *Bloomberg*

25   Stefan Nicola, 'Merkel's Other Crisis Spurs German Quest for Energy Holy Grail,' *Bloomberg*, August 26, 2012

26   'Eon Dividend Tipped to Suffer in 2013,' *Utility Week*, February 8, 2013

27   'E.On Puts German Natural Gas-Fired Electricity Plants in Cold Reserve,' *ICIS*, November 13, 2012

28   'How to Lose Half a Trillion Euros,' *The Economist*, October 12, 2013

29   Freya Roberts, 'Renewables Growth in Europe: Good News for Wholesale Electricity Prices?,' *The Carbon Brief*, November 12, 2012

30   James Murray, 'Moody's: Renewables Boom Poses Credit Risk for Coal and Gas Power Plants,' *Business Green*, November 6, 2012

31   Frank Dohmen and Alexander Neubacher, 'Merkel's Switch to Renewables: Rising Energy Prices Endanger German Industry,' *Der Spiegel*, February 24, 2012

32   Review & Outlook, 'Berlin's Green Welfare,' *The Wall Street Journal*, August 15, 2012

33   David Talbot, 'The Great German Energy Experiment,' *Technology Review*, July-August 2012

34   *ibid*

35   Dieter Bohme, ‚Development of Renewable Energy Sources in Germany 2011,' Bundesministerium für Umwelt, Naturschutz und Reaktorsicherheit, July 2012, Page 17

36   Alexander Neubacher, 'Solar Subsidy Sinkhole: Re-Evaluating Germany's Blind Faith in the Sun,' *Der Spiegel*, January 18, 2012

37   James Murray, 'Moody's: Renewables Boom Poses Credit Risk for Coal and Gas Power Plants,' *Business Green*, November 6, 2012

38   David Crossland, 'Doubts Rising over German Switch to Renewables,' *Der Spiegel*, July 17, 2012

39   Osha Gray Davidson, 'Can the U.S. Create Its Own German-Style Energy Revolution?,' *Bloomberg*, November 26, 2012

40   *op. cit.*, 'How to Lose Half a Trillion Euros,' *The Economist*

41   Matthew Day, 'Germany Facing Power Blackouts,' *The Telegraph*, October 15, 2012

42   'Germans Grow Wary of Switch to Renewables,' *Der Spiegel*, October 15, 2012

43   Melissa Eddy, 'Energy Price Increases Pose Challenge for Merkel,' *The New York Times*, October 16, 2012

44   '2010 Solar Technologies Market Report,' *National Renewables Energy Laboratory*, November 2011, Page 1

45   'Average Sunshine a Year in Germany,' *Current Results*

46   Daniel Greenfield, 'Electric Poverty and Germany's Green Energy Disaster,' *Frontpage Magazine*, October 20, 2012

47   'CEO of Energy Giant RWE: "The Nuclear Power Chapter Has Come to an End",' *Der Spiegel*, June 29, 2012

48   Erik Kirschbaum, 'Germany Sets New Solar Power Record, Institute Says,' *Reuters*, May 26, 2012

49   Charles Hawley, 'The World from Berlin: Germany Hits Brakes on Race to Renewable Energy Future,' *Der Spiegel*, August 28, 2012

50   Matt McGrath, 'Can Germany Afford Its "Energy Bender" Shift to Green Power?,' *BBC*, July 9, 2013

51   *op. cit.*, 'How to Lose Half a Trillion Euros,' *The Economist*

52   Steve Leone, 'Germany's Day in the Sun: Solar Hits 22 GW Mark,' *Renewable Energy World*, May 29, 2012

53   Juergen Baetz, 'German Wind Power Installation Up 26 Percent,' *Bloomberg Business Week*, August 1, 2012

54   David Crane and Robert F. Kennedy Jr., 'Solar Panels for Every Home,' *The New York Times*, December 13, 2012, Page A35

55   'Corrections: December 15, 2012,' *The New York Times*, December 14, 2012

56   Phil Plait, 'Robert F. Kennedy Jr.: Anti-Vaxxer,' *Slate*, June 5, 2013

57   Frank Dohmen, Nils Klawitter and Wolfgang Reuter, 'Solar Industry Fights to Save Subsidies,' *Der Spiegel*, April 22, 2010

58   Table 5A. Residential Average Monthly Bill by Census Division, and State 2011, *Energy Information Administration*

59   Joel Stonington, 'A Mere Breeze: Era of Fast Growth Ends for Wind Energy in Europe,' *Der Spiegel*, February 8, 2013

60 See the high cost profile of solar PV at 'Levelized Cost of New Generation Resources in the Annual Energy Outlook 2011,' *Energy Information Administration*

61 Alexander Neubacher, 'Solar Subsidy Sinkhole: Re-Evaluating Germany's Blind Faith in the Sun,' *Der Spiegel*, January 18, 2012

62 *ibid*

63 Alexander Neubacher and Catalina Schröder, 'Germans Cough Up for Solar Subsidies,' *Der Spiegel*, July 4, 2012

64 Jens Lubbadeh and Anselm Walderman, How Effective Are Renewables, Anyway?,' *Der Spiegel*, December 16, 2009

65 Ted Nordhaus and Michael Shellenberger, 'Going Green? Then Go Nuclear,' *The Wall Street Journal*, May 22, 2013

66 'Rising Energy Prices: Germans Grow Wary of Switch to Renewables,' *Der Spiegel*, October 15, 2012

67 'Germany's Energy Poverty: How Electricity Became a Luxury Good,' Der Spiegel, September 4, 2013

68 'German Renewable Surcharge to Rise by 47 Percent: Source,' *Reuters*, October 10, 2012

69 Laura Gitschier and Christian Schwägerl, 'Revolution Threatens to Falter: Is Germany's Green Energy Plan Faltering?,' *Der Spiegel*, October 11, 2011

70 Spiegel Staff, 'Germany's Energy Poverty: How Electricity Became a Luxury Good,' *Der Spiegel*, September 4, 2013

71 *op. cit.*, 'Table 5A. Residential Average Monthly Bill by Census Division 2011,' *EIA*

72 Spiegel Staff, 'Merkel's Blackout: German Energy Plan Plagued by Lack of Progress,' *Der Spiegel*, October 10, 2012

73 Siobhan Dowling, 'Germany Battles Over the Future of Solar Energy,' *Global Post*, February 20, 2012

74 Daniel Wetzel, ,Die Krassen Fehlprognosen beim Ökostrom,' *Die Welt*, October 25, 2012

75 *ibid*

76 Tritten is infamous for once approving a Greens party platform position document that advocated legalization of pedophilia. See for instance AFP, 'German Greens Party's Jürgen Trittin Expresses Regret over Child-Sex Views,' *South China Morning Post*, September 18, 2013

77 Daniel Wetzel, 'Lies, Damn Lies and Green Statistics,' *The Global Warming Policy Foundation*, October 25, 2012

78 *ibid*

79 *ibid*

80 *ibid*

81 Electricity Prices for Domestic Consumers, Second Half 2008 to First Half 2013, Bi-Annual Data, Price in Euros, All Taxes Included, Euros per Kilowatt-Hour, *Eurostat*, European Commission; Dollar-Euro exchange rate data from *Yahoo Finance* based upon exchange rate at middle of each half of bi-annual period

82 Table 5A. Residential Average Monthly Bill by Census Division 2012,' *Energy Information Administration*

83 John Daly, 'Germany's Rising Cost of Going Green,' *Oil Price*, February 25, 2012

84 'Levelized Cost of New Generation Resources in the Annual Energy Outlook 2012,' *Annual Energy Outlook 2012, Energy Information Administration*, July 12, 2012

85 'IEA Wind 2012 Annual Report,' *International Energy Agency*, July 2013, Page 5

86 34.0% divided by 17.34% = 1.96 or 96% more

87 'Germany's Energy Policy: Man-Made Crisis Now Costing Billions,' *Institute for Energy Research*, October 30, 2012

88 'Big Gift to Big Business: Berlin to Exempt 1,550 Firms from Electricity Surcharge,' *Der Spiegel*, December 24, 2012

89 Jörg Schindler and Gerald Traufetter, 'Tax Breaks and Subsidies for Industry Divide Germans,' *Der Spiegel*, October 26, 2012

90 *ibid*

91 Tino Andresen and Julia Mengewein, 'RWE Said to Drop Two Coal-Fired Power Contracts,' *Bloomberg*, December 23, 2013

92 Frank Dohmen, Christoph Pauly and Gerald Traufetter, 'War on Subsidies: Brussels Questions German Energy Revolution,' *Der Spiegel*, May 29, 2013

93 *ibid*

94 William Boston and Alessandro Torello, 'EU Probes German Grid-Fee Exemptions,' *The Wall Street Journal*, March 6, 2013

95 Electricity Prices for Consumers, from 2007 Onwards, Bi-Annual Data, *Eurostat*

96 *ibid*

97 Compound annual growth rate between January 2008 and July 2012. See *op. cit.*, 'Monthly Energy Review — October 2012,' *EIA*, Table 9.8 Average Retail Prices of Electricity, Page 127

98   G. Allen Brooks, 'Germany's Clean Energy Problems Gaining Visibility in U.S.,' *Downstream Today*, October 15, 2013
99   Jerry Taylor and Peter Van Doren, 'The Green Jobs Myth,' *Forbes*, April 11, 2011
100   Janina Ketterer, 'The Impact of Wind Power Generation on the Electricity Price in Germany,' IFO Working Paper No. 143, *Leibnitz Institute for Economic Research*, 2012
101   'Germany's Green Energy Destabilizing Electric Grids,' *Institute for Energy Research*, January 23, 2013
102   *op. cit.*, Jerry Taylor and Peter Van Doren, 'The Green Jobs Myth,' *Forbes*
103   *op. cit.*, 'Germany's Energy Policy: Man-Made Crisis Now Costing Billions,' *Institute for Energy Research*
104   *op. cit.*, Guenter Traumann, ,Wenn Das Geld Nicht Mehr Zum Heizen Reicht,' *Focus*
105   Fiona Harvey, 'UK Cuts Feed-In Tariff for Solar Power,' *The Guardian*, August 1, 2012
106   Tony Czuczka, 'Germany Cuts Solar Aid to Curb Prices, Panel Installations,' *Bloomberg*, March 29, 2012
107   Stefan Nicola and Tino Andresen, 'Merkel Curbs Renewables to Limit Voter Anger on Power Bills,' *Bloomberg Business Week*, October 12, 2012
108   Christopher Booker, 'Germany's Wind Power Chaos Should Be a Warning to the UK,' *The Telegraph*, September 22, 2012
109   Frank Dohmen and Alexander Jung, 'Stress on the High Seas: Germany's Wind Power Revolution in the Doldrums,' *Der Spiegel*, December 30, 2011
110   Tino Andresen, 'Power Links for Unbuilt Windmills Cost Consumers, TenneT Says,' *Bloomberg*, October 12, 2012
111   Stefan Schultz, 'Power Failures: Germany Rethinks Path to Green Future,' *Der Spiegel*, August 29, 2012
112   Matthias Land and U. Mutschler, 'BNetzA and German Cartel Office Present Joint Electricity and Gas Monitoring Report 2012,' *German Energy Blog*, November 28, 2012
113   'Germany's Energy Supply Transformation Has Already Failed,' *Europäisches Institut für Klima und Energie*, January 9, 2012, Page 9
114   *ibid*, Page 11
115   *op. cit.*, Spiegel Staff, 'Merkel's Blackout: German Energy Plan Plagued by Lack of Progress,' *Der Spiegel*
116   *op. cit.*, 'Germany's Energy Supply Transformation Has Already Failed,' *Europäisches Institut für Klima und Energie*, Page 10
117   'Rising Offshore Wind Electricity Capacity to 'Crash' German Power Prices at Night, Says Analyst,' *ICIS*, December 10, 2012
118   'Q&A: Europe's Carbon Trading Scheme,' *BBC*, December 20, 2006
119   Harriet Torry, 'Indecision in Berlin Clouds Climate Goals,' *The Wall Street Journal*, April 12, 2013
120   Nina Chestney, 'Update 3-EU Climate Fight Hit by New Record Low Carbon Price,' *Reuters*, November 30, 2012
121   James Murray, 'European Carbon Price "Inching Ever Closer to Zero",' *The Guardian*, February 7, 2013
122   'Carbon Price Under EU Emissions Trading System Hits All-Time Low,' *BBC*, January 21, 2013
123   Joel Stonington, 'Wake-Up Call: A Disastrous Week for Carbon Trading,' *Der Spiegel*, January 25, 2013
124   *ibid*
125   'Tilting at Windmills,' *The Economist*, June 15, 2013. The *Economist* attributes Germany's environmental zeal to "a culture that values earnest efforts to do good." The editors must have skipped over the 20th century.
126   Stanley Reed, 'Europe Vote Sets Back Carbon Plan,' *The New York Times*, April 16, 2013
127   Christian Teevs, 'Failed Emissions Trading Reform: "The End of a European Climate Policy",' *Der Spiegel*, April 17, 2013
128   *op. cit.*, Sean Carney, 'Vote Leaves EU Emissions Trading in Tatters,' *The Wall Street Journal*
129   Art Patnaude, 'EU Votes to Revamp Carbon-Trading Program,' *The Wall Street Journal*, July 3, 2013
130   Alessandro Vitelli and Mathew Carr, 'Carbon Drops to Second-Lowest Close After EU Permit Sale Fails,' *Bloomberg*, March 12, 2013
131   Jan Hromadko, 'Utility CEOs Slam EU Energy Policy,' *The Wall Street Journal*, May 22, 2013
132   Review & Outlook, 'Cap and Trade Collapses,' *The Wall Street Journal*, April 19, 2013
133   *BP Statistical Review of World Energy 2012*,' Page 6
134   Otto J. Reich, 'In Venezuela, Plenty of Oil, Not Enough Food,' *The Wall Street Journal*, February 11, 2013
135   See for instance Saul Hudson, 'Power Blackout in Venezuelan Capital, Oil Province,' *Reuters*, September 1, 2008; see also 'Venezuela's Most Populated Areas Suffer Another Major Blackout,' *Merco Press*, April 11, 2011; see also Francisco Toro, 'The Possum Ate My Cable,' *Los Angeles Times*, June 21, 2012; see also Patricia Rey Mallén, '70% of Venezuela Suffers Electricity Blackouts; 9th Largest Oil Producer in Serious Energy Trouble,' *International Business Times*, September 5, 2013
136   Associated Press, 'Venezuela Hopes to Wipe Out Toilet Paper Shortage by Importing 50M Rolls,' *The Guardian*, May 16, 2013; see also 'Venezuela Orders Temporary Takeover of Toilet Paper Factory,' *Reuters*, September 20, 2013

137   Rowena Mason, 'The Great Carbon Trading Scandal,' *The Telegraph*, January 30, 2011

138   Alexander Jung, 'Hot Air: The EU's Emissions Trading System Isn't Working,' *Der Spiegel*, February 15, 2012

139   Joel Stonington, 'Cutting Carbon: Is Europe's Emissions Trading System Broken?,' *Der Spiegel*, October 26, 2012

140   Manuel Frondel, Nolan Ritter, Christoph Schmidt and Colin Vance, 'Economic Impacts from the Promotion of Renewable Energy Technologies: The German Experience — Ruhr Economic Papers #156,' *Rheinisch-Westfälisches Institut für Wirtschaftsforschung*, Essen, Germany, November 2009, Page 13

141   'Energy Policies of IEA Countries: Germany 2007 Review,' *International Energy Agency*, OECD, 2007, Page 40

142   Review & Outlook, 'Europe's Return to Coal,' *The Wall Street Journal*, May 17, 2012

143   Nick Grealy, 'The Dirty Coal Behind Germany's Clean Energy,' *The Christian Science Monitor*, July 16, 2013

144   Alexander Neubacher, 'Reality Check: Germany's Defective Green Energy Game Plan,' *Der Spiegel*, October 25, 2013

145   Stefan Nicola and Tino Andresen, 'Merkel's Green Shift Force Germany to Burn More Coal,' Bloomberg, August 20, 2012

146   *ibid*

147   James Conca, 'Germany — Insane of Just Plain Stupid,' *Forbes*, August 31, 2012

148   Stanley Reed, 'Volatility of Renewables Pushes Europe Back Toward Dependence on Coal,' *The New York Times*, October 31, 2012

149   'How Less Became More: Wind, Power and Unintended Consequences in the Colorado Energy Market,' *Bentek Energy LLC*

150   'Europe's Dirty Secret: The Unwelcome Renaissance,' *The Economist*, January 5, 2013

151   *ibid*

152   Anselm Waldermann, 'Climate Change Paradox: Wind Turbines in Europe Do Nothing for Emissions-Reduction Goals,' *Der Spiegel*, February 10, 2009

153   Renuka Rayasam, 'Woodland Heists: Rising Energy Costs Drive Up Forest Thievery,' *Der Spiegel*, January 17, 2013

154   *ibid*

155   Nektaria Stamouli and Stelios Bouras, 'Greeks Raid Forests in Search of Wood to Heat Homes,' *The Wall Street Journal*, January 11, 2013

156   Spiegel Staff, 'The Price of Green Energy: Is Germany Killing the Environment to Save It?,' *Der Spiegel*, March 12, 2013

157   *ibid*

158   'Primeval Beech Forests of the Carpathians and the Ancient Beech Forests of Germany,' *United Nations Educational, Scientific and Cultural Organization*, 2011

159   *op. cit.*, Anselm Waldermann, 'Climate Change Paradox: Wind Turbines in Europe Do Nothing for Emissions-Reduction Goals,' *Der Spiegel*

160   Richard L. Strout, 'Chamber of Commerce Challenges Reagan on Soviet Pipeline,' *Christian Science Monitor*, February 22, 1982

161   Mohammad I. Aslam, 'Putin's Gazprom: An Unhealthy Mix of Business and Politics,' *The Independent*, April 17, 2012

162   Robert Johnston and Leslie Palti-Guzman, 'The Foreign Policy Uses of an Energy Bounty,' *The Wall Street Journal*, January 9, 2013

163   'BP Explores Nord Stream Extension to UK,' *Pipeline & Gas Journal*, January 2013

164   Neil Buckley, 'Gazprom Reduces Price of Gas to Poland,' *Financial Times*, November 6, 2012

165   Gerrit Wiesmann, 'Europe's Fears Over U.S. Energy Gap,' *Financial Times*, November 9, 2012

166   *ibid*

167   *ibid*

168   *ibid*

169   'Building German Natural Gas Electricity Plants Could Be "Politically Driven" – Analyst,' *ICIS*, September 26, 2012

170   'Europe Brent Spot Price FOB,' *Energy Information Administration*, Price per Barrel (Dollars per Barrel), October 2009

171   Stefan Nicola, 'Germany's $263 Billion Renewables Shift Biggest Since War,' *Bloomberg*, March 19, 2012

172   'E.On Puts German Natural Gas-Fired Electricity Plants in Cold Reserve,' *ICIS,* November 13, 2012

173   *ibid*

174   Jan Hromadko, 'Shale Boom a Bust for Europe's Gas Plants,' *The Wall Street Journal*, May 8, 2013

175   See for instance the triumphal boasts from German government advisor and chair of the Scientific Advisory Board of the Federal Finance Ministry Kai Konrad at 'A Plea for a New Climate Strategy: Europe Shouldn't Try So Hard to Save the Planet,' *Der Spiegel*, December 6, 2012

176 'Irony of Ironies: Europe Switches to Coal as U.S. Gas Glut Reduces Emissions,' *Energy Tribune*, July 12, 2012

177 Alex Morales, 'Ignoring "Fantastic Opportunity" of Gas Is Foolish: Lomborg,' *Bloomberg*, October 18, 2012

178 *op. cit.*, Stefan Nicola, 'Germany's $263 Billion Renewables Shift Biggest Since War,' *Bloomberg*

179 *op. cit.*, Anselm Waldermann, 'Climate Change Paradox: Wind Turbines in Europe Do Nothing for Emissions-Reduction Goals,' *Der Spiegel*

180 Walter Russell Mead, 'In Green Europe, It Takes an Economic Disaster to Reduce Emissions,' *The American Interest*, April 30, 2013

181 Benny Peiser, 'Cooling on Global Warming,' *The Wall Street Journal*, December 16, 2008

182 Marita Noon, 'Europe Climate Bailout Scheme Shows They Think We're Clowns,' *Frontpage Magazine*, December 18, 2011

183 Bret Stephens, 'Myth and Reality in the EU,' *The Wall Street Journal*, June 12, 2005

184 Daniel Halper, 'Claim: Germany Spends $110 Billion to Delay Global Warming by 37 Hours,' *The Weekly Standard*, March 30, 2013

185 See for instance proposals to tax carbon at the border at Daniel Gros and Christian Egenhofer, 'Climate Change and Trade: Taxing Carbon at the Border,' *Center for European Policy Studies*, 2010; see also a critical analysis of BCA structures that was ignored by collectivist engineers who authored HR 2454 at Christopher L. Weber and Glen P. Peters, 'Climate Change Policy and International Trade: Policy Considerations in the U.S.,' *Energy Policy*, Volume 37, November 7, 2008, Pages 432-440; see also a paper advocating BCAs as part of "preferential trade agreements" as opposed to unilaterally-imposed sovereign trade rules at Keteryna Holzer and Nashina Shariff, 'The Inclusion of Border Carbon Adjustments in Preferential Trade Agreements: Policy Implications,' *Inter-American Development Bank*, October 19, 2012

186 See H.R. 2454, Title IV, Subtitle A., Section 401 (2) "to prevent an increase in greenhouse gas emissions in countries other than the United States as a result of direct and indirect compliance costs incurred under this title" at 'H.R. 2454 (111th): American Clean Energy and Security Act of 2009, 111th Congress, 2009-2010, *Gov.Track*; see GAO advisory to the Senate Finance Committee at Loren Yager, 'Climate Change Trade Measures,' *Government Accountability Office*, GAO09-724R, July 8, 2009

187 Valerie Volcovici, 'Obama Shields U.S. Airlines from EU Carbon Fees,' *Reuters*, November 27, 2012

188 Jasmine Wang, 'EU Vows to Keep Airline-Emission Levies as China-India Opposition Mounts,' *Bloomberg*, February 13, 2012

189 'EU to Keep Carbon Tax on Airlines,' *Phys Org*, March 8, 2012

190 Richard Black, 'Top China Airlines to Ignore EU Carbon Tax, Body Says,' *BBC*, January 5, 2012

191 Barbara Lewis, 'Update 4-EU Commission Freezes Airline Carbon Law,' *Reuters*, November 12, 2012

192 *op. cit.*, Richard Black, 'Top China Airlines to Ignore EU Carbon Tax, Body Says,' *BBC*

193 'China "Blocks Airbus Deals" in EU Carbon Levy Spat,' *BBC*, March 8, 2012

194 Doug Cameron, 'U.S. Airlines Seek Action on EU Carbon Tax,' *The Wall Street Journal*, March 27, 2012

195 'China Retaliates to EU Carbon Tax, Blocks Airbus Orders,' *The China Post*, March 9, 2012

196 Richard Black, 'Countries Rally Against EU Carbon Tax on Airlines,' *BBC*, February 21, 2012

197 *ibid*

198 Elisabeth Rosenthal, 'Your Biggest Carbon Sin May Be Air Travel,' *The New York Times*, January 26, 2013

199 *ibid*

200 Sonia van Gilder Cooke, 'Will Austerity Derail Europe's Clean-Energy Movement?,' *Time*, February 10, 2012

201 Steve Goreham, 'Wind Turbines Clutter the North German Countryside,' *The Washington Times*, August 28, 2013

202 See 'Abraham Lincoln: Vampire Hunter (2012),' *Internet Movie Database*

203 Review & Outlook, 'Europe's Green Central Planning,' *The Wall Street Journal*, May 9, 2013

204 Jonathan Stearns, 'EU Said to Plan Duties Up to 67.9% on China Solar Panels,' *Bloomberg*, May 9, 2013

205 Angeline Benoit and Ben Sills, 'Spain Has EU's Largest Deficit, Undermining Rajoy Pickup,' *Bloomberg*, April 22, 2013

206 'Spanish Unemployment Hits Five Million: Record Rise Leaves an Incredible One Quarter of the Population Unemployed,' *The Daily Mail*, March 4, 2013

207 Europa Press, 'El 'Lobby Bancario' Cree que la Economía Española se Contraerá un 2% en 2013,' *El Economista*, April 22, 2013

208 Joel Stonington, 'A Mere Breeze: Era of Fast Growth Ends for Wind Energy in Europe,' *Der Spiegel*, February 8, 2013

209 op. cit., Alexander Neubacher, 'Solar Subsidy Sinkhole: Re-Evaluating Germany's Blind Faith in the Sun,' *Der Spiegel*

210 Jan Hromadko, 'EU Energy Chief Wants to Prioritize Affordability,' *The Wall Street Journal*, April 10, 2013

211 'EU Energy Chief Oettinger Warns of Deindustrialization,' *Reuters*, July 16, 2012

212 Dow Jones Newswire, 'EU Says 2020 Renewable Energy Target Still Unachievable,' *Fox Business*, March 27, 2013

213 Robert Stokes, 'EU Climate Policy "Costs Billions and Risks Jobs",' *Utility Week*, June 14, 2012

214 *op. cit.*, Stanley Reed, 'Europe Faces a Crisis in Energy Costs,' *The New York Times*

215 Peter C. Glover, 'The World Is Not Running Out of Oil — But Europe Is,' *The Energy Tribune*, May 14, 2013

216 Benjamin J. Phrampus and Matthew J. Hornbach, 'Recent Changes to the Gulf Stream Causing Widespread Gas Hydrate Destabilization,' *Nature*, Volume 490, October 25, 2012, Pages 527-530

217 'Ice That Burns May Yield Clean, Sustainable Bridge to Global Energy Future,' *Science Daily*, March 24, 2009

218 Matthew Kaminski, 'Europe's Indispensible Nation,' *The Wall Street Journal*, December 13, 2012

CHAPTER 9

1 'President Jackson's Veto Message Regarding the Bank of the United States,' *The Avalon Project at Yale Law School*, July 10, 1832

2 'Assembly Bill 32: Global Warming Solutions Act,' *California Environmental Protection Agency*, Air Resources Board

3 'Renewable Portfolio Standard Policies,' Database of State Incentives for Renewables & Efficiency, U.S. Department of Energy

4 See for instance Melissa Anders, 'Michigan Proposal 3: Voters Reject 25 by 25 Renewable Energy Mandate,' *Michigan Live*, November 6, 2012

5 Barack Obama, 'Securing Our Energy Future: Remarks of Senator Barack Obama, Resources for the Future,' Washington, DC, September 15, 2005

6 Barack Obama, 'Energy Security Is National Security Speech,' Washington, DC, February 28, 2006

7 Barack Obama, 'A Secure Energy Future Speech,' Dayton, Ohio, *The American Presidency Project*, July 11, 2008

8 Public Law 110-140, 'Energy Independence and Security Act of 2007, *U.S. Government Printing Office*, December 19, 2007

9 Fuels and Fuel Additives, 2012 RFS2 Data, Cellulosic Biofuel (D3), *Environmental Protection Agency*

10 'Assembly Bill No. 32, Chapter 488,' *Official California Legislative Information*, Legislative Counsel, State of California

11 op. cit., 'Assembly Bill 32: Global Warming Solutions Act,' *California EPA*

12 Review & Outlook, 'The Price of Green Virtue,' *The Wall Street Journal*, July 6, 2012

13 'Low Carbon Fuel Standard Program Background,' *California Environmental Protection Agency*, Air Resources Board

14 'Updated Economic Analysis of California's Climate Change Scoping Plan,' Staff Report to the Air Resources Board, *California Environmental Protection Agency*, Air Resources Board, March 24, 2010, Page ES-6

15 Andrew Chang & Company, LLC, 'The Fiscal and Economic Impact of the California Global Warming Solutions Act of 2006 — Executive Summary,' *California Manufacturers & Technology Association*, June 2012, Page 3

16 Andrew Chang & Company, LLC, 'The Fiscal and Economic Impact of the California Global Warming Solutions Act of 2006,' *California Manufacturers & Technology Association*, June 2012, Page 6

17 *ibid*, Page 8

18 *ibid*, Page 12

19 *ibid*, Page 81

20 Daniel Foster, 'Western Promises,' *National Review*, June 17, 2013

21 Maggie Creamer, 'Pacific Coast Producers Worried About Effects of Global Warming Legislation,' *The Lodi News-Sentinel*, September 8, 2012

22 *ibid*, Page 83

23 *ibid*, Page 85

24 Allysia Finley, 'The Reverse-Joads of California,' *The Wall Street Journal*, March 3, 2013

25 *ibid*, Page 83

26 Daniel Weintraub, 'Air Board Will Do the Real Work on Global Warming,' *Sacramento Bee*, October 5, 2006

27 WSPA Administrators, 'Boston Consulting Group Study Measures Impacts of Climate Change Policies,' *Western States Petroleum Association*, June 19, 2012

28 'Understanding the Impact of AB 32,' *The Boston Consulting Group*, June 19, 2012, Page 3

29 Review & Outlook, 'California's Green Gas Shortages,' *The Wall Street Journal*, October 7, 2012

30 *ibid*, Page 3

31 Joseph Vranich, 'Calif. 'Disinvestment Events' Reach New High As Companies Opt for Other States, Nations,' *The Business Relocation Coach*, April 13, 2011

32 Katy Grimes, 'Gov. Brown Needs a Reality Check: Rebutting "State of the State" Address,' *California Political Review*, January 19, 2012

33 'Electric Power Monthly with Data for December 2012,' Table 1.6.B. Net Generation, Table 5.4.B. Retail Sales of Electricity to Ultimate Customers by End-Use Sector, *Energy Information Administration*, February 2013

34 Margot Roosevelt, 'State Acts to Limit Use of Coal Power,' *Los Angeles Times*, May 24, 2007

35 Max Schulz, 'California's Potemkin Environmentalism,' *City Journal*, Volume 18, No. 2, Spring 2008

36 *ibid*

37 *ibid*

38 Rachel Konrad, 'Rolling Power Blackouts Darken California,' *CNET News*, January 17, 2001

39 Jeff McMahon, 'Initiative Would Shutter California Nuclear Plants for Decades While Feds Ponder Waste,' *Forbes*, February 8, 2013

40 Electricity: Detailed State Data, 2001-Present, Net Generation by State by Type of Producer by Energy Source, *Energy Information Administration*

41 'SCE to Close San Onofre Nuclear Power Plant,' *CBS Los Angeles*, June 7, 2013

42 'California's Energy Future — Powering California with Nuclear Energy,' *California Council on Science and Technology*, 2011

43 Ian Tuttle, 'Gold Into Dross,' *National Review*, June 3, 2013

44 'The Other California Tax Grab,' *The Wall Street Journal*, November 14, 2012

45 *ibid*

46 Associated Press, 'Money from California Carbon Auction Less Than Expected,' *San Jose Mercury News*, November 22, 2012

47 'California's First Greenhouse Gas Emissions Auctions Sells Near Minimum Price,' *Energy Information Administration*, December 21, 2012

48 Rory Carroll, 'Big Banks Weigh Risks, Rewards of California's New CO2 Market,' *Reuters*, September 7, 2012

49 Review & Outlook, 'California's Cap-and-Tax Grab,' *The Wall Street Journal*, June 17, 2013

50 *ibid*

51 Nathaniel Gronewald, 'Europe's Carbon Emissions Trading - Growing Pains or Wholesale Theft?,' *The New York Times*, January 31, 2011

52 'Carbon Credit Fraud Causes More Than $5 Billion Euros Damage for European Taxpayer,' *Europol*, December 9, 2009

53 Fiona Harvey and Stephen Fidler, 'Industry Caught in Carbon "Smokescreen",' *Financial Times*, April 25, 2007

54 Anne C. Mulkern, 'Offsets Could Make Up 85% of Calif.'s Cap-and-Trade Program,' *The New York Times*, August 8, 2011

55 Chris Noble, et. al., 'Carbon Credit Fraud: The White Collar Crime of the Future,' *Deloitte*, November 2009

56 David R. Baker, 'Jerry Brown Wants to Raise Renewable Target to 40%,' *San Francisco Chronicle*, April 14, 2011

57 Review & Outlook, 'Another California Dream,' *The Wall Street Journal*, April 5, 2010

58 Robert Bryce, 'The High Cost of Renewable-Electricity Mandates,' *The Manhattan Institute*, February 10, 2012, Page 2

59 '33% Renewables Portfolio Standard: Implementation Analysis Preliminary Results,' *California Public Utility Commission*, June 2009

60 'Guide to State and Local Census Geography — California: Basic Geography,' *U.S. Census Bureau*, Page 1, California Population of 37,253,956

61 Daniel B. Wood, 'Green Power May Ruin Pristine Land in California,' *Christian Science Monitor*, April 24, 2007

62 See for instance the example of NRG that is building several massive solar energy generating projects in California that will provide the company a 25% return on equity throughout the 20-year life of the projects at Eric Lipton and Clifford Krauss, 'A Gold Rush of Subsidies in Clean Energy Search,' *The New York Times*, November 11, 2011

63 Adam Nagourney, 'Shortfall in California's Budget Swells to $16 Billion,' *The New York Times*, May 12, 2012

64 'California's "Unexpected" $16 Billion Deficit,' *Investors Business Daily*, May 14, 2012

65 Michael B. Marois and William Selway, 'Calif. Governor Prepares "Terrible Cuts" to Close Deficit,' *Bloomberg*, May 11, 2010

66 Associated Press, 'California Lawmakers Approve Billions of Dollars to Start Nation's First High-Speed Rail Line,' *The Washington Post*, July 6, 2012

67 George F. Will, 'A Golden State Train Wreck,' *The Washington Post*, August 8, 2012

68 John Fund, 'Train to Nowhere: Full Speed Ahead,' *National Review*, July 9, 2012

69 Nannette Miranda, 'Assembly Approves Funding for High-Speed Rail Project,' *KSFN-TV ABC Local*, July 5, 2012

70 Table 5B. Residential Average Monthly Bill by Census Division, and State 2010, *Energy Information Administration*, February 2011

71 Table 5B. Residential Average Monthly Bill by Census Division, and State 2012, *Energy Information Administration*, December 2012

72   Table 5B. Residential Average Monthly Bill by Census Division, and State 2012, *Energy Information Administration*, September 2013

73   Jason Burwen and Yuliya Shmidt, 'Green Rush: Investor Owned Utilities' Compliance with the Renewables Portfolio Standard,' *Division of Ratepayer Advocates*, California Public Utilities Commission, February 2011, Page 8

74   'Levelized Cost of New Generation Resources in the Annual Energy Outlook 2011,' *Energy Information Administration*, November 2010

75   *op. cit.*, Jason Burwen and Yuliya Shmidt, 'Green Rush,' *Division of Ratepayer Advocates*, Page 8

76   *ibid*, Page 9

77   Garance Burke and Jason Dearen, Associated Press, 'Analyst: Bills Rising Due to Overpriced Renewables,' *San Diego Union-Tribune*, November 12, 2011

78   *op. cit.*, 'Electric Power Monthly September 2013,' *Energy Information Administration*, Table 5.6.A

79   Holman W. Jenkins, Jr., 'Green Energy's Baptists and Bootleggers,' *The Wall Street Journal*, January 15, 2013

80   'DRA Troubled By Continued CPUC Approval of Overpriced Renewable Projects,' *California Division of Ratepayer Advocates*, November 10, 2011

81   'Staff Report" Initial Statement of Reasons - Advanced Clean Cars,' *California Environmental Protection Agency Air Resources Board*, December 7, 2011, Page 3

82   'Governor Brown Announces $120 Million Settlement to Fund Electric Car Charging Stations Across California,' *Office of Governor Edmund G. Brown, Jr.*, March 23, 2012

83   Review & Outlook, 'A Green Car Named Desire,' *The Wall Street Journal*, September 18, 2013, Page A16

84   See for instance John Voelcker, 'Tesla Makes Money on Model S: $35K per Car Selling ZEV Credits,' *Green Car Reports*, May 7, 2013; Megan Durisin and Alan Ohnsman, 'Tesla Rises After Posting Surprising Quarterly Earnings,' *Bloomberg*, August 8, 2013

85   Stephen Edelstein, 'Tesla Says It Will Raise Model S Prices, But Won't Say How Much,' *Digital Trends*, November 26, 2012

86   *op. cit.*, Review & Outlook, 'A Green Car Named Desire,' *The Wall Street Journal*

87   Alex Taylor III, 'Chevy Volt vs. Nissan Leaf: Who's Winning?,' *Auto Pacific*, September 15, 2011

88   *op. cit.*, Review & Outlook, 'A Green Car Named Desire,' *The Wall Street Journal*

89   John Howard, 'Brown Taps Cap-and-Trade Money,' *Capitol Weekly*, May 14, 2013

90   David Zahniser, 'Villaraigosa Celebrates Los Angeles DWP Milestone: 20% of Power from Renewable Sources,' *Los Angeles Times*, January 13, 2011

91   *ibid*

92   Ralph Vartabedian, 'Rise in Renewable Energy Will Require More Use of Fossil Fuels,' *Los Angeles Times*, December 9, 2012

93   Review & Outlook, 'California's Coming Green-Outs,' *The Wall Street Journal*, March 29, 2013

94   'Public Must Face True Cost of Unreliable Renewables,' *Investors Business Daily*, December 11, 2012

95   'Green Energy Has a Brownout Problem,' *Investors Business Daily*, February 27, 2013

96   'Report: Increased Rolling Blackouts in Store for California This Summer,' *CNN*, May 16, 2001; see also *op. cit.*, Rachel Konrad, 'Rolling Power Blackouts Darken California,' *CNET News*

97   Justin Scheck and Ianthe Jeanne Dugan, 'Wood-Fired Plants Generate Violations,' *The Wall Street Journal*, July 23, 2012

98   *ibid*

99   Justin Scheck, 'Massachusetts Tightens Rules on Biomass Plants,' *The Wall Street Journal*, August 21, 2012

100   Thomas Walker, et. al., 'Biomass Sustainability and Carbon Policy Study,' *Manomet Center for Conservation Sciences*, June 2010

101   Madera Power, LLC Company Website

102   'Overview of Greenhouse Gases: Nitrous Oxide Emissions,' *Environmental Protection Agency*

103   *op. cit.*, Justin Scheck and Ianthe Jeanne Dugan, 'Wood-Fired Plants Generate Violations,' *The Wall Street Journal*

104   Tom Gray, 'California Needs a Crude Awakening,' *City Journal*, Summer 2012, Vol. 22, No. 3

105   *ibid*

106   Mark Mills, 'California Could Be the Next Shale Boom State,' *The Wall Street Journal*, January 15, 2013

107   'Information on Shale Resources, Development, and Environmental and Public Health Risks,' GAO-12-732, *U.S. General Accountability Office*, September 2012, Page 21

108   Victor Davis Hanson, 'California Here We Stay,' *City Journal*, Autumn 2012, Vol. 22, No. 4

109   *op. cit.*, Tom Gray, 'California Needs a Crude Awakening,' *City Journal*

110   Petroleum and Other Liquids, Spot Prices, WTI – Cushing, Oklahoma Crude Oil, January 3, 2012 to November 6, 2012, *Energy Information Administration*

111 'State Tax and Royalty Rates and Production of Oil and Natural Gas in Top Producing States,' *New Mexico Area Community Colleges*, Page 8

112 *op. cit.*, Mark Mills, 'California Could Be the Next Shale Boom State,' *The Wall Street Journal*

113 Kenneth P. Green, 'Viewpoints: Implementing AB32 Will Increase Unemployment, Household Expenses,' *The Sacramento Bee*, August 16, 2012

114 Steven Greenhut, 'Californians Want Oil's Tax Revenue Without the Oil,' *Bloomberg*, March 10, 2013

115 'Democrats Block California's "Economic Miracle",' *Investors Business Daily*, May 31, 2013

116 Alison Vekshin, 'California Lawmakers Turn Down Moratorium on Fracking,' *Bloomberg*, May 30, 2013

117 Review & Outlook, Fracturing in California,' *The Wall Street Journal*, June 7, 2013

118 *ibid*

119 *op. cit.*, 'Democrats Block California's "Economic Miracle",' *Investors Business Daily*

120 Ed DeSeve, 'Report of the State Budget Crisis Task Force: California Report,' *State Budget Crisis Task Force*, September 2012 Page 30

121 *ibid*, Page 31

122 Steven Greenhut, 'California, Unsaved, Speeds Toward a Wall of Debt,' *Bloomberg*, January 16, 2013

123 Conn Carroll, 'Can Conservatives Prevent the U.S. from Becoming California?,' *The Washington Examiner*, November 17, 2012

124 *ibid*

125 *op. cit.*, Mark Mills, 'California Could Be the Next Shale Boom State,' *The Wall Street Journal*

126 Victor Davis Hanson, 'The California Mordida,' *National Review*, March 7, 2013

127 *op. cit.*, Conn Carroll, 'Can Conservatives Prevent the U.S. from Becoming California?,' *The Washington Examiner*

128 *op. cit.*, 'Democrats Block California's "Economic Miracle",' *Investors Business Daily*

129 James MacPherson, 'ND Becomes Nation's Second-Leading Oil Producer,' *Associated Press*, May 15, 2012

130 'Regional and State Employment and Unemployment — March 2013,' *Bureau of Labor Statistics*, April 18, 2013, Table A., Page 3

131 'Widespread Economic Growth in 2012,' *Bureau of Economic Analysis*, June 6, 2012

132 National Income and Product Accounts, *Bureau of Economic Analysis*, Table 1.1.6 Real Gross Domestic Product, Chained Dollars, Seasonally Adjusted at Annual Rates)

133 *op. cit.*, 'Widespread Economic Growth in 2012,' *Bureau of Economic Analysis*, Tables 1-4

134 Associated Press, '$1.6 Billion: ND Budget Surplus Continues to Zoom,' *CBS News*, September 20, 2012

135 Michael Warren, 'Frack to the Future,' *The Weekly Standard*, Volume 18, No. 39, June 24, 2013

136 'Enterprising States: Getting Down to Small Business,' *U.S. Chamber of Commerce*, April 2013

137 Mark J. Perry, 'Middle-Class Stagnation? Jobless Recovery? Falling Incomes? Not in America's "Economic Miracle State" of North Dakota,' *American Enterprise Institute*, May 16, 2013

138 Executive Order S-3-05 by the Governor of the State of California, *California Department of Transportation*, June 1, 2005

139 Justin Gerdes, 'How Will California Slash Greenhouse Gas Emissions 80% by 2050?,' *Forbes*, February 27, 2013

140 'California's Energy Future — The View to 2050,' *California Council on Science and Technology*, 2011

141 'California's Energy Future — The View to 2050,' *California Council on Science and Technology*, May 2011, Page 1

142 *ibid*, Page 15

143 *ibid*, Page 15

144 *ibid*, Page 16

145 *ibid*, Page 16

146 'Energy Almanac,' Database of California Power Plants, Plants Greater Than 0.1 Megawatt, *California Energy Commission*, November 6, 2012

147 *op. cit.*, 'SCE to Close San Onofre Nuclear Power Plant,' *CBS Los Angeles*

148 'Thermal Discharges – Cooling Water Intake Structures: Power Plants That Are Affected,' *State Water Resources Control Board*, California EPA

149 *op. cit.*, Ralph Vartabedian, 'Rise in Renewable Energy Will Require More Use of Fossil Fuels,' *Los Angeles Times*

150 'Fact Sheet: Once-Through Cooling Policy Protects Marine Life and Insures Electric Grid Reliability,' *State Water Resources Control Board*

151 'State Water Resources Control Board Resolution No. 2010-0020,' *State Water Resources Control Board*, May 4, 2010

152 'California Moves to Ban Once-Through Cooling,' *World Nuclear News*, May 6, 2010

153 John Forsythe and Matthew Trask, 'Electric Grid Reliability Impacts from Regulation of Once-Through Cooling in California,' Prepared for California Ocean Protection Council and State Water Resources Control Board, *ICF Jones & Stokes*, April 2008, Page 3

154 *ibid*, Table 3-1

155　'2012 Summer Loads and Resources Assessments,' *California Independent System Operator*, March 15, 2012, Table 2, Page 4

156　*ibid*, Page 1

157　'The Myth of Wind and Solar Energy: They Are Not Free,' *Institute for Energy Research*, December 21, 2012

158　*op. cit.*, Ralph Vartabedian, 'Rise in Renewable Energy Will Require More Use of Fossil Fuels,' *Los Angeles Times*

159　David Bailey, 'Assessment of Cooling Water Intake Structure Impacts to California Coastal Fish and Fisheries,' *Electric Power Research Institute*, December 2007, Page vi

160　*ibid*, Page vi

161　*ibid*, Page vii

162　Allysia Finley, 'Joel Kotkin: The Great California Exodus,' *The Wall Street Journal*, April 20, 2012

163　*op. cit.*, Victor Davis Hanson, 'The California *Mordida*,' *National Review*

164　Victor Davis Hanson, 'California Doesn't Exist — It's Now Two States,' *Investors Business Daily*, August 17, 2012

165　Victor Davis Hanson, 'Bankrupt California,' *National Review*, October 9, 2012

166　*op. cit.*, Victor Davis Hanson, 'California Here We Stay,' *City Journal*

167　Review & Outlook, 'A Downgrade for Illinois,' *The Wall Street Journal*, August 29, 2012

168　William McGurn, 'McGurn: Jerry Brown vs. Chris Christie,' *The Wall Street Journal*, May 14, 2012

169　Charlotte Allen, 'Decline and Fall,' *The Weekly Standard*, Volume 18, No. 10, November 19, 2012

170　Norimitsu Onishi, 'Californians Back Taxes to Avoid Education Cuts,' *The New York Times*, November 7, 2012

171　'California Voters Approve Corporate Tax Hike for Budget, Clean Energy,' *The Sacramento Bee*, November 6, 2012; see also Marc Lifisher, 'For Prop. 39, a Quiet but Decisive Victory,' *Los Angeles Times*, November 10, 2012

172　Felicity Barringer, 'How to Choose Between Fish and Farmers?,' *The New York Times*, December 15, 2010

173　Norimitsu Onishi, 'Some in California Skirt a Ban on Foie Gras,' *The New York Times*, August 12, 2012

174　Jim Sanders, 'Lawmaker Wants California to Push for National Bill of Gay Rights,' *The Sacramento Bee*, August 6, 2012

175　Cory Brown, 'Calif. Lawmakers Mull Adjusting Family Structure,' *The Washington Times*, July 4, 2012

176　Bills in the California State Legislature (2011-2012),' *Open Government*

177　Regional and State Employment and Unemployment Archived News Releases, Bureau of Labor Statistics, January 2009 to April 2012

178　Forest Jones, 'Arthur Laffer: Obama's Tax Strategies Are Guaranteed to Fail,' *Money News*, April 18, 2012

179　*op. cit.*, Victor Davis Hanson, 'California Here We Stay,' *City Journal*

180　*ibid*

181　*op. cit.*, Victor Davis Hanson, 'California Doesn't Exist — It's Now Two States,' *IBD*

182　*op. cit.*, Regional and State Employment and Unemployment Archived News Releases, BLS

183　Arthur Laffer and Stephen Moore, 'Laffer and Moore: A 50-State Tax Lesson for the President,' *The Wall Street Journal*, April 20, 2012

184　See for instance Review & Outlook, 'California Ugly,' *The Wall Street Journal*, May 13, 2012; see also John Seiler, CA Business Exodus Accelerates, *Cal Watchdog*, April 14, 2011

185　J.P. Donlon, 'Best/Worst States for Business 2011,' *Chief Executive*, May 3, 2012

186　Carolyn Jones, 'Vallejo Votes to Declare Chapter 9 Bankruptcy,' San Francisco *Chronicle*, May 7, 2008

187　'Mammoth Lakes, California Files for Bankruptcy,' *Reuters*, July 3, 2012

188　Steven Church and Alison Vekshin, 'Stockton, California, To File for Bankruptcy,' *Bloomberg*, June 27, 2012

189　Michael Marois, 'San Bernardino, California, Weighs Chapter 9 Bankruptcy,' *Bloomberg*, July 10, 2012

190　Ronald Grover and Jim Christie, 'City of Compton May Declare Bankruptcy by September: Officials, *Reuters*, July 18, 2012

191　Phil Wilson, Catherine Saillant and Abby Sewell, 'Rising Costs Push California Cities to Fiscal Brink,' *Los Angeles Times*, July 12, 2012

192　'Ken Grubbs: California Is Not Too Big to Fail,' *The Weekly Standard*, March 5, 2013

193　*CNBC* notes that Compton's auditors have resigned, refusing to sign off on the city's financial reports. Speculation increases that Riverside may join San Bernardino into Chapter 9. See Jane Wells, 'The Ripple Effect of California's Bankruptcies,' *CNBC*, July 13, 2012

194　Dan Walters, 'State Auditor: California's Net Worth at Negative $127.2 Billion,' *The Sacramento Bee*, March 28, 2013

195　*ibid*

196　Table B-4A.1, Personal Income Tax Statistics for Resident Tax Returns, Tax Year 2009, *Franchise Tax Board*, State of California; Table B-4A.1, Personal Income Tax Statistics for Resident Tax Returns, Tax Year 2007, *Franchise Tax Board*, State of California

197　Dan Walters, 'California's High-Income Taxpayers Dropped Sharply,' *The Sacramento Bee*, February 13, 2012

198　Mark Steyn, 'The Downfall of Detroit,' *National Review*, July 19, 2013

199   Gary Heinlein, 'Ingham County Judge Rules Detroit Bankruptcy Be Withdrawn; Schuette Appeals,' *The Detroit News*, July 19, 2013

200   Katie McHugh, 'Judge Orders Detroit Bankruptcy to Be Withdrawn, Claims It's "Not Honoring the President",' *The Daily Caller*, July 19, 2013

201   Steven Rattner, 'We Have to Step In and Save Detroit,' *The New York Times*, July 19, 2013

202   *op. cit.*, Mark Steyn, 'The Downfall of Detroit,' *National Review*

203   Robin Emmott and John O'Donnell, 'Debt Crisis: Finland Warns of Euro Exit Rather Than Pay Debts of Others,' *The Independent*, July 6, 2012

204   Editorial Board, 'California's Climate-Change Experiment,' *The Washington Post*, December 30, 2012

CHAPTER 10

1   H. Sterling Burnett, 'Commentary: Rare Earth Dependence,' *KERA Public Radio*, August 19, 2011

1   'Obama's Plan for More Energy Dependence on China,' *Institute for Energy Research*, March 21, 2012

2   Barack Obama, 'Remarks in Portsmouth, New Hampshire: "Real Leadership for a Clean Energy Future",' *The American Presidency Project*, October 8, 2007

3   See for instance the case advocated by Thomas L. Friedman, 'What They Really Believe,' *The New York Times*, November 17, 2009

4   'Energy Sources Have Changed Throughout the History of the United States,' *Energy Information Administration*, July 3, 2013

5   'Rare Earth Elements are Vulnerable to Supply Disruptions When China Controls 97% of the World's Production,' *Institute for Energy Research*, February 17, 2010

6   U.S. Code, Title 10, Subtitle A, Part IV, Chapter 173, Subchapter III, § 2924, *Cornell University of Law*

7   Martin Zimmerman, 'California Metal Mine Regains Luster,' *Los Angeles Times*, October 14, 2009

8   *ibid*

9   Keith R. Long, 'The Future of Rare Earth Elements — Will These High-Tech Industry Elements Continue in Short Supply?,' *U.S. Geological Survey*, 2011, Page 6

10   Lindsey Hilsum, 'Environmentalists Dirty Little Secret, Rare Earth Elements *Channel 4, You Tube*, December 7, 2009

11   *ibid*

12   Lindsey Hilsum, 'Chinese Pay Toxic Price for a Green World,' *The Times*, December 6, 2009

13   John J.C. Kopera, 'Inside the Nickel Metal Hydride Battery,' *Cobasys*, June 25, 2004

14   Wayne M. Morrison and Rachel Tang, 'China's Rare Earth Industry and Export Regime: Economic and Trade Implications for the United States,' *Congressional Research Service*, April 30, 2012, Page 1

15   Statement of W. David Menzie, Chief of Global Minerals Analysis, National Minerals Information Center, U.S. Geological Survey, U.S.-China Economic and Security Review Commission hearing on 'China's Global Quest for Resources and Implications for the United States,' January 26, 2012

16   James T. Areddy, 'China Moves to Strengthen Grip Over Supply of Rare-Earth Metals,' *The Wall Street Journal*, February 7, 2011

17   Tom Vulcan, 'Mark Smith: Why Rare Earth Metals Matter,' *Hard Assets Investor*, May 14, 2009

18   'Critical Materials Strategy,' *U.S. Department of Energy*, December 2010, Page 11

19   Cindy Hurst, 'China's Rare Earth Elements Industry: What Can the West Learn?,' *Institute for the Analysis of Global Security*, March 2010, Page 12

20   *op. cit.*, Cindy Hurst, 'China's Rare Earth Elements Industry: What Can the West Learn?,' *Institute for the Analysis of Global Security*, Pages 12-13

21   Jeffrey St. Clair, 'The Saga of Magnequench,' *Counterpunch*, April 7-9, 2006

22   *ibid*

23   *ibid*

24   *op. cit.*, Tom Vulcan, 'Mark Smith: Why Rare Earth Metals Matter,' *Hard Assets Investor*

25   *op. cit.*, Jeffrey St. Clair, 'The Saga of Magnequench,' *Counterpunch*

26   John J. Tkacik, Jr., 'Magnequench: CFIUS and China's Thirst for U.S. Defense Technology,' *The Heritage Foundation*, May 2, 2008

27   *ibid*

28   See for instance Keith Bradsher, 'China Plans to Reduce Its Exports of Minerals,' *The New York Times*, October 18, 2010; see also You Tube Video, 'China to Restrict Exports of Strategic Rare Earth Metals – CCTV 090509,' *CCTV-9 on You Tube*, May 9, 2009; Keith Bradsher, 'China Consolidates Grip on Rare Earths,' *The New York Times*, September 15, 2011

29   Amy Oliver, 'Green Technology that Pollutes the Planet,' *Townhall*, December 24, 2011; see also Justin Paul

and Gwenette Campbell, 'Investigating Rare Earth Element Mine Development in EPA Region 8 and Potential Environmental Impacts,' *U.S. Environmental Protection Agency*, Washington, DC, August 15, 2011, Document-908R11003, page 6

30   Reed Livergood, 'Rare Earth Elements: A Wrench in the Supply Chain?,' *Center for Strategic & International Studies*, No. 22, October 5, 2010

31   Hepeng Jia, 'Proposed Rare Metal Ban Unlikely to Impact Market,' *Chemistry World*, October 2009

32   'Molycorp Shares Yoyo on China Rare Earth Quota Cut,' *Reuters*, December 28, 2010

33   Eric Martin and Sonja Elmquist, 'U.S. to File WTO Complaint Over China Rare-Earth Export Caps,' *Bloomberg*, March 13, 2012

34   Wang Zhuoqiong, 'Export Quota for Rare Earths to Stay the Same,' *China Daily*, December 20, 2012

35   *ibid*

36   Emilio Godoy, 'China's Grip Tightens on "Green" Metals,' *Asia Times*, June 30, 2009

37   Paul Mason, 'Rare Earth: The New Great Game,' *BBC*, November 18, 2009

38   *op. cit.*, Cindy Hurst, 'China's Rare Earth Elements Industry: What Can the West Learn?,' *Institute for the Analysis of Global Security*, Page 27

39   *ibid*

40   See Mark A. Smith, 'Rare Earth Minerals: The Indispensable Resource for Clean Energy Technologies,' *Molycorp Presentation*, January 28, 2010, Page 5

41   Matthew Hill, 'Rare Earth Demand to Surge 33% by 2016, Says Kingsnorth,' *Mining Weekly*, February 3, 2012

42   Michael A. Riley and Ashlee Vance, 'China Corporate Espionage Boom Knocks Wind Out of U.S. Companies,' *Bloomberg*, March 15, 2012

43   Tom McGregor, 'West Hypes "China Threat" for Profit,' *China Daily*, October 18, 2012

44   James A. Lewis, 'China's Economic Espionage,' *Foreign Affairs*, November 13, 2012

45   David E. Sanger, et. al., 'Chinese Army Unit Is Seen as Tied to Hacking Against U.S.,' *The New York Times*, February 18, 2013

46   Michael Auslin, 'China's Wall Crumbles,' *National Review*, February 20, 2013

47   Siobhan Gorman and Jared A. Favole, 'U.S. Ups Ante for Spying on Firms,' *The Wall Street Journal*, February 21, 2013

48   *op. cit.*, 'Critical Materials Strategy,' *U.S. Department of Energy*

49   Blake Hounshell, 'Is China Making a Rare Earth Power Play?,' *Foreign Policy*, September 23, 2010

50   Cahal Milmo, 'Precious Metals That Could Save the Planet,' *The Independent*, January 2, 2010

51   *ibid*

52   Wayne M. Morrison and Rachel Tang, 'China's Rare Earth Industry and Export Regime: Economic and Trade Implications for the United States,' *Congressional Research Service*, April 30, 2012, Page 1

53   'Baotou Rare Earth Development and Future Direction of (a),' *China Magnet*, June 28, 2007

54   'Molycorp, Inc. at Goldman Sachs Global Metals & Mining/Steel Conference,' November 28, 2012, Page 24

55   Wang Zhuoqiong, 'Largest Rare Earth Producer Halts for 3rd Month,' *China Daily*, December 26, 2012

56   *op. cit.*, Tom Vulcan, 'Mark Smith: Why Rare Earth Metals Matter,' *Hard Assets Investor*

57   Peter C. Dent, 'High Performance Magnet Materials: Risky Supply Chain,' *Advanced Materials & Processes*, August 2009

58   Keith Bradsher, 'Prices of Rare Earth Metals Declining Sharply,' *The New York Times*, November 16, 2011

59   'Obama's Plan for More Energy Dependence on China,' *Institute for Energy Research*, March 21, 2012

60   'China Mulls Plans to Curb Rare Earth Smuggling,' *China Daily*, September 14, 2009

61   Lucy Hornby, 'China Aims to Shake Up Rare Earths Trade,' *Reuters*, October 29, 2010

62   'News: Declaration: about Reuters Lucy Horney Report on Interview with Mr. Lin Donglu, the Secretary-General of CSRE,' *The Chinese Society of Rare Earths*, October 29, 2010

63   *op. cit.*, James T. Areddy, 'China Moves to Strengthen Grip Over Supply of Rare-Earth Metals,' *The Wall Street Journal*

64   'Ames Laboratory to Lead New Research Effort to Address Shortages in Rare Earth and Other Critical Materials,' *U.S. Department of Energy*, January 9, 2013

65   *op. cit.*, Cindy Hurst, 'China's Rare Earth Elements Industry: What Can the West Learn?,' *Institute for the Analysis of Global Security*, Page 6

66   *ibid*, Pages 5-6

67   Lisa Margonelli, 'Clean Energy's Dirty Little Secret,' *The Atlantic*, May 2009

68   'Molycorp, Inc. v. U.S. Environmental Protection Agency,' No. 98-1400, *United States Court of Appeals for the District of Columbia Circuit*, December 17, 1999

69   Molycorp forecasts 40,000 metric tons of rare earth oxide production by mid-2013. See *op. cit.*, 'Molycorp, Inc. at Goldman Sachs Global Metals & Mining/Steel Conference,' Page 9

70   'Rare Earth Materials in the Defense Supply Chain,' *U.S. Government Accountability Office*, April 1, 2010, Page 22

71   *ibid*, Page 10

72   Judith Chegwidden and Dudley J. Kingsnorth, 'Rare Earths — An Evaluation of Current and Future Supply,' 2011, Page 17

73   *ibid*, Page 24

74   Mitch Jacoby and Jessie Jiang, 'Securing the Supply of Rare Earths,' *Chemical & Engineering News*, Volume 88, Number 35, August 30, 2010

75   Peter Foster, 'Rare Earth: Why China is Cutting Exports Crucial to Western Technologies,' *The Telegraph*, March 19, 2011

76   'Molycorp's History,' Molycorp Corporate Website

77   Robert Manor, 'Chevron Texaco, Unocal to Merge,' *Chicago Tribune*, April 5, 2005

78   Jim Jelter, 'CNOOC Bids $18.5 Billion for Unocal,' *Market Watch*, June 23, 2005

79   'China Oil Firm in Unocal Bid War,' *BBC*, June 23, 2005

80   David Barboza and Andrew Ross Sorkin, 'Chinese Oil Company Offers $18.5 Billion for Unocal,' *The New York Times*, June 22, 2005

81   Eugene Gholz and Daryl G. Press, 'Energy Alarmism: The Myths That Make Americans Worry About Oil,' *Cato Institute*, April 5, 2007, Page 9

82   Steve Lohr, 'Unocal Bid Denounced at Hearing,' *The New York Times*, July 14, 2005

83   Steve Lohr, 'Who's Afraid of China, Inc.?' *The New York Times*, July 24, 2005

84   Ross Kelly, 'Australia Delays Ruling on China Rare-Earth Investment,' *The Wall Street Journal*, September 4, 2009

85   *op. cit.*, Cindy Hurst, 'China's Rare Earth Elements Industry: What Can the West Learn?,' *Institute for the Analysis of Global Security*, Page 14

86   Alex Wilson, 'Lynas Turns to Market for Funds After China Deal Sours,' *The Wall Street Journal*, September 30, 2009

87   'U.S., EU and Japan Challenge China on Rare Earths at WTO,' *BBC*, March 12, 2012

88   Doug Palmer and Sebastian Moffett, 'U.S., EU, Japan Take on China at WTO over Rare Earths,' *Reuters*, March 13, 2012

89   Keith Bradsher, 'China Files W.T.O. Case Against Europe,' *The New York Times*, November 5, 2012

90   'President Obama Announces China Rare Earth Trade Case,' *BBC*, March 13, 2012

91   David Saleh Rauf and Darren Samuelson, 'Obama Hits China's Hold on Minerals,' *Politico*, March 13, 2012

92   Walter T. Benecki, 'Permanent Magnet Industry Outlook — 2013,' *Magnetics Business & Technology*, December 2012

93   *ibid*

94   See for instance recent 15-year estimates for the lifespan of a typical Chinese rare earth mine at Dudley J. Kingsnorth, 'Rare Earths: Facing New Challenges in the New Decade,' *SME Annual Meeting 2010*, Page 5

95   David Biello, 'Solar Power Lightens Up with Thin-Film Technology,' *Scientific American*, October 20, 2008

96   Ken Zweibel, 'The Impact of Tellurium Supply on Cadmium Telluride Photovoltaics,' *Science*, Volume 328, May 7, 2010, Pages 699-701

97   A micron is a millionth of a meter.

98   Kevin Bullis, 'What Happened to First Solar?,' *Technology Review*, May 8, 2012

99   'Polycrystalline Thin-Film Materials and Devices R&D,' Photovoltaics Research, *National Renewable Energy Laboratory*, October 6, 2011

100   Gao Zitan and Frank Fang, 'Game Over for China's Photovoltaic Manufacturers,' *The Epoch Times*, December 30, 2012

101   Marc Roca and Ben Sills, 'Solar Glut Worsens as Supply Surge Cuts Prices 93$: Commodities,' *Bloomberg*, November 10, 2011

102   Ben Sills and Marc Roca, 'Solar's 80% Plunge Hurts Utilities from Hawaii to Spain,' *Bloomberg*, March 20, 2012

103   Todd Woody, 'What Solyndra's Bankruptcy Means for Silicon Valley Solar Startups,' *Forbes*, August 31, 2011

104   Tim Worstall, 'Solyndra Sues Chinese Solar Makers: Entire Nonsense,' *Forbes*, October 15, 2012

105   Steven Mufson, 'Commission Imposes Low Duties on Chinese Solar Panels,' *The Washington Post*, March 20, 2012

106   Andrew Beebe, 'Inside a U.S.-China Solar Trade War,' *The Wall Street Journal*, March 28, 2012

107   Alexander Neubacher, 'Solar Subsidy Sinkhole: Re-Evaluating Germany's Blind Faith in the Sun,' *Der Spiegel*, January 18, 2012

108   Keith Johnson and Cassandra Sweet, 'U.S. Imposes Tariffs on China Solar Panels,' *The Wall Street Journal*, May 18, 2012

109   Brian Wingfield, 'U.S. Sets Anti-Dumping Duties on China Solar Imports,' *Bloomberg*, October 10, 2012

110   Jesse Jenkins, et. al., 'Beyond Boom & Bust: Putting Clean Tech on a Path to Subsidy Independence,' *Brookings Institution*, April 2012, Page 6

111 Christopher Martin, 'GE Picks Colorado for $300 Million Solar Panels Production Plant,' *Bloomberg*, October 13, 2011

112 Syanne Olson, 'GE Suspends Construction of Colorado Solar Panel Manufacturing Facility,' *PV Tech*, July 10, 2012

113 Tom Konrad, 'Updated: GE Solar Laying Off Employees in Colorado,' *Forbes*, July 3, 2012

114 *op. cit.*, Kevin Bullis, 'What Happened to First Solar?,' *Technology Review*

115 See for instance 'Solar Manufacturers Slowly Closing Up Shop in U.S.,' *Institute for Energy Research*, August 22, 2011; see also 'More Solar Firms Fall into Bankruptcy,' *Institute for Energy Research*, March 14, 2012

116 Eric Wesoff, 'Solar Power Year in Review,' *Seeking Alpha*, December 22, 2011

117 *op. cit.*, Mitch Jacoby and Jessie Jiang, 'Securing the Supply of Rare Earths,' *Chemical & Engineering News*

118 *op. cit.*, 'Critical Materials Strategy,' U.S. Department of Energy, December 2010, Page 20

119 *ibid*, Page 42

120 *ibid*, Pages 28-29

121 *op. cit.*, Barack Obama, Real Leadership for a Clean Energy Future Speech, Portsmouth, New Hampshire, October 8, 2007

122 H.R. 6 (110th): Energy Independence and Security Act of 2007, Senate Vote #226, *Gov Track*

123 H.R. 6 (110th): Energy Independence and Security Act of 2007, House Vote #40, *Gov Track*

124 John M. Broder, 'Bush Signs Broad Energy Bill,' *The New York Times*, December 19, 2007

125 Public Law 110-140, 'Energy Independence and Security Act of 2007, *U.S. Government Printing Office*, December 19, 2007

126 *ibid*, Section 321 Efficient Light Bulbs

127 Peter Whoriskey, 'Light Bulb Factory Closes; End of Era for U.S. Means More Jobs Overseas,' *The Washington Post*, September 8, 2010

128 Consider the views advocated by the odious climate fraudster Peter Gleick at Peter H. Gleick, 'Renewable Energy, Climate Change, and the Difficulty of Major Transitions,' *Yahoo Finance*, February 4, 2013

129 Ian M. London, 'The Delicate Supply Balance and Growing Demand for Rare Earths,' *Avalon Rare Metals Inc.*, January 27, 2010, Page 28

130 *op. cit.*, Peter Foster, 'Rare Earth: Why China is Cutting Exports Crucial to Western Technologies,' *The Telegraph*

131 Ryan Wiser and Mark Bolinger, '2011 Wind Technologies Market Report,' *Energy Efficiency & Renewable Energy*, U.S. Department of Energy, August 2012, Page v

132 *ibid*

133 Elisa Alonso, et. al., 'Evaluating Rare Earth Element Availability: A Case with Revolutionary Demand from Clean Technologies,' *Environmental Science & Technology*, Volume 46, No. 6, February 3, 2012, Pages 3406-3414

134 'In a Hole?,' *The Economist*, March 17, 2012

135 Annual Energy Outlook 2013 Early Release Overview, *Energy Information Administration*, December 5, 2012, Table A1 Total Energy Supply and Disposition Demand

136 See EIA's Annual Energy Outlook reports from 2003 onwards

137 *ibid*

138 Catherine Ngai, 'Replacing Oil Addiction With Metals Dependence?,' *National Geographic*, October 1, 2010

CHAPTER 11

1 Jim Wiegand, 'Big Wind & Avian Mortality (Part II: Hiding the Problem),' *Master Resource*, March 15, 2013

2 Simon Parry and Ed Douglas, 'In China, the True Cost of Britain's Clean, Green Wind Power Experiment: Pollution on a Disastrous Scale,' *The Daily Mail*, January 26, 2011

3 See for instance an absurd opinion that if external costs of coal usage were properly allocated, solar power would already be competitive with coal at Paul Krugman, 'Here Comes the Sun,' *The New York Times*, November 6, 2011; Krugman, in his usual disingenuous manner, suggests that fracking imposes extensive external costs from trucking that damages roads. But he fails to acknowledge that truckers pay road use excise taxes on diesel fuel that are more than adequate to pay for the marginal cost of road damage the trucks cause. Malfeasance of the political class he adores is responsible for failure to utilize road use taxes in the lawful manner for which they were intended.

4 Alison Benjamin, 'Stern: Climate Change a "Market Failure",' *The Guardian*, November 29, 2007

5 See for instance this wild-eyed leftist's plea for a massive increase in Soviet-style central planning that worked so marvelously during the Stalin era at Naomi Klein, 'Capitalism vs. the Climate,' *The Nation*, November 28, 2011

6 See the *American Recovery and Reinvestment Act*, H.R. 1, January 2009

7 Review & Outlook, 'Michael Mann's Climate Stimulus,' *The Wall Street Journal*, January 20, 2010

8 David A. Fahrenhold, 'One Grower's Grapes of Wrath,' *The Washington Post*, July 8, 2013

9   Ben Machol and Sarah Rizk, 'Economic Value of U.S. Fossil Fuel Electricity Health Impacts,' *Environmental International*, Volume 52, February 2013, Pages 75-80

10   'Electric Power Monthly with Data for December 2012,' Table 5.6.B Average Retail Price of Electricity to Ultimate Customers by End-Use Sector, by State, Year-to-Date through December 2012, *Energy Information Administration*, February 2013

11   Justin Gerdes, 'How Much Do Health Impacts from Fossil Fuel Electricity Cost the U.S. Economy?,' *Forbes*, April 8, 2013

12   John W. Dawson and John J. Seater, 'Federal Regulation and Aggregate Economic Growth,' *Journal of Economic Growth*, Volume 18, Issue 2, Pages 137-177

13   Julia Huscher and Diana Smith, 'The Unpaid Health Bill: How Coal Power Plants Make Us Sick,' *Health and Environment Alliance*, March 2013, Page 5

14   'The Hidden Costs of Energy: Unpriced Consequences of Energy Production and Use,' *National Academy of Sciences*, 2010, Page 6

15   *ibid*, Page 8

16   Bjørn Lomborg, 'The End of the EU's Cap-and-Trade Affair,' *The Wall Street Journal*, April 21, 2013

17   Gordon Hughes, 'Why is Wind Power So Expensive?: An Economic Analysis,' *University of Edinburgh*, July 2011

18   Daniel Simmons, 'Corporate Welfare Masquerading Under an Environmental Rainbow,' *Institute for Energy Research*, September 29, 2011

19   CBO estimates an 8% CO_2 reduction estimate at 'Effects of a Carbon Tax on the Economy and the Environment,' *Congressional Budget Office*, May 2013, Page 1; see also actual estimated future CO_2 emission data at 'International Energy Outlook 2013,' Table A10 World Carbon Dioxide Emissions by Region, Reference Case, 2005-2040, *Energy Information Administration*, July 25, 2013

20   Friedrich A. Hayek, *The Fatal Conceit*: *The Errors of Socialism*, Chicago, Illinois: The University of Chicago Press, 1991

21   Severin Borenstein, 'Making the Wrong Case for Renewable Energy,' *Bloomberg*, February 13, 2012

22   Severin Borenstein, 'The Private and Public Economics of Renewable Electricity Generation,' *Energy Institute at Haas*, September 2011

23   Jennifer Koons, 'Exxon Mobil Pleads Guilty to Killing Migratory Birds,' *The New York Times*, August 13, 2009

24   'ExxonMobil Pleads Guilty to Killing Birds,' *ABC News*, August 13, 2009

25   *op. cit.*, Jennifer Koons, 'Exxon Mobil Pleads Guilty to Killing Migratory Birds,' *The New York Times*

26   Associated Press, 'ExxonMobil Pleads Guilty to Killing Protected Birds,' *Fox News*, August 13, 2009

27   James Conca, 'Wind Energy Gets Away,' *Forbes*, September 22, 2013

28   Stephen Moore, 'The Obama Promise: Then and Now,' *The Wall Street Journal*, September 15, 2011

29   Peg Mackey, 'U.S. to Overtake Saudi as Top Oil Producer: IEA,' *Reuters*, November 12, 2012

30   'U.S. Expected to Be Largest Producer of Petroleum and Natural Gas Hydrocarbons in 2013,' *Energy Information Administration*, October 4, 2013

31   See Russell Gold and Daniel Gilbert, 'U.S. Is Overtaking Russia as Largest Oil-and-Gas Producer,' *The Wall Street Journal*, October 2, 2013; see also 'U.S. Surges Past Saudis to Become World's Top Oil Supplier - PIRA,' *Reuters*, October 15, 2013

32   Crude Oil Production, Petroleum & Other Liquids, *Energy Information Administration*

33   ND Monthly Production Statistics, *North Dakota Department of Mineral Resources*, Bismarck, North Dakota

34   Mona Charen, 'The Volt Administration,' *Townhall*, December 13, 2011

35   Kate Bommarito, 'Criticism Continues to Mount Against U.S. Attorney Tim Purdon,' *Plains Daily*, September 9, 2011

36   Andrew Malcolm, 'Politicizing Justice? Obama Names DNC Member Tim Purdon as a U.S. Attorney,' *Los Angeles Times*, February 5, 2010; see also 'Obama Nominee Under Fire for Political Connections, Lack of Experience,' *Fox News*, February 27, 2010

37   Review & Outlook, 'A Bird-Brained Prosecution,' *The Wall Street Journal*, September 29, 2011

38   Kate Bommarito, 'Oil Companies Arraigned in Federal Court for 28 Bird Deaths in ND,' *Plains Daily*, September 22, 2011

39   Fidelity Exploration & Production Co. pleaded guilty and paid a $1,500 fine for killing a single sandpiper. See James MacPherson, Associated Press, 'Oil Company to Plead Guilty in ND Bird Death,' *Deseret News*, October 26, 2011; Slawson Exploration Co. pleaded guilty and agreed to pay $12,000 in fines for killing 12 birds. See AP Wire Story, 'Oil Firm Agrees to Plead Guilty in ND Bird Deaths,' *World Oil*, October 25, 2011

40   Stephen Moore, 'Green Jobs vs. Real Jobs,' *The Wall Street Journal*, September 2, 2011

41   See for instance *Curry v. U.S. Forest Service*, 988 F. Supp. 541, Western District of Pennsylvania, 1997 which held that the MBTA was an improper statutory basis upon which to contest a timber sale that resulted in the loss of migratory birds from logging activity. See also *Mahler v. U.S. Forest Service*, 927 F. Supp. 1559, South Dakota

District, 1996 where the court ruled that a logging program approved by the federal government resulting in habitat destruction during nesting season did not constitute a violation of the MBTA. See also *Citizens Interested in Bull Run, Inc. v. Edington*, 781 F. Supp. 1502, Oregon District, 1991 where logging that diminished spotted owl habitat did not constitute a taking under MBTA.

42 See *United States v. Ray Westall Operating, Inc.*, No. CR 05-1516-MV, 2009 U.S. District of New Mexico, Lexis 130674, February 25, 2009

43 See *U.S. v. Brigham Oil and Gas, et. al.*, Case No. 4:11-po-005,U.S. District Court for the District of North Dakota, Northwestern Division, January 17, 2012, Page 16

44 *op. cit.*, Review & Outlook, 'A Bird-Brained Prosecution,' *The Wall Street Journal*

45 Dina Cappiello, Associated Press, 'Wind Farms Get Pass on Eagle Deaths,' *WTOP*, May 14, 2013

46 K. Shawn Smallwood, 'Comparing Bird and Bat Fatality-Rate Estimates Among North American Wind-Energy Projects,' *Wildlife Society Bulletin*, Volume 37, Issue 1, March 26, 2013, Pages 19-33

47 *op. cit.*, Review & Outlook, 'A Bird-Brained Prosecution,' *The Wall Street Journal*

48 J.H.B. Benner, J.C. Berkhuizen, R.J. de Graaff, and A.D. Postma, 'Impact of Wind Turbines on Birdlife: Final Report No. 9247,' *Consultants on Energy and the Environment*, Rotterdam, The Netherlands, 1993

49 'A Roadmap for PIER Research on Avian Collisions with Wind Turbines in California,' *California Energy Commission*, December 2002, Page 12

50 'AWEA U.S. Wind Industry Fourth Quarter 2012 Market Report,' *American Wind Energy Association*, January 30, 2013, Page 8

51 Matt Ridley, 'Let's Shatter These Five Myths About Fracking,' *The Times*, August 15, 2013

52 'IEA Wind: 2012 Annual Report,' *International Energy Agency*, July 2013, Table 2, Page 5

53 Andrew Darby, 'Deaths of Rare Eagles Rise,' *Sydney Morning Herald*, November 17, 2010

54 James Delingpole, 'Wind Industry Big Lies No 3: Wind Turbines Are Eco-Friendly,' *The Telegraph*, January 5, 2013

55 Michael Bastasch, 'Study: Feds Underestimated How Many Birds Get Killed by Wind Turbines,' *The Daily Caller*, July 23, 2013

56 Jim Wiegand, 'Big Wind & Avian Mortality (Part II: Hiding the Problem),' *Master Resource*, March 15, 2013

57 *ibid*

58 *op. cit.*, Dina Cappiello, Associated Press, 'Wind Farms Get Pass on Eagle Deaths,' *WTOP*

59 Albert M. Manville II, 'Towers, Turbines, Power Lines, and Buildings — Steps Being Taken by the U.S. Fish and Wildlife Service to Avoid or Minimize Take of Migratory Birds at These Structures,' *Proceedings of the Fourth International Partners in Flight Conference*, 2010, Pages 262-272

60 Mark Jaffe, 'Phil Anschutz and Wind Energy in Wyoming: Entrepreneur's Latest $9 Billion Idea,' *The Denver Post*, January 20, 2013

61 *ibid*

62 Robert Bryce, 'The Latest Wind-Energy Outrage,' *National Review*, May 16, 2013

63 Associated Press, 'Calif. Wind Farm Eagle Protection Plan Released,' *San Francisco Chronicle*, September 27, 2013

64 Peter Fimrite, 'Windmill Farm Seeks Permit to Kill Eagles,' *San Francisco Chronicle*, September 26, 2013

65 Fish and Wildlife Service, 'Golden Eagles: Programmatic Take Permit Application; Draft Environmental Assessment; Shiloh IV Wind Project, Solano County, California,' *Federal Register*, Volume 78, No. 188, September 27, 2013, Page 59710

66 Bob King, 'Dustup Over Florida Wind Farm,' *Politico*, June 1, 2011

67 Giannis Skarpathiotakis, 'Vulture Accident,' *YouTube*, at the 1 minute 58 second mark

68 Clive Hambler, 'Wind Farms vs. Wildlife,' *The Spectator*, January 5, 2013

69 Lawrence Hurley, 'Obama Admin Sweats Legal Response as Turbines Kill Birds,' *Environment & Energy Daily*, January 26, 2012

70 Beth Daley, 'Audubon Review Supports Wind Farm,' *The Boston Globe*, March 29, 2006

71 'RSPB Takes First Step Towards Climate Action at its HQ,' *Royal Society for the Protection of Birds*, July 16, 2012

72 Simon Johnson, 'Birdwatchers See Rare Swift Killed by Wind Turbine,' *The Telegraph*, June 27, 2013

73 *op. cit.*, Dina Cappiello, Associated Press, 'Wind Farms Get Pass on Eagle Deaths,' *WTOP*

74 Clive Hambler and Mark Duchamp, 'The Tip of the Iceberg,' *World Council for Nature*, July 1, 2013

75 Will Robinson, 'Rare Bird Last Seen in Britain 22 Years Ago Reappears — Only to be Killed by Wind Turbine in Front of Horrified Crowd of Birdwatchers,' *The Daily Mail*, June 27, 2013

76 James Delingpole, 'This Bird Rare Enough for You, Greenies?,' *The Telegraph*, June 27, 2013

77 James Delingpole, 'RSPB Makes a Killing … from Windfarm Giants Behind Turbines Accused of Destroying Rare Birds,' *The Daily Mail*, April 6, 2013

78 'Wind Turbine Proposal,' *Royal Society for the Protection of Birds*, April 10, 2012

79 *ibid*

80   *op. cit.*, Clive Hambler, 'Wind Farms vs. Wildlife,' *The Spectator*

81   Doug Leslie, et. al., 'Altamont Pass Wind Resource Area Bird Fatality Study, Bird Years 2005-2010,' *Alameda County Community Development Agency*, November 2012, Pages 1-2

82   Dina Cappiello, Associated Press, 'Wind Farms Get Pass on Eagle Deaths,' *WTOP*, May 14, 2013

83   John Ritter, 'Wind Turbines Taking Toll on Birds of Prey,' *USA Today*, January 4, 2005

84   Noaki Schwartz and Jason Dearen, Associated Press, 'BLM's Eagle Worries Stymie Wind Projects,' *The Spokesman-Review*, December 14, 2010

85   Maxim Lott, 'Climate Models Wildly Overestimated Global Warming, Study Finds,' *Fox News*, September 12, 2013

86   Randy LoBasso, 'How Wind Energy Is Sucking the Life Out of Our Bat Population,' *Philadelphia Weekly*, May 23, 2012

87   *op. cit.*, Clive Hambler, 'Wind Farms vs. Wildlife,' *The Spectator*

88   Ingemar Ahlén, et. al., 'Behavior of Scandinavian Bats during Migration and Foraging at Sea,' *Journal of Mammalogy*, Volume 90, No. 6, December 2009, Pages 1318-1323

89   *ibid*

90   'California Condor Recovery Program,' *California Condor*

91   Michael Woodbridge, 'Wild Condor Population in California Reaches 100 Total Birds,' *U.S. Fish & Wildlife Service*, Pacific Southwest Region, October 6, 2010

92   *ibid*

93   Todd Woody, 'Wind vs. Bird,' *Forbes*, January 16, 2012

94   'Feds Give Wind Farms License to Kill,' *Institute for Energy Research*, May 20, 2013

95   Louis Sahagun, 'Companies Won't Face Charges in Condor Deaths,' *Los Angeles Times*, May 10, 2013

96   Chris Clarke, 'Killing a Condor is Okay at Wind Project, Feds Say in About-Face,' *KCET*, May 14, 2013

97   *ibid*

98   *op. cit.*, Chris Clarke, 'Killing a Condor is Okay at Wind Project, Feds Say in About-Face,' *KCET*

99   Chris Clarke, 'Ivanpah Solar Project Reaches Construction Halfway Point,' *KCET*, August 8, 2012

100   Judy Miller, 'The Great Green Rush: Desert Solar Energy Leaving Tortoise in the Dust?,' *KCET*, January 20, 2012

101   *ibid*

102   Travis Fisher, 'FERC Order 1000: Cost Socialization for 'Green' Energy (NRDC, AWEA Rejoice),' *Master Resource*, April 8, 2013

103   Paul Driessen, 'Stop Subsidizing the Slaughter,' *Townhall*, December 15, 2012

104   Ryan Tracy, 'Wind and Solar Projects Advance on a Fast Track,' *The Wall Street Journal*, January 2, 2012

105   Kristin Fisher, 'Woodpecker-Saving Girl's Mother Gets Fined $500,' *WUSA*, August 3, 2011

106   Paul Driessen, 'Charles Manson Energy Butchery,' *The Washington Times*, January 13, 2012

107   Michael Bastasch, 'Feds Give Wind Farms the OK to Kill Eagles for 30 Years,' *The Daily Caller*, December 6, 2013

108   Barack Obama, 'Remarks in Portsmouth, New Hampshire: "Real Leadership for a Clean Energy Future",' *The American Presidency Project*, October 8, 2007

109   Ralph B. Alexander, *Global Warming False Alarm: The Bad Science Behind the United Nations' Assertion That Man-Made CO_2 Causes Global Warming*, Royal Oak, Michigan: Canterbury Publishing, 2009, Page 102

110   Energy Department Finalizes Loan Guarantee to Support California Solar Generation Project, *Loan Programs Office*, U.S. Department of Energy, September 30, 2011

111   *ibid*

112   See The Financing Force Behind America's Clean Energy Economy, *Loan Programs Office*, U.S. Department of Energy, September 30, 2011

113   Cadmium Telluride — The Good and the Bad, Solar Facts and Advice

114   Green Job Hazards, *Occupational Safety & Health Administration*, U.S. Department of Labor

115   Annual Industrial Capabilities Report to Congress, Office of Under Secretary of Defense Acquisition, Technology & Logistics, Office of Manufacturing & Industrial Base Policy, U.S. Department of Defense, September 2011, page 10

116   Eric Wesoff, 'Solar Power Year in Review,' *Seeking Alpha*, December 22, 2011

117   Lindsey Hilsum, 'Environmentalists Dirty Little Secret, Rare Earth Elements, *Channel 4* on *You Tube*, December 7, 2009

118   *ibid*

119   Simon Parry and Ed Douglas, 'In China, the True Cost of Britain's Clean, Green Wind Power Experiment: Pollution on a Disastrous Scale,' *The Daily Mail*, January 26, 2011

120   See for instance Sui-Lee Wee, 'China Cancer Village Tests Law Against Pollution,' *Reuters*, January 16, 2012; see also Jonathan Watts, 'China's "Cancer Villages" Reveal Dark Side of Economic Boom,' *The Guardian*, June

6, 2010; see comprehensive treatment of the subject at Lee Liu, 'Made in China: Cancer Villages,' *Environment*, March-April 2010

121 Tan Ee Lyn, 'China's "Cancer Villages" Bear Witness to Economic Boom,' *Reuters*, September 16, 2009

122 Dan Griffiths, 'China's "Cancer Villages" Pay Price,' *BBC*, January 17, 2007

123 Donna L. Hoyert and Jiaquan Xu, 'National Vital Statistics Reports: Deaths - Preliminary Data for 2011,' *Centers for Disease Control and Prevention*, Volume 61, No. 6, October 10, 2012, Table B., Page 4

124 See the World Bank report providing a low estimate of 460,000 premature deaths from cancer at 'Cost of Pollution in China: Economic Estimates of Physical Damages,' Conference Edition, *The World Bank*, February 2007; Accusations that the Chinese government forced the World Bank to whitewash its cancer casualty estimate is covered at John Laumer, 'Pollution Estimated to Cause 750,000 Premature Deaths Each Year in China,' *TreeHugger*, July 3, 2007

125 'World Bank Death-by-Pollution Figures Baseless: China,' *Reuters*, July 17, 2007

126 'China Acknowledges "Cancer Villages",' *BBC*, February 22, 2013

127 *ibid*

128 Amy Oliver, 'Clean Energy's Dirty Secret: Cancer,' *Townhall*, October 23, 2011

129 Review & Outlook, 'China's Toxic Rice Bowl,' *The Wall Street Journal*, May 22, 2013

130 *ibid*

131 *op. cit.*, Tan Ee Lyn, 'China's "Cancer Villages" Bear Witness,' *Reuters*

132 Joseph Kahn and Jim Yardley, 'As China Roars, Pollution Reaches Deadly Extremes,' *The New York Times*, August 26, 2007

133 *ibid*

134 Cindy Hurst, 'China's Rare Earth Elements Industry: What Can the West Learn?,' *Institute for the Analysis of Global Security*, March 2010, Page 17

135 Cindy Hurst, 'The Rare Earth Dilemma: China's Rare Earth Environmental and Safety Nightmare,' *The Cutting Edge*, November 15, 2010

136 *ibid*

137 *op. cit.*, Cindy Hurst, 'China's Rare Earth Elements Industry: What Can the West Learn?,' *Institute for the Analysis of Global Security*, Page 16

138 Li Jiabao and Liu Jie, 'Rare Earth Industry Adjusts to Slow Market,' *China Daily*, September 7, 2009

139 *ibid*

140 *op. cit.*, Li Jiabao and Liu Jie, 'Rare Earth Industry Adjusts to Slow Market,' *China Daily*

141 *op. cit.*, Cindy Hurst, 'China's Rare Earth Elements Industry: What Can the West Learn?,' *Institute for the Analysis of Global Security*

142 Tom McGregor, 'News: Environmental Hypocrisy Over Rare Earth Quotas,' *The Chinese Society of Rare Earths*, July 7, 2011

143 *op. cit.*, Barack Obama, Real Leadership for a Clean Energy Future Speech

144 'Technical Support Document - Technical Update of the Social Cost of Carbon for Regulatory Impact Analysis Under Executive Order 12866,' *Council of Economic Advisors*, May 2013

145 Review & Outlook, 'The "Social Cost of Carbon" Gambit,' *The Wall Street Journal*, June 27, 2013

146 Michael Greenstone, et. al., 'Estimating the Social Cost of Carbon for Use in U.S. Federal Rulemakings: A Summary and Interpretation,' *MIT Center for Energy and Environmental Policy Research*, May 2011, Page 23

147 David Wagner, Paulina Nusinovich, and Esteban Plaza-Jennings, ' The Effect of Proposed MY 2017-2025 Corporate Average Fuel Economy (CAFE) Standards on the New Vehicle Market Population,' *National Automobile Dealers Association*, February 13, 2012

148 Based upon a figure of 166,440 liters a year where one mole weighing 44 grams of CO_2 occupies 22.4 liters at 0° Celsius and 24.5 liters at 25° C at 'Q&A; Burden of Breathing,' *The New York Times*, August 14, 1990

149 Robert P. Murphy, 'Rolling the DICE: William Nordhaus' Dubious Case for a Carbon Tax,' *The Independent Review*, Volume 14, No. 2, Fall 2009, Pages 197-217

150 Famed climate change economist Richard S.J. Tol surveys 14 academic estimates performed by leading researchers. All but one of the estimates in Figure 1 on page 35 of his paper show substantial net benefits up to and, for some, even beyond a 2 °C atmospheric temperature increase. See Richard S.J. Tol, 'The Economic Effects of Climate Change,' *Journal of Economic Perspectives*, Number 2, Spring 2009, Pages 29-51

151 Review & Outlook, 'The Continuing Climate Meltdown,' *The Wall Street Journal*, February 16, 2010

152 Robert Zubrin, 'The Greens' Attack on Mariculture,' *National Review*, January 3, 2013

153 See for instance Simon Read, '24,000 Die in Winter as Fuel Poverty Climbs,' *The Independent*, November 30, 2012; see also Sam Marsden, David Barrett and Robert Mendick, 'Drawn-Out Winter May Have Caused Thousands of Extra Deaths,' *The Telegraph*, March 24, 2013

154 Robert Murphy, 'White House Revises Dubious "Social Cost of Carbon",' *Institute for Energy Research*, June 6, 2013

155 'The President's Budget for Fiscal Year 2014,' *Office of Management and Budget*, Historical Tables, Table 7.1—Federal Debt at the End of the Year: 1940–2018 and Table 15.4—Total Government Expenditures by Major Category of Expenditure: 1948–2012

156 Phil Gramm and John Taylor, 'The Hidden Costs of Monetary Easing,' *The Wall Street Journal*, September 11, 2012

157 Daily Treasury Yield Curve Rates, 1990 to Present, *U.S. Department of the Treasury*

158 *op. cit.*, 'The President's Budget for Fiscal Year 2014,' *Office of Management and Budget*

159 *ibid*

160 *ibid*

161 *ibid*

162 'S&P 500,' Total Annual Return, S&P Dow Jones Indices, *McGraw Hill Financial*

163 'Effects of Federal Tax Credits for the Purchase of Electric Vehicles,', *Congressional Budget Office*, September 2012, Page 11

164 'Circular No. A-94 Revise,' *Office of Management and Budget*, October 29, 1992

165 'Circular No. A-4 Revise,' *Office of Management and Budget*, September 17, 2003

166 'Technical Support Document: Technical Update of the Social Cost of Carbon for Regulatory Impact Analysis Under Executive Order 12866,' *Interagency Working Group on Social Cost of Carbon*, May 2013, Page 3

167 Mark Drajem, 'Obama Quietly Raises "Carbon Price" as Costs to Climate Increase,' *Bloomberg*, June 12, 2013

168 Daniel Kruger, 'Treasury Auction Bids Drop to Weakest Since 2009 as Yields Rise,' *Bloomberg*, June 27, 2013; see also Karen Brettell, 'Treasuries - Yields Rise Before Five-Year Note Sale,' *Reuters*, June 25, 2013

169 David Rose, 'Office Report Quietly Released … and Here Is the Chart to Prove It,' *The Daily Mail*, October 16, 2012

170 'Climate Expert von Storch: Why Is Global Warming Stagnating?,' *Der Spiegel*, June 20, 2013

171 Robert Murphy, 'Why the "Social Cost of Carbon" Matters,' *Institute for Energy Research*, June 13, 2013

172 See for instance the absurd opinion posted by the NRDC of *Alar* infamy that preposterously urges a number of $266 at Laurie Johnson, 'New Study (Part II of II): Feds Underestimate Costs of Carbon Pollution, Low-Balling Climate Change's Impact on Our Children and Grandchildren,' *Switchboard*, September 17, 2012

173 Russ Roberts, 'Pindyck on Climate Change,' *Library of Economics and Liberty*, August 5, 2013

174 CV, 'Robert S. Pindyck,' Bank of Tokyo-Mitsubishi Professor of Economics and Finance, *MIT Sloan School of Management*, January 2013

175 Dennis Prager, 'On Comparing Global Warming Denial to Holocaust Denial,' *Townhall*, February 13, 2007

176 Robert S. Pindyck, 'Climate Change Policy: What Do the Models Tell Us?,' *National Bureau of Economic Research*, Working Paper 19244, July 2013

177 *ibid*

178 *ibid*, Pages 12-13

179 Robert Murphy, 'MIT Economist on Bogus Climate Damage Functions,' *Institute for Energy Research*, August 21, 2013

180 'Global Climate Change: A Warming World,' *NASA Goddard Institute for Space Studies*, National Aeronautics & Space Administration

181 Robert Zubrin, 'The Cost of Carbon Denial,' *National Review*, July 31, 2013

182 Kimberly A. Strassel, 'Obama's Keystone Debacle,' *The Wall Street Journal*, June 27, 2013

183 David Anthoff, Richard S. J. Tol, and Gary W. Yohe, 'Discounting for Climate Change,' *Economics: The Open-Access, Open-Assessment E-Journal*, Vol. 3, 2009, Pages 1-22

CHAPTER 12

1 Barack Obama, 'Remarks in Portsmouth, New Hampshire: "Real Leadership for a Clean Energy Future",' *The American Presidency Project*, October 8, 2007

1 Kenneth P. Green, 'Why Obama's "Green Jobs" Plan Won't Work,' *The American*, November 7, 2008

2 Wayne Winegarden, 'Today's Energy Crisis: Too Much, Not Too Little, Fossil Fuel,' *Investors Business Daily*, July 24, 2013

3 Mortimer Zuckerman, 'A Jobless Recovery Is a Phony Recovery,' *The Wall Street Journal*, July 15, 2013

4 See for instance the obsequious genuflection from Bryan Walsh, 'What Is a Green-Collar Job, Exactly?,' *Time*, May 2008

5 'Barack Obama's Acceptance Speech,' *The New York Times*, August 28, 2008

6 'Current and Potential Green Jobs in the U.S. Economy,' *U.S. Conference of Mayors*, October 2008, Page 2

7	Bob Lutz, 'The Green Jobs Scam,' *Forbes*, August 7, 2012

8	'Green Jobs: Towards Decent Work in a Sustainable, Low-Carbon World,' *UN Environment Programme*, September 2008, Page 306

9	John Maynard Keynes, *The General Theory of Employment, Interest, and Money*, Amherst, New York: Prometheus Books, May 1997

10	See for instance the evidence compiled at John F. Cogan and John B. Taylor, 'Stimulus Has Been a Washington Job Killer,' *The Wall Street Journal*, October 3, 2011

11	The President's Budget for Fiscal Year 2013, Historical Tables, *Office of Management and Budget*, Table 1.2— Summary of Receipts, Outlays, and Surpluses or Deficits (-) as Percentages of GDP: 1930–2017

12	See for instance an Obama-Biden campaign position paper promising to create 5 million new jobs at 'Barack Obama and Joe Biden: New Energy for America'

13	*op. cit.*, Barack Obama, 'Remarks in Portsmouth, New Hampshire,' *The American Presidency Project*, October 8, 2007

14	Jeanne Cummings, 'Can Green Jobs Save Us?,' *Politico*, October 14, 2008

15	Barack Obama, 'New Energy for America,' *The American Presidency Project*, Lansing, Michigan, August 4, 2008

16	*ibid*

17	Gabriel Calzada Alvarez, et. al., 'Study of the Effects on Employment of Public Aid to Renewable Energy Sources,' *Universidad Rey Juan Carlos*, Volumen VII, Número 1, Primavera 2010. ISSN: 1697-6797-13, March 2009, Page 28

18	*ibid*, Page 2

19	*ibid*, Page 1

20	'Spain: Highest Unemployment Rate in EU at 18.7%,' *Seeking Alpha*, July 6, 2009

21	Matthew Sparkes, Eurozone Unemployment Hits Record High of 11.7 Pc,' *The Telegraph*, November 30, 2012

22	Denise Roland, 'Spanish Unemployment at Record High,' *The Telegraph*, January 24, 2013

23	Giles Tremlett, 'Spain: The Pain of Austerity Deepens,' *The Guardian*, December 31, 2012

24	George F. Will, 'A Quixotic Pursuit: Green Energy Jobs,' *The Washington Post*, June 25, 2009

25	Spain Unemployment Rate, Google Public Data

26	*ibid*

27	Harmonised Unemployment Rate by Sex, *Eurostat*

28	AFP, 'Spanish Unemployment Rate at Record 27.16%,' *France24*, April 25, 2013

29	*op. cit.*, Gabriel Calzada Alvarez, et. al., 'Study of the Effects on Employment,' Page 25

30	*ibid*, page 30

31	*ibid*, page 30

32	Peter Fairley, 'Largest Solar Thermal Storage Plant to Start Up,' *IEEE Spectrum*, Publication of the Institute of Electrical and Electronics Engineers, October 2008

33	*ibid*

34	Todd Woody, 'Solar Millennium Files for Bankruptcy as Solar Shakeout Continues,' *Forbes*, December 21, 2011

35	David Biello, 'How to Use Solar Energy at Night,' *Scientific American*, February 18, 2009

36	Press Release, 'German Consortium Holds Inauguration Ceremony for the Andasol 3 Solar Thermal Power Plant,' *RWE Innogy*, September 30, 2011

37	'Andasol Solar Power Station, Spain,' *Power Technology*

38	'Levelized Cost of New Generation Resources in the Annual Energy Outlook 2009,' *Energy Information Administration*, July 2009

39	Andasol Solar Power Station, *Wikipedia*

40	Willem Post, 'Impact of CSP and PV Solar Feed-In Tariffs in Spain,' *The Energy Collective*, November 8, 2010

41	*ibid*

42	'Spain Halts Feed-In Tariffs for Renewable Energy,' *Institute for Energy Research*, April 9, 2012

43	William Boston, et. al., 'Germany and Spain Move to Curb Green-Energy Supports,' *The Wall Street Journal*, February 14, 2013

44	Tracy Rucinski and Jose Elias Rodriguez, 'Exclusive: Foreign Investors Set to Sue Spain over Energy Reform,' *Reuters*, February 14, 2013

45	*ibid*

46	Ben Sills, 'Spain's Solar Deals on Edge of Bankruptcy as Subsidies Founder,' *Bloomberg*, October 18, 2010

47	*ibid*

48	*ibid*

49	Ben Sills, 'Spain Halts Renewable Subsidies to Curb $31 Billion of Debts,' *Bloomberg*, January 27, 2012

50	*op. cit.*, Tracy Rucinski and Jose Elias Rodriguez, 'Exclusive: Foreign Investors Set to Sue Spain over Energy Reform,' *Reuters*

51 Alex Morales and Ben Sills, 'Spain Ejects Clean-Power Industry with Europe Precedent: Energy,' *Bloomberg*, May 30, 2012

52 Charles Penty, 'Spanish Banks Bleeding Cash Cloud Bailout Debate: Euro Credit,' *Bloomberg*, September 17, 2012

53 Mark Thompson, 'Europe's Jobless Lines Keep Growing,' *CNN Money*, November 30, 2012

54 *op. cit.*, Giles Tremlett, 'Spain: The Pain of Austerity Deepens,' *The Guardian*

55 *op. cit.*, Tracy Rucinski and Jose Elias Rodriguez, 'Exclusive: Foreign Investors Set to Sue Spain over Energy Reform,' *Reuters*

56 Richard Marsh and Tom Miers, 'Worth the Candle?: The Economic Impact of Renewable Energy Policy in Scotland and the UK,' *Verso Economics*, March 2011

57 'New Study: Green Sector Costs More Jobs Than It Creates,' *BBC News*, Reprinted in The Global Warming Policy Foundation, February 28, 2011

58 Peter C. Glover, 'Europe's Renewables Hype Implodes As German Solar Goes Belly Up,' *Energy Tribune*, June 24, 2013

59 *ibid*

60 Robert Mendick and Edward Malnick, 'True Cost of Britain's Wind Farm Industry Revealed,' *The Telegraph*, June 15, 2013

61 Luciano Lavecchia and Carlo Stagnaro, 'Are Green Jobs Real Jobs? The Case of Italy,' *Instituto Bruno Leoni*, May 2010

62 *ibid*, Page 40

63 Kenneth P. Green, 'The Myth of Green Energy Jobs: The European Experience,' *American Enterprise Institute*, No. 1, February 2011

64 Eboom Staff, 'EU Member States Must Submit Binding National Renewable Energy Action Plans,' *Energy Boom Policy*, June 30, 2009

65 Eboom Staff, 'The Netherlands Cuts Renewable Energy Subsidies, Looks to Nuclear,' *Energy Boom Policy*, February 11, 2011

66 *ibid*

67 Richard S.J. Tol, Economic and Social Research Institute, Dublin, Ireland, 'The Costs and Benefits of EU Climate Policy for 2020,' *Copenhagen Consensus Center*, June 1, 2010

68 Bjørn Lomborg, 'The EU's Response to Global Warming is a Costly Mistake,' *The Telegraph*, July 2, 2010

69 'Electricity Prices for Domestic Consumers, from 2007 Onwards - Bi-Annual Data, Euros per kWh, 2013 First Half,' *Eurostat*

70 For wind energy output, see 'IEA Wind: 2012 Annual Report,' *International Energy Agency*, July 2013, Table 2, Page 5; for total electricity consumption, see International Energy Statistics, Total Electricity Net Consumption (Billion Kilowatt-hours), *Energy Information Administration*

71 'Wind Energy: The Case of Denmark,' *Center for Politiske Studier*, Copenhagen, Denmark, September 2009

72 David J. White, 'Danish Wind: Too Good to be True?,' *The Utilities Journal*, July 2004, Page 37

73 International Energy Statistics, Electricity Exports % of Wind Electricity Net Generation, *Energy Information Administration*

74 Andrew Gilligan, 'An Ill Wind Blows for Denmark's Green Energy Revolution,' *The Telegraph*, September 12, 2010

75 *op. cit.*, International Energy Statistics, Electricity Imports % of Wind Electricity Net Generation, *EIA*

76 *op. cit.*, 'Wind Energy: The Case of Denmark,' *CEPOS*

77 Manuel Frondel, Nolan Ritter, and Colin Vance, 'Economic Impacts from the Promotion of Renewable Energies: The German Experience — Final Report,' *Rheinisch-Westfälisches Institut für Wirtschaftsforschung*, Essen, Germany, October 2009, Page 6

78 *ibid*, Page 22

79 *ibid*, Pages 6-7

80 For a critique of Frédéric Bastiat's "Broken Window Theory" of unanticipated events, see Louis Carabini, 'Bastiat's "The Broken Window": A Critique,' *Journal of Libertarian Studies*, Volume 21, No. 4, Winter 2007, Pages 151-155; see examples of the slow-learning Obama administration's window breaking efforts at Caroline Baum, 'Cash for Clunkers is Just a Broken Windshield,' *Bloomberg*, August 4, 2009

81 Roger Bezdek, 'Renewable Energy and Energy Efficiency: Economic Drivers for the 21st Century,' *American Solar Energy Society*, 2007, Page iv

82 'Annual Energy Outlook 2012: With Projections to 2035,' *Energy Information Administration*, June 2012, Table A2., Energy Consumption by Sector and Source, Pages 133-134

83 'Monthly Labor Review, *U.S. Department of Labor*, Volume 135, No. 1, January 2012, Table 2.1 Employment by Major Industry Sector

84 Jerry Taylor and Peter Van Doren, 'The Green Jobs Myth,' *Forbes*, April 11, 2011

85   Robert Murphy, 'Energy Sector Jobs,' *Institute for Energy Research*, July 18, 2012

86   Annual Energy Review 2012, Total Energy, *Energy Information Administration*, Table 1.2 Primary Energy Production by Source, 1949-2011, Quadrillion BTUs

87   Employment data by energy source is supplied by NaturalGas.org; see 'Millions of Jobs from Natural Gas – and More Possible,' *NaturalGas.org*

88   Donald Harker and Peter Hans Hirschboeck, 'Green Job Realities: Quantifying the Economic Benefits of Generation Alternatives,' *Public Utilities Fortnightly Magazine*, May 2010

89   *ibid*

90   Charles Cicchetti, 'Inflated Numbers; Erroneous Conclusions: The Navigant Wind Jobs Report,' *American Energy Alliance*, March 2013

91   *op. cit.*, Manuel Frondel, et. al., 'Economic Impacts from the Promotion of Renewable Energies,' *RWI*, Page 4

92   Review of the RWI Study available at 'Green Jobs,' *Institute for Energy Research*

93   'Germans Grow Wary of Switch to Renewables,' *Der Spiegel*, October 15, 2012

94   *op. cit.*, Review of the RWI Study available at 'Green Jobs,' *Institute for Energy Research*

95   Table 1.1.6 Real Gross Domestic Product, 2005 Chained Dollars, *Bureau of Economic Analysis*, All NIPA Tables

96   *op. cit.*, Review of the RWI Study available at 'Green Jobs,' *Institute for Energy Research*

97   *ibid*

98   *op. cit.*, Roger Bezdek, 'Renewable Energy and Energy Efficiency,' *ASES*, Page 15

99   Stephen Evans, 'Will Sun Still Shine on Germany Solar Power Industry?,' *BBC*, March 12, 2012

100   Alexander Neubacher, 'Solar Subsidy Sinkhole: Re-Evaluating Germany's Blind Faith in the Sun,' *Der Spiegel*, January 18, 2012

101   Stefan Schultz, 'Twilight of an Industry: Bankruptcies Have German Solar on the Ropes,' *Der Spiegel*, April 3, 2012

102   *ibid*

103   'Solar Panel Maker Q-Cells to File for Bankruptcy,' *BBC*, April 2, 2012

104   Josephine Moulds, 'Siemens Pulls Out of Loss-Making Solar Power Business,' *The Guardian*, October 22, 2012

105   Spiegel Staff, 'The Sun Rises in the East: German Solar Firms Eclipsed by Chinese Rivals,' *Der Spiegel*, September 7, 2011

106   *ibid*

107   Jonathan Stearns, 'EU Hits China with Solar-Panel Duties in Dumping Dispute,' *Bloomberg*, June 5, 2013

108   'A Trade Escalation Perilous for Europe,' *Financial Times*, June 10, 2013, Page 8

109   Review & Outlook, 'The New Solar Rules,' *The Wall Street Journal*, July 28, 2013

110   Jim Brunsden and Jonathan Stearns, 'China-EU Solar Panel Deal Avoids Tariffs With Import Cuts,' *Bloomberg*, July 28, 2013

111   Review & Outlook, 'The "Green Jobs" Myth,' *The Wall Street Journal Europe*, December 10, 2008

112   'Over 10,000 Metal Workers Protest EU Climate Plans,' *Agence France-Presse*, December 2, 2008

113   Office of White House Communications, Memo to Interested Parties, The Obama-Biden Economic Plan: Creating Jobs, Strengthening the Economy for Massachusetts Families, Washington, DC, April 22, 2009

114   *ibid*

115   *ibid*

116   *ibid*

117   Erin Allworth, 'Evergreen Solar to Shift Some Operations to China,' *The New York Times*, November 4, 2009

118   Keith Bradsher, 'Solar Panel Maker Moves Work to China,' *The New York Times*, January 14, 2011

119   Greg Turner and Jerry Kronenberg, 'Evergreen Solar Files for Bankruptcy, Plans Asset Sale,' *The Boston Herald*, August 15, 2011

120   Debra Saunders, 'The Trouble With "Green Jobs" Approach,' *Real Clear Politics*, February 6, 2011

121   Patrice Hill, ' "Green" Jobs No Longer Golden in Stimulus,' *The Washington Times*, September 9, 2010

122   Russ Choma, 'Overseas Firms Collecting Most Green Energy Money,' *Investigative Reporting Workshop at American University*, October 29, 2009

123   'American Taxpayer Investment, Foreign Corporation Benefit,' *Energy and Commerce Committee*, U.S. House of Representatives, Volume 2, Issue 1, January 17, 2013, Pages 2-3

124   Recovery Act, 1603 Program: Payments for Specified Energy Property in Lieu of Tax Credits,' *U.S. Department of Treasury*

125   *op. cit.*, 'American Taxpayer Investment, Foreign Corporation Benefit,' *Energy and Commerce Committee*

126   John Lee, 'The Greening of China a Mirage,' *The Australian*, September 19, 2011

127   'Green Jobs: A Review of Recent Studies,' *Center for Energy Economics*, Bureau of Economic Geology, The University of Texas at Austin, December 2008

128   *ibid*, Page 3

129   Robert Michaels and Robert P. Murray, 'Green Jobs: Fact or Fiction? An Assessment of the Literature,' *Institute for Energy Research*, January 2009

130   Robert Pollin, et. al., 'Green Recovery: A Program to Create Good Jobs and Start Building a Low-Carbon Economy,' *Political Economy Research Institute*, University of Massachusetts, September 2008, Page 9

131   $34.5 billion under Section 1703 Program, $34.5 billion under Section 1705 and $34.5 billion under the Advanced Technology Vehicles Manufacturing Program at Loan Programs Office, *U.S. Department of Energy*

132   Recovery Act, 1603 Program: Payments for Specified Energy Property in Lieu of Tax Credits,'. *U S. Department of Treasury*

133   Robert Pollin, 'Response to "Seven Myths about Green Jobs" and "Green Jobs Myths",' *Political Economy Research Institute*, March 2009, Page 2

134   It is exceedingly curious that Pollin chose to wade into the controversy over 2010 research by Carmen Reinhart and Kenneth Rogoff after one of Pollin's graduate students detected errors in the R&R analysis. Pollin suggested that R&R had deliberately fudged the numbers to reinforce their case. See Thomas Herndon, Michael Ash and Robert Pollin, 'Does High Public Debt Consistently Stifle Economic Growth? A Critique of Reinhart and Rogoff,' *Political Economy Research Institute*, April 15, 2013. If anyone was fudging numbers, it was Pollin in his discredited 'green jobs' work which has now been thoroughly debunked in the academic literature. At least R&R issued a revision to their work. Pollin had not as of the date of these pages being written.

135   Employed Persons, Seasonally Adjusted, *Bureau of Labor Statistics*

136   Labor Force Statistics from the Current Population Survey, Employed, Usually Work Part Time, *Bureau of Labor Statistics*

137   Total Nonfarm Payrolls, Seasonally Adjusted, *Bureau of Labor Statistics*

138   Gürcan Gülen, 'Economic Analysis of the Promise of "Green Jobs",' *Copenhagen Consensus Center*, February 2011

139   Alister Doyle, ' "Green" Job Creation Risks Backfiring: Lomborg,' *Reuters*, February 6, 2011

140   Hilliard G. Huntington, 'Creating Jobs With 'Green' Power Sources,' *Energy Modeling Forum*, Stanford University, April 2009

141   *ibid*, page 12

142   *ibid*, page 12

143   Nina Chestney and Jackie Cowhig, 'German Nuclear Cull to Add 40 Million Tonnes CO_2 per Year,' *Reuters*, May 31, 2011

144   Jeff McMahon, 'Wind Power May Not Reduce Carbon Emissions as Expected: Argonne,' *Forbes*, May 30, 2012

145   Nina Chestney and Jackie Cowhig, 'German Nuclear Cull to Add 40 Million Tonnes CO_2 per Year,' *Reuters*, May 31, 2011

146   *op. cit.*, Hilliard G. Huntington, 'Creating Jobs With 'Green' Power Sources,' *Energy Modeling Forum*, Page 14

147   Christina Romer and Jared Bernstein, *The Job Impact of the American Recovery and Reinvestment Plan*, Council of Economic Advisors, Office of the Vice President-Elect, January 9, 2009, Page 4

148   Labor Force Statistics from the Current Population Survey, Unemployment Rate, *Bureau of Labor Statistics*

149   Daniel Halper, 'Former White House Economist Admits "Clean Energy" Firms Don't Create Many Jobs (Updated),' *The Weekly Standard*, April 5, 2012

150   Andrew P. Morriss, et. al., 'Green Jobs Myths,' *University of Illinois College of Law*, University of Illinois Law and Economics Research Paper Series No. LE09-001, 2009, Page 50

151   *ibid*, Page 5

152   *ibid*, Page 49

153   Examiner Editorial, 'Waxman-Markey Cap-and-Trade Bill Stuffed Full of Unpleasant Surprises,' *The Washington Examiner*, May 21, 2009

154   Barack Obama, Remarks in Jacksonville, Florida, *American Presidency Project*, November 3, 2008

155   Philip Matera, et. al., 'High Road or Low Road?: Job Quality in the New Green Economy,' A Report by *Good Jobs First*, February 3, 2009

156   Aaron Glantz, 'Number of Green Jobs Fails to Live Up to Promises,' *The New York Times*, August 18, 2011

157   Mark Muro, 'Sizing the Clean Economy: A National and Regional Green Jobs Assessment, '*The Brookings Institute*, July 13, 2011

158   Mark Muro, Jonathan Rothwell and Devashree Saha, 'Sizing the Clean Economy: A National and Regional Green Jobs Assessment,' *The Brookings Institution*, July 13, 2011, Page 4

159   Randal O'Toole, 'Does Rail Transit Save Energy or Reduce Greenhouse Gas Emissions,' *Cato Institute*, April 14, 2008, Page 4

160   Nicholas Riccardi, AP, 'Mitt Romney's Green-Jobs Criticism Carries Risks,' *Bangor Daily News*, August 7, 2012

161   Sunil Sharan, 'The Green Jobs Myth,' *The Washington Post*, February 26, 2010

162   *ibid*

163   'The Green Jobs Myth,' *Institute for Energy Research*, September 12, 2012

164 Brian Hughes, 'Green Energy Jobs Far Short of Obama Goal,' *The Washington Examiner*, May 26, 2012

165 BLS discovered 333 classifications of existing jobs that could be re-classified as 'green jobs'

166 Diana Furchtgott-Roth, 'The Expensive, Elusive Green Job,' *Manhattan Institute*, No. 20, September 2012

167 'Green Goods and Services News Release,' *Bureau of Labor Statistics*, March 22, 2012

168 'Table 1. Green Goods and Services (GGS) Employment by Industry Sector, 3rd Quarter 2011 Annual Averages,' *Bureau of Labor Statistics*, March 22, 2012

169 See for instance 'The Employment Situation — September 2011,' *Bureau of Labor Statistics*, October 7, 2011, Summary Table A. Household Data Seasonally Adjusted, Employed Persons, Page 4

170 Max Schulz, 'Don't Count on "Countless" Green Jobs,' *The Wall Street Journal*, February 20, 2009

171 Veronique de Rugy, 'Assessing the Department of Energy Loan Guarantee Program,' *Mercatus Center at George Mason University*, June 19, 2012

172 *op. cit.*, Jerry Taylor and Peter Van Doren, 'The Green Jobs Myth,' *Forbes*

173 'June 19, 2012 - Oversight & Investigations Subcommittee Hearing on "The Federal Green Jobs Agenda",' *YouTube*, June 19, 2012

174 Free Beacon Staff, 'Obama Administration Program Spent $10B to Create 355 Jobs Per Year,' *The Washington Free Beacon*, June 20, 2012

175 'Loan Programs Office,' *U.S. Department of Energy*, 1703 Program

176 Carol D. Leonnig and Steven Mufson, 'Obama Green-Tech Program that Backed Solyndra Struggles to Create Jobs,' *The Washington Post*, September 14, 2011

177 Ira Boudway, 'The 5 Million Green Jobs That Weren't,' *Bloomberg Business Week*, October 11, 2012

178 Marshall Goldberg, et. al., 'Preliminary Analysis of the Jobs and Economic Impacts of Renewable Energy Projects Supported by the §1603 Treasury Grant Program,' *National Renewable Energy Laboratory*, April 2012, Page iv

179 *ibid*, Page v

180 Ed Feulner, 'The Green-Jobs Fallacy,' *The Heritage Foundation*, October 4, 2011

181 'The Financing Force Behind America's Clean Energy Economy,' *Loan Programs Office*, U.S. Department of Energy, May 2013

182 'DOE's $11 Million Jobs,' *Institute for Energy Research*, May 8, 2013

183 See his 2008 campaign promise at Barack Obama, 'A Serious Energy Policy for Our Future,' American Presidency Project, Las Vegas, Nevada, June 24, 2008

184 'The Empty Promise of Green Jobs: The Costly Consequences of Crony Capitalism,' *House Committee on the Budget*, September 22, 2011

185 *op. cit.*, Robert Pollin, et. al., 'Green Recovery: A Program to Create Good Jobs and Start Building a Low-Carbon Economy,' *Political Economy Research Institute*

CHAPTER 13

1 Carl Sagan, 'Cosmos,' Episode Number 12, *PBS*, December 14, 1980

2 Elana Schor, 'Gore Calls for End of Using Fossil Fuels for Electricity in U.S. by 2018,' *The Guardian*, July 17, 2008

3 'Energy Sources Have Changed Throughout the History of the United States,' *Energy Information Administration*,, July 3, 2013

4 Annual Energy Review 2011, *Energy Information Administration*, September 2012, Table 10.1 Renewable Energy Production and Consumption by Primary Energy Source, Selected Years, 1949-2011, Page 279

5 'AWEA U.S. Wind Industry Fourth Quarter 2012 Market Report,' *American Wind Energy Association*, January 30, 2013, Page 8

6 Dan Charles, 'Renewables Test IQ of the Grid,' *Science*, Volume 324, Number 5924, April 10, 2009, Page 172

7 *ibid*

8 'Loss of Wind Causes Texas Power Grid Emergency,' *Reuters*, February 27, 2008

9 'Texas Prepares for Soaring Power Demand, Urges Conservation,' *Reuters*, June 25, 2012

10 'ERCOT Planning: 2012 Long-Term Demand and Energy Forecast,' *Electric Reliability Council of Texas*, December 31, 2011, Page 9

11 'Report on the Capacity, Demand and Reserves in the ERCOT Region,' *Electric Reliability Council of Texas*, December 2011, Page 3, "Effective Load Carrying Capability (ELCC) of Wind Generation — The amount of wind generation that the Generation Adequacy Task Force (GATF) has recommended to be included in the CDR. The value is 8.7% of the nameplate capacity …"

12 'Wind Energy Facts: Texas,' *American Wind Energy Association*, January 2012

13 Elizabeth Souder, 'ERCOT May Initiate More Blackouts Wednesday Night, Thursday Morning,' *The Dallas Morning News*, February 2, 2011

14 Robert Bryce, 'Texas Wind Energy Fails, Again,' *National Review*, August 29, 2011

15   Associated Press, 'Mexico Provides Electricity to Ice Storm-Hit Texas,' *The Statesman*, February 2, 2011

16   'Texas Grid Sets June Power Record, Urges Conservation,' *Reuters*, June 25, 2012

17   'Texas Electricity Market Faces Summer Challenges,' *Today in Energy*, U.S. Department of Energy, July 9, 2012

18   'Wind Energy and Climate Change,' *American Wind Energy Association*; 5,000 mWh of energy ÷ 1.67 mW nameplate capacity = 2,994 mWh per 1 Mw nameplate capacity rating. And 2,994 mWh ÷ 8,766 hours per year = 34.2% ELCC. The number 8,766 accounts for leap years.

19   'Making Sense of Levelized Costs,' *Institute for Energy Research*, December 22, 2011

20   AEO2013 Early Release Overview: Levelized Cost of New Generation Resources in the Annual Energy Outlook 2013, Energy Information Administration, January 2013

21   Electricity: Detailed State Data, Net Generation by State by Type of Producer by Energy Source 2001-Present, *Energy Information Administration*

22   *ibid*

23   *ibid*

24   *ibid*

25   'IEA Wind: 2011 Annual Report,' *International Energy Agency*, July 2012, Page 172

26   Ryan Wiser and Mark Bolinger, '2011 Wind Technologies Market Report,' *Energy Efficiency & Renewable Energy*, U.S. Department of Energy, August 2012, Page 38

27   *op, cit.*, 'IEA Wind: 2011 Annual Report,' *International Energy Agency*, July 2012, Page 5

28   Robert Dropkin, 'PJM Wind Power Statistics,' December 2012

29   Doug Leslie, et. al., 'Altamont Pass Wind Resource Area Bird Fatality Study, Bird Years 2005-2010,' *Alameda County Community Development Agency*, November 2012, Pages 1-2

30   Brendan Kirby, et. al., 'California RPS Integration Cost Analysis-Phase I: One Year Analysis of Existing Resources,' *California Wind Energy Collaborative*, December 2003, Page 32

31   *op. cit.*, Electricity: Detailed State Data, Net Generation by State, *EIA*

32   David Dixon, 'Wind Generation's Performance During the July 2006 California Heat Storm,' *Energy Pulse*, September 8, 2006

33   *ibid*

34   Ralph Vartabedian, 'Rise in Renewable Energy Will Require More Use of Fossil Fuels,' *Los Angeles Times*, December 9, 2012

35   *op. cit.*, 'AWEA U.S. Wind Industry First Quarter 2012 Market Report,' *AWEA*, Page 7

36   Daniel Simmons, 'California's Flex Alert: A Case Study in Intermittent Energy,' *Institute for Energy Research*, August 13, 2012

37   *ibid*

38   *ibid*

39   'Accommodating High Levels of Variable Generation,' *North American Electric Reliability Corporation*, April 2009, Page 16

40   Patrick Jenevein, 'Wind-Power Subsidies? No Thanks,' *The Wall Street Journal*, April 1, 2013

41   'IEA Wind 2012 Annual Report,' *International Energy Agency*, July 2013, Page 5

42   *ibid*

43   Output of 449,400 gigawatt-hours divided by average yearly capacity of 221.3 GW [(203+239.6)/2] x 366 days x 24 hours

44   IEA Wind Annual Reports from 2002 to 2012

45   IEA's 10-year capacity yield averaged 23.7% between 2003 and 2012

46   Simon Parry and Ed Douglas, 'In China, the True Cost of Britain's Clean, Green Wind Power Experiment: Pollution on a Disastrous Scale,' *The Daily Mail*, January 26, 2011

47   Christopher Booker, 'It's Payback Time for Our Insane Energy Policy,' *The Telegraph*, March 23, 2013

48   Christopher Booker, 'George Osborne's CO2 Tax Will Double UK Electricity Bills,' *The Telegraph*, September 29, 2012

49   *ibid*

50   David Derbyshire, 'Wind Farms Don't Work in the Cold: Why It's No Use Waiting for Turbines to Keep Us Warm as the Snow Returns,' *The Daily Mail*, January 8, 2011

51   Paul Hudson, 'Coal Takes the Strain … Again,' *BBC*, January 11, 2011

52   Christopher Booker, 'The Great Wind Delusion Has Hijacked Our Energy Policy,' *The Telegraph*, August 11, 2012

53   *ibid*

54   Michael Lockwood, et. al., 'Are Cold Winters in Europe Associated with Low Solar Activity?,' *Environmental Research Letters*, Volume 5, Number 2, 2010

55   *ibid*

56   Mark Kinver, 'Low Solar Activity Link to Cold UK Winters,' *BBC*, April 14, 2010

57   Kerry Picket, 'Wind Turbines Fail in Minnesota's Cold Weather,' *The Washington Times*, February 1, 2010

58   Ed Morrissey, 'Minnesota Wind Turbines Won't Work in Cold Weather,' *Hot Air*, January 30, 2010

59   Dr. Klaus L.E. Kaiser, 'Electricity "Generating Capacity",' *Canada Free Press*, August 31, 2010

60   'Ontario's Most Pristine Locations Are Being Sacrificed for Wind Farms – Vic Fedeli,' *Net News Ledger*, July 6, 2012

61   'Wind Generation in Ontario,' *Independent Electricity System Operator*, 58 Mw Between 10:00 PM and 11:00 PM on August 13, 2012

62   'Offshore Wind Energy Potential Boosted During Heat Wave, Data Shows,' *Knoxville News Sentinel*, July 30, 2011

63   Consider the *WSJ* story by Jennifer Levitz who falsely claimed that Cape Wind is "expected to produce as much as 468 megawatts" of power. It is expected to produce only a fraction of this amount. The reporter defended her mistake in an email exchange, declining to file a correction. See Jennifer Levitz, 'Cape Cod Wind Farm Tiptoes Ahead,' *The Wall Street Journal*, August 10, 2012

64   Shawn Shaw, et. al., 'Status Report on Small Wind Energy Projects Supported by the Massachusetts Renewable Energy Trust,' *The Cadmus Group*, November 10, 2008

65   E. Thomas McClanahan, 'Let the Wind-Power Tax Credit Expire,' *The Kansas City Star*, March 24, 2012

66   Mark Glaess, 'A Historic State Assembly Shift,' *Minnesota Rural Electric Association*, December 2010

67   Tom Steward, 'Rural Electric Customers Pay the Price for Renewable Energy Mandate,' *Minnesota State News*, April 18, 2012

68   Katie O'Connell, 'Comments of the Minnesota Department of Commerce, Division of Energy Resources Docket No. E999/CI-11-852,' Division of Energy Resources, *Minnesota Department of Commerce*, January 25, 2011

69   'Milford Wind Corridor Overview,' *First Wind*, February 2012

70   Laura Hancock, 'BLM OKs Milford Wind Project,' *Deseret News*, October 21, 2008

71   'Millard County: County Profile,' Economic Development Corporation of Utah, Page 3

72   'Giant New Utah Wind Farm Will Power Los Angeles Homes,' *Environment News Service*, November 11, 2009

73   'Assembly Bill 32: Global Warming Solutions Act,' *California Environmental Protection Agency*, Air Resources Board

74   Robert Bryce, *Power Hungry: The Myths of "Green" Energy and the Real Fuels of the Future*, New York: Public Affairs, 2010, Page 90

75   'Exhibit A: LADWP Board Approval Letter, *Los Angeles Department of Water and Power*, September 17, 2007, Page 11

76   *op. cit.*, Robert Bryce, *Power Hungry*, Page 12

77   *op. cit.*, Levelized Cost of New Generation Resources, U.S. Department of Energy

78   Based upon a phone interview with Long-Term AEO Renewables Analysis & Forecasting expert Chris Namovicz, *Energy Information Administration*, June 11, 2012

79   'UK Electricity Generation Costs Update,' *Mott MacDonald*, June 2010

80   Gordon Hughes, 'Why is Wind Power So Expensive?: An Economic Analysis,' *University of Edinburgh*, July 2011, Page 1

81   Gerald Warner, 'Fueling an Inconvenient Delusion that Spells Ruin for Scotland,' *The Scotsman*, March 11, 2012

82   *ibid*, Page 1

83   Because there is a cost of capital, the "real" rate of return is a negative number. A June 2010 consultant report submitted to the UK's Department of Energy and Climate Change purporting to measure the full life-cycle costs of a variety of competing energy technologies utilized a 10% per year cost of capital figure. See 'UK Electricity Generation Costs Update,' *Mott MacDonald*, June 2010

84   *ibid*, Page 2

85   *ibid*, Page 2

86   Business Green Staff, 'EU Carbon Price Plumbs New Depths on Weak Emissions Data,' *Business Green*, April 3, 2012

87   Mike Anderson, 'EU Carbon's Record Low Lures Buyers in Australia: Energy,' *Bloomberg*, December 5, 2012

88   'Impact of Wind Power Generation in Ireland on the Operation of Conventional Plant and the Economic Implications,' *ESB National Grid*, February 2004, Page 36

89   'Wind, Coal and Gas in Colorado,' *Bentek Energy LLC*

90   Electricity: Detailed State Data, *Energy Information Administration*, Net Generation by State by Type of Producer by Energy Source 2001-Present

91   'How Less Became More: Wind, Power and Unintended Consequences in the Colorado Energy Market,' *Bentek Energy LLC*

92   'How Less Became More: Wind, Power and Unintended Consequences in the Colorado Energy Market,' *Bentek Energy LLC*, April 16, 2010, Page 8

93   Synapse Energy Economics, Inc.

94   Bob Fagan, et. al., 'The Net Benefits of Increased Wind Power in PJM,' *Synapse Energy Economics, Inc.*, May 9, 2013

95   *ibid*, Page 5

96   'PJM Wind Power Statistics,' Page 2

97   'Intense Storms Called a "Derecho" Slam 700 Miles of the U.S.,' *AccuWeather*, July 2, 2012

98   Operational Analysis, Wind Generation 2012, *PJM Interconnection*

99   *op. cit.*, Bob Fagan, et. al., 'The Net Benefits of Increased Wind Power in PJM,' *Synapse Energy Economics*, Page 5

100   *ibid*, Page 2

101   Based upon 35% marginal federal corporate tax rate and an average marginal state corporate tax rate of 9.1% in the MD, NJ, PA region

102   Wholesale Market Data, Wholesale Day Ahead Prices at Selected Hubs, Peak in $ per Megawatt-Hour 2012, *Energy Information Administration*

103   See for the devastating critique of integrated assessment models used by climate hysterics to justify their wildly inflated measures of "the social cost of carbon" at Robert S. Pindyck, 'Climate Change Policy: What Do the Models Tell Us?,' *National Bureau of Economic Research*, Working Paper 19244, July 2013

104   Roger Highfield, 'An Inconvenient Truth Exaggerated Sea Level Rise,' *The Telegraph*, September 4, 2008

105   *op. cit.*, Bob Fagan, et. al., 'The Net Benefits of Increased Wind Power in PJM,' *Synapse Energy Economics*, Page 4

106   Operational Analysis, Capacity by Fuel Type 2013, *PJM Interconnect*

107   *op. cit.*, Bob Fagan, et. al., 'The Net Benefits of Increased Wind Power in PJM,' *Synapse Energy Economics*, Page 12

108   *op. cit.*, Robert Dropkin, 'PJM Wind Power Statistics,' December 2012

109   *op. cit.*, Electricity: Detailed State Data, Net Generation by State by Type of Producer by Energy Source 2001-Present, *Energy Information Administration*

110   *op. cit.*, Bob Fagan, et. al., 'The Net Benefits of Increased Wind Power in PJM,' *Synapse Energy Economics*, Page 12

111   Ryan Wiser and Mark Bolinger, '2012 Wind Technologies Market Report,' *Lawrence Berkeley National Laboratory*, U.S. Department of Energy, August 2013, Page vii

112   *ibid*

113   *op. cit.*, Bob Fagan, et. al., 'The Net Benefits of Increased Wind Power in PJM,' *Synapse Energy Economics*, Page 12

114   Henry Hub Gulf Coast Natural Gas Spot Price, 2010 to August 2013, *Energy Information Administration*

115   See the charts and analysis in Chapter 20

116   Sally Bakewell and Marc Roca, 'Renewable Subsidies "Unaffordable" at $725 Billion, Bank Says,' *Bloomberg*, November 12, 2012

117   Herman K. Trabish, 'Study: Doubling Wind Will Cut Rates for PJM Customers,' *Green Tech Media*, May 15, 2013

118   Guenter Traumann, ,Wenn Das Geld Nicht Mehr Zum Heizen Reicht,' *Focus*, November 2, 2012

119   Editorial, 'A Breath of Stale Air from GOP,' *Los Angeles Times*, December 26, 2012

120   Ralph Vartabedian, 'Rise in Renewable Energy Will Require More Use of Fossil Fuels,' *Los Angeles Times*, December 9, 2012

121   Annual Energy Outlook 2013 Early Release Overview, Levelized Cost of New Generation Resources in the Annual Energy Outlook 2013, *Energy Information Administration*, January 28, 2013

122   *op. cit.*, Electricity: Detailed State Data, Net Generation by State by Type of Producer by Energy Source 2001-Present, *EIA*

123   'AWEA U.S. Wind Industry Fourth Quarter 2012 Market Report,' *American Wind Energy Association*, January 30, 2013, Page 3

124   Based upon a 29.7% ELCC for 2002-2011 derived from *op. cit.*, Electricity: Detailed State Data, Net Generation by State by Type of Producer by Energy Source 2001-Present, *EIA*

125   *op. cit.*, Annual Energy Outlook 2013 Early Release Overview, Levelized Cost of New Generation Resources in the Annual Energy Outlook 2013, *Energy Information Administration*

126   *op. cit.*, 'AWEA U.S. Wind Industry Fourth Quarter 2012 Market Report,' *American Wind Energy Association*, Page 3

127   Jay Lehr, 'The Rationale for Wind Power Won't Fly,' *The Wall Street Journal*, June 17, 2013

128   George Taylor and Thomas Tanton, 'The Hidden Costs of Wind Electricity,' *American Tradition Institute*, December 2012

129   *op. cit.*, 'How Less Became More,' *Bentek Energy*

130   *op. cit.*, Gordon Hughes, 'Why is Wind Power So Expensive?: An Economic Analysis,' *University of Edinburgh*

131   *op. cit.*, George Taylor and Thomas Tanton, 'The Hidden Costs of Wind Electricity,' *American Tradition Institute*

132   '20% Wind Energy by 2030: Increasing Wind Energy's Contribution to U.S. Electricity Supply,' *National Renewable Energy Laboratory*, July 2008, Page 169

133   Gordon Hughes, 'The Performance of Wind Farms in the United Kingdom and Denmark,' *Renewable Energy Foundation*, 2012

134   *ibid*, Page 6

135   Andrew Mills, Ryan Wiser, and Kevin Porter, 'The Cost of Transmission for Wind Energy: A Review of Transmission Planning Studies,' *Lawrence Berkeley National Laboratory*, February 2009

136   'German Electricity Distribution Grid in Need of Significant Expansion by 2030,' *DENA German Energy Agency*

137   Paul Kaiser, 'Solving the Transmission Dilemma,' *Wind Systems Magazine*, February 2010

138   Kate Galbraith, 'Texas Approves a $4.93 Billion Wind-Power Project,' *The New York Times*, July 19, 2008

139   Kate Galbraith, 'Cost of Texas Wind Transmission Lines Nears $7 Billion,' *The Texas Tribune*, August 24, 2011

140   Pam Radke Russell, 'New Transmission Lines to Link Texas Cities with Future Wind Farm Development,' *Engineering News-Record*, April 16, 2012

141   Emily Pickrell, 'Cost of West Texas Power Lines Could Shock Ratepayers, Author Says,' *Fuel Fix*, October 17, 2013

142   Steve Goreham, 'Offshore Wind: The Enormously Expensive Energy Alternative,' *Energy Tribune*, June 10, 2013

143   'Department of Public Utilities Approves Contract for Offshore Wind Power,' *Massachusetts Office of Energy and Environmental Affairs*, November 22, 2010

144   Composite price in 2012 at the NEPOOL Mass Hub at 'Wholesale Market Data 2012,' *Energy Information Administration*

145   Jay Lindsay, Associated Press, 'Wanted: Buyer for Controversial Cape Wind Energy,' *The San Diego Union-Tribune*, December 19, 2010

146   Electric Power Monthly, Detailed State Data, Net Generation by State by Type of Producer by Energy Source 2001-Present, *Energy Information Administration*

147   National Income and Product Accounts, *Bureau of Economic Analysis*, Table 1.1.5 Gross Domestic Product, Seasonally Adjusted at Annual Rates

148   Annual Energy Review 2011, *Energy Information Administration*, October 19, 2011

149   'Wind and Solar Power Will Continue to Erode Thermal Generators' Credit Quality,' *Moody's Investor Service*, November 6, 2012

150   James Murray, 'Moody's: Renewables Boom Poses Credit Risk for Coal and Gas Power Plants,' *Business Green*, November 6, 2012

151   'Wind Energy: The Case of Denmark,' *Center for Politiske Studier*, Copenhagen, Denmark, September 2009

152   Andrew Gilligan, 'An Ill Wind Blows for Denmark's Green Energy Revolution,' *The Telegraph*, September 12, 2010

153   Electricity Prices for Domestic Consumers, from 2007 Onwards - Bi-Annual Data, Euros per kWh, 2013 First Half,' *Eurostat*

154   Torsten Fagerholm, 'Proposed EU Rules May Thwart New Norway-Europe Power Cables,' *Bloomberg*, December 10, 2012

155   Toby Price, 'A First as Hydrogen-Hybrid Power Station Commissioned,' *Renewable Energy Magazine*, November 4, 2011

156   'Anatomy of a Wind Turbine,' *American Wind Energy Association*

157   'Renewable Fuels Module of the National Energy Modeling System: Model Documentation 2012,' *Energy Information Administration*, October 2012

158   *op. cit.*, 'Accommodating High Levels of Variable Generation,' *North American Electric Reliability Corporation*, Page 16

159   Paul L. Joskow, 'Comparing the Costs of Intermittent and Dispatchable Electricity Generating Technologies,' *Center for Energy and Environmental Policy Research*, September 2010

160   Paul L. Joskow, 'The Difficult Transition to Competitive Electricity Markets in the U.S.,' *Center for Energy and Environmental Policy Research*, MIT, May 2003, Table 3

161   Electricity, *Energy Information Administration*, Table 2.1.A, Net Generation by Energy Source by Type of Producer, 1999 through 2010

162   Paul L. Joskow, 'Capacity Payments in Imperfect Electricity Markets: Need and Design,' *Utilities Policy*, Volume 16, No. 3, September 2008, Pages 159-170

163   *op. cit.*, Paul L. Joskow, 'Capacity Payments in Imperfect Electricity Markets: Need and Design,' *Utilities Policy*

CHAPTER 14

1   'Water Implications of Biofuels Production in the United States,' *National Academy of Sciences*, October 2007

2   Alex Rindler, 'More Corn Ethanol Means Environment, Consumers Lose Out,' *Environmental Working Group*, August 19, 2013

3   'H.R. 5263 (95th): Energy Tax Act,' *GovTrack*

4   'Federal & State Incentives & Laws: Key Federal Legislation,' Alternative Fuels & Advanced Vehicles Data Center, U.S. Department of Energy

5   James W. Weaver, Linda R. Exum and Lourdes M. Prieto, 'Gasoline Composition Regulations Affecting LUST Sites,' *U.S. Environmental Protection Agency*, EPA 600/R-10/001, January 2010, Page 3

6   Methyl Tertiary Butyl Ether (MTBE): Drinking Water,' *Environmental Protection Agency*

7   *op. cit.*, J. W. Weaver, et. al., 'Gasoline Composition Regulations Affecting LUST Sites,' EPA

8   See Methyl Tertiary Butyl Ether (MTBE): Drinking Water,' *Environmental Protection Agency*; see also 'Drinking Water Advisory: Consumer Acceptability Advice and Health Effects Analysis on Methyl Tertiary Butyl Ether,' *Environmental Protection Agency*, EPA-822-F-009, December 1997; see also American, 'Oil Companies Pay Santa Monica MTBE Cleanup Costs,' *Environment News Service*, February 17, 2005

9   Public Law 109-58, 'Energy Policy Act of 2005, U.S. Government Printing Office, August 8, 2005

10   Public Law 110-140, 'Energy Independence and Security Act of 2007, *U.S. Government Printing Office*, December 19, 2007

11   See 'Energy Policy Act of 2005,' Alternative Fuels & Advanced Vehicles Data Center, *U.S. Department of Energy*; see also EPAct Transportation Regulatory Activities, *U.S. Department of Energy*

12   'Renewable Fuel Standard (RFS),' *Environmental Protection Agency*

13   'Energy Independence and Security Act of 2007,' Alternative Fuels & Advanced Vehicles Data Center, *U.S. Department of Energy*

14   'Certain Biofuel Mandates Unlikely to Be Met by 2022; Unless New Technologies, Policies Developed,' *Science Daily*, October 4, 2011

15   *ibid*

16   'U.S. Energy Leaders Decry New Biofuels Mandate,' *ICIS News*, December 14, 2007

17   Ucilia Wang, 'U.S. Won't Meet Its Own Biofuel Mandate,' *Green Tech Media*, December 17, 2008

18   Senator Barack Obama, 'Energy Security is National Security Speech,' U.S. Senate, Washington, DC, February 28, 2006

19   There are 42 gallons in a barrel of crude, which expands to about 45 gallons of finished product when refined. Thus 7.5 million barrels/day x 365 days/year x 42 gallons per barrel x 1.0715 expansion coefficient = 123.2 billion gallons of fossil fuel per year. But ethanol is only 65.6% as energetic as gasoline on a thermodynamic basis. So 123.2 divided by 65.6% is 187.8 billion gallons of ethanol.

20   Senator Barack Obama, 'Energy Independence and the Safety of Our Planet,' Chicago, Illinois, April 3, 2006

21   'Witnesses Blast EPA Decision to Allow Higher Ethanol Blends,' *Committee on Science, Space and Technology*, U.S. House of Representatives, July 7, 2011

22   'U.S. Decision Awaited on 2010 Cellulosic Biofuels Mandate,' *Recharge News*, January 12, 2010

23   'EPA Announces E15 Partial Waiver Decision and Fuel Pump Labeling Proposal,' *U.S. Environmental Protection Agency*, October 2010

24   'Ford and Toyota Blast EPA for Forcing Ethanol Blends on Public,' *Daily Tech*, July 6, 2011

25   Sebastian Blanco, 'Critics Sound Off on EPA's E15 Decision, Say It's the Work of the "Ethanol Promotion Agency",' *Auto Blog*, October 14, 2010

26   'NPRA Criticizes EPA Decision to Increase Ethanol in Gasoline,' *PR Newswire*, October 13, 2010

27   'EPA Grants E15 Fuel Waiver for Model Years 2001 - 2006 Cars and Light Trucks/Agency Continues Review of Public Comments for an E15 Pump Label to Help Ensure Consumers Use the Correct Fuel,' U *U.S. Environmental Protection Agency*, January 21, 2011

28   Press Release, 'EPA to Allow 15 Percent Renewable Fuel in Gasoline/Agency Approves First Applications for Registration of Ethanol to Make E15,' *U.S. Environmental Protection Agency*, April 2, 2012

29   John Fund, 'E-Mail Scandal at the EPA,' *National Review*, January 5, 2013

30   'Ethanol Industry Has EPA as Ally in Battle Against Big Oil,' *The Washington Examiner*, July 19, 2013

31   Judson Berger, 'Attorney Claims EPA Chief Resigned Over Alias Email Accounts,' *Fox News*, December 27, 2012

32   Rolf Westgard, ' "Blend Wall" Decision on Ethanol Will Have Multiple Side Effects,' *Minneapolis Post*, May 26, 2010

33   John Voelcker, 'E15 Ethanol Fuel Can Damage Engines, New Automaker Study Says,' *Green Car Reports*, May 16, 2012

34   David Shepardson, 'AAA Urges EPA to Halt Approval of E15 for Vehicles,' *The Detroit News*, November 15, 2012

35   Gary Strauss, 'AAA Warns E15 Gasoline Could Cause Car Damage,' *USA Today*, November 30, 2012

36   Michael Green, 'New E15 Gasoline May Damage Vehicles and Cause Consumer Confusion,' *American Automobile Association*, November 30, 2012

37   Mark Perry, 'Production of Corn Ethanol as an Automotive Fuel Source Should Cease,' *American Enterprise Institute*, January 16, 2013

38   Nash Keune, 'Ethanol Promotion Agency,' *National Review*, July 5, 2012

39   *op. cit.*, 'Ford and Toyota Blast EPA for Forcing Ethanol Blends,' *Daily Tech*

40   Charles T. Drevna, 'EPA Approval of E15 Hurts Consumers,' *The Hill*, January 15, 2011

41   Ami Cholia, 'EPA Sued By Oil Industry and Farm Groups Over Increase in Ethanol Blend,' *Alt Transport*, November 15, 2010

42   Ken Thomas, Associated Press, 'Automakers Sue EPA Over Plan to Sell 15% Ethanol Gas,' *USA Today*, December 20, 2010

43   Eric Loveday, 'Oil Refiners File Lawsuit to Overturn EPA's E15 Approval for 2001-2006 Vehicles,' *Auto Blog*, March 23, 2011

44   Jason Mick, 'EPA Calls Automakers Liars, Says Cars Can Handle Higher Ethanol Blend,' *Daily Tech*, July 8, 2011

45   Lawrence Hurley, 'Legal Fliers Flock to Challenge and Defend EPA Climate Regs,' *The New York Times*, November 15, 2010

46   Nash Keune, 'Ethanol Promotion Agency,' *National Review*, July 5, 2012

47   *op. cit.*, John Voelcker, 'E15 Ethanol Fuel Can Damage Engines, New Automaker Study Says,' *Green Car Reports*

48   John O'Dell, 'Controversial E15 Fuel Blend Is on the Way,' *Edmunds*, May 29, 2012

49   'E15: Misfueling Mitigation Plans,' Fuels and Fuel Additives, *U.S. Environmental Protection Agency*

50   Bill Summary & Status, 112th Congress (2011-2012), H.R.4345 Domestic Fuels Protection Act of 2012

51   H.R. 1214: Domestic Fuels Protection Act of 2013, *GovTrack*

52   Steven F. Hayward, 'Bureaucratic Gas,' *The Weekly Standard*, April 2, 2012

53   'Gasoline Markets: Special Gasoline Blends Reduce Emissions and Improve Air Quality, but Complicate Supply and Contribute to Higher Prices,' GAO-05-421, *U.S. Government Accountability Office*, June 2005

54   *op. cit.*, Steven F. Hayward, 'Bureaucratic Gas,' *The Weekly Standard*

55   Andrew P. Morriss and Donald J. Boudreaux, 'A Coca-Cola Solution to High Gas Prices,' *The Wall Street Journal*, August 21, 2012

56   *op. cit.*, 'Gasoline Markets: Special Gasoline Blends,' GAO, Page 5

57   *op. cit.*, Steven F. Hayward, 'Bureaucratic Gas,' *The Weekly Standard*

58   Editorial, 'Clean Green Fraud,' *The Washington Times*, February 8, 2012

59   Timothy B. Wheeler, 'Perry Hall Man Convicted in Biodiesel Fraud Case,' *The Baltimore Sun*, June 25, 2012

60   Ron Kotrba, 'Biodiesel Scammer Rodney Hailey Found Guilty on All Counts,' *Biodiesel Magazine*, June 25, 2012

61   Review & Outlook, 'Clean Green Scam,' *The Wall Street Journal*, July 13, 2012

62   *op. cit.*, Doris de Guzman, 'Biofuel Battle Heats Up,' *The Energy Collective*

63   *op. cit.*, Review & Outlook, 'Clean Green Scam,' *The Wall Street Journal*

64   'Baltimore-Area Executive Convicted in Biodiesel Scam,' *Baltimore Business Journal*, June 26, 2012

65   Ann E. Marimow, 'Maryland Man Convicted in Biodiesel Scam,' *The Washington Post*, June 25, 2012

66   Ben Evans, 'Biodiesel Producers to Meet With Lawmakers, Administration Officials: Industry Leaders to Call for RFS Growth, Tax Incentive,' *National Biodiesel Board*, June 5, 2012

67   'AFPM Criticizes EPA's Decision to Continue Advancing Phantom Fuel Mandate,' *American Fuel & Petrochemical Manufacturers*, May 25, 2012

68   *op. cit.*, Deroy Murdock, 'EPA in Wonderland,' *National Review*

69   Michal Conger, 'EPA Waives Fee Requests for Friendly Groups, Denies Conservative Groups,' *The Washington Examiner*, May 14, 2013

70   Bryan Walsh, 'This Year's Gulf of Mexico Dead Zone Could Be the Biggest on Record,' *Time*, June 19, 2013

71   David A. Dzombak, et. al., 'Mississippi River Water Quality and the Clean Water Act: Progress, Challenges, and Opportunities,' *National Research Council*, 2008, Page 172

72   Dave Juday, 'A Mess We Made: The Biofuels Fiasco,' *CBS News*, October 28, 2011

73   'NOAA-Supported Scientists Find Changes to Gulf of Mexico Dead Zone,' *National Oceanic and Atmospheric Administration*, August 9, 2010

74   Seth Borenstein, *AP* Science Fiction Writer, 'Floodwaters to Widen "Dead Zone" in Gulf of Mexico,' *USA Today*, June 20, 2008

75   Juliet Eilperin, 'Gulf Oil Spill Could Cause Lasting Damage to Fish Populations, Study Finds,' *The Washington Post*, September 26, 2011

76   Leslie Patton, 'Gulf of Mexico "Dead Zone" Grows as Spill Impact is Studied,' *Bloomberg*, August 12, 2010. Bloomberg uses a misleading headline while acknowledging in the fine print below that the Gulf oil spill was not the cause of the dead zone.

77   'The Dead Zone Will Worsen Unless Agriculture Cleans Up,' *Environmental Working Group*, Fact Sheet, Page 2

78   Carol Kaesuk Yoon, 'A Dead Zone Grows in the Gulf of Mexico,' *The New York Times*, January 20, 1998

79   Diana Furchtgott-Roth, 'The Focus on Green Jobs is Misplaced,' *Market Watch*, September 6, 2012

80   Bryan Walsh, 'The Gulf's Growing "Dead Zone",' *Time*, June 17, 2008

81   John Senn, 'Giving New Life to the Dead Zone,' *It's Our Environment*, U.S. Environmental Protection Agency, April 19, 2012

82   David Bailey, 'Environmental Groups Sue EPA Over Gulf Dead Zone,' *Reuters*, March 14, 2012

83   See for instance Nathanael Greene, 'Getting Biofuels on the Green and Narrow Path,' *NRDC Switchboard*, February 15, 2011; see also Nathanael Greene, 'How to Make the End of 2011 and the Corn Ethanol Tax Credit the Beginning of Real Alternatives to Oil,' *NRDC Switchboard*, December 23, 2011

84   See for example Bruce A. Babcock, 'High Crop Prices, Ethanol Mandates, and the Public Good: Do They Coexist?,' *Iowa Ag Review*, Volume 13, No. 2, Spring 2007; see also Robert Hahn and Caroline Cecot, 'The Benefits and Costs of Ethanol: An Evaluation of the Government's Analysis,' Working Paper 07-17, *AEI-Brookings Joint Center for Regulatory Studies*, November 2007

CHAPTER 15

1   Barack Obama, 'Remarks in Portsmouth, New Hampshire: "Real Leadership for a Clean Energy Future",' *The American Presidency Project*, October 8, 2007

2   Letter to President George Bush and Congressional Leaders, February 7, 2008

3   Wolfram M. Kürschner, Zlatko Kvacek and David L. Dilcher, 'The Impact of Miocene Atmospheric Carbon Dioxide Fluctuations on Climate and the Evolution of Terrestrial Ecosystems,' *Proceedings of the National Academy of Sciences*, Volume 105, January 15, 2008, Pages 449-453

4   Colin P Osborne and David J Beerling, 'Nature's Green Revolution: The Remarkable Evolutionary Rise of C4 Plants,' *Philosophical Transactions of the Royal Society*, Volume 361, January 29, 2006

5   Colin P. Osborne, 'Atmosphere, Ecology and Evolution: What Drove the Miocene Expansion of C_4 Grasslands?,' *Journal of Ecology*, Volume 96, January 2008, Pages 35-45

6   'The Miocene Epoch,' University of California Museum of Paleontology

7   Gregory J. Retallack, 'Cenozoic Expansion of Grasslands and Climatic Cooling,' *The Journal of Geology*, Volume 109, 2001, Pages 407-426

8   Caroline A.E. Strömberg, 'Evolution of Grasses and Grassland Ecosystems,' *Earth and Planetary Sciences*, Volume 39, May 2011, Pages 517-544

9   Christine M. Janis, et. al., 'The Origins and Evolution of the North American Grassland Biome: The Story from the Hoofed Mammals,' *PALAEO (Paleogeography, Paleoclimatology, Paleoecology)*, Volume 177, January 2002, Pages 183-198

10   M. Soledad Domingo, et. al., 'Resource Partitioning Among Top Predators in a Miocene Food Web,' *Proceedings of the Royal Society*, Volume 280, January 2013; see also 'Study Sheds Light on How Miocene Predators Shared Space and Food,' *Sci-News*, November 7, 2012

11   *op. cit.*, Wolfram M. Kürschner, et. al., 'The Impact of Miocene Atmospheric Carbon Dioxide Fluctuations on Climate and the Evolution of Terrestrial Ecosystems,' *Proceedings of the National Academy of Sciences*

12   'Scientists Find That Grasslands Can Act as "Carbon Sinks",' *Science Daily*, January 15, 2001

13   See for instance W.S. Benedict and Earle K. Plyler, 'Absorption Spectra of Water Vapor and Carbon Dioxide in the Region of 2.7 Microns,' *Journal of Research of the National Bureau of Standards*, Volume 46, No. 3, March 1951, Pages 246-265; see also Phillip G. Wilkinson and Herrick L. Johnson, 'The Absorption Spectra of Methane, Carbon Dioxide, Water Vapor and Ethylene in the Vacuum Ultraviolet,' *Journal of Chemical Physics*, Volume 18, No. 190, 1950

14   See 'Directive 2003/30/EC of the European Parliament and of the Council of 8 May 2003 on the Promotion of the Use of Biofuels or Other Renewable Fuels for Transport,' *Official Journal of the European Union*, L123/45, May 17, 2003

15   'Renewable Energy: Targets by 2020,' *European Commission*

16   Elisabeth Rosenthal, 'Once a Dream Fuel, Palm Oil May Be an Eco-Nightmare,' *The New York Times*, January 31, 2007

17   Press Release, 'Commission Publishes Its 2009 Progress Report on Renewable Energy,' IP/09/639, April 24, 2009

18   'Renewable Energy: Biofuels and Other Renewable Energy in the Transport Sector,' *European Commission*

19   AFP, 'Apocalyptic Scenes as Smog Engulfs Singapore,' *France24*, June 30, 2013

20   *op. cit.*, Rosenthal, 'Once a Dream Fuel, Palm Oil May Be an Eco-Nightmare,' *The New York Times*

21   International Energy Statistics, Total Primary Energy Consumption (Quadrillion BTUs in 2010), *Energy Information Administration*

22   *ibid*

23   'PEAT-CO2: Assessment of CO_2 Emissions from Drained Peatlands in SE Asia,' *Wetlands International and Delft Hydraulics*, December 7, 2006

24   Britt Childs and Rob Bradley, 'Plants at the Pump: Biofuels, Climate Change, and Sustainability,' *World Resources Institute*, 2008, Page 12

25   *ibid*

26   *op. cit.*, Rosenthal, 'Once a Dream Fuel, Palm Oil May Be an Eco-Nightmare,' *The New York Times*

27   Tad W. Patzek, 'How Can We Outlive Our Way of Life?,' Paper prepared for the *20th Round Table on Sustainable Development of Biofuels*, OECD, Paris, September 11-12, 2007, Page 14

28   Susan E. Page, et. al., 'The Amount of Carbon Released from Peat and Forest Fires in Indonesia During 1997,' *Nature*, Volume 420, November 7, 2002, Pages 61-65

29   *ibid*

30   'Three Rare Elephants Found Dead in Indonesia,' *Agence France-Presse*, June 2, 2012

31   Caroline Behringer, 'Habitat Loss Drives Sumatran Elephants Closer to Extinction,' *World Wildlife Fund*, January 23, 2012

32   Alok Jha, 'Endangered Tigers Found in Indonesian Jungle Allocated to Agriculture,' *The Guardian*, October 30, 2007

33   *Associated Press*, 'Rare Sumatran Orangutans Dying as Fires Rage in Indonesian Swamp Forest,' *The Guardian*, March 28, 2012

34   'Endangered Sumatran Rhinoceros Born in Captivity,' *BBC*, June 23, 2012

35   Press Release, 'New Figures; Palm Oil Destroys Malaysia's Peatswamp Forests Faster Than Ever,' *Wetlands International*, February 1, 2011

36   *op. cit.*, *Associated Press*, 'Rare Sumatran Orangutans Dying as Fires Rage in Indonesian Swamp Forest,' *The Guardian*

37   Jonathan Watts, 'Sumatran Elephant Upgraded to Critically Endangered Status,' *The Guardian*, January 24, 2012

38   See for instance Nick Sundt, 'U.S. Agency Projects Widening Gap Between U.S. Carbon Emissions from Fossil Fuel and Reduction Commitments,' *World Wildlife Fund*, January 23, 2012; see also Lou Leonard, 'Renewable Energy Can Phase Out Fossil Fuels in 40 Years,' *World Wildlife Fund*, February 3, 2011

39   James Kanter, 'E.U. to Announce Tighter Controls on Biofuels,' *The New York Times*, June 7, 2010

40   'Report from the Commission on Indirect Land-Use Change Related to Biofuels and Bioliquids,' *Europa EUR-LEX*, Access to European Union Law, COM/2010/0811 final, Brussels, December 22, 2010

41   In addition to those sources cited above, see also Dr. H.-D.V. Boehm and Dr. F. Siegert, 'Monitoring Land Cover and Impacts, Remote Sensing (RS) and GIS Used for Kalteng and Sarawak,' *Kalteng Consultants*, Remote Sensing of Kalimantan, March 30, 2002

42   'Opinion of the EEA Scientific Committee on Greenhouse Gas Accounting in Relation to Bioenergy,' *European Environment Agency*, September 15, 2011

43   Michael Grunwald, 'The Clean Energy Scam,' *Time*, March 27, 2008

44   See for instance David Pimentel and Tad W. Patzek, 'Ethanol Production Using Corn, Switchgrass, and Wood; Biodiesel Production Using Soybean and Sunflower,' *Natural Resources Research*, Volume 14, No. 1, March 2005, Pages 65-76; see also Tad W. Patzek, 'Thermodynamics of the Corn-Ethanol Biofuel Cycle,' *Critical Reviews in Plant Sciences*, 23(6):519-567 (2004), Department of Civil and Environmental Engineering, University of California, Berkeley, August 14, 2005; see also Tad W. Patzek, 'A First-Law Thermodynamic Analysis of the Corn-Ethanol Cycle,' *Natural Resources Research*, Vol. 15, No. 4, December 2006; see also 'Study: Ethanol Production Consumes Six Units of Energy to Produce Just One,' *Science Daily*, March 29, 2005

45   Alexander E. Farrell, et. al., 'Ethanol Can Contribute to Energy and Environmental Goals,' *Science*, Volume 311, January 27, 2006

46   An example of this rationale can be found at David Zilberman, et. al., 'Indirect Land Use: One Consideration Too Many in Biofuel Regulation,' *Agricultural and Resource Economics*, Volume 13, No. 4, March-April 2010

47   See for instance Kevin Bullis, 'Do Biofuels Reduce Greenhouse Gases?,' *Technology Review*, May 20, 2011

48   Tara Hudiburg, et. al., 'Production of Biofuel from Forests Will Increase Greenhouse Emissions,' *OSU University Relations & Marketing*, October 24, 2011

49   Tara W. Hudiburg, et. al., 'Regional Carbon Dioxide Implications of Forest Bioenergy Production,' *Nature Climate Change*, October 23, 2011, Pages 419-423

50   Tara Hudiburg, et. al., 'Carbon Dynamics of Oregon and Northern California Forests and Potential Land-Based Carbon Storage,' *Ecological Applications*, Volume 19, No. 1, 2009, Pages 163-180

51   'Production of Biofuel from Forests Will Increase Greenhouse Gas Emissions, Study Finds, *Science Daily*, October 26, 2011

52   William K. Jaeger and Thorsten M. Egelkraut, 'Biofuel Economics in a Setting of Multiple Objectives and Unintended Consequences,' *Renewable and Sustainable Energy Reviews*, Volume 15, Issue 9, December 2011, Pages 4320-4333

53 'Cost-Effectiveness of Biofuels and Their Ability to Cut Fossil Fuel Use Questioned,' *Science Daily*, November 29, 2011

54 'Annual Energy Outlook 2012: With Projections to 2035,' *Energy Information Administration*, Table A11. Liquid Fuels and Disposition, Page 153

55 *ibid*

56 'Biofuels — At What Cost?: Government Support for Ethanol and Biodiesel in the United States,' *International Institute for Sustainable Development*, 2006, Page 54

57 Finn Danielsen, et. al., 'Biofuel Plantations on Forested Lands" Double Jeopardy for Biodiversity and Climate,' *Conservation Biology*, Volume 23, No. 2, 2008, Pages 348-358

58 'Biofuels Could Hasten Climate Change,' *Science Daily*, April 15, 2009

59 Editorial, 'Kill King Corn,' *Nature*, Volume 449, October 11, 2007

60 Jerry M. Melillo, et. al., 'Indirect Emissions from Biofuels: How Important?,' *Science*, Volume 326, No. 5958, October 22, 2009, Pages 1397-1399

61 'Biofuel Displacing Food Crops May Have Bigger Carbon Impact Than Thought,' *Science Daily*, October 25, 2009

62 Jerry M. Melillo, et. al., 'Unintended Environmental Consequences of a Global Biofuels Program,' *MIT Joint Program on the Science and Policy of Global Change*, Report No. 168, January 2009

63 Thomas W. Hertel, et. al., 'Effects of US Maize Ethanol on Global Land Use and Greenhouse Gas Emissions: Estimating Market-mediated Responses,' *BioScience*, Volume 60, No. 3, March 2010, Pages 223-231

64 'More Maize Ethanol May Boost Greenhouse Gas Emissions.' *Science Daily*, March 12, 2010

65 'European Biofuels Are as Carbon Intensive as Petrol, New Study Suggests,' *Science Daily*, November 8, 2011

66 Chris Malins, 'Indirect Land Use Change in Europe – Considering the Policy Options,' *International Council on Clean Transportation*, November 2011

67 Chris Malins, 'A Model-Based Quantitative Assessment of the Carbon Benefits of Introducing iLUC Factors in the European Renewable Energy Directive,' *Global Change Biology*: *Bioenergy*, September 1, 2012

68 James Murray, 'Carbon Traders Deliver Record Activity During 2012, But Market Value Plummets,' *Business Green*, January 3, 2013

69 Charlie Dunmore, 'Exclusive: EU to Limit Use of Crop-Based Biofuels — Draft Law,' *Reuters*, September 10, 2012

70 Damian Carrington, 'Biodiesel Industry Dealt a Major Blow by EU Policy Changes,' *The Guardian*, September 21, 2012

71 *op. cit.*, Charlie Dunmore, 'Exclusive: EU to Limit Use of Crop-Based Biofuels — Draft Law,' *Reuters*

72 Arthur Neslen, 'Biodiesels Pollute More Than Crude Oil, Leaked Data Show,' *EurActiv*, January 27, 2012

73 Damian Carrington, 'Leaked Data: Palm Biodiesel as Dirty as Fuel from Tar Sands,' *The Guardian*, January 27, 2012

74 Alister Doyle, 'Biofuels Cause Pollution, Not as Green as Thought — Study,' *Reuters*, January 7, 2013

75 OGJ Editors, 'Chatham House Report Warns Against Expansion of UK Biofuels,' *Oil & Gas Journal*, April 16, 2013

76 *ibid*

77 *ibid*

78 Rob Bailey, 'The Trouble with Biofuels: Costs and Consequences of Expanding Biofuel Use in the United Kingdom,' *Chatham House*, April 2013

79 *ibid*

80 Matt McGrath, 'Biofuels: "Irrational" and "Worse Than Fossil Fuels",' *BBC*, April 14, 2013

81 Sally Bakewell, 'Biofuels to Cost UK Motorists $707 Million, Chatham House Says,' *Bloomberg*, April 14, 2013

82 Tim Wallace, 'Analysts Fear Biofuel Increase in EU Will Harm Environment,' *City A.M.*, April 15, 2013

83 *op. cit.*, Sally Bakewell, 'Biofuels to Cost UK Motorists $707 Million, Chatham House Says,' *Bloomberg*

84 Rob Bailey, 'The Trouble with Biofuels: Costs and Consequences of Expanding Biofuel Use in the United Kingdom,' *Chatham House Programme Paper*, April 2013, Page 9

85 Review & Outlook, 'Floored by Carbon,' *The Wall Street Journal Europe*, April 18, 2013

86 Sean Carney, 'Vote Leaves EU Emissions Trading in Tatters,' *The Wall Street Journal*, April 16, 2013

87 Christopher Booker, 'George Osborne's CO2 Tax Will Double UK Electricity Bills,' *The Telegraph*, September 29, 2012

88 Rupert Darwall, 'The Green Energy Mirage Will Cost the Earth,' *The Telegraph*, March 5, 2013

89 Press Release, 'New Figures; Palm Oil Destroys Malaysia's Peatswamp Forests Faster Than Ever,' *Wetlands International*, February 1, 2011

90 'Oil Palm Surging Source of Greenhouse Gas Emissions,' *Science Daily*, April 26, 2012

91 *op. cit.*, Rosenthal, 'Once a Dream Fuel, Palm Oil May Be an Eco-Nightmare,' *The New York Times*

92   Tad W. Patzek, 'How Can We Outlive Our Way of Life?,' Paper prepared for the *20th Round Table on Sustainable Development of Biofuels*, OECD, Paris, September 11-12, 2007, Page 14

93   *op. cit.*, Rosenthal, 'Once a Dream Fuel, Palm Oil May Be an Eco-Nightmare,' *The New York Times*

94   Kimberly M. Carlson, et. al., 'Committed Carbon Emissions, Deforestation, and Community Land Conversion from Oil Palm Plantation Expansion in West Kalimantan, Indonesia,' *Proceedings of the National Academy of Sciences*, April 20, 2012

95   Kimberly M. Carlson, et. al., 'Carbon Emissions from Forest Conversion by Kalimantan Oil Palm Plantations,' *Nature Climate Change*, October 7, 2012

96   'Oil Palm Plantations Are Clearing Carbon-Rich Tropical Forests in Borneo, Researchers Show,' *Science Daily*, October 7, 2012

97   'A Price on Carbon Not Enough to Save Rainforests,' *Science Daily*, December 23, 2008

98   Timothy Searchinger, et. al., 'Use of U.S. Croplands for Biofuels Increases Greenhouse Gases Through Emissions from Land-Use Change,' *Science*, Volume 319, No. 5867, February 7, 2008, Pages 1238-1240

99   Joseph Fargione, et. al., 'Land Clearing and the Biofuel Carbon Debt,' *Science*, Volume 319, No. 5867, February 7, 2007, Pages 1235-1238

100 Elisabeth Rosenthal, 'Biofuels Deemed a Greenhouse Threat,' *The New York Times*, February 8, 2008

101 'GREET Model,' *Argonne National Laboratory*, Transportation Technology R&D Center, U.S. Department of Energy

102 Michael Q. Wang and Zia Haq response to Searchinger, et. al., 'Ethanol's Effects on Greenhouse Gas Emissions,' *Science*, August 12, 2008

103 Food and Agricultural Policy Research Institute, *U.S. Baseline Briefing Book: Projections for Agricultural and Biofuels Markets* (FAPRI-MU Report #-3-08, University of Missouri, March 2008

104 *ibid*

105 Timothy Searchinger response to Wang & Haq, 'Response to M. Wang and Z. Haq's E-Letter,' *Science*, August 12, 2008

106 Alan Zarembo, 'Biofuel May Raise Carbon Emissions,' *Los Angeles Times*, February 8, 2008

107 'Re: New Research on Biofuels,' Letter to President George Bush and Congressional Leaders, February 7, 2008

108 Public Law 110-140, 'Energy Independence and Security Act of 2007, *U.S. Government Printing Office*, December 19, 2007, Section 201, (1)(H) Lifecycle Greenhouse Gas Emissions

109 John Barrasso, 'The EPA Needs a New Broom. Will It Get One?,' *The Wall Street Journal*, April 10, 2013

110 Susan Tarka Sanchez, et. al., 'Accounting for Indirect Land-Use Change in the Life Cycle Assessment of Biofuel Supply Chains,' *Journal of the Royal Society Interface*, June 7, 2012, Pages 1105-1119

111 Deborah Zabarenko, 'Food-Based Biofuels Can Spur Climate Change,' *Reuters*, February 7, 2008

112 Susanne Retka Schill, 'FTC: U.S. Ethanol Market Remains Unconcentrated in 2012,' *Ethanol Producer Magazine*, November 27, 2012

113 Josef Herert, Associated Press, 'Study: Ethanol May Add to Global Warming,' *USA Today*, February 8, 2008; the basis for the 20% greenhouse gas reduction claim comes from a May 2011 paper at Michael Q. Wang, 'Energy and Greenhouse Gas Emission Effects of Corn and Cellulosic Ethanol with Technology Improvements and Land Use Changes,' *Biomass and Bioenergy*, Volume 35, No. 5, May 2011, Pages 1885-1896; that finding merely reiterated a 19-21% reduction claim published by Wang in 2007 in *ERL* at Michael Wang, et. al., 'Life-Cycle Energy and Greenhouse Gas Emission Impacts of Different Corn Ethanol Plant Types,' *Environmental Research Letters*, May 22, 2007

114 'Biofuel Crops Increase Carbon Emissions,' *Environmental News Network*, February 12, 2008

115 *op. cit.*, Wang and Haq response to Searchinger, 'Ethanol's Effects on Emissions,' *Science*

116 'Carbon Calculator for Land Use Change from Biofuel Production (CCLUB): Users' Manual and Technical Documentation,' *Argonne National Laboratory*, September 2013, Page 11

117 Michael Wang, et. al., 'Well-to-Wheels Energy Use and Greenhouse Gas Emissions of Ethanol from Corn, Sugarcane and Cellulosic Biomass for U.S. Use,' *Environmental Research Letters*, Volume 7, No. 4, December 13, 2012

118 Ron Gecan, et. al., 'The Impact of Ethanol Use on Food Prices and Greenhouse-Gas Emissions,' *Congressional Budget Office*, April 2009, Page 13

119 Seungdo Kim and Bruce E. Dale, 'Indirect Land Use Change for Biofuels: Testing Predictions and Improving Analytical Methodologies,' *Biomass and Bioenergy*, Volume 35, No. 7, July 2011, Pages 3235-3240

120 Michael O'Hare, et. al., 'Comment on "Indirect Land Use Change for Biofuels: Testing Predictions and Improving Analytical Methodologies" by Kim and Dale; Statistical Reliability and the Definition of the Indirect Land Use Change (ILUC) Issue,' *Biomass and Bioenergy*, Volume 35, No. 10, October 2011, Pages 4485-4487

121 *op. cit.*, Kevin Bullis, 'Do Biofuels Reduce Greenhouse Gases?,' *Technology Review*

122 *ibid*

123 Holly K. Gibbs, et. al., 'Carbon Payback Times for Crop-Based Biofuel Expansion in the Tropics; The Effects of Changing Yield and Technology,' *Environmental Research Letters*, July 9, 2008

124 See Michael Himmel, et. al., 'Biomass Recalcitrance: Engineering Plants and Enzymes for Biofuels Production,' *Science*, Volume 315, No. 5813, February 9, 2007, Pages 804-807; see also Daemon Fairless, 'Biofuel: The Little Shrub that Could — Maybe,' *Nature*, October 10, 2007

125 Daniel C. Nepstad, et. al., 'Interactions Among Amazon Land Use, Forests and Climate: Prospects for a Near-Term Forest Tipping Point,' *Philosophical Transactions of the Royal Society*, 2007; see also Jason Hill, et. al., 'Environmental, Economic, and Energetic Costs and Benefits of Biodiesel and Ethanol Biofuels,' *Proceedings of the National Academy of Sciences*, June 2, 2006

126 *Sustainable Bioenergy: A Framework for Decision Makers*, United Nations Food & Agricultural Organization, 2007; see also 'World Energy Outlook 2006,' *International Energy Agency*

127 Lee R. Lynn, et. al., 'How Biotech Can Transform Biofuels,' *Nature Biotechnology*, Volume 26, 2008, Pages 169-172; see also *op. cit.*, Daemon Fairless, 'Biofuel: The Little Shrub that Could — Maybe,' *Nature*

128 M. Johnson and T. Holloway, 'A Global Comparison of National Biodiesel Production Potentials,' *Environmental Science Technology*, December 1, 2007, Pages 7967-7973; see also Annie Dufey, ' *Production, Trade and Sustainable Development: Emerging Issues*, London: International Institute for Environment and Development, 2006

129 Lian Pin Koh and David S. Wilcove, 'Is Palm Oil Agriculture Really Destroying Tropical Biodiversity?,' *Conservation Letters*, May 15, 2008; see also Douglas C. Morton, et. al., 'Cropland Expansion Changes Deforestation Dynamics in the Southern Brazilian Amazon,' *Proceedings of the National Academy of Sciences*, July 27, 2006

130 William F. Laurance, 'Switch to Corn Promotes Amazon Deforestation,' *Science*, Volume 318, No. 5857, Page 1721, December 14, 2007; see also *op. cit.*, Lian Pin Koh and David S. Wilcove, 'Is Palm Oil Agriculture Really Destroying Tropical Biodiversity?,' *Conservation Letters*

131 'Measuring the Indirect Land-Use Change Associated with Increased Biofuel Feedback Production: A Review of Modeling Efforts,' *Economic Research Service*, U.S. Department of Agriculture, February 2011

132 *op. cit.*, Holly K. Gibbs, et. al., 'Carbon Payback Times for Crop-Based Biofuel Expansion in the Tropics; The Effects of Changing Yield and Technology,' *Environmental Research Letters*

133 *op. cit.*, Daemon Fairless, 'Biofuel: The Little Shrub that Could — Maybe,' *Nature*

134 'Distribution of Expected CERs from Registered Projects by Host Party,' *UN Framework Convention on Climate Change*, September 30, 2013

135 'Trading the Absurd,' *Carbon Trade Watch*, November 17, 2005

136 See for instance 'Validation Report: Hubei Lichuan Qiyueshan Wind Power Project in China,' *Det Norsk Veritas*, August 30, 2011, Page 26

137 Robin Bravender, 'Biomass Industry Sees "Chilling Message" in EPA's Greenhouse Gas Emissions Rule,' *The New York Times*, May 17, 2010

138 Ben Geman, 'EPA Delays Climate Rules for Biomass Energy,' *The Hill*, January 12, 2011

139 Ben Geman, 'Green Groups Challenge EPA on Biomass Climate Exemption,' *The Hill*, August 15, 2011

140 Matthew Wald, 'Court Overturns E.P.A.'s Biofuel Mandate,' *The New York Times*, January 25, 2013

141 *ibid*

142 Andrew Zajac, 'EPA Delay on Greenhouse Gas Biofuel Rules Tossed by Court,' *Bloomberg*, July 12, 2013

143 Mica Rosenberg, 'U.S. Court Says Biofuel Producers Must Face Carbon Emission Rules,' *Reuters*, July 12, 2013

144 International Energy Statistics, Total Oil Supply (Thousands of Barrels Per Day), *Energy Information Administration*

145 T.A. Kiefer, 'Twenty-First Century Snake Oil: Why the United States Should Reject Biofuels as Part of a Rational National Security Energy Strategy,' *Waterloo Institute for Complexity & Innovation*, No. 4, January 2013, Page 15

146 Henry Fountain, 'A Rogue Climate Experiment Outrages Scientists,' *The New York Times*, October 18, 2012

147 Naomi Klein, 'Geoengineering: Testing the Waters,' *The New York Times*, October 27, 2012

148 Martin Lukacs, 'World's Biggest Geoengineering Experiment "Violates" UN Rules,' *The Guardian*, October 15, 2012

149 Martin Lukacs, 'Canadian Government "Knew of Plans to Dump Iron Into the Pacific",' *The Guardian*, October 17, 2012

150 Robert Zubrin, 'The Greens' Attack on Mariculture,' *National Review*, January 3, 2013

151 Jeff Tollefson, 'Ocean-Fertilization Project off Canada Sparks Furore,' *Nature*, October 23, 2012

152 John Vidal, 'Rogue Geoengineering Could "Hijack" World's Climate,' *The Guardian*, January 8, 2013

153 Martin Lukacs, 'U.S. Businessman Defends Controversial Geoengineering Experiment,' *The Guardian*, October 19, 2012

154 ETC Group at http://www.etcgroup.org/

155 *op. cit.*, Martin Lukacs, 'World's Biggest Geoengineering Experiment "Violates" UN Rules,' *The Guardian*

156 Adam Corner, 'Profitable Climate Fixes Are Too Tempting for Rogue Geoengineers to Resist,' *The Guardian*, October 19, 2012

157 David Roberts, 'An Excerpt from a New Book by George Monbiot,' *Grist*, September 20, 2006

158 Clearing forest, pasture or wetland for new cropland to produce biofuels results in decomposition of organic carbon and elevated GHG emissions, creating a "carbon debt" which may take many years for biofuel consumption to "pay down." See 'Biofuels and the Environment: Triennial Report to Congress,' *Environmental Protection Agency*, 2011, Pages 5-9

159 Fertilizer applications increase emissions of nitrous oxide, a far more potent greenhouse gas than carbon dioxide. In 2011, nitrous oxide accounted for about 5% of all US GHG emissions, and nitrous oxide molecules stay in the atmosphere for an average of 120 years. See 'Overview of Greenhouse Gases: Nitrous Oxide Emissions,' *Environmental Protection Agency*

160 'Renewable Fuel Standard Program (RFS 2) Regulatory Impact Analysis,' *Environmental Protection Agency*, 2010

161 Scott Faber, 'Hearing on Overview of the Renewable Fuel Standard: Stakeholder Perspectives,' *House Energy and Commerce Committee*, July 24, 2013

162 *op. cit.*, Jeff Tollefson, 'Ocean-Fertilization Project off Canada Sparks Furore,' *Nature*

163 *op. cit.*, Henry Fountain, 'A Rogue Climate Experiment Outrages Scientists,' *The New York Times*

164 Victor Smetacek, et. al., 'Deep Carbon Export from a Southern Ocean Iron-Fertilized Diatom Bloom,' *Nature*, Volume 487, July 19, 2012, Pages 313-319

165 Damian Carrington, 'Dumping Iron at Sea Can Bury Carbon for Centuries, Study Shows,' *The Guardian*, July 18, 2012

166 Robert Rapier, 'Who Loses from Rising Natural Gas Prices?,' *Energy Tribune*, May 29, 2013

167 *op. cit.*, Robert Zubrin, 'The Greens' Attack on Mariculture,' *National Review*

168 Robert Zubrin, 'Carbon Emissions Are Good,' *National Review*, April 3, 2012

169 Becky Oskin, 'Carbon Dioxide Greening Deserts,' *Live Science,* May 31, 2013

170 Randall J. Donohue, et. al., 'CO2 Fertilisation Has Increased Maximum Foliage Across the Globe's Warm Arid Environments,' *Geophysical Research Letters*, May 2013

171 'Elevated Carbon Dioxide Making Arid Regions Greener,' *American Geophysical Union*, AGU Release No. 13-24, May 31, 2013

CHAPTER 16

1   'Future of Alcohol in the Industries,' *The New York Times*, August 5, 1906

2   'Ford Predicts Fuel from Vegetation,' *The New York Times*, September 20, 1925, Page 24

3   Editorial, 'Ethanol's Promise,' *The New York Times*, May 1, 2006

4   Katie Fehrenbacher, '11 Companies Racing to Build U.S. Cellulosic Ethanol Plants,' *Giga OM*, June 3, 2008

5   'DOE Invests $385 Million in Six Cellulosic Ethanol Projects,' Energy Efficiency & Renewable Energy Office, U.S. Department of Energy, February 28, 2007

6   'DOE Awards Up to $385 Million to Six Cellulosic Ethanol Plants; Total Investment to Exceed $1.2 Billion,' *Green Car Congress*, February 28, 2007

7   *Associated Press*, 'Gasification May Be Key to U.S. Ethanol,' *WPVI-TV6 Action News*, March 4, 2007

8   'DOE Awards $23 Million to Five Cellulosic Ethanol Conversion Projects,' *Energy Efficiency & Renewable Energy Office*, U.S. Department of Energy, March 27, 2007

9   'Kansas Gets First U.S. Cellulosic Ethanol Plant,' *Environment News Service*, August 28, 2007

10 'Abengoa Starts Building Cellulosic Ethanol Plant,' *Hay & Forage Grower*, September 21, 2011

11 Amy Bickel, 'Ethanol Plant is Big Business for Area,' *The Hutchinson News*, March 11, 2012

12 Eric Durban, 'Biomass or Bust: Kansas Ethanol Plant Seeks Higher Ground,' *KVNO News*, February 14, 2012

13 'Current State of the U.S. Ethanol Industry,' *Office of Biomass Programs*, U.S. Department of Energy, November 30, 2010, Page 5-1

14 'Commercial Cellulosic Ethanol Still Coming, Execs Say,' *Argus Media*, February 24, 2012

15 Kris Bevill, 'Next Up,' *Ethanol Producer Magazine*, January 11, 2012

16 Art Hovey, 'Abengoa's $500 Million Vision Could Take Shape in York County,' *The Lincoln Journal-Star*, October 27, 2011

17 'Abengoa Plans Temporary Shutdown of Two Ethanol Plants,' *Chemicals-Technology.com*, December 21, 2011

18 *op. cit.*, 'DOE Invests $385 Million in Six Cellulosic Ethanol Projects,' DOE

19 'Alico Selected for a Department of Energy Grant,' *PR Newswire*, March 1, 2007

20 Lindsey Irwin, 'Cellulosic Wave Set in Motion,' *Ethanol Producer Magazine*, May 22, 2007

21 Katie Fehrenbacher, 'Alico Abandons Cellulosic Ethanol Plans,' *Giga OM*, June 4, 2008

22 Susan Salisbury, 'Start-Up Takes Over Abandoned Ethanol Project,' *The Palm Beach Post*, June 3, 2008

23   'Alico to Discontinue Ethanol Efforts,' *PR Newswire*, June 2, 2008

24   Jim Lane, 'INEOS New Planet BioEnergy Aims for 8 Mgy Cellulosic Ethanol Plant in Florida,' *Biofuels Digest*, February 15, 2010

25   'INEOS Bio Produces Cellulosic Ethanol at Commercial Scale,' *INEOS Bio*, July 31, 2013

26   Ben Messenger, 'INEOS Bio Begins Commercial Production of Biofuel from Wastes in Florida,' *Waste Management World*, August 5, 2013

27   *op. cit.*, 'DOE Awards Up to $385 Million' *Green Car Congress*

28   'Bluefire Renewables, Inc. – Form 10-K, *U.S. Securities & Exchange Commission*, April 7, 2011, Page 6

29   *ibid*, Page 22

30   *ibid*, Page 24

31   'Form 10-Q for Bluefire Renewables, Inc., May 16, 2012, *U.S. Securities & Exchange Commission*

32   Kerry A. Dolan, 'Mr. Ethanol Fights Back,' *Forbes*, November 24, 2008

33   Sam Abuelsamid, 'Broin Companies to Add Cellulosic Ethanol Production to Iowa Plant,' *Auto Blog Green*, November 21, 2006

34   *op. cit.*, 'DOE Awards Up to $385 Million' *Green Car Congress*

35   *op. cit.*, Kerry A. Dolan, 'Mr. Ethanol Fights Back,' *Forbes*

36   Rod Swoboda, 'Iowa a Step Closer to Cellulosic Ethanol Production,' *Farm Progress*, July 12, 2011

37   Dave Dreeszen, 'Seven Questions About Project Liberty,' *Sioux City Journal*, July 24, 2011

38   David Shaffer, 'Poet Adds Dutch Partner to Cellulosic Ethanol Venture,' *Minneapolis Star Tribune*, January 23, 2012

39   *ibid*

40   Dave Dreeszen, Poet Partners With Dutch Firm in Northwest Iowa Cellulosic Venture,' *Sioux City Journal*, March 4, 2012

41   Meghan Sapp, 'U.S. Senate Nixes Biodiesel, Cellulosic Biofuels Credit Extension,' *Biofuels Digest*, March 20, 2012

42   Jodi Schwan, 'Poet, Dutch Firm "Writing History Together",' *Sioux Falls Business Journal*, June 22, 2012

43   Iogen Corporation corporate website

44   Maurice Hladik, 'Cellulose Ethanol Is Ready to Go,' *Iogen Corporation*, Presentation to the Emerging Energies Conference, University of California Santa Barbara, February 10-11, 2006

45   Kathleen Schalch, 'Canadian Dreams of Ethanol Distilled from Grass,' *National Public Radio*, May 16, 2006

46   Public policy dissonance among *NPR*'s loyal followers is displayed in a June 2012 web page carrying a banner advertisement for a Toyota Plug-In Electric Hybrid *Prius* alongside a report covering a Senate vote upholding EPA rules on emissions, measures that will shutter 25% of the nation's coal-fired power plants (screen capped for posterity by author). All five contributors in the comments section hail the vote in celebratory fashion, oblivious to the self-contradiction. How will they power plug-in cars when coal-fired power stations are closed? See Tamara Keith, 'Senate Votes to Keep Mercury Limits on Power Plants,' *National Public Radio*, June 20, 2012. The EPA rules will remove 35 gigawatts of electrical power from the grid with no ready replacement. See Phil Kerpen, 'The Crony War on Coal,' *National Review*, July 16, 2012

47   Hope Deutscher, 'Cellulosic Ethanol: Ready, Set, Go,' *Ethanol Producer Magazine*, June 3, 2009; a hilarious anecdote in Deutscher's story concerns a publicity stunt by Green Alternative Motorsports race driver Steve Zadig who wanted to burnish his 'green' credentials for a 2007 race in Willows, California. So the environmentally conscious Zadig ordered 800 gallons of cellulosic E85 from Iogen's Ottawa, Ontario plant, the only place he could find cellulosic ethanol. A typical tank truck traveling 2,911 road miles each way from Ottawa to Willows could expect to burn about 970 gallons of diesel fuel on the round trip movement liberating about three tons of CO_2 in the process. The Earth's atmosphere would have been far better served with Zadig burning fossil fuel. It is a classic 'green left example of the primacy of style over substance.

48   Katie Fehrenbacher, 'Iogen Suspends U.S. Cellulosic Ethanol Plant Plans,' *Giga OM*, June 4, 2008

49   'Shell and Iogen Corporation Announce Further Investment to Accelerate Commercialization of Cellulosic Ethanol,' *Iogen News*, June 3, 2010

50   'Shell Boosts Stake in Iogen Cellulosic Ethanol,' *Reuters*, July 15, 2008

51   Shawn McCarthy, 'Canada's Ethanol Boom, Minus the Boom,' *The Globe and Mail*, June 10, 2010

52   Shawn McCarthy, 'Shell-Iogen Plant Cancellation Raises Doubts About New Biofuel Technology,' *The Globe and Mail*, April 30, 2012

53   'Iogen Energy to Refocus Its Strategy,' *Iogen News*, April 30, 2012

54   Dan Chapman, 'Plant Closure Bursts Ga.'s Biomass Bubble,' *The Atlanta Journal-Constitution*, February 15, 2011

55   'DOE Announces Up to $200 Million in Funding for Biorefineries,' *U.S. Department of Energy*, May 1, 2007

56   'U.S. Department of Energy Selects First Round of Small-Scale Biorefinery Projects for Up to $114 Million in Funding,' *U.S. Department of Energy*, January 29, 2008

57   'DOE Selects 3 Small-Scale Biorefinery Projects for Up to $86 Million of Federal Funding in Maine, Tennessee and Kentucky,' *U.S. Department of Energy*, April 18, 2008

58   Ryan C. Christiansen, 'The Cellulosic Ceiling,' *Ethanol Producer Magazine*, July 8, 2009

59   'DOE to Provide Up to $40 Million in Funding for Small-Scale Biorefinery Projects in Wisconsin and Louisiana,' ' *U.S. Department of Energy*, July 14, 2008

60   *op. cit.*, Ryan C. Christiansen, 'The Cellulosic Ceiling,' *Ethanol Producer Magazine*

61   Gregory H. Friedman, 'Follow-Up Audit of the Department of Energy's Financial Assistance for Integrated Biorefinery Projects,' DOE/IG-0893, *U.S. Department of Energy*, September 2013, Page 2

62   *ibid*

63   Katie Fehrenbacher, 'Biofuel Firm KiOR Closes Flat in IPO,' *Giga OM*, June 24, 2011

64   Andrew Herndon, 'KiOR Unchanged After Pricing IPO at 29% Below Top of Range,' *Bloomberg*, June 24, 2011

65   KiOR, Inc. Historical Prices, Intra-Day High Price on September 29, 2011, *Yahoo Finance*

66   Ucilia Wong, 'Vinod Khosla: Greentech Has Generated Huge Profits,' *Giga OM*, September 27, 2011

67   Tristan R. Brown, 'KiOR: No Revenue, No Problem … For Now,' *Seeking Alpha*, August 15, 2012

68   *Associated Press*, 'KiOR Rises on Manufacturing Plant Update,' *The Sacramento Bee*, August 14, 2012

69   *op. cit.*, Tristan R. Brown, 'KiOR: No Revenue, No Problem … For Now,' *Seeking Alpha*

70   'KiOR's CEO Discusses Q2 2012 Results – Earnings Call Transcript,' *Seeking Alpha*, August 14, 2012

71   Associated Press, 'KiOR 4Q Loss Nearly Doubles on Plant Startup Costs,' *Yahoo Finance*, March 18, 2013

72   'Katie Fehrenbacher, 'KiOR to Start Up Next-Gen Biofuel Plant Next Month,' *Giga OM*, August 14, 2012

73   ''KiOR Receives Fuel Registration from EPA for Renewable Gasoline,' *NASDAQ*, July 24, 2012

74   *ibid*

75   Tristan R. Brown, 'KiOR Passes a Major Hurdle; Still Faces Several More,' *Seeking Alpha*, July 24, 2012

76   Robert Rapier, 'Who Loses from Rising Natural Gas Prices?,' *Energy Tribune*, May 29, 2013

77   See for instance 'Law Offices of Howard G. Smith Announces Class Action Lawsuit Against KiOR, Inc.,' *Yahoo Finance*, September 4, 2013; see also 'Hagens Berman Advises KiOR Investors of Oct. 21, 2013, Class-Action Deadline and Continuing Investigation,' *Yahoo Finance*, September 4, 2013

78   'EPA Finalizes 2013 Renewable Fuel Standards,' *Environmental Protection Agency*, August 2013

79   Gerard Wynn, 'Column-U.S. Advanced Biofuel Targets Inflated Expectations: Wynn,' *Reuters*, September 3, 2013

80   *ibid*

81   Kris Bevill, 'API Sues EPA Over Cellulosic Biofuel Mandate,' *Ethanol Producer Magazine*, March 13, 2012

82   Ayesha Rascoe, 'U.S. Court Blocks 2012 Cellulosic Biofuel Target,' *Reuters*, January 25, 2013

83   Daniel Kish, 'EPA's Ethanol Mandates Are Costing Consumers,' *U.S. News & World Report*, February 7, 2013

84   Steven Mufson, 'Government's Plan to Expand Biofuel Use Runs Into Multiple Bumps in the Road,' *The Washington Post*, February 1, 2013

85   Lisa Jackson, 'Regulation of Fuels and Fuel Additives: 2013 Renewable Fuel Standards,' *Environmental Protection Agency*, January 31, 2013 Page 9

86   *ibid*

87   Stone Phillips, 'A Simple Solution to Pain At the Pump,' *MSNBC*, May 7, 2006

88   'Venture Capitalist and Business Analyst Predict Rapid Expansion of Biofuels Industry, Dramatic Reductions in Carbon Emissions,' *Business Wire*, March 22, 2007

89   Christopher Doering, 'Cellulosic Ethanol Output Could "Explode",' *Reuters*, January 9, 2009

90   Susanne Retka Schill, 'Blue Sugars Claims First Cellulosic RIN, Extends Petrobras Deal,' *Ethanol Producer Magazine*, July 3, 2012

91   *ibid*

92   *op. cit.*, Fuels and Fuel Additives, 2012 RFS2 Data, Cellulosic Biofuel (D3), Monthly Data *Environmental Protection Agency*

93   Erin Voegele, 'Western Biomass Energy Receives BCAP Funding,' *Ethanol Producer Magazine*, November 11, 2009

94   Robert Rapier, 'First Commercial Cellulosic Ethanol Plant in U.S. Goes Bankrupt,' *Financial Sense*, March 20, 2013

95   Susanne Rethka Schill, 'Western Biomass Energy in Chapter 11 Reorganization,' *Ethanol Producer Magazine*, February 12, 2013

96   *op. cit.*, Susanne Retka Schill, 'Blue Sugars Claims First Cellulosic RIN, Extends Petrobras Deal,' *Ethanol Producer Magazine*

97   Public Law 110-140, December 19, 2007, Energy Independence and Security Act of 2007, Section 202 Renewable Fuel Standard, (2) Applicable Volumes of Renewable Fuel, (B) Applicable Volumes, (III) Cellulosic Biofuel, *U.S. Government Printing Office*

98   Henri Braconnot, 'Mémoire Sur la Nature des Corps Gras,' *Annales de Chimie*, March 15, 1815

99   'Energy Efficiency and Renewable Energy, Dilute Acid Hydrolysis,' *U.S. Department of Energy*

100 Rufus Frost Herrick, *Denatured or Industrial Alcohol*, New York: John Wiley & Sons, 1907, Page 307

101 John K. Brachvogel, *Industrial Alcohol: Its Manufacture and Use*, New York: Munn & Co., 1907, Page 13

102 E.C. Sharrad and F.W. Kressman, 'Review of Processes in the United States Prior to World War II,' *Industrial & Engineering Chemistry*, January 1945, Pages 5-8

103 E.C. Sherrard and F.W. Kressman, 'Review of Processes in the United States Prior to World War II,' *Industrial and Engineering Chemistry*, Volume 37, No. 1, 1945, Pages 5-8

104 Robert Rapier, 'Why Sugarcane Bagasse is the Most Promising Pathway for Cellulosic Ethanol,' *Consumer Energy Report*, August 20, 2012

105 'Ford Predicts Fuel from Vegetation,' *The New York Times*, September 20, 1925, Page 24

106 'Launching of a Great Industry: The Making of Cheap Alcohol,' *The New York Times*, November 25, 1906, Section III Page 3

107 "The New Cheap Illuminant," *The New York Times*, May 25, 1906

108 *ibid*

109 'Future of Alcohol in the Industries,' *The New York Times*, August 5, 1906

110 *ibid*

111 See for instance Matthew L. Wald, 'New Technology Turns Useless Agricultural Byproducts Into Fuel for Autos,' *The New York Times*, October 25, 1998; see also Editorial, 'Ethanol's Promise, *The New York Times*, May 1, 2006; Kate Galbraith, 'Ethanol Industry Hoping for Surge,' *The New York Times*, March 30, 2011; Matthew L. Wald, 'Fuel from Waste, Poised at a Milestone,' *The New York Times*, November 13, 2012

112 Rudolf Diesel, 'The Diesel Oil Engine,' *Engineering*, Volume 93, 1912, Pages 395-406

113 Rudolf Diesel, 'The Diesel Oil Engine and Its Industrial Importance Particularly for Great Britain,' *Proceedings of the Institute of Mechanical Engineers*, 1912, Pages 179-280

114 Michael Köpke, et. al., 'The Past, Present, and Future of Biofuels,' Chapter in Marco Aurelio Dos Santos Bernardes, Editor, *Biofuel Production-Recent Developments and Prospects*, InTech, ISBN: 978-953-307-478-8, 2011, Page 452

115 Thomas Midgley, 'Discussion of Papers at Semi-Annual Meeting,' *SAE Journal*, October 1921, Page 269. Reprinted in Bill Kovarik, 'Henry Ford, Charles Kettering and the "Fuel of the Future",' *Radford University*, 1998

116 Midgley, inventor of the refrigerant freon, worked at General Motors in the early 1900s. He and his boss Charles Kettering patented use of tetra ethyl lead in gasoline. Midgley's research team discovered that addition of the lead compound to gasoline reduced engine knock and boosted performance. Midgley later poisoned himself trying to demonstrate the safety of the dangerous compound, fleeing to Europe in 1925 to receive medical treatment.

117 *op. cit.*, 'Energy Efficiency and Renewable Energy, Dilute Acid Hydrolysis,' *U.S. Department of Energy*

118 W.L. Faith, 'Development of the Scholler Process in the United States,' *Industrial and Engineering Chemistry*, Volume 37, No. 1, 1945, Pages 9-11

119 'Early Days of Coal Research,' *U.S. Department of Energy*

120 *ibid*

121 Lee R. Lynd, et. al., 'Fuel Ethanol from Cellulosic Ethanol,' *Science*, Volume 251, No. 4999, March 15, 1991, Pages 1318-1323

122 'Cellulosic Ethanol Technology on Track to Being Competitive with Other Transportation Fuels,' *National Renewable Energy Laboratory*, February 2011

123 'Novel Biomass Conversion Process Results in Commercial Joint Venture,' *National Renewable Energy Laboratory*, June 2010

124 Ling Tao and Andy Aden, 'The Economics of Current and Future Biofuels,' *In Vitro Cellular & Developmental Biology*, Volume 45, No. 3, June 2009, Pages 199-217

125 D. Sandor and R. Wallace, 'Understanding the Growth of the Cellulosic Ethanol Industry,' *National Renewable Energy Laboratory*, April 2008

126 'Research Advances in Cellulosic Ethanol: NREL Leads the Way,' *National Renewable Energy Laboratory*, March 2007

127 Robert Wallace, et. al., 'Feasibility Study for Co-Locating and Integrating Ethanol Production Plants from Corn Starch and Lignocellulosic Feedstocks,' *National Renewable Energy Laboratory*, January 2005

128 A. Aden, et. al., 'Lignocellulose Biomass to Ethanol Process Design and Economics Utilizing Co-Current Dilute Acid Prehydrolysis and Enzymatic Hydrolysis for Corn Stover,' *National Renewable Energy Laboratory*, June 2002

129 Wooley, R., et. al., 'Lignocellulosic Biomass to Ethanol Process Design and Economics Utilizing Co-Current Dilute Acid Prehydrolysis and Enzymatic Hydrolysis Current and Futuristic Scenarios,' *National Renewable Energy Laboratory*, July 1999

130 Christopher Martin and Mario Parker, 'BP Cancels Florida Ethanol Plant, Extends Renewable Exit,' *Bloomberg*, October 25, 2012

131   Kevin Bullis, 'BP Plant Cancellation Darkens Cellulosic Ethanol's Future,' *Technology Review*, November 2, 2012

132   *ibid*

133   *ibid*

134   'Clean Cities Alternative Fuel Price Report,' *U.S. Department of Energy*, October 2013, Page 3

135   Christopher Helman, 'Same Moonshine, Different Name: Welcome to the Age of Cellulosic Ethanol,' *Forbes*, September 4, 2013

136   Tom Capehart, 'Cellulosic Biofuels: Analysis of Policy Issues for Congress,' *Congressional Research Service*, RL34738, November 7, 2008, Page 7

137   David Rotman, 'The Price of Biofuels,' *Technology Review*, December 18, 2007

138   *ibid*

139   'Wood: The Fuel of the Future,' *The Economist*, April 6, 2013

140   'Typical Calorific Values of Fuels,' Biomass Energy Centre, *UK Forestry Commission*

141   *op. cit.*, A. Aden, et. al., 'Lignocellulose Biomass to Ethanol Process Design and Economics Utilizing Co-Current Dilute Acid Prehydrolysis and Enzymatic Hydrolysis for Corn Stover,' *National Renewable Energy Laboratory*, Page 13

142   Petroleum & Other Liquids, Supply and Disposition, Motor Gasoline, Annual 2011 in Thousand Barrels of 3,188,709 KBbls, *Energy Information Administration*

143   'Transportation Energy Data Book, 30th Edition,' *U.S. Department of Energy*, Appendix B. Conversions, Table B.4, Heat Content for Various Fuels, Page B-5, Conventional Gasoline = 115,400 BTU per gallon vs. Ethanol = 75,700 BTU per gallon

144   Calculation performed by the author based upon a distance estimate of 93 million miles from Sun to Earth

145   Calculation performed by the author based upon an estimate of 7,918 miles diameter of the Earth

146   'Minnesota's Forest Resources, 2011,' *Northern Research Station*, Forest Service, U.S. Department of Agriculture

147   *ibid*

148   *op. cit.*, Alan Rudie, 'Producing Ethanol from Wood,' *Forest Products Laboratory*

149   J.Y. Zhu and X.J. Pan, 'Woody Biomass Pretreatment for Cellulosic Ethanol Production: Technology and Energy Consumption Evaluation,' *Bioresource Technology*, Volume 101, December 6, 2009, Pages 499-5002

150   'Annual Energy Review 2011,' Petroleum Products Supplied by Type (Thousand Barrels per Day), *Energy Information Administration*, Page 141

151   Dave Juday, 'The Ethanol Mandate to Nowhere,' *The Weekly Standard*, November 23, 2009

152   'Wisconsin's Forest Resources, 2011,' *Northern Research Station*, Forest Service, U.S. Department of Agriculture

153   'Iowa's Forest Resources, 2011,' *Northern Research Station*, Forest Service, U.S. Department of Agriculture

154   'Illinois' Forest Resources, 2011,' *Northern Research Station*, Forest Service, U.S. Department of Agriculture

155   'Indiana's Forest Resources, 2011,' *Northern Research Station*, Forest Service, U.S. Department of Agriculture

156   'North Dakota's Forest Resources, 2011,' *Northern Research Station*, Forest Service, U.S. Department of Agriculture

157   'South Dakota's Forest Resources, 2011,' *Northern Research Station*, Forest Service, U.S. Department of Agriculture

158   'Missouri's Forest Resources, 2011,' *Northern Research Station*, Forest Service, U.S. Department of Agriculture

159   'Kansas' Forest Resources, 2011,' *Northern Research Station*, Forest Service, U.S. Department of Agriculture

160   'Nebraska's Forest Resources, 2011,' *Northern Research Station*, Forest Service, U.S. Department of Agriculture

161   'Vermont's Forest Resources, 2011,' *Northern Research Station*, Forest Service, U.S. Department of Agriculture

162   'EPA's Report on the Environment: Highlights of National Trends,' *U.S. Environmental Protection Agency*, 2008, Page 31

163   Vaclav Smil, '21st Century Energy: Some Sobering Thoughts,' *OECD Observer*, Volume 258-259, December 2006

164   S. David Freeman, *Winning Our Energy Independence: An Energy Insider Shows How*, Layton, Utah: Gibbs, Smith, 2007

165   See for instance Christian Anton and Henning Steinicke, 'Bioenergy — Chances and Limits,' Leopoldina Nationale Akademie der Wissenschaften, 2012, Page 5; In Chapter 16, we saw how Woods Hole researcher Jerry Melillo found that N_2O emissions from fertilizer are forecasted to overtake CO_2 in their greenhouse potential in the 21st century. See Jerry M. Melillo, et. al., 'Unintended Environmental Consequences of a Global Biofuels Program,' *MIT Joint Program on the Science and Policy of Global Change*, Report No. 168, January 2009

166   Vaclav Smil, *Enriching the Earth: Fritz Haber, Carl Bosch, and the Transformation of World Food Production*, Cambridge, Massachusetts: MIT Press, 2001

167   Steve Savage, 'Moving Towards Fossil-Energy-Independent Nitrogen Fertilizer,' *Science 2.0*, April 2, 2013

168   'Inventory of U.S. Greenhouse Gas Emissions and Sinks: 1990-2011,' *U.S. Environmental Protection Agency*, April 2013, Page ES-3

169   'Biofuels from Switchgrass: Greener Energy Pastures,' *Oak Ridge National Laboratory*

170   Robert Bryce, 'The Cellulosic Ethanol Delusion,' *Counterpunch*, March 30, 2009

171   Scott Malcolm and Marcel Aillery, 'Cellulosic Ethanol From Crop Residue Is No Free Lunch,' *Amber Waves*, Volume 7, Issue 4, U.S. Department of Agriculture

172   Rich Keller, 'Cellulosic Ethanol from Corn Stover Ready to Blast Off,' *Ag Professional*, May 17, 2012

CHAPTER 17

1   Govinda Timilsina, et. al., 'World Oil Price and Biofuels: A General Equilibrium Analysis,' *The World Bank*, June 2011

2   Govinda Timilsina, 'How Global Biofuel Expansion Could Affect the Economy, Environment and Food Supply,' *The World Bank*, June 27, 2011

3   Barack Obama, 'Real Leadership for a Clean Energy Future Speech,' Portsmouth, New Hampshire, October 8, 2007

4   Robert Murphy, 'Nobel Laureate Agrees: Federal Support for Ethanol Must End,' *Institute for Energy Research*, August 3, 2012

5   'USDA Agricultural Projections to 2022,' OCE-2013-1, Office of the Chief Economist, U.S. Department of Agriculture, February 2013

6   Randy Schnepf and Brent Yacobucci, 'Renewable GFuel Standard (RFS): Overview and Issues,' *Congressional Research Service*, March 14, 2013, Page 22

7   'Renewable Fuel Standard Assessment: Agricultural Sector Impacts,' *Energy & Commerce Committee*, U.S. House of Representatives, April 18, 2013

8   *ibid*

9   Bryan Walsh, 'Why Biofuels Help Push Up World Food Prices,' *Time*, February 14, 2011

10   *ibid*

11   Michael Grunwald, 'The Clean Energy Scam,' *Time*, March 27, 2008

12   Jack Hough, 'Rising Corn Prices and Your Grocery Bill,' *Smart Money*, July 18, 2012

13   *op. cit.*, Kerry A. Dolan, 'Mr. Ethanol Fights Back,' *Forbes*

14   Monica Davey, 'Searing Sun and Drought Shrivel Corn in Midwest,' *The New York Times*, July 4, 2012

15   See for instance Jack Farchy and Gregory Meyer, 'World Braced for New Food Crisis,' *Financial Times*, July 19, 2012; see also Jack Farchy, 'Food Crisis Fears as U.S. Corn Soars,' *Financial Times*, July 13, 2012; see also 'Grains – Soybeans Hit Record High, Corn Up Daily Limit on Dry U.S. Weather,' Reuters, July 9, 2012

16   'World Agricultural Supply and Demand Estimates,' U.S. Department of Agriculture, July 11, 2012, Page 2

17   *Reuters*, 'USDA Slashes Corn Outlook; Forecast Sends Prices Surging,' *CNBC*, July 11, 2012

18   'U.S. Corn, Soy Prices Hit Records as Drought Lingers,' *France 24*, August 22, 2012

19   *op. cit.*, Bryan Walsh, 'Why Biofuels Help Push Up World Food Prices,' *Time*

20   Emiko Terazono and Javier Blas, 'U.S. Slashes Corn Production Forecast,' *Financial Times*, July 11, 2012

21   *op. cit.*, Jack Farchy, 'Food Crisis Fears as U.S. Corn Soars,' *Financial Times*

22   Scott Irwin and Darrel Good, 'U.S. Corn Exports — The Rest of the Story,' *Farm Doc Daily*, University of Illinois, Department of Agricultural and Consumer Economics, College of Agricultural, Consumer and Environmental Sciences, September 29, 2011

23   *op. cit.*, Jack Farchy and Gregory Meyer, 'World Braced for New Food Crisis,' *Financial Times*

24   Bill Tonson, 'USDA Rolls Out Drought Help,' *Agriculture*, August 1, 2012

25   Tim Searchinger, 'How Biofuels Contribute to the Food Crisis,' *The Washington Post*, February 11, 2011

26   *ibid*

27   'Grains – U.S. New-Crop Corn, Soy Hit Contract Highs on Weather Woes,' *Reuters*, July 16, 2012

28   C. Larry Pope, 'The Ethanol Mandate is Worse Than the Drought,' *The Wall Street Journal*, July 26, 2012

29   *ibid*

30   See for instance Obama's remarks at a town hall on energy where he repeated the phrase he had used dozens of times previously and since at Barack Obama, Town Hall on Energy, Elkhart, Indiana, August 6, 2008

31   Hans Bader, 'Ethanol Mandates Cause Thousands of Deaths from Hunger in Poor Countries,' *The Examiner*, October 22, 2011

32   Christine Hall, 'ActionAid, CEI Target Ethanol Fuel Programs in EPA Filing: EPA Fails to Consider Full Impact on World Hunger,' *Competitive Enterprise Institute*, October 13, 2011

33   Kristin Sundell, 'Ethanol Mandates Impairing Food Aid,' *Financial Times*, May 28, 2013, Page 8

34   Derek Headey and Shenggen Fan, 'Reflections on the Global Crisis,' *International Food Policy Research Institute*, 2010

35   Govinda Timilsina, 'How Global Biofuel Expansion Could Affect the Economy, Environment and Food Supply,' *The World Bank*, June 27, 2011

36 Govinda Timilsina, et. al., 'World Oil Price and Biofuels: A General Equilibrium Analysis,' *The World Bank*, June 2011

37 *op. cit.*, Jack Farchy, 'Food Crisis Fears as U.S. Corn Soars,' *Financial Times*

38 'USDA Slashes Corn Yield Forecast,' *Fox Business*, August 10, 2012

39 Review & Outlook, 'Ethanol vs. the World,' *The Wall Street Journal*, August 10, 2012

40 Mario Parker, 'Lower U.S. Corn Doesn't Justify Ethanol Waiver, RFA Says,' *Bloomberg*, August 10, 2012

41 Dean Reynolds, 'Livestock Farmers Hurt by Soaring Grain Prices,' *CBS News*, July 30, 2012

42 Alan Bjerga, 'Ranchers Send Cows to Slaughter as Drought Sears Pasture,' *Bloomberg*, August 10, 2012

43 Lee Mielke, 'Milk, Dairy Prices Climb as More Dairy Cattle Move to Slaughter,' *The Farmer's Exchange*, August 10, 2012

44 Anne Lowrey and Ron Nixon, 'Severe Drought Seen as Driving Cost of Food Up,' *The New York Times*, July 25, 2012

45 Mark Peters, 'Crops Hurt, but Farmers Will Still Get Paid,' *The Wall Street Journal*, July 31, 2012

46 Vincent Ryan, 'Earnings May Shrivel Along With the Corn Stalks,' *CFO Magazine*, August 10, 2012

47 Jeff Cox, 'Why $9 Corn Could Be a Big Problem for the Economy,' *CNBC*, August 8, 2012

48 Mark Peters and Owen Fletcher, 'Prices Surge as Drought Stunts Corn Crop,' *The Wall Street Journal*, August 10, 2012

49 Mario Parker and Roger Runningen, ''Obama Administration Looking at Ethanol Rules, as Drought Spurs Corn Prices,' *The Washington Post*, August 10, 2012

50 Doug McKelway, 'EPA is Pressured to Drop Ethanol Mandate While Drought Drives Corn Prices Up,' *Fox News*, August 16, 2012

51 Charles Abbott, 'Drought Crop Damage Worsens, Ethanol Waiver Urged,' *Reuters*, August 11, 2012

52 Marlo Lewis, 'Pressure Grows on EPA to Suspend Ethanol Mandate,' *Global Warming*, August 13, 2012

53 'U.S. Corn, Soy Prices Hit Records as Drought Lingers,' *France 24*, August 22, 2012

54 Tennille Tracy, 'EPA Denies Request to Waive Ethanol Mandate for Gas,' *The Wall Street Journal*, November 16, 2012

55 Environmental Protection Agency, 'Request for Comment on Letters Seeking a Waiver of the Renewable Fuel Standard,' *Federal Register*, Volume 77, No. 169, August 30, 2012, Page 52715

56 OGJ Editors, 'EPA Denies Texas' Waiver Request,' *Oil & Gas Journal*, August 7, 2008

57 'U.S. EPA Denies Texas Waiver Request; Biofuel Mandates Remain 9B Gallons for 2008, 11.1B for 2009,' *Green Car Congress*, August 7, 2008

58 'EPA Decision on Texas Request for Waiver of Portion of Renewable Fuel Standard (RFS),' *U.S. Environmental Protection Agency*, EPA420-F-08-029, August 2008

59 *ibid*

60 *ibid*

61 *op. cit.*, EPA, 'Request for Comment on Letters Seeking a Waiver of the RFS,' *Federal Register*

62 Betsy Blaney, 'EPA Denies Texas Governor's Ethanol Waiver Request,' *USA Today*, August 7, 2008

63 'EPA Decision to Deny Requests for Waiver of the Renewable Fuel Standard,' *U.S. Environmental Protection Agency*, November 2012, Page 2

64 Christopher Doering, 'Request to Waive Ethanol Mandate Denied by EPA,' *Des Moines Register*, November 17, 2012

65 Stephen E. Schatz, 'National Council of Chain Restaurants to Unveil New PwC U.S. Study on the Impact of the Renewable Fuel Standard,' *National Retail Federation*, November 19, 2012

66 Rob Green, 'A Mandate to Raise Food Prices,' *The Wall Street Journal*, November 27, 2012

67 *ibid*

68 Marlo Lewis, 'The EPA vs. State Economies,' *National Review*, November 19, 2012

69 Environmental Protection Agency, 'Greenhouse Gas Emissions Standards and Fuel Efficiency Standards for Medium- and Heavy-Duty Engines and Vehicles,' *Federal Register*, Volume 75, No. 249, December 29, 2010, Page 81952

70 *op. cit.*, Marlo Lewis, 'The EPA vs. State Economies,' *National Review*

71 *ibid*

72 Environmental Protection Agency, 'Standards of Performance for Greenhouse Gas Emissions for New Stationary Sources: Electric Utility Generating Units,' *Federal Register*, Volume 77, No. 72, April 13, 2012, Page 22392

73 *ibid*, Page 22430

74 Matt Ridley, ' Our Fading Footprint for Framing Food,' *The Wall Street Journal*, December 21, 2012

75 *ibid*

76 Indur M. Goklany, 'Unintended Consequences,' *The New York Times*, April 23, 2007

77 *ibid*

78 The Fiscal Times, 'Could Midwest Drought Cause Global Crisis?,' *MSN Money*, August 1, 2012

79 Indur Goklany, 'Economic Development in Developing Countries: Advancing Human Well-Being and the Capacity to Adapt to Global Warming,' in Patrick J. Michaels, Editor, *Climate Coup: Global Warming's Invasion of Our Government and Our Lives*, Cato Institute, Washington, DC, 2011, Page 181

80 Terry Macalister, 'U.S. Slashes Corn Production Forecast as Drought Raises Crisis Fears, *The Guardian*, August 10, 2012

CHAPTER 18

1 Barack Obama, New Energy for America Speech, Lansing, Michigan, August 4, 2008

2 See Table HINC-01. Selected Characteristics of Households, by Total Money Income in 2011, *U.S. Census Bureau*

3 George F. Will, 'Have We Got a Deal for You,' *Townhall*, June 7, 2009

4 Tom Gantert, 'Chevy *Volt* Costing Taxpayers Up to $250K per Vehicle,' *Michigan Capitol Confidential*, December 21, 2011

5 'Effects of Federal Tax Credits for the Purchase of Electric Vehicles,', *Congressional Budget Office*, September 2012, Page 11

6 Barack Obama, Real Leadership for a Clean Energy Future, Portsmouth, New Hampshire, October 8, 2007

7 Marita Noon, 'Renewable Energy's Reversal of Fortune,' *Townhall*, June 2, 2013

8 'Most States Have Renewable Portfolio Standards,' *Energy Information Administration*, February 3, 2012

9 *ibid*

10 Electric Power Monthly, Table 1.1 Energy Source Total – All Sectors (Thousand Megawatt-Hours), *Energy Information Administration*

11 'Statement of Eugene M. Trisko,' *Committee on Oversight and Government Reform*, February 14, 2013, Page 15

12 Electric Power Monthly, Table 5.6.A. Average Retail Price of Electricity to Ultimate Customers by End-Use Sector by State (Cents per Kilowatt-Hour), *Energy Information Administration*

13 Local Area Unemployment Statistics, *Bureau of Labor Statistics*; Renewable Portfolio Standards Map, *Energy Information Administration*

14 *ibid*

15 Bill Ritter, Jr., 'Gov. Bill Ritter: Advancing Colorado's New Energy Economy,' *The Denver Post*, March 11, 2010

16 Joel Kotkin, 'America's Red State Growth Corridors,' *The Wall Street Journal*, February 25, 2013

17 Robert J. Michaels, 'A Federal Renewable Electricity Requirement: What's Not to Like?,' *Cato Institute*, No. 627, November 13, 2008

18 *ibid*, Page 10

19 *op. cit.*, Electric Power Monthly, Table 5.6.A. Average Retail Price of Electricity to Ultimate Customers by End-Use Sector by State, *Energy Information Administration*; see also *op. cit.*, Electric Power Monthly, Table 1.1 Energy Source Total — All Sectors, *Energy Information Administration*

20 National Income and Product Account Tables, *Bureau of Economic Analysis*, Table 1.1.5. Gross Domestic Product (A) (Q)

21 National Income and Product Account Tables, *Bureau of Economic Analysis*, Table 1.1.6. Real Gross Domestic Product, Chained Dollars (A) (Q)

22 'Impacts of a 25-Percent Renewable Electricity Standard as Proposed in the American Clean Energy and Security Act Discussion Draft,' *Energy Information Administration*, April 2009, Page v.

23 Barbara Alexander, 'Renewable Energy Mandates: An Analysis of Promises Made and Implications for Low Income Customers,' *Oak Ridge National Laboratory*, June 2009

24 *ibid*

25 Lest one think the designation "unhinged" is idle polemics, consider that Roberts advocates Nuremberg-style show trials for anyone accused of climate change thought crimes. See David Roberts, 'An Excerpt from a New Book by George Monbiot,' *Grist*, September 20, 2006

26 David Roberts, 'Tea Party Dim Bulbs Go After Renewable Energy Standard in Kansas,' *Grist*, February 12, 2013

27 'Economic Benefits, Carbon Dioxide (CO2) Emissions Reductions, and Water Conservation Benefits from 1,000 Megawatts (MW) of New Wind Power in Kansas,' *National Renewable Energy Laboratory*, June 2008

28 'Electricity: Detailed State Data,' Net Generation by State by Type of Producer by Energy Source, 2001-Present, *Energy Information Administration*

29 *ibid*

30 Alan Claus Anderson, et. al., 'The Economic Benefits of Kansas Wind Energy,' *Polsinelli Shugart*, November 19, 2012, Page 8

31 *op. cit.*, 'Electricity: Detailed State Data,' Net Generation by State by Type of Producer by Energy Source, 2001-Present, *EIA*

32   Electric Power Monthly with Data for December 2012, Table 5.6B Table 5.6.B. Average Retail Price of Electricity to Ultimate Customers by End-Use Sector, by State, Year-to-Date through December 2012 (Cents per Kilowatt-hour), February 2013, and Electric Power Monthly with Data for December 2008, March 2009, *Energy Information Administration*

33   *ibid*

34   Incentives/Policies for Renewables & Efficiency, Renewable Electricity Production Tax Credit (PTC), Database of State Incentives for Renewables & Efficiency, U.S. Department of Energy

35   *op. cit.*, 'Electricity: Detailed State Data,' Net Generation by State by Type of Producer by Energy Source

36   Tim Carpenter, 'Kansas Considers Pulling Plug on Renewable Energy Standards,' *The Topeka Capital-Journal*, February 10, 2013

37   Analysis by author of the impact of a 1.7% surcharge upon $4.1 billion Kansas electricity cost between December 2011 to November 2012 derived from EIA data of all-sector cost and generation quantity.

38   Economic analysis of conventional vs. wind energy cost differentials performed by author.

39   *op. cit.*, Alan Claus Anderson, et. al., 'The Economic Benefits of Kansas Wind Energy,' *Polsinelli Shugart*

40   George Taylor and Thomas Tanton, 'The Hidden Costs of Wind Electricity,' *American Tradition Institute*, December 2012

41   'How Less Became More: Wind, Power and Unintended Consequences in the Colorado Energy Market,' *Bentek Energy LLC*

42   Gordon Hughes, 'The Performance of Wind Farms in the United Kingdom and Denmark,' *Renewable Energy Foundation*, 2012

43   Associated Press, 'Otter Tail Power Wants to Increase Wind Energy Surcharge,' *WDAZ*, February 24, 2010

44   David G. Tuerck, Paul Backman and Michael Head, 'The Economic Impact of the Kansas Renewable Portfolio Standard,' *The Beacon Hill Institute*, July 2012, Page 2

45   *ibid*

46   'Renewable Energy Mandates Have Negative Economic Consequences for Citizens,' *Kansas Policy Institute*, July 16, 2012

47   Bob Weeks, 'Brownback, Moran Wrong on Wind Tax Credits,' *Wichita Liberty*, March 19, 2012

48   Review & Outlook, 'Republicans Blow With the Wind,' *The Wall Street Journal*, March 7, 2012

49   Cluck Stinnet, 'PSC Rejects Wind Surcharge,' *Evansville Courier & Press*, October 21, 2009

50   Based upon an annual cost of $1,600,365,328 per 1,000 mW times the factor 2.346, the actual amount of Kansas wind capacity in 2012

51   Review & Outlook, 'The Great Transmission Heist,' *The Wall Street Journal*, November 7, 2010

52   Levelized Cost of New Generation Resources in the Annual Energy Outlook 2012, *Energy Information Administration*, July 2012

53   Fact Sheet, 'Order No. 1000: Final Rule on Transmission Planning and Cost Allocation by Transmission Owning and Operating Public Utilities,' *Federal Energy Regulatory Commission*, July 21, 2011

54   David B. Raskin, et. al., 'Analysis of FERC Order No. 1000,' *Steptoe & Johnson LLP*, August 3, 2011

55   Review & Outlook, 'The Great Transmission Heist,' *The Wall Street Journal*, November 7, 2010

56   18CFR Part 35, 'Transmission Planning and Cost Allocation by Transmission Owning and Operating Public Utilities, *Federal Energy Regulatory Commission*, Docket No. RM10-23-00; Order No. 1000, July 21, 2011, Page 15

57   Review & Outlook, 'The Wind Power Tax,' *The Wall Street Journal*, February 10, 2013

58   'Transmission Projects: At a Glance,' *Edison Electric Institute*, March 2013, Page iii

59   Travis Fisher, 'FERC Nominee Ronald Binz: Another Anti-Energy Czar?,' *Institute for Energy Research*, July 15, 2013

60   Travis Fisher, 'FERC Order 1000: Cost Socialization for 'Green' Energy (NRDC, AWEA Rejoice),' *Master Resource*, April 8, 2013

61   'CFTP's Sue Sheridan Discusses FERC Transmission Order, 2013 Congressional Energy Agenda In Focus Washington Interview,' *PR Newswire*, November 5, 2012

62   Green media boosters prefer the euphemism "access to the grid" as a way of advocating for inordinate costs solely attributable to far-flung solar and wind projects should be spread to all ratepayers. The term "access" sounds better than "free-loading." They proclaim that "it's complicated." But it's not. It's just free-loading. That's easy to understand. See some embarrassing examples of hagiographic coverage by the FERC Chairman's groupie press spokesperson, who pretends to be a reporter at Erica Gies, 'New Federal Rules Boost Grid Access for Wind, Solar Storage,' *Forbes*, June 29, 2012; see also Erica Gies, 'Clean Energy: It's Complicated,' *Grist*, April 7, 2011; see also Eric Gies, 'Making the Consumer an Active Participant in the Grid,' *The New York Times*, November 29, 2010

63   PR Newswire, 'Federal Energy Regulatory Commission Dismisses Interstate Power,' *Bloomberg*, April 16, 2009

64   See for instance Barack Obama, Speech in Chester, Pennsylvania, October 28, 2008

65   Solar Reserve, LLC (Crescent Dunes), Loan Guarantee Program, *Loan Programs Office*, U.S. Department of Energy

66   Zachary Tracer, 'Solar Reserve Wins $737 Million Guarantee for Solar Thermal Plant,' *Bloomberg Business Week*, September 28, 2011

67   'DOE Finalizes $737 Million Loan Guarantee to Tonapah Solar Energy for Nevada Project,' Loan Programs Office, *U.S. Department of Energy*, September 28, 2011

68   Solar Reserve Corporate Website; see About Us link for investment partners

69   Pacific Corporate Group, corporate website

70   Mark Hemingway, 'Crony Capitalism: $737 Million Green Jobs Loan Given to Nancy Pelosi's Brother-In-Law,' *Weekly Standard*, September 29, 2011

71   Andrew Stiles, 'The Solyndra Mess Gets Messier,' *National Review*, September 29, 2011

72   Joel Gehrke, 'Solyndra Director Tied to $737 Million Loan Guarantee,' *The Washington Examiner*, September 28, 2011

73   Andrew Stiles, 'The Solyndra Mess Gets Messier,' *National Review*, September 29, 2011

74   'Crescent Dunes: Project Overview,' Solar Reserve corporate website

75   Jennifer Robinson, 'Going Green Not Cheap for NV Energy,' *Las Vegas Review-Journal*, July 15, 2010

76   Marc Gunther, 'Solar Reserve Banks on Storing Heat from the Sun,' *Green Biz*, July 5, 2011

77   Electric Power Monthly, February 2013, Table 5.6.B. Average Retail Price of Electricity to Ultimate Customers by End-Use Sector, by State, *Energy Information Administration*

78   *op. cit.*, Marc Gunther, 'Solar Reserve Banks on Storing Heat from the Sun,' *Green Biz*

79   *ibid*

80   Electric Power Monthly, Table 5.6.B. Average Retail Price of Electricity to Ultimate Customers by End-Use Sector, by State, Year-to-Date 2003 to 2012, *Energy Information Administration*

81   *ibid*

82   *op. cit.*, Jennifer Robinson, 'Going Green Not Cheap for NV Energy,' *Las Vegas Review-Journal*

83   *ibid*

84   *ibid*

85   Robert Bryce, 'The High Cost of Renewable-Electricity Mandates,' *Manhattan Institute for Policy Research*, No. 10, February 2012

86   *op. cit.*, Jennifer Robinson, 'Going Green Not Cheap for NV Energy,' *Las Vegas Review-Journal*

87   *ibid*

88   Ryan Tracy and Cassandra Sweet, 'New Push to Securitize Renewable-Power Pacts,' *The Wall Street Journal*, March 14, 2013

89   'Jet Fuel-Gate Is Obama's New Solyndra,' *Investors Business Daily*, December 13, 2011

90   Stephen Singer, 'New England Renewable Energy a Hard Sell in Region,' *Associated Press*, April 1, 2013

91   *ibid*

92   Mackenzie Weinger, 'AP Boss: Sources Won't Talk Anymore,' *Politico*, June 19, 2013; *AFP*, 'U.S. Seizure of Journalist Records Called "Chilling",' *France24*, June 19, 2013

93   *op. cit.*, Ryan Tracy and Cassandra Sweet, 'New Push to Securitize Renewable-Power Pacts,' *The Wall Street Journal*

94   Ben Sills, 'Spain Halts Renewable Subsidies to Curb $31 Billion of Debts,' *Bloomberg*, January 27, 2012

95   Jan Hromadko and Andreas Kissler, 'Germany Plans to Cap Renewable Subsidies,' *The Wall Street Journal*, January 29, 2013

96   'Update 2 — Italy Set to Cut Solar Incentives – Sources,' *Reuters*, March 28, 2012

97   Konrad Krasuski, 'Poland Plans to Cut Subsidy for Renewables as Deficit Grows,' *Bloomberg*, April 9, 2013

98   ČTK, 'President Zeman Supports Efforts to Cut Solar Subsidies,' *Prague Daily Monitor*, March 29, 2013

99   Michael Kanellos, 'France Set to Cut its Feed-In Tariff for Solar by 12 Percent,' *Green Tech Media*, August 24, 2010

100   Sumi Somaskanda, 'Renewable Energy Losing Its Shine in Europe,' *USA Today*, March 23, 2013

101   Agnieszka Flak, 'South Africa Cuts Proposed Green Energy Subsidies,' *Reuters*, March 23, 2011

102   Ben Willis, 'Japan Feed-In Tariff Faces 10% Cut,' *PV Tech*, March 11, 2013

103   Christopher Martin, 'U.S. States Turn Against Renewable Energy as Gas Plunges,' *Bloomberg*, April 23, 2013

104   See for instance the preposterous finding of Synapse that wildly concluded wind power would lower customer bills in the PJM Interconnection service territory if wind power were to be quadrupled at Bob Fagan, et. al., 'The Net Benefits of Increased Wind Power in PJM,' *Synapse Energy Economics, Inc.*, May 9, 2013

105   'Analysis - States' Bids to Slash Renewables Targets Slows U.S. Progress,' *Wind Power Monthly*, May 14, 2013

106   Electric Power Monthly, Detailed State Data, Net Generation by State by Type of Producer by Energy Source 2001-Present, *Energy Information Administration*

107 'Levelized Cost of New Generation Resources in the Annual Energy Outlook 2011,' *Energy Information Administration*

108 *op. cit.*, Electric Power Monthly, Table 5.6.A. Average Retail Price of Electricity, *EIA*

109 *ibid*

110 Patrick Sawer, 'Promoters Overstated the Environmental Benefit of Wind Farms,' *The Telegraph*, December 20, 2008

111 A 51% wind cost premium applied to a $0.0251 per kilowatt-hour cost premium for all California electricity over non-RPS all-sector consumers in 2011 distributed over 7.752 million megawatt-hours of wind energy divided by 3,333,290 metric tons of abated CO_2 yields a cost per metric ton of $88.10.

112 Ricardo Lopez, 'California's First Carbon-Credit Auction Raises $290 Million,' *Los Angeles Times*, November 20, 2012

113 Will Nichols, 'MEPs Reject Backloading Plan, Carbon Price Drops Below €3,' *Business Green*, January 25, 2013

114 *ibid*

115 James Murray, 'European Carbon Price "Inching Ever Closer to Zero",' *The Guardian*, February 7, 2013

116 Timothy Considine and Edward Manderson, 'Powering California: Balancing Fiscal, Energy, and Environmental Concerns,' *American Enterprise Institute*, June 2012, Pages 20-21

117 'Growing Wind: Final Report of the NYISO 2010 Wind Generation Study,' *New York Independent Operator System*, September 2010, Page i

118 *ibid*

119 Paul L. Joskow, 'Comparing the Costs of Intermittent and Dispatchable Electricity Generating Technologies,' *Center for Energy and Environmental Policy Research*, September 2010, Page 9

120 'Issues in Focus,' Annual Energy Outlook 2013, *Energy Information Administration*, April 15, 2013

121 *ibid*, Figure 15

122 Todd Woody, 'How Renewable Energy Could Beat Natural Gas to the Future,' *Quartz*, April 30, 2013

123 See the hyper-ventilating claims made by one green cheerleader at Todd Woody, 'When the U.S. Government Says Your Next Car Will Run on Biofuel, Don't Take It Too Seriously,' *Quartz*, April 26, 2013

124 See the error-riddled hymn sung by Woody in his preposterous boast that wind and solar could overtake natural gas on a cost-competitiveness basis at *op. cit.*, Todd Woody, 'How Renewable Energy Could Beat Natural Gas to the Future,' *Quartz*

125 Annual Energy Review 2011, *Energy Information Administration*, Table 8.2a Electricity Net Generation: Total (All Sectors),1949-2011, September 2012

126 'Levelized Cost of New Generation Resources in the Annual Energy Outlook 2013,' *Energy Information Administration*, January 28, 2013

127 See for instance Richard S.J. Tol, 'An Analysis of Mitigation as a Response to Climate Change,' *Copenhagen Consensus Center*, 2009; see also Bjørn Lomborg, 'The End of the EU's Cap-and-Trade Affair,' *The Wall Street Journal*, April 21, 2013

128 *op. cit.*, 'Effects of Federal Tax Credits for the Purchase of Electric Vehicles,', *Congressional Budget Office*, Page 18

129 *ibid*

130 Gordon Hughes, 'Why is Wind Power So Expensive?: An Economic Analysis,' *University of Edinburgh*, July 2011, Page 1

131 Joel Stonington, 'Wake-Up Call: A Disastrous Week for Carbon Trading,' *Der Spiegel*, January 25, 2013

132 *op. cit.*, Gordon Hughes, 'Why is Wind Power So Expensive?: An Economic Analysis

133 Dr. Manuel Frondel, Nolan Ritter, and Prof. Colin Vance, Ph.D., 'Economic Impacts from the Promotion of Renewable Energies: The German Experience — Final Report,' *Rheinisch-Westfälisches Institut für Wirtschaftsforschung*, Essen, Germany, October 2009, Page 6

134 Joel Stonington, 'Cutting Carbon: Is Europe's Emissions Trading System Broken?,' *Der Spiegel*, October 26, 2012

135 'Cost-Effectiveness of Biofuels and Their Ability to Cut Fossil Fuel Use Questioned,' *Science Daily*, November 29, 2011

136 'Biofuels — At What Cost?: Government Support for Ethanol and Biodiesel in the United States,' *International Institute for Sustainable Development*, 2006, Page 54

137 Chris Malins, 'Indirect Land Use Change in Europe – Considering the Policy Options,' *International Council on Clean Transportation*, November 2011

138 'Effects of a Carbon Tax on the Economy and the Environment,' *Congressional Budget Office*, May 2013, Page 1

139 'International Energy Outlook 2011,' Table A10 World Carbon Dioxide Emissions by Region, Reference Case, 2006-2035, *Energy Information Administration*, September 19, 2011

140 James Delingpole, 'Climate Change: We Really Don't Need to Waste All This Money,' *The Telegraph*, May 27, 2013

141 'Executive Summary of the Stern Review: The Economics of Climate Change,' *HM Treasury*, National Archives, October 30, 2006

142 Jason Pontin, 'Vinod Khosla: A Veteran Venture Capitalist's New Energy,' *Technology Review*, March 12, 2007

143 Wilson Clark, *Energy for Survival: The Alternative to Extinction*, Garden City, NY: Anchor Books, 1974, Page 364

144 Abengoa Solar, Inc. (Solana), *Loan Programs Office*, U.S. Department of Energy

145 Dylan Smith, 'World's Largest Solar Plant Slated for Gila Bend,' *Tucson Sentinel*, July 3, 2010

146 Analysis by author of a $2 billion capital cost with 8% interest rate for 25 years on a 250 megawatt capacity plant

147 Ryan Randozzo, 'Plant to Brighten State's Solar Future,' *The Arizona Republic*, February 21, 2008

148 Composite wholesale electricity price in 2010 at the Palo Verde hub available at 'Wholesale Market Data 2010,' *Energy Information Administration*

149 Analysis of Gila Bend project financials by author based upon DoE state all-sector electricity rate and consumption data

150 *ibid*

151 Veronique de Rugy, 'Assessing the Department of Energy Loan Guarantee Program: Testimony Before the House Committee on Oversight and Government Reform,' *Mercatus Center*, June 19, 2012

152 'Updated Capital Cost Estimates for Utility Scale Electricity Generating Plants,' *Energy Information Administration*, April 2013, Table 2-5, Page 2-10 for Solar Thermal Technology

153 Peter E. Glasser, 'Solar Energy,' *Science*, May 21, 1965, Page 1127

154 Barry Commoner, *The Poverty of Power*, New York: Alfred A. Knopf, 1976, Page 151

155 Jimmy Carter, 'The President's Proposed Energy Policy.' *Public Broadcasting System*, April 18, 1977, Vital Speeches of the Day, Volume XXXXIII, No. 14, May 1, 1977, pp. 418-420

156 Renewable Energy Industry, Joint Hearing Before the Subcommittees of the Committee on Energy and Commerce, U.S. House of Representatives, 98th Congress, 1st Session, *Government Printing Office*, 1983, Page 52

157 K. Wells, 'As a National Goal, Renewable Energy Has An Uncertain Future,' *The Wall Street Journal*, February 13, 1986, Page 19

158 Scott Sklar, Solar Energy Industries Association Quoted in Solar Power, Hearing Before the Subcommittee on Energy and Power of the Committee on Energy and Commerce, House of Representatives, 100th Congress, 1st Session Washington, DC, *Government Printing Office*, 1987, Page 12

159 'Monthly Energy Review March 2013,' Table 1.1 Primary Energy Overview (Quadrillion BTUs) vs. Table 1.2 Primary Energy Production by Source, *Energy Information Administration*, March 27, 2013

160 Allen R. Myerson, 'Solar Power for Earthly Prices,' *The New York Times*, November 15, 1994

161 'Will Renewables Become Cost-Competitive Anytime Soon?,' *Institute for Energy Research*, April 1, 2009

162 *op. cit.*, Barack Obama, Real Leadership for a Clean Energy Future, Portsmouth, New Hampshire, October 8, 2007

163 The $139 billion figure comes from the following: $34.5 billion for DoE Section 1703 projects, $34.5 billion for DoE Section 1705 projects, $34.5 billion for Advanced Technology Vehicle Manufacturing projects, $17.2 billion for Treasury Section 1603 projects plus $4.2 billion per year in RPS renewable energy surcharges over 4 and a half years.

164 Neil King, Jr. and Stephen Power, 'Times Tough for Energy Overhaul,' *The Wall Street Journal*, December 12, 2008

CHAPTER 19

1 From a speech by Ben Bernanke to the Japan Society of Monetary Economics, May 31, 2003 in 'Notable & Quotable,' *The Wall Street Journal*, April 30, 2013

2 Annual Energy Review 2011, Table 1.1 Primary Energy Overview, *Energy Information Administration*, September 2012

3 *ibid*

4 *ibid*

5 Annual Energy Review 2011, Table 10.1 Renewable Energy Production and Consumption by Primary Energy Source, *Energy Information Administration*, September 2012

6 Office of the White House Press Secretary, Remarks by the President on Energy, University of Miami, Miami, Florida, February 23, 2012

7 'Green Jobs: Towards Decent Work in a Sustainable, Low-Carbon World,' *UN Environment Programme*, September 2008

8 See for instance Robert Bryce, *Power Hungry: The Myths of "Green" Energy and the Real Fuels of the Future*, New York: Public Affairs, 2010

9   Malcolm Keay, 'CO2 Emissions Reduction: Time for a Reality Check?,' *Oxford Institute for Energy Studies*, February 2005

10 International Energy Statistics, Total Carbon Dioxide Emissions from the Consumption of Energy (Million Metric Tons), *Energy Information Administration*

11 Jesse Ausubel, 'The Future Environment for the Energy Business,' *APPEA Journal*, July 2007, Page 493

12 *ibid*

13 *ibid*

14 Robert Bryce, *Power Hungry: The Myths of "Green" Energy and the Real Fuels of the Future*, Public Affairs, Philadelphia, PA, 2007, Page 86

15 Roscoe Wind Energy Complex, *E.On* at http://eoncrna.com/contentProjectsRoscoe.html

16 *ibid*

17 Candace Lombardi, 'Texas Completes $1 Billion Wind Energy Complex,' *C-Net*, October 1, 2009

18 Electricity: Detailed State Data, Net Generation by State by Type of Producer by Energy Source 2001-Present, *Energy Information Administration*

19 Power Plants: Palo Verde, *Arizona Public Service*

20 State Nuclear Profiles, Arizona Nuclear Profile 2010, *Energy Information Administration*

21 Tony Rose and Michael J. Economides, 'Wind Energy: The Truth Blows,' *The Energy Tribune*, October 20, 2010

22 'Winning a Prudence Audit,' *Office of Science*, U.S. Department of Energy

23 See for instance 'Accommodating High Levels of Variable Generation,' *North American Electric Reliability Corporation*, April 2009, Page i

24 'How Less Became More: Wind, Power and Unintended Consequences in the Colorado Energy Market,' *Bentek Energy LLC*

25 Robert Mendick, 'Wind Farm Turbines Wear Sooner Than Expected, Says Study,' *The Telegraph*, December 30, 2012

26 Barack Obama, 'A Secure Energy Policy for Our Future Speech,' Las Vegas, Nevada, June 24, 2008

27 Thomas L. Freidman, 'Foreign Affairs; The Secret Oil Talks,' *The New York Times*, September 8, 2000

28 'History of Railroads and Maps,' *The Library of Congress*, American Memory Project

29 'Timeline: History of the Electric Car,' *PBS*

30 Chris Bedford, '115-Year-Old Electric Car Gets Same 40 Miles to the Charge as Chevy *Volt*,' *The Daily Caller*, October 14, 2011

31 David Biello, 'Intoxicated on Independence: Is Domestically Produced Ethanol Worth the Cost?,' *Scientific American*, July 28, 2011

32 Rufus Frost Herrick, *Denatured or Industrial Alcohol*, New York, John Wiley & Sons, 1907, Page 307

33 Mathew Sathyajith, *Wind Energy: Fundamentals, Resource Analysis and Economics*, Heidelberg, Springer, 2006, Pages 1-9

34 'Timeline: The History of Wind Power,' *The Guardian*, October 17, 2008

35 Windmill Light & Power Company Advertisement, *Harper's New Monthly Magazine*, No. 565, June 1897

36 Robert Bryce, 'Get Dense,' *City Journal*, Volume 22, No. 1, Winter 2012

37 *ibid*

38 Matt Ridley, 'Our Fading Footprint for Framing Food,' *The Wall Street Journal*, December 21, 2012

39 Jesse H Ausubel, et. al., 'Peak Farmland and the Prospect for Land Spaing,' *Population and Development Review*, Volume 38, 2012

40 Dan Charles, 'Peak Farmland? Some Researchers Say It's Here,' *National Public Radio*, December 19, 2012

41 'New USDA Data Offers In-Depth Look at Organic Farming,' *National Agricultural Statistics Service*, U.S. Department of Agriculture, February 3, 2010

42 Steven D. Savage, Ph.D., 'A Detailed Analysis of U.S. Organic Crops,' *Scribd*

43 Bryan Walsh, 'Whole Food Blues: Why Organic Agriculture May Not Be So Sustainable,' *Time*, April 26, 2012

44 *ibid*

45 Verena Seufert, Navin Ramankutty and Jonathan A. Foley, 'Comparing the Yields of Organic and Conventional Agriculture,' *Nature*, Volume 485, May 10, 2012, Pages 229-232; see also Natasha Gilbert, 'Organic Farming is Rarely Enough,' *Nature*, April 25, 2012

46 Jon Entine, 'Organic Industry's Credibility Eroded by Misinformation About GE Foods,' *American Enterprise Institute*, May 20, 2013

47 Maria Rodale, 'Organic Can Feed the World,' *PCC Natural Markets*, September 2010

48 James McWilliams, 'Organic Crops Alone Can't Feed the World,' *Slate*, March 10, 2011

49 Barbara Kingsolver, *Animal, Vegetable, Miracle: A Year of Food Life*, New York: Harper Perennial, 2008

50 Christopher L. Weber and H. Scott Matthews, 'Food-Miles and the Relative Climate Impacts of Food Choices in the United States,' *Environmental Science & Technology*, Volume 42, No. 10, April 16, 2008, Pages 3508-3513

51   *ibid*, Page 3508

52   Steve Sexton, 'The Inefficiency of Local Food,' *Freakonomics*, November 14, 2011

53   Anna Lappé, *Diet for a Hot Planet: The Climate Crisis at the End of Your Fork and What You Can Do About It*, New York: Bloomsbury Press, 2010

54   Philip and Erin Ackerman-Leist, *Rebuilding the Foodshed: How to Create Local, Sustainable, and Secure Food Systems*, White River Junction, Vermont: Chelsea Green Publishing, 2013

55   'APL Plans 30% Reduction of CO2 Emissions,' *Ship & Bunker*, December 11, 2013

56   'Brown Introduces Bill to Expand Markets for Framers and Increase Access to Local Foods,' *Senator Sherrod Brown*, November 1, 2011

57   'Geographic Preference Option for the Procurement of Unprocessed Agricultural Products in Child Nutrition Programs,' *Federal Register*, Volume 76, No. 78, April 22, 2011, Pages 22603-22608

58   One might be tempted to wonder aloud who would oppose a law called The Healthy, Hunger-Free Kids Act of 2010. See 'USDA Rule Encourages Local Food for School Meals,' *Food Safety News*, April 29, 2011. They might also wonder who could oppose something called the Patient Protection and Affordable Care Act. That is better known as Obamacare.

59   *op. cit.*, Robert Bryce, 'Get Dense,' *City Journal*

60   *ibid*

61   Bryan Walsh, 'Why Biofuels Help Push Up World Food Prices,' *Time*, February 14, 2011

62   International Energy Statistics, Total Petroleum Consumption, Thousand Barrels per Day, *Energy Information Administration*

63   Levelized Capital Cost of New Generation Resources in the Annual Energy Outlook 2012, *Energy Information Administration*, July 2012

64   'Renewable Energy Country Attractiveness Indices,' *Ernst & Young*, Issue 29, May 2011, Page 5

65   *ibid*

66   *ibid*

67   Daily Treasury Yield Curve Rates, U.S. Department of the Treasury, 10 Year Treasury Note on May 31, 2012

68   Hugo Duncan, ' "Beware a Rerun of the Great Panic of 2008": Head of World Bank Warns Europe is Heading for "Danger Zone" As World Markets Suffer Bleakest Day of Year So Far,' *The Daily Mail*, June 1, 2012

69   *Reuters*, 'U.S. Benchmark 10-Year Yield Hits New Lows,' *CNBC*, July 22, 2012; see also *Associated Press*, 'Treasury Yields Sink to Record Low on Europe Fears,' *The Houston Chronicle*, July 24, 2012

70   'Interest Expense on the Debt Outstanding,' Treasury Direct, *U.S. Department of the Treasury*

71   'The Daily History of the Debt Results,' Treasury Direct, *U.S. Department of the Treasury*, Public Debt on October 1, 2010 vs. September 30, 2011

72   Phil Gramm and John Taylor, 'The Hidden Costs of Monetary Easing,' *The Wall Street Journal*, September 11, 2012

73   'Average Interest Rates: June 30, 2012,' Treasury Direct, *U.S. Department of the Treasury*

74   'Fiscal Year 2012, Analytical Perspectives, Budget of the U.S. Government, *Office of Management and Budget*, 2012, Page 68

75   *ibid*, Page 150

76   See for instance John Doukas, 'The ECB's Policy of Printing Money Will Not Lead to Wealth Creation. Instead It Will Inevitably; see also *Reuters*, 'ECB Prepares to Open Spigot Again in Debt Crisis,' *CNBC*, February 26, 2012

77   Simon Goodley, 'Dare Nine Men Defy the Siren Call of Christine Lagarde?,' *The Guardian*, June 2, 2012

78   Jim Efstathiou Jr., 'Obama to Press Congress for $2 Billion Clean-Energy Fund,' *Bloomberg*, March 15, 2013

79   *op. cit.*, 'Fiscal Year 2012, Analytical Perspectives, Budget of the U.S. Government, Page 150

80   Felicity Carus, 'Obama Calls for $2bn from Oil and Gas Revenues to Fund Clean Energy Research,' *PV Tech*, March 15, 2013

81   Charles Krauthammer, 'Obama: The Fall,' *The Washington Post*, May 2, 2013

82   Congressman Tim Griffin unearthed a memo from Charles Brown at the U.S. Department of Agriculture ordering staffers to inflict maximum disruption, U.S. House of Representatives

83   $34.5 billion in DoE Section 1703 projects, $34.5 billion in Section 1705 projects, $34.5 billion in Advanced Technology Vehicle Manufacturing projects and $17.2 billion in Treasury Section 1603 projects

84   Daily Treasury Yield Curve Rates, *U.S. Department of the Treasury*, U.S. Treasury Rates on June 1, 2012

85   *op. cit.*, 'Fiscal Year 2012, Analytical Perspectives, Budget of the U.S. Government, Page 150

86   'Transcript: Al Gore's Speech,' *National Public Radio*, August 28, 2008

87   U.S. Imports by Country of Origin, Monthly Thousand Barrels, *Energy Information Administration*

88   National Income and Product Accounts, *Bureau of Economic Analysis*, Table 1.1.6 Real Gross Domestic Product, 2005 Chained Dollars

89   National Income and Product Accounts, Table 1.1.6. Real Gross Domestic Product, Chained Dollars, *Bureau of Economic Analysis*

90   The issue gained notice with a 2008 paper published by NBER submitted by a pair of Harvard economists available at Carmen M. Reinhart and Kenneth S. Rogoff, 'This Time is Different: A Panoramic View of Eight Centuries of Financial Crises,' NBER Working Paper No. 13882, *National Bureau of Economic Research*, March 2008; the authors expanded their paper into a book-length manuscript in 2009 published by Princeton University Press. See Carmen M. Reinhart and Kenneth S. Rogoff, *This Time is Different: Eight Centuries of Financial Folly*, Princeton, New Jersey: Princeton University Press, 2009; R&R developed a model correlating economic growth rate reductions to external debt levels in a 2010 paper that suggested austerity measures combined with structural reform is recommended over increased fiscal stimulus at Carmen M. Reinhart and Kenneth S. Rogoff, 2010. 'Growth in a Time of Debt,' *American Economic Review*, Volume 100(2), Pages 573-578, May 2010; a graduate student at the University of Massachusetts discovered some methodological errors in the Harvard study which led the authors to correct their analysis but which left their main thesis intact. See Edward Crudy, 'How a Student Took on Eminent Economists on Debt Issue — and Won,' *Reuters*, April 18, 2013; R&R responded at Carmen M. Reinhart and Kenneth S. Rogoff, 'Debt, Growth and the Austerity Debate,' *The New York Times*, April 25, 2013; for an excellent summary that places the entire affair in its proper context, see Anders Aslund, 'Reinhart-Rogoff Austerity Case Still Stands,' *Financial Times*, April 19, 2013

91   Tyler Durden, 'Total U.S. Debt to GDP: 105%,' *Zero Hedge*, April 26, 2013

92   Morgan Korn, 'The Real Reason the U.S. Economy Won't Take Off,' *Yahoo Finance*, April 9, 2013

93   Robert Zubrin, 'Obama's Energy Plan: Impoverish America,' *National Review*, June 29, 2013

94   Review & Outlook, 'The Growth Deficit,' *The Wall Street Journal*, April 28, 2013

95   'Fed Balance Sheet Grows to Record Again in Latest Week,' *Reuters*, April 26, 2013

96   Review & Outlook, 'Debt and Growth,' *The Wall Street Journal*, April 29, 2013

97   Morgan Korn, 'Niall Ferguson to Paul Krugman: You're Still Wrong About Government Spending,' *Daily Ticker on Yahoo Finance*, April 30, 2013

98   Michael Pento, *The Coming Bond Market Collapse: How to Survive the Demise of the U.S. Debt Market*, New York: Wiley & Co., 2013

99   Aaron Task, 'The "Most Overpriced, Oversupplied, Over-Owned Market in History,' *Daily Ticker on Yahoo Finance*, May 1, 2013

100   Total Private Payrolls, *Bureau of Labor Statistics*

101   Employed Persons and Civilian Noninstitutional Population, *Bureau of Labor Statistics*

102   Employment-Population Ratio from the Current Population Survey, *Bureau of Labor Statistics*

103   'The Employment Situation — August 2013,' *Bureau of Labor Statistics*, Page 2

104   Don Lee and Alexie Koseff, 'U.S. Adds 195,000 Jobs in June,' *Los Angeles Times*, July 6, 2013

105   Jeffrey Bartash, 'U.S. Economy Creates 195,000 Jobs in June,' *Market Watch*, July 5, 2013

106   Patrick Rizzo, 'U.S. Economy's Job Creation Revved Up in June,' *NBC News*, July 5, 2013

107   The Employment Situation — June 2013, Table B-3. Average Hourly and Weekly Earnings of All Employees on Private Nonfarm Payrolls by Industry, *Bureau of Labor Statistics*, July 5, 2013

108   Household Data Table A-9 Selected Employment Indicators, *Bureau of Labor Statistics*

109   Kevin G. Hall, 'Most 2013 Job Growth Is in Part-Time Work, Survey Suggests,' *McClatchy Papers*, August 2, 2013

110   Full-Time Employed vs. Part-Time Employed from the Current Population Survey, *Bureau of Labor Statistics*

111   *ibid*

112   Mortimer Zuckerman, 'A Jobless Recovery Is a Phony Recovery,' *The Wall Street Journal*, July 15, 2013

113   Civilian Labor Force and Civilian Non-Institutional Population, *Bureau of Labor Statistics*

114   *op. cit.*, Mortimer Zuckerman, 'A Jobless Recovery Is a Phony Recovery,' *The Wall Street Journal*

115   *ibid*, Employed Persons Change, August 2013 Minus January 2009, *Bureau of Labor Statistics*

CHAPTER 20

1   Paul Johnson, *National Review*, June 29, 1984

2   'University Report: Ethanol Reduced Gas Prices $0.89 in 2010,' *Renewable Fuels Association*, May 2, 2011

3   'New University Study: Ethanol Reduced Gas Prices by More Than $1 in 2011,' *Renewable Fuels Association*, May 15, 2012

4   Review & Outlook, 'How Ethanol Causes Joblessness,' *The Wall Street Journal*, August 17, 2012

5   Cindy Zimmerman, 'RFA Ads Tout Ethanol Reducing Gas Prices,' *Domestic Fuel*, July 26, 2011

6   Cindy Zimmerman, 'Ag Secretary Wants Biofuels Support in Farm Bill,' *Domestic Fuel*, October 26, 2011

7   News Transcript, 'Agriculture Secretary Vilsack on Priorities for the 2012 Farm Bill,' *U.S. Department of Agriculture*, Release No. 0458-11, October 24, 2011

8   Bob Dinneen, 'U.S. Ethanol Industry Helps Households Make Ends Meet,' *Ethanol Producer Magazine*, June 12, 2012

9   'New University Study: Ethanol Reduced Gas Prices by More than $1 per Gallon in 2011,' *Market Watch*, May 15, 2012

10   Cindy Zimmerman, 'Report Shows Ethanol Kept Gas Prices Lower in 2011,' *Domestic Fuel*, May 15, 2011

11   Ethanol demand of 4.5 billion bushels of corn at Mario Parker, 'Ethanol Drops on USDA Corn Estimate,' *Bloomberg*, August 10, 2012; corn production of 10.8 billion bushels at Mark Peters and Owen Fletcher, 'Prices Surge as Drought Stunts Corn Crop,' *The Wall Street Journal*, August 10, 2012

12   Examiner Editorial, 'To Protect Ethanol, Obama Seeks to Inflate Meat Prices,' *The Washington Examiner*, August 14, 2012

13   NREL is a Department of Energy agency that promotes renewable energy use as its full-time occupation and occasionally does research into making it slightly less impractical.

14   McKinsey and Company, 'The Impact of Ethanol Blending on U.S. Gasoline Prices,' *National Renewable Energy Laboratory*, November 2008, Page 4

15   Xiaodong Du and Dermot J. Hayes, 'The Impact of Ethanol Production on U.S. and Regional Gasoline Markets: An Update to May 2009,' *Center for Agricultural and Rural Development*, Iowa State University, April 2011

16   *ibid*, page 1

17   David Biello, 'Intoxicated on Independence: Is Domestically Produced Ethanol Worth the Cost?,' *Scientific American*, July 28, 2011

18   Annual Energy Review, September 2012, *Energy Information Administration*, Table 5.24 Retail Motor Gasoline and On-Highway Diesel Fuel Prices, 1949-2011

19   Annual Energy Outlook 2012 Early Release Overview, *Energy Information Administration*, January 23, 2012, Table 11 Liquid Fuels Supply and Disposition

20   *ibid*

21   'U.S. Total Motor Gasoline Exports Down Slightly from Last Year but Still at High Levels,' *Energy Information Administration*, August 14, 2012

22   Marlo Lewis, 'MIT Study Debunks RFA/Vilsack Claims on Ethanol, Gas Prices,' *Global Warming Blog*, July 17, 2012

23   'USA Plants,' Existing Ethanol Plants as of April 8, 2012, *Ethanol Producer Magazine*

24   Christopher R. Knittel and Aaron Smith, 'Ethanol Production and Gasoline Prices: A Spurious Correlation,' *MIT Center for Energy and Environmental Policy Research*, July 2012

25   Steven F. Hayward, 'Energy Fact of the Week: Debunking the Rosenfeld Curve,' *American Enterprise Institute*, October 27, 2011

26   *ibid*, Page 15

27   Bruce A. Babcock, 'Updated Assessment of the Drought's Impacts on Crop Prices and Biofuel Production,' *Center for Agricultural and Rural Development*, August 2012

28   'Notice of Decision Regarding Requests for a Waiver of the Renewable Fuel Standard,' *U.S. Environmental Protection Agency*, November 16, 2012

29   'New Flex Fuel Vehicles,' Fuel Economy Website, *U.S. Dept. of Energy* and *Environmental Protection Agency*, November 2012

30   'The Renewable Fuels Association (RFA) Organized an Information Awareness Campaign in Washington DC,' Abengoa Corporate website

31   Bernice Napach, 'Gas Prices Will Continue to Rise Until U.S. Builds More Refineries: Gas Buddy Analyst,' *CNBC*, August 17, 2012

32   'New York Harbor RBOB Regular Gasoline Future Contract 1,' *Energy Information Administration*, August 13, 2012

33   National Weekly Ethanol Summary, USDA *Livestock & Grain Market News*, U.S. Department of Agriculture, August 17, 2012

34   Ethanol is only 66% as energetic as gasoline. See BNSF Rate Book 4024-A for current BNSF railroad ethanol tank car rates and surcharges; see Marina R. Denicoff, 'Ethanol Transportation Backgrounder: Expansion of U.S. Corn-Based Ethanol from the Agricultural Transportation Perspective,' *U.S. Department of Agriculture*, September 2007 for various assumptions about average tank car lading sizes

35   Today in Energy, Daily Prices, *Energy Information Administration*, July 19, 2013

36   'Clean Cities Alternative Fuel Price Report,' *Energy Efficiency & Renewable Energy*, U.S. Department of Energy, January 2013, Page 3

37   'Clean Cities Alternative Fuel Price Report,' *Energy Efficiency & Renewable Energy*, U.S. Department of Energy, April 2013, Page 3

38 'Clean Cities Alternative Fuel Price Report,' *Energy Efficiency & Renewable Energy*, U.S. Department of Energy, July 2013, Page 3

39 Lihong McPhail, Paul Westcott and Heather Lutman, 'The Renewable Identification Number System and U.S. Biofuel Mandates,' *U.S. Department of Agriculture*, November 2011, Page 12

40 Gregory Meyer, 'U.S. Ethanol Credits Surge 1,400% This Year,' *Financial Times*, March 6, 2013

41 Robert Wagner, 'Ethanol RIN Prices Up 2,740% Year to Date,' *Seeking Alpha*, July 19, 2013

42 Monthly Energy Review February 2013, Table 3.5 Petroleum Products Supplied by Type, *Energy Information Administration*

43 *ibid*

44 *ibid*

45 Dan Strumpf, 'Lawmakers Examine Ethanol Credits' Affect [*sic*] on Gas Prices,' *The Wall Street Journal*, March 14, 2013

46 Annual Energy Outlook 2013 Early Release, Table 11. Liquid Fuels Supply and Disposition Balance, *Energy Information Administration*

47 Review & Outlook, 'The Ethanol Gas-Pump Surcharge,' *The Wall Street Journal*, March 11, 2013

48 'Will the U.S. Hit the Blend Wall?,' *Institute for Energy Research*, March 20, 2013

49 'Editorial: The Ethanol Bubble,' *The Washington Times*, March 15, 2013

50 Gregory Meyer, 'Cut in Fuel Use Reignites Ethanol Debate,' *Financial Times*, March 11, 2013

51 'A Question Worth Billions: Why Isn't the Conventional RIN Price Higher?,' *Food and Agricultural Policy Research Institute*, December 2012

52 *op. cit.*, 'The Ethanol Gas-Pump Surcharge,' *The Wall Street Journal*

53 Review & Outlook, 'The Ethanol Tax,' *The Wall Street Journal*, July 19, 2013

54 *op. cit.*, Dan Strumpf, 'Lawmakers Examine Ethanol Credits' Affect on Gas Prices,' *The Wall Street Journal*

55 *ibid*

56 'U.S. Ethanol Production and the Renewable Fuel Standard RIN Bank,' *Energy Information Administration*, June 5, 2013

57 *op. cit.*, Review & Outlook, 'The Ethanol Tax,' *The Wall Street Journal*

58 Review & Outlook, 'An Ethanol Spring,' *The Wall Street Journal*, April 16, 2013

59 Amy Harder, 'Ethanol Mandate to be Debated for Two Days Before House Panel,' *National Journal*, July 22, 2013

60 Robert Wagner, 'Understanding the EPA's RFS2, Its Future, RINs and the Ethanol Blend Wall — Part 1,' *Seeking Alpha*, August 18, 2013

61 Jason A. Flower, et. al., 'Fraudulent Identification Numbers Issued Under EPA's Renewable Fuel Standard: Buyer Beware,' *Martindale-Hubbell*, May 2, 2012

62 Dave Juday, 'Bipartisanship and Biofuels: A Volatile Mix,' *The Weekly Standard*, Volume 19, No. 4, September 30, 2013

63 Bob Dinneen, 'Hearing on Overview of the Renewable Fuel Standard: Stakeholder Perspectives,' *House Energy and Commerce Committee*, July 23, 2013

64 Robert Murphy, 'Ethanol Proponents Mislead on Gas Prices,' *Institute for Energy Research*, April 22, 2013

65 Tom Buis and Bob Dinneen, 'Setting the Record Straight on U.S. Gas Prices,' *Politico*, April 16, 2013

66 *ibid*

67 Today in Energy, Daily Prices, *Energy Information Administration*, April 16, 2013

68 Public Law 110-140, December 19, 2007, Energy Independence and Security Act of 2007, Section 202 Renewable Fuel Standard, (2) Applicable Volumes of Renewable Fuel, (B) Applicable Volumes, (III) Cellulosic Biofuel

69 *op. cit.*, Dan Strumpf, 'Lawmakers Examine Ethanol Credits' Affect [*sic*] on Gas Prices,' *The Wall Street Journal*

70 Juliet Eilperin, 'EPA Issues New Fuel-Efficiency Standard; Autos Must Average 54.5 MPG By 2025,' *The Washington Post*, August 28, 2012

71 Maxx Chatsko, 'This Bill Wants to Cut Ethanol Production in Half,' *The Motley Fool*, May 11, 2013

72 Maxx Chatsko, 'Why KiOR Is Not Range Fuels,' *The Motley Fool*, January 28, 2013

73 *ibid*

74 Drew Johnson, 'Who Really Gets Rich Off High Gas Prices?,' *The Wall Street Journal*, August 2, 2012

75 *ibid*

76 *op. cit.*, Robert Wagner, 'Understanding the EPA's RFS2, Its Future, RINs and the Ethanol Blend Wall — Part 1,' *Seeking Alpha*

77 Editors, 'End the Ethanol Mandate,' *Bloomberg*, August 16, 2012

78 James M. Griffin and Mauricio Cifuentes Soto, 'U.S. Ethanol Policy: The Unintended Consequences,' *Mossbacher Institute*, Texas A&M University, Volume 3, Issue 1, 2012

79 *ibid*

80 *op. cit.*, 'Clean Cities Alternative Fuel Price Report,' *Energy Efficiency & Renewable Energy*, DoE, January 2013,

April 2013, July 2013, January 2014; biofuel volume from Monthly Energy Review February 2014, Table 3.1 Petroleum Overview, *Energy Information Administration*

81 National Income and Product Accounts, Table 1.1.6. Real Gross Domestic Product, Chained Dollars, *Bureau of Economic Analysis*

82 CO_2 emission data from International Energy Statistics, *Energy Information Administration*, Total Carbon Dioxide Emissions from the Consumption of Energy (Million Metric Tons)

83 Editorial, 'Ethanol's Promise,' *The New York Times*, May 1, 2006

84 Steve A. Yetiv,' Is the Energy Boom a Mirage?,' *The New York Times*, September 4, 2012

CHAPTER 21

1 Richard F. Fullenbaum and John W. Larson, 'America's New Energy Future: The Unconventional Oil and Gas Revolution and the U.S. Economy,' *IHS Global Insights*, September 2013

2 Barack Obama, 'Energy Security Is National Security Speech,' Washington, DC, February 28, 2006

3 Barack Obama, Energy Independence and the Safety of Our Planet Speech, Chicago, Illinois, April 3, 2006

4 *ibid*

5 Petroleum and Other Liquids, U.S. Imports by Country of Origin, Total Crude Oil and Products; Petroleum and Other Liquids, Exports by Destination, Total Crude Oil and Products, *Energy Information Administration*

6 Günther H. Oettinger, 'The Energy Roadmap 2050 - Commissioner Günther H Oettinger,' *Science Omega*, September 12, 2012

7 'Energy Roadmap 2050,' foreword by Günther H. Oettinger, *European Commission*, December 15, 2011, Page 1

8 *ibid*, Page 6

9 'Energy Technology Perspectives 2012: Pathways to a Clean Energy System – Executive Summary,' *International Energy Agency*, 2012, Page 1

10 *ibid*

11 Alice Waltham, 'Powerful Targets: Exploring the Relative Cost of Meeting Decarbonisation and Renewables Targets in the British Power Sector,' *AF-Mercados UK*, March 4, 2012

12 Alexander Neubacher, 'The Latte Fallacy: German Switch to Renewables Likely to Be Expensive,' *Der Spiegel*, July 27, 2011

13 Dr. Manuel Frondel, Nolan Ritter, and Prof. Colin Vance, Ph.D., 'Economic Impacts from the Promotion of Renewable Energies: The German Experience — Final Report,' *Rheinisch-Westfälisches Institut für Wirtschaftsforschung*, Essen, Germany, October 2009

14 Based upon an exchange rate of $1.3084 USD per 1 €uro; See Electric Power Monthly, December 2012, Table 5.6.A. Average Retail Price of Electricity to Ultimate Customers by End-Use Sector, *Energy Information Administration*, Average residential rate of $0.1162 per kilowatt-hour

15 Electric Sales, Revenue and Average Price, Table 5A. Residential Average Monthly Bill by Census Division, and State, *Energy Information Administration*, Average residential monthly bill of $110.14 in 2011

16 A. Denny Ellerman and Barbara K. Buchner, 'The European Union Emissions Trading Scheme: Origins, Allocation, and Early Results,' Review of Environmental Economics and Policy, Volume 1, 2007, Pages 66-87

17 Climate Action: Emission Trading System (EU ETS), *European Commission*

18 'Breathing Difficulties: A Market in Need of a Miracle,' *The Economist*, March 3, 2012

19 Alexander Jung, 'Hot Air: The EU's Emissions Trading System Isn't Working,' *Der Spiegel*, February 15, 2012

20 *op. cit.*, 'Breathing Difficulties: A Market in Need of a Miracle,' *The Economist*

21 'Funding Shortage Threatens Germany's Energy Revolution,' *Der Spiegel*, February 13, 2012

22 Review & Outlook, 'Europe's Return to Coal,' *The Wall Street Journal*, May 17, 2012

23 Siobhan Hall, 'EU Climate Chief Mulls Changes to Timing of ETS Carbon Auctions,' *Platts*, April 20, 2012

24 Karel Beckman, ' "Replace Emission Trading Scheme With a Carbon Tax",' *European Energy Review*, May 10, 2012

25 'Emissioni di CO2: Una Carbon Tax e Una Soluzione Preferibile all'ETS,' *Instituto Bruno Leoni*, May 9, 2012

26 Matthew Carr, 'Obama May Levy Carbon Tax to Cut U.S. Deficit, HSBC Says,' *Bloomberg*, November 7, 2012

27 Lee E. Ohanian and John B. Taylor, 'What Economic Recovery?,' *Defining Ideas*, September 18, 2013

28 Adele Morris, 'The Many Benefits of a Carbon Tax,' *The Brookings Institution*, February 26, 2013

29 Robert Murphy, 'Brookings Study Misleads on Carbon Tax,' *Institute for Energy Research*, March 15, 2013

30 Chip Knappenberger, 'Analysis of U.S. and State-by-State Carbon Dioxide Emissions and Potential "Savings" in Future Global Temperature and Global Sea Level Rise,' *Science & Public Policy Institute*, April 10, 2013, Page 2

31 'Economic Outcomes of a U.S. Carbon Tax: Full Report,' *National Association of Manufacturers*, February 26, 2013

32 Derrick Morgan, 'Conservatives for a Carbon Tax?,' *National Review*, June 3, 2013

33 *ibid*

34 See for instance the counter-factual boosterism at Billy Parish, 'U.S. Can't Afford to Cede Green Energy Industry to its Competitors,' *The Christian Science Monitor*, July 15, 2013

35 'Transcript: Obama's State of the Union Address,' *National Public Radio*, January 25, 2011

36 Joseph E. Aldy, et. al., 'Willingness to Pay and Political Support for a U.S. National Clean Energy Standard,' *Nature Climate Change*, Volume 2, May 13, 2012, Pages 596-599

37 Based upon a population estimate of 315,091,138 persons at 'Census Bureau Projects U.S. Population of 315.1 Million on New Years Day 2013,' *U.S. Department of Commerce*, December 28, 2012

38 Alex Fitzsimmons, 'Green Energy Subsidies Do Nothing to Curb CO2 Emissions,' *Institute for Energy Research*, July 16, 2013

39 William D. Nordhaus, et. al., 'Effects of U.S. Tax Policy on Greenhouse Gas Emissions,' *National Academy of Sciences*, 2013

40 *ibid*, Page 7

41 *ibid*, Page 70

42 *ibid*, Page 70

43 Based upon 2012 CO_2 emission estimate of 5,621.8 million metric tons in 'International Energy Outlook 2011,' Table A10 World Carbon Dioxide Emissions by Region, Reference Case, 2006-2035, *Energy Information Administration*, September 19, 2011

44 *op. cit.*, Billy Parish, 'U.S. Can't Afford to Cede Green Energy Industry to its Competitors,' *The Christian Science Monitor*

45 Petroleum & Other Liquids, Crude Oil Imports by Area of Entry, Annual Thousand Barrels; Crude Oil Exports, Annual Thousand Barrels, *Energy Information Administration*

46 *ibid*

47 U.S. International Natural Gas Receipts vs. International Natural Gas Deliveries, Million Cubic Feet, *Energy Information Administration*

48 Between the year 2000 and 2007, domestic natural gas consumption exceeded production by an average of about 2.7 trillion cubic feet.

49 *op. cit.*, .S. International Natural Gas Receipts vs. International Natural Gas Deliveries, *EIA*

50 U.S. Product Supplied for Crude Oil and Petroleum Products, Thousand Barrels per Day; Crude Oil Production, Thousand Barrels, *Energy Information Administration*

51 *ibid*

52 *op. cit.*, U.S. Natural Gas Marketed Production, Million Cubic Feet; Natural Gas Consumption by End Use, Million Cubic Feet, *Energy Information Administration*

53 *op. cit.*, Natural Gas Consumption by End Use, Million Cubic Feet, *Energy Information Administration*

54 U.S. Natural Gas Prices, Imports Price $ per Thousand Cubic Feet, *Energy Information Administration*

55 Analysis by author based upon EIA data

56 *Investors Business Daily*, 'Petroleum Exports Soar to New High in Economic Boost,' *Yahoo News*, February 8, 2013

57 *ibid*

58 *ibid*

59 Foreign Trade, 'U.S. International Trade in Goods and Services (FT900),' *U.S. Census Bureau*, December 2013

60 'Monthly Energy Review, December 2013,' *Energy Information Administration*, Table 3.1 Petroleum Overview

61 *ibid*, Foreign Trade, 'U.S. International Trade in Goods and Services (FT900),' *U.S. Census Bureau*

62 Petroleum & Other Liquids, Texas Field Production of Crude Oil, *Energy Information Administration*

63 *ibid*

64 Review & Outlook, 'A Tale of Two Oil States,' *The Wall Street Journal*, May 5, 2013

65 Russell Gold, 'Oil and Gas Boom Lifts U.S. Economy,' *The Wall Street Journal*, February 8, 2012

66 'The Economic Impacts of the Oil and Natural Gas Industry on the U.S. Economy in 2009: Employment, Labor Income and Value Added,' *PricewaterhouseCoopers LLP*, May 2011, Page 16; Full Disclosure — the author worked as a management consultant for the consulting division of PwC between 1999 and 2002. That division was sold to IBM.

67 'The Economic Contributions to the U.S. National and State Economies by the Oil and Natural Gas Industry,' *PricewaterhouseCoopers LLP*, January 15, 2007, Page 12

68 'The Contributions of the Natural Gas Industry to the U.S. National and State Economies,' *IHS Global Insight*, September 2009, Page 9

69 'Energy for Economic Growth: Energy Vision Update 2012,' *World Economic Forum*, 2012, Page 15

70 *ibid*

71 *ibid*

72   'USTA Study: Eagle Ford Generated Over $61B for South Texas in 2012,' *Oil & Gas Financial Journal*, March 26, 2013

73   Jonathan Tirone, 'Voestalpine Chooses Texas for Record $718 Million Pellet Plant,' *Bloomberg*, March 13, 2013

74   Nicole Lundeen, 'Voestalpine to Open Direct Reduction Plant in Texas,' *The Wall Street Journal*, March 13, 2013

75   *op. cit.*, Jonathan Tirone, 'Voestalpine Chooses Texas for Record $718 Million Pellet Plant,' *Bloomberg*

76   Daniel Yergin, 'Energy's Unexpected Jobs Boom,' *CNN*, September 5, 2013

77   'Cheniere Developing More Gulf Liquefaction in Corpus Christi,' *Oil & Gas Journal*, December 20, 2011

78   PR Newswire, 'Cheniere Developing Liquefaction Project in Corpus Christi, Texas,' *Alaska Dispatch*, December 16, 2011

79   Review & Outlook, 'Natural Gas Exports, Maybe,' *The Wall Street Journal*, May 20, 2013

80   'M&G Moving Ahead With Investment of Its 1 Million Ton PET and 1.2 Million Ton PTA Plants at Corpus Christi, Texas,' *PR Newswire*, September 12, 2012

81   Frank Esposito, 'M&G Group Looks at Markets for Planned 2.2 Billion Pound PET Plant,' *Plastics News*, April 18, 2013

82   Matthew V. Veazey, 'Corpus Christi Project Could Yield Nearly 4,000 Jobs,' *Downstream Today*, September 12, 2012

83   Mike Mazoni, 'Gregory Pipe Mill to Create Hundreds of Jobs,' *KRIS-TV*, January 2, 2013

84   Mike Collette, 'Steel Company's Arrival at Port Corpus Christi Raises Possibilities for Tianjin Pipe,' *The Corpus Christi Caller-Times*. March 17, 2013

85   'Economic Impact of the Eagle Ford Shale,' *University of Texas at San Antonio*, March 2013, Page 62

86   'Linde Strengthens Petrochemical Hub in the U.S.,' *The Linde Group*, June 3, 2013

87   Molly Ryan, 'Linde Invests $200M in La Porte Plant Expansion,' *Houston Business Journal*, May 30, 2013

88   op. cit., 'USTA Study: Eagle Ford Generated Over $61B for South Texas in 2012,' *Oil & Gas Financial Journal*

89   Tim Daiss and Michael J. Economides, 'There's Oil Flowing Again in Texas: Corpus Christi's Oil & Gas Boom,' *The Energy Tribune*, May 18, 2013

90   'Texas Shale 'Gusher' Shows Why Fracking Is Important,' *Investors Business Daily*, May 8, 2012

91   Daniel Yergin, 'The Real Stimulus: Low-Cost Natural Gas,' *The Wall Street Journal*, October 23, 2012

92   Matthew Kaminski, 'Annise Parker: The Modern American Boomtown,' *The Wall Street Journal*, May 17, 2013

93   *ibid*

94   Wayne Slater, 'President Obama's Press Secretary on the Middle-Class Jobs Tour: Why Visit Texas? Why Not?,' *The Dallas Morning News*, May 8, 2013

95   'Rick Perry: Texas "Right Place" for Obama to Tout Economic Growth,' *United Press International*, May 9, 2013

96   Aman Batheja, 'Obama's Austin Visit to Start With Perry Meeting,' *The Texas Tribune*, May 9, 2013

97   Summary Table A. Household Data, Seasonally Adjusted, Employed Persons, 'The Employment Situation — July 2013,' *Bureau of Labor Statistics*, August 2, 2013 vs. Table A. Major Indicators of Labor Market Activity, Seasonally Adjusted, Employed Persons, 'The Employment Situation: January 2009,' *Bureau of Labor Statistics*, February 6, 2009

98   Table 3. Civilian Labor Force and Unemployment by State and Selected Area, Seasonally Adjusted, 'Regional and State Employment and Unemployment —July 2013,' *Bureau of Labor Statistics*, August 19, 2013 vs. Table 3. Civilian Labor Force and Unemployment by State and Selected Area, Seasonally Adjusted, 'Regional and State Employment and Unemployment —January 2009,' *Bureau of Labor Statistics*, March 11, 2009

99   BLS prepares two surveys each month, the Household Survey and the Institutional Survey

100 Table B-1. Employees on Nonfarm Payrolls by Industry Sector and Selected Industry Detail, *op. cit.*, 'The Employment Situation: January 2009,' *BLS* vs. Table B-1. Employees on Nonfarm Payrolls by Industry Sector and Selected Industry Detail, *op. cit.*, 'The Employment Situation — July 2013,' *BLS*

101 *op. cit.*, Table 3. Civilian Labor Force and Unemployment by State, 'Regional and State Employment and Unemployment —July 2013,' *BLS* vs. Table 3. Civilian Labor Force and Unemployment by State, 'Regional and State Employment and Unemployment —January 2009,' *BLS*

102 Table B-3. Average Hourly and Weekly Earnings of All Employees on Private Nonfarm Payrolls by Industry Sector, Seasonally Adjusted, *op. cit.*, 'The Employment Situation — July 2013,' *BLS*

103 *op. cit.*, Table B-1. Employees on Nonfarm Payrolls, 'The Employment Situation — July 2013,' *BLS*

104 *op. cit.*, Table B-3. Average Hourly and Weekly Earnings, 'The Employment Situation — July 2013,' *BLS*

105 Editorial Board, 'Rick Perry's Tour Markets More Than Texas: Our View,' *USA Today*, October 28, 2013

106 Paul Krugman, 'The Texas Unmiracle,' *The New York Times*, August 14, 2011

107 'Regional and State Employment and Unemployment: February 2009,' *Bureau of Labor Statistics*, March 27, 2009 Table 3. Civilian Labor Force and Unemployment by State and Selected Area, Seasonally Adjusted vs. 'Regional and State Employment and Unemployment — July 2013,' *Bureau of Labor Statistics*, August 19, 2013

108 Population Level from the Current Population Survey, Seasonally Adjusted, *Bureau of Labor Statistics*

109 Employment Level from the Current Population Survey, Seasonally Adjusted, *Bureau of Labor Statistics*
110 *op. cit.*, 'Regional and State Employment and Unemployment: February 2009' vs. 'Regional and State Employment and Unemployment — July 2013' *BLS*
111 *op. cit.*, Employment Level from the Current Population Survey, Seasonally Adjusted, *Bureau of Labor Statistics*
112 Regional Real GDP in 2005 Chained Dollars, 2007 to 2012, *Bureau of Economic Analysis*
113 'Local Area Personal Income: New Estimates for 2012; Comprehensive Revisions for 2001-2011,' *Bureau of Economic Analysis*, November 21, 2013
114 David G. Lenze, 'State Personal Income 2012,' *Bureau of Economic Analysis*, March 27, 2013, Table 1. Personal Income, Population, and Per Capita Personal Income, by State and Region, 2011-2012
115 'Estimating the State-Level Impact of Federal Wind Energy Subsidies,' *Institute for Energy Research*, December 2013, Page 13
116 Frontier Associates LLC, 'Texas Renewable Energy Resource Assessment,' *Texas State Energy Conservation Office*, December 2008, Page 4-17
117 *op. cit.*, Fullenbaum and Larson, 'America's New Energy Future, *IHS Global Insights*, Page 1
118 Mark P. Mills, 'Unleashing the North American Energy Colossus: Hydrocarbons Can Fuel Growth and Prosperity,' *Manhattan Institute*, July 9, 2012, Page 10
119 National Income and Product Accounts, *Bureau of Economic Analysis*, Table 1.1.5 Gross Domestic Product
120 Katie Holliday, 'Brent Crude at $80? It Could Happen by Year-End,' *CNBC*, February 15, 2013
121 Spot Prices for Crude Oil and Petroleum Products, Europe Brent Spot Price FOB (Dollars per Barrel), *Energy Information Administration*
122 Patti Domm, 'Power Shift: Energy Boom Dawning in America,' *CNBC*, March 18, 2013
123 *ibid*
124 Andrew Peaple, 'Oil Demand Growth Could Seep Away,' *The Wall Street Journal*, March 27, 2013
125 'Shale Oil: The Next Energy Revolution,' *PricewaterhouseCoopers LLC*, February 2013, Page 1
126 Richard Engel and Robert Windrem, 'U.S. Oil, Gas Boom Could Rattle Global Order,' *CNBC*, April 1, 2013
127 Peter C. Glover and Michael J. Economides, 'The Coming Arab Winter,' *The Energy Tribune*, May 1, 2013
128 Peter C. Glover, 'The End of OPEC Despotism,' *Energy Tribune*, June 29, 2012
129 Roger Altman, 'Prepare to Celebrate OPEC's Demise,' *Financial Times*, May 21, 2012
130 International Energy Statistics, Total Oil Supply (Thousands of Barrels Per Day), *Energy Information Administration*
131 Leonardo Maugeri, 'The Coming Oil Glut,' *The Wall Street Journal*, November 6, 2012
132 Patrice Hill, 'China Poised to Top U.S. as Top Oil Buyer; Increased Car Sales Spur Jump,' *The Washington Times*, March 14, 2013
133 *ibid*
134 Rick Newman, 'Peak Driving Is Looking Like a Myth,' *Yahoo Finance*, July 3, 2013
135 *ibid*
136 Mike Ramsey and Neal Boudette, 'Global Car Sales Seen Rising to 85 Million in 2014,' *The Wall Street Journal*, December 16, 2013
137 'The Experts: How the U.S. Oil Boom Will Change the Markets and Geopolitics,' *The Wall Street Journal*, March 27, 2013
138 Associated Press, 'Promises, Promises: Oil Imports May Fall by Half, But Economy Will Still Need Mideast Oil,' *The Washington Post*, April 8, 2013
139 Ángel González, 'Expanded Oil Drilling Helps U.S. Wean Itself from Mideast,' *The Wall Street Journal*, June 27, 2012
140 *op. cit.*, Associated Press, 'Promises, Promises: Oil Imports May Fall by Half, But Economy Will Still Need Mideast Oil,' *The Washington Post*
141 *ibid*

CHAPTER 22

1 'Former Greenpeace Founder Slams Green Extremists,' *Nuclear Engineering International*, February 23, 2005
2 Jonathon M. Seidl, 'Greenpeace Founder Questions Man-Made Global Warming,' *The Blaze*, January 20, 2011
3 Joseph Cotto, 'Patrick Moore on the Facts and Fiction of Climate Change,' *The Washington Times*, August 9, 2012
4 'The End of India's Green Revolution?,' *BBC*, May 29, 2006
5 John Pollack, 'Green Revolutionary,' *Technology Review*, December 18, 2007
6 Paul Ehrlich, *The Population Bomb*, New York: Balllantine Books, 1968, Page 1
7 Robert Zubrin, 'Debating Phil Cafaro,' *National Review*, June 7, 2013
8 *ibid*

9   See for instance his Carter-era quackery in Paul R. Ehrlich, Anne H. Ehrlich, and John P. Holdren, *Ecoscience*: *Population, Resources Environment*, San Francisco: W. H. Freeman and Co., 1977

10   Paul Ehrlich, *The Population Bomb*, New York: Balllantine Books, 1968, Page 146

11   John Tierney, 'Flawed Science Advice for Obama?,' *The New York Times*, December 19, 2008

12   Ed Regis, 'The Doomslayer,' *Wired*, Volume 5, No. 2, February 1997

13   Ronald Bailey, 'Science and Public Policy,' *Reason*, February 4, 2004

14   Paul Ehrlich, *Ramparts*, September 1969, Pages 24-28

15   Paul R. Ehrlich and Anne H. Ehrlich, *The Population Explosion*, New York: Simon & Schuster, 1990

16   Indur M. Goklany, *The Improving State of the World: Why We're Living Longer, Healthier, More Comfortable Lives on a Cleaner Planet*, Washington, DC: Cato Institute Press, 2007

17   See for instance the softballs, slobbery wet kisses and hosannas heaped upon Ehrlich in this cringe-inducing press release masquerading as an interview — it's more accurately a love sonnet — authored by a love-struck Ehrlich fan club member at the *Los Angeles Times* at Patt Morrison, 'Paul R. Ehrlich: Saving Earth,' *Los Angeles Times*, February 12, 2011

18   Canadian columnist Dan Gardner wrote a book in 2010 that draws upon the research of psychologist Philip Tetlock who undertook decades of research on why the public often places so much trust in the future predictions of "experts" when they were about as accurate as dart-throwing monkeys. Ehrlich comes under special scrutiny as his past prediction accuracy is in inverse proportion to his celebrity. Garner concludes that a deeply rooted human need for future certainty accounts for why the public can so easily dismiss cranks and charlatans like the Ehrlichs and return to them repeatedly for advice even after their past predictions have left a lengthy track record of epic failure. See Dan Gardner, *Future Babble: Why Expert Predictions Fail — and Why We Believe Them Anyway*, Toronto: McClelland & Stewart, 2010

19   John Tierney, 'Betting on the Planet,' *The New York Times*, December 2, 1990

20   Julian L. Simon, *The Ultimate Resource*, Princeton, New Jersey: Princeton University Press, 1981

21   John Tierney, 'Economic Optimism? Yes, I'll Take That Bet,' *The New York Times*, December 27, 2010

22   Graham Chedd, 'Some Are Paying Heed …,' *New Scientist*, September 16, 1971, Page 636

23   Together with fellow Malthusian quack John Holdren, Ehrlich selected a group of five strategic metals — tungsten, copper, nickel, tin and chromium — that they were certain would all be higher in price by 1990 due to global depletion. In 1990, the prices of all five metals were much lower than in 1980 for the exact reasons enumerated by Simon. Ehrlich was publicly humiliated. Simon, an economist who had extensively researched the topic, understood the impact of resource substitution on changing demand patterns and technological advancement which opened previously uneconomic supply sources. Ehrlich paid the debt, announcing he would continue to issue doomsday predictions in future but would never again wager his own money.

24   Julian Simon, *The Ultimate Resource II*, Princeton, New Jersey: Princeton University Press, 1998

25   Jonathan V. Last, 'Book Review: "The Bet" by Paul Sabin,' *The Wall Street Journal*, August 30, 2013

26   Lee Ferran, 'Michelle Obama: "Let's Move" Initiative Battles Childhood Obesity,' *ABC News*, February 9, 2010

27   Paul Sabin, The Bet, New Haven, Connecticut: Yale University Press, 2013

28   Edwin J. Feulner, 'The Man Who Dissected "The Liberal Mind",' The Wall Street Journal, June 30, 2013

29   Kenneth Minogue, 'Notable & Quotable,' *The Wall Street Journal*, June 30, 2013

30   Maxim Lott, 'Eight Botched Environmental Forecasts,' *Fox News*, December 30, 2010

31   Ronald Bailey, 'Cracked Crystal Ball: Environmental Catastrophe Edition,' *Reason Magazine*, December 30, 2010

32   Bernard Dixon, 'In Praise of Prophets,' *New Scientist*, September 16, 1971, Page 606

33   *ibid*

34   Boyce Rensberger, '14 Million Acres a Year Vanishing as Deserts Spread Around the World,' *The New York Times*, August 28, 1977, Page A1

35   *Newsweek*, September 19, 1977, Page 80

36   Julian L. Simon, 'Resources, Population, Environment: An Oversupply of False Bad News,' *Science*, Volume 208, No. 4451, June 1980, Pages 1431-1437

37   Peter Gwynne, 'The Cooling World,' *Newsweek*, April 28, 1975, Page 64

38   Indur M. Goklany, 'Unintended Consequences,' *The New York Times*, April 23, 2007

39   *ibid*

40   Justin Gillis, 'A Warming Planet Struggles to Feed Itself,' *The New York Times*, June 4, 2011

41   David Lam, 'How the World Survived the Population Bomb: Lessons From 50 Years of Extraordinary Demographic History,' *Demography*, Volume 48, November 2011, Pages 1231-1262

42   Onkar Ghate, 'Eco-Terrorism's War on Man,' *Frontpage Magazine*, January 25, 2006

43   Walter E. Williams, 'Clues About the Progressive Agenda,' *Richmond Times-Dispatch*, June 8, 2013

44   William Aiken, 'Ethical Issues in Agriculture,' in *Earthbound: New Introductory Essays in Environmental Ethics*, Tom Regan, Editor, New York: Random House, 1984, Page 269

45   *op. cit.*, Walter E. Williams, 'Clues About the Progressive Agenda,' *Richmond Times-Dispatch*

46   Christopher C. Horner, 'In Gaia We Trust,' *National Review*, January 16, 2003

47   Marita Noon, 'Environmentalists Are Hurting the U.S. Economy,' *The Energy Tribune*, May 10, 2013

48   Paul Ehrlich, 'An Ecologist's Perspective on Nuclear Power,' Public Issue Report, *Federation of American Scientists*, May-June 1978

49   'All the President's Men,' *Fox News*, May 14, 2010

50   John Tierney, 'Betting on the Planet,' *The New York Times*, December 2, 1990

51   'Why Our Economy Is Killing Our Planet and What We Can Do About It,' *New Scientist*, October 18, 2008, Page 40

52   Tim Jackson, 'What Politicians Dare Not Say,' *New Scientist*, October 18, 2008, Page 43

53   Craig Offman, 'Jail Politicians Who Ignore Climate Science: Suzuki,' *National Post*, February 7, 2008

54   David Suzuki and Jo Merchant, 'We Should Act Like the Animals We Are,' *New Scientist*, October 18, 2008, Page 44-45

55   Herman Daly, 'On a Road to Disaster,' *New Scientist*, October 18, 2008, Page 47

56   George F. Will, 'On Immigration, Charles Dickens Matters,' *The Washington Post*, May 10, 2013

57   Gustave Speth and Liz Else, 'Swimming Upstream,' *New Scientist*, October 18, 2008, Page 48

58   James Gustave Speth, *The Bridge at the Edge of the World: Capitalism, the Environment, and Crossing from Crisis to Sustainability*, New Haven: Yale University Press, 2009

59   Aggregate emissions of six common pollutants declined by 59% between 1990 and 2010. Airborne lead emissions declined by 99% between 1970 and 2002. Airborne mercury emissions declined by 52% from 1990 to 2002. Benzene concentration levels decreased by 55% between 1994 and 2006. Acid rain components SO_2 decreased 37% and NO_x decreased 17%. See 'EPA's Report on the Environment: Highlights of National Trends,' *U.S. Environmental Protection Agency*, 2008, Page 31; see also 'Our Nation's Air — Status and Trends Through 2010,' *U.S. Environmental Protection Agency*

60   John Tierney, 'Use Energy, Get Rich and Save the Planet,' *The New York Times*, April 20, 2009

61   Jesse Ausubel, et. al., 'Returning Forests Analyzed With the Forest Identity,' *Proceedings of the National Academy of Sciences*, Volume 103, November 14, 2006, Pages 17574-17579

62   Peter Dauvergne, *The Shadows of Consumption: Consequences for the Global Environment*, Cambridge: MIT Press, 2010

63   Paul Farhi, 'After Crime, Blame Game Picks Media,' *The Washington Post*, January 11, 2011

64   Jeffrey D. Sachs, *Common Wealth: Economics for a Crowded Planet*, New York: Penguin Books, 2009

65   Kate Soper, 'The Good Life,' *New Scientist*, October 18, 2008, Page 54

66   Richard Heinberg, *The End of Growth: Adapting to Our New Economic Reality*, Gabriola Island, British Columbia: New Society Publishers, 2011

67   'World Economic Outlook Update,' *International Monetary Fund*, July 9, 2013. The IMF reports global economic growth of 3.9% in 2011 and 3.2% in 2012. It projects another 2.9% in 2013 and 3.6% in 2014. The world will have achieved a 14.3% increase in economic activity since his 2010 base period in just four years.

68   Annual Energy Outlook 2013, Table 1.1 Primary Energy Overview, *Energy Information Administration*

69   Table 1.1.6. Real Gross Domestic Product, Chained Dollars, *Bureau of Economic Analysis*

70   Steven F. Hayward, *2011 Almanac of Environmental Trends*, San Francisco: Pacific Research Institute, April 2011, Page 19

71   Kenneth P. Green and Steven F. Hayward, 'Back to the 1970s: Let's Get Small!,' *The American*, April 2, 2010

72   Justin Gillis, 'To Stop Climate Change, Students Aim at College Portfolios,' *The New York Times*, December 4, 2012

73   Stanley Kurtz, 'Fossil-Fuel Divestment — Part 2,' *National Review*, March 4, 2013

74   See how Klein's bizarre plan was carried out in the 1950s by Mao Zedong at Jung Chang and Jon Halliday, *Mao: The Unknown Story*, London: Jonathan Cape, 2005

75   William Shawcross, *Sideshow: Kissinger, Nixon and the Destruction of Cambodia*, New York: Simon & Schuster, 1979, Page 240

76   *ibid*

77   See for instance Craig Etcheson, *After the Killing Fields*, New York: Praeger, 2005, Page 119; see also Sydney Schanberg, 'The Death and Life of Dith Pran: A Story of Cambodia,' *The New York Times Magazine*, January 20, 1980; see also William Shawcross, *The Quality of Mercy: Cambodia, Holocaust and Modern Conscience*, New York: Touchstone, 1985, Pages 115-116; see also Marek Sliwinski, *Le Génocide Khmer Rouge: Une Analyse Démographique*, Paris: L'Harmattan, 1995, Pages 41-48, 57

78   Klein claims that "climate change isn't 'the issue.' In fact, it isn't an issue at all. Climate change is a message, one that is telling us that many of our culture's most cherished ideas are no longer viable." see Naomi Klein, 'Capitalism vs. the Climate,' *The Nation*, November 28, 2011

79   *ibid*

80   *ibid*

81   'Mayor Bloomberg's Urge to Rule Makes Him a Tyrant,' *Investors Business Daily*, March 26, 2013

82   Pascal Bruckner, *The Fanaticism of the Apocalypse: Save the Earth, Punish Human Beings*, Malden, Massachusetts: Polity Press, 2013

83   Pascal Bruckner, 'Apocalyptic Daze,' *City Journal*, Volume 22, No. 2, Spring 2012

84   Michael Barone, 'The Great Global-Warming Disappointment,' *National Review*, September 27, 2013

85   *op. cit.*, Pascal Bruckner, 'Apocalyptic Daze,' *City Journal*

86   *ibid*

87   Friedrich A. Hayek, *The Fatal Conceit: The Errors of Socialism*, Chicago, Illinois: The University of Chicago Press, 1991

88   Fred Barnes, 'The Lost Era of Economic Growth,' *The Weekly Standard*, Volume 18, No. 23, April 1, 2013

89   *op. cit.*, Herman Daly, 'On a Road to Disaster,' *New Scientist*

90   Alexandra Jaffe, 'Greens Get Billionaire Ally, Money,' *The Hill*, April 3, 2013

91   Kimberly A. Strassel, 'Obama's Keystone Regrets,' *The Wall Street Journal*, June 18, 2013

92   Ronald Reagan, 'A Time for Choosing,' *Reagan Library at the University of Texas*, October 27, 1964

CONCLUSION

1   From an address at the 1955 Fall meeting of the National Academy of Sciences given by Richard P. Feynmann, 'The Value of Science,' *California State University at Berkeley*

2   Phillip Handler, Interview in *U.S. News and World Report*, January 18, 1971, Page 30

3   Vaclav Klaus, *Blue Planet in Green Shackles: What Is Endangered: Climate or Freedom?*, Washington, DC: Competitive Enterprise Institute Press, 2008

4   Dr. Timothy Ball, 'Global Warming: The Cold, Hard Facts?,' *Canada Free Press*, February 5, 2007

5   Gregg Marland and Bob Andres, 'Total Carbon Emissions from Fossil-Fuels in Million Metric Tons of Carbon,' *Carbon Dioxide Information Analysis Center*, Oak Ridge National Laboratory

6   Joseph Cotto, 'Patrick Moore on the Facts and Fiction of Climate Change,' *The Washington Times*, August 10, 2012

7   Naturally-occurring methane traps heat also. It is far more efficient at doing this than CO_2. Methane seeps out of decaying organic matter in wetland swamps — and gets "liberated" by flatulent animal species.

8   Sandrine Bony, et. al., 'How Well Do We Understand and Evaluate Climate Change Feedback Processes?,' *Journal of Climate*, Volume 19, August 1, 2006 Pages 3445-3482

9   Garth Paltridge, Albert Arking and Michael Pook, 'Trends in Middle- and Upper-Level Tropospheric Humidity from NCEP Reanalysis Data,' *Theoretical and Applied Climatology*, Volume 98, Numbers 3-4, February 26, 2009, Pages 351-359

10   Paula J. Brown and Arthur T. DeGaetano, 'Trends in U.S. Surface Humidity, 1930-2010,' *Journal of Applied Meteorology and Climatology*, Volume 52, Issue 9, September 2012

11   'Climate Change 1995: The Science of Climate Change,' *UN Intergovernmental Panel on Climate Change*, 2nd Assessment Report, Working Group 1 Report, Page 16

12   *op. cit.*, Paula J. Brown and Arthur T. DeGaetano, 'Trends in U.S. Surface Humidity, 1930-2010,' *Journal of Applied Meteorology and Climatology*

13   Assessment Report 4, *UN Intergovernmental Panel on Climate Change*, Working Group 1, The Physical Science Basis, Chapter 8, 2007, Figure 8.14, Page 631

14   'Climate Change 2007: The Physical Science Basis,' *UN Intergovernmental Panel on Climate Change*, Chapter 8 Climate Models and Their Evaluation, Box 8.1: Upper-Tropospheric Humidity and Water Vapour Feedback, Page 632

15   See for instance the testimony of John R. Christy, Ph.D. to the House Energy and Commerce Committee, Subcommittee on Energy and Power, March 8, 2011

16   See for instance Roy W. Spencer, *The Great Global Warming Blunder: How Mother Nature Fooled the World's Top Climate Scientists*, Encounter Books, 2010

17   See for instance Benjamin A. Laken and Enric Palle, 'Understanding Sudden Changes in Cloud Amount: The Southern Annular Mode and South American Weather Fluctuations,' *Journal of Geophysical Research*, Volume 117, July 4, 2012; see also 'Trends in Middle- and Upper-Level Tropospheric Humidity from NCEP Reanalysis Data,' *Theoretical and Applied Climatology*, Volume 98, Issue 3-4, September 2009, Pages 351-359

18   'Climate Expert von Storch: Why Is Global Warming Stagnating?,' *Der Spiegel*, June 20, 2013

19   *ibid*

20   A case in point is the expletive-laced incendiary tirade of Al Gore at an Aspen Institute speech in 2011 where

he completely lost his composure, shouting foul language at the idea that the science is not entirely settled. See Darren Hunter, 'Al Gore's Expletive Laced Tirade Causes Alarm,' *The Examiner*, August 9, 2011

21   James Hansen, Makiko Sato and Reto Ruedy, 'Perception of Climate Change,' *Proceedings of the National Academy of Sciences*, August 6, 2012

22   Cliff Mass, 'Climate Distortion,' *Cliff Mass Weather Blog*, August 9, 2012

23   See for instance Paul Farrell's psychotic claim, offered in complete seriousness, that humanity will be extinct in 50 years due to CO_2 discharge. See Paul B. Farrell, 'Big Oil is Earth's Public Enemy No. 1,' *Market Watch*, August 3, 2012. Accorded a prominent place among *Market Watch* contributors, Farrell is best known for writing a book recommending astrology as a guide for investment selections.

24   Consider the vitriol heaped upon fast food chain Chick-fil-A by leftists, and the counter-reaction appeals to reason by conservative voices, and all because the CEO of the company admitted he supports a traditional definition of marriage at John Roberts, 'Chick-fil-A Appreciation Day Brings Out Supporters, Protestors,' *Fox News*, August 1, 2012

25   Todd Shepherd, 'CO: Academic to Conservatives: We're Liberal Because We're Smarter Than You,' *Colorado Watchdog.org*, July 30, 2012

26   Drew Westen, 'What Happened to Obama?,' Sunday Review, *The New York Times*, August 6, 2011

27   Dan Gainor, 'On CNN, Informal Obama Advisor, Professor Claims Fox News Audience is "Ignorant",' *Fox News*, October 22, 2012

28   Leo Hickman, 'James Lovelock: Humans Are Too Stupid to Prevent Climate Change,' *The Guardian*, March 29, 2010

29   Emily Esfahani Smith, 'Survey Shocker: Liberal Profs Admit They'd Discriminate Against Conservatives in Hiring, Advancement,' *The Washington Times*, August 1, 2012

30   'Academia Nuts: The Left's Bias Against Conservatives is Real,' *Investors Business Daily*, August 21, 2012

31   Emily K. Shuman, MD, 'Global Climate Change and Infectious Disease,' *New England Journal of Medicine*, Volume 362, March 25, 2010, Page 1061

32   Theda Skocpol, 'Naming the Problem: What It Will Take to Counter Extremism and Engage Americans in the Fight Against Global Warming,' *Harvard University*, January 2013

33   *ibid*, Page 7

34   *ibid*, Page 64

35   *ibid*, Page 20

36   See for instance a similar recital of the so-called crisis of public acceptance about climate change at Amy Luers, 'Rethinking U.S. Climate Advocacy,' *Climatic Change*, June 6, 2013

37   *ibid*, Page 22

38   Keith Johnson, 'Climate Politics: Forget the Carrots, Grab the Sticks,' *The Wall Street Journal*, March 18, 2009

39   *ibid*, Page 29

40   Brad Plumer, 'Why Has Climate Legislation Failed? An Interview with Theda Skocpol,' *The Washington Post*, January 16, 2013

41   See for instance Robert Murphy, 'White House Revises Dubious "Social Cost of Carbon",' *Institute for Energy Research*, June 6, 2013

42   'Climate Models Predict Heat That Hasn't Occurred,' *Investors Business Daily*, June 11, 2013

43   'Annual Energy Outlook 2013,' Market Trends - Emissions, Energy-Related Carbon Dioxide Emissions Remain Below Their 2005 Level Through 2040,' *Energy Information Administration*, April 15, 2013

44   'Effects of a Carbon Tax on the Economy and the Environment,' *Congressional Budget Office*, May 2013, Page 1

45   'International Energy Outlook 2013,' Table A10 World Carbon Dioxide Emissions by Region, Reference Case, 2005-2040, *Energy Information Administration*, July 25, 2013

46   Chip Knappenberger, 'Carbon Tax: Climatically Useless,' *Master Resource*, December 3, 2012

47   *ibid*

48   Michael J. Economides and Peter C. Glover, 'Fracking Energy Mess: Deconstructing the Green Agenda,' *Energy Tribune*, June 11, 2013

49   *op. cit.*, 'Climate Expert von Storch: Why Is Global Warming Stagnating?,' *Der Spiegel*, June 20, 2013

50   'Global Fossil-Fuel Carbon Emissions,' *Carbon Dioxide Information Analysis Center*, Oak Ridge National Laboratory

51   Steven F. Hayward, 'Political Attacks, Circa 1800,' *The New York Times*, April 20, 2011

52   Michael Barone, 'The Pros and Cons of Partisan Divide,' *National Review*, August 2, 2012

53   'The Caning of Senator Charles Sumner: May 22, 1856,' *United States Senate*, Historical Minutes

54   Even Britain's bible of leftist progressivism has noticed the shameful intolerance asking why liberals are so rude to their ideological opponents at Leften Wright, 'Why Are Liberals So Rude to the Right?,' *The Guardian*, May 27, 2013

55 Jonathan Haidt, *The Righteous Mind*: *Why Good People are Divided by Politics and Religion*, New York: Pantheon Books, 2012

56 'The Environment: A Growing Concern,' *BP*

57 John Browne, 'Addressing Global Climate Change (Part 1),' *BP*, May 19, 1997

58 Saeed Shah, 'BP Looks "Beyond Petroleum" With $8bn Renewables Spend,' *The Independent*, November 29, 2005

59 'BP to Invest $8 Billion in Alternative Energy Through 2015,' *Biofuels Digest*, April 15, 2010

60 *ibid*

61 Marita Noon, 'BP: Back to Petroleum and Beyond Puff-Power,' *Energy Tribune*, April 10, 2013

62 William M. Connolley, 'In Defence of Exxon,' *Science Blogs*, May 20, 2008

63 Paul Roberts, 'It's Not Easy Being Green,' *Mother Jones*, November-December 2006

64 Holman W. Jenkins, Jr., 'Beyond "Beyond Petroleum",' *The Wall Street Journal*, June 9, 2010

65 Jeffrey Ball, 'Exxon Chief Makes a Cold Calculation on Global Warming,' *The Wall Street Journal*, June 14, 2005

66 For a book-length narrative on BP's follies over the years that was prompted by the Deepwater Horizon disaster, see Loren C. Steffy, *Drowning in Oil: BP and the Reckless Pursuit of Profit*, New York: McGraw-Hill, 2011, Page 259

67 Maryann Tobin, 'BP CEO Tony Hayward: The Most Hated Man in America,' *The Examiner*, June 5, 2010

68 Steve Goreham, 'Using Energy and Happy About It,' *The Washington Times*, February 27, 2013

69 Electric Universe, Commonwealth Edison

70 'Monthly Energy Review September 2013,' Table 1.1 Primary Energy Overview (Quadrillion Btu) Page 3 vs. Table 2.2 Residential Sector Energy Consumption (Trillion Btu) Page 25, *Energy Information Administration*, September 25, 2013

71 Mark Drajem, 'Sierra Club Spurns $30 Million Gift as Fracking Turns Toxic,' *Bloomberg*, March 14, 2012

72 Robert W. Howarth, et. al., 'Methane and the Greenhouse-Gas Footprint of Natural Gas from Shale Formations: A Letter,' *Climatic Change*, March 13, 2011

73 Andrew C. Revkin, 'A Fresh Scientific Defense of the Merits of Moving from Coal to Shale Gas,' *The New York Times*, February 29, 2012

74 David Deming, 'What the Oil Business Could Learn from the NRA,' *The Wall Street Journal*, February 28, 2013

75 Joe Carroll, 'Chesapeake CEO Resigns After Scrutiny on Personal Loans,' *Bloomberg*, January 30, 2013

76 Selwyn Raab, 'Donovan Cleared of Fraud Charges By Jury in Bronx,' *The New York Times*, May 26, 1987

77 Brent Summers, 'Campus Divestment Fight Resonates in the East,' *The New York Times*, December 12, 2012

78 Beth Daley, 'Harvard Students Vote to Support Fossil Fuel Divestment,' *The Boston Globe*, November 20, 2012

79 Stanley Kurtz, 'Fossil-Fuel Divestment,' *National Review*, March 4, 2013

80 'International Energy Outlook 2013,' Table H12. World Total Net Electricity Generation by Region and Country, *Energy Information Administration*, July 25, 2013

81 'IEA Wind 2012 Annual Report,' *International Energy Agency*, July 2013, Page 5

82 Robert Bryce, 'Harvard Needs Remedial Energy Math,' *The Wall Street Journal*, December 16, 2012

83 Paul Denholm, et. al., 'Land-Use Requirements of Modern Wind Power Plants in the United States,' Technical Report NREL/TP-6A2-45834, *National Renewable Energy Laboratory*, August 2009, Page 10; Naturally NREL neglects to apply actual wind yield calculations. Instead it used only nameplate capacity figures for its estimate of wind sprawl. In 2009, the year of the NREL report, wind turbines in the U.S. generated only 28.62% of nameplate capacity. So NREL's estimate must be boosted by a factor of 3.5 to adjust for actual wind energy output.

84 Dry biomass of live trees 1-inch diameter or larger, Forest Resources 2012, Forest Service, *U.S. Department of Agriculture*

85 Petroleum & Other Liquids, Product Supplied 2013, *Energy Information Administration*

86 Vaclav Smil, '21st Century Energy: Some Sobering Thoughts,' *OECD Observer*, Volume 258-259, December 2006

87 Robert Wilson, 'Bill McKibben Gets the Math Wrong on Fracking,' *The Energy Collective*, April 4, 2013

88 Simon Read, 'Fuel Poverty Deaths Three Times Higher Than Government Estimates,' *The Independent*, February 28, 2012

89 See the World Bank report providing a low estimate of 460,000 premature deaths from cancer at 'Cost of Pollution in China: Economic Estimates of Physical Damages,' Conference Edition, *The World Bank*, February 2007; Evidence that the Chinese government forced the World Bank to whitewash its cancer casualty estimate is covered at John Laumer, 'Pollution Estimated to Cause 750,000 Premature Deaths Each Year in China,' *TreeHugger*, July 3, 2007

90 See for instance Darryl Fears, 'Wind Farms Under Fire for Bird Kills,' *The Washington Post*, August 28, 2011; see also 'Eagle Deaths Investigated at LADWP Wind Power Generation Site,' *Los Angeles Times*, August 2, 2011

91 'How Less Became More: Wind, Power and Unintended Consequences in the Colorado Energy Market,' *Bentek Energy LLC*

92 See for instance Shuguang Ji, et. al., 'Electric Vehicles in China: Emissions and Health Impacts,' *Environmental*

Science and Technology, Volume 46, 2012, Pages 2018-2024; see also 'Electric Transport With Wind in Its Sails,' *Science Daily*, September 13, 2013

93   Elisabeth Rosenthal, 'Your Biggest Carbon Sin May Be Air Travel,' *The New York Times*, January 26, 2013

94   See for instance Alok Jha, 'Endangered Tigers Found in Indonesian Jungle Allocated to Agriculture,' *The Guardian*, October 30, 2007; see also *Associated Press*, 'Rare Sumatran Orangutans Dying as Fires Rage in Indonesian Swamp Forest,' *The Guardian*, March 28, 2012; see also 'Endangered Sumatran Rhinoceros Born in Captivity,' *BBC*, June 23, 2012; see also Caroline Behringer, 'Habitat Loss Drives Sumatran Elephants Closer to Extinction,' *World Wildlife Fund*, January 23, 2012

95   Govinda Timilsina, 'How Global Biofuel Expansion Could Affect the Economy, Environment and Food Supply,' *The World Bank*, June 27, 2011

96   Diana Furchtgott-Roth, 'If Climate Change Is Happening Now, What Do We Do?,' *Manhattan Institute*, Testimony Before the Senate Environment and Public Works Committee, July 18, 2013, Page 10

97   *op. cit.*, Leo Hickman, 'James Lovelock: Humans Are Too Stupid to Prevent Climate Change,' *The Guardian*

98   Office of the White House Press Secretary, 'Remarks by the President on Climate Change,' Georgetown University, Washington, DC, June 25, 2013

99   'United States Overview,' *The World Bank*

100 'Toward a Sustainable Energy Future for All: Directions for the World Bank Group's Energy Sector,' *The World Bank*, July 17, 2013, Page v.

101 Anna Yukhananov and Valerie Volcovici, 'World Bank to Limit Financing of Coal-Fired Plants,' *Reuters*, July 16, 2013

102 Lisa Friedman, 'U.S. to Abstain on South African Coal Plant,' *The New York Times*, April 8, 2010

103 Lisa Friedman, 'South African Coal Plant Proposal Strains "Culture" of World Bank,' *The New York Times*, April 5, 2010

104 Sandrine Rastello, 'Kim Says World Bank Can't Reject Coal If People Freeze,' *Bloomberg*, April 17, 2013

105 Jigar Shah, 'Kosovo Is a Test for the World Bank's Support of Clean Energy,' *Green Tech Media*, May 31, 2013

106 Visitors can spot a mounted surf board inscribed with a line that few locals fully understand, the immortal "Charlie Don't Surf" uttered by the surfing enthusiastic Air Cavalry Lt. Col. Kilgore in the movie after which the club was named.

107 'Summary Sheet: Thai Binh 2 Coal-Fired Power Plant,' *Petro Vietnam*

108 'Vietnam Power Sector Reform Development Policy Operation,' *The World Bank*, March 17, 2010

109 *ibid*

110 The World Bank announced a second stage of the power sector initiative in March 2012, the expected outcome being "strengthening of electricity supply security and moving to efficient and competitive electricity prices [which would] deliver reliable and good quality electricity supply to support economic growth." See 'Vietnam Power Sector Reform DPO2,' *The World Bank*, March 2, 2012

111 Doug Palmer, 'Update 1 - Ex-Im Bank Won't Finance Vietnam Coal-Fired Power Plant,' *Reuters*, July 18, 2013

112 World Data Bank, Rwanda GDP (Current U.S. $ in Millions), *World Bank*

113 'Electrification Project Lights up Lives, Boosts Incomes in Rwanda,' *World Bank*, February 5, 2013

114 Robert Zubrin, 'The Cost of Carbon Denial,' *National Review*, July 31, 2013

115 *op. cit.*, World Data Bank, Rwanda GDP (Current U.S. $ in Millions), *World Bank*

116 'Project Paper on a Proposed Additional Credit in the Amount of SDR 39.0 Million to the Republic of Rwanda for an Electricity Access Scale-Up and Sector-Wide Approach (SWAP) Development Project,' *The World Bank*, January 22, 2013, Page 11

117 'World Bank Encourages Energy Poverty in the Name of Sustainability,' *Institute for Energy Research*, July 31, 2013

118 Daniel Yergin, 'The Puzzle of Energy Transitions' in 'Energy Vision 2013 — Energy Transitions: Past and Future,' *World Economic Future*, January 2013, Page 2

119 Review & Outlook, 'Climate of Uncertainty,' *The Wall Street Journal*, September 30, 2013

120 *op. cit.*, Gregg Marland and Bob Andres, 'Total Carbon Emissions from Fossil-Fuels in Million Metric Tons of Carbon,' *Carbon Dioxide Information Analysis Center*

121 Trends in Atmospheric Carbon Dioxide, Mauna Loa Annual Mean Data 1998-2012 in Parts per Million, Earth System Research Laboratory, *National Oceanic and Atmospheric Administration*

122 Monte Morin, 'Global Warming "Hiatus" Puts Climate Change Scientists on the Spot,' *Los Angeles Times*, September 22, 2013

123 *op. cit.*, Analysis by author based upon carbon emission data from *Carbon Dioxide Information Analysis Center*, Oak Ridge National Laboratory

124 Hayley Dixon, 'Wind Farms Could Become "Monuments of a Failed Civilization", Top Environmentalist Claims,' *The Telegraph*, February 4, 2013

125 Bjørn Lomborg, 'Comment: Global Warming Needs a More Innovative Solution,' *Financial Times*, November 25, 2011

126 Bjørn Lomborg, 'The Folly of Rio,' *Slate*, June 20, 2012

127 See for instance how this editorial bemoans the fact that developing nations make fossil fuel affordable to poor citizens in developing nations rather than promoting unreliable and unaffordable renewable energy schemes like wind and solar at Amar Toor, 'Saudi America: The Dangerous Fallacy of U.S. Energy Independence,' *The Verge*, December 6, 2012

128 Bjørn Lomborg, 'The Poor Don't Need Solar Panels,' *The Week*, July 6-13, 2012, Page 12

129 *ibid*

130 *ibid*

131 'Global Prevalence of Vitamin A Deficiency,' Micronutrient Deficiency Information System Working Paper No. 2, *World Health Organization*, Geneva, 1995

132 See for instance Kraken, 'A123 System's New Battery Won't Stave Off Bankruptcy, *Seeking Alpha*, June 18, 2012; see also Michelle Malkin, 'Another Corporate Welfare Recipient Teeters on Bankruptcy,' *Front Page Magazine*, April 3, 2012; see also Abby W. Schachter, 'Another Day, Another Solyndra,' *The New York Post*, June 1, 2012

133 Joseph Cotto, 'Patrick Moore on How to Stop Worrying and Love Mother Earth2' *The Washington Times*, August 10, 2012

134 Sue Horton, et. al., 'Micronutrient Supplements for Child Survival: Vitamin A and Zinc,' *Copenhagen Consensus Center*, 2009

135 Between May 2008 and May 2012, First Solar lost 96% of its capitalization value. See FSLR, *Yahoo Finance*

136 Bjørn Lomborg, 'The Smartest Ways to Save the World,' *Copenhagen Consensus Center*, May 16, 2012

137 *ibid*

138 Fact Sheet, 'Indoor Air Pollution,' *World Health Organization*, September 2011

139 Finn E. Kydland, 'Doing Good Efficiently,' *Project Syndicate*, June 2008

140 *ibid*

141 Bjørn Lomborg, 'Take Your Vitamins,' *Foreign Policy*, April 18, 2007

142 See for instance V. Ermert, et. al., 'The Impact of Regional Climate Change on Malaria Risk Due to Greenhouse Forcing and Land-Use Changes in Tropical Africa,' *Environmental Health Perspectives*, Volume 120, January 2012, Pages 77-84; see also Willem J.M. Martens, et. al., 'Sensitivity of Malaria, Schistosomiasis and Dengue to Global Warming,' *Climatic Change*, Volume 35, 1997, Pages 145-156; see also S.W. Lindsey and Willem J.M. Martens, 'Malaria in the African Highlands: Past, Present and Future,' *Bulletin of the World Health Organization*, Volume 76, 1998, Pages 33-45; see also P. Martens, et. al., 'Climate Change and Future Populations at Risk of Malaria,' *Global Environmental Change*, Volume 9, October 1999, Pages S89-S107

143 'Memorandum by Professor Paul Reiter, Institut Pasteur; Paris: The IPCC and Technical Information Example: Impacts on Human Health,' *UK Parliament*, March 31, 2005

144 Flemming Rose and Bjørn Lomborg, 'Will Al Gore Melt?,' *The Wall Street Journal*, January 18, 2007

145 Bjørn Lomborg, 'Climate Change and Malaria in Africa,' *The Wall Street Journal*, November 1, 2009

146 '10 Facts on Malaria,' *World Health Organization*, April 2012

147 'Hunger Statistics,' *UN World Food Programme*, 2013

148 'Maternal and Child Nutrition,' *The Lancet*, June 6, 2013

149 'Two Minutes to Learn About: School Meals,' *UN World Food Programme*, May 2012

150 Based upon 140,089 gigawatt-hours of wind energy generation at 'Electric Power Monthly with Data for December 2012,' Table 1.17.B Net Generation from Wind, by State by Sector, Year-to-Date through December 2012, *Energy Information Administration*, February 2013

151 Phillip Stevens, 'Diseases of Poverty and the 10/90 Gap,' *International Policy Network*, November 2004

152 Nigel Bruce, et. al., 'The Health Effects of Indoor Air Pollution Exposure in Developing Countries,' *World Health Organization*, Geneva, 2002

153 Jane A. Leggett, 'Funding for Federal Climate Change Activities, FY2008 to FY2012,' *Congressional Research Service*, April 26, 2012, Page 7

154 Caroline May, 'Federal Government Spent Nearly $70 Billion on "Climate Change Activities" Since 2008,' *The Daily Caller*, May 17, 2012

155 'World Health Report 2002,' *World Health Organization*, Geneva, 2002

156 *op. cit.*, Bjørn Lomborg, 'Climate Change and Malaria in Africa,' *The Wall Street Journal*

157 *op. cit.*, 'Memorandum by Professor Paul Reiter, Institut Pasteur; Paris, *UK Parliament*

158 Peter W. Gething, et. al., 'Climate Change and the Global Malaria Recession,' *Nature*, Volume 465, 2010, Pages 342-345

159 Richard S.J. Tol and Hadi Dowlatabadi, 'Vector-Borne Diseases, Development & Climate Change,' *Integrated Assessment*, Volume 2, Issue 4, October 2001, Pages 173-181

160 *ibid*

161 Robert E. Davis, 'Global Warming and Human Health,' in Patrick J. Michaels, editor, *Climate Coup: Global Warming's Invasion of Our Government and Our Lives*, Cato Institute, Washington, DC, 2011, Page 201

162 Mike Pflanz, 'Africa's Energy Consumption Growing Fastest in World,' *The Christian Science Monitor*, January 1, 2012

163 Bjørn Lomborg, 'Global Warming's Dirty Secret,' *Copenhagen Consensus Center*, 2007

164 Interview with Amy Goodman at 'Bolivian President Evo Morales on Climate Debt, Capitalism, Why He Wants a Tribunal for Climate Justice and Much More,' *Democracy Now*, December 17, 2009

165 *ibid*

166 Bjørn Lomborg, 'Kyoto's Misplaced Priorities,' *Copenhagen Climate Consensus*, 2005

167 Associated Press, 'EU Hails Climate Deal as Example for the World,' *The Jakarta Post*, December 13, 2008

168 'EU Leaders Reach New Climate Deal,' *BBC*, December 12, 2008

169 Richard S.J. Tol, Economic and Social Research Institute, Dublin, Ireland, 'The Costs and Benefits of EU Climate Policy for 2020,' *Copenhagen Consensus Center*, June 1, 2010

170 *op. cit.*, Bjørn Lomborg, 'Global Warming's Dirty Secret,' *Copenhagen Consensus Center*

171 Richard S. J. Tol, 'Why Worry About Climate Change? A Research Agenda,' *Environmental Values*, Volume 17, 2008, Pages 437-470

172 Alexander Neubacher, 'Solar Subsidy Sinkhole: Re-Evaluating Germany's Blind Faith in the Sun,' *Der Spiegel*, January 18, 2012

173 Rachel Morison, 'German Vote Won't Cut 20 Billion Euro Renewables Bill, BNEF Says,' *Bloomberg*, September 17, 2013

174 Daniel Halper, 'Claim: Germany Spends $110 Billion to Delay Global Warming by 37 Hours,' *The Weekly Standard*, March 30, 2013

175 Georg Ehring, ,Definitiv Eine Weniger Starke Erwärmung, Als Wir Erwartet Haben,' *Deutschland Radio*, September 9, 2013

176 Matt Ridley, 'Dialing Back the Alarm on Climate Change,' *The Wall Street Journal*, September 13, 2013

177 Mark J. Perry, 'Don't Divest from Energy Stocks,' *The Detroit News*, December 27, 2012

APPENDIX

1 TenneT Actual Wind Power Feed-In Data for December 2011 to November 2012

2 *Source*: TenneT Actual Wind Power Feed-In Data for December 2011 to November 2012

3 *Source*: TenneT Actual Wind Power Feed-In Data for December 2011 to November 2012

4 *ibid*

5 TenneT Actual Wind Power Feed-In Data for December 2011 to November 2012

6 TenneT Actual Wind Power Feed-In Data for December 2011 to November 2012

7 TenneT Actual Wind Power Feed-In Data for September 23, 2011 to November, 30, 2011

8 Based upon assumption that 108 Mw would provide power to 116,000 homes 'EWE, Enove Form JV to Develop Riffgat Wind Park Offshore Germany,' *Power Engineering*, May 11, 2008 and 'Off-Shore Wind Farm "Riffgat": Start of Construction 2012,' *ENOVA*

9 *ibid*

10 Holger Gassner, 'Challenge Energy Transition: Managing Volatility and Integrating Renewables into the Energy System,' in *Energiewende: Aspekte, Optionen, Herausforderungen*, Berlin, March 2012, Page 125

11 'Germany's New Energy Policy,' *Federal Ministry of Economics and Technology*, Page 19

12 Transnet BW Actual Wind Energy Feed-In Data for September 23, 2011 to November, 30, 2011

13 Warren Katzenstein, et. al., 'The Variability of Interconnected Wind Plants,' *Energy Policy*, Volume 38, Issue 8, August 2010, Pages 4400-4410

14 'AWEA U.S. Wind Industry Fourth Quarter 2012 Market Report,' *American Wind Energy Association*, January 30, 2013, Page 8